ALSO BY DICK MORRIS

Bum Rap on America's Cities:
The Real Causes of Urban Decay

Behind the Oval Office

BEHIND
THE
OVAL OFFICE

GETTING REELECTED AGAINST
ALL ODDS

Dick Morris

RENAISSANCE BOOKS
Los Angeles

Library of Congress Cataloging-in-Publication Data is available.
ISBN: 1-58063-053-7

10 9 8 7 6 5 4 3 2 1

Distributed by St. Martin's Press
Manufactured in the United States of America
Second Edition

For Eileen McGann

and Eugene Morris

"If you can meet with Triumph and Disaster

and treat those two impostors just the same."

—RUDYARD KIPLING

Contents

The Bill Clintons I Know: What Makes Them Tick

This book was written in 1996 as a memoir of one of the greatest comebacks in American political history—the reelection of President Bill Clinton, who emerged from the depths of powerless irrelevance after his party lost control of Congress in 1994 to win an astonishing victory two years later.

As this new introduction is written in October of 1998, the very man who was so victorious two years ago is now the third American president in our long history to face impeachment proceedings. How has this incredible reversal of fortune come to pass? As I ponder the twenty-two years of my relationship with Clinton, I recall episodes, fragments of memories, snippets of conversation which, taken together, show a man

---

* After I first used the Sunday-morning Clinton/Saturday-night Bill dichotomy to refer to Clinton in my column in the *New York Post* several months ago and it was quoted by Maureen Dowd in the *New York Times,* Monica Lewinsky herself apparently picked it up and referred to it in her grand jury testimony. I suspect that anyone who knows Bill Clinton well will see the resonance of this characterization in their own experiences of the man.

at war with his own dark side. The seeds of the deadly crop of revelations which have poisoned his presidency, though largely undetected, were already taking root in the late 1970s. This is the story of how I saw them yield their gruesome harvest over the years.

Bill Clinton is, without a doubt, one of the most complex figures in contemporary American politics. Like many brilliant and successful people, his personality is intricate, with both highly attractive and equally unattractive qualities. But unlike most people, the gulf between those two opposite sides of Clinton's character is enormous. In fact, it is a chasm.

The Sunday-morning President Clinton is the one we have all seen so often on television. Pious, optimistic, brilliant, principled, sincere, good-willed, empathetic, intellectual, learned, and caring, he is the president for whom America voted in 1992 and again in 1996. But the Saturday-night Bill who cohabits within him is pure id—willful, demanding, hedonistic, risk-taking, sybaritic, headstrong, unfeeling, callous, unprincipled, and undisciplined. The Sunday man adores his family. The Saturday-night counterpart risks its destruction. The Sunday President Clinton reads history and yearns for an exalted place in its pages. But Saturday-night Bill courts destruction and infamy by craving danger and excitement. On Sunday morning, Clinton values the reassurance of safe, moral ground. But on Saturday night he covets stimulation and seeks the thrill of potential disaster without any concern for the consequences.

Yet each side of Clinton seems unaware of the other and will vehemently deny, deride, and mock the very idea that the other half exists. The Sunday-morning President Clinton's denials of a Saturday-night side are forceful, clear, crisp, and eminently convincing. But they are untrue. The manifest evidence clearly indicates a dark side to the sunny, Sunday Clinton. The Saturday-night Bill assumes that to err is just an inevitable by-product of the flesh and that to deny it is unrealistic and not mentally healthy.

This division of Clinton's personality makes him hard to comprehend. He can be generous and warm one moment, withholding and angry the next. He can be insightful and accepting one day, petulant and accusatory the next. He is enigmatic. At times lately, his dark side seems to overshadow the goodness within him and take over more and more of his soul. The wall of denial he maintains permits no aeration of his private failings and, hence, no cure. Combined with the isolation of the presidency and the sycophancy of his aides and closest advisers, he rarely has to confront his unattractive and generally hidden side. Clinton noir lets in no sunshine and stays locked in the bosom of his psyche—unrepentant, unreformed, and even unrecognized by the daylight Clinton.

Saturday-night Bill has the nervous system of a shark, dividing everyone he meets into two categories—edible and inedible—depending on whether the person meets one of his needs or does not. As a consequence of this unique dichotomy, Saturday-night Bill lives in one of only two alternative states of being: caught or not caught. He avoids the former at all costs and seeks the latter by any means necessary.

Saturday-night Bill maintains an up-to-date mental inventory of who might have compromising information about him. He always works hard at staying on the good side of anyone who does, so that they won't turn on him by telling what they know. Clinton's frantic efforts to get Monica Lewinsky a job and stay in her good graces as she was called to testify at the Paula Jones deposition seem to have been just a continuation of Clinton's normal pattern of behavior.

Clinton's political career has been marked by incredible highs and unbelievable lows as the heedlessness of his private risk-taking has led him into trouble over and over again. The alternation between victory and defeat—between vindication and ominous threat—stems from the duality of Clinton's persona. Now we are driven to ask if he will be one of two men to be forced from the presidency or if he will be well remembered by history for his many achievements.

The possibilities of exceptional triumph and inconceivable disaster have both seemed quite real from the moment he first held public office in Arkansas.

In 1994 the president and the First Lady invited a hundred guests to dine and to watch the Paul Newman movie *The Hudsucker Proxy.* My wife, Eileen McGann, and I sat behind the First Couple, Newman, and Joanne Woodward in the White House theater, watching the movie's hero rise from the mail room to the head of his corporation, fall back down again, and then rise once more. As the president left the auditorium afterwards, he joked to me, "It sounded like my political career."

I was next to Clinton for much of the up-and-down roller-coaster ride of his political career. I first met him in 1977 when he was a thirty-one-year-old, longhaired, sideburned Arkansas attorney general. We worked together the next year on his successful bid to become the youngest governor in America. Our relationship was interrupted when he fired me in 1979 after I had counseled him not to risk his neck by raising taxes during his first term as governor.

I next heard from the Clintons when Hillary, then of dark hair and thick Coca-Cola eyeglasses, called in a panic a few days before the 1980 election to say that Bill was in trouble and to ask for my help. After reviewing the situation, I told her that it was too late. The tax increase had killed his chances. The day after his defeat, the Clintons hired me to help him regain office.

Clinton won the governorship again in 1982 as he and I developed a decade-long political collaboration. Due to an altercation during his 1990 race for governor, described in this book, I decided not to accept his offer to serve on his 1992 presidential campaign. We remained friendly but distant until Clinton again met disaster, this time losing both houses of Congress to the GOP in 1994.

The president and the First Lady hired me in late 1994 to turn their fortunes around in time for the 1996 presidential election. Until I was toppled by scandal in late August of 1996 during the Democratic National Convention, I had piloted the president's reelection bid.

This book is about the journey of those two years. This new introduction reflects on the disturbing story of the increasing ascendancy of Saturday-night Bill in the battle for Clinton's psyche. The presidency brings out the best in many people. As the rest of this volume indicates, it has catalyzed enormous positive growth in Bill Clinton, obvious to anyone who knows him. But it has also brought out his worst aspects. I have watched the battle between Sunday-morning President Clinton and Saturday-night Bill rage over the years, and I have followed its ebb and flow. At this writing, the presidency clearly belongs to Sunday-morning Clinton. But the man is dominated by Saturday-night Bill.

Friends never know quite how to act around alcoholics or addicts. To join in a conspiracy of silence or a chorus of defense only helps their self-destructive denial to prevent rehabilitation or change. To condemn and expose them seems disloyal, but, ultimately, it is the only way to help protect them from themselves. For too long, Bill Clinton's friends and associates, myself among them, have held their tongues and kept his secrets. We were doing him no favors. Unless this president breaches his inner wall of denial and conquers his dark side, he will destroy his own administration while he tries to hide from himself. His auspicious first six years in office and his inner abilities would make such a fate truly tragic.

After all, the Sunday-morning Clinton is a very good president of the United States. Almost every major problem that America had been facing at the time he took office has been ameliorated materially during his years in office. Consider his achievements:

- The economy is better.
- American competitiveness is way up.
- The gap between the rich and the poor has narrowed.
- Child support collections have significantly increased.
- Crime is down and police forces have grown.
- Teen pregnancy has dropped.
- Drunk driving deaths have dropped.
- Smoking is down.
- Infant mortality is lower.
- NAFTA passed and a global cycle of protectionism has been averted.
- Hospital stays are shorter and medical-cost inflation is lower.
- The budget is balanced.
- Taxes are dropping, particularly for the working poor.
- The minimum wage is higher.
- Much more college scholarship aid is available.
- Headstart programs have more than doubled.
- Child immunization is virtually universal.
- The Brady Law stops thirty thousand felons and fugitives a year from buying guns.
- Assault rifles are banned.
- Prosecutions of teenage gangs are much more extensive.
- Freedom of choice is protected and the abortion pill is en route to approval and use.
- Deportations of illegal aliens have almost tripled.
- Drug use is down.
- New AIDS infections are decreasing rapidly and, thanks to federal research dollars, AIDS deaths have dropped in half.
- Student-loan interest rates and default rates have both dropped substantially.
- Private pensions are much better protected by the government. TV-rating systems and the V-chip have been implemented and more educational television for children is required.
- Family and medical leave has been passed.
- The cleanup of superfund sites has accelerated appreciably.
- Half of all children not previously covered are now covered by health insurance.
- Educational standards and test scores are up.
- The environment is cleaner.
- National parks have been expanded and are much better protected than previously.

xviii   Behind the Oval Office

- Peace has come to Bosnia, Haiti, South Africa, and Cambodia.
- China is more open.
- The situations in Northern Ireland, Iran, and North Korea have improved.

Clinton's is one of the most successful presidencies of our time.

Only in the areas of the global currency crisis, campaign finance reform, nuclear proliferation, Kosovo, containment of Iraq, instability in Russia, and teen smoking and drug-use are the trends disturbing.

Saturday-night Bill must have begun as a playful character, following the ethics and ethos of the '60s, when sex was abundant, unrestricted, and uncensored. The only sin apparent to the Me Generation was to leave needs unfulfilled or any life experience untried. In this atmosphere, Saturday-night Bill must have merely been the happy-go-lucky, off-duty soulmate of his self-righteous alter ego.

In the White House sat Sunday-morning Clinton's inspiration, role model, and hero, President John Fitzgerald Kennedy. As Saturday-night Bill came of age, he doubtless had heard the stories about Kennedy's sexual life with Marilyn Monroe, a mobster's girlfriend, and a host of others. Saturday-night Bill must have concluded that these sexual perks came as a side benefit to a life of public service and sacrifice.

His identification with JFK was particularly evident to me in 1995 when Clinton returned from a President's Day interview with the media where he was asked, "If you could ask your idol, John Kennedy, one question and only one question, what would it be?"

"I'd want to ask him, you know, how did you do it?" Clinton jokingly confided. "How did you get away with it? But I couldn't say that, so instead I said I'd ask what it was like to be president before Americans got alienated from their government."

When Clinton entered the national stage, with its intrusive press corps, Saturday-night Bill learned the increasing importance of lying to all concerned, all the time. Rather than reevaluate his Saturday-night side, Clinton just buried it further underground and developed his skills of camouflage and concealment into an art form.

Sunday-morning Clinton felt no hypocrisy in marrying Hillary Rodham. Indeed, he probably saw marrying for brains as a notch above marrying for glamour as Kennedy had done. It mimicked more closely the behavior of his other role model, FDR, who betrothed to Eleanor but tarried with Lucy Mercer.

One wonders if Hillary understood all along that while she was married to Sunday-morning Clinton she was at least an inadvertent in-law of Saturday-night Bill. If Clinton's sexual conduct was shrouded from her view, she had to have at least known of it by the time talk of his infidelities became commonplace in the late '80s in Arkansas.

But the high ground Hillary might otherwise have held in the marriage was compromised by her own vulnerabilities. Raised in a middle-class Illinois home, Hillary found herself living in a small state, married to a husband who was paid a constitutionally set ceiling of $35,000 as governor. She resented the financial sacrifice. She was never greedy, but she did feel that she lacked financial security, a fear which loomed larger as she became a mother. She became deeply involved in questionable transactions on the futures market and has been accused of possible illegal activity on behalf of the Madison Guaranty Savings and Loan Association. Her handling of the family investment in Whitewater has been investigated for years.

By the time Saturday-night Bill's escapades had begun to cause political damage, she and he had developed their matching set of his-and-hers potential scandals. From that, there developed a mutual pattern of enabling and concealment between the Clintons. Neither asked the other probing questions or sought real answers. Each looked the other way. As long as Clinton attested to his wife's financial integrity, she would attest to his fidelity. They both brushed aside inconvenient facts and damaging evidence. On this shaky foundation, their marriage and careers thrived.

As Americans learn of the financial and legal shenanigans of the Clintons during the Arkansas years, they need to remember the permissive environment within which it happened. The newspapers in Arkansas were notoriously lax in their scrutiny of public figures and the TV stations were even less vigilant. All the investigative agencies were controlled by the Democratic political machine and there was nobody to blow the whistle if there was reason to do so. What would have been impossible to get away with in other states was the norm in the one-party system of Clinton's Arkansas in the '80s.

Within this opaque cocoon, the Clintons learned how far they could go and still get away with it. If Saturday-night Bill used this protective layer of insulation from scrutiny to shelter his sexual promiscuity, Hillary used it to make the money she felt she needed for her family's future.

While the Clintons' marriage has always appeared to me to be much more than a mere a business relationship, its subtext clearly requires sharing the power they attain through their joint efforts. Throughout their lives, power has flowed back and forth between Bill and Hillary. When Clinton began his political odyssey they were a typical two-career couple, meeting at night over dinner and pleasantly exchanging stories of the day, swapping advice and counsel. Politics was Bill's career and law was Hillary's.

Once Bill lost the governorship in the surprise upset of 1980, after only two years in office, Hillary realized she had to move in and take over the management of her husband's career. Out of office, down on his luck, facing political oblivion, Bill turned to Hillary for rescue.

She seemed to maintain a loving attitude toward her husband's political shortcomings. "Bill is just too nice and too decent for his own good," she would explain. "He thinks everybody means what they say and says what they mean and he can't get used to the fact that this isn't true. It just isn't true." She was the realist, anxious to go on the attack and to rain down negatives on her husband's opponents.

When Clinton regained the governorship in 1982, Hillary did return to her own career, but also remained closely involved with her husband's. She had helped him win back the state House and was determined to acquire political power as a reward. She used it well, designing an extraordinary program of educational reform which included increased teacher pay and higher school standards. She had the dominant voice in her husband's political councils, playing the same active role in the state House as she later did in the White House.

By the mid-'80s, Saturday-night Bill began to chafe under Hillary's domination. The leash was too tight around his neck. Hillary's surrogate Bill-watcher, chief of staff Betsey Wright, had alienated him, perhaps by pulling him out of too many bedrooms or possibly because she had confronted him too directly about the threat that Saturday-night Bill posed to his career. He kicked her upstairs by making her Arkansas state party chairman and installed a compliant staff in her place.

Hillary found herself increasingly shut out of her husband's political life. She began to spend more time at the Rose Law Firm. No longer did she attend the morning strategy sessions, but would leave early for work, pausing only briefly at the foot of the stairs in the Governor's Mansion to bid everyone a cheery adieu.

Hillary came back to power during the 1992 presidential race when Gennifer Flowers announced that she had conducted a twelve-year affair with Clinton. Saturday-night Bill was unmasked and introduced to America. It almost destroyed the campaign, but Hillary came to the rescue. Standing by her man in the pivotal *60 Minutes* television interview, Hillary vouched for Bill. The nation shrugged as if to say, "If she forgives him, why shouldn't we?"

Having rescued her husband from political oblivion for the second time, Hillary stuck around to enjoy her new power. Grateful for her help, Clinton gave Hillary a huge role in the new White House.

Unfortunately, she showed surprisingly terrible judgment. Virtually every appointee that Hillary pushed got into trouble. Guinier, Kennedy, Hubbell, Foster, Nussbaum, Livingstone, and Magaziner were each in turn discredited and forced out.

Her foray into healthcare reform failed. She was insistent on secrecy in her task force's deliberations as they developed the proposal; her critics demanded more openness. At first they issued press releases. Then they sued in court and eventually won with a stinging reprimand from a federal judge against Hillary's conduct of the task force. When Hillary finally did unearth her healthcare package, it sank, inch by agonizing inch, into the mud at the bottom of the congressional pond and with it went her reputation.

When Hillary's financial and legal transactions from the Arkansas years were called into question, she was forced onto the defensive.

As Republican sharks closed in, the Clintons erected a wall to protect Hillary from partisan bricks and stones, surrounding themselves with a staff having special skills in handling opposition attacks. When a charge was leveled against the Clintons, the instant-response team would swing into action, denying the accusation, attacking the accusers, and spinning the exchange to the president's and First Lady's benefit.

This protective wall sheltered Hillary, but it also provided the ideal hiding place for Saturday-night Bill.

Crucial to this protective wall was the "secret police," private detectives hired to protect both Hillary and Saturday-night Bill. The secret police quietly made their first entry into Clinton's life, according to published sources, when detectives helped dig up dirt on Clinton's opponent in the 1990 race for governor, Sheffield Nelson. In the same year, newspaper accounts suggest that the Clinton campaign hired private detective Terry Lenzner to investigate then New York state governor Mario Cuomo, the favorite for the Democratic presidential nomination two years hence.

The secret police came out in full force during the 1992 presidential campaign. The *Washington Post* reported in early 1992 that Betsey Wright had used federal campaign funds to engage the services of San

Francisco private detective Jack Palladino to investigate women who were rumored to have been involved sexually with Clinton and to discredit their stories. Reportedly, detectives led by Lenzner continued to use these tactics to discourage women from testifying accurately in the Paula Jones sexual harassment lawsuit.

There is even some evidence of possible physical intimidation to terrify women so that they would keep their own counsel. Kathleen Willey, who reluctantly accused President Clinton of groping her in the Oval Office, reported that her cat was kidnapped and the tires of her car were slashed. She said that a few days later, while jogging, a man ran up beside her, referred to her cat, and implied that her children might be in danger.

A former Miss America, in an interview with the *New York Post,* tells a similar story. She relates how Clinton aide Mickey Kantor met with her theatrical agent and helped arrange bookings for her in return for a statement, which she later recanted, denying a sexual relationship with Clinton. When she and her husband were on vacation she says that men in suits broke into their room and ransacked it, but didn't take the $2,000 in cash or the expensive watch that were on the bureau. She suspects they were looking for tapes that they thought she might have made describing her sexual encounter with Clinton.

These tactics and others remind one of the tactics of Segretti and McCord during the Nixon era. The secret police, like the plumbers of the '70s before them, cater to the worst in their boss, enabling his defects to shape his behavior in such a way as to lead to his self-destruction. Would Saturday-night Bill have felt as free to roam if the secret police were not there to clean up after him?

Saturday-night Bill had at last found a safe haven. Having emerged victorious after the Gennifer Flowers scandal, he had survived his first brush with public exposure. Saturday-night Bill began to take greater risks. The Sunday-morning Clinton could no longer subdue him by warning that his conduct would bring them down. Flowers had made her charges, which Clinton later partially admitted to be true, and Saturday-night Bill had overcome them with the help of his new friends and staff.

Now he could prowl as he wished from his Oval Office lair. With limitless opportunities for sex close at hand, protected by a bodyguard of press aides to counter bad publicity and detectives to dig up dirt on women who got out of line, Saturday-night Bill felt safe. He had found his niche.

As I entered the White House to renew my relationship with Clinton in 1994 after four years at a distance, I was shocked by the changes that had taken place in the man I thought I had known so well in the '80s. I had trouble recognizing him.

The affable extrovert of the '80s had become a sullen, withdrawn introvert. Instead of talking his decisions out in public, he seemed to withdraw into himself to come to his conclusions. Paranoia had replaced openness, as if the process of being president had beaten out of him his normally gregarious nature. Clinton had learned to run the White House silently. He had become a master at management by indirection.

Clinton had been so burned by his openness and loquacity in the first two years in the White House that he had learned to play his cards close to his vest. By 1995 there were no more staff bull sessions where he and the group he called, contemptuously, "the children who helped me get elected" would kick around ideas. A strict hierarchical chain of command was in place with Chief of Staff Leon Panetta at the top. Spontaneity had vanished and discipline had taken its place. Leaks to the press were cut off and the president achieved a separation from his staff.

Clinton had developed a new style of management. He rarely told anyone what to do. He almost never gave direct instructions or orders. Instead, he surrounded himself with able, smart people whom he knew intimately. With his unbelievably acute powers of observation, his radar-like sensitivity to the moods and thoughts of others, he knew well how each of his key staff people would respond to any situation.

All he had to do was drop the right hint to the right person and he knew exactly how they would fill in the blanks. If they succeeded he could make their efforts his own. If they floundered he could distance himself by denying that he ever instructed them to do anything like that in the first place. Without clear verbal or written instructions, he could not be quoted or, if things screwed up, blamed.

For example, he knew that his deputy chief of staff, Harold Ickes, would move heaven and earth to raise money for his candidacy for reelection. All he needed to do was drop the hint and leave it in Harold's lap. Did he realize that Harold might cut corners? How could he not? But did he tell him to? Likely not. Clinton didn't want to know how Harold was raising the money, just as long as he raised it.

He realized that George Stephanopoulos would spin the press. He need never give an instruction, only hint at his concerns and George would do the rest. Chief of Staff Leon Panetta could be depended upon to smooth relations with the Democratic congressional barons. I would suggest centrist policies, poll all of Clinton's options at each turn, and use my Republican ties to help the president. We each had our roles and he knew how to push our buttons perfectly.

He is a bit like a Freudian psychiatrist whose blank face and silence lead his patients to project onto him their own neuroses. One patient finds the doctor consumed with envy, another believes he is coming on to her sexually, a third thinks he's aggressively hostile. The psychiatrist is, in fact, none of these things. He just lets the patient project onto him his own feelings.

At the time I worked for Clinton, I wondered if the modern presidency forces its occupants to behave as self-protectively as Clinton does. Do the scrutiny, the pressure, and the looming presence of special prosecutors all combine to inhibit presidential free speech? Do we force presidents to be introverts, keeping their own counsel lest their inner thoughts leak or are revealed to a grand jury?

But with the hindsight of recent revelations about the president's private life, it is clear that this strategy of management by indirection, passivity, and silence protected not only the president but Saturday-night Bill as well. Shrouded in privacy, sheltered from his staff, he could fulfill the dictates of his darker side without adequate check. He could distance himself from any damaging acts of his aides and yet profit if they succeeded. It was not that this style of leadership had been forced on the institution of the presidency, but rather that this president had voluntarily chosen it because it suited the convenience of Saturday-night Bill.

On a deeper plane, it became clear that denial had taken root at the heart of Clinton's persona. In the '80s he had been a fair judge of himself, ready to take blame when appropriate or credit when deserved. Only when directly confronted with accounts of Saturday-night Bill's sexual escapades did he resort to obfuscation and denial. But when I met Clinton again as president, in 1994, he was constantly trying to escape blame for anything. Denial spread into a ubiquitous pattern where everything that went wrong was somebody else's fault. Never his.

Why did he snap at that reporter on the train going to the Democratic Convention in 1996? "Of course I snapped at her," he explained to me. "Every time I get a free minute somebody is sticking a microphone in my face. I can't think. I can't rest. They let anybody in here to talk to me who wants to. It's a wonder I didn't snap at more of them."

Why did he screw up in a Houston speech in 1995 and say that he thought that he had raised taxes too much in 1993, a remark which drove the Democrats, who were defeated for backing the tax increase, up the wall? "What do you expect," he told me, "when they over-schedule me like that? Make me stay up 'til midnight one night and get up at six the next morning and I'll screw up every time. Every single time. Anybody would. But do they learn? No. They just keep on scheduling me until I crack like I did in Houston." But we both knew full well, even as he spoke, that it was usually at his insistence that his staff added extra events to his schedule.

Why didn't he move to the political center earlier? Again the staff was at fault. "Every time I get up there to speak, they put this liberal stuff in front of me. I try to balance it, but it's hard to do it right up there on your feet."

Why did the *New York Times* editorial board criticize him so frequently? Not because he deserved it, he explained to me carefully, but "because Hal Raines [the editor] resents me. Unlike him, I'm a southerner who didn't have to move north to make good."

Why was the press so frequently critical of him and Hillary? "They resent us because we are the same age as they are, we're all baby boomers, and they're just jealous and envious."

Why was General Colin Powell riding so high in late 1995? Because the press "is a bunch of guilty white liberals who want to make him president, so they won't ask him the kind of tough questions I get asked all the time."

Most incredible was his explanation of why he chose to push his proposal to let gays serve in the military so soon after he took office. "Bob Dole forced me to do it," he explained. I still wonder what he meant by that.

The essence of his new style was denial of responsibility through management by indirection and denial of fault through blaming others.

Sheltered behind denial, Saturday-night Bill came to dominate Clinton's personality. Denial is, of course, the prerequisite of irresponsible personal conduct. If the left hand knows what the right hand is doing, it usually intervenes and stops it. Only by pretending that things are not happening, even though they are, will the conscience let them proceed.

Taking his cue from Clinton's insistence on distance between himself and his staff, Deputy Chief of Staff Erskine Bowles rearranged the president's schedule so that Clinton had lots of free, unstructured office time every afternoon. His official day usually ended at 2:00 P.M., giving him time for phone calls, reading, or thinking until his evening schedule kicked in at 6:00. Inadvertently, Bowles, an upstanding man of great integrity, had freed Clinton from not only some of the demands of the job, but from some of its discipline as well. This liberty gave Saturday-night Bill full opportunity to get into trouble.

At the very moment in late 1995 that Clinton's entire political career hung in the balance, he apparently began his relationship with Monica Lewinsky. The Sunday-morning president was standing up to the Contract With America, battling against legislation that would have sharply cut environmental protection, eviscerated Medicare and Medicaid, and ended any real federal role in education. But Saturday-night Bill was endangering it all for illicit sex in the Oval Office. As Clinton inched up in the polls, and as his strongest performance in office helped him recapture the political viability he had lost the year before, his Saturday-night side was risking it all.

I can only imagine the struggle, the daily and hourly battle, that must rage within Clinton's mind as Saturday-night Bill fights the constraints that Sunday-morning Clinton would impose. It must be like an alcoholic trying to stay on the wagon or a drug addict wanting to go drug-free. Moral condemnation is not the appropriate response; empathy and compassion are. Saturday-night Bill likely acts out to quench the raging fires of his compulsion, not to seek joy or pleasure.

Most Americans may be inclined to forgive the sex on a personal level, but it is harder to forgive the lying and deception which accompany it and harder still to forgive the intimidation and discrediting of innocent witnesses who inadvertently stray into harm's way.

Where does Saturday-night Bill come from? I'm no psychologist, but from my observations, certain aspects of his behavior and personality may offer a clue.

I believe that Saturday-night Bill's roots go to Clinton's basic lack of self-sufficiency as a person. While many people tap into an internal energy source, often spiritual, Clinton derives his stimulation only externally, from his environment. In this respect, he is more like a roadside reflector than a car's headlight. Unable to provide his own energy, he reflects the lights of oncoming vehicles offering illumination only so long as he basks in their glow. In the warm rays of a crowd, or even in the dangerous heat of political combat, he is empowered and shines. But when alone in a dark room, he is like a cold lump of metal with neither glow nor warmth.

As a result, he craves stimulation. He cannot stand his own emptiness when left in solitude. He lives from high to high. Like a chimpanzee swinging from branch to branch, he goes from one stimulus to the next, desperately needy. It is as if he can only be truly alive when reacting to outside stimulation.

He has, of course, chosen a career which provides almost as much stimulus as a person could ever want. From adoring crowds to dangerous press conferences to sensitive diplomatic missions to high-stakes legislative gambles, there is so much in politics to keep the blood flowing, the nerves tingling, and the senses alert and ready. Boredom is normally not one of its risks.

But sometimes, even for a president, the band stops playing. At night the crowds go home, the press leaves, and the White House is empty. Many times I have seen him stay up late into the night playing solitaire, mechanically shuffling the cards as his mind goes blank.

Mood swings come upon Clinton frequently. Far from the affable, kinetic figure he shows in public, he is most often morose in private. When deprived of stimulation, Clinton turns dour, surly, sullen, mopey, and aloof. Doubtless, he dislikes himself in these unattractive moods as much as do those around him.

In private he is often distracted, working on a crossword puzzle or doodling during a meeting. Eye contact is so rare that if he looks up and looks at you, you notice it. In meetings he will often sit quietly for half an hour, deep within himself, seemingly disconnected from the discussion swirling around him.

On the phone at night, when he speaks to those who know him well, he rarely wants to chat and never exchanges civilities. He never asks after your health or your family. He answers the phone, typically, with a laconic and peremptory "yes!" which invites no intimacy. The only emotion he regularly shows is anger.

Even reading offers Clinton no real companionship. He attacks books, rather than curling up with them. He turns the pages as fast as he can, skimming with remarkable energy and seeming to suck the contents out of the volume. Rather than savor the language or the writer's style or irony, he treats these trappings as a waste of his time as he plunges into the book to extract the meat and move on. He doesn't watch TV, rarely listens to music, only occasionally follows sports, and watches movies only at staged White House events. He has no hobbies other than golf. And you can't golf at night.

Perhaps illicit sex might seem to him as exciting as an adoring crowd, its danger as energizing as political combat. Possibly he finds there the stimulation necessary to get his system functioning again, to feel truly alive. Warm-blooded animals carry within them the ability to adjust their body temperatures, but cold-blooded creatures need outside warmth from the sun to keep them warm inside. Does Clinton require outside radiance before he can shine within?

This sullen and silent behavior of the private Clinton likely deadens his relationship with Hillary as well. While she appears to be genuinely in love with him, even dependent upon him emotionally, she's married to a maddeningly remote and elusive man. Clinton's difficulties in expressing, or even feeling, emotion make him a hard man to love. Rather than affection, he uses elusiveness and the denial of either thanks or praise as tools to get the most from others. He is rarely grateful or emotive with anyone, and I suspect he is not with Hillary either. In all my private moments with the Clintons, the ones beyond the ears or eyes of even a small group, I have very rarely, if ever, seen him express emotion or love toward Hillary. The handholding and hugging are for public display. Hillary is not cold, remote, or, as some have suggested, gay. It's Bill who frosts the relationship over.

But if Clinton is not faithful to Hillary, he is loyal. He never blames Hillary for anything and always defends her. But from the way he talks about her, you wouldn't know they were married.

His private aloofness toward her is chilling. Eileen and I attended a White House dinner and movie on the day that the story of Hillary's winnings in the futures market was first reported in the *New York Times*. Although they sat next to each other throughout the movie, they did not exchange a glance or even a word. Each stared straight ahead as if they were strangers.

Earlier, during dinner, the president had taken me aside and inquired anxiously, "What are we going to do about Hillary?" From his tone, it was as if she were a crisis and a threat to his future, not a wife about whom he cared deeply.

In early 1996 Clinton was enraged by a derogatory comment that *New York Times*' columnist Bill Saffire had made about Hillary. Asked for his reaction at a press conference, Clinton lost it and said that he wanted to punch Saffire in the nose. I noted a drop in his ratings. Concerned, I mentioned to him that his strong defense of his wife seemed to make her problems into his problems.

"You're the one on the ballot," I reminded him, cautioning against using his own reputation to defend hers. Somewhat callously, I advised him to stop using the pronoun "we" in responding to questions about allegations against Hillary. "Just say 'she,'" I advised.

The president didn't say anything, but I never heard him speak of "we" again in public.

Each week, in my polling, I would ask voters who was more responsible for the scandals of the Clinton administration—Bill or Hillary? Back then, before Saturday-night Bill's sex scandals dominated the environment, voters always answered that she was more at fault than he was. I would report these numbers to Clinton each week and note with alarm any slippage in his rating or any gain in hers. He never told me to stop and always treated the data objectively. As long as the public didn't blame him, Hillary's scandals, while unfortunate, were her problem.

The fact is that Hillary is almost totally dependent on her husband for political power. When he is going strong politically, her lack of power—or, one suspects, even access—is pathetic.

During much of 1995 and 1996, Hillary had little visible role in the reelection campaign. Despite press leaks that she was in charge, she never participated openly in any of the major decisions before the summer of 1996. But what was the story behind closed doors? I wondered.

In the summer of 1995 I realized how little power Hillary really had when her husband chose not to give her any. She began to call to urge me to support the appointment of her dear friend Ann Lewis to the post of White House communications director. I was horrified. Liberal Massachusetts congressman Barney Frank's sister as communications director in a White House that needed to move to the center?

At Hillary's urging, I met with Lewis—at a group meeting of Hillary and her staff—and found her innocuous enough. She was not the crusading liberal I had feared, but neither was she the last word in creative thinking. I ended up fashioning a compromise which permitted my friend and ally Don Baer to serve as communications director in the White House while Lewis occupied a similar, less important post in the campaign. Baer served with great distinction. Lewis did no harm.

But what shocked me was that Hillary couldn't get Lewis appointed on her own. She called me six or eight times to push for Ann's appointment, lobbying at every opportunity. She felt grateful for Lewis's support during the Whitewater hearings and was concerned that her good friend was losing her job at Planned Parenthood in a staff shakeup. But she couldn't get her appointed without coming to me! Her husband was president, but she was calling me to talk to him for her!

This experience gave me a different understanding of the role that Hillary plays in her husband's life. Their marriage, too, must have its Sunday-morning and Saturday-night phases.

The Sunday-morning marriage is based on their shared and genuine commitment to progressive values. Their relationship has always been a partnership that promoted human decency, opportunity for children, compassion for the poor, and help for average people. They are sincere in their dedication to their ideals and always have been. One can picture the two idealistic kids meeting at Yale and carrying their convictions with them throughout life.

But there is also a Saturday-night side of mutual enabling. Like the moon, Hillary only shines or—one suspects—receives affection, when her husband is most luminous. She seems most brilliant when Saturday-night Bill has strayed, gotten caught, and needs his wife to rescue him before an irate public. Then, when he needs her to stand by him, this self-involved man gives her what she can't get at other times. Does Hillary, at some level, want to enable the Saturday-night Bill to prowl so that he will need her, reach out to her, give her affection, and accord her power? Does Saturday-night Bill know this and see it as a way to act out without getting hurt? Do the two of them perpetuate a destructive cycle to feed their own needs?

All of this is not to say that Hillary is, in the least, anesthetized to Saturday-night Bill's adultery. In 1992 I had a brief insight into the pain that public disclosure must bring her when I spoke with Clinton about their television appearance on *60 Minutes*, where he and Hillary fought back against the accusations of Gennifer Flowers. I suggested to Clinton that he admit on the program that he had not always been faithful, apologize to Hillary, and say that he felt remorse and was trying as hard as he could to become a better husband and father.

I said he should add that "Franklin Roosevelt was not always faithful to his wife, Dwight Eisenhower was not always faithful to his wife, John Kennedy was not always faithful to his wife, and Lyndon Johnson was not always faithful to his wife." Then I said that he should go on to express the hope that "his past sins would no more interfere with his ability to serve the nation than it had interfered with these other great presidents'."

His answer spoke volumes. "That's a good line, but if I said it I'd have to find a new place to live." Clearly, Hillary was not ready to accept a public admission of his infidelities and, perhaps he did not feel able to tell her the truth.

I saw more of the pain that Saturday-night Bill caused Hillary in 1995, when the David Maraniss biography of Clinton was published. Its scandalous highlight was the admission attributed to Betsey Wright that Clinton had used Arkansas state troopers to procure women. The president was in obvious rage and pain as he spoke with me about the book. I suggested various steps to defuse its potential for political damage, but these did not do much to ease his concern. He told me that Hillary was furious. As he went on about the personal difficulties the story was causing him, I came to realize that it was his marital situation, more than his political health, that was concerning him.

We got Betsey to issue a vague denial and Clinton intervened in the baseball strike to distract public attention. He didn't do much to settle the strike, but he did blunt the coverage of the trooper story. Yet Clinton continued to raise the issue long afterwards. I gathered that the book caused a uniquely personal pain in his relationship with Hillary, perhaps because Hillary trusted Betsey and would tend to believe her story.

The president never spoke of his chagrin that he had done things to bring pain to Hillary, he just railed against his misfortune at its coming out. Nowhere was there any contrition for the adultery—just a furious rage that the world was making trouble for him in his marriage.

What is clear and tragic is that the Sunday-morning president is losing his battle with Saturday-night Bill. Introversion, pragmatism, denial, indirection, dissembling and enabling become more and more the modus operandi of the Clinton presidency. The powers and pressures of the presidency have unleashed a side of Clinton that was always there but rarely important. What had been a sidelight in an attractive public figure has become the central and deadly flaw in his character—the defect around which everything else orbits.

Henry Kissinger recounts in his memoirs how much the process of wiretapping his aides and unfriendly reporters came to consume his time. Unable to trust a secretary with the task of reviewing the tapes from his secret wiretaps, he had to listen to them personally. Before long he was spending most of his day listening to the mundane and trivial conversations that had been intercepted.

The sheer magnitude of the task of protecting Clinton's presidency from the ravages of Saturday-night Bill is devouring his administration. To permit Saturday-night Bill to do as he pleases, everyone in the White House must now work to shield his behavior from discovery and scrutiny. It is far more the Saturday-night Bill than the Sunday-morning president who today lives at 1600 Pennsylvania Avenue.

Can Bill Clinton change? Yes. Anybody can if they but first acknowledge that they have absolutely no choice. But can Clinton overcome the denial, secrecy, and self-justification that have surrounded his lifelong misbehavior like a protective, enabling cocoon? Can he avoid believing in the false, siren songs of his lawyers and staff who would offer obfuscation, distraction, and deceit as alternatives to real self-examination and reform? And can Hillary recognize her own failure to break the cycle of sin/apology/reconciliation/relapse which has characterized xxxii   Behind the Oval Office

their years together? Can she change her own attitudes so that they facilitate his reform rather than just enable him to repeat the pattern again?

The history of the American presidency is replete with administrations in which the dark side of the president took over. We have watched Hoover's isolation amid the depression, Johnson's self-pity as Vietnam entrapped him, and Nixon's paranoia as his enemies closed in. The growth of Clinton noir threatens to join these lamentable examples. But in each of these other three models of failure, an outside circumstance—like an economic depression or a foreign war—impelled the negative turn in the president's attitude. Even in Nixon's case, the burglary at the heart of Watergate was executed, and presumably planned, by others. But for Clinton it is the enemy within that eats away at his presidency like the cancer of which John Dean warned Nixon. It is the Saturday-night Bill who threatens to consume the Sunday-morning president.

Unfortunately, in the short run, Saturday-night Bill's escapades will obscure from view the brighter sides of Sunday-morning Clinton's legacy. Undoubtedly, the archaeology of history will, in time, dig beneath the scandals and retrieve his record of achievement for the American people. What he has done to help the United States and its citizens is too sweeping and too profound to remain buried for all time.

He should not and will not be removed from office for his Saturday-night side. America will not tolerate the removal of a president for purely personal conduct, no matter how laden with subsequent and resulting perjury, obstruction of justice, or witness tampering. Only evidence of intimidation of innocent people by Clinton's secret police has the power to force him from office. If no further evidence emerges, Bill Clinton will likely serve out his term and go on to a retirement where he faces his demons, most likely alone.

The same public that lets him serve in office without demanding that he change assures that he never will change and that he will dwell forever in the private hell of compulsive and self-destructive behavior. This fate, not his shame or the threats that hover over his administration, is his true punishment.

As Frank Harris, Oscar Wilde's biographer and best friend, wrote of Wilde in 1916, "If a man yields habitually to a weakness, he will one day go much further than he ever intended and be punished much more than he ever deserved."

Preface

This is a report of an overwhelming experience, two years working with President Clinton as he struggled to save his presidency and win the support of the American people for a second term. But it is also the story of how a presidential campaign operates in the nineties and how a new moderate consensus has formed in America.

The center of the narrative is Bill Clinton himself—who he is, what drives this complex man, how his thinking works, and what we can expect of him. Reelected, vindicated, omnipresent, he is still largely unknown. His attractive face and compelling cadences, his intellect and his vision, invite our curiosity. I believe he regained his power by finding his true voice. As readers know more about the man, I hope they will observe Clinton's manifest passion to do well for the country, a passion that many politicians share, despite all the charges of cynicism made against them.

▲

I consider Bill Clinton a good friend. Our intense mercurial relationship in the din of battle during the last two years is the climax of twenty years of working together in election campaigns. We share a mutual passion for politics, for staying up late at night talking about issues, writing ads, deconstructing opinion polls, arguing, and dreaming. The difference is, of course, that he was elected by the people and I was a hired hand.

Strategic advisers, pollsters, and advertising and public-relations specialists are part of the modern electoral process. Some find this distasteful, suspecting a manipulation of the democratic process by "spin doctors." I was not a spin doctor—I was concerned with policy in ways I will describe—and I hope my description of the process advances public discussion and removes some of the confusion. The strategies that helped Bill Clinton were not just tactical moves on a chessboard. They reflected key conclusions about what America wants. The move to the center—triangulation—articulated a deeper and broader consensus in America than we have seen for decades. No matter who runs for office in the future or where events take us, this new consensus will continually reassert its domination of our politics. I try to explain how it arose and what it means for the future of our country.

It has been suggested that I decided to write this book only in the wake of my resignation. This is not true. I had always intended to write after the end of the 1996 campaign. The scandal precipitated my resignation, but not my resolve to describe my experiences. There is nothing exceptional in a participant writing about government or a presidential campaign. A long tradition of accountability has led very many political figures to write their memoirs soon after leaving office. Others will certainly follow me and give their perspective on the first term of the Clinton presidency. In telling this story, I should make it clear that I have had no access to classified information and have violated no government restrictions. I have reconstructed conversations from memory. When in doubt about specific language, I have paraphrased.

The president knows about this book. In August he reasonably asked that I wait to write it until after the election. He said then, "I realize that our relationship is a subject of legitimate historical interest. It's probably unique in American history." After my resignation, we spoke again and he reaffirmed our understanding; he said he was looking forward to reading what I wrote.

In this book, I acknowledge political misjudgments in my career, as well as my grave lapse of moral standards. All my well-known mistakes are real. But no one is merely the sum of her or his mistakes. My desire for political progress is as genuine as my love of politics. It is more than a game to me. Everything else I have ever written was a speech, an ad, a memo, a tract—all text with a mission to convert, a goal to persuade. This is simply the truth about my role in a series of extraordinary events.

▲

The press has given me much credit for President Clinton's triumph in 1996. It will become obvious throughout this narrative that the mind behind the victory was that of President William Jefferson Clinton.

A Personal Note from the Author

Dear Reader,

I owe my wife, Eileen, President Clinton, Vice President Gore, and my colleagues in the White House a public apology.

I took every manner of security precautions when I joined the president. I discouraged press inquiries. I said nothing to the White House staff about my discussions with the president. I sent my discarded writings to a shredder. I used an alphabet code of names in cellular phone calls (Dole was "P" for pineapple).

But then I talked to a prostitute at night. What was I thinking? I wasn't thinking.

I was in blind denial, out of control, driven by my ego. I could not bring myself to imagine the consequences of what I was doing. To do so would be to admit that I would have to curb my behavior. Anything but that!

Now I have come back to earth without a parachute to break my fall. I am, I suppose, merely the latest example of the Greek aphorism, "Those whom the gods would destroy they first make mad with power." Having won a struggle within the White House to help the president get back on his true course, I felt omnipotent. My downfall occurred in my room at the Jefferson Hotel in June 1995 when I was flush with victory after the president's highly successful balanced-budget speech, for which I felt myself largely responsible in the wake of considerable opposition from the White House.

I cannot excuse my behavior. But perhaps I can explain it and learn from it. Before I took on the commitment to work with President Clinton, I had rarely been away from Eileen for more than one or two nights a week. I sometimes traveled a thousand miles to be with her for a night. I needed her. She is my center of gravity. But, during my months at the Clinton White House, my priority became Bill Clinton. I was away from home almost every night. Doing a good job counted for more than being at home. Plenty of people are away from their loved ones for a long time; in the high-pressure world of official Washington, I was simply not mature enough to handle it. Early in my tenure, she told me that she understood how much was at stake and how hard I had to work. For a while she herself took no new clients in her legal work so she could come to Washington four or five nights a month to be with me. Eileen McGann is an extraordinary woman whom I love and respect. Her sensitivity and intuition made her my best friend as well and my best guide to this strange new Washington world with its bitter rivalries and infighting.

But I could not cope with the inevitable periods of solitude. Walls close in on me when I'm alone. I don't do well. So I sought out, through the most dishonorable kind of relationship, someone to spend the night with me. Foolishly, I trusted this woman and even deluded myself to the point of thinking of her as a friend, though like all men who have paid for sex I am guilty of exploiting the woman involved.

Many of the published recollections of the affair are correct. Some are fanciful. I did not share any state secrets with her. I didn't, in any event, know any. To spare people unnecessary pain, not to justify my conduct, I must correct some of the allegations.

- As I have confirmed under oath, I never said Hillary Clinton was responsible for the administration looking into the FBI files of Republicans. I said that polling data showed that people held Hillary responsible for much of this, but I did not know the facts of the case and still don't. I do not think Hillary was responsible, but to have mentioned the polling data at all was reprehensible.

- I did not let my companion eavesdrop on my conversations with the president on an extension phone. What I did, when I let my inflated ego get the better of me, was to put my phone to her ear for a moment or two so she could hear his voice. I had behaved in a similarly immature way with my brother-in-law and my uncle. It was just a stupid thing to do.

I deeply violated the president's trust in me, as well as Eileen's. Sometimes one has to lose almost everything to gain the beginning of self-knowledge and truly accept responsibility for one's conduct. It may take a lifetime to repair the damage I have done, but I have learned from my fall and I will try.

Sincerely,

Dick Morris

Behind the Oval Office

O n e

The President Calls

"We'll carry Ridgefield, we'll split Ansonia and Derby, but I don't see any way we avoid getting killed in Wilton," the big man with big hands, walrus mustache, and a big voice boomed at me across a battered card table in his storefront campaign headquarters. Outside, the union-printed banner read MALONEY FOR CONGRESS. Inside, Jim Maloney, Democratic candidate from Danbury, in the fifth congressional district of Connecticut, was reviewing his prospects, town by town, on September 14, 1994. The town names blurred for me as I struggled to look interested. My vibrating pager interrupted. The page was from the White House.

In the past two years, I'd spoken with Hillary Rodham Clinton frequently and with the president six or seven times as I presumed on our relationship of nearly seventeen years to offer advice, more often disregarded than followed. I still felt the electric jolt, the wonderful high, the temporary sense of being summoned to a cloud above when one of them returned my call—a few days later—on my pager. But, I hadn't called them. *They* were calling me. The high went higher.

"What number are you calling from?" the nasal voice of the White House operator asked.

I answered.

"What town is that in?" she asked.

Again I answered.

"Is that D-A-N-B-U-R-Y or B-E-R-Y?" she probed, maddeningly denying me the one piece of information I needed: Who the hell was calling me, her or *him*?

Then mechanically, routinely, she said, "Hold for the president."

The *president.* What did he want? Get ready, I coached myself. He hasn't called you in the year since his election. Brace yourself. Remember how smart he is and how strong he comes on. Get up, get up, *get up!* You've got to meet him straight on. Don't let him ride over you.

The people in the storefront faded. My body was there, but my mind walked on a high plain somewhere else, somewhere I longed to be. For one phone call, I was going to be there. A fix, rushing, warming, stimulating, enticing, addicting.

"Hello, how are you?" is not Bill Clinton's style when he needs you; that's only for when he needs to court you. Now he began, "I've got to speak on TV about invading Haiti, what arguments should I use?"

Haiti was not a town in the fourth congressional district of Connecticut. Change focus. My first, silent reaction was, What do I know? I don't know anything about Haiti. Then, a nanosecond later, came the second reaction. This isn't about Haiti; it's about American politics a month before the 1994 election. And you do know elections, so go for it.

In nearly seventeen years with Clinton, I'd learned this: If at this moment you temporized or sounded conditional, he'd never call again. If he met the friction of another idea or the crosscurrent of a different perspective, he'd be back. And did I want him to call back.

Now, on the phone, it seemed in an instant that our old relationship was back. That voice, the tone of that question, the urgency, and the openness rekindled for me more than a decade of memories and experiences.

"You shouldn't invade Haiti at all," I heard myself say. "You're invading the wrong goddamn island," I went on, referring to Cuba. "Racism and isolationism are the two most deadly, poisonous forces in our politics, and by suffering casualties in Haiti, you will be offending them both at once, and you'll never recover."

The president took refuge in idealism and detail, his favorite defense when he wasn't ready to talk about the politics. He ticked off the abuses, the rapes, the killings, the death squads, the midnight raids.

I knew this was a dress rehearsal. It wasn't the real reason, either. I *knew* the real motivation. It was buried in our past together. In 1979, a young, anxious-to-please Governor Bill Clinton acceded to President Jimmy Carter's urgent request that Arkansas agree to take some Cuban refugees from Florida facilities and house them at Fort Chaffee. Carter couldn't afford to lose Florida. He needed to get the Cubans out. But then Carter had reneged on what Clinton believed was a promise to move them out of Arkansas before the 1980 election. "He screwed me," Clinton had told me the following year over dinner at New York's Four Seasons restaurant as he recounted the tale. Clinton partially blamed the refugees for his defeat.

President Clinton didn't need Haitian refugees swarming over our beaches. He knew how refugees could hurt you. A successful U.S. invasion, which would restore democratic rule, would keep the potential refugees at home.

"I know you're afraid of the refugees," I said, "but why would you ever invade an island? Just surround it and blockade it. You could force the Dominicans to let us police their side of the border as a condition for letting goods enter their side of the island."

"We'd starve too many innocent people whom we want to help," he answered. "Besides, I don't think the Dominicans would agree, and our allies wouldn't like it."

I retreated to familiar ground: "Look, I'm no expert on Haiti, but there'll be hell to pay if you incur American casualties in Haiti."

We explored the option of sending troops offshore and then negotiating, a modern version of the gunboat diplomacy Theodore Roosevelt had used with great success in the Caribbean. Clinton had earlier been humiliated when he sent a small, lightly armed force that fled in the face of Haitian attack. Now, I argued, we needed "a massive force a few miles out. Then try diplomacy. When they feel the heat, they'll see the light," I said, recalling a maxim of the late Illinois senator Everett Dirksen.

Silence on the line. Others might have been put off. "What do you think?" or "So?" one might have asked. But I knew Clinton's silences. They meant "I'm working on it. I'll take it to my bed tonight to think about. Go on."

For the speech, I advised him to center his comments much more on the moral outrages against Haitian women and children on the island than on the practical threat of the refugees who might come to the United States if Haiti didn't become democratic. "You've got to get off the refugee issue and onto the human rights and values issues. You look weak when you are trying to stop refugees from flooding us, but you look strong when you are protecting children abroad."

This is a theme I have developed from listening to the American people speak in the political polling I do. I am convinced that the American people want a foreign policy based on *values,* whereas the foreign policy advisers and the NSC (National Security Council) people always want a policy based on *interests.*

The phone call didn't end; it just faded. I heard the president speaking with someone else in the room. Absentmindedly, he remembered I was still talking, and he said into the receiver, "Bye." It reminded me of the time he called from Arkansas late at night and we talked for an hour or so. His replies became less frequent, his words became indistinct, and then silence. He had fallen asleep. All night my line stayed busy and I couldn't make calls. When I picked up the phone, all I heard was snoring. Mischievously, I'd put the receiver to my ear now and then to monitor his snoring. In the morning, my dial tone returned. He had awakened and hung up.

Anyway, Maloney still had to carry Wilton. But I felt intoxicated. I wanted more and more and more. I called Clinton day after day. I left messages. He didn't return the calls, but he could see that I was reaching out. By accepting the invitation implied by the Haiti call, I indicated my availability.

As a political consultant, I was among America's highest paid migrant workers. Like those who follow the harvest, I moved around the country according to a seasonal schedule, this one the schedule of political primaries and elections; I had worked for candidates in forty different states since my start in 1977. Bill Clinton had been my first client and my best one.

Politics has been my whole life. I first worked for a presidential candidate in the fourth grade of elementary school, when I helped elect the president of the student council. His name was Mark Zarro. Capitalizing on the popular TV show of the time, my slogan was naturally THE Z THAT STANDS FOR ZORRO. I love winning, but more compelling for me is the process. Figuring out a campaign strategy is pure pleasure. Like other consultants, I am often called a mercenary, which is fair enough, though I sometimes get involved for free in hometown Connecticut races just because it is fun to help. I have worked for both Democrats and Republicans, which strikes some people as the height of cynicism. I would refute that. I do have political convictions, as will become apparent in this narrative, but I am not an ideologue in search of a candidate. I am happiest when I can put my technical skills at the service of someone I admire, someone who can make a contribution irrespective of party label. And these technical skills are essentially democratic: I am a specialist in figuring out how politicians can advance issues that move voters and win elections. I have, I admit, made mistakes of judgment in accepting assignments, but I was right in believing that Clinton had the highest potential. He has a genuine passion to improve the lot of Americans, and he has the greatest political skills I've ever seen. I was thrilled when he told me in 1987 that he was probably going to run for president the next year. Here was the chance I had waited for, the chance to project on a national level the ideas we had developed together. I sent strategy memos, planned the race, and even drafted his announcement speech. Bill Clinton was my ticket up. But he flinched in 1988. I was depressed for months. Bill Clinton, I concluded, was no ticket to anywhere, he was a dead end, a man without the guts to pull the trigger.

Others beckoned. Republican Congressman Trent Lott of Mississippi asked me to help him win a U.S. Senate seat. Just as Michael Dukakis was winning the Democratic nomination for president that Clinton could have had, Lee Atwater, George Bush's campaign manager, began to call. In 1978, I'd run the campaign for Ed King that succeeded in toppling Dukakis from the Massachusetts governorship in a dramatic upset primary victory. "You're the world's expert on how to defeat Dukakis," Atwater said. "Come work for us." I'd felt Dukakis had been a bad governor. He'd be a worse president. So I joined the Bush campaign in 1988.

At the point I came on board, the Bush people were attacking Dukakis as a liberal big spender and taxer. They accused him of being "soft on defense," an accusation that goaded him to pose in a tank looking ridiculous.

I told Atwater, "Stop running attacks that Dukakis will deny. He'll never agree that he's a big spender or in favor of a weak defense." At the time, Dukakis had a higher favorability rating than Bush. "People will believe him, not you. You'll spend your whole time running around trying to make your charges stick, playing pin the tail on the donkey."

Instead, I suggested the campaign zero in on issues on which Dukakis admitted his disagreement with Bush—the death penalty, for example. "Here he'll stand up and debate you. You won't have to prove he is against capital punishment; you'll just have to show that he's wrong."

Atwater switched his tactics and went on an all-out offensive on crime. The big transforming moment came in the debate with Bush, when Dukakis was asked how he would feel if his wife were raped and murdered. He expressed no shock at the idea and gave a technical response about the death penalty being wrong, which made him appear cold and bureaucratic. It was the beginning of the end for Dukakis.

Throughout the 1988 campaign, I kept Clinton closely posted on my work for Bush and counseled him on the lessons of the campaign. "Dukakis will never answer an attack," I reported. "He won't even run attacks of his own."

Clinton agreed. "I keep telling him to go on the attack, to answer the charges, but he just doesn't get it. He just thinks it's beneath him and the public won't believe the attacks on him. Bullshit they won't believe them. Look at how bad his poll numbers are."

My impatience backfired in 1992. Bill Clinton, the "dead end" I had abandoned, won the Democratic nomination and the presidency. I was not at his side. Initially, I did not believe he was really going to run. Then I didn't think he'd win. When I realized that I should have had more faith in him and that he was, indeed, a serious candidate, it was too late. He had his consultants all set, and it made no sense to try to dislodge them. That was a fight I'd never win. Besides, they had had the courage to bet on Clinton and I hadn't, so they deserved the right to win.

With the generosity of a victor, Clinton never alluded to my having given up on him. "I need you to help me govern," he said when he called me thirty-six hours after he had been elected. "I never would have been president without you," he said graciously. Yet we both knew the truth. I had nothing to do with his winning the presidency; I was involved only with his string of gubernatorial victories. I settled into my seat in the bleachers to watch his presidency, writhing in self-inflicted frustration.

I was hardly in touch with Clinton in the first eighteen months. I watched his health-care program fail so badly it never even made it out of the Senate committee. His poll ratings fell. He seemed to have lost his grip on America.

A good time to call him. A good time to be available again. That fall, like the elusive Rochester in the life of Jane Eyre, Clinton would unpredictably, suddenly flit into and out of my life.

My pager vibrated its summons again in early October 1994, after the success of the Haitian operation. The president: "I want you to do a poll for me. I'm not satisfied that I know how to handle what the Republicans are doing to me. I'm not getting the advice I need."

The Republicans? I was one of them. My candidates in that year's midterm election included Republican Massachusetts governor Bill Weld and Mississippi senator Trent Lott, both seeking a second term, and Don Sundquist of Tennessee and Tom Ridge of Pennsylvania, two Republican gubernatorial candidates.

"Mr. President, that would be a conflict of interest. If you want me to do political work for you, you'll have to ask me after the November election." That's what I didn't say. You don't say no to the president. Besides, I needed the fix too badly. I agreed to do the polling.

All four of my candidates won that November, and I helped them to the end.

▲

From the beginning of our relationship, in 1977, polls have been my common frame of reference with Bill Clinton. We used polling not to determine what positions he would take but to figure out which of the positions he had already taken were the most popular. I would always draw the distinction between deciding on policy and identifying certain issues for emphasis by telling Clinton, "You print the menu of the things you want. Then I'll advise which dish to have for dinner tonight."

In that October 1994 survey, we polled 800 voters distributed across the country in proportion to each state's share of the national vote. It defies logic that interviews with 800 Americans will accurately mirror the opinions of 250 million of their countrymen. But many laws of science seem crazy. The fact is that if you got a phone book of the entire United States, from *a* to *z,* and you pulled out every 312,500th name and interviewed that person, the resulting 800 interviews would accurately reflect—within a margin of error—the opinions of everybody who is listed in the phone book. I've seen it time and again. The final poll results accurately state the final election results. It's eerie. Of course, polls can go wrong:

- Polls give you an accurate sample of the database you choose. But the database had better be right. For example, if you use a phone book, what about unlisted numbers? If you use a list of registered voters, what about new registrants? If you poll by phone, what about people with no phones? You have to make allowances for these and other factors.
- If you ask the wrong question, you get the right answer to the wrong question. One Texas pollster asked, "Have you decided to vote for

candidate X?" Only about half the people who planned to vote for his man actually answered yes. He got the right answer to the wrong question. He would have gotten a more accurate response had he asked, "If the election were held tomorrow and the candidates were X and Y, for whom would you vote?"

I have a lot of faith in polling. But polling shouldn't determine what a political leader does. Much of the time he has to go against what the polls say the people want. But polls can help a leader figure out which arguments will be the most persuasive.

The point of this survey was to read the voters a lengthy list of Clinton accomplishments to find out which would help his case more in the November '94 congressional elections. With all the seats in the House of Representatives and a third of the seats in the Senate at stake, the president had a lot at risk. For the first time, Republicans had "nationalized" their campaigns, running not on local issues, as was customary, but on national themes and issues presented in the Contract with America. Chief among their themes was Clinton as a "liberal" for his support of a health-care overhaul and as a "taxer" for his deficit-reduction tax increase. To counter these effective jabs, Clinton wanted to explain his record to the voters. But which aspect of the record did it make sense to highlight?

The polling technique on which we settled was to read each respondent the accomplishments Clinton felt entitled to claim, asking first whether he or she believed the accomplishment had actually been achieved, then whether Clinton deserved the credit, and finally, whether it made the respondent more likely to vote for the Democratic congressional candidates Clinton was backing.

In our Arkansas days together, Clinton would spend hours reviewing each detail of a questionnaire before we gave it to the interviewers to field. Surely now that he was president, his review would be more cursory. That's what I thought when I took Clinton's call. But after two hours of reviewing each question, I realized that Bill Clinton's need for the micromanagement of polling had not lessened as his responsibilities had increased. He lovingly detailed each of his achievements, citing to the nearest thousand the number of jobs that had been created while he served as president, the amount by which the deficit had been reduced, the number of trade agreements that had been signed, the amount by which the default rate on student loans had dropped and the collection rate on child-support judgments had risen.

And after each accomplishment came the president's plaintive refrain, "of course, nobody knows we did this" or "we'll never get the credit we deserve on this one" or "the newspapers never printed that we got this one done." Aching from what he considered neglect of his record, Clinton needed not only recognition of his achievements, but praise as well. Typically, much of Bill Clinton's self-image comes from the feelings reflected by others around him. In a room, he will instinctively, as if by a canine sense of smell, find anyone who shows reserve toward him, and he will work full time on winning his or her approval and, if possible, affection. My wife, Eileen McGann, for one, is ambivalent about Clinton, and he senses it. She likes him and agrees with his programs, but she resents him for some of the potholes that blemished my relationship with him while he was governor. Each time he calls and Eileen answers or when they meet at a reception, he focuses his six feet two inches of oozing charm on her—though usually with little effect.

America is the ultimate room for Clinton. For him, a poll helps him sense who doesn't like him and why they don't. In the reflected numbers, he sees his shortcomings and his potential, his successes and his failures. For Bill Clinton, positive poll results are not just tools—they are vindication, ratification, and approval—whereas negative poll results are a learning process in which the pain of the rebuff to his self-image forces deep introspection. Intellectually, polls offer Clinton an insight into how people think. He uses polls to adjust not just his thinking on one issue but his frame of reference so that it is always as close to congruent with that of the country as possible.

I was shocked when I read the poll's results. Voters believed that the president had not accomplished much and didn't stand for anything. President Clinton was in deep, deep trouble. I briefed him and Hillary over the phone. The accomplishments of which they were so proud—a smaller budget deficit, more jobs, rising exports—met a solid wall of rejection. Most voters believed they weren't true. Those who agreed they were accurate denied Clinton credit. Those who gave him credit said it had no impact on their likelihood of voting for his candidates in the 1994 congressional election.

The president debated the eight hundred people in my sample with all his skill and effectiveness. "But what do they say when we tell them we've created millions of jobs and cut the deficit for two years in a row? They can't deny that. It's a fact."

"They can, and they do," I answered. "Every day the papers are filled with stories of layoffs or companies closing."

"But those are the big companies," he replied. "It's the small businesses that are creating the jobs, and nobody writes about that."

"Look," I answered, "if you were asking them about the good works we have been doing in Guam, then you could tell them what we've done, and they might believe it. But this is about the economy that's right in front of them. If they don't agree that you've created jobs or they believe you shouldn't get the credit, you'll never convince them otherwise. Never. It's a total waste of money to try."

A lot of politicians believe that if they have enough money, they can persuade voters that anything is true. In Clinton's case, he had the added virtue of having facts on his side. I told him, "Don't confuse me with the facts. You'll never get them to believe you."

Hillary took up my point. "Bill, when I go out and speak about these jobs we say we've created, you can tell they don't believe it," she emphasized. In the Arkansas years, at the end of every discussion, it always fell to Hillary to tell her husband the political facts of life. This apparently hadn't changed.

"But there is good news," I added. My job was to say what could be done, not what couldn't. "They are prepared to believe in your smaller achievements, and these are enough, more than enough, to move their votes back to you."

I elaborated: "They believe you delivered family and medical leave, and they love you for it. They believe you named pro-choice judges to the Court. They buy that you set up direct student lending and that this is lowering rates. The Brady bill, the assault-rifle ban, Americorps—these are what they know you did."

Clinton wasn't interested. "But I *did* create those jobs, and the deficit *is* down. Why won't they believe it? You mean we just have to forget all these things? Just like that?"

"Stop trying to get elected for the right reasons. Just try to get elected," I answered. "The jobs and the deficit news are too new. If it happens for four years, maybe they'll begin to buy it, but now you can't make them believe it's true."

"But it is true."

"So what? Jesus Christ," I said in exasperation, "there is a perfectly good and fine list right here of bite-size achievements that they can and will digest—give you credit for—and that will move up your ratings. Why not embrace them? Why not run on them?"

Hillary joined in. "Bill, these things work. They're important to people. I know the response I get when I talk about them. Dick's right."

This was the beginning of a discussion among the three of us that continued for two years: the importance of incremental achievements. These steps, which I called "bite size," were of enormous magnitude to the individual families of America. Hillary sensed it immediately, but the president was initially too focused on the big scale, more traditional in Washington. He cared deeply about issues like keeping handguns off the street or adding extra police, but he wasn't prepared to put them center stage in his list of achievements. As he became more comfortable with a step-by-step process toward helping people and moved away from the dramatic big program initiatives like health-care reform, he grasped how well these issues could work.

I sometimes thought that Bill Clinton had two mind-sets: the Boy Scout and the politician. In the Boy Scout mode, he sees his own goodness and focuses, with lofty dignity, on doing good in the world. He abstains from practical political calculations. In this mode, he usually wants nothing to do with me or any pragmatic consideration. He feels intensely idealistic emotions, but is often detached from the realities of American politics. He spurns the process and criticizes it. He feels he can rise above it to meet his goals.

During his first term as governor of Arkansas, Clinton wanted to improve the roads in order to keep a campaign pledge and to win favor with highway contractors, who sustain political treasuries in the state. To finance his program, he doubled car-license fees. He honestly couldn't imagine that people would hold it against him. "It's such a small amount of money," he argued, "and why shouldn't the motorists pay for the roads? They're the ones who use them."

While I agreed with him on the merits, I told him my polls suggested that the increase could kill his chances for reelection. He couldn't believe it and even resented my intrusion into the sphere of public policy. So he fired me, alienated by my overstepping my boundaries. I was from the politician world. Now that he was governor, he had no need of such advice.

Less than two years later he lost the election, largely over the license-fee increase. Afterward I heard stories from people who had driven two hours over bad roads to bring their license plates in for renewal, people who had the exact amount in their pocketbooks and jeans but no more. When they got to the Department of Motor Vehicles and were charged twice their usual fee, many of them had to drive back home, get more money, and drive back again. This gave them approximately six hours in which to decide how much they hated this boy governor from Yale.

When Clinton faces political adversity, he switches into his politician mode. In this mind-set, he doesn't spurn the process; he tries to win. While still faithful to his basic principles, he becomes an astute and acute political warrior. I used to sense that he dislikes himself in this mode and didn't like me much, either, for embodying it. When he needs to be a politician, he is, but he enjoys the Boy Scout role so much more. And he constantly separates his idealist and politician modes, consciously keeping the purity of the one apart from the pragmatism of the other. (Psychiatrists call it splitting when someone fails to integrate good and bad in a unified, coherent personality.)

In the politician mode, Clinton recaptured the governorship in 1982. The reason there are so many comebacks in Clinton's career is the alternation of these two mind-sets. In 1994, Eileen and I were invited to the White House to watch the Paul Newman movie, *The Hudsucker Proxy,* which traces the career of a mailroom clerk who rises to be the chief of the company on the strength of his invention of the Hula Hoop in the 1950s. After a scandal, he plunges to the depths and then comes back and lands on top again. When the lights came on after the film finished, Clinton turned to me and joked, "It sounds like my political career."

In October 1994, he was in his Boy Scout mode: he would get elected two years later for the right reasons or not at all. But as our conversation drew to a close, he began to embrace my views, rephrasing them to see how they sounded in his voice. He hadn't yet made the words his own. They were foreign. He was still a Boy Scout.

The president told me his advisers were pressing him to attack the Gingrich-inspired Contract with America as the campaign theme. I felt this wouldn't work. The items in the Contract were popular—balancing the budget, cutting taxes, deregulation; it was what you had to do to pay for them—the budget cuts—that would in time become unpopular. To attack the Contract itself when it first came out seemed to me to be a flawed strategy.

Besides, the issue was Clinton, not the Contract. "You're the one on the griddle," I told him. "It's your record that's under attack. It's your record you need to defend. Use the strategy of publicizing these bite-size achievements, which are so important to people. They are credible, and they're enough to bring enough votes to avert a disaster."

Later the president shared his recollection of how the '94 disaster unfolded: "I got your poll, and I agreed with it. Hillary did too. We told them"—I assumed he meant his political advisers, James Carville,

Harold Ickes, and George Stephanopoulos, but he didn't say—"that we wanted it followed. But I had to go to the Middle East, and they were all hot about attacking the Republican Contract with America. I agreed with you that the Contract was initially pretty popular and that this wasn't the way to campaign. But they were there and I wasn't, and they kept attacking the Contract and it didn't work, just like you said it wouldn't."

I don't believe Clinton was being candid with himself. If he had wanted to campaign on these "bite-size" issues, he would have done so. No adviser would have stopped him. The problem was that these achievements weren't enough for him. They were not nearly enough. He had done great things, and he wanted to be approved of for those great things.

Throughout October, Clinton skillfully used the office of the president. Having successfully restored democratic rule in Haiti without loss of American life, he traveled to the Middle East to oversee the signing of a peace treaty between Israel and Jordan. Clinton acted as peacemaker and it resonated throughout the United States. His approval ratings rose steadily.

On Monday, October 31, right after his return from the Middle East, the president called to ask what he should do in the remaining week to capitalize on his new, broader public-approval ratings. How could he translate these better ratings into congressional and senatorial victories? In which states should he campaign?

"Go back to the Middle East," I said facetiously. "Don't campaign for anyone; it will lower your approval ratings, and you will drag everyone down to defeat."

I was constantly giving Clinton blunt advice with what I hoped was a touch of humor. Never once did he acknowledge the irony or resent the bluntness. He would focus on the advice, and that was it. "But my ratings are high enough now that I'm not going to hurt anyone I campaign for," he protested. "It wasn't like before, when I couldn't have helped them." In September and October, the president's approval ratings were so low that any candidate for whom he campaigned would have been hurt politically. Now his ratings were up, and he felt he could be an asset. "I've got to help them after what they did for me, voting for my economic plan and my health-care package," he exclaimed.

"That's just it," I replied. "Your ratings are up because they don't see you as a politician; the voters see you as president. Now if you start campaigning again, you'll become a politician again. It will be a short-term help to whomever you're campaigning for, but in the long run it will kill dozens of your candidates when your ratings drop."

Intellectually, he may have agreed with my prescription for noninvolvement, for staying presidential, above the battle. But emotionally, he needed the crowds, the cheers, the mirror. After being defeated on health-care reform, he naturally felt battered. Public approval bound his wounds and soothed his spirit, as it would have for anyone.

The president later told me that he had wanted to do less campaigning in this last week but was "horrified" at the heavy schedule his staff had set for him when he got back from the Middle East. But Clinton always says that. When his schedule is light, he complains. When his staffers add events, he's resentful of the full schedule, and he still complains of overwork, but then he goes out and loves every minute of it.

As predicted, his approval ratings skidded again. After a heady week for the Democrats at the end of October, when their polls showed improvement as they rode the president's successes in Haiti and the Middle East, they lost their momentum in the first week of November. This baby-kissing, hand-shaking, hamburger-eating politician was not the president who had led the Middle East to peace the week before. As the president dropped, so did his candidates.

"You're going to lose the Senate and the House," I said to a worried President Clinton four days before election day in 1994.

"Not the House, no way," he answered.

"And the House," I repeated. "And by significant margins."

"No way, no way. Not the House," he replied. "Not the House. You're wrong. You really think so? You're wrong."

I was annoyed that the president had once more blown a chance to get out of his funk, so I replied combatively, "Just in case what you're sure won't happen happens, I'll fax you the statement I think you should give when the returns come in."

He grunted and hung up.

In our relationship, I always spoke frankly when I thought Clinton was making a mistake. I adopted this style in dealing with him because I knew he appreciated it. He told Todd Purdum, a *New York Times* writer, that I've "always been very straightforward and honest, the bad news as well as the good, and, if possible, the bad news first." Severe in his self-criticism, Clinton distrusts those who are more considerate of his feelings.

The day after election day in 1994, I didn't need an alarm clock. The phone rang early. It was Clinton. He had just witnessed the greatest debacle the Democratic Party had suffered in a midterm election since 1946, losing both the Senate and the House. Yes, the House.

"You were right," he began generously. "You saw I gave your statement. What should I do?"

Well, I thought to myself, I've been waiting for all of my forty-seven years for a president of the United States to ask me this question. To the president, I said, "Let's get together and talk about it." We talked for the next twenty-two months.

T w o

My Return

Clinton and I talked a lot during the first few weeks of November 1994, as he sought to find his balance amid the Republican landslide. Although his term of office had two more years to run, the press had already written him off as a lame-duck president, serving out his time until he too would fall under the Republican steamroller. He was labeled "irrelevant" by Washington commentators, a fallen president.

I could feel that he was going to ask me to come back to work for him, and this posed a crucial question about the direction of my career—which was, to a great extent, my life. I'd climbed to the top of the heap among the Republican consultants, and I had been happy working mostly for Republican candidates. If I worked with the president again, I would have to give up my chances of ever returning to the Republican party. But I was intrigued with the idea of working for Bill Clinton in the White House.

There is so little contact across party lines that there is a real chasm between them. The parties in our country might as well be different worlds. Even top-level politicians are distrustful of and misguided about the other party's motivations and beliefs. Democrats in particular have trouble understanding my nonpartisanship. They don't really know many Republicans well and often imagine them to be secretly evil. Politicians like these remind me of the character Daddy Warbucks in a scene from the Broadway play *Annie*. Warbucks, a lifelong Republican, is so upset about the Depression ("When I'm not making money, nobody's making money") that he decides to call FDR and invite him for dinner to tell him how bad things have gotten. But he is flustered by the idea of dining with the opposition, and so he instructs his secretary to "call Al Smith and find out what Democrats eat."

I don't work exclusively for candidates of one party or the other because like most intelligent voters, I don't vote that way. I voted for Humphrey in '68, McGovern in '72, Carter in '76, Reagan in '80, Reagan in '84, Bush in '88, and Clinton in '92. Sometimes I vote Democrat and sometimes Republican. About 40 percent of the American electorate responds the same way. It's only in Washington, where everything is either on the Democratic side of the aisle or the Republican side that this behavior is considered weird.

So my clients tend to reflect my own political outlook: moderate or middle of the road. Most of them in both parties have been moderates, including Republican Senator Warren Rudman of New Hampshire, Governor Bill Weld of Massachusetts, Governor Pete Wilson of California, and Governor Tom Ridge of Pennsylvania and Democratic Senator David Pryor of Arkansas, Senator Jeff Bingaman of New Mexico, Governor Mark White of Texas, and Clinton. I've also worked for liberals, like Senator Howard Metzenbaum (Ohio) and Congresswoman Bella Abzug (New York) and for conservatives, like Senator Trent Lott of Mississippi, Senator Dan Coats of Indiana, and Senator Paula Hawkins of Florida.

I liked Metzenbaum, Abzug, Lott, Coats, and Hawkins for the same reason: they had something good to say—Metzenbaum, about oil-company rip-offs; Abzug, about Vietnam; Coats, about using tax credits to encourage people to care for an elderly relative at home or to adopt a child; and Hawkins, about missing and abused children. Lott is a populist, a former Democrat, and I love his feisty, shit-on-the-shoes style.

On a personal level, a great many of the Republicans I worked for are kinder and more generous than many of the Democrats I've handled. Dan Coats, for example, is a gentle man with deeply held religious principles. One of his aides was made to resign in 1990 because he had used

Coats's office to send out mailings for a House candidate in another district, a relatively minor offense as political scandals go. It was clear Coats neither benefited from the mailing nor knew anything about it. Yet he was depressed and traumatized for a year. He even hinted that he would retire. He has little tolerance for the moral ambiguity of politics. He opposes higher taxes because he is genuinely grieved to see working people give up their pay to bureaucrats who don't care. He's against school busing not because he's racist but because he empathizes with what a six-year-old goes through at a strange new school and doesn't want to make a child's life more difficult by busing the child to a faraway school in a neighborhood where he or she has no friends.

Coats had a big impact on Clinton's program. We swiped Coats's idea for an adoption tax credit, and it was signed into law. Our proposal for a tax incentive for hiring welfare recipients also came from Coats. Had I remained with Clinton, other ideas of Coats's would probably have been proposed to Congress.

▲

Not all my clients were so admirable. I made a mistake in working for Jesse Helms in his 1990 North Carolina reelection campaign. Jesse Helms is a bad senator. He is really from the mold of the old Southern senators who were intolerant of anyone who is not like them—American, male, and heterosexual. I misjudged him and shouldn't have worked for him.

Republican party leaders were suspicious of my Democratic past, and I went to work for Helms largely to show them my loyalty. I guess I saw it as an initiation ritual—necessary to put up with once but not, I hoped, the norm. I was also very moved by a personal story from Helms's life.

One night around Christmas in the '60s, before he entered politics, Jesse Helms and his wife, Dot, were watching TV at home in North Carolina. A program came on that featured interviews of children at a camp for orphans. One child was a four- or five-year-old with, I believe, cerebral palsy. In any case, he couldn't walk. The kid was asked what he wanted most for Christmas, and he answered, "A mother and a father." Jesse and Dot drove up to the camp the next day and six weeks later adopted the boy. They raised him as one of their children, paid hundreds of thousands of dollars for surgery that ultimately enabled the boy to walk. Helms would not permit this story to be aired in his state in an ad or as a news item, even when threatened with defeat for reelection.

When I thought about working with Helms, I was also swayed by how right his warnings had been. The drug use that he outspokenly condemned presaged the widespread addiction that led to so many personal tragedies. The policy of increased defense spending that he long advocated did actually hasten the demise of communism when the Soviet economy proved incapable of competing with the United States. But when I wanted Helms to campaign on these ideas, I was badly disappointed. Helms and his opponent dueled with ads on issues like the death penalty, education, and the environment. I didn't feel I could quit a campaign midway, but I should have. When I was fired, Helms's manager called me in and said, "We appreciate your advice, but now we feel that we have to win this race the old-fashioned way." After I left, the central theme of the Helms campaign became attacks on the Democratic candidate's acceptance of support from gay groups and his alleged support for racial quotas. I was glad not to have been involved.

But politics is not just good guys versus bad guys. The lines are often blurred by factors more apparent to those who really know the men and the women involved than to those who don't but write about them. Is it wrong for a Democratic political consultant to work for Bill Weld but OK for him to work for George Wallace? Was it right to work for Trent Lott, Phil Gramm, and Ronald Reagan when they were Democrats? Did it become wrong when they turned Republican? Life's not that black and white.

My decision to leave the Republican party and go to work for Clinton came down to one simple fact: You never say no to a president. You may think you will, you may think you can, but you can't. He's the president. You also can't say no to a man you've known and advised for almost two decades, not when he's down and facing the battle of his life.

I knew that I would have to leave normal political consulting and take my chances with Bill Clinton. I'd alienated a lot of Democrats by working for some Republicans, and now I'd alienate the Republicans by working for Clinton.

As I look back on my arrival in Washington, I think of a scene from the recent movie *Independence Day* when everybody is fleeing Washington as the space aliens hover menacingly overhead, waiting to destroy the city. Not a lot of people were going *to* Washington in those days to join up with Clinton, and a lot of Democratic congressmen were becoming Republicans. Everyone else was sure he was dead politically, and I suspected he might be. The president put it well himself in the spring of '96: "It looks like a smart thing Dick is doing now [working with me], but it didn't look so smart when he joined me in 1994."

I gave Clinton my decision and touched on the personal risks I was taking when we met in November 1994 in the ornate splendor of the White House Treaty Room. It's a room Clinton uses as his office when he's in the East—residential—Wing rather than the West Wing, where the Oval Office is found. We sat in facing wing chairs, with a couple of his predecessors on the walls. President William McKinley, who stood in this room to accept the surrender of Spain in the Spanish-American War, looked down on us from one huge painting as we sat across a coffee table inlaid with the presidential seal. Clinton had a view of George P. A. Healy's *Lincoln and His Generals.*

"There are only two people who are genuinely, permanently screwed if you lose," I said. "You and me. Everybody else has a new line on his résumé. But you're out of a job, and I'm permanently out of work. I left the Democratic party, so they won't have me back, and now I'm about to alienate the entire Republican party, so they'll never let me back. And when you're a political consultant and it's a two-party country, it's not very good to alienate both parties."

That basic commitment impressed the president. I had no agenda other than victory.

Often while waiting for the president to arrive for a meeting, I would walk around the room, and I would study the Lincoln painting. Lincoln and Clinton, it seemed to me, had a lot in common. Each was a dark-horse candidate from a small western state (as Illinois was at the time). Neither had much Washington experience: Clinton had served as a staffer on Capitol Hill as a teenager, and Lincoln had served two years in the House of Representatives. Each was elected with a bit more than 40 percent of the vote in a three-way race.

Most important, neither was at the center of his party. Each was deeply suspected by his own party and shunned by the opposition. In response, each man, deeply self-confident, hired for his Cabinet (in Lincoln's case) or his White House staff (in Clinton's) people who served him but also served as the president's access to other power centers in the party. In Lincoln's Cabinet were three rivals for the presidential nomination of the infant Republican party (Secretary of State William Seward, Secretary of War Edwin Stanton, and Secretary of the Treasury Salmon Chase). On Clinton's staff, he had loyal and true servants who were also ambassadors to other realms of the party. Leon Panetta, the White House chief of staff, was a link to the hierarchy of barons in the

House Democratic leadership. George Stephanopoulos had always been a link to House leader Dick Gephardt, for whom he once worked. Deputy Chief of Staff Harold Ickes was a link to labor, the left, and Jesse Jackson. Mack McLarty, Clinton's former chief of staff, was a link to the business community, as is Erskine Bowles, the new chief of staff who was then deputy chief. Secretary of Commerce Ron Brown was a link to blacks, the party's national structure he once headed, and the business world. Secretary of Housing and Urban Development Henry Cisneros is Clinton's link to the Hispanic community. All ambassadors, all devoted to the president, but all, in his eyes, tethered to his often fractious allies in the party as well.

I had no links in the party. I made it clear I would not stay for a second term. I would be out on election day, and I had only one goal: to win. It was an agenda Clinton could share.

▲

I went to the White House secretly in early December to meet the president and the First Lady in the Treaty Room. Hillary had been my principal link to the president during the 1992–94 period. I had tried to offer her advice on her own work and on her own political style, advising incremental steps in health care and urging greater stress on cost-containment measures. We spoke once or twice each month. Much of the time I passed ideas on to the president through the First Lady. But since Clinton, in my view, had erred by setting out on a path of one-party government in 1993, I felt there was not much my day-to-day tactical advice could do to correct the major problems the administration faced.

When I reconnected with Clinton after the '94 elections, I looked forward to working closely with Hillary, as I had in past years. But the highly pragmatic woman I knew in the '80s was not the woman in the headlines of the '90s.

I tend to do little to prepare for meetings. The more I think about them in advance, the more nervous I get. I find that too much advance planning and focus impairs my spontaneity and just limits my creativity and imagination. So because of the importance of this meeting—I knew it was perhaps the most important one of my career—I deliberately tried not to think about it. I had probed my beliefs about what Clinton had done wrong in the past and how things could be made right again, but I avoided rehearsing my lines. My aim was to be loose, limber, quick, flexible, adaptive, and focused. These are the qualities one needs for a meeting with one Clinton, let alone for a meeting with both.

But I did choose my suit and tie with care. Was this tie too flamboyant? Did this one smack of staid thinking? Did this one make me seem too arrogant? Clinton loves clothing. As governor, he once looked at my alligator shoes (politically incorrect, but I like them anyway) and said, "If I became a political consultant, do you think I could wear shoes like that?" He usually comments on ties.

The meeting went well.

"I want you to come back and do the things for me here that you did back in Arkansas," Clinton said. "I need new ideas and a new strategy. I'm not getting what I need here, and I want you to come in. I've lost confidence in my current team."

We joked about the parallel to my resuscitation efforts in 1982. Hillary teased her husband saying, "You know, you have to stop having to be rescued like this."

The president raised his hands defensively and said, "Last time, I swear."

I said that I needed to be assured that he would give me the tools I needed. "If we lose because I'm not good enough or you're not good enough, OK. But I know you, and I know me, and I'll take that chance. But I won't be in a position where we lose because I don't get the tools I need to win." I set three conditions for my return.

First, I wanted total control of the polling for the campaign. I asked that Clinton hire Doug Schoen from the firm of Penn and Schoen to do the work. Schoen, a professorial type, balding on top, thickening in the middle, with a ponderous way of judgmentally reciting the points he wants to make, has been a friend of mine since he was seventeen. He and his wife spent weekends at their home a few miles from ours in Redding, Connecticut. They were close friends with both Eileen and me. He was our drummer, pounding out a steady beat to show us where we needed to go and always laboring to keep us in step. More conservative than I, he focused on the alienated Democratic voter, the people we had to get back.

At the beginning, though, the president didn't trust Schoen. Doug had polled for his former nemesis, who was now the president's supporter and his successor as governor, Jim Guy Tucker. Clinton wondered whether Schoen's polling for Tucker had been accurate, and he squirmed at the notion of bringing Schoen into his confidence. He was especially worried about leaks, since they had driven him to distraction during the first two years of his presidency. He once told me, "I have learned never to say anything—anything—in a meeting larger than three people."

I assured him on both counts, and he hired Schoen on my say-so.

Second, I wanted a member of the White House staff to work with me. "You aren't changing a single person on your staff after they helped lead you to the biggest defeat in history," I said. "That's OK. I'm not asking you to. But you've got to give me somebody on the inside." I asked the president to hire Bill Curry, the Democratic candidate who lost the Connecticut gubernatorial race in 1984.

Curry is a Tory egghead. Tall, intelligent, and very Irish, he moves with the ethereal quality of a lord of the manor, with his head in the clouds. He rarely enunciates a sentence of fewer than thirty words and makes his points so artfully that I—and, I suspect, he—often forget how they started. But I needed Curry's deft sensitivity to the motives and reactions of others and his skill in formulating new issues and ideas.

The president asked instead whether I would work with an existing member of his staff. He suggested Bruce Lindsey, whom I had known since the 1978 David Pryor campaign. I insisted that I needed my own person. The president had been impressed with Curry when he campaigned with him in Connecticut and especially praised his ideas on using health-care purchasing pools to lower insurance costs. So the president initially agreed to appoint Curry but later hedged when Panetta questioned the need for another staffer. After weeks of pressure, Clinton called Curry and offered him the job, making no reference to me or our intra–White House battles.

Third, I told Clinton that I wanted to have weekly meetings with him. I said that I needed them to be held every seven days no matter what. I knew that Bill Clinton can be elusive. He'll just disappear on you. One minute you think he's right there on your wavelength, and the next minute you're turning your head to look for him. He gets distracted, disenchanted, bored, or annoyed and stops the meetings or the phone calls that are a consultant's lifeline. I'd seen it in Arkansas, when weeks would go by without a meeting or even a returned phone call. I'd call Betsey Wright and ask why he had forgotten I was alive. "He's not ready to think about politics" was her usual answer. I wasn't going to let that happen here. The stakes were too high.

The president's agreement to the weekly meetings was the central step in organizing his campaign. At the time, it was one of several meetings that were rumored to be taking place regularly. It was said that a group of senior political advisers met every week, and speculation was that among those at the meetings were Mack McLarty, the president's old chief of staff and lifelong friend; former governor Ned McWherter of Tennessee; and former Democratic National Committee chairman Bob Strauss. I never knew. The old consulting team was said also to meet regularly with Stephanopoulos and Political Affairs Director Doug Sosnik. Again, I don't know whether it did.

In any case, our meetings became the ones that counted. They began in December and continued every week (with few exceptions) until I left the campaign, at the end of August 1996. They became the central forum for campaign strategy and decisions.

They were almost always held in the residence of the White House, where they were legally permissible (since our purpose was political, we could not meet in the business part of the White House). At first, the meetings involved only the president, the First Lady, and me. By early January, Hillary had stopped attending, and I was meeting with Clinton alone. In the first few months of 1995, we added Doug Schoen to the meetings. In March, the president brought in Leon Panetta, Al Gore, and Deputy Chiefs of Staff Harold Ickes and Erskine Bowles. By the end of August '96, the meetings included more than twenty people.*

I chaired the meetings and always prepared an agenda that summarized the advice the consultants and I were planning to give the president at that meeting. In the early days, this agenda ran to five or six pages; by the end, it was usually twenty-five to thirty pages. I was perhaps a little flamboyant in my dress for these meetings. My floral ties in bold colors became the object of considerable White House ribbing.

At first, both the president and I wanted the relationship to be secret. Neither of us was sure how it was going to work out. We had been close enough in the '80s, but had not really worked together in four years, and I had no institutional experience with the presidency. For Clinton, the desire for secrecy stemmed from his having no clear sense that I could handle the job at that level.

---

* The following was a typical guest list for the later White House strategy meetings: the president; the vice president; Leon Panetta, chief of staff; Harold Ickes, deputy chief of staff; Evelyn Lieberman, deputy chief of staff; George Stephanopoulos, senior adviser; Don Baer, director of communications; Doug Sosnik, political affairs director; Ron Klain, vice president's chief of staff; Sandy Berger, deputy national security adviser; Senator Chris Dodd of Connecticut; John Hilley, legislative director; Maggie Williams, First Lady's chief of staff; Mike McCurry, press secretary; Henry Cisneros, secretary of Housing and Urban Development; Mickey Kantor, secretary of Commerce; Mack McLarty, adviser and former chief of staff; Peter Knight, campaign manager; Ann Lewis, deputy campaign manager and director of communications; Ron Brown, secretary of Commerce, until his death; Erskine Bowles, deputy chief of staff, until his departure; Jack Quinn, vice president's chief of staff until his appointment as White House counsel; Dick Morris, consultant; Doug Schoen, consultant; Mark Penn, consultant; Bob Squier, consultant; Bill Knapp, consultant.

In my case, I had a long way to fall if it were publicly announced that I was working for this Democratic president and was then fired. This was no ordinary Democrat. He was the object of the Republican party's fixation and hatred. Being convicted of working for Clinton would mean capital punishment for a Republican operative. So the secrecy, for me, was temporary protection.

I never asked for a commitment or a guarantee. I never asked for the political equivalent of tenure. I always assume that clients can and will fire me whenever they want to. I was especially worried that Clinton had not fired anyone on his staff. "I don't want to scapegoat anyone," he explained.

I thought, *Damn it, these are the guys you told me had screwed up health care, messed up Whitewater, and delivered the most crushing midterm defeat imaginable. Fire any of them? Of course not. How ridiculous.*

But I understood why he was reluctant to fire people. Bill Clinton has a deep sense of personal loyalty to people who have worked for him. He forms bonds with them that he finds hard to break. He was determined to assume full personal responsibility for his 1994 defeat and his persistent, harsh, and nagging superego would not permit him to share the blame for the disaster with others.

In spite of my misgivings, I said calmly, "That's up to you, Mr. President. I'll play the hand you deal me." He never really fired any of the consultants who helped him win in 1992. Mandy Grunwald, his former media adviser, was shifted over to the First Lady's staff, to give Hillary advice on TV appearances. James Carville remained for the entire campaign, as far as I know, on the Democratic National Committee— DNC—payroll but had little real direct role in the campaign from 1994 through 1996. Paul Begala moved to Texas. Stan Greenberg, his pollster, remained the DNC's pollster, did work on the fringes of the campaign, and labored long and hard to appear in the newspapers as the president's pollster long after I replaced him. With the old consultants likely gone (but poised offstage to return at any moment) but the old staff in place, I felt like a French revolutionary entering the palace at Versailles to try to work with the lords and ladies of the *ancien régime*.

In any event, neither Clinton nor I was prepared to bet our hides that this would last. So I became Charlie. That was my self-selected code name. I would call the Oval Office or the usher's office in the White House residence and announce that Charlie was on the phone. Nancy Hernreich, the president's chief administrative assistant and an old pal of mine from Arkansas days, and Betty Currie, from Mississippi, were in on the secret. They would transfer the call to the president's private line, and we would talk.

Nancy, tall, beautiful, and bright with long blond hair, looks a decade or two younger than her still young years. She is clearly the person in the White House the president trusts the most. She is able and empathic, but very firm, and she knows him well. Sometimes she would intercept a call I had made to Clinton, asking "Do you have to speak with him right now? He hasn't really slept in three days, and he'll be zonked if we don't put him to bed." She keeps the president's business totally confidential. When she dies, her epitaph should read SHE KNEW EVERYTHING AND SHE LEAKED NOTHING.

Why Charlie? Some have speculated that it was a takeoff on *Charlie's Angels,* the television series in which various beautiful female operatives receive their instructions from an unseen Charlie. No way—I've never seen *Charlie's Angels* in my life; I use my TV set for viewing political ads and for watching Sunday-night movies with Eileen. It was really a code name I chose after my favorite Republican political consultant, Charlie Black, to whom I'd been very close. I got a kick out of using the name of a top Republican in my dealings with the Democratic president.

In part, the code-name business was a carryover from my earlier work with Clinton. Secrecy had been part of my method in Arkansas. During all of Clinton's races there, my name almost never appeared in the Arkansas press. Nobody knew I was there, and nobody could try to stop me. I was always way behind the scenes. It was ideal. My private life has always been very important to me. Perhaps I realized that publicity could destroy me—as it ultimately did. Instinctively, I avoided the stage and left before the cameras arrived. It was my style, and Clinton loved it.

Clinton was also delighted that nobody knew I was working for him in Washington. He'd whisper into the phone so that others in the Oval Office couldn't hear. He'd go out into the private library adjacent to his office to take my calls, always on the private line, so nobody could eavesdrop.

Once, during the winter of '95, I called to speak to the president. He was meeting with Leon Panetta, Harold Ickes, and a few other White House staffers, and sent word that he'd call me back. When he phoned, half an hour later, he said, conspiratorially, "I called you as soon as I got rid of those guys." He was never happier working with me than he was in the Charlie days. It remains something of a miracle that the press didn't catch on until April '95 that since the previous December I had been the closest political adviser to the president.

▲

To turn the president's misfortune around, we needed to start with a clear idea of how he had fallen. What had gone wrong to make his administration fall so low in the public's esteem? In my opinion, it dated back to the initial assumptions—flawed assumptions—that Clinton made in November and December of 1992, days after winning the election.

It all had to do with the president-elect's memory of the last Democrat in the White House, Jimmy Carter. To Clinton, Carter's administration was marked by the inability to get things *done,* sniping from the Democratic Congress, bumbling, and lack of cohesion. Carter's mistakes haunted Clinton.

The parallels between the two men were stark. Neither could find his way around Washington without a map when he took office. Both were governors, not senators, from primarily rural southern states, not big northern state capitals. Each was elected outside his party's mainstream: Kennedy wouldn't run, so Carter got nominated; Cuomo wouldn't run, so Clinton won the nomination. Each superimposed a Democratic victory on a Republican era, Carter because of Watergate and Clinton because of the recession. Both beat incumbents who had never emerged from the shadow of their makers, Gerald Ford from Nixon's and George Bush from Reagan's. And most of all, neither would have received 5 percent of the votes from the Democratic caucus of either House when he started his race. These men were not creatures of the establishment; they were stand-ins who filled a vacuum in presidential leadership in a party dominated by its congressional wing.

Yet Clinton had big plans: economic stimulus, health-care reform, welfare overhaul, Americorps, direct student loans, family and medical leave, environmental initiatives, and now, grafted on top, deficit reduction. But when his big proposals collided with the absence of the relationships necessary to implement them, Clinton became seriously alarmed.

At first, they had called: George Mitchell, Tom Foley, Dick Gephardt, one after another. The lions of Congress calling on the cub about to enter the White House. Their message: We're with you. We're behind you. We'll get it *done* for you. No Jimmy Carter–Tip O'Neill relationship this time. We're there for you. And when he had his first meeting with them, on November 15, 1992, he looked at them as if they were an offensive line: big, big, big men willing to block and tackle to protect their quarterback, to keep him whole and well.

But will they follow my program? Clinton asked himself.

"Yes," they swore. Never men with long personal agendas, they were there to get the job done for him. Whatever he wanted, wherever he wanted to go.

Oh, there were a few no-no's. Campaign-finance reform was a touchy issue; their colleagues depended on contributions to keep their seats. As with civil rights in the early days of the Kennedy administration, the president was willing to put finance reform in the backseat so as not to disturb his congressional allies.

To the congressional leaders, it must have been a relief to find that this outsider president was practical and willing to work with them. As for Clinton, he felt that his charm had worked, that he had reached out and found the answer to the Jimmy Carter question. There would be no bills that wouldn't pass, no congressional sniping. Instead, a united wall of blockers would protect him, shelter him.

There was a price, however—a huge one. This freelancer was accepting that he would be tethered to a desk. This scrambling quarterback, used to living by his wits and his intellect, whose style was improvisation and whose credo was flexibility, would now have to stay within the shelter formed by his blockers. And within this shelter, he couldn't move. He was locked into a game he had never played before. He had led teams, but he had never before led one that demanded the kind of parochialism that would ultimately cripple him.

In Arkansas, when he had to—for example, to implement his proposed mandatory competency testing of schoolteachers—he reached beyond the traditional Democratic constituencies, bringing in Republican and independent support. But now, bound to the Democratic congressional majority, he had lost his ability to maneuver.

"Your supporters will become your jailers," I warned him at our December 2, 1992, meeting at the governor's mansion in Little Rock as he prepared his transition. "Their protection will become your parole. They're in good faith," I conceded; "they want to help you, but they can't, and in the process they'll limit your mobility and drag you down. You think you're their candidate, but you'll become their hostage."

When the president asked me to elaborate, I said that it took sixty votes to get a bill passed in the Senate. "The concept of a fifty-one-vote majority is dead," I noted. Long since, in the days when Senate Majority

Leader Mitchell was trying to frustrate President Bush's legislative initiatives, the filibuster had become automatic; the need for sixty votes to cut off debate, crucial. But Clinton and Mitchell didn't have sixty votes. There were only fifty-six Democrats—not enough. In the House, where majority rule sufficed, the Democratic margin was only 256–178—slim, easily fractured.

"You will spend all day every day rounding up each member of each liberal caucus looking for unanimity. They'll make you tack on amendments, and each of these amendments will become its own controversy. You'll find yourself taking positions that you don't really mean, and you'll become a caricature of yourself as you defend them to keep your majority for your basic premise.

"Play the whole field," I urged. "Put Republicans in your Cabinet." I suggested former governor Tom Kean of New Jersey and former senator Warren Rudman of New Hampshire. "Reach out to all one hundred senators and all four hundred thirty-five congresspeople. Then you can temper the Democratic left with the fear that you will deal with the centrist Republicans and leave them high and dry."

But Clinton wasn't buying it. Later I came to understand why. After I came back to work for him, he offered an explanation during a one-on-one chat in the Treaty Room. "They [the Republicans] never saw my presidency as legitimate," he complained. "They see me as accidental, illegitimate, a mistake in a three-way race. They want to destroy me; they don't want to work with me. I've made every kind of overture I can think of, but no response."

He was right. Typical of the Republican attitude toward his presidency was that of Senator Bob Dole, who virtually declared his candidacy for president immediately after election day in 1992. These Republicans saw Clinton as a brief interruption in their rule, which would resume in 1996.

As the president talked with me, he played hand after hand of solitaire, mechanically arranging the cards, dealing himself new ones, merging and separating columns, and shuffling the deck. His hands moved to their own rhythm as if disembodied, ceaselessly moving, moving, moving. In his mouth was a cigar, unlit. When on rare occasion he removed it, the end he'd had between his teeth was dry and unmolested.

Despite the GOP rejection of his administration, I basically disagreed with the president's premise that any offer of cooperation would be rejected. Republicans were not of one mind on the subject. His intellect and charm could have brought around enough Republicans to make bipartisan cooperation work—but not enough to pass every detail of every bill. And that was the real problem. He couldn't parse his program. He couldn't see how to do a portion of it. If the first step of the ladder were removed, how could he keep the rest intact?

This stubbornness came not from pride but from perfectionism. He wanted to do what he thought was right. He had reasoned out what he felt was the best course for the country, and he was determined to see it through. He would rather have the full loaf from the Democrats than half a loaf from a bipartisan majority. But he did not foresee the result: that he would be pulled further and further to the left to round up every last Democratic vote. "You won't be able to recognize yourself in a year," I predicted.

Still, I felt that he was comfortable in the quarterback's pocket, comforted by his majority, sheltered by its leadership. He was eager to have a home among his Washington peers and was happy to find a place at the head of their table. This, though, was the fundamental error. He became president of the Democratic party. Once he was bound to its credos, his ability to pass bills was restricted by the party's voting strength in Congress, and he began to flounder.

For example, he wanted to switch the budget from one based on bureaucratic spending to one based on strategic investments in education, research, and technology. For that, though, he needed lower interest rates to help fund the new businesses he hoped to generate.

And for that, he needed the bond market to drive down rates.

And for that, he had to cut the budget deficit.

And for that, he had to have enough Democratic votes to pass a budget.

And for that, he had to raise taxes and at the same time pass a stimulus package to get the economy moving.

And for that, he had to cram the stimulus package with pork-barrel projects for the cities that met the needs of urban Democratic liberal congresspeople.

So the president who wanted to invest in education, research, and technology found himself defending tax increases and pork-barrel spending to round up every last Democratic vote.

He also wanted to pass an anti-crime bill that stipulated more federal crimes punishable by the death penalty, provided funds for one hundred thousand additional police officers, and imposed stricter gun-control measures. But for that, he again needed every last Democratic vote, so he had to tack on a "crime-prevention package" that would pay for basketball courts that stay open till midnight to occupy kids and lower the crime rate. Yet that sounded a lot like the stimulus package, which sounded a lot like more pork. So the issue became "midnight basketball," not the cops and not the death penalty.

By the end of 1994, Clinton had indeed become a caricature of himself, fighting battles far from his preferred centrist base, trapped by the demands of the most liberal Democrats in his caucus.

And the public got the point. This was not the reformist, New Democrat Bill Clinton they had elected in 1992. Where was campaign-finance reform? (Buried to appease Democratic incumbents.) Why the tax increases? (Because the Democratic caucus would not vote to reduce the deficit by means of spending cuts alone. It demanded tax hikes as well.) Why the pork-barrel spending programs? (To satisfy the president's urban Democratic supporters.) The president became a prime minister, rounding up legislative majorities, dependent on their largesse and subservient to their wishes. He was stuck, fused with the Democratic caucus. His popularity decreased. His ratings dropped.

At first, the leaders of the caucus stayed with him, protecting the pocket. They wouldn't let him scramble out with moderate programs, but they did continue to pass the bills they and he wanted. Then, though, the shelter caved in. Discouraged or frightened by the president's loss of popularity and lower approval ratings, Democrats in the House and, particularly, in the Senate began to abandon their quarterback. Even the leaders—loyal to the end—could not deliver the votes. The shelter imploded under the pressure of Clinton's faulty health-care reform. The entire party soon followed.

There was a silver lining, however. Amid the total rubble of a destroyed Democratic congressional majority, there was no need to compromise with the past. Once the obsolete structure collapsed, the president could rebuild, not just renovate or modernize. He could now construct a new centrist program, as the Japanese and the Germans had constructed modern auto plants on the foundations of their countries' wartime rubble.

The 1994 defeat devastated Clinton. He grieved for each member of Congress who lost his or her seat while loyally backing him. He would talk about them as he might have talked of family members who had passed away. He later told me, "I needed to buy time to get back on my feet, and I think it pleased the American people that I showed up for work every day and kept at it."

He would talk about the defeat endlessly, ruminating on what had gone wrong. He would forlornly second-guess his every move:

"I shouldn't have run against the Contract with America."

"We never ran a truly national campaign; they had a national campaign."

"They had a two-word message: 'less government.' Our message took an hour to recite."

The explanations ran on and on and on.

▲

A curious duality dominates the way President Clinton handles bad news or defeat. In public, even with just a handful of intimate staff or advisers, he appears to deflect blame easily. Even in private, he says that when something goes wrong, it is someone else's fault. On the train trip to the Democratic convention in 1996, he snapped at a reporter who was asking about welfare reform. That night he told me over the phone, "My damn staff is scheduling me so tightly, every minute of every day, that I don't get enough sleep. Anytime I look up, somebody's putting a camera or a mike in my face. No wonder I was so tired that I almost took that reporter's head off."

But I learned by my close association with him as he coped with the two major defeats of his life, those of 1980 and 1994, that he doesn't really blame others for his own errors. Bill Clinton savages himself for his mistakes. He doesn't articulate his responsibility because his mind is so filled with self-criticism. This brutal self-criticism became evident in 1980 and again in 1994, when he explored his own failings and concluded that he faced permanent political defeat.

Clinton has a knack for sensing danger. When he believes things are going badly or feels the need to change course, he complains loudly to anyone who will listen. Invariably, he predicts disaster and continues in this vein until he feels the situation is getting under control. At such times, he exhibits anxiety, restlessness, even insomnia. Sometimes he becomes ill.

He is almost always on target in his analysis of danger. Many of us will not speak of a difficulty unless we have a clear idea of how to solve it. We find it too threatening to recognize a danger before we can articulate, even if only to ourselves, a route of escape. Not Clinton. Before he has any idea of what to do to solve a problem, he emphasizes the looming adversity. He doesn't immediately suggest ways out but simply complains and in this way sometimes finds an answer to his dilemma.

His awareness of danger sets those around him scurrying for ways to deal with the difficulty. They also serve to mobilize his own thoughts.

Together, the resulting suggestions, from others or from within himself, usually point to a solution.

Once he perceives a solution, he is decisive and even bold in following it.

In early December 1994, Clinton was groping for answers as I laid out my strategy for recovery in an evening meeting in the Treaty Room. I based my argument on a paradox of recent political history. It is commonly assumed that elected officials are always brought down by their failures. I think they often can be brought down by their successes: they become vulnerable when they have done what they said they would do. Their mandate runs out and the public no longer has a pressing reason for voting for them.

The classic instance I cited was that of Winston Churchill. Named prime minister so that Great Britain could win World War II, he accomplished his task. But his very success made him expendable when Labour candidate Clement Attlee seemed to have a better idea of how to go about the post-war reconstruction. Had the war continued, Churchill never would have lost to Attlee.

In the United States, President Lyndon Johnson was elected to pass the civil rights bill and to implement Great Society programs. Once he succeeded, he became expendable and ultimately lost his popularity because of his decision to deepen U.S. involvement in the Vietnam War.

President Jimmy Carter, elected in Watergate's aftermath, had a popular mandate to restore integrity to government. After four relatively scandal-free years, Carter had fulfilled his mandate, making him expendable as well. He was defeated for failing to free the American hostages in Iran.

President George Bush, elected to wrap up the Cold War and establish a "new world order," fulfilled his charge. This then made his foreign policy experience largely irrelevant to the election of 1992 and enabled Bill Clinton to defeat him over the economy and the recession.

Bringing the argument full circle, I said that while Clinton had seemingly been defeated mid term by his mismanagement of health-care reform and by his tax increases of 1993, he had been exposed and vulnerable to these attacks only because the economy was no longer a big issue in 1994, which was largely due to his success in helping to end the Bush recession.

Clinton was intrigued by this argument. He probed its historical antecedents. He cited the example of how Reagan had been laid low by the Iran-contra hearings, unable to keep the nation's focus on his stance against big government after he had defused the issue by cutting taxes early in his term.

So how was he to get back? Clinton asked.

I had been browsing through his library while we talked. Over the years, we had swapped books and recommended books to each other, and our libraries had dozens of volumes in common. Clinton reads a lot faster than I do, but I guess I had a bit more time than he usually did.

He has a shelf of books on Kennedy and a vast collection of biographies. Earlier, while waiting for him to start our meeting, I had found a book that I had read and enjoyed, the biography of French president François Mitterrand by Wayne Northcutt. Now I took it down from the shelf and handed it to him. "You can come back," I said, "by doing what Mitterrand did in 1985."

He cocked his head and knit his brow, and in response I explained what I meant. I noted that some said his comeback should be cast in the mold of Democratic President Harry Truman's 1947 slashing denunciation of the "do-nothing" Republican Congress. Others wanted him to emulate Republican President Dwight Eisenhower's benign passivity in working with a Democratic Congress headed by future president Lyndon Johnson and Speaker Sam Rayburn.

I rejected both. I said that the Truman model would merely lead to partisan deadlock, taking away the potential for progress during half of Clinton's presidency. I warned that in 1996 he would face a right wing determined to move in for the kill and a nation yearning for a real chance to give the right wing's simple solutions a try if he adopted this course.

With the Eisenhower model, he would let Gingrich and Dole walk all over him, and he would barely be evident in the Oval Office. "You can't be a doughface," I said, referring to the passive, timid, almost invisible presidents who occupied the office without distinction between 1848 and 1860.*

But look, I said, at the record of Mitterrand between 1985 and 1987, when he shared power with his rival, the current French president, Jacques Chirac. France elects a president directly and a prime minister through the vote of its legislative branch, the National Assembly. If the same party controls both offices, all works well, but in 1985 conservative, hardheaded Jacques Chirac took over the National Assembly while

---

* Presidents Zachary Taylor, Millard Fillmore, Franklin Pierce, and James Buchanan, each more likely to be found in a game of Trivial Pursuit than in a history book.

the Socialist François Mitterrand remained as president. All expected a collision leading to Chirac's election as president in the 1987 elections. The parallels with Clinton were there.

Chirac is much like Newt Gingrich, a born leader who likes to march his followers into battle against big government. His main goal was to denationalize the businesses Mitterrand had nationalized when he came to power.

I had briefly worked with some of Chirac's people early in the '80s. At that time, their election poster featured a voter stripped naked: UNDER SOCIALISM, I HAVE NOTHING LEFT!

The way Mitterrand handled Chirac's majority was superb. First, he ignored those who advised him to appoint a moderate rightist as prime minister instead of Chirac. He said, in effect, that the people voted for Chirac, and Chirac it will be. On the other hand, he ignored those who proposed he fight Chirac for every foot of ground. Instead, he let Chirac pass his program and privatize most of the French businesses that had been nationalized. "He fast-forwarded Chirac's agenda," I said, "passing enough of it to relieve the frustrations that led to Chirac's victory." He helped Chirac succeed, thereby rendering irrelevant the issues that had rendered Chirac's victory possible.

"Chirac lost in 1987," the president recalled.

"So what we must do is relieve the frustrations that impelled the election of the Republican Congress in 1994 by helping to address the issues on which they ran. Let the wave wash over the shore so that its energy is spent," I added.

The president was intrigued. The thought flitted through my mind that if this man could bring to bear his considerable intellect, he might then become the great president he is capable of becoming. But as we talked, I saw clearly that he was overwhelmed by detail, as he often is, and starved for concepts.

I had prepared a series of principles that I felt should guide our comeback in the face of the Republican victory. I read them aloud and then handed him a copy. At our first few meetings, I always brought a copy of this document with me to remind him of the broad strategic overview as we focused on specifics.

1.   Fast-forward the Gingrich agenda so that the deficit is reduced, welfare is reformed, the size of government is cut, and regulations are reduced. This will make the Republican issues less appealing since they will be on their way to solution.

2.   Present a Democratic way of achieving this agenda. Cut the deficit not by slashing programs Republicans urge [cutting] but by protecting the programs people need and Democrats value and cutting the others. Reform welfare in a way that helps welfare recipients move up, not which punishes them. Use Gore's [reinventing government] program to cut the public sector's size rather than [doing] the wholesale dismantlement Republicans urged.

3.   Use executive branch actions to show leadership in a positive direction. Develop an executive-order strategy to move the country forward that is not dependent on Congress.

4.   Use foreign policy situations to demonstrate your strength and toughness to the American people. Show by your actions in foreign situations, where you have control unfettered by Congress, that you are in charge and the boss.

5.   Don't add to the damaging perception that you have flip-flopped on issues. It is never worth the price. If we've said something before, we're bound by it. We won't change it. The American people aren't against you because of your positions nearly so much as because of their perception of weakness and indecision. Don't ever, ever change your mind.

At each point in this presentation, he would interrupt and describe his vision of what I was discussing. After my point about moving toward the goals of the Gingrich agenda but using progressive means of reaching them, he alluded to his success in achieving the conservative goal of raising Arkansas's education standards not just by testing teachers' competence but also by insisting on a big raise in teachers' pay.

He said that his administration had done a poor job of making sure that important executive actions by the Cabinet agencies were announced at the White House level. He suggested that Bill Curry be placed in a position to harness these initiatives so they were seen as his initiatives, not just those of Cabinet members. I supported the idea, but made it clear that I needed Curry to work directly with me to implement the entire strategy, not just a piece of it.

When we came to the part about not flip-flopping, Clinton agreed strongly. For months afterward, any position anyone proposed on an issue could be killed if there was evidence that we had taken the opposite position in the past. "If we never flip-flop again," I said, "there's an even chance we can get this perception down by '96, but just one will bring it all back."

Then our discussion turned to the First Lady. My polling showed clearly that Bill and Hillary were locked in a sort of zero-sum game. The more powerful she seemed, the weaker he seemed. The voters who protested Hillary's power, telling our pollsters, "Who elected her?" were the same ones who five minutes later described the president as "weak, wishy-washy, ineffective."

I urged that Hillary withdraw from overt participation in White House staff meetings and politics so that the impression of secret hidden power not sap her husband's image and undermine perceptions of his strength. But I did not feel Hillary Clinton should be silent. That would be a big mistake. The more often people heard Hillary speaking out for her beliefs, the better they would like her. They needed to see Hillary *in public* so they wouldn't spend their time morbidly imagining what she was doing *in private*.

It took a seventeen-year relationship with the Clintons to allow me to give advice so frankly. Obviously, one of Bill Clinton's problems was the public image of Hillary Clinton. Normally, a consultant would hesitate before addressing a president about the First Lady. But I knew I didn't have to be careful. Both the president and Hillary wanted the best advice I could give. The more candid the better.

President Clinton is deeply supportive of Hillary. He believes in his soul that she is one of the best people he knows and is unshakably of the opinion that she can do no wrong. He makes no concessions at all to the claims of many Americans that she is untrustworthy. But he and she are willing to listen endlessly to practical advice about how she should handle herself and what missteps she might be making.

Generally, I gave such advice directly to the president, who then passed it along to the First Lady. He would dispassionately note what I was urging, usually without comment, and tell Hillary about it later. Unfortunately, Hillary took the advice too much to heart and stopped attending the weekly strategy meetings. She never came to one after January of 1995. I missed her. Her input was always helpful, and she is a sound, practical thinker.

The president was not at all sorry to see Hillary absent herself from the White House political and strategy meetings. He just switched to asking her advice in private. He routinely took to Hillary each week's written "agenda" (a summary of the polling data and advice on strategy, and she read every word. I know they talked at length about it in private, because she showed intimate familiarity with every bit of it.

President Clinton never, ever criticizes Hillary in public or in private. He criticizes himself all the time and goes after everyone else when he's angry. But he never says a negative thing about his wife. This is a strength and it's a blind spot, but it's how he is.

▲

Reporters like to use the word "spin" to describe what political consultants do. But the word implies no change in the substance, just in the rotation or presentation of the issue or the candidate. That is the exact opposite of what I do. I don't "spin" anything, I put new substance and ideas before the voters.

When I enter a campaign, the candidate probably has several hundred "positions" on issues he has already articulated and hundreds more about which he would speak if anyone asked. Only a handful of these issues are typically already before the public. Rather than change the packaging or spin on those positions that are already out there, I reach into the candidate's issue basket and pull out positions he's already taken, but not publicized, and try to use them to win the election. Often, I take the general themes from the candidate and then find new specific issues to illustrate them. This is not spin. It's substance.

With President Clinton, our strategy went even further. We really sought to redefine the job of president in such a way that he was uniquely qualified to fill it. Under Reagan, the presidency was redefined by ideology. In the second half of Clinton's first term, it was defined by compromise, reconciliation, values, and healing—skills at which this president was awfully good.

We won in 1996 by a new definition of the job and by new substance, not by spinning, as I will explain.

Those who look in this book in search of illumination of the Whitewater, FBI-file, travel-office, Paula Jones, Gennifer Flowers, and other Clinton-era scandals will find none. I'm not holding anything back, I just don't know anything. I worked hard at staying as far away from these issues as I could. When the president talked to me about them, protesting his innocence or expressing his outrage at his accusers, I tried to divert the discussion to politics—or to anything else. I didn't want to get involved in *that*. I focused intently on how to escape political damage from the allegations, but I never worked on replies to accusations or even asked for the facts.

Once in a phone conversation, Clinton declared, "I get the sense that you're not interested in talking about Whitewater with me."

"Damn right I'm not," I replied, "I'm here to help you get reelected, and I'll deal with political responses to the situation as it plays out. You have other people to help you with other aspects of the situation. I'll do my job, and I hope they do theirs."

As we parted that evening, I felt that the president was more relaxed and happier than he had been since the congressional defeat. It was then that he—for the first and the last time—criticized his former pollster, Stan Greenberg, whom I had replaced. His comment: "Greenberg never told me what to do!"

I left the White House and departed through the side residence gate so as not to be seen by any members of the press who might have been lingering in front of the West Wing, near the president's Oval Office. As I walked into the winter Washington night, I wondered where this journey would lead me. It seemed so simple to speak to this man.

But how were we to act on these strategic principles? I knew nothing about the workings of the executive branch. What role did the president truly play? Could he just push a button and make it happen? Was he really agreeing with me, or was he just listening, as he does with so many friends who offer advice?

Arkansas Roots

It had been nineteen years since I first met Bill Clinton and started my career in national politics. Back then only a few people made their living running political campaigns. Most who worked professionally in politics had full-time jobs at corporate polling firms or advertising agencies and did the political work as a sideline, usually as a favor for a client with close links to the candidate. When my parents pestered me to tell them what I was doing for a living, no easy term sprang to mind. "I help people win elections," I explained inadequately. I was sure I was no good at anything else. *But,* I asked myself, *is it a full-time job?* I was reminded of the scene in *Butch Cassidy and the Sundance Kid* where Newman and Redford, having failed at farming in Bolivia, have gone back to robbing banks. Sundance, lamenting the resumption of their life of crime, asks Cassidy, "Hey, Butch, how come everything we're good at is illegal?"

Since I knew of no occupation concerned solely with getting people elected, I resolved to invent one. I would try to work exclusively for political customers. To get clients, I called every Democrat in the United States who was running for senator or governor in 1978. I made sixty attempts that year and ultimately found three clients. Bill Clinton was the first. Most incumbent senators and governors wouldn't even talk to me. They didn't understand what a political consultant was, and many of them had gotten along quite nicely without one for decades. I found, though, that I had a shot with the challengers.

The hard part was getting in the door. Generally, if you tell a staff person that you are going to make a special trip to his state capital to meet him and his boss, he won't let you come. It's not that you are asking them to pay for the trip, but that they don't want to feel responsible for the money you are likely to waste on your ticket. So I made up some nonsense about having to be in Little Rock on other business and tried the line out on Steve Smith, Bill Clinton's chief of staff. Clinton had been elected attorney general of Arkansas the year before and was considering a race for governor or senator. Smith was impressed that someone from New York City would be interested in an Arkansas candidate, and he agreed to let me come by his boss's office.

In New York City, where I grew up, I was already well-known among political operatives. As the only child of a prominent trial lawyer and a professional writer, I had developed verbal skills early. My parents didn't much like the company of children, but they loved the companionship of young adults. So my childhood was truncated. I began reading *The New York Times* regularly when I was eight because commenting on international affairs was the only way for me to get my parents' attention.

When I was twelve, I dressed in a jacket and tie and canvassed my seventeen-floor apartment building on Eighty-fifth Street and West End Avenue, on Manhattan's Upper West Side, on behalf of John Kennedy's presidential campaign. I visited each of the sixty-four apartments, speaking to tenants for five minutes at a time about why they should vote for my candidate. On weekends, I spoke about my hero from Democratic club sound trucks parked on street corners. Twice during the campaign I got Kennedy's autograph on my student-government card. I soon learned, however, that to get anywhere in the local Democratic clubs, you had to wait your turn. I was too impatient for that. I'd still be there waiting if I'd taken that route.

As a teenager, I set up political organizations in the city's high schools and colleges. I struck bargains with the brightest kids I could find in each school: I would help them win election to their student government—by writing their speeches, advising them on campaign themes, explaining how to organize their supporters—if they would recruit their followers to work with me. With my classmates from Stuyvesant High School and Columbia University, I organized my own political machine in the area. Using the political organizing tools of the activist Saul Alinsky, author of the famous *Rules for Radicals,* we ran draft clinics to help boys stay out of the Vietnam War, painted park benches, collected cans and bottles for recycling, set up big-brother and big-sister programs for low-income children, and bused thousands of students to the peace marches in Washington.

The goal of this adolescent political organizing was to take political control of the West Side, a one-party area, by challenging the Democratic party district leaders in primary contests. In 1969, at age twenty-one, I ran seven successful challenges for the post of Democratic party district leader. Never has a more meaningless job been invented than that of Manhattan district leader. With no pay, no real duties, and little real power, it exists as a vestige of the Tammany Hall days, when district leaders chose judges and distributed patronage. Where political machines are still in power, district leaders have considerable leverage, but in Manhattan, where the machine has long since disappeared, the job is an anachronism.

But it's *there.* Those who climb the political ladder still vie for it in primary contests because it is the lowest elective office in the city and can presage a race for the state legislature or even Congress. And because it is there, it is highly coveted, and I was determined that my candidates would win these races. After two years of campaigning and thousands of hours of work, my confederates and I prevailed and established a toehold in New York City politics.

After my followers and I took power, we began to elect our people to public office. Congressman Jerrold Nadler and New York State assemblyman Richard Gottfried began their tenures in local office as part of our organization. We advocated a more militant left than the regular Democratic organization wanted. Our group became the nucleus of the McGovern campaign apparatus in New York in 1972 and served as the focus of statewide efforts to strengthen tenants' rights at the expense of landlords.

Ironically, one of my staunchest opponents in this drive for power was Harold Ickes, son of FDR's famous secretary of the Interior and my chief rival in the Clinton White House. Ickes and I both backed Eugene McCarthy for president in 1968 and supported George McGovern in

'72. We dueled for control of each man's New York State campaigns. Ickes ran the McCarthy campaign, but my organization took over the McGovern operation. We opposed each other in the fratricidal hand-to-hand combat typical of New York liberal Democratic politics. The animosity between Ickes and me began early.

Now I was in Arkansas, about to meet my first out-of-state client, Attorney General Bill Clinton. I was thirty and he was thirty-one. I had never before met a candidate my own age with sideburns and hair as long as mine and with an attitude toward the Vietnam War that was the same as mine. What wasn't the same were our bodies. His six feet two inches—compared to my five feet six inches—were folded behind his desk but still towered over it.

He was, though, the only thing in sight that was impressive. His attorney general's office could have been the recreation room at the local Knights of Columbus. It had false walnut paneling, folding tables, and the kind of metal chairs that usually have MUSIC DEPARTMENT stenciled on the back.

I'd also never before met a southerner who talked fast. The accent was all there, but he spoke as rapidly as any New Yorker. We began by discussing Arkansas politics. In 1977, before I met Bill Clinton, I had gone to Arkansas in search of business from Governor David Pryor, who was lining up a race for the U.S. Senate. I came away from that meeting impressed by Pryor's geniality but not impressed by his decisiveness or his strength. He was expected to run for the Senate and was perceived as a shoo-in. Opposing him in the Democratic primary was a young congressman, Jim Guy Tucker, Clinton's immediate predecessor as attorney general. Tucker was an obvious threat to Clinton's ambitions for higher office.

The attorney general asked me whether I thought Pryor had the race locked up. I said that I doubted it and that Tucker had a real chance to win.

"But Pryor's so popular," Clinton argued.

I answered that the country was in a nasty, angry mood after Vietnam, Watergate, and the oil-price increases. Voters were no longer necessarily supporting people they liked. Now they sometimes voted for candidates they thought would take on their enemies for them.

With Dick Dresner, my future partner, I had recently served as an adviser to Howard Metzenbaum, who defeated Bob Taft in Ohio's 1976 senatorial election. In that race, I told Clinton, most Ohioans believed that Taft was a nice guy and that Metzenbaum was a son of a bitch. Metzenbaum had taken such extensive deductions on his tax returns that in 1969 he paid no taxes at all despite an income of $241,000. Ruthless and determined to buy the Senate seat with his personal fortune, he made quite a contrast to the honorable but reserved incumbent, the grandson of President William Howard Taft.

"Our basic campaign theme," I explained, "was that Taft was too nice to be a senator, that you needed to send a tough, mean guy to Washington to deal with the big oil companies and government bureaucrats. Niceness in a time of anger is a disqualification if you play against it right."

"I agree with you," Clinton said, leaning forward. "Nobody else here does, but I do. David's too nice, and Tucker can clean his clock. That's my problem. In the long run, Tucker's competition for me. We're both young, smart guys. Do you think Pryor can win?"

"If he wages the right kind of campaign, of course he can," I said.

"What do you think I should do?" Clinton asked.

"Well, I gather you'd rather be senator than governor," I began carefully.

"I'd like to be governor; I feel there's a lot I can do here. But the real action is in Washington," he said.

"So let's poll to see if you can win the Senate race," I suggested. The Arkansas talent was all in the Senate race. If Clinton ran for governor, it would be easy to win.

"How do you figure that out?" he asked.

"The wrong way to do it is to ask how people feel about a candidate. This is the South: everybody's very polite, and the candidates all get good ratings, but once the campaign starts, none of this matters," I replied. "What you do instead is compose all the ads and all the arguments each candidate will use. Then you read them to the voters and see how it affects them."

"You mean you actually write out the whole campaign for each candidate and then ask the voters how they'll vote?" he asked.

I explained that I got this idea from the polling my friend Dick Dresner had done for the movie industry. Before a new James Bond movie or a sequel to a film like *Jaws* came out, a film company would hire Dresner to summarize the plot and then ask people whether they wanted to see the movie. Dresner would read respondents proposed PR blurbs and slogans about the movie to find out which ones worked the best. Sometimes he even read them different endings or described different places where the same scenes were shot to see which they preferred.

"And you just apply these techniques to politics?" Clinton asked.

I explained how it could be done. "Why not do the same thing with political ads? Or speeches? Or arguments about the issues? And after each statement, ask them again whom they're going to vote for. Then you can see which arguments move how many voters and which voters they move."

We talked for almost four hours and ate lunch at his desk. I showed the attorney general sample polls I'd done.

He was fascinated by the process. Here was a tool he could use, a process that could reduce the mysterious ways of politics to scientific testing and evaluation. Implicit in his and my calculation was the idea that elections are won by issues, not by images, a thought that would shape our collaboration for nearly two decades.

"It isn't mood or image or vibes that elect a candidate; it's issues," I said.

"Kennedy won on image," he responded.

"I think America fell in love with its politicians in the fifties and sixties, when we first saw them on TV," I answered. "Eisenhower was Dad; Kennedy was handsome; Johnson, our uncle; Nixon, the small-town banker. We were innocents. We were newlyweds, and our men could do no wrong. Then came Vietnam, Watergate, lines at gas stations, the bribery scandals of the seventies. Suddenly, our politicians were human beings like us; we became alienated. We got our divorce. We weren't going to be taken in again for a time.

"These days," I concluded, "we want to know where a candidate stands—the issues and just the issues. Don't ask us to fall in love; just tell us where you stand, and we'll vote for you. We won't bet our hearts on you, but we'll give you our votes until you screw up."

Clinton probed, "So you use the issues you care about to show your personality. If you want to clean up nursing homes, that suggests you must be compassionate. If you are for schools, you might be a person who likes kids."

"That's right." I elaborated: "But you can't go out there and say, 'I love children.' Voters sense that's baloney. You can't even say, 'I'm for education.' Voters know you incur no risks with such a bland position. But if you say, 'I want to raise taxes to help schools,' then voters can believe you really care about kids because they see you're willing to take heat to help them."

We were a match. I had found a client who could delve into the strategy with me, and he had found a rational approach to the mystery of winning elections. I had my first client, and he had his first consultant. Back then Clinton was not the suave sophisticate he is now. He was country. I was city. I hadn't met many people like him. He had, of course, been to Georgetown, Yale, and Oxford, but I got the feeling I seemed odd to him.

At that first marathon meeting, as I got up to leave, I asked to use the bathroom. Clinton showed me to it, and as I closed the door behind me, I was confronted by a full-length pinup of a blonde in a bikini. When I returned to Clinton's office, I gravely asked whether he thought it was a good idea to have such a thing on his bathroom door.

"Don't you know who that is?" the young attorney general asked impishly.

"No," I said, feeling foolish. "We haven't been introduced."

"That's Dolly Parton."

"Who?"

That was 1977, and I should have known. He whistled and said, "Man, you really are from New York."

In early 1978, Eileen and I visited Arkansas to watch as Clinton filmed the first commercial of his gubernatorial campaign, a biographical ad that was meant to introduce him to the voters. It was to feature his mother and his first-grade teacher talking about his childhood. When we met the two women, we were taken aback by their appearance—false eyelashes, rouged cheeks, mink stoles. I took Clinton aside and suggested that his mom and his teacher dress "a little more like typical Arkansans."

"Let me take care of it," he said, and he walked the two performers back into the house. Twenty minutes later they emerged, scrubbed of most of the makeup and denuded of their minks.

When President Clinton's mother died, I sent him a note recalling the episode. He replied in a handwritten card, "I, too, remember the scene from the 1978 filming. After that, she dressed as she pleased."

▲

My poll showed that Clinton could likely have won the Senate seat, but it was iffy, so he decided to run for governor. He told Pryor that he wouldn't run for Senate if Pryor did but that he would run for governor instead. He also asked Pryor to hire me to run his campaign. Pryor was grateful to have his most serious competition for the Senate bow out and said he'd put me on his team.

He did, but much to my frustration, he ignored my advice. I told him—and Clinton told him too—that Tucker was running a campaign very much like the one Dresner and I had helped create for Howard Metzenbaum. Still, he ran soft, feel-good image ads showing himself as one of the boys. Tucker, aided by rival consultant David Sawyer (who died recently—tragically and prematurely—of cancer), ran a skillful campaign whose slogan was "The Difference Is Leadership."

Pryor dropped twenty points in the polls. In Arkansas, if no candidate wins a majority in the primary, the top two contenders face each other in a runoff. Pryor came in just one tenth of a percentage point ahead of Tucker, and now the conventional wisdom held that Tucker would win the runoff, having almost beaten Pryor in the first round.

Clinton and I went to work as a consulting team, designing hard-hitting ads for Pryor. The attorney general suggested using Pryor's strong stand against a firefighters' strike and his threat to call out the National Guard as positive accomplishments.

Then Eileen noticed *Congressional Quarterly*'s report on Tucker's poor attendance record in Congress.

"Of course he was absent. He was running for the Senate then," I responded.

"So what?" she argued. "Shouldn't he have to show up and vote? He's still a congressman, and that's what we're paying him to do, not run for higher office."

Eileen and I had met when she was president of the Consumer Federation of America, the nation's top consumer group. An early public-interest lobbyist and a frequent ally of Ralph Nader's, she has always helped me see the outsider perspective. Born into a political family, I am sometimes too accustomed to the ways of politics to see things as the voters do.

So I wrote an ad in which a dull-voiced clerk calls the names of the Arkansas congressmen.

"How does the House vote? Congressman Thornton?"
   "Aye."
   "Congressman Hammerschmidt?"
   "Nay."
   "Congressman Alexander?"
   "Aye."
   "Congressman Tucker? . . . Congressman Tucker? . . . Is Jim Guy Tucker here? . . . Will someone please check the cloakroom. . . . Mr. Tucker? . . . Mr. Tucker?" While continuing his frantic search, the announcer explained how often Tucker was absent and concluded by turn-

ing the Tucker slogan on its head, saying, "You can't lead if you're not there."

The ad got lots of laughs and lots of votes. Pryor won handily. After the election, an *Arkansas Gazette* editorial cartoon summarized the campaign theme Clinton and I had designed—the need to show toughness. It was a takeoff on the familiar *Peanuts* cartoon in which Lucy holds a football for Charlie Brown as he fruitlessly attempts a successful kick-off. Before each try, Lucy takes the ball away at the last moment, and Charlie Brown ends up on the ground. But here Charlie Brown has David Pryor's face, and Lucy watches in astonishment as the football soars aloft. She says, "David Pryor, you kicked the ball!"

Pryor's comeback earned me Bill Clinton's respect. My theories seemed to work.

▲

My early career was marked by an emphasis on negative advertising. In the '70s, I was one of the first consultants to use such ads. They mirrored the anger of the times and the public's disappointment with a generation of politicians who had brought on the disasters of Vietnam and Watergate.

In the trenches, I was a necessary evil. But once Clinton had been elected governor, my style seemed undignified. So in 1979, he fired me. Clinton had decided it would be inappropriate for the governor to use the same polling and campaign tactics that had helped him get elected.

He was in an Eagle Scout mode (Boy Scout squared). He probably felt like an Olympic pole vaulter who had just soared twenty feet through the air with the aid of a fiberglass pole. I was the pole, useful for making it over the bar but expendable once it had been cleared.

When he fired me, he said, "You do as well as or better than I do what I do best: politics. And that is an assault on my vanity."

He lost his very next election. His increase in car-license fees, which I had advised against, and his opening of Fort Chaffee to Cuban refugees had combined to put him in a vulnerable position. In the final days of the 1980 débâcle, Hillary phoned Eileen: "We need Dick down here right away. Bill's losing the race badly." I was in Orlando, working hard to elect Paula Hawkins, who would shortly became the first woman in U.S. history ever to be elected to the Senate on her own, without the help of a father or husband who had held the office previously.

Eileen asked me whether the Clintons' reaching out for me again soothed my hurt at having been fired. It sure did. I hastened to Arkansas, but it was too late. Clinton had let his Republican opponent, Frank White, pound him while he, keeping to the high road, refused to return the fire. By making Clinton the issue, White hadn't needed to prove he could be a better governor; he only had to show that Clinton had done badly. Indeed, my polling showed that few voters thought Clinton would lose, but they were backing White to teach Bill Clinton a lesson: not to ignore their opinion. When we asked whether they would vote for Frank White if doing so meant that Clinton would lose, enough said no to tip the election back to Clinton. But Clinton hadn't wanted to admit that he was in trouble. With only a week left, we couldn't turn it around.

Without a goal, Bill Clinton tends to become disorganized. He ignores political projects that he has planned carefully. His attention span shrinks. He loses focus. His worst trait is a tendency toward intellectual clutter. It causes him to lose track of political priorities, especially if he already lacks a clear goal and a well-planned strategy. It allows him to be easily seduced by the last idea he heard, so that he will meander aimlessly in pursuit of it. It means that when he tries to return to the task at hand, he can't distinguish the core necessities from the irrelevances. The multiplicity of alternatives paralyzes him. But when he recovers enough to shape his strategy, he becomes devastatingly effective.

After the 1980 election, Hillary called again. "Bill needs you right now, and you've got to help him see how he can get his career back on track."

I found him in this state of confusion when I returned, right after election day, to begin a two-year drive to restore him to power. I saw that it would be futile to talk him out of his depression. He seemed so out of place, a big man cramped into a little office in a local law firm, walking out to the corridor to see whether he could borrow a secretary to do his typing for him. Evicted from the spacious governor's mansion, which had been decorated by former governor Winthrop Rockefeller, he and Hillary had rented a small yellow frame house with built-in bookcases and heavy, Germanic furniture. He mentioned that it seemed odd to do his own laundry now, after two years in the mansion. He needed a goal and a game plan to keep him on a straight track. I knew that once he felt the tug of a goal, order and good judgment would return to his life.

Sensing his mood, Hillary had also approached her old friend Betsey Wright, who had served as political director for AFSME—the labor union for government workers—and asked her to manage Bill's 1982 reelection campaign. Betsey set about restoring order to Clinton's life. For six years, she lent structure to his life and enforced discipline. She almost seemed to wake him up and tell him when to go to bed at night. She tried to schedule his every meal and his every meeting. Eventually, she became too rigid and restricted his capacity for growth and self-discipline. In 1988, he fired Betsey and installed her as chairman of the state Democratic party. But during his disorganized first two years as president, I often thought of how he needed Betsey back. Had she been in the White House in 1993 and '94, she would have taken the president to boot camp all over again and restored his focus.

▲

I approached Clinton's comeback in 1981 with the idea that he had to communicate with the voters early and directly through paid advertising. At that time, many candidates still did not use television advertising at all, and those who did used it only in the few weeks before election day. To use the medium in February 1982, almost a year before the general election, was unprecedented. But Clinton instantly grasped the importance of communicating directly with the voters early in the race to explain his failures of 1980 and to prepare for his comeback. By going over the heads of the press, he could say what he needed to say without a filter.

In those days, Clinton was inclined to grumble and brood over perceived slights in the columns of the Arkansas newspapers. I told him that instead he should be out raising money. Betsey then structured a fund-raising plan that brought in enough money to allow us to get our message out without depending on the goodwill of the press.

This emphasis on advertising foreshadowed the second rescue plan that I devised and implemented for Clinton. In 1995, White House staffers, including Harold Ickes, who had not been in there the first time, were aghast that we were advertising sixteen months before election day. They didn't know that in 1982 we began putting out our ads ten months before the election. But, as we shall see, Clinton remembered, and he let me roll the dice on a massive, early advertising effort in 1995, as he had before.

In 1981–82, the message was rooted in the 1980 pre-election poll: we had to get back those voters who liked Clinton, wanted him to remain as governor, but had voted for Frank White to teach Clinton a lesson, so he would be a better governor in the future. We wanted them to understand that he had heard them, gotten the point, knew he had erred, and wouldn't repeat the mistake.

Arkansans saw Bill Clinton as a young man filled with promise who had gone astray—off to Georgetown, off to Oxford, off to Yale. He had shown how disconnected he was from their lives by raising their taxes. Not just any taxes but fees for car licenses, known in the vernacular as car tags. Now the electorate, which had intended only to teach Bill Clinton a lesson, was saddled with a new governor, Frank White. He was a conservative, a populist, but most of all, a cretin. He was pudgy and pompous, and when he spoke, he sounded dumb. His big initiative was to require that the biblical version of Creation be taught in Arkansas public schools on equal footing with Darwinian evolution, which he deeply distrusted. For that, the *Arkansas Gazette* depicted him in its editorial cartoons as a monkey eating a banana.

I told Clinton to begin the campaign with an apology for raising car-tag fees.

But Clinton didn't want to apologize. "It's not me; it's not my style. How was I going to improve roads without getting the money from someplace?" he pleaded.

I was forceful and pointed out that forgiveness could start only with an apology. "It has to start with an act of contrition," I preached, "an apology."

Clinton's friends scoffed at the idea. "Why call attention to the negative?" said one. "You'll look weak," warned another.

But then he read the 1979 poll results again and got my point. Disregarding the kibitzers in his camp, Clinton agreed that he needed to address the issue head-on. Still, he wouldn't apologize.

In December of '81, Clinton came to New York City to shoot his first ad for the 1982 campaign. We were working with Tony Schwartz, who originated modern political advertising. In 1964, it was his ad that pictured a little girl picking a daisy while an announcer counted down to zero, after which an atomic mushroom cloud filled the screen. The ad ran only once before a panicked Johnson campaign pulled it off the air, but that one airing so chilled America that Barry Goldwater dropped in the polls dramatically and permanently, making his election as president impossible.

Tony is agoraphobic and rarely leaves his old town house on Fifty-sixth Street and Tenth Avenue, but candidates, including Hubert Humphrey, Jimmy Carter, and Walter Mondale, have come to him. Clinton asked for the bathroom before we started and returned chuckling at Tony's two toilets, one labeled REPUBLICANS and the other, DEMOCRATS.

Serious and all business, the former governor sat down to work on my proposed script for his apology ad. "I'll do it your way except for the apology," he explained as he was about to do his first take. "The apology you'll have to leave to me, but I think you'll like it."

Tony turned on the camera, and Clinton, the prodigal son, looked soulfully into the lens and began: "In a few days I will formally announce my candidacy for governor.

"But before I do, I want to speak directly with you to share some of what I've learned not only as governor but from my defeat in the last election.

"All across this state, many of you have told me you were proud of some things I did as governor.

"But you also think I made some big mistakes, especially in increasing the car-license and title-transfer fee.

"When I became governor we had serious problems with our streets and roads, and I did support those increases to try to solve the problems. But it was a mistake because so many of you were hurt by it. . . . And—"

So far, OK. I held my breath to see how he was going to apologize.

Clinton continued:

"I'm really sorry for that.

"When I was a boy growing up my daddy never had to whip me twice for the same thing.

"And now I hope you'll give me another chance to serve as governor because our state has many problems and opportunities that demand strong leadership.

"If you do, I assure you I won't try to raise the car licenses again.

"But I will build on my experience as governor, and from my defeat, to be the best governor our state could have."

I was amazed, just amazed. The line about his daddy was folksy and descriptive. Clinton has a genius for saying powerful things in homey language. I could never have scripted such lines. And he had stayed within his principles. He wouldn't lie; he wouldn't apologize. He thought it was *right* to have raised the car-tag fees, damn it. But the voters would feel that they had heard an apology when he apologized for their pain and told his homespun story. "This guy could be president," I distinctly remember thinking.

The *Arkansas Gazette,* which had previously caricatured Clinton in a baby carriage, now drew him as a monk in sackcloth and ashes. Voters had never heard anything like it, a politician who said he had been wrong. The ad had an immediate impact throughout the state. Unfortunately, it was not the one I had anticipated. In my next poll, his rating dropped ten points. I feared I had killed Clinton's career. I thought the ad would work, but now he seemed dead because he had listened to me. I flew to Arkansas like a prisoner about to receive his sentence. I met Hillary at the airport, and we drove to a meeting where Bill was speaking. On the way, I told her about the poll but brashly and confidently predicted that he would soon rise again. "It's like getting a smallpox shot," I explained with bravado. "You get a little sick, but you don't get the disease when you are exposed to it for real." I boldly proclaimed that Clinton was now "invulnerable to negative ads" because the voters had heard him apologize and had forgiven him. And I prayed I was right.

As we watched Clinton speak, I said to Hillary, "He could be president." In those days, her eyes and hair were brown, and she wore glasses with Coke-bottle lenses. She looked at me through them and said, "We have to get him elected governor first."

Oh—that!

When Bill finished speaking, I did my routine on him. I must have sounded like the lawyer who had lost his client's case in court but was promising great things on appeal. The Clintons probably didn't believe me but decided to stick around to see what would happen.

Then the gods of politics answered my prayers. Clinton moved up and up and up. His chief primary opponent, his nemesis, Jim Guy Tucker, attacked him on car-tag fees, crime, taxes, schools, and anything else he could think of, but none of it worked. It all just bounced off. Why? "He apologized," voters would tell me in my polls.

Clinton won. As he rolled over his opponents, the *Gazette* changed its caricature once again. Clinton was back in a baby bonnet inside his carriage, but the carriage had treads and a turret. It was a tank.

I owe my political instincts to heredity and environment. My granduncle was Judge Albert Cohn, who ran the Jewish parts of the Bronx, a borough of New York City, for the Democratic party organization headed by the legendary boss Ed Flynn. Promoted through the ranks, Cohn became a judge in the appellate division, the second highest court in New York State. I remember meeting him only once, at the celebration of my cousin's bar mitzvah, when I was eight. Judge Cohn asked me whether I was having a good time, and in reply I said, "I didn't like the show."

His son was Roy Cohn, who became known nationally when he was in his twenties and serving as chief counsel to Joseph McCarthy's Senate committee investigating alleged Communist infiltration of the U.S. government. Famous for his brash and ruthless tactics, Roy was anathema to my mother, who had been a borderline Communist during the '30s, when she was in her teens. My parents and their New York City friends would dump on him constantly, all the more so because as Jews they saw him as a traitor to their religion's tradition of political liberalism. My dad was fond of saying, "It is an unalterable fact that Roy Cohn is my cousin." Cohn ultimately became one of America's most famous attorneys, representing Aristotle Onassis and handling mob and other cases that many other lawyers wouldn't touch.

I didn't know him well personally. My mother always held Roy up as an example of something *not* to become. My father told a story about how Roy's parents had hired a tutor to teach him after school when Roy was in his very early teens. He hated the tutor and hated having to study. He tried everything he could think of to get his parents to suspend the lessons, but without success. Finally, in desperation, he accused the tutor of sexually molesting him and got the poor man fired.

My father, Eugene J. Morris, was heavily involved in Bronx politics as a young man. Called Judge by his friends, Gene Morris was slated for high political office. But he left elective politics at my mother's insistence and became one of the country's most distinguished real estate attorneys. Still, he remained a politician at heart. He wrote dozens of real estate textbooks and articles but was respected primarily for the legal and political work he did to help create dozens of middle-income housing projects, containing tens of thousands of apartments in all, that now dot the New York City skyline. He knew the political system intimately and worked closely with New York's political bosses to get his housing projects approved.

We bonded on our walks through Central Park on weekends to get to his midtown office. On these walks, he would explain how the political favor system worked or how patronage was distributed. I learned early on that he loved politics and that success at politics was the best way to win his approval. I may possess some of his energy, his penchant for hard work, and his singleness of purpose.

Temperamentally, my mother, Terry Morris, was my father's opposite. She was a brilliant student who came from an illiterate Hungarian immigrant family. She skipped every other grade in school and so entered Hunter College in New York City at the age of fourteen and, to her great embarrassment, still had knee socks on. Her career as a successful magazine writer spanned three decades. She was a founder and president of the American Society of Journalists and Authors and became well-known for her articles on psychology and medicine. One, in *Redbook* magazine, publicized the horrors of Tay-Sachs disease, a hereditary disorder that affects descendants of eastern European Jews and causes death in early childhood. As a result of the article, the Tay-Sachs Foundation was established and the disease was eventually controlled. Throughout my childhood, I was proud of her pathbreaking stories on schizophrenia, nervous breakdowns, and other topics in psychiatry. She had creativity, a gift for language, and a sense of possibility, and if I have any of these qualities, they come from her.

Nonetheless, I grew up with a chip on my shoulder. Born in 1947 three months prematurely, I began life weighing only two pounds, eleven ounces, and spent my first three months in incubators, untouched by anyone, even my mother. Only after years of therapy did I begin to understand how this early deprivation affected my personality thereafter. I learned that much of my need to bond closely with people came from that experience.

Always a small child (at the age of one year, I weighed eleven pounds), I was well behaved, shy, and fearful. But my parents believed in challenging that timidity. They sent me to a sleep-away camp for eight weeks when I was six years old. For five years, I returned annually to this desolate camp on the lonely Maine shore, with its almost British-public-school-style severity. In retrospect, I suspect I was mildly autistic. I walked late, learned to talk late, read late, wrote late. My interests were captured, as a child, by access points that came to fascinate me. At three, I was given a book on bridges and soon learned the dimensions, construction style, and design of fifty major bridges in the world. At five, an Indian tepee in my bedroom led to my similarly encyclopedic knowledge of every tribe and its history. When I was eight, my parents gave me statues of the presidents. I toyed with them, arranged them, ranked them, and memorized them. They were my entry into politics. By the fifth grade, I'd written, in my chicken-track scrawl, a biography of each president.

Like Clinton, I was entranced by John Kennedy. At camp, I listened to the radio under the blankets on the summer night in 1960 when he won the Democratic nomination at the convention in Los Angeles. When Wyoming put him over the top, I cheered silently, fearful of attracting a counselor's attention. Kennedy's death, when I was sixteen, left me devastated. Depression turned to anger as I watched Lyndon Johnson drag us further into the blood of Vietnam.

I participated in all the major East Coast anti-war protests, inhaling the radicalizing odors of tear gas while chanting slogans at cops. My visit to Chicago for the convention that nominated Bill Clinton in 1996 was my second visit to a Democratic national convention in the Windy City: in 1968, I worked as a volunteer on the political staff of George McGovern as he sought to translate the political momentum of the assassinated Bobby Kennedy into an upset nomination. When the Daley-Humphrey machine rolled over my dreams, I joined the demonstrators in the streets to protest its arrogance and autocracy.

I was perfectly suited to the negative politics of the late '70s and early '80s. Enraged myself, I had no difficulty empathizing with voters' anger and no inhibitions about doing negative advertising. In my early career as a consultant, I became well-known in political circles for contributing to upset defeats of Senate or gubernatorial incumbents in New Mexico, Texas, California, Massachusetts, New Hampshire, Florida, and in 1982, Arkansas.

The idiot savant became the *enfant terrible.*

The political work I did then was all volunteer. For pay, I worked for the New York Citizens Budget Commission, a civic watchdog group dedicated to improving productivity and efficiency in city and state services. In this way—by writing critiques of management procedures—I learned about sanitation truck routes, police patrols, fire truck manning, city fiscal policy, school administration, social services, and welfare programs. I saw the massive inefficiency of government. In my study of sewage treatment, I found plants that had been under construction for twenty years and had still not been completed. Sanitation trucks had three men when they needed only two, a result of union featherbedding. It took longer to build a New York City school in the 1970s than it had taken to build the Empire State Building at the end of the '20s. In my critiques of city and state services, I discovered that government was not a good instrument for social progress, and I came to challenge a central premise of the Democratic party: that government can run programs and run them well.

Bored with the minutiae of local political clubs, I left the Budget Commission after five years and used the knowledge I'd gained to offer "issue advice" to Democrats in New York State. I worked for future mayors Ed Koch and David Dinkins and for gubernatorial candidate Howard

J. Samuels, New York State assembly speaker Stanley Steingut, Manhattan borough president Percy Sutton, Congresswoman Bella Abzug, and many others. My advice reflected my revisionist thinking and helped each candidate find issues that spoke to the growing disillusionment with government that I shared with much of the rest of America.

In 1977, I wrote my only other book, *Bum Rap on America's Cities: The Real Causes of Urban Decay.* In it, I showed how urban problems in the North were the product of a federal bias against the Northeast, whose cities' disproportionately high tax revenues pay for an equally disproportionate subsidy of the Sunbelt. In a chapter entitled "The Pentagon, a Five-Sided Building That Faces South," I showed how defense spending subsidized the Sunbelt. In one called "Let's Get the Middle Class Off Welfare," I noted that 80 percent of the "welfare" budget subsidizes landlords, doctors, hospitals, and administrators. Only one dollar in five goes to the poor.

My political persona, like Clinton's, was also split between bad-pragmatic and good-substantive sides. In the early years, I showed Clinton only the pragmatic side, but as our relationship matured and my own rage ebbed, I showed the substantive side as well.

In 1974, I met Eileen when we worked together on Howard Samuels's unsuccessful race for governor. She was our consumer adviser, and I hounded her daily for fact sheets and position papers. My persistent nagging was not the right way to make friends, and we parted coldly after Samuels's loss. The next year, Bess Myerson, the consumer advocate and former Miss America, was eyeing the mayoral race and so asked me to brief her on city issues. Bess, who knew Eileen, suggested that we work together on a proposal for consumer intervention in the lawsuits relating to the AT&T monopoly. Eileen made clear her dislike of me. "I'll do all the work, and he'll take all the credit," she replied.

But she gave me a chance and came to my office. I got a haircut and did my best to be charming. "I'll draft the proposal and send it by your office. You make any changes you want, and I'll send it out. We'll split the money evenly," I said. This gallantry earned me dinner and a chance to live down my reputation.

My marriage to Eileen in 1977 expanded my focus beyond election day. I changed from a Spartan to an Athenian. I wore suits, blow-dried my hair, and began to feel my anger subsiding. Under Eileen's influence, I learned to appreciate Impressionist painters, Vivaldi, and long evenings at home with friends.

As Eileen and my therapist, Dr. Elizabeth Hauser, softened my rage and brought me inner peace for the first time in my life, I decided to abandon negative advertising as a métier. The baby boom generation was maturing, moving from left to right, forgoing its anger. As the country mellowed in the warmth of the Reagan years, I began to see ways to win that were not necessarily destructive. I remained a hired gun, but I became more strategist than assassin. I began to depend on issues, not negatives, to win elections—not standard issues but new ones, new ideas that attracted new constituencies and led to political victories. In Texas, I helped the Democratic candidate for governor, Mark White, reach Independent voters by promising to end automatic utility-rate hikes by instituting a fuel-adjustment pass-along. In New Hampshire, I encouraged Warren Rudman in his move to become the first successful Senate candidate in the United States to reject political action committee—PAC—funds. In his ads, we asked, "Wouldn't it be nice to have a senator we could call our own?" In New Mexico in 1982, I guided Jeff Bingaman to an upset defeat of lunar astronaut Senator Jack Schmitt. I had come so far from my old negative campaigns that the commercial that helped defeat Schmitt was almost nonpartisan: "Do you believe we should drill for oil in national parks? Jack Schmitt says yes because we need the oil. Jeff Bingaman says no because we may need the oil, but we need our heritage more. Two good men running for Senate. On election day, vote for the one who agrees with you."

This issue-based campaign style became my new professional trademark, and it strengthened my relationship with Clinton. He saw me more as a colleague, a partner, not just in winning elections but in developing the philosophical underpinnings of his strategy for governing as well. When our political visits were over, I'd hang around the governor's mansion. We'd wander over to the massive kitchen, with its industrial-size refrigerator. I'd usually sit on the counter, with my legs dangling, while he'd lean against the stove and munch on a sandwich. Instead of basketball, we talked about recent political history. We were both obsessed with, and enjoyed talking about, the common experiences of the American people since Kennedy's death: the failure of the Great Society to reduce poverty, the mangled war in Vietnam, and the scandal of Watergate. We explored how these examples of government's incapacity to manage successfully left progressives without a tool for implementing social progress. From these talks came our common agenda of using government to stimulate change but not to administer programs. The agenda of providing opportunity while demanding responsibility emerged as we talked, taking the place of the old government handouts.

These ideas first materialized in Clinton's educational reforms in Arkansas. I latched on to an issue Hillary Clinton had suggested: that teachers be tested for competence. This issue came to distinguish Bill Clinton from the special-interest advocates of the Arkansas Education Association, the teachers' union, and made clear that Clinton's commitment to schools was motivated by a love of children, not an affection for teachers' campaign money. He raised teachers' pay, but he wanted results. He increased funding but demanded that students pass certain tests to get promoted. Clinton saw early that the economic problems of his small, undeveloped state could be solved only by major improvements in public education. This link between schools and good jobs was a mainstay of his state political career and became a theme we deployed in his White House years. As Clinton prepared for a possible presidential race in 1988, our talks intensified and we developed the idea of a "new partnership" as the campaign's theme, an idea that evolved into the New Covenant that animated the '92 race.

We both wanted to merge Democratic compassion with the Republican notion of responsibility. When I urged him to run in 1988, I drafted an announcement statement that read, "We need a new partnership between our government and our people. We can't continue to ignore people's problems as President Reagan's administration has. They don't go away. They just grow. But we can't just pass out aid and hand out checks as we did in the New Deal and the New Frontier and the Great Society because when the money is spent, the problems remain, unsolved and festering. Instead, we need a new partnership where government helps people if they are willing to help themselves, where government renders aid but demands standards and performance and commitment to self-help in return."

That speech was never delivered, however, and in 1988 I faced a dismal array of traditional Democrats as potential clients. I turned in frustration to the Republicans and went to work with then congressman Trent Lott of Mississippi and George Bush's campaign manager, Lee Atwater.

Two years later, when Clinton ran again for governor, I agreed to handle his campaign out of loyalty, despite the disappointment of his failure to run for the presidency in 1988. It was to mark a turning point in our relationship.

▲

Bill Clinton had been deeply ambivalent about running for reelection in 1990. It would be his sixth race for a job which he had already held for ten years. He was bored in the governor's office and was toying with the idea of a race for president in 1992.

But his prospects for 1992 seemed remote in late 1989. His path to the nomination was barred by the likely candidacy of New York's popular governor, Mario Cuomo. And with George Bush's popularity at a high, the opposition seemed formidable. Bush's roller-coaster ride in favorability—from the highs of the Gulf War to the lows of the recession—had not yet begun, and America liked its speedboat-racing president with his down-to-earth wife and his appealing aversion to broccoli. When Clinton considered running for president, he was inclined not to seek the governorship again. Like Jimmy Carter in 1974, he was tempted to leave office to campaign for the nomination full-time. But he remembered hauntingly how Governor Dukakis became impaled on his state budget crisis just as he was in the midst of his race for president. "I don't want to have to come back here," he told me, "and raise taxes to bail myself out of a fiscal jam when I'm out there running in '92."

But Bush's popularity presented Clinton with a dilemma: if he didn't run for president in 1992 but left the governorship in 1990, what would he do in the meantime? I felt his prospects against Bush were dim and did not want to see his political career fade away. As governor, he could skip the '92 race if it looked impossible and run for president in '96.

He decided to run for governor again.

In the Democratic primary, he faced Tom McRae, a little-known but very bright opponent who had written about state issues for years from his post with the Rockefeller Foundation. McRae seemed to have no chance at election, but he hired Mike Shannon, a skilled Texas consultant, to run his campaign. Shannon used effective negative ads that satirized Clinton's tenure in office by showing Salvador Dalí clocks stretching out time surrealistically. Other ads featured Clinton loyalists at the airport waving good-bye as Bill took off on yet another out-of-state trip in pursuit of the presidency.

My polls showed McRae gaining steadily. There was a real chance of him defeating Clinton in the primary, thereby ending the governor's political career.

"Your favorability is going up each week, but your vote share is going down," I reported.

"How can that be?" my client asked.

"They're ready to give you a gold watch for your retirement, but they want a new governor. They think you've served them well but that you've been in office too long," I explained.

I said, "We have to transform this from a referendum on you to an election between you and McRae." Hillary came up with a good way for starting the rebuttal campaign. She suggested that she appear at McRae's next press conference and challenge him directly for misstating her husband's record and for not articulating any solutions of his own. "If I take him on," she said to her husband at a meeting with me, "it will get a lot of publicity, but it won't necessarily signal a deep concern about the race by you. It will just be your wife expressing her anger at attacks on her husband."

We agreed to Hillary's suggestion, and she went to the McRae press conference and directly challenged him. The effect was just as she had envisioned. McRae's gain slowed. But more was needed.

I proposed an ad in which we rebutted Shannon's attacks on Clinton for his out-of-state trips. Our defense of these journeys was that they had brought new business to Arkansas and that, in his foreign trips, Clinton had concluded export deals for Arkansas products. Polling showed that people believed that the economic purposes of his travels justified the governor's absence. Our ad showed workmen building a brick wall that rose higher and higher as the announcer spoke of Clinton's success in bringing jobs to Arkansas through his explorations outside the state. Citing McRae's criticism of these trips, the ad concluded, "Don't let McRae build a wall around Arkansas." To film the ad, our media creator, David Watkins, built a shoulder-high brick wall down the middle of his swank Little Rock office and filmed the workmen adding each layer of brick. We began to air the ads in early May as the primary loomed four weeks away.

Clinton's race was not the only election I was handling in Arkansas. Betsey Wright, now state Democratic chairman, had asked that I work on four or five key state legislative races to defeat long-term incumbents who had always opposed Clinton's programs. If the governor were to run for president, Betsey explained, he'd need to have a loyal legislature so he could campaign around the country without fear of embarrassment in his home state. Most of these races were primary fights, and they too were reaching their peak of activity in May.

One morning in early May, just as our rebuttal ad started to air, I underwent dental surgery in New York after several days of pain. Because of the difficulties Clinton was facing in Arkansas, I left the dentist's chair to fly to Little Rock for an early-evening meeting with the governor. As often happened, Clinton had to postpone the meeting until later that night because of last-minute additions to his schedule. I had not taken pain-killers because I wanted to be clearheaded for the meeting, and in some discomfort I awaited his return to the Arkansas governor's mansion.

At about midnight, Clinton joined Hillary, Gloria Cabe, his campaign manager, and me in the cozy breakfast room off the kitchen. My polling showed that McRae's offensive had dropped Clinton's vote share to a meager 43 percent. Generally, when an incumbent's share of the vote sinks below 50 percent in the polls, it means he is likely to lose. Our ads had yet to take effect, and the situation looked bleak.

Clinton's temper got the better of him. Exhausted, worried, and angry, he exploded. "You got me into this race," he screamed, "so you could make some extra money off me. That was the only reason. And now you give me no attention, no attention at all. I'm about to lose this election, lose this primary, against a nobody, and you're too busy with the little legislative races that Betsey got you to give me any attention at all. I pay your expenses and you come down here and you work on Bet-sey's races, not on mine. You've forgotten me. You've dismissed me. You don't care about me. You've turned your back on me. I don't get shit from you anymore. You're screwing me! You're screwing me!"

Clinton has a terrible temper. That's the bad news. He gets over it very quickly. That's the better news. Hillary helps him keep it in check. That's the best news.

These charges, though, were unfair. I was working very hard on his race and had taken on the other races only to help purge the legislature of his enemies. I faced extensive criticism from my Republican clients for working for Clinton and the other Arkansas candidates, my only Democratic clients in the nation. I had told the Republicans that I had always said I would handle Clinton's 1990 campaign because of my prior commitments to him, but they were no less angry about it.

In pain and facing this harsh and unjustified criticism, I lost my temper too. If he was too hasty in his criticism, I was too sharp in my reply. Storming out of the breakfast room through the kitchen toward the door to the outside, I railed, "Thank you, thank you, thank you. You've just solved my problem. I'm getting shit from Atwater and shit from [Trent] Lott for working for you, and now I can solve my problem. Go fuck yourself. I'm quitting your goddamn campaign, and now I'm a free agent. I can be a fifty-state Republican and don't have to take your shit."

Clinton charged up behind me as I stalked toward the door, grabbed me from behind, and wrapped his arms around me to stop me from leaving. I slipped to the floor. Hillary helped me to my feet. The moment I stood up, Clinton became apologetic. "Don't go, don't go, I'm sorry. Don't go, I'm sorry," he said as I walked out the door, slamming it behind me. Hillary ran after me to calm me down. She put her arm around my shoulders and walked me around the grounds of the mansion. "Please forgive him," she pleaded. "He's under so much pressure. He didn't mean it. He's very sorry. He's overtired, he hasn't slept well in days. He's not himself. He values you. He needs you," she repeated.

I calmed down enough to drive to my hotel, and I called Eileen, shaking in rage. Later Hillary called and said how much Bill wanted me back. Then he came on the line to apologize. I phoned my fellow consultant Ray Strother, a longtime friend (so I thought), to tell him what had happened and to seek consolation.

I couldn't leave Clinton three weeks before his primary, but from then on I dealt with him in a formal, almost frosty way. I stopped calling him Bill, always addressed him as Governor, and left when our meetings were over rather than hang around and chat. I think the incident weighed heavily on his mind too and that he sincerely regretted his behavior that night.

I have never talked about it in public since, but Ray Strother has, endlessly. When he was working for Bob Kerrey's presidential candidacy in 1992, Strother leaked his version of the story to several newspapers, hoping to undermine Clinton. And author David Maraniss in his biography of Clinton, *First in His Class,* also reports the incident, citing former Clinton campaign manager Gloria Cabe as his source. Despite numerous entreaties from the press, I refused to be interviewed on the subject. One enterprising reporter from the *Los Angeles Times* came to Connecticut to interview me about the Los Angeles riots. Showing up at my door with no appointment at six forty-five in the morning, it turned out that he just wanted to know what had happened in the governor's mansion that day. I would not comment.

Clinton is given to emotional excesses that lead him to rages. He controls them well, and none has affected his capacity to serve as president. I relate the Arkansas incident here not because it seems relevant to his ability to serve in office but because it did affect our relationship for the next few years and because it's time to put the exaggerations to rest. By 1994, the story had been transformed to the point that Clinton was supposed to have punched me.

"If you had," I joked to him, "I'd have decked you."

He replied that he hadn't punched me. "I was just trying to stop you from leaving," he recalled.

▲

The rebuttal ads we did worked, Clinton won his primary, and it seemed he had the general election wrapped up. Sheffield Nelson, the Republican nominee, spent a huge amount of his personal wealth on his campaign but was hobbled by reports of questionable dealings with Arkla, the giant utility company he had headed. Throughout the race, polls showed that the governor held about 55 percent of the votes.

Eileen and I were celebrating the end of the election season at the home of a friend in New York when, late in the evening, I remembered that I had fielded a poll for Clinton and realized I had better call for the results before the polling staff went home. It was eleven o'clock, and I was lucky my call was answered. Peter Bakalia, the owner of the interviewing house, told me he had his coat on and was about to lock the place up. I mumbled an apology, and he read me the data: "Clinton, forty-five percent."

"Wait a sec," I said, instantly alert. "Say that again."

"Clinton, forty-five percent," he said in a monotone.

"Peter, he was at fifty-five percent three nights ago. Your poll must be screwed up."

He promised to "check the data" and call me back. His return call elevated my anxiety a few more notches. "Clinton, forty-five percent," he repeated.

Why had Clinton dropped ten points in three days? The best way to find out was to examine voters' responses to inquiries like "Please tell me in your own words what you like most and what you like least about Bill Clinton." I decided not to call the governor until I knew more and could give him both the cause and the cure along with the bad news.

Eileen and I left the party. When I got home, at one that morning, there was a lump in my throat. I called Peter again, and he read me two hundred voters' responses over the phone. The answers came back "taxes," "he raised taxes," "he said he wouldn't, but he raised my taxes," "he just wants to raise and spend."

"Raise and spend"—*damn it,* I thought, *that's the text of Nelson's latest ad, the one he had started to run only after I'd done my last poll.* It featured Clinton's own voice saying the words "raise and spend." It went like this:

"What did Bill Clinton do to us in 1979?"

"Raise and spend."

"And what did he do to us in 1983?"

"Raise and spend."

"And what did he do to us last year?"

"Raise and spend."

"And what will he do to us next year if we reelect him?"

"Raise and spend."

This ad had clearly caused the massive drop. A good negative ad at the end of a race can do that. It was now time to call Clinton. So at two in the morning—one o'clock Arkansas time—I called the governor's mansion. The state trooper who answered said, "The governor is asleep." I asked him to wake the governor up, and after some emphatic urging, he agreed to do so. While I waited for Clinton to come to the phone, I remembered how New York's governor, Thomas E. Dewey, the Republican candidate for president, had gone to bed on election night of 1948 confident that he had been elected. When the returns shifted against him right before dawn, the story goes, the trooper guarding his door told a campaign aide who wanted to see him, "The president-elect is still asleep," to which the aide replied, "Well, when the president-elect wakes up, tell him he is not the president-elect anymore."

Governor Clinton came to the phone, groggy and sleepy. "Yes, what's up?"

"Sorry to wake you up," I began, "but we're in tough shape. We've fallen ten points since Wednesday; we're at forty-five percent."

"It's that raise-and-spend ad," he said before I could. "I knew it, I can feel it, I can feel it. It's cutting on us out there. I was speaking yesterday, and I could feel it working." In an acute crisis, Clinton wastes no energy or time on anything that's not absolutely related to solving the problem at hand. He does not despair. He is sharp, alert, quick, and decisive.

Most candidates react to bad news from polls in four stages: denial, depression, plans for recovery, and when they have fixed the problem, euphoria. Bill Clinton simply skipped all but the planning stage—no denial, no depression, and no euphoria.

"The answers suggest that it's definitely the raise-and-spend ad," I agreed. "We've got to answer it right away."

"Call me back with a draft in forty-five minutes, at the studio," he said. He hung up, got out of bed, dressed, and drove right to the TV studio.

I wrote out a reply ad and called him with it. He made a few changes in my text and made the spot. This was the text:

> This is Bill Clinton. You've probably seen Sheffield Nelson's negative ad using my own voice saying the words "raise and spend." But here's what I actually said in my speech to the legislature three years ago. "Unlike our friends in Washington, who can write a check on an account that is over-drawn, we can't. We can't just spend; we have to raise and spend." I was fighting for a balanced budget, not pushing higher taxes. But Nelson got out his scissors and edited the tape to give you the wrong impression. You can't trust Sheffield Nelson.

By dawn, Clinton had dozens of drivers pick up tapes of the ad from the studio and drive them to television stations throughout Arkansas. He stopped his slide, recovered, and won. Most of his enemies in the legislature were defeated as well. Governor Clinton was kind enough to call me on election night in 1990 to say, "You saved my bacon twice this year." But when he asked me to handle his 1992 race for president, our late-night encounter in the governor's mansion was still very raw in my mind. I had built important relationships with Republicans, and frankly I didn't think much of his chances of winning. So I turned him down. As New York City's former mayor Fiorello La Guardia said, "When I make a mistake, it's a beaut!"

When I turned Clinton down, he asked me whom he should hire in my place, and I suggested James Carville.

I've known Carville since the late 1970s. I think he is at his best when he faces a typical Democrat-versus-Republican fight, where the traditional arguments of each party are in opposition. He is a dogged fighter and a true populist. He is like an artillery piece. If the enemy is in front of him, within a certain range, his fire will be deadly. But he's not a tank. If the enemy isn't where he is supposed to be, he can't adjust to a different kind of fight. Clinton didn't know Carville, but I felt he would do a good job—and he did. The Cajun's energy and passion were what Clinton needed. James liked to preach "money discipline and message discipline"—stay with your message, and save your money for TV. That sounded like good medicine for Clinton.

I spent the years of 1991–94 on the periphery of Clinton's life, election, and administration, except at one crucial time. During the 1992 New Hampshire primary, when Eileen and I were vacationing in Paris at a small Left Bank hotel, a ringing phone shattered our sleep at seven o'clock one morning. It was a distraught and nervous Bill Clinton. The primary was only a week or so away, and he had been shaken badly, first by Gennifer Flowers's claim of having had an affair with him and then by reports that he had evaded the draft. He apologized for waking me. "It's one o'clock here," he said. "I stayed up as late as I could so I wouldn't wake you up too early." He asked for advice on how to handle the draft issue in New Hampshire.

His mind was full of the usual data, recommendations from others, bits of polling numbers, and articles he had read. This accumulation tends to litter his brain, like half-eaten sandwiches and uncovered take-out coffee cups found in a campaign headquarters the morning after election night—never assimilated, never rejected, just sitting there, waiting to be put in their proper places. What I think I've done for Clinton has been to help him see patterns and priorities amid this clutter, fresh loads of which are brought in daily by his photographic memory, his hunger for information, and his lightning-fast speed-reading. I've helped him see where to put what and how the pieces fit together. I've helped him process and prioritize his data so that he can get where I know he wants to go.

In New Hampshire, he was in free-fall, with his poll numbers dropping daily as the charges of draft evasion took effect. The Flowers episode did not hurt Clinton nearly as much as the draft issue.

I told him the key thing was not to spend his energy answering the draft charges; he should let his staff handle that. He needed to get his positive-issue message out. He had to revisit the ideas that had captured the lead in New Hampshire in the first place: welfare reform, opportunity and responsibility, the New Democratic agenda. "Put out a positive, exciting message, and I think you can come in second," I said.

I suspect I wasn't the only one suggesting this course of action, but I was heartened to see that Clinton followed it, and he survived the ordeal, as I hoped, with a strong second-place finish.

It was not the last time Bill Clinton would have to stage a comeback.

F   o   u   r

A Secret Channel Opens: Trent Lott

In 1994, as soon as I felt I would be working with president Clinton again, I picked up the phone and called Senator Trent Lott in Mississippi, my main Republican client. "I have to see you after the election," I said, without explanation. "Come on Thursday," he said. That would be thirty-six hours after the polls closed. "We've got a lot to talk about."

We sure did. Lott was considering a race for Senate majority whip, the number two spot in the Senate leadership, right behind Bob Dole. I was looking at becoming the strategist for the Democratic president. Interesting possibilities.

Lott and I had become close during his first election to the Senate in 1988, when he faced Democratic Congressman Wayne Dowdy. At the start of the campaign, Dowdy ran an advertisement in which a Trent Lott lookalike was seated in the backseat of a chauffeur-driven limousine. As the limo whizzed through the countryside, it passed an old lady groping futilely in her mailbox for a check that had not come. The announcer attacked Congressman Lott for supposedly voting to cut Social

Security benefits (he hadn't), and then upbraided him for having a chauffeur at public expense. The ad concluded, "Let's cut Trent Lott's chauffeur, not Social Security."

As I set off to meet Lott that Thursday after the Republican triumph, I recalled sitting with him in his congressional office with the fuzzy crew-cut Republican media creator Bob Goodman. When we first heard of the Dowdy ad I ran into the next room to a typewriter (the Stone Age was still with us) and wrote with Goodman at my shoulder. The ad featured Lott's "chauffeur," in reality a black security officer named George Awkward, in shirtsleeves with his shoulder holster and gun prominently visible. Its text:

> I'm George Awkward. I've been a member of the Washington, D.C., police force. Since an attempted terrorist bombing of the Capitol, Congress voted to provide security protection for its leaders. My job is to guard House Minority Whip Trent Lott. Now, in a negative ad in Mississippi, Wayne Dowdy is saying I'm Trent Lott's chauffeur. Mr. Dowdy, I'm nobody's chauffeur. Got it?

The ad destroyed Dowdy's candidacy instantly. All over Mississippi, kids on the basketball courts were saying, "Got it?" Lott loved the ad and our relationship was off to a great start.

That Thursday, in November 1994, right after the Republican landslide that transformed Lott's own prospects, he and I sat on wicker rockers on the sunlit front porch of his white antebellum home in Pascagoula. We had a lot to talk about. For my part, as he discussed his own position, I wondered how to break the news to him that I was about to sign up with the enemy. Lott is the kind of Republican I like. Republicans come in two versions—elitists and populists. The elitists usually come from wealthy families and often inherit their power. I am not drawn to these blue bloods, the likes of Dan Quayle, Lowell Weicker, and Steve Forbes. I prefer the down-and-dirty populist Republicans. Born poor, most are former Democrats who became Republicans when they saw the Hollywood and academic elites supplanting Main Street values in the Democratic party. Phil Gramm and Trent Lott are the kind of populists who can't get into a country club but are more true-blue Republican than the members.

Lott began talking right away about whether he should run for majority whip. Trent clearly relished the prospect of serving as part of a legislative majority after two decades in Congress. He had scores to settle with the Democrats. In the Senate, he had missed the hurly burly of the House, where he had been Republican whip and was succeeded, when he went to the Senate, by his protégé, Newt Gingrich. Lott's dilemma was that he would have to run against the veteran senator Alan Simpson of Wyoming, known for his acid wit, who was contemplating retirement when his Senate term expired in two years. Lott and I counted the votes and figured out he could beat Simpson by at least a three- or four-vote margin. "Go for it," I urged. "You'll never have this clear a shot at the job. If you wait for Simpson to retire, you'll be in a four- or five-way race, everybody will want the job, and you won't have the clear shot at it that you want." From his days leading legislative panty raids against the House Democrats, Trent had acquired a loyal coterie of former House Republicans who were now in the Senate. Frustrated by its decorum and traditions, they wanted a feisty leader like Gingrich to rally them to combat. Lott, with his spirit and partisan flair, was their man.

Lott had already shown that he would attack a politician ahead of him who was on the verge of retirement. He had won his Senate seat in the first place by declaring that he would oppose the ninety-three-year-old Mississippi Senator John Stennis, who had been in Congress since 1953. Nearly senile, Stennis was planning to run until he died. Lott was tired of waiting and made it clear to Stennis that he would have a tough fight on his hands if he wished to use the Senate as his nursing home. Stennis retired.

Now, once again, he was going to pounce and force the retirement of another elderly senator. His calculation was that nobody else would have the guts to take on Simpson. If he won, he would win it all. He could slide into the majority leader's chair when Dole retired, won the presidency, or was defeated. If he lost, he'd lose it all. The chance appealed to Lott, a gambler who would have done well on the casino riverboats that moor along the Gulf coast.

When Trent told me he would likely take the risk, I told him my news: that the president was asking me to come back and I thought I was going to work with him. I waited for the reaction.

"He sure could use you," he began cautiously. "All those liberals up there have gotten him into some tough sledding. But I guess you're just the person to turn all that around. Think he'll listen to you?"

"Always has," I answered. "He knows that I'm going to offer him good advice and urge him to move to the center. If he doesn't want to go that way, he won't hire me."

"You think you can handle those Sandinistas up there?" Trent asked, using his favorite term for Ickes, Stephanopoulos, and Panetta.

"Yeah," I answered. "If the president's with you, it's funny how easy it is to win."

"Hey," he said, "that'll be fun. You'll run the White House, and I'll run the Senate." Then a frown came over his face. "You haven't answered the real question: what about Hillary?"

"She likes me; I helped her husband win," I answered.

Trent grunted skeptically, and talked about the president.

"I like him," he said. "He's from Arkansas, and we both came from poor backgrounds. I kind of like him. Don't like his politics. Do like him." Then Trent the politician gave way to the statesman. "Besides, I'm old-fashioned: he's the president, and we only have one at a time, and if I can help him, I'll do it. But don't ask me to get mixed up with his wife.

"We'll have to be careful," he said, speculating on how the relationship might work. "If you're seen as too close to me, it will hurt you. They'll suspect you anyway because you've been a Republican."

"Same for you," I replied. "I won't be very popular in the party when I jump over to Clinton. My being for Clinton could hurt you since I've worked for you. If you want to call me a son of a bitch, I won't mind."

"I do that now," Lott reminded me. "I'll have to think of something stronger."

We agreed to stay in close touch.

▲

Lott went to work lining up votes. He got his old House buddies—Hank Brown of Colorado, Connie Mack of Florida, Dan Coats of Indiana, and Judd Gregg of New Hampshire—to help him persuade other senators to vote for him. Phil Gramm of Texas jumped on board, figuring he could use Lott to upset Dole as he fought the Kansas senator for the presidential nomination.

Trent almost got Strom Thurmond's vote. Strom had told Trent months ago that he'd be for him, but age caught up with the ninety-two-year-old South Carolina senator, and he forgot his pledge and signed on with Simpson. "I gave my word," he told Trent in explaining his vote for Simpson.

New York's Alfonse D'Amato wanted, like Rodney Dangerfield, to get respect and figured that he could do so as chairman of the Republican Senate Campaign Committee—the campaign manager for Senate

Republicans. Lott promised him his support if D'Amato voted for Lott for whip.

I persuaded Trent to cancel a yachting trip he had scheduled before he'd decided to make the race. He worked hard instead of sailing and needed every spare minute to nail down votes. But he was less than appreciative of my urging him to cancel the vacation while I talked to him by phone from a balcony of the Lugarno Hotel overlooking the Arno in Florence, where Eileen and I were vacationing.

Trent entered the secret-ballot voting with a four-vote margin over Simpson. Then Bob Dole went to work for Simpson, determined to re-elect his handpicked ally. Dole brought in key senators and pushed them, one-on-one, to repudiate their commitments to Lott. Some of those with weaker knees, like Tennessee senator Fred Thompson, who had earlier told me how much he admired Trent, caved in to the pressure. But enough held firm to elect Lott by one vote.

As majority whip, Trent served Dole loyally, overcoming his resentment at Dole's attempt to defeat him.

When Congress began its new session in January 1995, I visited Lott in his Senate office. Eileen had cautioned me to remember that "Trent is going to want to talk about his career, not Clinton's or yours." But after Lott and I chatted about how he could win over the people who had voted against him, he shifted in his high-backed Senate office chair behind his massive desk in his massive room and said: "I don't need you to tell me what to do in the Senate. What *else* do you want to talk about?"

I got the hint and brought him up-to-date on my moves inside the White House. I asked him how he wanted to work our liaison.

"Very close and very secret" was his answer.

I proposed that I tell him everything relevant to him and keep the president posted on the relationship. The idea was to create a kind of bipartisan back channel through which the president and Lott could coordinate their views, should they care to. I made it clear that I would do this only with the president's agreement and full knowledge. Trent agreed but repeated, "Be careful."

Why did Trent agree? Because in politics, power and information are everything. If he could dovetail his moves with those that Clinton was likely to make, he could benefit enormously. For example, early on he asked me whether I thought the regulatory reform package, which cut back on environmental and consumer protections, was likely to pass. "No way," I said. "It'll never survive the Democratic filibuster, and if it does, Clinton will veto it in a minute."

"How about welfare reform?" he asked.

"Yes," I said. "I'll bet that passes and Clinton eventually signs it. He wants welfare reform, and he'll eventually get a bill he can sign."

"Telecommunications?" he asked, referring to the massive restructuring of phone and cable service now pending before Congress.

"Gore wants that," I reported, "and Clinton will let Gore take the lead on it. I think it's got a good chance."

So acting on that information, Trent focused on the telecommunications and welfare-reform bills, where success was likely.

The president's initial inclination was to shy away from Lott because he was the leader of the conservative wing of the Senate Republicans. Dole's core supporters—including senators like Bill Cohen of Maine, John Chafee of Rhode Island, and Bob Packwood and Mark Hatfield of Oregon—were seen as more moderate. Clinton's natural reaction was to work with the moderates since they seemed closer ideologically to his position.

"It's a mistake," I said. "Lott's much more in touch with what is going on in the Senate." Most Democrats instinctively feel greater kinship with Republican moderates than with the conservatives, but they are wrong. "The Republican moderates won't stand up for you," I said to a surprised president; "they are usually the ones with character defects." I explained: "They're the guys who are usually too rich or too drunk to be taken seriously—guys like Packwood. Nobody takes them seriously. They always cave when Dole pressures them. They have no relationships in the House, so they know that if they stay with you, they'll be isolated. Above all, they don't want to bother. They don't want the hassle.

"If you want to deal with the Republicans," I said, "you have to go through Lott. He's active, he wants to get things done, and he'll keep his word. He can also work with Gingrich when he needs to."

I kept the president well informed of my dealings with Lott, and with the president's full knowledge, I kept Lott informed of the president's thinking. Clinton encouraged the use of this channel. Always suspicious of formal communications, he wanted another dimension in his understanding of the Republicans in the Congress. He was eager for information and wanted to understand where at least one legislator on the other side of the aisle was coming from.

Trent Lott is straight, but he's not boring. His values and approach are square—family, God, country. What saves him from pomposity is his wit. His quips and laugh are dry, southern, and cool, and they prevent him from taking things too seriously. Though conservative, he's no right-wing crazy. His stance is due neither to wealth nor to ideological or religious zeal. His head is not really into the social Christian right. He's pro-life and all that, but more as a matter of southern culture than as a matter of evangelical politics. He comes from a state and a culture where conservatism is the accepted norm. What is right-wing for America is down the middle in the white community of Mississippi. Lott is a politician first and a conservative second. He sees ideology as a guideline, not as a straitjacket, and wants to pass laws, not stand true to dogma.

Lott is probably the only politician I've ever worked for who will say with a straight face, and meaning every word, "It's the right thing for the country." He's unabashed about his patriotism and looks to duty before he looks at either politics or ideology. He figures that he's a good enough politician to be able to get away with idealism.

He was born lower middle class and worked his way through college. He's made very little money in his life and basically accepts that he's chosen a career in which he won't make much. He sides with big business only when it's in his state's interest to do so for local industries, like the shipbuilders. Basically, he'd rather fight to repeal taxes on social security beneficiaries than to live or die over the capital-gains tax.

Both Trent Lott and Bill Clinton are part of the new South. The big difference between the men stems from their home states. Arkansas has historically had a moderate-left orientation. William Fulbright, who led the opposition to the Vietnam War in the Senate, is a prime example of an Arkansas politician. Mississippi has historically been much more conservative. James Eastland, who led the battle for segregation in the Senate, is a typical example of a Mississippi politician.

The two men come from neighboring southern states and from similar economic backgrounds, but they differ also in that Trent is a creature of Washington. He's been there for almost three decades—as a staffer to a congressman, as a congressman, as House minority whip, as a senator, as Senate majority whip, and now as Senate majority leader.

Lott switched parties when it became clear that the national Democratic party of George McGovern had moved too far to the left to be acceptable in Mississippi. His views didn't change; the party that articulated them did. Trent Lott is basically a mainstream politician who happens to come from a conservative southern state.

Initially wary of him, the president warmed to the Mississippi senator. After two years of Gingrich's charming chatter but rigid ideology and Dole's timidity in the face of the Republican right, Clinton finds it a relief to deal with a senator who controls events and doesn't let ideology or his party control him. Above all, he *trusts* Lott to keep his word and to keep their dealings under wraps.

When Clinton came to town in 1993, Lott was suspicious of him, as all insiders are of all outsiders. He wondered at the president's naïveté as he blundered through his first year in office. He bridled at the high-profile role Hillary assumed. He wondered whether Clinton's head was screwed on right. But as he came to see Clinton in 1995–96 and, particularly, as he began to see the president from my inside point of view, he came to understand him and like him.

For my part, I consciously played the role of matchmaker, selling each man to the other. I knew ultimately that they would have to govern together and did all I could to prepare the way. I met Lott every few weeks and called him more often. When I had not spoken with him for a while, he would gently chide me by answering my call with "Hello, stranger."

When I met with Lott and talked to his staffers, they welcomed me as a good man gone awry. Many remembered the frantic days of the 1988 campaign, when I would commandeer a desk and type out an ad or a speech for the congressman in his race for the Senate. They had a hard time figuring out what I was doing with Clinton, but if it was OK with the boss, it was OK with them.

Sipping my ever present diet Pepsi, I'd be called into Lott's office. He would gesture for me to sit to the left of his desk, facing him in his high-backed Senate chair. Often these meetings led to awkward situations. The president paged me in the middle of one, and I returned the call while Lott looked on, smiling indulgently. Another time, Lott was having a particularly difficult time persuading a Republican senator to back a bill the administration was supporting, so he called the man and said he was going to put a "staff member" of his on the phone. I got on and, without giving my name, tried to persuade the Republican of the administration's position. I failed.

Clinton wanted me to stay in touch with Lott and avidly welcomed the information I brought back. As the Clinton-Dole and Clinton-Gingrich relationships hardened into adversarial postures, this connection provided the president with his only real opportunity for a conversation with a congressional leader.

Lott always saw our meetings as part of his job. "If the Republican legislative leaders don't talk to the president's advisers, what use are they?" he'd ask. Good question.

Unlike Dole, Trent does not live to move up and run for president or vice president. The southern senatorial tradition is to stay put, win re-election term after term, and become more and more powerful in the Congress. Sometimes southern senators do make the switch and go for national office, as Lyndon Johnson did. Trent may go in that direction, but that's far in the future. His goal in the Senate is to prove that the Republican party can govern and pass laws. He wants to eradicate the "Charge of the Light Brigade" image that Gingrich and Dole pinned on the party in 1993–94. If he can look back on a balanced-budget deal and on a welfare-reform program that worked, he'll be a happy senator in 1998. He'll be even happier if his record permits him to solidify control of the Senate for the next decade.

By the end of 1996, Clinton's relationship with Lott proved crucial in the passage of the welfare-reform, health-care, and minimum-wage legislation. The final judgment on Trent Lott's role in the Clinton administration came from the president himself in a phone conversation with me in early October 1996, a month after I left his campaign. Clinton said, "Trent really came through in the budget deal we worked out. He's a stand-up guy, and he puts his country first."

Triangulation

"It's from the president of the United States," I tried to explain to the late-night desk man, who spoke no English, at the Hôtel Régine, an old Right Bank hotel across from the Louvre.

He asked incredulously—the president himself?

"Yes, the president himself," I answered, trying to make the clerk understand why it was important for him to pay attention to the hotel fax machine at four in the morning (ten in the evening, Washington time) as the president and I faxed each other drafts of his forthcoming TV address to the nation.

Duly impressed by the president and gratified by the two-hundred-franc note I handed him, the clerk trooped up to my room and back down to his desk every half hour to deliver or receive and send the latest fax. Months later I asked the president for an autograph on his behalf, which I presented to the bemused clerk on my next visit to Paris.

This was the president's first major speech on my watch, in mid-December 1994, and my participation in it gave the term *ghostwriter* a new meaning. I was alone in Paris on a previously scheduled trip. I'd had no idea before I left that the president was about to address the nation for the first time since the débâcle of the '94 elections.

He had to give the speech. Ever since Gingrich's rise to power, a single question had dominated the press: Is the president any longer relevant? "How can Bill Clinton get back in the game?" John McLaughlin roared as he announced the topic for discussion on his Sunday talk show. *Lame duck, term server, walking wounded* were among the milder phrases used to describe the president now that his allies on Capitol Hill were reduced to serfdom in the new congressional hierarchy. It was like a scene from a Western in which the prisoner hears the sound of the gallows being constructed outside his barred window.

I imagined what it was like for him. All the trappings of office—the White House, the receptions, the staff—all of it was a grim reminder that many now thought he was finished.

In our early December 1994 meetings, I had groped for a way to explain how he could get back into the game. Parroting the rhetoric of the congressional Democrats—who opposed all things Republican— would merely be sharing the storm cellar with them, waiting until the Republican twister passed safely by. Adopting the Republican agenda begged the basic question, What is the relevance of Clinton? I wanted to suggest that the president take a middle course, but not one that just split the difference between the two parties. The president needed to take a position that not only blended the best of each party's views but also transcended them to constitute a third force in the debate.

I blurted out the strategy I proposed in a single word: *triangulate.* I found myself shaping my fingers into a triangle, with my thumbs joined at the base and my forefingers raised to meet a point at the top.

"Triangulate, create a third position, not just in between the old positions of the two parties but above them as well. Identify a new course that accommodates the needs the Republicans address but does it in a way that is uniquely yours," I counseled.

I saw triangulation as a way to change, not abandon, the Democratic party. When political activists or public officials seek to change the orientation and policies of their party, they normally work from within through persuasion or, more combatively, through primary challenges to those who espouse the orthodox view. But a president can step out ahead of his party and articulate a new position. The triangle he forms between the orthodox views of the two parties at each end of the base and his views at the apex is temporary. Either he will be repudiated by the voters and slink back into the orthodox positions or he will attract support and, eventually, bring his party with him.

To demonstrate this point, I stood in front of the president with my feet apart to represent the traditional views of the two parties. Then I stepped forward with my left foot to illustrate the new position he was shaping. "This is a temporary triangle as the older and less enlightened members of the Democratic party hang back. But soon it will resolve itself into a new bipolar divide between the two parties with the Republicans back where they have always been and the Democrats fully committed to the new positions you have articulated."

Not as addicted to Euclid as I was, the president ignored my vocabulary. "Like I did when I announced my candidacy in '92, like in my Georgetown speeches, a new force, new solutions," he said in response. I agreed.

For his first effort at triangulation in this new political world, he had decided to propose a tax-cut program of his own, scooping the major item in the Republican Contract with America.

Tax cuts are a sensitive subject with Clinton. During the '92 election, he had promised to cut middle-class taxes, and his failure was a most visible weakness. At least, he had tried to keep his promise on health-care reform, but he hadn't even attempted or proposed a middle-class tax cut. Clinton said that deficit reduction had to take priority and promised that when the economy was moving again, generating revenue as it should, he would cut taxes.

The Democratic Congress abhorred tax cuts, particularly if they led to spending cuts. To orthodox congressional liberals, the idea that we would cut spending on important programs to fund a reduction in taxes, especially for the wealthy, was heresy. Nestled in the shelter of the '93–94 Democratic Congress, Clinton had not been about to invite excommunication by trying to cut taxes. Now, however, with the Republican majorities, Clinton felt able to propose tax cuts and keep his '92 election promise. But he wanted them to be *his* tax cuts, *his* vision, *his* initiative, not the Republicans'.

To distinguish between his tax-cut plan and Gingrich's, he thought about triangulating along the lines of class distinctions: "Let Democrats say, 'No tax cuts,' " he explained; "let Republicans say, 'Tax cuts for the wealthy.' But I'll say, 'A middle-class tax cut.' "

I disagreed with triangulation based on class; I said it must be based on substance. "Class warfare doesn't work in America," I told the president. "When I go shopping in the supermarket, I love to buy no-brand, generic paper towels or toilet paper. I think I'm being really smart by paying less for an equally good product that simply lacks a brand name. But call it 'poor people's paper towels' or 'poor people's toilet paper' and I wouldn't be caught dead in the aisle."

"Americans are conditioned to think optimistically," Clinton agreed. "They always say, 'The economy might fall apart in the future, but I'm going to be better off than ever before.' The Republicans overcome their numerical disadvantage by selling the hope of wealth and keeping the voters in line through their expectations."

I referred him to the survey I had conducted in October '94. "Remember, we asked people if they paid capital-gains taxes?" I asked. "And they all were sure they were a lot richer than they are?"

"And forty percent said they pay capital-gains taxes, but less than ten percent ever do," Clinton answered, drawing on his photographic memory. "Even a lot of low-income people think they pay capital-gains taxes," he added. "So if we differentiate ourselves from the Republicans by saying we are for the middle class and they are for the rich, we won't get the break we think we will."

Clinton noted that the real difference between his views and the Republicans' was that he wanted to target the tax cuts at people who are assuming responsibility for their own lives and need an opportunity to get ahead, people saving for homes, trying to go to college, raising kids, creating jobs. But the Republicans just wanted to give everybody who invests money in anything a tax break, whether what they're doing is important or just speculation designed to make a killing. "Why should we reward some investor who gets rich quick?" he said.

I agreed: "So I think the key here is not which income level gets the tax cut but what they have to do to get it." I reconfigured the idea he had expressed. "The Democrats say, 'No tax cuts.' The Republicans say, 'Tax cuts for everyone.' We say, 'Tax cuts if you are going to college or raising children or buying a first home or saving for retirement.' That's the difference: triangulate by functional differences, not by economic classes."

"But I promised a middle-class tax cut," the president responded, "so I have to aim it somewhat at the middle class. We also don't have the money to cut everybody's taxes even if we wanted to. I mean, I don't know where they [the Republicans] think they're going to get the money for this huge tax cut of theirs; I really don't. But if we have to decide who gets it and who doesn't, we probably need some upper-income limit."

Clinton wasn't ready to abandon class warfare to distinguish him from the Republicans, but he was willing to triangulate according to both class and behavior. So the speech, like much of his rhetoric during the next four months, was a hybrid. Part was shaped around the traditional Democratic attacks on the rich and a professed love of the middle class. But part was the New Democrat theme based on rewarding those who assume personal responsibility by helping to provide them with opportunity. Those who went to college would get tax cuts to help with tuition. Those who saved for retirement or for a first home could do so tax free. But those who weren't taking special steps to assume responsibility for self-improvement could just go on paying their taxes.

This push-pull between the traditional class-warfare language and the new language of opportunity-responsibility was to dominate the rest of the winter of 1994–95. Whenever Stephanopoulos or Panetta would introduce class differences into a Clinton speech, I would urge the president to take it out and instead put in opportunity-responsibility language. He usually did both to satisfy the two camps. But since the press understood class warfare and was slow to get the opportunity-responsibility concept, reporters always covered the soak-the-rich language and ignored the new theme.

Clinton's decision, in which I did not participate, to give a major national address proposing a plan for tax cuts was my first exposure to the way policy was to be formulated. I waited for instructions. And waited. And waited. No instructions came. No orders. No phone calls. So I decided to see whether I should take the first step. I called the president and suggested that we formulate the speech the same way we used to do it in Arkansas: he would tell me what he wanted to say and what he was thinking of proposing, I would test it in a poll, we would analyze the results together, and then I would draft a speech. He agreed.

Still, I was waiting for a buzzer to go off that would warn in authoritative tones, "*Wait!* This is not how it's done *here*. This is the White House. *This* is how it must be done." But no buzzer sounded. The president seemed fully at ease with my process. I was as yet unknown to any other person in the White House except the First Lady and the president's closest personal assistant. On the phone, I was still Charlie.

Bill Clinton uses polls in an important and unique way. It's not the way many suppose it to be: "What should I be for? What should I do?" He knows that already. He wants to know how to get there, and he uses a poll to help him find out.

The best metaphor I can think up is that of a sailboat. You can't just decide to go from here to there in a straight line. This is a democracy—you have no motor; you can't just order a tax cut or any other major program. So you combine two elements to calculate how to go from here to there: where do you want to go? and where does public opinion—metaphorically, the wind—want you to go?

A demagogue does not need to make such a calculation. He simply goes where the wind of public opinion dictates. He irresponsibly raises his sails without seeking to dictate direction and catches as much wind as he can to go as fast as he can. A dictator just starts his motor and goes. An inept politician ignores the wind, sets his rudder according to principle alone, and capsizes valiantly.

Clinton is none of these. He tacks. He consults polls as if they were giant wind socks that tell him which way the wind is blowing. And then he asks the pollster to help him determine which current he should try to harness to move him closer to his destination. He sails with that air current until he has gone too far to the left of his destination. He polls again, reverses his tack, and this time aims a little to the right. And he gets there. He ends up where he wanted to be, in the middle. He always gets there.

To the journalist covering the news of the day as it occurs, without the advantage of perspective, it looks like zigzagging. That's what tacking is. But it's not the zigzag of a flip-flop. These zigs and zags bring you ever closer to the place you want to be.

For him, the mandate was to set the objective, review the plan, and carry his message to America.

For me, it was to help chart a course, help conceptualize it, assist in explaining it to America, and then integrate it into a coherent strategy and plan.

So we talked about what he wanted to achieve. He had reviewed the Republican Contract with America and found its proposal for a $500-per-child tax credit interesting. He felt it would give parents more to spend on their children. But the Republican proposal was too expensive. So Clinton asked me to explore how he could cut it down to the $50–$100 billion range. What cuts would leave the most popular elements of the program in place?

Again, he was tacking. He wanted a tax cut. He wanted one that wouldn't increase the deficit or necessitate horrendous cuts in important programs, so how could he get from here to there? For that, he needed a poll.

Our polling showed that voters didn't care much if the proposal were capped at families making $70,000 a year. But more interestingly, we also found that about 85 percent of parents with a child under eighteen living with them also had a child under thirteen living with them. So, Clinton reasoned, if we just gave the tax credit for families with children under thirteen, we'd hit 85 percent of the families with children—and it would cost about a third less.

I formulated a questionnaire that tested all the tax cuts the president was considering, including capital-gains tax cuts, income-tax rate cuts, and others. We reviewed the questionnaire together by phone.

Clinton had a new idea he wanted included in the poll, an idea that had come from Labor Secretary Robert Reich: let people deduct college tuition from their income taxes. I thought it a sound idea.

Reich, short, feisty, and free spirited, is a wonderful source of inspiration. He is a one-man think tank, constantly suggesting new ways to advance his social agenda of upward mobility for America's workers. He is a pragmatist inside the shell of an idealist. I came to admire him immensely and listen closely to his suggestions.

After hours of carefully reviewing each question on the poll, haggling with me over every word, and adding dozens of extra questions, the president then demanded immediate poll data. I tried to accommodate his impatience. In this case, the firm of Penn and Schoen, which I used to take the survey, made the necessary changes in the poll questionnaire, found 800 people willing to answer the questions in the poll, completed the interview with them, entered the results in the computer, and printed out the results in the ten hours between three P.M. on December 17 and one A.M. on December 18. On the afternoon of December 18, I was on the phone briefing the president on the results, only twelve hours after we had agreed on the questionnaire.

The results showed that Reich's idea for tax deductions for college tuition had resonated deeply with the public at a visceral level, with 55 percent saying they strongly supported it and another 25 percent somewhat supporting it, far better numbers than any other tax-cut proposal we'd tested.

As usual, Washington was totally disconnected from the public's thinking. In the capital, only two questions mattered: How large would the tax cut be, and which income groups would benefit the most? But the people were asking a different question: Which tax cut would benefit the nation most? This was the opposite of pocketbook politics. Voters were not asking, Which will help *me* the most? but, Which will do the most good for *all* the country?

Republicans and Democrats had missed the point. The Republicans hoped that by passing out broad-based tax cuts to everybody, they would induce the people to vote their self-interest. But they showed no sign of doing that. Instead, they wanted the tax cuts that most appealed to their sense of justice and progress. The Democrats attacked the tax cut as favoring the rich. But the people didn't care who got the tax cut as much as they cared about what they had done to deserve it.

This early survey foreshadowed the 1996 presidential victory in two crucial respects. First, it identified for the president and me a shift in American attitudes from self-interest to public spirit. As we polled further, we realized that the average American felt that his or her own personal well-being was impaired more by the dysfunction of society as a whole than by a lack of money for themselves in particular. It was their worries about crime; discipline and values of the young; violence on television; teen smoking, drinking, and drug use; the environment; the affordability of college; and other such issues that constituted the gravest threats to their well-being—not a lack of income. This was the basis for our initiatives concerning values that dominated our agenda in 1996.

If the 1980s were the "me" decade, we realized the 1990s were the "we" decade.

Second, the poll showed us how wrong a tax cut that appealed to self-interest would be. People wanted a tax cut to go to those who merited it and needed it to do good things like raise children or go to college. In August of 1996, when Dole decided to base his entire campaign on the idea of an across-the-board 15 percent tax cut, we had only to refer back to this survey in December of 1994 to see how mistaken the proposal was. Thus, President Clinton opposed the Dole tax-cut plan with his own targeted cut, relying on our polling data.

The tax-deduction plan suggested by the poll was the beginning of a long series of ideas the president would fashion to accomplish Democratic ends with Republican means—in this case, using the Republican means of cutting taxes to accomplish the Democratic end of helping families meet the cost of a college education. In the old days of big government, he would have done it through a national scholarship program, with grants and a bureaucracy. Now, in the age of smaller government, it makes sense to cut taxes so as to accomplish the same goal—sending people to college.

So now what? I wondered. How does the president get from poll to speech? It was the night before the speech was to be delivered on national TV. There wasn't time to wait for instructions. So once again I took the initiative: "Would you like me to set down a few words you might find helpful in the speech?" I asked by phone from Paris.

"Yes, please do," he answered. "Fax them directly to me or to Nancy [Hernreich]. Don't go through the staff," he cautioned.

I called Eileen in Connecticut. We discussed the ideas in the speech, and she said she thought it needed a "wrapper," a slogan by which the public could come to know this speech. I told her that I was using the metaphor of the GI Bill of Rights, the program adopted in 1944 to enable soldiers returning from the war to go to college free. She suggested we call this program the Middle-Class Bill of Rights.

The president liked the idea and used it.

I wrote a first draft on my laptop and faxed it to the White House residence at ten in the evening, Washington time—four o'clock in the morning for me in Paris! I called the usher's office in the residence and asked someone there to be sure the president got it. Half an hour later, after I'd gone to bed, the desk clerk called to announce that Clinton was calling.

"I liked it, but I want a little more about the IRA proposal," Clinton said. In the speech, he proposed extending the use of individual retirement accounts—IRAs—beyond their traditional purpose: a tax-free way to put aside money for retirement. His plan called for allowing people to use these tax-free savings accounts to meet certain other needs: education, medical expenses, or the purchase of a first home.

He tinkered with each word over the phone and finally faxed back to me my draft with his extensive handwritten notes. The president is left handed. I had never before seen a lefty's check marks, which start with a downward stroke and then go up and out to the left instead of to the right. I couldn't figure out what they were. In my next call that night, I asked him, and he chuckled, saying, "That's the correct way to make a check."

Eventually, we had a clean draft.

I later learned from Don Baer, the president's chief speechwriter and my early ally, that he had received this draft from Clinton the next morning, the day of the speech. He called it the Immaculate Conception speech since as far as he could tell, it had come from nowhere. He knew nothing about Charlie.

I was not about to let my first speech for the president air without my watching it, even though that meant my third night of interrupted sleep.

Fortunately, CNN broadcasts live in France, so I was able to see the speech, but unfortunately (for me) I had nobody to share it with. I know it should have been enough to watch the speech and share in the triumph silently, but somehow it wasn't. This experience and the feeling that it inevitably evoked would recur in the following months and came to be both familiar and maddening. Ultimately, my desire for an audience for my increasingly bloated ego led to the self-destructive, immature behavior that cost me my job. Ego is the occupational disease of politics. It infects idealism and turns it into self-righteousness. It distorts a desire to make positive change into a search for power. It lured me out of my lifelong desire for anonymity and led me to lose my sense of reality.

Eager to show the president how well triangulation would work, I had scheduled a poll to be conducted in the hour after the end of the speech, with viewers of the speech as the respondents. Doug Schoen kept his New York–based interviewers busy until one in the morning phoning viewers on the West Coast. Jubilantly, I called the president at one-thirty Washington time—at his direction—to report on the results.

"Forty percent of America watched the speech," I told a bleary Bill Clinton, who was desperate for his first good news in two months, "and your approval rating among those who saw it rose nine points." Triumph.

Then I went back to sleep. It was nearly eight in the morning in Paris. No museums today, I thought.

This was the first step back to recovery. The speech restored the president's ratings to where they had been on his return from the Middle East at the end of October. No all-time highs, but at least movement, movement up. So we can move the numbers, these dismal, dismal numbers, I thought to myself. Maybe this guy can pull it off after all. For all my bravado since the '94 elections, this was the first time I ever felt that maybe we really had a chance to win, or at least to avert a landslide defeat.

Charlie

We were alone in the White House residence, and nobody knew I was there. As the president stood and looked over my shoulder, I worked at the typewriter on his 1995 State of the Union address. When I looked up, he seemed to loom over me like a sequoia. I turned fully around to look up at him, way up, and said, "Mr. President, you know, I've dreamed of doing exactly this in exactly this way ever since I was eight years old."

He replied, "So did I," and left the room.

The president's first goal that day was to produce a speech that reflected a triangulated response to the Republican Contract with America. His second goal was to do it in complete secrecy so that no one else on his staff knew that I was involved at all.

The president had given me a sheet of white lined paper on which he had made notes about the order of the speech. Had the speech appeared on the White House computer network, the presence of an outsider would have been obvious, so we had to hunt for a typewriter for me to use. After a room-to-room search, a White House usher located an old IBM, dusted it off, and lugged it upstairs to the Treaty Room.

From that point, Clinton's method was simple. I sat in the Treaty Room on the second floor of the White House residence while the president sat two doors down, in the yellow dressing room off his bedroom. As I completed a page, I brought it down the hall to him. He sat at his desk, an unlit cigar in his mouth, and wrote his version of the speech in longhand. Why longhand? Because his staff knew that he couldn't type, and had he produced a typed speech, the involvement of another person would have been evident.

At one point, we walked together from the dressing room back to the Treaty Room after I'd delivered a few pages to him. We discussed how he could continue to conceal my involvement. He said he was keeping his speechwriters over in his office—in the West Wing—while we worked in secret in the East Wing. "I like subterfuge," he said. "That's why I like you." Then he seemed embarrassed and hastily added, "One of the reasons."

Why the secrecy? At the time, I thought he was protecting me, taking into account my desire to see how things worked out before I burned my Republican contacts by announcing my full commitment to him. But now I suspect the real reason was that he wanted to keep me for himself and not share me with his staff. This president was very independent of his staff. Most staffers had loyalties not just to the president, but also to a faction of the party. He wanted me to empower *him* in his dealings with his staff rather than let staffers use my ideas to thereby empower *them* in their dealings with him.

Lott, of course, knew all about my role with Clinton, but none of the other Republicans knew. I didn't want them to until I had decided that I would have enough impact on Clinton's strategy to make staying with him worthwhile.

▲

This State of the Union Address was critically important to the president. It was his response to the dramatic challenge that the GOP had mounted in the aftermath of its 1994 victory, which gave the party control of both houses of Congress for the first time since 1952. The Republicans had come on like the German war machine invading Russia in 1941. In their headlong advance they bypassed such heavily defended issues as gun control and abortion just as the Germans had bypassed heavily defended cities in their rush to gain territory. The Republicans kept their focus on their main objective: the repeal of sixty years of government growth, stretching back to the New Deal. They called for reductions in environmental protection, cuts in meat and poultry inspections, in food and drug regulation, cuts in Medicaid guarantees of care for the poor, cuts in nursing-home standards, cuts in nutrition programs like free school lunches and food stamps, cuts in any federal role in education, and cuts in the middle-class entitlement of Medicare.

On some issues, like welfare reform and deficit reduction, they were backed by popular majorities. On others, they left their political backing way behind. But the Republican blitzkrieg smashed ahead, paying little heed to their lack of the political equivalent of logistical support: popular backing.

Meanwhile, the Democratic congressional leaders acted as if the last election had never happened. They stubbornly defended every inch of bureaucracy so that I wondered whether they imagined their defeat had been a mere typographical error. It was as if they were waiting for a recount to restore their mandate to continue the growth of the federal government. To every cut, they said "No, no, and no again." Their strategy seemed foolish to me. The electorate had spoken. To ignore this sentiment was suicidal. But as the Republican program unfolded, it became clear that it too would never sell in America as a single package. It completely flouted the most deeply held aspects of what the president came to call the "common ground" of the American people.

The president was truly enraged by what the Republicans were doing. He always personalized the harm of their proposals by citing an imaginary child who couldn't get a hot lunch at school or a teenager whose college scholarship had been cut. His liberalism on these issues was elemental; it was not intellectually driven. It reflected the experience of a poor boy from Arkansas dependent on public largesse for his education and much else in his early life. Sometimes, even when Clinton and I were alone and he didn't have to convince me, he would wave his fist in the air as he bellowed out a point about the Republicans' cuts. I was reminded of Queen Victoria's comment about Prime Minister William Gladstone, that he addressed her as if she were a public meeting.

But in assessing where the progressive programs of the past had gone wrong, the president and I shared common experiences. We discussed, for example, the failings, for all its achievements, of Johnson's Great Society programs: student loans that were not repaid; welfare recipients who were trapped in a lifetime of dependency rather than spurred to self-reliance; antipoverty programs that became job-training centers and then drug-rehabilitation clinics, changing with each fad while their salaried bureaucrats remained, as did the poverty.

We drew on our conclusions in Arkansas about the introversion and narcissism of the '80s. The public ignored social problems and measured progress only by private gain. Now we sought a combination of the intentions of the Great Society and the "tough love" concepts of discipline, standards, and responsibility that underscored the realism with which the Republicans addressed the government's social programs.

In Arkansas, Clinton had reached for a new approach on the central issue of education, embracing both Republican calls for discipline and standards and Democratic demands for higher teacher pay. As Clinton watched the success of this program from the political stage, he came to see it as the forerunner of a national agenda. When Clinton had flirted with entering the 1988 presidential race, he and I had debated the ideas in Daniel Yankelovitch's 1981 book, *The New Rules*. Yankelovitch traces America through three phases of social ethics in the last fifty years. First, the years of self-denial by our GI-generation parents who put off self-fulfillment, sacrificing for their children. Second, the self-fulfillment ethic of our boomer youth that made consumption a moral duty. Self-denial was seen as neurotic and a dangerous repression of one's impulses. Through the sexual revolution of the sixties, the "me" decade of the seventies, the yuppie adventures in hedonism, and into the indulgent, selfish, money-hungry eighties, we tested life to its limits. But Yankelovitch suggested a third social ethic had begun to evolve, one of commitment. He cites as evidence declining sexual promiscuity, drops in drug and alcohol use, a decrease in divorce. Clinton and I came to see the ethic of commitment as the father of a new political force: liberalism with standards. Give to the needy, but exact performance and responsibility in return. To my mind, the ethic of "give but demand" combines the generosity of liberalism with the realism of conservatism.

This new force in our politics became the opportunity-responsibility-community theme of Clinton's 1991 announcement of his campaign for the presidency and then metamorphosed into the "new social covenant" he articulated when he accepted the 1992 Democratic nomination.

The Democratic party was having none of this. "Give me the old-time religion; it's good enough for me," the Democrats seemed to sing as they repeated every mistake that had led to electoral rejection in the first place. They ignored not only the rejection of 1994, but those of 1988, 1984, 1980, and 1972 as well.

In January 1995 I urged the president to play off this intractability by showing an eagerness to work with the new Republican leaders of Congress. I urged him to appear to be as open as possible to the Republican leadership to show that *they* were outside the consensus with *their* extremism, not that *we* were flouting the popular will with *our* intransigence.

The president agreed and made the key decision not to stand with the Democratic left in total rejection of all that the Republicans were attempting to do. His decision was courageous and wise and ultimately saved the Democratic party from itself. While others attacked all the Republican legislation as extreme, the president mixed criticism with approval of the better parts of the Republican program. And he followed through, first by signing a Republican-sponsored bill subjecting Congress to the laws it passes to regulate the private sector and then by approving legislation blocking federal unfunded mandates on the states.

▲

To prepare for the State of the Union Address, the president had asked me to take the mother of all polls, a huge national survey that tested every aspect of the Republican offensive. The aim was to clarify the specifics of Clinton's opportunity-with-responsibility program.

The survey was 259 questions long. It had to be divided into five parts, since no one would willingly stay on the phone for the hours it would have taken to answer every question. It was by far the longest poll I had ever done, and we followed its results throughout the year in battling over the Republican budget proposals.

I was very excited when I went to meet the president on Thursday, January 19, 1995, to brief him fully on the results. It took five hours. Here was the anvil for the hammer blow of policy.

The core of the strategy that emerged from the poll results was to embrace parts of the Republican initiative and reject others. We would work to eliminate the deficit, require work for welfare, cut taxes, and reduce the federal bureaucracy. Indeed, the president had already gotten a deficit-reduction package through Congress without Republican support, which has helped cut the deficit by 60 percent and reduced the federal workforce by 250,000 jobs, more than 10 percent. But we would reject emphatically and inflexibly the efforts to cut Medicare benefits, eliminate Medicaid guarantees, weaken environmental-protection laws, and reduce federal aid to schools. As I noted in my memo to the president, "Medicare cuts are your single biggest weapon against the Republicans. They are hated by the public, old and young."

We met all day Monday, January 23, to work on the speech. As we wrote, the president became especially frustrated by our inability to reduce our position to a thirty-second rationale. "The Republicans can do it; I can't. They say, 'We're for less government, lower taxes, welfare reform, deregulation, curbs on immigration, and core social values. We stand for scaling back government's role in people's lives. Government is the problem, not the solution.' See," he said, proud of his ad-libbed theme statement for the other side, "I'm pretty good at their rationale. I've got it down pat. But what's mine?"

"It's opportunity and responsibility," I said.

"Doesn't grab me like theirs does," he answered gloomily.

After hours of work, he summoned me to his dressing room, where he continued critiquing the speech as he finished dressing for a bill-signing ceremony. "It's too long. . . . It's not human enough. . . . It's not doing anything for my political base. . . . It's not presidential enough."

Another speechwriter would have been suicidal—or homicidal. But I'd worked with Clinton long enough to know that no sooner has he decided what to do than he harshly criticizes his own conclusions. He will be withering in subjecting it to argumentation, ridicule, scorn, and derision. Anyone listening to him will swear that he won't do what he had decided to do yesterday—and will in fact do tomorrow. But all he's doing is venting his own doubts aloud to see how they sound. Silently he is articulating the case for it, but you'd never know that from listening to him. My years of experience told me that every word of criticism meant that he liked the speech.

When he returned from the bill signing, we got back to work on the draft, and then—and only then—did he sit down with his speechwriters to ponder his speech text. Later Don Baer said once more how eerie it was to have this new draft, unrelated to any previous one, descend from on high with no fingerprints or other identifying marks. First there had been the Immaculate Conception speech. Now he said, "It was like watching the planet Neptune. You couldn't see Pluto, but with Neptune acting the way it was, you could be pretty sure that Pluto was out there."

Baer's remarks confirmed nobody knew who this mysterious Pluto was.

What emerged was really two speeches, one a tightly written and well-delivered forty-minute message explaining where the president embraced Republican goals and where he differed from them sharply. Its tone was eloquent and its phrases sometimes ringing. It was the first speech since the '94 defeat in which the president had laid out the opportunity-responsibility doctrine as the alternative to the no-government agenda of the Republicans. "We must not ask the government to do what we should do for ourselves. We should rely on government as a partner to help us do more for ourselves and for each other."

Bravo.

In the final version of that first speech, he and Don Baer had taken my words to another plane. They were lofty, presidential, an expression of national leadership that I was only beginning to grasp. So far, very good.

The second part of the speech, however, was a thirty-minute self-indulgent, rambling monologue. But perhaps the nation understood what was happening in those final thirty minutes better than I did or better than the press did. Here was a man who had been savaged in the election now basking in the national spotlight, relishing the rounds of applause that washed over him. In that moment, I saw a man at ease, enjoying himself, indulging in public approbation—but not giving a speech. In those final thirty minutes, the public saw Clinton at his best, without artifice or pretense, genuinely enjoying his talk with them; they were settling back in a booth at McDonald's chatting over a hamburger and a cup of coffee with their president. The informal language, the familiar style, his obvious enjoyment at having a chance to speak with them was deeply comforting to the American people, no matter how tedious it seemed to me.

At the time, I was horrified. The next day I told him he was like a rabbi at Friday-night services who has so longed for an audience in his empty synagogue all week that he could not bring himself to end his sermon.

Clinton defended himself against the press's accusation that the speech was too long by saying, "It was really only a forty-minute speech. I just had no idea they'd applaud so much." I dismissed his explanation, calling it "an accountant's defense," but admitted that the country liked the speech, and his ratings rose as a result.

One way or another, it worked. The poll numbers had finally begun to move. When I had joined the president in early November, he was losing a race to Dole in my polling by 33–49. Now he had inched up a few points. Not much, but a change nonetheless. His ratings were higher than they had been for months. My early hopes flared again. Perhaps there was a way out.

▲

Or perhaps not. The president left the podium in triumph after delivering his centrist message, and walked into the frigid embraces of his liberal staff and the Democratic House leadership, which called the shots in the White House that February and March of 1995.

And his ratings dropped right back to where they'd been—dismal.

Each week in February and March the House Republicans, shaped into a phalanx by Newt Gingrich's discipline, passed bill after bill to implement their Contract with America. Democrats and the White House seemed to oppose every step in some of the rawest partisan fighting that Washington had seen in decades. Tempers flared, insults flew, but the march of legislation went on without any break in ranks: the Republican crime bill, the deregulation bill, the balanced-budget amendment, their appropriations bills to slice spending on the environment and education, tort reform, and on and on. The president was largely irrelevant as the House drove the government.

February and March were truly the Gingrich administration. Even Dole was an afterthought in the Republican revolution who couldn't keep pace with his House colleague. Clinton was invisible. The nation watched the Republican Congress grind on with its agenda. It was a withering sight.

During this time, I was still Charlie, unknown to all but the president. We continued our weekly meetings. On February 8, Doug Schoen joined us. The president had overcome his worries about the pollster and now saw him as a reliable, politically acute observer and adviser.

I felt like an outsider, cut off as I was from the White House staff. Each week I would give the president the same advice: move to the center. Each week I criticized the president's speeches for not offering a positive alternative to his attacks on the Republicans' budget cuts. I argued that as long as we lined up with the congressional Democrats and just sniped at cuts in school lunches and Medicare, we would get nowhere. "These guys in Congress [the Democrats] just want to refight the '94 elections and make them come out right this time. It won't happen," I predicted. I pleaded with the president to stake out an alternative rather than just blindly condemn the Republican budget cuts.

The president said he agreed with me. He too sensed that he looked weak and liberal in his failure to follow through on the new directions he had mapped out in his State of the Union. He spoke increasingly of the need to move toward a more balanced and less partisan critique of the Republican initiatives, and I would go home happy. But week after week his speeches seemed simply to echo the partisan die-hard opposition to the Republican budget proposals being voiced each day on the House floor by Democratic leaders Dick Gephardt and David Bonior.

When I complained, the president would cite bipartisan references in his speeches and show me quotes from the script—which the news media ignored—where he had dedicated himself to the goals of cutting taxes, reducing government, and balancing the budget, but doing so in ways that differed from the Republicans' methods. Indeed, if a speech were 90 percent bipartisan and positive but 10 percent sharply critical of a Republican proposal, it was covered as a negative attack on Gingrich, and all the positives would go unreported. I began to see these speeches as inky water—ninety-nine parts water and only one part ink but still too inky to drink.

The president's poll ratings fell to pre–State of the Union levels during February '95, as did the Democratic party ratings, but by March the ratings of the Republicans in Congress were heading south too. What was going on? The downturn in the GOP popularity heartened the liberals in the administration and in Congress. Now they had turned the corner, they figured. I was sure they were as wrong in their diagnosis as in their remedy. I argued that the drop in ratings suggested the public was fed up with both Clinton's passivity and Republican extremism. They reflected frustration over the inability of both Congress and the White House to move ahead, frustration that would cripple the incumbent president, too, in the long run. "You can't win if the country thinks things are going to hell," I told Clinton on March 16. "You're still the incumbent. In that sense, you and the Republicans are joined at the hip. We go up or down together as the country thinks the government is working or not. You are part of the government before you are a Democrat, and when government becomes partisan and accomplishes nothing, everybody's ratings drop."

The president complained that his speeches were too liberal. "I get up there, and all I have in front of me is liberal, populist, partisan stuff. I need more balance back in these speeches."

I was confused. Why don't you just write it in? I wanted to ask. It's your mouth and it's your voice. I didn't say that because it seemed too obvious.

The truth, which I learned only as the months passed, was that President Clinton was in chronic conflict with his staff, and he was very dissatisfied. He told me, in the privacy of his residence office, that "I spent all my time before I took office choosing my Cabinet. Richard Neustadt [the presidential historian] was in here the other day and told me that I have the best Cabinet since Jefferson. It's a great Cabinet. But I didn't spend the time I should have choosing my staff. I just reached out and took the people who had helped get me elected and put them on the staff. It was a mistake."

Time and again he would derisively refer to his staff as "the children who got me elected." He would plead for more "adults" in the White House. Why didn't he fire a bunch of them and bring in new people? Indeed, he kept them all, even though they were responsible for the greatest midterm election defeat for an incumbent president since 1946. He didn't even change his Congressional Relations staff once the Republicans were running Congress.

Perhaps he was afraid that anyone he fired might turn on him—might denounce him or leak damaging information and turn into an adversary. When I asked him why he didn't fire his staffers, he referred with pride to his success in ousting David Dreyer, a White House aide from before my time. He said Dreyer had been a huge leaker of stories to the newspapers. "It took me months to get him moved out of the White House," Clinton confessed. Why the president couldn't simply call up Panetta and say "Fire Dreyer" I never really understood. I guess it just wasn't his way.

The White House staff was run by Leon Panetta, the ultimate insider. A former congressman, Panetta respected the institutions of government, the established protocols of process, and abhorred circumvention. He mistrusted spontaneity. Deeply loyal to his Democratic congressional buddies, he at first seemed to me to be a liberal. "Leon's no liberal," Clinton would say. This was true. He just *was* the establishment.

Panetta had two deputy chiefs of staff, Harold Ickes and Erskine Bowles. They were total opposites. Ickes was the street fighter I had opposed on the West Side of Manhattan decades ago. Practical, hard, unflappable, ruthless, stubborn, he is a warrior. Erskine, a wealthy and genteel southern gentleman, was a successful businessman who entered politics an ingenue. As a businessman, he made sure things ran well. As a politician, he learned quickly but, at the beginning, had a long way to go. Erskine was the president's loyal servant. Inexperienced and non-ideological, he was a blank slate who faithfully mirrored, and competently executed, the president's priorities.

Behind all three was the driving intellectual force of the staff—George Stephanopoulos. Friendly, affable, charming, and brilliant, George's ideas and George's suggestions drove the process before I arrived. A dedicated liberal, he combined an often maddeningly fixed ideology with an infinitely fluid and subtle approach to tactics.

In the conflict between the president and his staff, each side had its powers.

The staff's foremost weapon was the ability to select the information the president received. Clinton didn't really read the newspapers. He got a collection of clips every day from more than a dozen newspapers: *The Washington Post, The New York Times, USA Today, The Wall Street Journal, The Washington Times,* the *Chicago Tribune,* the *Los Angeles Times, The Miami Herald, The Boston Globe, The Hartford Courant,* the *Arkansas Democrat Gazette,* and a few others. The clipping file also included a summary of the previous night's network news shows.

I don't think he read the clips much. Dozens of times I would mention a front-page story of great importance in *The New York Times* or *The Washington Post,* the first two papers in the file, and he had not seen them. He almost never knew what was on the nightly news. In my weekly meetings, I began including a summary of the content of the TV news and the frequency of front-page mentions of topics in twenty-five of the nation's newspapers. It was all new information to him.

But he did not underrate the power of the press. "The people don't get it that the press runs the government," he said in March 1995. He thinks of the press in highly personal terms, seeing each story as a reflection of the biases of the writer or reporter. "They love to destroy people. That's how they get their rocks off." From inside the White House, it did often seem that there was a confusion of skepticism, which is a necessary vigilance, with a cynicism that is corrosive. Some reporters seem to think that the real story is never the candidate's idea, but always the motivation to improve his or her political status. The terror of being conned tends to ensure a negative response to any initiative or innovation. Were the same suspicions applied to business, where the profit motive takes the place of the electoral one, stories might read like this:

> General Motors, in a cynical effort to boost profits, today announced that it had developed a car that would run without gasoline and would perform as well as the traditional internal combustion engine. Fearful of losing its competitive position and under fire for bad management in the past, observers said the GM announcement was timed to have maximum impact on its stock prices. In the past few months, investors have grown wary. . . .

Clinton did read magazines and op-ed articles regularly. If you wanted your views to reach the president, the way to do it was through the op-ed pages of *The New York Times* and *The Washington Post* or through articles in *Harper's, The New Yorker,* the *New Republic, The Atlantic,* and a few other magazines.

The staff made sure he saw certain articles but not others and could spend all day steaming him up about a topic that underscored the need for confrontation with the Republicans while keeping from him any item that argued for moderation and compromise.

The president knew that his inability to read all the papers—due to demands on his time—made him exceedingly vulnerable to staff censorship. He tried to overcome it by making dozens of phone calls each week to FOBs—friends of Bill—who would share their views with him. The journalists Sidney Blumenthal, Mort Zuckerman, and E. J. Dionne were constant favorites, as were former governor Ned McWherter of Tennessee, Governor Evan Bayh of Indiana, Senator John Breaux of Louisiana, Senator Joe Lieberman of Connecticut, Al Fromm, head of the moderate Democratic Leadership Council, and others.

The staffers also controlled the president's schedule. He very often had no time to think or to act on his own and, unfortunately, very little time for sleep. Clinton could not resist a meeting with local politicians or an opportunity to give a speech. When he traveled, they would cram his day and evening with wall-to-wall meetings with every local leader or fund-raiser they could scrape up. He would leave the White House at six in the morning and typically not return until one the following morning. On trips of several days' duration—such as to the West Coast, which he visited frequently—he would keep such a schedule for two or three days in a row.

Clinton willingly agreed to each new meeting and demanded even more speeches and more stops on each new trip. The president would so exhaust himself with all these events that he would be, in Nancy Hernreich's words, a "basket case" when he returned.

Despite claims to the contrary, Clinton, like most people, does not function well with little sleep. He requires a great deal of rest to function coherently. After a trip to the West Coast or overseas, three or four days would pass before he performed at his best. I estimate that during the period I worked closely with the president, he was exhausted, seriously depleted, and sometimes even ill about one quarter of the time. Add another quarter for the days he was out of town all day and all night—including the postmidnight returns to the White House—and he was able to function at top speed in the Oval Office only about half the time. Of course, his half speed was like top speed for the rest of us.

While the president was his own worst enemy in permitting the overscheduling, he bitterly complained about it: "Every time I look up, there's someplace else I've got to go or someone else I've got to see." I contributed to this problem with my demands for paid advertising, which imposed the particularly heavy burden of fund-raising.

As 1995 progressed, Erskine Bowles, as Clinton's calm and effective deputy chief of staff, used his business experience to clear the president's day sufficiently to give him more time to think. Thanks to Erskine's intervention—at Clinton's request—the president had more time to read and talk on the phone, and it was then that he regained command of his presidency.

When he wasn't being driven to exhaustion, the president recovered by taking off more time than was commonly acknowledged. He would sneak in an afternoon of golf on a weekday and kept a relatively light schedule most weekends, except during the campaign period. He tended to hang around the White House or go golfing on weekends, only infrequently going to Camp David for a more thorough rest.

Sometimes the staff drowned the president in far too many details that clouded his view of an overall situation. Overwhelmed by information and specifics, Clinton couldn't help himself as he pursued the intricacies of each problem and learned each statistic. Here the president's greatest strength very often hurt him.

So often when we spoke, the president would begin with a detail when I thought he should have been looking at the overall concept. But I was an adviser, and he was the president. An adviser can afford to focus on the big picture, but a president has to take actions every day whose "details" can cause huge misery or great relief, so I came to understand, and empathize with, his focus on specifics.

Clinton is uniquely swift and effective at encoding, storing, and retrieving a vast amount of information. But he is not nearly as adept at prioritizing, categorizing, conceptualizing, and analyzing the material in his possession. Thus, he tends to be immobilized by the mass of material he consumes, rather than empowered by it.

The president did realize that he was drowning in information, and he reached out to me frequently to download seriatim, bit by bit, all the new material he had acquired. He was like a pelican eating the fish he carried in his beak. He would ask me to assess its relevance to our overall plan. He would quote an op-ed piece, a magazine article, and a phone conversation that made three different points. I'd offer my views on how I thought they fit or didn't fit our basic thrust.

The staff's most pernicious weapon was to shackle the president by leaking stories that tied up his options. Frequently Clinton would ponder his position, and suddenly a news article would announce that "informed sources" indicated he had decided on a course of action. Then the reaction for or against the supposed decision became a factor to reckon with in whatever course he eventually chose. If he "reversed" the decision he had actually never made, he was likely to be accused of flip-flopping.

In the spring of 1996, for example, Wisconsin passed a far-reaching welfare-reform bill designed to move welfare recipients into jobs. To implement its legislation, however, the state needed a waiver from the Department of Health and Human Services in Washington. The department was averse to most welfare-reform proposals and regarded the Wisconsin plan as anathema, whereas the president wanted to approve the Wisconsin welfare waiver. He said so in a radio address shortly after the bill was passed and repeated it several times. But the waiver was complex, since the bill had to be squared with many federal statutory requirements, some of which the president had no authority to waive. As he was considering these legal complexities, *The New York Times* ran a front-page story, based on Health and Human Services Department leaks, that said the president was likely to turn down the Wisconsin waiver request, an option the president had emphatically rejected. He resolved the situation when he signed the welfare-reform bill Congress passed in August '96, making the Wisconsin issue moot. But the *Times* story made the decision seem like a flip-flop.

At one of our intermittent Oval Office meetings during 1993, before I came back on board, the president was livid because a story had leaked on April 15 that he was considering a value-added tax as a way of paying for health-care reform. Clinton was determined not to raise taxes again that year, after having taken unending heat for raising them earlier in 1993. He also felt that a value-added tax was dishonest because the tax is hidden in the price of the product rather than being added on at the time of its sale. But the story made the headlines on the strength of its source, Health and Human Services Secretary Donna Shalala.

Leakers also undermined the president by assuming credit for something he had done and explaining, in minute detail to the press, why it was a bold and brilliant strategic move. The effect was to elevate the leaker in the eyes of the journalist while making the president seem conniving and politically driven in what had often been a very principled and nonpolitical decision. The president felt that these leaks robbed him of the credit due him for many of the courageous things he had done by making them appear to have been politically calculated when they weren't.

Once, when I strayed over the line and he felt I was taking credit in this way, he let me know how he felt. He was red-faced as he yelled, "I will do this race alone, alone, alone if I have to"—his voice now reaching a higher octave—"to avoid having done to me what was done to me every week, ev—er—y week, in 1993 and 1994 by my staff and my consultants. I will not have decisions that I make"—his fist now pounding his chair arm, keeping time with his words—"that take guts, that take courage, where I'm really risking everything, and have them transformed into"—his lips curling in a sneer—"seamy, seedy, political decisions so some staff member or some consultant can blow his own horn to look oh so smart and oh so good to some journalist. I'll do the race alone first."

OK, I think I got the point. Nonetheless, I later sent him a note saying that my father had often yelled at me when I was a child, so that my blood froze when someone yelled at me. I asked him not to do it again.

Tom Freedman, my sensitive and poetic chief of staff, showed me a passage from a Jewish prayer about the need to make allowances for the weaknesses of others. I enclosed it with the note. In return, I received a handwritten apology in which the president noted that "I might have done well to have read the prayer you sent me before I spoke so harshly with you."

In view of the president's legitimate concerns about press leaks, how do I defend writing a book that chronicles so many of his words, thoughts, relationships, and ideas while he is still in office? I discussed this question with the president in August 1996, just about ten days before I resigned in disgrace. He took a broad view of the issue: "I know we both have a duty to history to talk about this relationship," he said. "It's very likely unique in American history for a relationship like this to exist. I just ask two things as you write or talk about it. First, that you do so after the election is over. Second, that it be right for you and right for me." He paused a few moments and repeated, "Right for Bill Clinton and right for Dick Morris."

I hope I've satisfied both conditions.

The president felt his staffers had deliberately tied his hands. In October '96, he had told me over the phone that "it's gotten a little bit better lately, but I still have to watch them." It was precisely because he felt these staff control tactics—slanting the flow of information, overscheduling, and leaking information to the press—were deliberate that he brought me in to advise him and kept me apart from the staff.

One big reason that he sought to circumvent his staffers rather than replace them is that he chose them, as noted earlier, as ambassadors from various Democratic factions. It was his patience, among other things, in dealing with staffers who represented priorities of labor or minorities or Congress that spared him a primary fight and won him an unopposed nomination.

Without the help of his staff—and certainly if it opposes him—it is very difficult for a president to move, no matter what his personal views. To articulate a policy or an initiative requires coordination and cooperation. Facts have to be assembled. Discordant voices in the administration have to be stilled or mollified. Most of all, proposals or ideas have to be vetted by White House and Cabinet department staffs to see whether they are legal, make sense, are affordable, and won't anger key constituency groups. The president owns his voice but not his government.

President Clinton's style is not to give direct orders or instructions. He has an almost Oriental way of waiting until the forces move, as they naturally will, in the direction he prefers. His actions are dictated more by his sense of timing than by bullying his way through. If he feels the force is with him and time is on his side, he'll wait for the force to produce results on its own. If he feels things are moving against him, he'll usually wait then too, to see whether they reverse themselves of their own accord. Only when all else fails does he take direct, personal action.

It is odd that a president seen, correctly, as an "activist" is so passive in his political method. But the more I worked for Clinton, the more I understood and began to admire and adopt his practice of letting historic forces do what they would, on their own, without attempting to intervene.

His style was to send out signals—to me, to Panetta, to his Cabinet, to Gore, to Hillary—and wait for us to get the point, however gradually. Sometimes this procedure seems passive as he avoids giving orders, but he always knows where he wants to go and finds the right time to get there.

There is a spiritual side to Bill Clinton that I was not often privileged to meet. Like a ship captain searching for icebergs in the Arctic Ocean, I mostly saw what was above the water—his rational, logical mind and his keen ambition. But beneath lay a vast and somewhat mystical spirituality that has a great deal to do with what he does and how he thinks. Not really devoted to formal religion, Clinton works hard at encoding in his memory religious insights he uses as a daily guide to his behavior.

For example, once he told me a story he had heard from Andrew Young, former Atlanta mayor and colleague of Dr. Martin Luther King

Jr. As a child, King had been stabbed perilously close to the aorta and his life was saved. He was left, Young told Clinton, with a scar in the shape of a cross on his chest and each morning, as he shaved, he looked at the scar and asked the mirror what he was going to do this day to deserve the life God had saved for him.

His grousing about partisan polarization—to which his speeches were contributing—grew louder every day as March 1995 progressed. On some fronts—like the nomination of Henry Foster to be surgeon general—he fully agreed with the strategy of all-out conflict. He was angered when the Republicans tried to disqualify this highly successful black doctor from this largely symbolic post because he had performed a handful of abortions in the past. He was determined to dig in and fight. I cheered him on; anything that focused attention on abortion and underscored Republican extremism on the issue would help our ratings. But he was upset by his failure to reach independent voters in his repeated opposition to Republican budget cuts. "I'm sounding more like Gephardt every day," he complained.

Exit Charlie, Enter Dick

The president loved the idea of Charlie the Anonymous. I loved the shadows even more than he did. Once I had decided to work for the president, forsaking my Republican relationships, I no longer needed anonymity, but I still wanted it. It suited me to come and go secretly, unsuspected, even by the press.

I have always had what some have called "a passion for anonymity." While others may find publicity fulfilling, I enjoy the thrill of *not* being seen. On election nights, I would leave the victory parties early and wander outside hearing the noise and jubilation and say to myself, "You helped to create that, but nobody suspects it." The thrill of being a hidden hand, an unheard voice, appealed to a romanticism in my soul. To avoid publicity, I never took an official campaign position and never worked for public agencies. That way, I was not obligated to reveal myself to the public.

In 1984, Eileen and I celebrated Halloween in our home in the old town section of Key West, Florida. We watched the "fantasy festival" costume parade down Duval Street. I put on a Ronald Reagan mask and "campaigned," shaking hands along the parade route. This liberal and partially gay community enjoyed the joke and flocked to me as I shook every hand in sight. When it got too hot to wear the mask, I'd take it off and walk normally down the street, enjoying the creative costumes all around me. I told Eileen that "becoming famous is like wearing a mask, but you can never take it off."

Eventually, the press revealed my work with the president. Then, after the scandal erupted, my privacy was gone forever. The mask had now become my skin, and I was forced to confront failings that I had managed to ignore until now. Inwardly, the scandal forces me to try to rectify these flaws in my character. Outwardly, I am defined by what the public thinks of me, whereas in the past, by choosing obscurity I had paid no attention to what others might think.

Media expert Tony Schwartz once spoke to me of primitive societies where those who break the rules are forced by shame to change, die, or leave. "In the modern media age," Tony said, "you can't leave. The media is everywhere." My choice, therefore, is change or die.

The second worst sin I committed against Eileen after betrayal was to deprive her, without her consent, of her privacy. As much as my betrayal and adultery, it is this offense that I regret most. At least I chose to jeopardize my privacy by working for a president. Then I compounded the danger by living recklessly. She did nothing, but suffered the loss of her anonymity, just as I did.

My desire for secrecy served another need. I had a lot to hide. I had fathered a daughter by a woman to whom I was not married and I knew that were I to become well known, the story could eventually leak out.

Early in my tenure with Clinton, Erskine Bowles approached me and asked that I tell him anything "the president needs to know" about my past. Determined not to mislead the president, I told him about my daughter, and said that I paid four thousand dollars a month for child support. I told Erskine that I was under no court obligation to do so but knew it was my duty.

▲

Throughout 1995, I struggled with the difficulties of being both a newcomer to Washington and an outsider in the White House. When the president hired me, he granted me no specific authority. He wanted my advice on a regular basis but gave me no title and no staff. I had to win these on my own. The president also gave me no special access to information, except for daily clippings from seven or eight newspapers. He wanted me to live off the land like a guerrilla fighter, recruiting allies as I went and accumulating information in any way I could.

When Eileen entered law school, a friend sent her a quote describing the first year of law school as "like being parachuted into China with only a phrase book." I felt like this as I groped my way toward power in the administration. I have never been a Washington insider. Because I worked for candidates I liked in either party, the Washington establishment ostracized me. I didn't live there and I didn't intend to stay. I didn't know anyone there. I knew no one in the media, the government, or the social scene and I had no phone numbers.

Most of my work had been outside Washington, in Massachusetts, Texas, California, and Arkansas, helping to elect governors and senators. I tended not to follow my clients to Washington when they were elected. Washington has its own consensus, and I knew nothing of it. My ideas come from the country, not from the capital. This was an advantage, but it left me vulnerable to the ways of Washington.

I would leave my room at the Jefferson Hotel, arrive at the White House gate to see the president, and enter through the East Wing, where the tours commence. I would show my photo identification—my drivers' license—and I would have to have a specific appointment with a specific person at a specific time in order to get a visitor's pass. Upon entering, I often felt that within the building lived my one and only ally in this cold city. I walked through the halls to the Map Room, where I waited until the president was ready to see me. While I waited, I studied the walls. Over the fireplace, was a small map of Europe—probably two feet by two feet—with red circles and blue and red markers. The plaque beside it says that this was the last situation map of the Allied and Axis armies that Franklin Roosevelt saw before his death, a few weeks before the Nazi surrender.

My presence amid such grandeur seemed incongruous as I mused on my doubts about my usefulness to the president. Then, Bill Clinton would send for me, and I'd enter the Treaty Room and see him sitting there, usually dressed in a T-shirt and jeans, sometimes with his favorite hand-tooled Texas cowboy boots, just as I had seen him a hundred times before in Arkansas. Same man, different surroundings.

It was lonely work, and at the end of January 1995 I suffered a disastrous break in my relations with Hillary. It arose from quotes written in what is, to date, the definitive biography of the president by *The Washington Post* reporter David Maraniss. Maraniss had covered Clinton for the *Post* during the 1992 election. Before the president summoned me to Washington, Maraniss had interviewed me. I respected his professionalism—and still do—and decided to answer questions on my work for Clinton when he was governor of Arkansas.

▲

When I advised Governor Clinton in the 1980s, I avoided, as usual, any press exposure. I visited the Arkansas governor's mansion twenty to thirty times a year and was never mentioned in either of the state's daily newspapers. Clinton liked it that way, and so did I. I'm not the message, I'm not the candidate, I'm not the issue—he is. I'm only an adviser. The governor and, now, the president makes all the decisions. It was in the interests of us both that I not become like Pierre, the spy, a character described by the comedian Danny Kaye. With a thick French accent, Kaye noted that "Pierre was very successful; he was very famous; wherever he went, people would stop, point, and say, 'Look there goes Pierre, the spy.' "

But I didn't like being entirely left out of history, either. Many books had been published about Clinton in Arkansas and I was not mentioned in any of them. I decided, therefore to wait for a legitimate historical work before I talked about our relationship.

When the book appeared at the very end of January 1995, Hillary was annoyed. I had told the story of how she and I had discussed installing a swimming pool in the governor's mansion. The segment in Maraniss's book, *First in His Class,* that describes the incident is this:

> Some people sensed a growing resentment in Hillary that she had to take on so many private duties in the partnership while at the same time, she was being asked, unfairly, she thought, to sacrifice material things. In 1985, Hillary told consultant Dick Morris that she wanted to build a swimming pool on the mansion grounds. She said among other things it would be great for Chelsea. "I said, 'How could you even think of that? You'll get killed for that!' " Morris recalled. "And she said, 'Well, it's really not for us, the mansion is for all future governors of the state and they'll all be able to use it.' And I said, 'You'll never be able to sell that argument. The next time you fly over Little Rock, look down and count the number of swimming pools you see.' She said, 'Well a lot of people have swimming pools.' I got really sarcastic with her and said, 'On the next poll, do you want me to ask whether people have swimming pools?' She was really mad. Very angry. She said, 'Why can't we lead the lives of

normal people?' I saw in that flash the resentment from a lot of those issues, the sacrifices they made staying in public life."

I had worked closely with Hillary for seventeen years. In 1980 and in 1994, she was key to the decision to bring me back to work for her husband. In the 1993–94 period, I spoke with her every few weeks about her own career, and she also passed my ideas on to the president. But when she saw the Maraniss quote she became annoyed. I had left out of the story the fact that the pool was not to have been paid for with taxpayer money at all. Understandably, she was upset. I wrote her notes of apology. I was very contrite.

Hillary is usually a very, very warm person. She is loving and caring, quite the opposite of her sometimes strident public image. For example, in 1993, my mother and father visited her in the White House. My mother, seventy-nine at the time, was an ardent admirer of Eleanor Roosevelt, a dedicated feminist, and a great fan of Hillary. The First Lady graciously received them and spent half an hour with them though only five minutes had been allocated on her schedule for the visit. Her only reason was kindness. There was nothing my parents could ever do for her in return. This was probably the happiest moment in the last year of my mother's life.

A few months later, when my mother was dying, Hillary called often to console me and share the experiences of her own father's death the year before. She was a major support in my grief and I can never forget that. On the very day my mother died she received a warm and comforting note from Hillary.

But when Hillary is stung, she reacts viscerally and closes up. After the Maraniss incident, she ostracized me. There is no colder feeling on the planet. She is intensely human and sensitive and feels every slap and aches with every blow. Her stoic exterior masks enormous pain. Although I felt she was overreacting to my comments to Maraniss, I understand her reaction. It came at a time when her adversaries were hurting her and I was truly sorry to have added to her pain.

During the blackout period, I communicated with Hillary through the president. I continued to urge her not to fade from view, as others had suggested, and advised her to tackle new projects she cared about: the inadequacy of the government's response to Gulf War disease and the need for more widespread use of mammography for elderly women. Hillary's influence on the Gulf War–disease issue encouraged scientific investigations that confirmed that many U.S. troops were exposed to dangerous toxins when American planes bombed Iraqi storage sites.

I was always puzzled by Hillary's mistakes in the health-care debate of 1993–94. I spoke with her many times about the issue, always stressing the importance of using cost-containment measures to lower health-care expenditures. But she became fascinated by the idea of a complete reworking of the health-care system and fashioned a white elephant that wouldn't sell and undermined the president's credibility.

I vividly remember one phone conversation we had in early September 1994, immediately after it became clear that the president didn't have the votes even to get the health-care bill out of the Senate committee to which it had been assigned. I warned Hillary that the failure to pass any health reform at all would seriously injure the administration in general and her reputation in particular. I suggested that she back a limited bill to ensure that workers could take health insurance with them when they changed jobs and that pre-existing conditions could not be used as an excuse to deny coverage. It was legislation like that in the Kennedy-Kassebaum bill that Congress passed late in 1996. Bob Dole had endorsed such a concept. I said that if the Clintons backed the Dole bill as an alternative, Dole would be forced to support it since it was his bill, even though he was reluctant to pass anything at all that summer, hoping to use Clinton's failure to reform health care as a campaign issue.

Hillary was adamant that she would not back such a bill, because "you can't fix part of the problem. If you do this over here, it causes this bad reaction over there. You've got to do it all or do nothing." She also worried that the legislation I was suggesting might lead to higher premiums.

I felt that Hillary had been convinced after a year's study of health care that nothing short of utopia would work. Long gone was the pragmatic Hillary I knew in the '80s and would meet again later in 1995.

After the election defeat of 1994, she was far less certain of herself. She regretted not having backed a compromise health-care bill and wondered if she had made a mistake. To be sure, she also justifiably blamed the tens of millions of dollars that the insurance industry lobbyists spent to defeat the bill—whereas I wondered why an administration capable of raising tens of millions of dollars itself let the insurance ads go largely unanswered.

▲

My relationship with Hillary did not improve until May 1995, almost five months after the Maraniss book was published. The turning point was an odd one.

After my mother's death, my father got a call from Blanche Funk, his high-school and college sweetheart. The Jewish immigrant neighborhood of 156th Street in the East Bronx, where he lived in a tenement and she in a slightly more ritzy semi-attached house, assumed they were going to marry. Then along came la femme fatale, Terry Lesser, my mother. Bohemian in her ways, seductive in her feisty independence, she lured my father away. After their sixty-two-year tryst ended with her death, my father took Blanche's call, and they had dinner. Nine months later, they married. He was eighty-three; she, seventy-nine. I wondered why, at that age, they waited so long.

It so happens that Blanche's oldest and dearest friend is Florence Thomases, the mother of one Susan Thomases. Blanche and Florence had met as Hunter College freshmen, and Blanche has known and loved Susan since she was a baby. And Susan, of course, is Hillary Clinton's closest friend and adviser.

Everybody assumed that Susan and I would be at loggerheads. Susan, the core of the liberal wing in Clinton's circle, was my natural adversary. But she and I felt a bond because of Blanche's marriage to my dad. Though we were acquainted and each of us heard nice things we had said about each other, a rarity in politics, we had never been close during the Arkansas years.

After the marriage, I called Susan and suggested we meet. "You're basically my half sister," I said.

"We're certainly *mishpachah,*" she answered, using the Yiddish word for extended family.

We met for lunch on May 30 at her law office in the Citicorp Center in Manhattan. I'm sure she had heard awful stories about me, and I had certainly heard such stories about her. But the Susan I met that day and since is warm and generous, more motherly than ruthless. She made her points firmly but clearly and she had a very subtle grasp of politics. We got along fine.

As we chatted, Hillary called. Susan put me on the line, and Hillary and I talked directly for the first time since January. She made no reference to our estrangement, although I did use the opportunity to apologize to her for the fifth time, this time directly. The message implied by the circumstances of her call was clear: You're back. Don't screw it up. Susan's my main person.

The major storm over the Maraniss book came not from my remarks about the swimming pool but from the fact that Betsey Wright, Hillary's friend and Clinton's chief of staff and campaign manager in the Arkansas years, had supposedly told friends that she had been "covering up for him [Clinton] for years" and that "she was convinced some state troopers were soliciting women for him and he for them." Maraniss did not attribute these quotes directly to Betsey but to unnamed "friends" of hers whom he had interviewed.

The president was beside himself when he read these accusations. "How is my daughter going to feel when she reads these lies, this horseshit?" he screamed into the phone to me at the end of January. He was livid at Betsey and felt betrayed. He kept saying, "How could she do this to me?" But I pointed out that the quotes weren't Betsey's.

Betsey's lawyer issued a statement giving Betsey's account of what she knew. She denied that she had any knowledge of troopers' soliciting women for Clinton. Instead, she said, the troopers were using their status as Clinton's bodyguards to solicit women for themselves. This statement quieted the story somewhat, and Clinton got over his rage. But the pain for Clinton lingered for weeks, for months. I felt that it left deep scars that took months to heal.

Clinton's major concern was about how the book would hurt Hillary and Chelsea. As a husband and father he wanted to protect them from pain, not always an easy task when you are president. He was consumed with concern. When he realized that there was really little he could do to shield them, he became very angry. His face became raw, red, and angry as he railed against the injustice and the violation. He wouldn't stop. On and on he would talk, into the night, pounding his fist, elaborating his resentment, voicing his anger.

His anger deeply disturbed me, all the more so given his normal self-possession and dignity. I watched him as if I were a small child watching a father lose control—frightening in its intensity and its revelation of a father's essential humanity, a discovery no less disquieting when it is a president of the United States.

A year or more later, I met with Maraniss and told him of the intensity of Clinton's hurt. He was genuinely surprised that the president had responded to the book so emotionally. Having suffered exposure by the press, I am astonished that journalists are so unaware of the pain they cause. Perhaps they should not refrain from such journalism; they have a responsibility to the public. But as people, they should weigh the suffering they inflict.

In the weeks following the publication of the Maraniss book, I suggested that Clinton divert public attention from it by focusing on hard-news events. The president had been long upset by the prolonged base-ball strike. I suggested he try to settle it.

After a night-long effort to bring the sides together, the president complained to me that "this is not really a labor-management negotia-tion at all. It's more like a partners' meeting in a law firm at the end of the year. You have three hundred owners, counting all the principals on all the teams, and about six hundred players. These nine hundred rich men are trying to divide two billion dollars in revenues." He noted that his labor negotiator, William Usery, who was struggling to end the strike, "had been in coal strikes where men murdered each other, but told me he had never seen such bitterness at the bargaining table as he saw here." Ultimately, the National Labor Relations Board—the NLRB—stopped the strike by ruling the owners' attempt to impose a unilateral wage cap was illegal. The president received no public credit though it was really his action and that of his appointees on the NLRB that settled the strike.

The president was thoroughly frustrated in this period. He was not getting the credit for what he did but was being blamed for a liberal line he did not endorse. His frustration with the liberal direction in which the staff was leading him was what finally forced him to widen the circle of my contacts in the administration. At first, in February, we added only pollster Schoen to the weekly meeting with the president. In March, the president invited his chief of staff, Leon Panetta. Shortly afterward, Vice President Gore joined with his chief of staff, Jack Quinn, and the president's deputy chiefs of staff, Erskine Bowles and Harold Ickes, my old adversary from New York politics. At the first meeting they at-tended, I explained that I wanted no publicity and sought to remain out-side the spotlight. Ickes grinned, and, wickedly I thought, said, "The one thing I can guarantee you, Dick, is that you won't be secret for long." Perhaps it was his fault that I wasn't. Soon after that meeting, Jane Mayer of *The New Yorker* magazine (formerly of *The Wall Street Journal*), who happened a year later to write a flattering article about Ickes, got wind of my role and called me soon after our enlarged group meetings began. I tried to discourage the story but saw that I couldn't. I refused to be interviewed face-to-face, but did speak briefly to her by phone. I soon learned not to do on-the-record interviews with reporters who were writing stories about me. Since I discouraged press attention I believed that most stories about me were the result of leaks or plants by my adversaries in the White House or in the Republican party. Mayer's piece ran in mid-April 1995 and featured a caricature of the president listening on the telephone with rapt attention to me speaking at the other end. It was the first public mention of my role. Shortly afterward, *The Washington Post* and *The New York Times* ran front-page stories announcing my existence.

The president was displeased by the publicity but understood that I had not generated it and had tried my best to avoid it. I didn't realize that merely doing what I did in Arkansas, on the federal level, would result in such massive publicity. I didn't consider myself newsworthy. I was simply doing what I had been doing quietly for seventeen years.

So, between September 15, 1994—when I got the first phone call from the president about Haiti—until mid-April 1995, I worked with the president without anyone outside the White House knowing about it. It was the happiest time of my life. I wish it could have gone on forever.

When I suddenly became the object of scrutiny, the press happened upon a life that had not been lived with an eye to how it would look in public.

Coming from the shadows, I was blinded by the bright and searching light of media attention. Eventually I grew accustomed to it, but I couldn't adjust my destructive obsessions to my new notoriety and this eventually led to my downfall.

The experience of becoming suddenly well known is the strangest I have ever had. I felt a bit as though I were Forrest Gump, suddenly appearing with this or that famous person, brought in to make the movie set seem real. Sam Donaldson was calling me. Pulitzer Prize–winner Bob Woodward wanted an interview that I summoned the courage to refuse. (A few months before, I would have settled for his autograph.) Rita Braver advised me to meet privately, off-the-record with the press so that I did not become an object of such mystery that I would invite vilification. Rita invited me to address a gathering of the CBS News Washington Bureau staff. Faces that I watched on the news as I sat at home in my pajamas were now watching me—in a suit. The world was the same, but suddenly I was in the picture myself and I felt very odd. I grew to accept the situation, but never liked it and always feared it.

The basic fact was that I couldn't change it.

I felt like a stranger in a strange building in a strange city. I needed allies desperately, and the vice president came to my rescue. By late winter of 1995, at one of their weekly lunch meetings, the president had discussed with Gore my role in the administration. Sensing my isolation, Clinton urged me to see the vice president, and I immediately set up an appointment.

We met in mid-March in the office of Jack Quinn, Gore's chief of staff at the time and later White House counsel. Gore sat in a wing chair, and I sat at the corner of the couch next to him. I explained my ideas and theories for about half an hour with little or no interruption. I could sense that the vice president agreed with most of what I was saying. He listened intently. I stressed that I needed his help to get anything done and underscored how frustrated I had been.

He grasped what I was saying at once and offered his full support, subject to two conditions: first, that I respect his priorities, such as the environment, and include them in my planning and second, that I promise not to divulge anything related to the campaign to Lott. I readily agreed to both, and made clear that my talks with Lott only focused on government issues, not on campaign plans.

Gore told me that he had been increasingly troubled by the drift of the White House and badly shaken by the defeat in '94. He said that he had tried, in vain, to move the administration toward the center, but the White House staff had shut him out. He said that he had only recently heard of my involvement and did not know me at all. But, he said, "We need a change around here, a big change, and I'm hoping and praying that you're the man to bring it." We shook hands on our alliance.

As I got to know Vice President Gore well, I came to appreciate his warmth and humor. In many ways, he is the mirror image of President Clinton—a reflection, but reversed. In public, Clinton is deeply emotional, drawing deep feelings from his empathy with the sorrows or joys of those around him. But in private he is more shy and reserved, usually keeping his feelings within. Gore is the opposite. He seems frosty and rigid in public, often seeming to freeze on the stage. But in conversation, he reveals himself as a man of intense emotions.

On a platform, Bill Clinton comes alive with a humor and wit that is both spontaneous and genuine. But in private he rarely weaves humor into his business conversations. On occasion, he'll tell a joke, but it is a structured affair with a set punch line. He is not usually a man to get people laughing at a political strategy meeting. His private humor, when he shows it, is dry and subtle, often going over the heads of those around him. Gore, on the other hand, carries his humor everywhere except to the podium. In any sort of meeting, he can be very funny, often cloaking substantive points in satire and irony. Once he joked at his own expense and then turned to me, as if explaining, "Self-deprecating humor. You should try it sometime."

Gore's wit was in full view at one strategy meeting after I raised the idea of planning a press event celebrating the success of the Endangered Species Act, which Dole opposed, in assuring a healthy future for the bald eagle, the condor, the Florida panther, and other species on our planet. The vice president criticized the press for caring only about what he called "charismatic mammals" and pointed out that it is important to save all levels of life in our ecosystem. Following his lead, I never again asked Eileen how our dogs were doing when phoning home, but rather inquired after the health of our two beautiful blond golden retrievers by asking about the "charismatic mammals."

In describing the proposed media event, I told the president and the vice president that "behind you two, we'll have a buffalo grazing, a panther in a cage, and you'll release a bald eagle. No snail darters here." I was alluding to the bitter controversy over limiting commercial development to protect the snail darter, one of nature's less significant species. "You'll be like Noah on the ark, saving these species," I said, for once purposely using overblown rhetoric and, for once, aware that I was doing so.

Clinton turned to Gore, who was sitting on his right, and said, "You know, Al, there were no snail darters on the ark."

Gore's face turned rigid and stern. He moved his head ostentatiously to the left to face the president, keeping his body facing forward to exaggerate the neck motion. "Mr. President," he began with mock formality, "there were."

"Really," the president said, looking quizzical. "How can you tell?"

"They're *here*," the vice president said with the emphasis of a Baptist fundamentalist, his face right out of Grant Wood's *American Gothic.*

"Oh," said the president, comically deflated.

Gore turned forward again and emphatically nodded his head, once.

The struggle to rescue the president from his staff began in earnest and in the open in March. I discovered I had an eloquent ally in Clinton's speechwriter Don Baer—and a clever, stubborn opponent in Leon Panetta. My relationship with Leon began badly.

On March 16, I suggested that the president deliver what I called the Pile of Vetoes speech. It would be an overall response to the Republican agenda and would feature a disclaimer by the president that "I didn't come to Washington to issue a pile of vetoes" in response to partisan confrontation. And in the speech he would reach out to the Republicans and urge that they join him in finding common ground. The idea was to induce the opposition not to pursue a rightist agenda that would be dead on arrival at the White House door. I proposed a *tour d'horizon* in which the president would emphasize the aspect of the Republican program, in each substantive area, which he would accept and name the bills he would veto. I pressed this idea on the president in ever more urgent tones during the strategy sessions at the White House residence on March 23 and April 5.

The April 5 strategy session was the genuine turning point in the president's move to the center. I harshly criticized our position: "The vast bulk of our rhetoric is anti-Congress and anti-Republican. Getting involved in a zero-sum game with Congress is a very bad idea. Congress is winning the public relations war. Congress has a fifty-eight–thirty-five approval rating for the first hundred days, and by forty-nine to thirty-nine voters say Congress is not going too far in its budget cuts." I criticized our rich-versus-poor rhetoric and our almost total absence of any attempt to carve out a Clinton position that was separate and distinct from that of the congressional Democrats. "The new Clinton positions are receiving short shrift and are getting submerged in a two-way Democrat *v.* Republican fight," I complained.

More strategically, I warned that our current identification with the negativism of the House Democrats "demands vetoes that will undermine the central element of our strategy—that we pose a moderate alternative, a third way. Unless the president articulates third-way solutions in the crucible of the current controversies, he will become irrelevant, and this will lead to the miniaturization of the presidency."

Panetta argued strenuously against such a speech, proposing instead to focus on education policy during the month of April. The president should not break ranks with congressional Democrats, he said, when they were beginning to make progress in sullying the Gingrich image and blunting the offensive.

I argued that philosophical discussions of education would make the president even more irrelevant. We needed to strike out and fight for a triangulated third way.

Vice President Gore, who had recently joined the meeting, sat in silence, as did the president, while Panetta and I argued. Finally, the president turned to Gore and said, "What do you think, Al?"

Gore spoke as if he were writing an opinion for the Supreme Court. He reviewed the recent history since the '94 defeat and then made an exaggerated bow to Leon's position: "I fully realize how important it is for us to listen to Leon and not to break ranks with the rest of the party, and I fully appreciate how concerned Leon is that such a course might lead us to disaster and even greater trouble than we have now." Then came the long awaited *but:* "But I have to say that, on balance, I agree with Dick's point that we need now to emerge from the shadows and place ourselves at the center of the debate with the Republicans by articulating what we will accept and what we will not in a clear and independent way."

Bravo!

As I saw the byplay between Clinton and Gore, I began to understand how important the vice president was to the president. Gore is the single person in the world whose advice the president most values. He sees Gore as a junior president—not at the top yet, but good enough to serve when his time comes. When he wants a clear-eyed assessment, he turns to Gore, as he does when he wants something really important handled really well.

The president knew what Gore was going to say at our meeting and the tip of his hat to the vice president was a giveaway to his own thinking. He had pondered my recommendations for two weeks, while watching his presidency as it was sidetracked and identified with the orthodox Democratic position. He was ready for a change. As he spoke, I recalled my image of the scrambling quarterback imprisoned behind his offensive line, the Democratic leadership in Congress. Now he was breaking out.

"Leon, I want to do it Dick's way for now," he began. "I understand where you are coming from, but we've tried that way for two months now without much to show for it. I think that if I go out and talk about education, nobody's going to cover it or care what I say. I've got to get back in the game and I think Dick's speech is the way to do it."

Leon tried one last gambit. "Even if we do the speech," he protested, "we shouldn't do it Friday at the Newspaper Editors Convention in Dallas [where I had proposed we give the Pile of Vetoes speech]. It's too close to the hundred-days anniversary of the Republican takeover of Congress, and we will be ratifying that anniversary if we give the speech then. We'll be playing into their hands."

I argued that the opposite was true, that by choosing this date for the speech we would jam the Republican's celebration and show that now we were passing to the next phase of the debate, that of presidential leadership.

The president, tired of our wrangling, got up and examined books in his library as Leon spoke—his way of indicating he had made his decision. The meeting was over.

This president had taken charge.

Clinton asked me to meet with Don Baer the next day (Thursday) to draft the speech so he could get it in shape for the Friday convention in Dallas.

"You'll like Don," he predicted. "He thinks like you."

I was being brought in from the outside to work with the White House staff on a speech. It felt very good.

▲

Baer had been Bill Clinton's speechwriter for years. A former journalist at *U.S. News & World Report,* he had been on the White House staff since the beginning of the administration and had coined many of Clinton's classic formulations (including "opportunity, responsibility, and community"). He had detected a gravitational pull on the president's words in recent months, but didn't know that I was the source. When we were introduced, he made the connection at once.

He welcomed me almost tearfully. "I have been fighting a lonely fight here to get things moving this way. I'm getting sick of it and I've been planning to just leave. It's been affecting my spirit and even my health." He cited the names of former White House staffers who had quit in disgust at the "leftward" drift, including David Gergen and Bill Galston.

In the meantime, Bill Curry had been hired as a result of my pleas that the president honor his commitment to me. Panetta had dragged his feet and tried to divert Curry to some job outside the White House. I welcomed Curry's intellect and his Irish gift for phrase and words and his feel for the centrist issues as he, Baer, and I worked on the speech.

The three of us set to work by commandeering a desk in the downtown Washington office of Bob Squier—whom I wanted to hire as campaign media creator but so far hadn't been able to. Don Baer typed out a draft as Curry and I chimed in. I realized, as I heard Baer speak, that I did not know presidential language and was delighted to be introduced to its cadences and rhythms. Often I would propose a sharp line and Don would say, indulgently, "That would be good, but he can't say that. He's president."

Finally the speech was finished and Baer, Curry, and I went over to the residence for an evening meeting with Clinton. He made extensive changes, sharpening the words and changing the language to project exactly the third way he wanted to stake out.

Vice President Gore had suggested to me that I try to get the president to speak extemporaneously more often. "I've seen him do it and he does it so well," Gore said. I, too, remembered what a great speaker he had been without notes in the Arkansas years. I decided to talk to Clinton about giving this speech without a text in front of him.

"You don't need a text," I said. "I've seen you rattle off an hour's worth of text without having a line in front of you and you never miss a beat."

He acknowledged that he really didn't need a text.

"Could you have given the State of the Union speech without a text?" I asked.

"Of course," he answered casually, "of course I could have."

"Then how about it?" I asked. "How about just taking a bare outline with you up there tomorrow and give it a try?"

The president first said he'd think about it and, as I encouraged him further, he agreed to try it.

He had been burned so badly by ill-prepared decisions like the appointment of Lani Guinier or his early introduction of the gays-in-the-military issue, that he had tended to overprepare, unwilling to trust himself to ad-lib again. But I'd been there in Arkansas and I remembered how much better he was when he could write his speech as he went along, guided only by an outline of basic points.

I also realized how much his confidence had been shattered by the difficulties of his first two years and the devastating defeat of 1994. Getting him to discard a text and trust himself was a key step and I was determined to see him take it.

So, the Pile of Vetoes speech was delivered extemporaneously, as were many, many speeches that followed. The Dallas speech went over beautifully. Reporters commented on hearing an entirely new Clinton, one markedly different in style and content. He got equal time in the press with Gingrich's celebration of his first hundred days in office and was, at last, back on the playing field.

Panetta, having been defeated once, fought hard to resist any more moves to the center. He came on very friendly, with a constant smile and an ever ready nod. But his demeanor said nothing about what he was really thinking. Behind a mask of geniality and a seeming desire to please lurked an intense territoriality and suspicion of outsiders.

Elevated, at Al Gore's suggestion, from his post as director of the Office of Management and Budget to the chief of staff job, Panetta had united the White House staff and ended most of the destructive leaks that embarrassed the president and hurt his image in the first year of his term.

In fighting leaks, Leon relied on counterleaking. When a staffer anonymously placed an item in the press, Leon figured out who had done it. Who was friends with the journalist? Who was quoted on the record elsewhere in the same story? Whose name was mentioned favorably a few days later by the same journalist? In his personal court, Leon didn't require proof beyond a reasonable doubt. If he thought it was you, it was you.

Then Leon turned it over to his press secretary, Barry Toiv, a mustached, innocent-looking, baby-faced man who is known around the White House as "The Assassin." Barry would talk to a reporter, often from *The Wall Street Journal,* and soon an article would appear saying that a certain staff member was on the outs or that he had screwed up on something a few months ago and was on probation. It stopped the leaking.

So Leon exerted a control very much needed in the White House. But originality and innovation were not his strong suits. He had been part of the House leadership for years, principally as Budget Committee chairman, and he was joined at the skull to the House Democratic leaders much of the time. He wanted consensus and party unity. But party unity at this point was the last thing we needed. We needed to chart an independent third way rather than merge with the obsolete orthodoxies of the Democratic congressional leadership.

Face-to-face dealings with Leon were almost useless. He never really listened, and when he disagreed, he never let you know.

I have been told that Panetta put out an all-points bulletin to the staff, asking to be kept closely informed of any "Morris sighting," and gave orders to freeze me out as much as possible. He certainly went to great lengths to keep Bill Curry out of the White House mainstream, forgetting to invite him to meetings. He even once had his staff physically bar Curry's way when he showed up for one.

Clinton and I had discussed possible new policy initiatives in crime and immigration. At the May 16, 1995, meeting of our strategy group, at which Leon was present, I complained about the suppression of my ideas. "There are too many pulled teeth," I said, meaning ideas that had been killed.

At the urging of former Brooklyn district attorney Elizabeth Holtzman, I suggested cracking down on militias. We could require that weapons inventories be filed with local police, that notice of maneuvers and training be given to local police and the FBI, and that the president alert innocent citizens by publishing a list of organizations dedicated to domestic terror. This plan was killed by adverse reaction from the Justice Department, citing civil liberties.

I urged more aggressive attacks on Japanese trade policy but was stopped by the National Security Council staff, which then, posing as sentinals, leaked my proposals to the press.

Anxious to cope with national concern on illegal aliens, the president wanted to increase deportations, so I proposed that we urge states to deny illegal immigrants driver's licenses. Since our most frequent police contact is on the highway, I believed this would be an easy way to identify illegals: if people found to be driving without a license were citizens or legal immigrants, they would be ticketed; if they were here illegally, they could be sent to the Immigration and Naturalization Service—the INS—for deportation. But the INS killed this idea by saying that it didn't want to know of any more illegals since it couldn't deport those it already knew about—an odd response.

Even my idea of backing a zero tolerance for teen drinking and driving—whereby any amount of alcohol in a teen's bloodstream would constitute drunk driving (after all, teen drinking is illegal)—was shot down because we hadn't cleared it with the Democratic governors.

The White House staff blocked or delayed my proposals and were happy if every day we recycled Gephardt's leftover speeches attacking the Republican budget cuts. The staff seldom had ideas of their own.

Frustrated by these roadblocks, I asked sarcastically at a May 16 strategy meeting, "Why hurry? Just because we are below forty percent in vote share and under fifty percent in approval, why have any sense of urgency at all?"

Leon was angry and said he refused to "turn the White House over to a political consultant."

I countered that he would be turning it over to the Republicans a year and a half from now at the rate we were going.

I had earlier shared my concerns with Gore and implored him to help break the logjam. We were collecting gravestones in a cemetery of discarded ideas, but we needed these ideas to live.

For years Clinton and I had believed that issues are the paddle you use to power yourself through the political swamp. Others prefer images, photos, adjectives, and negatives. We believed it was through issues that the public learned who you really were.

It was with this in mind that I told Gore my efforts would be useless if they were continually blocked by Panetta and his White House operation. The vice president sympathized and noted how coldly the president's staff had received his own ideas in the past two years and how often he felt shut out.

The president said little as the argument intensified at our May 16 meeting, and he brought the combat to a close by saying he would address the conflict "later on."

After our May 16 strategy meeting, I asked to see the president and the vice president alone. We sat in the Treaty Room, the president between the vice president and me. We'll get him in stereo, I thought.

I began by elaborating my frustrations. "Look," I said, "you hired me to get you back and turn this race around. We've made some good progress, but not nearly enough. On a personal level," I said, "I've risked everything I have—my career, my ability to work in this field ever again—on being able to win this race. But I'm stymied, checkmated by a bureaucracy that just won't let it happen."

Gore spoke up for me and talked of his own frustrations in dealing with the staff on issues dear to him like reinventing government and protecting the environment.

The president responded lamely. "I haven't gotten over my jet lag from the trip to Russia," he said even though the trip had taken place two weeks before.

I interrupted him. "I don't want to talk about a specific event; I don't even want to talk about your staff. I want to talk about you," I said, pointing my finger directly at the president. "You're the biggest problem. You've lost your nerve," I shouted. "You're not the same man I worked for in Arkansas. That guy took risks. That guy took on issues. That guy knew that a good fight with a good enemy would build him a political base. That guy tested teachers. That guy took on the utilities. Where is that guy? He's the one I signed on to work for. I'd follow him to the end of the earth and back. I'd bet on him any day. Where in the hell is he?"

Gore motioned to me to lower my voice. Clinton smiled and said that if I talked any louder, the Secret Service agents would think I was killing him, and they'd come in with their guns.

I settled down.

The president turned serious. His hands were together in front of his chest, his long fingers almost touching as they moved outward in a gesture of expressing what was in his heart. He explained himself as he hadn't ever done before. "There used to be chaos around here. Every day we would have three, four meetings lasting hours and hours. I'd sit in them, and we'd make decisions like a committee. And every day I'd read about them in the papers. It got so that the public had an impression that I was indecisive. I wasn't. I just didn't have the luxury of making my decisions in private. Every step, every stage, every word was leaked.

"Then Leon came in, and he got some order here. And maybe it went too far. And maybe we need to let more get out." But still he was ducking the main issue—him.

"Sir," I said, "I can't help you get reelected unless you change. You're like Birch Bayh's cat," I said, alluding to a Mark Twain story that the famed Indiana senator used to tell in the days after the Vietnam War to counter the trend toward isolationism. "After a cat sits down on a hot stove lid, she learns never, never to sit down on a hot stove lid, but she won't sit down on a cold one, either.

"I know you got the living shit beaten out of you on health care. And I know that you got killed for raising taxes. And I know all about gays in the military, but goddamn it, we have to fight fights—the right fights. You have to take new positions—the right positions, the ones you believe in. You have to act boldly. You have to reposition yourself. Or it won't work. It just won't work."

In a gesture of near surrender, the president raised his hands and said, "I get it. I get it. I've been worrying about terrorism and Oklahoma City. I've been up all night working on Bosnia. I haven't been sleeping well. I get it. We'll get it done."

Whenever the president felt he had failed, he always looked for someone or something to blame. It seemed self-indulgent, but I also knew how hard he really was on himself. Usually, I let it go. This time, though, was too important.

I said I doubted any real change was going to be possible as long as Panetta stayed on as chief of staff. "He blocks everything," I said. "He's just locked into the liberal Democratic line coming out of Congress. And anything he doesn't oppose ideologically he opposes because it's a change in the way government operates. And anything he doesn't oppose because of that he opposes because it's my idea."

The president defended Panetta: "He's not a liberal. He's centrist. You're misreading him."

"I don't care whether he's liberal or he's part of the establishment or he's a bureaucrat or he's just contrary. I don't care what the reason is; he can't keep blocking the stuff I develop—at your behest—to move you to the center. When I'm wrong, OK, but I'm right *sometimes,* and I don't have another thirty ideas sitting around to replace the thirty he keeps shooting down."

Gore came to Leon's defense. "Dick, I know Leon. I was the one who urged that the president appoint him chief of staff. If we sit down with him and explain our concerns and it comes from the president, Leon will get it done, believe me."

The meeting ended, and Gore left. When we were alone, I said to the president, "Stop making excuses all the time about why you lost in '94. It's just like '80," I said, alluding to our experiences together after his 1980 defeat. "You're moping around blaming yourself for all those dead Democrats in 1994. You count their graves every night. Snap out of it. We've got an election to win. Let's get moving."

He stared at me impassively, apparently thinking about what I'd said. We were standing by his bookshelves on the far side of the Treaty Room. I put my hands on his upper arms and squeezed them. Then I looked straight at him and shook him harshly, violently. I said through clenched teeth, "Get your nerve back. Get your fucking nerve back." He looked at me through bloodshot, weary eyes and with his face downcast solemnly nodded yes.

Clinton wanted to move to the center, but wanted me to do it for him. He wasn't going to intervene unless he had to. Why use political muscle to achieve what I might be able to achieve on my own? But now, I'd said in effect that unless he got involved and made it happen, I wasn't going to stick around and watch the ship sink. People would never use the word "passive" to describe Clinton. But a lot of times he is passive.

Outside, in the cool night breeze, I walked along Pennsylvania Avenue toward my room at the Jefferson Hotel. I was relieved, energized, determined. I'd put it all on the line. I'd talked to Clinton in a way I'd never done before. But I hadn't had to before. There hadn't been this much at stake for him or for the country. I knew he'd either resent me permanently for this unspeakable intrusion or he'd understand that it was time to get it in gear.

A lot of things came together for Clinton between mid-April and mid-June of 1995. His speech at Oklahoma, his skill in his summit with Yeltsin, and the slip in Gingrich's popularity all contributed to an upsurge of energy. Our talk may also have contributed.

Fortunately, he got the message, and things changed in short order. He approved the balanced-budget speech, took on the tough issue of affirmative action, lashed out at tobacco companies, began to issue a string of executive orders, approved the bombing of Bosnia, approved a massive advertising campaign, and stood firm in the budget fight in the face of the Republicans.

It wasn't only because of our talk, but the change dated from that night. I've never really understood our relationship, and I never will completely, for he's not an emotionally extroverted person despite his public persona. I do know, though, that he walked differently and talked differently and acted differently after that night in May.

Nobody ever talks to a president as I had. One just doesn't. But I could do it because we had been together for so long in Arkansas. I didn't have to wait long for results, either. On Sunday, June 4, I was summoned to a special meeting at the White House residence with the president, the vice president, and Panetta. I'd been called down to Washington only the night before, while my wife and I were having dinner at Arrows, our favorite restaurant in Ogunquit, Maine. We had rented a house with a wonderful view of the ocean and pretended that our time was our own. The interruption spoiled that fantasy. The call was from the president. He said, "Al set up a meeting with Panetta. We have to have it Sunday. Where are you?"

"In Maine at our summer house," I answered tentatively.

"I'm sorry to mess up your weekend. We have to do it Sunday—"

"Sunday's fine," I interrupted.

"We'll do it late. How about nine-thirty?" He offered.

I said three in the morning was fine, any time he wanted.

We hung up.

Clinton is like that. At least with me, he was always considerate about interrupting family time; it was touching, especially when he thinks he's losing you, as he must have thought after our previous meeting.

It's remarkable how participants in regular, weekly meetings tend to assign themselves the same seats at every session, an unspoken and un-negotiated pecking order that everybody respects even though anyone can, in theory, sit anywhere. Such was the case with our meetings, which were then always held in the Treaty Room. So, true to habit this Sunday, the president sat in his wing chair with his back to his desk and the window, facing the narrow end of the rectangular coffee table with the presidential seal. I sat, as always, directly facing him, in a matching wing chair at the other end of the table. The vice president sat at the corner of the couch to the president's left, and Panetta sat facing the VP.

Gore began the meeting, obviously an arrangement he and the president had worked out ahead of time. He spoke of the difficulty all White House staffs have in integrating themselves with the election-year political teams. By painting the problem as generic rather than specific to Leon and me, he defused much of our anger and laid the basis for a solution. He said that we needed to meet now to clarify how the president wanted the staff and my political operation to work together.

Tom Freedman had prepared a memo for me summarizing the past controversies between the White House and the campaign operations in the '80 Carter, '84 Reagan, and '92 Bush reelection efforts. I had passed the memo to the vice president's staff and this may have served to make his focus more generic at this meeting.

At this point, the president jumped in: "Leon, I've chosen Dick to be my strategist. I've worked with him before, we know each other, and he and I have a track record together. I need to throw long, Leon. We've got a lot of yardage to make up here, and I've got to throw long. I'm bringing Dick in to throw long, and I need you to help him do it."

Leon nodded in acquiescence but then said huffily, "Mr. President, you can have my resignation before I will allow half-baked ideas to make it out of this building, before the experts who have spent their lives working in these areas have a chance to review them and modify them to make them work. We cannot just turn the White House staff and the Cabinet over to a political consultant."

"Leon," the president replied, "I know Dick can be pushy, very pushy. It's one of the things about him that I like. And I know he can come up with wild ideas, but he comes up with a lot of good ones. We've known each other and worked closely together for seventeen years. He knows my thinking, and he knows what I want. Sometimes we just find ourselves thinking in tandem, without even talking. I need this man to throw long."

"Leon," I pleaded, "I would be delighted—delighted—to work only through you. I would avoid all the end runs and do everything through channels if I could be assured of a vetting process that would keep ideas alive and not kill them. We need ideas to put points up on the board."

I had heard from the president the words I wanted to hear, and Leon had heard from me the words he wanted to hear. The meeting progressed substantively and amiably from then on. Leon was justly concerned that, after he had disciplined the staff and stopped everyone leaking to the press what he pleased, I was now going to reinject chaos into the process.

Leon changed that day. He kept his distance from me, but we tolerated each other and began to learn how to work together.

Still, we needed one more midcourse correction to make it right. The June 4 meeting left me with too much power, in Leon's eyes, to intervene with his staff. He didn't feel I was keeping my end of the bargain.

I took to walking the corridors of the West Wing—where the staff offices are—and tried to infuse what I felt to be the president's views in operations at all levels. As writers prepared statements, I would sometimes lean over their shoulders and add or delete words. Leon, who felt demoted by the early June meeting, triggered a "get even" meeting on Wednesday afternoon, June 28, in the Oval Office with the same gang of four. Again Gore took the lead, this time at Leon's prompting.

The vice president said how we had met three weeks before and discussed ways in which Leon might work with me, but now we must lay down the reciprocal arrangement—how I should work with Leon.

Panetta, irritated, spoke of how I was breeding anarchy and even disloyalty to him among the staff. "They don't know whom to take orders from, whom to listen to," he said. "I can't have—and I won't have—you roaming the halls of the West Wing, poking your head into each office and asking what's going on and giving instructions. I'll resign first." The *r* word was a serious threat for a president still unskilled in the ways of Washington and still in political danger.

Gore reinforced Panetta's point to say that we needed one organization with one leader, and that was to be Panetta.

The president said nothing.

I was inwardly furious at his silence and felt that he was letting both of us down.

Then, just as I was considering my own resignation, I had an idea. The president was sending me a message: put up with Leon's rules. The White House is an absolute monarchy and the king had spoken. I was the king's chief political adviser, and this was a political year. I did not need Leon's staff to keep things moving in the direction I wanted. My job was to persuade one man, and nothing could block my access to him except his disfavor.

The president was telling me to fold my hand and get out of the meeting alive. I did. I explained that I did not do well working with staffs or administering anything. I noted that I worked alone in my Connecticut home without staff and without an office. I really didn't even have a desk, only a computer. And I didn't have a secretary; I answered my own phone. I said that I was not used to bureaucracy and organization and that I had certainly never worked in government. "There's nothing like learning at the top," I joked to relieve some of the tension.

I then said that I appreciated Leon's points and would respect them.

Gore laid down rules that governed my tenure in the White House for at least the next eight or nine months. By 1996, things got a little looser, and trust developed. I would not go to the West Wing offices unless specifically invited to a meeting there. Before I saw any government official, the meeting had to be cleared by Leon or Erskine Bowles, with whom I worked well. Each week after the evening strategy meeting in the residence an implementation group would meet the next morning with the president—without me—to decide which ideas to accept and which to reject.

After that June 28 meeting, I never saw a public official in the executive branch without first going to Bowles for permission and Leon and I got along better when he saw that I was following the rules.

▲

A few weeks later I sat alone with the president in the Treaty Room late at night for about an hour. I wanted to test the conclusions to which I had come in the last meeting with the president, Gore, and Panetta. I began by saying "I think I've finally figured you out."

"Really," he replied, "tell me about it." He was dressed in slacks and a T-shirt and was cleaning up some papers that lay around his office. He kept at it as I spoke, using his housekeeping task to avoid looking at me while I covered potentially dangerous turf.

"I make all kinds of proposals at our meetings, and your usual reaction is a blank stare," I said to his back as he shuffled more papers. "I didn't know before, but now I think I know exactly what you mean by that blank stare."

"Go on," he encouraged.

"The blank stare says to me, 'I've known you for seventeen years. You know my mind, and you know where I want to go.' So the blank stare says, 'I want to do it if I can. Figure out how and let me know.' If it looks good to you, you climb out on it. If it doesn't, you don't."

I continued while he tidied up his desk and library shelves. "I used to wonder why you never tell me what your concerns are or why you aren't climbing out on the issue I work up. Then I realized that you're the president, and you've got a few other things to do."

He turned around, stopped fidgeting, and stared straight at me, looking blank. I continued: "You're basically saying to me, 'You are the same age as me. You are as good a politician. You can figure it out as well as I can, so go do your job, and I'll climb out on your issue when it's ready.' It's the same reason you don't elbow people aside for me and make my power base in the White House secure. You don't want to spend your political capital doing what I can probably do for myself anyway. You've got a few other things to spend your political capital on."

He stared at me for about twenty seconds while he sorted it out. Then he sat down in his wing chair and smiled in relief for some reason. "You finally got it right" was all he said. I nodded, said good night, and left.

I knew exactly where I stood. It was time to stop seeing Clinton as protecting me while I dispensed political advice in return. I had to put it together myself. He had done all he was going to do in that first talk with Panetta. He'd spent political capital then and wasn't about to spend any more. It was my turn.

Before I arrived, the White House was essentially run by a troika of Panetta, Deputy Chief of Staff Harold Ickes, and Senior Adviser George Stephanopoulos. Ickes was and would remain my dedicated opponent. He had a right to be. When I showed up, he was fully in control of the campaign—as he had been in control of the '94 disaster. Now I was crowding his turf. He was to remain in charge of relations with the party and labor, local politics, patronage, the field organization, fund-raising, and staff, but I took over the message and the media.

He was deeply opposed to the centrist course I had charted with the president. A longtime liberal and son of FDR's Interior Secretary, he had inherited many of his father's curmudgeonly traits.

Harold represented the old school of orthodox, labor-liberal Democratic dogmatism. He rarely spoke in our two- to three-hour strategy meetings and sometimes fell asleep, left early, or didn't bother to attend. He was not very articulate. Once he actually delivered a speech—about how we should handle our convention planning—reading it seemingly verbatim from typewritten notes. When he did speak, he usually asked questions, aggressively it seemed to me, and would always back down quickly when they were answered—or when their implications were refuted.

Behind the scenes, however, he was a real street fighter. He opposed everything I wanted to do in any way he possibly could, from arguing about my minibar charges at my hotel (only Diet Coke and orange juice were reimbursable; alcohol was not) to, I suspected, leaking stories to besmirch my reputation. When I confronted Ickes about press leaks, he adamantly denied any responsibility. I didn't and don't believe him. Harold was an unrelenting opponent.

Still, he wasn't much of a day-to-day threat. Early on the president told me, "I know Harold can't run the campaign." Clinton wondered about the anger that smoldered beneath the surface of this rawboned face, underscored by his unruly shock of red hair. "He always seems to be in a rage," the president said; "I don't know where it comes from." He said he hoped Harold would one day gain control of his anger before it destroyed him.

In a way, I didn't mind Harold. He had lost and had a right to be angry. The president gave me the role I sought, and I had no ambition to run the local politics or control the other parts of Harold's turf. His attacks were annoying and sometimes threatening, but I tended not to pay much attention. Only when he attempted to kill our advertising or contest my fee did I fight.

Ickes deserves credit for helping to avoid a primary challenge to the president by maintaining the bridges between Clinton and the labor unions on the one hand and minority spokespeople on the other. His eye was always on the needs of the left wing of the party and he managed it skillfully.

But Harold didn't have a lot to do with what I believe was the key reason the president avoided a challenge for the nomination from mainstream Democrats. (Speaker Dick Gephardt and Senators Bill Bradley, Sam Nunn, and Bob Kerrey had been mentioned as possible rivals.) What rescued Clinton from ambush was his ratings in the polls.

Clinton's swelling bank account may also have inhibited rivals, though a president's success at fund-raising had done little to deter past primary challenges to incumbent Democratic presidents, such as those mounted by Gene McCarthy and Ted Kennedy.

Still, my resentment should not obscure the fact that Ickes's outreach to liberals and minorities did a lot to avoid a "suicide" challenge from the left, such as Jesse Jackson, for example, might have offered. In this way, he performed an outstanding service for Bill Clinton and for the country.

▲

My relationship with George Stephanopoulos is a happier and more complex story. I first met him at Harold's invitation on May 17 over dinner at Kincaid's, the Washington restaurant favored by the staff because of its proximity to the White House and its late closing time. Harold had also invited Janice Enright, his personal assistant, whose desk was actually inside his office and who rarely left his side. Janice is sane and gentle and was a welcome presence when I had to deal with Harold.

At Kincaid's, Stephanopoulos and I talked for more than four hours, about political theory and strategy. He differed sharply with my view that we should endorse a balanced-budget plan early on. He warned about the impact of centrism on our political base in Congress.

I tried hard to win him over to my point of view. He patiently responded, showing where he agreed with me and where he didn't. I don't think I convinced him of anything, but at the end of dinner we each clearly knew where the other stood. Stephanopoulos's integrity in sticking with his position is remarkable and admirable.

Ickes and Enright had long since left us and, when the restaurant closed, we went to the bar. Over his whiskey and my cognac, the conversation loosened, and I felt a warmth toward him that continues still.

George is well known for his untamed bangs, very fine and jet-black. He is short, bright, and thirty-something (now only thirty-five). Most often he could be found in his little cubbyhole office next to the Oval Office, where he sat folded into his chair, feet on his desk, in the summer in his seersucker suit, working the telephones while surfing the TV channels with his remote control in a desperate search for news. He wanted to be the first to know anything.

His intensity matched mine, and our skills were complementary. He was Mr. Inside Washington while I was Mr. Outside Washington. He was highly sensitive to the Washington press and the congressional Democrats, two things I knew little about since my focus was voters' attitudes and public opinion in the country at large.

Stephanopoulos's strengths are managing today and tomorrow to avoid future slipups and keeping the news cycle positive. His management of the Rapid Response Team, which jumped all over any Dole attack, threw an already inept Republican campaign further off balance. At the height of the give-and-take with the Dole campaign, he told me, "We have to win every week, every day, and every hour." I admired that passion and focus.

George was little concerned with strategy but obsessed with tactics. He would get you through tomorrow; but he couldn't lead you in any particular direction over the year. I focused on long-term strategy and tried to achieve it day by day. Unfortunately, while I kept my eyes on the horizon in my absorption with strategic goals, I was apt to trip over any boulder that had been left in my path. I did not sufficiently appreciate the gravity of our short-term obstacles, and I tried to roll over them like a tank, whereas George knew how to maneuver around them.

Despite my admiration and affection, we disagreed a lot. George is an ideological liberal. He was my opponent in three identifiable episodes—the debate over the balanced-budget speech in May and

June of 1995, the disagreement over whether to offer a seven-year balanced-budget proposal in November of '95, and the discussion over whether to sign or veto the welfare-reform bill. But aside from these clashes we worked together easily. We conferred by phone five to fifteen times a day, and neither of us made a move without fully discussing it with the other. Every day would start with a phone call with George.

At the start of my tenure, the president regarded George with suspicion. He saw that he was young (one of the "children who helped get me elected") and felt that he and his consultants had adopted the worst possible strategy in 1994. He also suspected that he was the source of many press leaks. I gradually realized that my weekly meetings with the president were intentionally structured to exclude George.

Stephanopoulos's relationship with the vice president was even rockier. Before coming to the White House, George had been a top staffer of Congressman Richard Gephardt's—Gore's most likely Democratic rival for the presidential nomination in 2000.

But I knew—and the president knew as well—that George had to be involved if we were to win.

In July, I cornered George in the hallway of the Old Executive Office Building, the ornate structure next to the White House where most White House staffers had their offices and where most staff meetings took place, and ushered him into a vacant alcove. I didn't trust any office or phone line with this conversation. "What is your analysis of the power situation in the White House?" I began bluntly.

"You have all the power, and I don't have any," he replied genially.

"Want to change that?" I offered.

"Yes, how would I do that?" he asked warily.

"Come join me. Come work with me. My entire career is now staked on Bill Clinton's victory or defeat. I see my consulting operation as a meritocracy here. I don't care what you've done to me or I've done to you in the past. We were fighting for power and we were fighting over the balanced-budget speech. You fought fair, and so did I. It's over now. Come and join me—the two of us—and lead the operation with me. Equals, partners, allies." I meant every word. "When we disagree, we'll do it cleanly and with notice to each other. When it's settled, we'll be together again."

He said he'd think about it. A few minutes later he called me from his office and accepted the proposal. I don't know whether he liked it, but he lived by it.

I then set out to bring George and the president together again. I lobbied Clinton to include George in our weekly strategy meetings. I told him of our meeting, but the president didn't invite George to our strategy meetings. I also asked the vice president to support his inclusion.

As a result, George grew impatient. In early September, two months after our Executive Office Building chat, he told me that "we can't go on this way" and demanded that he be included in the meetings. I pressed the president very hard, and George was finally invited. Thereafter, George became one of the leading participants, along with the president and the consultants working with me.

Although his title was senior adviser on policy and strategy, George really controlled the White House staff. Panetta was in charge, but George could get Leon to do just about anything he wanted. As long as I didn't offend Leon and followed his rules, George saw to it that our efforts were in tandem. The rest of the White House staff settled in to cooperate with me once George had given his blessing.

Don Baer remained my closest ally among the core staff, but Bill Curry, the staff member with whom I was personally closest, was still frozen out of meetings, the casualty of my earlier secrecy and the abrasions it had left. During his tenure in the White House, his talents were ignored by the rest of the staff. He worked closely with me to develop policy initiatives that I passed on to the president, who greatly valued many of his ideas. But despite persistent efforts, I was never able to get him into our strategy sessions or other meetings with the president. It was the White House's loss that he was not more deeply integrated.

By the fall of 1995, my job had expanded beyond that of offering strategic advice to the president. I was in charge of the advertising war I describe in the next chapter and the polling and message development that went with it. But I also came to share with George the day-to-day operation of the White House "message machine," which produced a daily flow of speeches, issues, and proposals. When the day called for tactical responses to Republican thrusts or the exploitation of a weakness in the Republican position, George took the lead, with a lot of substantive help from Gene Sperling, the president's adviser on economics. With Baer, I oversaw the planned speeches, proposals, and initiatives that maintained our "lift and loft" during the fall budget mud-wrestling contest. George saved me from many pitfalls that I had overlooked due to my limited experience in Washington.

To manage the daily flow of public statements and presidential speeches, Panetta had set up a weekly "message meeting," usually chaired by him or by Erskine Bowles, with George and me in leading roles. This meeting served as a good way to coordinate the work of the other staffers, most of whom did not attend the strategy meetings.

When the post of White House communications director became vacant in the early summer of 1995, I worked hard to get Don Baer the job. It was very important that I have an ally who could run it without friction and could keep our message on target.

The president was willing, but the First Lady had her own ideas. In August, she called me at my weekend house. She was pushing Ann Lewis, the director of Planned Parenthood and a longtime friend of hers, for the position. She invited me to meet with Ann, herself, and the rest of her staff to discuss it.

Although Hillary and I had reestablished relations via the telephone in May, this was my first invitation to a meeting since the swimming pool mess. I eagerly accepted.

Hillary's crowd was at the meeting in the White House solarium, which served as unofficial headquarters for the girls' club, as she called her advisers. The room is airy and light and decorated with beautiful floral fabrics, which give it a more modern feel than can be found in the rest of the building, with its eighteenth-century furniture. With Hillary were Maggie Williams, her chief of staff; Melanne Verveer, the First Lady's friend since school and her issues director; and Ann Lewis. Mrs. Clinton was clad in a gray workout suit with tennis sneakers and no socks. She wore no makeup, and her hair was pulled back in a ponytail.

I appealed to the group for an alliance. I knew that "the boys," as they called Panetta, Ickes, and Stephanopoulos, had cut them out as surely as they had cut Gore's people out. "If we work together, we can turn things around and give the president a chance to win," I said.

Hillary complained that her people had no way of getting information about the staff's plans for the president. She was harshly critical of "the boys" for screwing things up, and she spoke vehemently about their lack of political savvy.

I said that I had always believed that Ickes was her person (the relationship between Harold and Susan Thomases had suggested it).

"He's not mine," Hillary said with a grin and added that she had privately "tried to get a few good people" into the White House staff but couldn't. She had urged Mike McCurry's selection as press secretary and for Bowles's elevation from director of the Small Business Administration to deputy chief of staff. Both were excellent choices, and I said so.

I promised the closest coordination with "the girls" and made clear that "whatever I'm doing, you'll know about it, we'll talk about it, and we'll do it together."

One outgrowth of this new alliance was that I began to meet privately with Hillary about every other week, to keep her posted on what was happening, answer her questions, and address her concerns. I felt she was as much my client as her husband was, and I needed to get instructions from her as well as from him.

As for Lewis, I felt she was grandmotherly but shrewd. She seemed to have a keen instinct for power and handled herself well. Hillary was indebted to her for her stand-up role in speaking out on the First Lady's behalf during the Whitewater scandals of the previous two years. I gathered that Lewis had had to leave Planned Parenthood and needed a job.

In view of Ann's ability as a spokesperson and her skill with the press, I suggested that she be *campaign* director of communications while Don Baer take the White House job, which is more of a background role. As the campaign press person, Lewis would deal with political charges and countercharges and could do what she did best: make no mistakes with aggressive reporters.

McCurry welcomed having someone to whom he could refer overtly political questions that he felt he should not address as White House press secretary. It worked out well, and both Lewis and Baer did well in their respective roles. Baer became my main collaborator in crafting a new message for the White House.

Maggie Williams and Melanne Verveer and I also worked closely. Maggie is motherly and kind with a gentle manner but a sharp instinct for getting her boss to hear new ideas. Melanne had a good sense of issues and policy and we collaborated on many issues.

I had essentially formed an alliance of the principals, but I had also formed an alliance of the outsiders. It is odd to call the president an outsider among his own staff. But like the vice president and Hillary, he remained often in disagreement with his staff, who marched to the beat of the liberal Democrats in Congress. The president, the vice president, and the First Lady were my key allies, united in their frustration with dealing with "the boys" of the White House staff.

The Secret Weapon:
Advertising

Why did Clinton win so easily in 1996? Why did his lead hardly vary? What was his strength with the voters that Dole could never shake?

In my opinion, the key to Clinton's victory was his early television advertising. There has never been anything even remotely like it in the history of presidential elections. In 1992, Clinton and Bush each spent about forty million dollars on TV advertising during the primary and general elections. In 1996, the Clinton campaign and, at the president's behest, the DNC spent upwards of eighty-five million dollars on ads— more than twice as much!

Very little reaches the outer fringes of the electorate unless it is advertised on television. From the moment I signed on with Clinton in 1994, I fought hard to persuade everyone that we would not win unless we started unconventionally early to fill the airwaves with our legislative priorities and issues. I hammered at this notion in every strategy meeting, always hearing derision from Ickes, who maintained that by the time the election came around in 1996, nobody would remember anything we said in 1995. I countered by predicting that if we brought legislative issues into every American's home through ads, the Republican issues would be dead before the race even started—which is what happened.

Week after week, month after month, from early July 1995 more or less continually until election day in '96, sixteen months later, we bombarded the public with ads. The advertising was concentrated in the key swing states: California, Washington, Oregon, Colorado, New Mexico, Louisiana, Arkansas, Tennessee, Kentucky, Florida, North Carolina, New Jersey, Pennsylvania, Ohio, Michigan, Wisconsin, Illinois, Minnesota, Missouri, and Iowa. During this period, television viewers in these states saw, on average, 150 to 180 airings of a Clinton or a DNC commercial, about one every three days for a year and a half. This unprecedented campaign was the key to success.

I knew that the ad campaign had to begin early, be continual, stress the same themes week after week, and above all, not be jammed or countered by the press (which we called the free media, in contrast to ads, which we called the paid media).

To achieve relative "secrecy"—an ironic term for an ad campaign that reached about 125 million Americans three times a week—we decided not to advertise in New York City or Washington, D.C., and to run ads only occasionally in Los Angeles. These are the cities where journalists live and work. If the ads had run there, the press would have grasped the magnitude of what we were doing. But if these cities remained "dark," the national press would not make an issue of our ads—of this we felt sure.

That we succeeded so well is a brutal comment on the free media's limitations in a country the size of America. One or two reporters—notably Alison Mitchell of *The New York Times*—realized in part what we were doing, but most had no idea. Teams of reporters covered every move, slip, misstep, speech, or cough by the president, Dole, or Gingrich, but not our daily bombardment of paid media messages. As the ads were shaping voters' attitudes, recasting the nation's views of Clinton, and reshaping its understanding of the budget fight, few newspapers ran articles, much less front-page articles, on the ads. Television—the very medium we were using—rarely mentioned the ads.

As election day approached, the free media began to cover the Clinton- and Dole-campaign ads with greater intensity. But by then, the early advertising had so locked the campaign into its basic pattern that the advertising—and the reports on it—had little impact. A given ad would produce a blip up or a blip down in the polls, but none realigned what had been set in place by our earlier ads. Thus, our best political reporters in print and television missed the top political story of 1995–96.

Each week, our polls showed huge differences between voters' attitudes in the swing states in which we were advertising and the solid Democratic or Republican states that we avoided. Typically, if our polls showed Clinton leading Dole nationally by seventeen points, the average lead in our 1996 polls, states where our ads had run showed a twenty-seven-point Clinton lead and states where no ads had run showed only a seven-point lead. Before we ran our ads, the difference between these two groups of states was only three points. As election day approached, the belief in a Clinton victory penetrated even those states where we had not advertised much, narrowing the gap between the states where we advertised and the rest. But in the early going, it was our ads more than anything else that created and held our lead.

I had always been interested in landmark changes in political communication. When FDR brought the president's voice home through his fireside chats, the effect was enormous. Eisenhower's use of national television helped bring about his landslide reelection. Kennedy's live press conferences and Johnson's use of negative political advertising were landmark changes in effective political communication.

In Arkansas, Clinton and I had pioneered a new kind of paid media advertising. Rather than advertising only in the weeks before an election and sending out messages only about the candidate, we advertised throughout the governor's tenure, not to promote his reelection but to publicize his views on important legislative issues. As a result, voters who might dislike Clinton found that they agreed with him on the issues and after a while became his increasingly enthusiastic supporters. The ads tended to make the elections anticlimactic.

The key was to advertise on legislative issues only, not to promote Clinton's candidacy. By focusing on these issues, Clinton could pass his program and build a vast base of support. I wanted to use such advertising to advance the president's legislative program at the expense of the Republicans, hoping to build national support as we had built local support in Arkansas.

No president had ever before used television advertising during legislative battles as lobbying groups have done for years on behalf of campaigns to confirm Judge Robert Bork, promote health-insurance reform, tort reform, and so on. But for the '96 election, unless we used TV to reach beyond the voters who normally follow legislative debates and congressional or budgetary issues, we would not make our case with the American people.

Everybody except the president and the vice president opposed early advertising but President Clinton knew what these legislative advocacy ads had done in Arkansas. His campaign for teacher testing worked its way through the Arkansas electorate via paid ads that appeared at times well before the election season. He'd watched these issues ads affect the legislature's deliberations as they strengthened the bond between himself and the electorate.

I wanted to do what we had done in Arkansas: hammer home the differences between the Democratic and the Republican legislative and budget proposals. I knew that once voters learned the specifics about the massive cuts in the Republican budget and saw that Clinton wanted to balance the budget too, but sensibly, they would reject the Republican plan. In this way we would win the political center. Having established a position of strength based on our legislative victories, we could deal later with the specifics of winning the election.

I met with campaign attorney Lynn Utrecht and Democratic National Committee lawyer Joe Sandler and explained the kind of ads I had in mind. Fortunately, they said the law permitted unlimited expenditures by a political party for such "issue-advocacy" ads. By the end of the race, we had spent almost thirty-five million dollars on issue-advocacy ads (in addition to about fifty million dollars on conventional candidate-oriented media), burying the Republican proposals and building a national consensus in support of the president on key issues.

To create and place the ads, I needed an advertising firm. I chose Bob Squier's agency, Squier, Knapp, Ochs. Sandy-haired, trim, and short, Squier is like a college senior at a party school. Despite his long history in political advertising—he had done Hubert Humphrey's ads—he retains an infectious boyish enthusiasm. He was close to the vice president, who was pleased by his appointment.

It was Squier's partner, Bill Knapp, who deserves the bulk of the credit for the ads we ran for Clinton. Knapp's creativity and managerial skills allowed us to run one of the most effective political-advertising campaigns in history. Knapp ran the paid media campaign, keeping all of its pieces together during the often chaotic and rushed pre-election months.

I also brought in Hank Sheinkopf of the New York firm of Austin-Sheinkopf and Marius Penczner from Memphis to help with the ads. Hank, an intense Russian Jew with wild hair and wilder ideas—and a former New York City cop—helped bring a raw, cutting emotional power to the advertising. Penczner, a mild, restrained, polite southerner, came from the world of country-music MTV, where he had produced videos for the Allman Brothers, Garth Brooks, and many others. Penczner brought us ideas that were well outside the mainstream of political advertising.

In Arkansas, Clinton and I had written most of his ads, and I had supervised the production of the spots, working closely with David Watkins of Little Rock. Now the president was not enthusiastic about Squier's firm. Clinton said he liked Squier, but was not especially impressed by his work. The First Lady was downright opposed to hiring him and echoed objections brought to her attention by Susan Thomases, who felt that Squier would take public credit for every successful move in the campaign and disappear from view if things turned bad.

I could not resolve the Squier situation through Erskine Bowles and confronted the president directly in a rare daytime Oval Office meeting. Clinton said he was grateful to the media creator Frank Greer, who had helped him in 1992. "Frank got screwed because he wouldn't talk to the press, so he let the other people who did my advertising in 1992 leak on him and knock him. Frank never answered in kind, and I feel I owe him." He wanted Greer to buy the media time, a function Squier was supposed to handle. I told him I would work only with Squier.

I was determined to avoid the chaos that had dominated the Clinton advertising effort in 1992, where media creators fought one another and every decision was a struggle. I wanted total control or none. I wouldn't take a middle position.

Clinton likes to divide his advisers so that he can understand which issues are truly important by watching the splits and cracks when they clash. These "seams" let him step in and take control, something he could not do in a homogeneous operation.

Greer is an ideological liberal, closely allied with Ickes. I did not want to see even part of the paid-media operation fall under Ickes's influence. I pointed out that we had decided to fire Greer in the 1990 Arkansas gubernatorial race because he wasn't following our guidance and gave us ads that we didn't want. "Let's not have to fire somebody twice," I said.

"But he did a great job buying media for me in '92; he got it very cheaply, cheaper than you guys can."

I was inflexible. "Either you let me have my team intact, as is, or you build your own without me. We can't have the factionalism of 1992. Media must be consistent, and it can't be with a patchwork team."

The president answered patiently: "Obviously, I have total faith in you. I've put myself and the whole campaign in your hands. Schoen? He seems OK, kind of a hard-nosed guy who pushes his ideas. Penn? Some interesting insights, some new ideas. I don't see what Squier does that's so different."

"The first part of your sentence is all you need," I replied. "If you have faith in me, give me the tools, and let me do the job. Hold me accountable; don't second-guess the way I get it done."

Then came the president's real objection: "If you control each aspect of the media and the polling, how can I control the process? How can I get different options and choices? How do I keep control?"

Control. The key word.

I answered, "You'll keep control, total control, the same way you have for seventeen years with me. You know I'll give you all the polling data, just as I've always done. You're better at reading polls than any pollster I know. I'll work with you the way I always have. I'll clear everything with you constantly. I'll talk with you when we develop the questionnaires for the polls, when we get the results back, when we script the ads, when we test them, and before we run them. You'll be right there every minute. You don't have to create a conflict between members of my team to have input; I'll bring it all to you all the time so you can have the control without the controversy."

The president agreed to use Squier, Knapp, Ochs temporarily. But the most permanent things in life are those we call temporary. This "temporary" arrangement continued until after the Democratic National Convention a year and three months later! By this time, Squier, Knapp, Sheinkopf, and Penczner had long since quieted the doubters with their mastery of television advertising. And the doubts about Squier that Susan Thomases had raised turned out to be groundless: Squier kept unusually quiet about his pivotal role in the race and was solidly available whenever the campaign needed him.

Despite their effective work, the president continued to gripe about Squier. During one period of intense fee negotiations between the consultants and Ickes, I raised the financial issues in question with the president during an Oval Office meeting.

"I don't mind paying you any amount of money you want," he said. By then, Clinton had assumed a commanding lead over Dole, something almost unthinkable at the start '95. "Nothing is too much to pay for a miracle. But why are you letting Squier make all that money?"

I explained that without Squier and Knapp, the media effort would never have been so effective and I wanted to be sure they were well compensated.

As a result of this and other Oval Office discussions, the president became the day-to-day operational director of our TV-ad campaign. He worked over every script, watched each ad, ordered changes in every visual presentation, and decided which ads would run when and where. He was as involved as any of his media consultants were. The ads became not the slick creations of admen but the work of the president himself. In that sense, they were much like the thirty-second speeches he had written to convey his views to the American people.

"Why don't you tell them that I cut taxes through EITC?" he would typically ask.

"Nobody knows what EITC [the earned-income tax credit] is," I would answer.

"You should say that it's a tax cut for fifteen million working families; that's really what it is."

Every line of every ad came under his informed, critical, and often meddlesome gaze. Every ad was *his* ad.

Our first ads were about the president's refusal to cave in to congressional Republicans and repeal the ban on assault rifles. These featured one police officer describing how his partner had been gunned down by an assault weapon, and another police officer talking about how he had been shot by one during a routine traffic stop. These ads, which Hank Sheinkopf—the former cop—largely created, sent a powerful message.

The effect was electrifying. Our approval ratings and voter share zoomed where we advertised. Still, Ickes discounted the results, arguing that we would lose these gains by election day. The ads would be forgotten.

"Not if we stay on the air," I predicted and pressed for more advertising money. In fact, as a result of these ads of early July '95, our ratings on "fighting crime" came to equal those of the Republicans, nullifying their historic advantage on this issue, and the ratings persisted throughout the pre-election period. Far from being forgotten, our early ads helped produce a massive base of voter support for our positions on the key issues before Congress.

In late August 1995, we began hitting Republican budget cuts in our ads and promoting the president's balanced-budget plan. These ads and their successors remained on the air, with only brief interruptions, until the Democratic Convention, after which our regular political ads picked up the slack. We created the first fully advertised presidency in U.S. history, which led to an extensive record of legislative accomplishment.

Penn and Schoen polled heavily to determine voters' views of the Republicans' proposed budget cuts. Drawing on this research, we identified which reductions mattered most. Broadly, cuts in Medicare, Medicaid, education, and environmental protection most upset the voters. Raising Medicare premiums and letting doctors bill patients for more than what Medicare would allow caused the greatest concern. The elimination of the Medicaid guarantee of free medical care to children under thirteen was very damaging to the Republicans, as were their proposed cuts in nursing-home standards and their proposed elimination of a guarantee of nursing-home beds to anyone eligible. Among the education cuts that troubled voters most were the reductions in college scholarships, the cuts in the president's expansion of Head Start, reductions in Title I aid, which would result in larger classes, and above all, the reduction of anti-drug-use programs in schools. Voters also distrusted cuts in funding for toxic-waste cleanup.

Our ads helped explain the Republican budget cuts. More important, they elaborated the president's balanced-budget proposal as an alternative. It would have been easy to publicize our opposition to the Republican cuts without doing any advertising. The press always comes to a fight, and a battle over cuts always makes the headlines. But our ads showed that Clinton had an alternative, a better way of balancing the budget and cutting taxes. The ads worked well because they challenged the Republicans' monopoly on balancing the budget. Now the fight was not whether to balance but how to balance.

Were our ads distorted? The Republicans charged that we were dishonest in calling cuts what were actually reductions in the rate of increased spending. But it was Republicans who first used the word in this sense to describe Clinton's failure to increase the defense budget in keeping with inflation. In defense budgeting, this use of the word *cut* is probably justified. In entitlement spending, for programs like Medicare and Medicaid, it is even more appropriate. If the cost of medical services and the number of patients in need of care increase at a certain rate while funding grows more slowly, it is obvious that fewer patients will be treated and the treatment each patient will receive will decline.

Any thirty-second ad on the budget is an oversimplification of complex questions. But we were quite meticulous in our choice of words. For example, White House staffer Gene Sperling once refused to let us characterize the Dole tax-cut proposal of 1996 as likely to "slow economic growth" since the consensus among economists was that it would speed it in the short term but slow it in the long term. Gene insisted on adding *in the long term* if we made this accusation.

Each ad we produced for almost a year hammered at these Republican cuts. While content and nuance varied they were substantially alike in hammering at these reductions and the distorted values that impelled them. And each ad explained President Clinton's proposals to balance the budget without these cuts. Say what you will about them, these ads, more than any other single factor, kept the Republicans from cutting Medicare, Medicaid, education, and environmental protection as they proposed.

Our ads were factual, emotional, and highly effective. We formulated each ad according to our polling. Mark Penn and Doug Schoen and I prepared the poll questionnaires. At first, we cleared each question's wording with the president, but soon he let us proceed on our own. The poll measured public reaction to each element of the president's legislative program and to that of the Republicans. After Penn, Schoen, and I explained where the public agreed with us on the issues, our media consultants wrote the ads. Two to three times a week, Bob Squier, Bill Knapp, Squier's associate Betsy Steinberg, Hank Sheinkopf, Marius Penczner, Bill Curry, Tom Freedman, and Democratic National Committee attorney Joe Sandler met with Mark Penn, Doug Schoen, and me to formulate copy. On the phone, we'd keep in close touch with White House staffers Rahm Emanuel and Gene Sperling to be sure our wording was accurate. I'd often run the wording by George Stephanopoulos. Author Naomi Wolf was sometimes with us. I myself met with Naomi every few weeks for nearly a year to get her advice on how to target women voters. She also gave me remarkably prescient analyses of the social-cultural trends in the country.

We prepared several different rough versions of the ads, called animatics, which Mark Penn would arrange to test at fifteen shopping malls around the nation. After the Republicans began to attack us in their own ads, Penn tested the opposition ad and our reply at the same time to measure their relative impact. Penn's staffers would set themselves up in a mall and invite shoppers one by one to fill out a short questionnaire about Clinton, Dole, and their own political views. Then they would show the voters the ad we wanted to test. Afterward the shopper would fill in the same questionnaire and Penn would measure any changes in opinion.

When I originally urged the president to hire the polling firm of Penn and Schoen, I planned to use only my old friend Doug Schoen. But I soon came to appreciate the skills of his partner, Mark Penn. Perpetually disheveled, even sloppy in appearance, largely devoid of personality, tact, or charm, he is all brain and became an increasingly important part of our consulting operation.

Based on the mall tests, we decided which ad to run and whether to combine it with elements from ads that did not do as well. We worked for hours to make the ad fit thirty seconds. Then we'd send the script to Doug Sosnik, the White House political director, who gave it to the president for his OK.

Particularly at the beginning of our ad campaign, we would then go to the Oval Office for a ten-minute meeting with the president and vice-president to win their approval. Nancy Hernreich watched closely to see that we left after the ten minutes were up. The president always suggested changes. Knapp, Penczner, Sheinkopf, and Steinberg then worked all day to produce the ad, always including some last-minute touch that made the ad work even better. To highlight Gingrich's cuts in education, for example, they were particularly good at finding film clips of him waving his hand no, as if rejecting dessert at a restaurant. Gore especially liked Knapp and Squier's ability to find footage of Dole creeping around behind Gingrich at a press conference. He compared it to a scene from *Jurassic Park* where a particularly mobile, kangaroo-like dinosaur, the Velociraptor, would maneuver for position in a hunt.

I'd worked in almost a hundred high-level political races, but never before had I worked with so many good consultants, and the thrill of it is hard to describe. I felt like a violinist suddenly surrounded by a great orchestra or a baseball player in an all-star lineup. Clinton gave us a virtually unlimited budget for polling and mall testing. We spent months in war games figuring out how to handle different budget-fight scenarios or different Republican attacks on issues. When the hypothetical became a reality, we had only to push a button on the computer, and the mall test and the poll for exactly that situation would pop up. As we sat one afternoon bouncing advertising copy back and forth among the laptops of Squier, Knapp, Sheinkopf, and me, analyzing the results of test ads, anticipating Dole's next move, I paraphrased a quote de Gaulle had used to describe the moment when the Germans were finally driven out of France—he said that he wanted to capture that moment and keep it suspended in time, never to change. I looked around me at our group, each outplaying his or her usual game, way above it, and wanted to be with them forever, in the middle of a campaign, writing ads. The élan of our group was palpable.

Clinton's skilled projection of his message via TV commercials is no less notable than Reagan's artful television image, FDR's radio personality, Woodrow Wilson's high-minded rhetorical style, or Lincoln's logical presentations in his open letters. Politics means making things happen, not just hoping for them. Clinton's effectiveness in using political spot advertising to promote his positions is one of his great strengths, and for that he deserves to be ranked as one of the great presidential communicators.

The president's media were based on issues, not on feel-good positives or character-assassination negatives. Clinton felt that the era of the negative ad was ending. He preferred to let the other side attack and then use his media to rebut and counterpunch.

In the late '70s and early '80s, Clinton and I explored the new area of negative advertising. These were ads that capitalized on voters' distrust of politics and used single-issue differences to bring down opponents. Our negative ads on utility rates were crucial in Clinton's 1982 comeback defeat of Governor Frank White, and so were the negative ads we helped prepare for David Pryor's 1978 defeat of Jim Guy Tucker.

Now, however, we believed that voters were suspicious of negative ads. They had been exposed to so many that they were jaded by them. From then on Clinton deeply believed in the rebuttal ad.

"Remember how we did it in Arkansas?" he asked me at a strategy meeting while the others looked on curiously. "We'd give the facts to rebut the negative ad first, always the facts up front, and then we'd counterpunch with our own negatives."

Clinton always loved the actual process of writing and designing ads. As involved as he was in the '95 and '96 ad campaigns, he missed actually sitting at the table, the way he had in Arkansas, and participating in the process. Once, as he wistfully contemplated the start of the actual campaign, he said, "I'll miss writing all those rebuttal ads. You'll have all the fun."

As the fall approached, it became more and more evident that everything depended on how well we could tell our story in the fight against the Republicans' proposed budget cuts.

"You never got your position across to the public in the '93 budget fight," I told the president in a private late-night session in early August.

"Your tax increase was almost exclusively on upper incomes, but the public believes that you increased taxes on everybody. You never got your point out in the health-care debate either. Your plan called for plenty of freedom to choose your own doctor, but the ads by the insurance companies gave the opposite impression and they beat you. Now, for once, it is absolutely crucial that you get your views on this budget fight out unfiltered, precisely, and repetitively through ads."

"We'll have the ads," he assured me wearily. But it was a long way from this almost whispered commitment to go ahead and find the money to run the ads. The decision had to be made in September.

I pressed the issue vigorously at a strategy meeting on September 7, 1995, in the Treaty Room. I believed then, and still do, that the entire fate of Clinton's presidency hinged on this key decision. Unless we could beat the Republican budget with our own and make America understand that we wanted to eliminate the deficit as much as Gingrich did, but in the right way, we would never win the '95 budget fight or the '96 election. "We will decide the outcome of the election right here and right now," I declared. "If we win now, we'll win later. If we lose now, we'll be dead no matter what we do."

In retrospect, the decision to advertise early and continually was, in fact, one of four keys to victory in '96. The first key was Clinton's decision to compete for the center by giving the balanced-budget speech in June '95, a decision that made winning possible. The second was the decision to advertise, which took us into 1996 with a lead over Dole. The third key was the State of the Union Address in 1996, which, coupled with our decisions on advertising, gave us a large and permanent lead. Finally, the president's decision to sign the welfare-reform bill in '96 eliminated the last real possibility of losing his lead.

In our September 1995 strategy meetings, I had to wage a giant battle with Ickes to convince the president to allow further advertising. The DNC had no cash on hand for such spending and eventually had to borrow much of the money.

Penn, Schoen, and I argued that advertising was vital to defeat the Republicans in the budget battle. "We will make the Republican proposals so unpopular and so unnecessary to balancing the budget that they will have to cave in long before the budget ever reaches your desk." I glibly predicted that by November the Republican unity would be shattered and the Republicans would be "split into hunter-gatherer groups" to be picked off one at a time.

In that prediction, I would turn out to be wrong. It wasn't until the spring of '96—a year later—that the hunter-gatherer groups formed, and it was every Republican for himself. Until then, the Republicans were determined to stick together, a determination that I badly underestimated. But I was right in predicting that their proposed budget would be the object of derision across the nation. I simply underestimated the capacity of the Republican party to stick to an unpopular position as it became more and more disliked by the public. I underestimated the capacity of Gingrich and Dole for political suicide.

Panetta and Stephanopoulos, normally Ickes's allies, intervened on my side to tilt the consensus toward going ahead with the advertising, but Erskine Bowles properly insisted that we project how much we wanted to spend through the end of the year rather than budget one week at a time. "What we had been doing," he complained, was "no way to run a business."

We agreed on a ten-million-dollar budget for the balance of 1995.

No president had ever advertised even remotely this far in advance of an election and none had used issue-advocacy ads, intended not to urge his reelection, but focus on the budget issues before Congress. Ten million dollars was about equal to what most presidents or candidates for the presidency spent on media ads for the entire primary season, from Iowa through the convention—yet here we were spending it on issue ads more than a year before the election year even began. I am sure I irritated everyone by repeating that if we spent money on ads, our polling numbers on the issues would rise, and those better numbers would generate more money. The president had seen this exact thing happen in our Arkansas days, but the numbers now showed one zero more than he was used to seeing.

Clinton complained bitterly at having to raise this much money. "You don't know, you don't have any remote idea," he said to me, "how hard I have to work, how hard Hillary has to work, how hard Al has to work to raise this much money." He didn't mean phone time. He rarely, if ever, had to pick up the telephone, as president, and ask for a campaign donation. But he did mean work. To raise a million dollars, he usually had to attend a massive fund-raiser, most often outside Washington, and shake hands with hundreds and hundreds of people.

Eileen and I went to a few of these events—paying our own way—and watched the trial by handshake as it grimly unfolded. We usually waited at the end of the receiving line since we were not eager to displace the customers. We stood—as Clinton had to—for hours while he shook each hand and posed, smiling, for each photo, chatting happily with each donor. Our feet ached. We shifted in place, leaned against the wall, looked at an empty chair as a thirst-crazed desert traveler would eye an oasis well. And still we stood. The line never seemed to ease up, much less end. The president went through this agony night after night after night. I began to see what those ads were going to cost him.

Only once did he complain to me about the pace of the fund-raising he had to endure: "I can't think. I can't act. I can't do anything but go to fund-raisers and shake hands. You want me to issue executive orders; I can't focus on a thing but the next fund-raiser. Hillary can't, Al can't— we're all getting sick and crazy because of it."

But the ads worked as voters began to reject the Republican budget. Slowly, week after week, we climbed in the polls and the Republicans dropped. The president's job-approval rating, in our polling, rose from 54 percent in August to 55 percent in September to 56 percent in October. Virtually all the gain took place where we advertised.

The ads were devastating. One, inspired by Marius Penczner, featured an EKG machine monitoring a patient's heartbeat as the announcer describes the premium increases and benefit cuts the Republicans planned for Medicare. Finally, the comforting beeps stop and we hear the terrifying, continuous monotone and see the flat line on the screen that means Medicare has died.

A second ad, inspired by Bob Squier's innocent joy at the birth of his first grandchild, Emma, shows Emma in her crib, playing with her toys beneath a mobile, while the announcer decries the Republican-proposed education cuts.

As the ads ran their course, voters came to prefer our budget plan to the Republican version by more than two to one and trusted Clinton to balance the budget "in a way that is fair to all" over the Republicans by twelve to fifteen points. We had invaded the heart of Republican territory, the very core—the advocacy of a balanced budget—and we were showing that we could do it better than they could.

The elderly became a solid phalanx of support for Clinton's budget proposals. Women over age sixty-five, in particular, were outraged at the Medicare cuts. One poll found that they backed Clinton by almost as much as such traditional Democratic constituencies as African Americans and Hispanics.

And yet the press continued to ignore our ads even though they were reshaping American politics. When stories did run, they were buried inside the paper. We got in under their radar by purchasing television time directly from local affiliates, rather than from the networks. The network news shows knew what we were doing but didn't grasp its meaning until long after the ads had run.

Through the ads, the country knew what the fight was about from our point of view, and wanted Clinton to stand firm. "For once, we've laid the groundwork for this free media spectacle with our paid media," I reassured Clinton as the government shutdown approached. "The country understands this fight and wants you to do just what you're doing."

What made the ads work? Was it just that we had money enough to run them a lot? Can anybody with enough money win an election? No. The graveyards are full of rich men and women who tried to buy their way into office and failed totally: Michael Huffington in California, Clayton Williams in Texas, Andy Stein in New York, Mitt Romney in Massachusetts, and for that matter, Ross Perot in the 1992 national race are all examples. The key is to advertise your positions only if the public agrees with them. If the public won't buy your basic premise, it doesn't matter how much you spend or how well your ads are produced; they won't work. Clinton's ads worked because his moderate budget plan made sense to the American people as a way to achieve a balanced budget without cutting popular programs. The Republican plan for massive spending cuts and huge tax reductions seemed wrong to voters.

From the beginning of our ad offensive, we all worried that the Republicans would retaliate. "Don't pick on somebody who has two or three times the money we have," Erskine Bowles warned in September when we were deciding whether to go with wall-to-wall media.

But incredibly, the Republicans didn't go on the air. Each week we monitored the TV stations. Once in a while, they would try to get press attention by running an ad on cable or by purchasing ad time in the Washington, D.C., media area and pretending that it was part of a national advertising buy. But they didn't go national.

At first, Clinton would ask me four times a week, "Are they on?"

Each time I would say, "No sir, thank God."

They didn't go on. They had plenty of money. Why did they wait?

As the weeks became months and then almost a year had passed and still our ads were running and they were "dark," I formulated all kinds of theories, sitting late at night with Clinton. He and I loved to speculate about what was going on. I suggested that maybe Dole and Texas senator Phil Gramm, Dole's major opponent at the time for the nomination, couldn't agree on a text and Republican National Committee chairman Haley Barbour wasn't willing to proceed on his own. I guessed that Barbour didn't want to compete with the fund-raising efforts of the various candidates for the Republican presidential nomination.

The Republicans had been burned by advertising too early in senatorial and gubernatorial races in the past, and Republican strategists were dead set against early ads in these statewide contests. They liked to hold their fire until closer to election day. But these strategists failed to understand that if the advertising concerned a current, ongoing fight—such as the one over the budget—voters would pay attention and the ads would be long remembered. Voters always remember what a president does in a major controversy.

In any event, once we were advertising heavily, no rational strategist should have failed to oppose our ads, especially ones so aggressively pointed at Dole's and Gingrich's issue positions. I kept telling myself, "They *have to* answer." But they never did. I made a point of never telling Trent Lott how mystified I was that they weren't on the air, but the thought hung over our meetings like the great unasked question it was. I was stumped.

Perhaps the Republicans could not believe that we intended to *stay* on the air for the entire year and a half. Perhaps they were waiting for us to stop, confident that our ads would then fade from memory without rebuttal. Had Ickes had his way, this would have been the case. But Clinton advertised through all of July, half of August, all of September, October, and November, and the first half of December in 1995. In 1996 we started in early January, and remained on the air with either issue-advocacy or regular ads through election day.

I believe that had the Republicans advertised early in the budget fight—in 1995—outspending us two or three to one, as they could have, they would have won the budget fight (either by forcing us to sign their budget or by getting enough conservative Democrats to override the president's veto). And I believe that they would have won the presidential election of 1996. Whoever killed their plans to advertise (or failed to draw them up) deserves the blame for their defeat.

By the end of 1995, the Clinton and DNC ads had run unopposed by any Republican paid media for most of six months. The effect was devastating. In swing states like Michigan and Wisconsin, where our ads had run, Clinton's lead over Dole was actually larger than in core Democratic states, like Rhode Island and New York. On the issues, the Republicans had let us convert their majority to our side.

▲

I was a lot less worried about the Republicans than I was about people like Ickes, who were supposedly on my side. It became a challenge to master the art of infighting, a skill I knew little about before I came to Washington. Generally, in my senatorial and gubernatorial races, I had worked directly with the candidate and didn't pay attention to the staff one way or another.

Now, however, I developed my own style of infighting: control through inclusion. I was secure in my position with the president and felt I would succeed better by using the carrot than the stick in dealing with the staffers. I took George Stephanopoulos into my confidence as well as other staff members who had opposed me in 1995. "You fought me clean and fair," I told Rahm Emanuel, "and I would love for you to work with me. I have no grudges, and I came to admire you as you opposed me, so I'd like to work with you." Emanuel, a short, thin former professional ballet dancer, had been a key Clinton fund-raiser in 1992. Now he ran crime, drugs, and immigration issues for the White House. He was one of the only sources of new ideas on the White House staff. He helped develop Clinton's tough anti-crime posture, stealing from the GOP a former monopoly on the issue.

Members of my consulting team asked why I was so generous with staff who had opposed us. Why did I insist we welcome them onto our team, making sure they had power and a role? "If we show that we're open and anxious to sign up all good people to our team, we'll get a lot less opposition."

The most interesting problem was handling the egos of the fellow consultants I had recruited. Each knew that he depended on me for his continued role in the race, but the line blurred as they became closer to the president and the president began to value their work as individuals, not just as associates of mine.

I had problems, in particular, with Mark Penn. Penn provided more original input than any other member of our team and played a central role in developing many of our core concepts. He is brilliant but his new status as an adviser to the president had gone to his head. Lured by the Washington power scene to move full time to the capital, he installed himself in a walk-in closet in Doug Sosnik's office. Sosnik, the White House political director, had become increasingly valuable to me as a way around Harold Ickes. Technically Ickes's deputy, Sosnik was competent and reasonable and helped me get approvals without my having to confront Ickes directly.

I suspected that Sosnik and Penn were getting too cozy and would form a coalition of technocrats who would position themselves between Harold and me; perhaps they thought that while Ickes and I fought, they would run the ship. I had no intention of letting Mark Penn operate independently. The president had hired me, and I was ultimately responsible for our success or failure. I became more suspicious when it became clear that Penn was going to White House meetings to which I had not been invited, as White House staff members tried to seduce Penn away from our team.

The situation with Penn worried each of the consultants on our team for political reasons as well. I spoke to the president about it and warned him of the danger of having a consultant with an office in the White House. I told the president about some of Penn's other projects, and said that critics might see a potential conflict of interest. I cited, specifically, his work as a consultant for AT&T while delicate negotiations on the telecommunications bill were going on. I also cited his work in foreign elections as a potential conflict. "It's OK for him to poll for us," I said, "but he shouldn't have a White House office."

The president, who was distressed at these possible conflicts, agreed and asked me to take care of it.

So I approached Penn and told him that he had to move out of his White House office and end his dealings with Sosnik and the rest of the staff. In return, I told him I would keep him close by my side and would bring him in on all my meetings and phone calls. I felt that this way I would elicit the best performance from him, while controlling his potential end runs around me. This solution worked well; Penn got more involved and more powerful as we worked more closely together.

While I waged my internal wars, the specter of General Colin Powell's presidential candidacy cost Bill Clinton sleep and, when he did sleep, doubtless haunted his dreams throughout October and early November of 1995. The president did not believe he could beat Powell.

"He'll take away blacks, he'll separate himself from the congressional Republicans, he'll run a great campaign, and he'll beat me bad," he predicted in late October as Powell-mania descended on America, with Powell's book, *My American Journey,* making him a national celebrity.

In June 1992, as Clinton prepared for his first run for the presidency, he conferred with me at some length on the selection of a vice president. I had urged that he choose Gore, arguing that he needed a vice president very much like himself. In eschewing the traditional notion of balancing the ticket with a vice president who is different, I said that Clinton had not fully explained to the voters who he, Bill Clinton, really was. Gore's similarity would make it easier for Clinton to tell voters more about himself.

In the course of these discussions, Powell's name had also come up. I said he would make an interesting choice.

Clinton said, "I know; I'd like him, but he won't do it."

I didn't probe and don't know whether Clinton actually offered the job to Powell or whether he just assumed that Powell would not run on Clinton's ticket because of his expressed desire to stay on active duty.

Now Clinton's fearful respect for Powell had not lessened. The president was upset about the adulatory attention Powell got. "They're giving him such a free ride; it's ridiculous. He comes on TV like a saint, and those white liberal guilty reporters are so awestruck that they won't ask him a damn question," he complained to me over the phone.

"He was against what we did in Bosnia," he said. "Powell would never have bombed Bosnia and stopped that war. He'd never send ground troops to keep the peace. But do they ask him that? Do they pin him down? No. No, they're too protective of their own creation. Powell is their candidate, the candidate of America's media establishment, so how do I beat him?"

Faced with a problem he didn't know how to solve, he would as usual complain until somebody showed him a way to get around it. He complained at every meeting, in every phone call, in every chat, endlessly and loudly.

I huddled with Penn and Schoen, who fielded a series of polls to see how to handle Powell. In an early-November strategy meeting, we reported that Powell, as a Republican, could indeed at that point beat the president. But he couldn't get the Republican nomination. And he couldn't beat the president if he ran as an independent. Checkmate.

The data were clear: Dole held a narrow lead over Powell in the Republican primary against a wide field of Republican candidates, but when the other candidates dropped out, leaving just Dole and Powell, the senator beat the general by more than two to one: deadly math for a Powell candidacy. Virtually any voters who supported either Gramm, Buchanan, Forbes, or Alexander in the primary preferred Dole to Powell.

The general's support of affirmative action, certain gun controls, and most of all, his pro-choice position, made him anathema in primaries where the religious right held sway. As Powell raced around the country speaking and signing books, I knew that he couldn't run and wouldn't try. The numbers weren't there. It remains to be seen whether the Republican primary voters will feel any more generous toward Powell in 2000, when he may face Jack Kemp.

When we got back the data suggesting that Powell couldn't get the Republican nomination, I saw the last major obstacle to Clinton's re-election removed. In our strategy meeting of early November I declared that the "election is now over." Across the rectangular coffee table, I said to the president, "Congratulations, you won." This prediction, delivered twelve months before the polls opened on election day, met with astonished silence, then derisive laughter from the twelve others in the room. But the president remained silent. He looked up at me over his reading glasses. Then, having silently calculated that I was probably right, he resumed reading his agenda book without saying a word. The outcome of the election, if not our actual margin of victory, was established that day and was never seriously in doubt afterward.

The Battle of the Budget

The darkest secret, the one truth the congressional Democrats would never admit was their profound belief that their program of social involvement and activism would never survive a balanced budget.

The Republicans sensed it. They realized that we had run a deficit almost every year since FDR brought government so thoroughly into the affairs of Americans. Under Eisenhower's shrinking military budget federal revenues matched the outflow of spending. But rarely has the budget been balanced in other years. Even as the Republicans tripled the national debt under Reagan and Bush by cutting taxes and raising military spending, the party rhetorically continued to worship at the altar of the balanced budget.

Democrats, too, pretended to support deficit reduction as they spoke vaguely of living within our means, but a zero deficit terrified them. And meanwhile, many liberal economists claimed that balancing the budget didn't matter. As long as the ratio of the deficit to the size of the economy dropped, we were OK. But a global shortage of capital, the inability of business to compete with the federal government at the loan window, and stubbornly high interest rates told a different story.

Politically, I felt that there were only five credible issues the Republicans could use to defeat the Democrats. First and second, they had a special bond of trust with most voters on fiscal issues and crime. Here their historic frugality and toughness gave them an innate advantage. Third, they had acquired, since Nixon's time, a special corner on welfare and other race-linked issues, like the reform of both affirmative action and immigration policy. Democrats were too tied to minorities on these issues to be fully trusted by conservative white voters. Fourth were the linked issues of foreign policy and defense. The Democratic failure in Vietnam and Bush's success in the Persian Gulf helped reenforce a perception of Republican superiority on military issues that probably started with Eisenhower. Clinton's lack of military experience strengthened that perception. The economy, the fifth issue, was up for grabs, depending on how it performed and who was in charge at the time. Fiscal matters, crime, welfare, foreign affairs and defense, and the economy: the Republicans had to win on those issues or lose control of the election.

I believed we needed to beat them on each one of these issues. If we could pose Clintonian alternatives in these five sectors, we could make their issues work for us. For example, opposition to gun control eroded the Republican advantage on the crime issue. The economy's fairly good performance blocked much of their traction in that area. But the Republicans still owned the fiscal, welfare, and foreign affairs–defense issues, and we had to attack their credibility in these sectors. We had to start by taking their claim to fiscal responsibility away from them by making the balanced budget Clinton's issue, not a Republican one.

It was President Clinton's monumental achievement to harness Democratic votes for a deficit-reduction package in 1993, shortly after he took office. But at least half of the reduction came from tax increases, not spending reductions. And by the time the program expired, there would still loom a deficit of hundreds of millions of dollars.

There is no political substitute for zero in the game of deficit reduction. For most Americans, it is an ethical issue: either you pay your way, or you don't. As long as the Republicans had an exclusive franchise as budget balancers, they could justify any cuts they wished.

Did this mean, therefore, that Republicans would cut Medicare too deeply? Were Medicaid guarantees of free care for the poor to be slashed? Were Head Start or college scholarships to be axed? Were environmental-protection laws to be weakened to the point of tokenism?

Unfortunate but necessary, in the public's view, if these cuts were needed to balance the budget. On the other hand, these cuts would be politically unforgivable if the budget could be balanced by other spending reductions, ones that did not sacrifice our core values.

From my first day on the job, I prodded the president to produce a balanced-budget proposal. Initially, he preferred not to make the first move. While constitutionally obliged to submit a budget proposal to Congress at the start of the year, he was unwilling to propose a balanced one. He felt that if he proposed cuts sufficient to balance the budget, he would provide political cover for the Republicans, from which they would suggest even deeper cuts. But if he submitted an unbalanced budget and made only marginal spending cuts, the Republican budget, including its gigantic cuts, would be exposed in the public glare. So the president proposed a budget that Republican critics said left two-hundred-billion-dollar deficits "as far as the eye can see."

The president's position was understandable. He had just suffered a huge defeat and lacked the political strength to assure the cuts needed to eliminate the deficit. To do so, he would have had to split his dwindling congressional supporters and likely provoke a primary challenge for the party nomination—all to no purpose. This Congress would not take his budget seriously but consider it a starting point for their cuts.

He was acutely conscious that he had impaled himself on a tax increase in 1993 in a well-intentioned and successful attempt to cut the deficit. He would get red in the face in private meetings when the subject came up and would slice the air in front of him with his forefinger as he yelled, "And I passed it without a single Republican vote. Not one. Not one. Not one." He'd swallowed his medicine once and it cost him the Congress; now it was *their* move.

The White House staffers, particularly Stephanopoulos and Panetta, were prepared to wait all year without proposing a balanced budget. The end of their wait was unclear. Sometimes they said we should hole up until after the Republicans passed their budget in both houses. At other times, they speculated that perhaps we should hold fire until after the Republicans' budget was out of the conference committee or maybe until it had passed both houses again, or even better until the president had vetoed it. Sometimes they didn't think it was safe to propose our alternative plan until after Clinton's veto had been sustained. Wait. Wait. Wait. They felt the president could continue to score political points by attacking the Republican cuts as long as he didn't propose a balanced budget on his own.

I argued that this path led to irrelevance: the press would not treat our criticism seriously until we produced an alternative. But most of all, I said the public wouldn't reject the Republican budget cuts unless it understood that there was a better, easier way to reduce the deficit.

The president suspected, and I agreed, that the Republicans were not cutting Medicare, Medicaid, education, and environmental protection—areas the president cared about—in order to balance the budget. They wanted to balance the budget *in order* to cut Medicare, Medicaid, education, and environmental protection.

It was important, I argued, for people to realize what the GOP was up to. The Republicans had opposed Medicare when it was first passed because it is not a needs-based program. The GOP was against federal aid to schools because they worried that education might be controlled by Washington, not locally. The right wing of the party had always opposed a federal role in environmental protection and wanted state regulators—whom businesses could more easily influence—to supervise clean-air and clean-water requirements. The Republicans wanted to balance the budget and cut taxes to give them a way to scale down these programs.

On the other hand, the Democrats were protecting these programs as an excuse *not* to balance the budget. Most congressional Democrats realized that these vital programs did not have to be cut in order to achieve balance. There were other ways to reach this goal, but they were unwilling to see programs cut. Behind every program is a government job. Behind every government job is a public-employee union. Behind every public-employee union is a campaign donation. And behind every campaign donation is a labor leader who will turn very cold very fast if his dues-paying ranks are thinned by budget cuts.

Each political party has its faithful supporters, but the Democrats can't exist without labor, and the Republicans can't make it without rich corporate donors. Just as the Republicans tend to take shelter behind free-market idealism as they protect the rich, so Democrats stand behind compassionate rhetoric when they avoid cuts that reduce the ranks of public employees. Public-employee unions, now the dynamic force in the labor movement, cannot abide big cuts in public spending.

To protect their financial saviors, both parties had promulgated a deception: that the only way to balance the budget without higher taxes is by cutting vital services in Medicare, Medicaid, education, or environmental protection. The Republicans depend upon this fiction to garner the majorities needed to cut these programs that they want to cut anyway. The Democrats relied upon the same deception to convince their constituents that the choice is raising taxes or deferring a balanced budget. What they really want to postpone are cuts in politically less popular programs that are equally essential to *their* political base, such as housing and energy subsidies, community development, legal-services aid, summer jobs, and job training.

Voters didn't believe that Democrats, Clinton included, wanted to balance the budget. At our May 16, 1995, strategy meeting, I said that on the budget, our polls showed that we had created a clear impression: "They believe you oppose a balanced budget," I explained. "You submitted a budget in deficit, oppose the balanced-budget amendment, and attack Republican plans to balance the budget. If it talks like a duck, walks like a duck, and looks like a duck, it's a duck. Voters think Clinton is a tax-and-spend liberal."

The White House staff was almost united in opposing a speech recommending a balanced budget. Except for Erskine Bowles, Bill Curry, Don Baer, and domestic adviser Bruce Reed, all others said no. "Just when we have the Republicans on the ropes," they argued, "why should we let them off by proposing cuts of our own?" The staff warned that senior citizen groups would turn on us since a balanced budget would have to include some cuts in Medicare. George Stephanopoulos said, "We'll lose our moral traction on this issue."

I replied that we could differentiate between our cuts, which required providers to lower their costs—and the Republican cuts—requiring fewer services or higher premiums for beneficiaries.

Opponents of the balanced-budget speech said that voters wouldn't take the president's proposals seriously because they obviously wouldn't pass. I countered that these proposals were a necessary definition of how we were different from both orthodox Democrats and Republicans. Triangulation, I said, was the key to winning the election.

Panetta and Stephanopoulos were particularly vigorous in arguing that such a speech would split us off from congressional Democrats. "They will go ballistic on the Hill," George predicted accurately. "They'll never forgive you," he added inaccurately.

But the president was inclined to give the speech. He felt uneasy without an alternative. He keenly felt his own irrelevance. "I can't just sit here passively and not play a role in this debate. I have to get into the argument. But until I have a plan, I can't join the debate." He was sure that the budget could be balanced without his core budget priorities being cut.

Vice President Gore backed a balanced-budget proposal. Without one, he said, we would have no standing in the current debate and no way to prove our fiscal moderation to swing voters.

I reached out to Hillary, drawing on our newly restored relationship. I asked for her help in convincing the president to resist the Panetta-Stephanopoulos line. In the years in Arkansas, Hillary was often my back channel when I wanted Clinton to do something but had turned him off with my nagging. Always pragmatic and shrewd, she would usually have come to some conclusion on her own, and would welcome my conversion to *her* position. This time was no exception. While she worried about the risks of alienating the Democratic left, she felt strongly that her husband had to speak out and advocate a balanced budget. "I think we've got to do this," she said in her usual emphatic style. "We just can't be left out of this debate. We've got to get into it. We've got to be on the map, to take a position."

Still the president hesitated to pull the trigger. He complained that he needed a full plan before he could possibly speak to the nation.

I argued that he could indicate his intention to balance the budget by a certain date, provide general numbers, and get on with it.

He rejected that: "I won't have any credibility if I don't present a full alternative budget." What worried me about this was the risk of pre-emption. "As you sit there and write your damn budget," I protested, "your staff will leak each cut day by day. By the time you give the speech, it will all have been covered, and the networks won't give you a prime-time address to the nation. It will be old news and you'll never get the credit you deserve." I added that my dire prediction of leaks might not be accurate; "It's just," I said intemperately, "that it has always happened before."

The president's determination to fill in all the lines of a full budget before he made a proposal to the nation reflected his intellectual style. He never sees concepts or wholes; he sees collections of detail. When he looks at the night sky, the president doesn't see a slice of the universe. He sees random stars. I would point out the constellation Orion. "See," I would say, "there's the belt—those three stars over there in a row—and there's his elbow, and those two stars are his legs."

The president would then quibble: "That can't be a belt; the three stars aren't arranged in a straight line; look how the middle star is a bit lower down." His perfectionism makes generalities hard to reach, unless all the specifics are arranged in exactly the right way.

Bill Clinton's intelligence is characterized by tremendous strengths punctuated by blind spots. He absorbs and retains data at incredible speeds with pinpoint accuracy and near total recall. He knows endless facts and perfectly encodes the exact advice he gets from each source, down to the slightest nuance. He carries these details in his brain while he works through a decision. But he finds it hard assigning relative importance to the various facts and opinions. He is slow to see patterns and slower still to process them to conclusions. His perfectionism does not permit the rough assumptions from which to build the general theories that are vital to decision making. Of course, once Clinton reaches a decision, he is superb at communicating it to the greatest of intellects and the least educated of people. He reaches them both.

Throughout his life, Clinton has usually had a person close by to help him process his information by noticing patterns, elaborating them into theories, and helping him reach conclusions based on those theories— but not an adviser in the traditional sense of the term. He needs someone to enter his thinking process and, like an enzyme, like insulin, assist in the digestion of the data and its transformation into a decision.

Hillary has usually helped him to see the larger picture, and occasionally I played this role as well. Particularly during the period of collaboration covered in this book, I tried to help him arrive at various hypotheses. We were a match because he works from the specific to the general, I work from the general to the specific. He is ruled by his data, I by my theories. His thinking is inductive, mine deductive. Our collaboration thrived on complementary strengths and weaknesses.

When he faced a decision, he would tell me the facts he considered crucial, the priorities that seemed right to him and then asked for advice. I would offer my theories about how to achieve his policy priorities, and would try to apply them to the decision at hand. He would subject these postulates to the exacting task of comparison with his data. When he was satisfied, the theories would serve as a basis for his decisions. Where they didn't, I would go back to my polling data and think again about how to modify the theory to fit his policy priorities and actual experiences. This ongoing dialogue between the specific and the general, between the facts and the strategic construct, ruled our relationship and helped make each of us more effective in the other's company. The press was naturally unaware of this process and came to think I exercised some strange powers over the president, like a Svengali or Rasputin. *The Boston Globe* reported that a White House staffer, having heard that Boris Yeltsin might be on mind-altering medicines, commented, "Look for Dick Morris."

So Clinton went about the task of devising a budget himself that combined the traditional Republican goal of eliminating the deficit with the Democratic goal of saving vital social programs.

He met every few days with his Office of Management and Budget (OMB) staff and his White House staff to design this balanced budget, program by program, agency by agency, line by line. On his yellow pad, he would sketch, in pencil, the decisions needed to balance the budget his way. Here was a president who knew the budget specifics as well as anyone in OMB. He peppered his staff with questions: What is the effect if we take nine years to balance the budget instead of seven? What if we reduce the increase in Medicare payments to hospitals by 1 percent below inflation? Can't we switch home care for the elderly out of the premium-supported part of Medicare and pay for it from general tax revenues? His intellect and minute understanding of the budget was astonishing as he wrote the first Democratic, activist, compassionate balanced budget in more than four decades.

My role in this process was to see where the budget numbers were leading him and, through polling, vet it politically. It became clear, for example, that he was unwilling to make cuts so drastic that we could balance the budget within the seven years the Republicans were promising. As I watched him agonize over these cuts and fail to reconcile them with his social priorities, I began to poll public attitudes on an appropriate date for a balanced budget. I found a large majority favored naming a specific date and favored year-by-year progress toward the goal, but I also found that voters didn't really care whether the budget was balanced in seven, eight, nine, or even ten years. It didn't matter to them as long as we moved in the right direction.

Each year's delay in reaching a zero deficit permitted the president to make the annual cuts less drastic. He was delighted that he had this leeway and at first wanted to balance the budget within ten years.

Another key question was how much economic growth was likely and how sharply medical costs would rise, a function of both inflation and the intrinsically higher costs of services. The OMB economists produced assumptions that were significantly more optimistic than those generated by the Congressional Budget Office (CBO) economists. The president obviously wanted to use the OMB's projections. Historically, they had proved more accurate—and, as it turned out, in this case as well they *were* much more accurate—than those of the CBO economists under the Republicans. Using the OMB assumptions would allow for less-drastic cuts, since the high economic growth would generate more tax revenues while reductions in the inflation rate would reduce spending on Medicare and Medicaid.

My polls showed that it was OK to use the more optimistic assumptions since they dovetailed with popular optimism about the economy, which was steadily growing.

Still the president hesitated about giving the speech. I was getting the blank-stare response again. I realized that he wanted advice on the politically tough choices that lay before him on the spreadsheet. Simply to say "We need to balance the budget" was not enough. The blank stare meant that he wanted to be told which cuts would hurt him politically and which he could live with.

This is not to say that these political judgments overrode his substantive views. That's not how it worked. He indicated the choices that were acceptable to him, which would eliminate the deficit, and then he sought advice on what made political sense. First came the policy and the math, then the polling and the politics.

George Stephanopoulos and I had agreed to disagree on whether the president should give a balanced-budget speech at this time. But I asked George to help outline the cuts that would least offend liberals, unions, elderly groups, minorities, and other key constituencies, in the hope that this information would help answer the president's political problems. Even though George disagreed with me on the strategy, he had agreed to help design the political parameters of a balanced budget. He realized that Clinton would make his own decisions, no matter what advice he gave. I remain very grateful to George for this decision. Had he been less forthcoming, we might not have been able to submit so successful a plan.

In three meetings, George and I took the numbers the president had given us and worked out the political options. Where we were unsure, we used polling to guide our recommendations. We came out against any cuts in education; indeed, we suggested an increase in keeping with the president's priorities. And we urged leaving environmental-protection programs, Gore's personal and political passion, untouched. He made it clear that he would tolerate no such cuts.

There were other programs the public did not at all mind our reducing. The traditional belief among politicians is that voters have no idea where they want cuts to fall: they know only what they don't want cut. On the contrary, in our surveys the voters indicated a distinct willingness to see most Housing and Urban Development—HUD—housing subsidies reduced, all energy-production incentives repealed, most

Commerce Department programs eliminated, and civilian jobs in the Defense Department cut.

As speculation mounted that the president was about to propose his own balanced budget, congressional leaders and their White House allies dug their heels in more deeply. They rained calls and arguments on the president and stepped up outside pressure.

From the press came repeated questions about where the president was headed. Amazingly, Panetta stopped leaks of the president's plans; they never appeared in the press, only on the president's spreadsheet. This lack of news drove the press crazy. On May 19, 1995, in an interview on a New Hampshire radio station, Clinton was asked whether he was going to commit himself to balancing the budget by a deadline. Clinton let it slip that he was planning to do so.

All hell broke loose.

The congressional Democrats bombarded him with complaints, and the White House staff acted as if he had confessed to war crimes. Facing intense internal pressure to recant and not ready to go forward with an alternative budget, he backtracked in a Rose Garden announcement choreographed by Panetta and Stephanopoulos.

Stories mysteriously appeared in newsmagazines that I had led the president astray but that cooler heads on the White House staff, like Ickes, Panetta, and Stephanopoulos, had pulled him back from disaster. Congressional Democrats and Republicans alike were relieved, the former because Clinton had not abandoned their orthodoxy and the latter because they feared seeing their issue preempted.

Clinton was upset with his indiscretion on the radio and also by the Rose Garden announcement. He said he had been hurried into the second statement, blaming his lack of sleep upon returning from Russia.

On May 25, he canvassed our weekly strategy meeting, reopening the whole issue of whether he should give the balanced-budget speech. I had just returned from the hospital bedside of my eighty-five-year-old father, who, except for my wife, is the central figure in my life. He was undergoing back surgery. Preoccupied with his condition, I boarded the Delta Shuttle from New York to Washington and in my disorganized state, I tried to compose my presentation for the meeting. Upon landing, I called the recovery room and learned that my dad had emerged in fine shape. He even spoke to me groggily to prove it.

If my elderly father could rally his resources, I could rally mine. Determined to press my case, I argued long and hard for the president to give the speech. Such a speech, I said, not only would be a good political move but would announce the start of a transformation of the Democratic party from big-government liberalism to policies that met the needs of the people within realistic constraints—an endorsement, in other words, of the takeover of the moderate wing of the Democratic party.

As the president sought out each opinion, he was largely silent. Panetta and Ickes led the opposition. Stephanopoulos had not yet been admitted to these meetings, but Panetta in effect spoke for him. After all had spoken, the president turned to Gore, as he so often did, and said, "What about it, Al?"

Gore, again as if issuing a Supreme Court opinion, traced the ancestry of the issue, recognizing opposite points of view, but finally said, "Mr. President, I think this is something we have to do."

The meeting broke up. The president decided to go with the speech. Now it was a question of timing.

I wrote the first draft, with help from Don Baer, Bill Curry, Bruce Reed, and Tom Freedman, and the president liked it. We reviewed and edited it in the Oval Office. Clinton sat behind his desk, while Gore, Baer, Curry, Panetta, Bowles, and I sat around it, working line by line.

Once again personal considerations intruded. My dad was fine, but my dog was not. In the midst of the Oval Office meeting, Eileen called to say that she had had to put to sleep our fifteen-year-old Siberian husky, Sasha. I returned to the desk and announced the sad news. Gore asked how old she was and I told him fifteen. The president quickly said, "That's one hundred and five years old," displaying once more that he is better with numbers than with emotion.

Clinton continued to receive scorching phone calls from the House and Senate Democratic leadership. He was shaken by the depth of their anger and their sense of betrayal. "We have the Republicans on the run, and you are letting them off scot-free," they yelled. Their message was not lost on the president: "You're on your own, buddy. You have no party anymore."

Then came calls from Senators John Breaux of Louisiana and Joe Lieberman of Connecticut. Each backed the president's plan to give the speech; each reassured him. Lieberman's call was especially important because it came right after the broadside from the congressional Democratic hierarchy. Lieberman's words fortified him as he took the biggest political gamble of his presidency.

Bill Clinton had decided to give the speech, but the networks had not yet decided to air it. The vice president called each network personally to get the speech run in prime time. As a result, about half of the American electorate watched the speech in full. Had it run only on the nightly news, only about a quarter of the electorate would have seen it, and only for a minute.

The final preparations for a Bill Clinton speech are not orderly. The president futzes with each draft line by line. On June 13, 1995, as we prepared to go on the air, we went through it once more an hour and a half before airtime. Squier, Stephanopoulos, Baer, Curry, Bowles, Panetta, and three or four others including myself crowded into the small vestibule off the Oval Office, where the president sat at a tiny desk near the door, pen in hand, still going over the speech. Another dozen aides gathered in the hallway outside the open door, trying to get in, to hear, to comment.

The president read each word for the tenth time. He thought he ought to be clearer still on the difference between his Medicare cuts on payments to providers of service—doctors and hospitals—and Republican cuts, which would force co-payments and higher premiums on beneficiaries.

Don Baer and I took the draft, cut and pasted it, and entered the alterations on a computer at forty minutes before airtime. Then came the phone call: Hillary had some ideas to add. I knew immediately that this was a test of our relationship. She had been instrumental in the birth of this speech, and now she wanted to see whether I would act like "one of the boys" and refuse to include the changes she wanted. As it happened, her proposed changes were excellent. She wanted, for example, more elaboration of the additional health benefits—mammograms and Alzheimer's care—that we proposed to add to Medicare. But even if her suggestions had been drivel, I would have gladly battled for their inclusion. I had waited five months to resume my relationship with the First Lady, and I was not about to blow it again.

At delivery minus twenty-five minutes, we gave the president a clean draft. I pointed out Hillary's changes, and he nodded. Instead of scooping up the pages and striding confidently into the Oval Office for five or six rehearsals, as I expected him to do, he sat down again, took out his pen, and made more changes. Finally, Bob Squier had had enough. "Mr. President," he said in his best it's-past-your-bedtime tone, "the speech is fine, fine. You just need time to get your act together and run through it a few times."

I chimed in: "Sir, no changes are nearly as important as rehearsal. You're not just the author of the speech, you're the one who has to deliver it too."

Bowing to our entreaties, he settled back to be made up. Clinton has prominent bags under his eyes. I like them. They remind me of JFK, but most people don't agree, and Bob Squier, one of the dissenters, had found a way to solve the problem. He knew a makeup artist who said she had a cream that would deflate the bags for an hour. The problem was to get the president to accept it. Ever the fraternity jock, Squier sent this attractive woman in to do the president's makeup. Innocently accepting the bait, Clinton offered no resistance.

The president was still editing the speech even as the makeup was being applied. He arrived in the Oval Office at D minus seven minutes, allowing barely enough time to read the speech through once on his TelePrompTer before going on the air.

I left the Oval Office to watch the broadcast from a set in the next room. I was desperately anxious since he had had virtually no time to prepare for the delivery, and I wondered whether he would stumble. He didn't. He was masterful. He explained why he was proposing a balanced budget and carefully drew the distinctions between his and the Republicans' plans to eliminate the deficit.

I thought back to the time when he filmed his apology ad in Tony Schwartz's town house to begin his gubernatorial comeback. Then too I had worried about how he would phrase his message. But with Bill Clinton, there is usually a time for consultants to just shut up, sit back, and watch a master perform. When the camera is running, no matter how short the preparation time has been, no matter how great the pressure, Bill Clinton comes through.

As the speech ended, Erskine Bowles—my close ally in promoting the speech to the president—and I hugged each other. "Until he started speaking, I couldn't be sure he was going to do it," said Bowles. Neither could I.

Immediately afterward, the networks ran a Republican response featuring Bob Dole. That the Republicans had no response—other than the old pieties—was evident when Dole finished. The public's response, though, was heartening: overwhelming approval—although some time would pass before this was reflected in the president's ratings. The press was largely positive. Only the Democrats on Capitol Hill dissented. For three days, CNN delighted in covering Democrats denouncing the president for his heresy, just as George and Leon had predicted they would. But nobody else cared. In the polls, Democrats, liberals, minorities all registered strong approval for the president's speech and budget plan.

For me, it was a moment of personal satisfaction. The newsmagazines' premature condemnation of my support for the speech following the New Hampshire radio interview and the Rose Garden retraction was now evidence that I had "won" this intra-White House battle. Such victories mean little to the nation but much to Washington, D.C., though I was increasingly losing the anonymity I preferred.

I had crossed a threshold and affected a major policy decision. I was proud, of course, but also felt inadequate. Was I right? Did I know what I was talking about? To convince the president, I had shown great confidence in my political wisdom, but did I *really* know? I had to pocket these doubts.

In the remaining fourteen months at the president's side, the doubts grew and I realized that I had to deal with them. I overcompensated. I became more and more arrogant. As my predictions came true, I began to believe in my perspicacity as it was reported in the press. I forgot the wonderful admonition by Rudyard Kipling that hung on the wall of my childhood bedroom: "If you can meet with Triumph and Disaster / And treat those two impostors just the same."

I found myself becoming more brusque and sharp with people, more dictatorial where once I had tried to be persuasive. Now I was impatient and often unkind.

My sense of triumph manifested itself in other, more self-destructive ways. Shortly after the balanced-budget speech, I began my relationship with the prostitute that led to the president's embarrassment and my fall. I could get away with anything, I felt. I wanted Clinton to win. To do that, I had to help change his course, as he had directed me to do. To do that, I needed power. But power corrupted me and became an addiction. I came to feel I could change all the rules.

I could say that pressure led me to risk my career so thoughtlessly. But plenty of people handle similar pressure with ease. I was not ready for Washington or for prime time.

I was taught a more immediate lesson about my frailty when I called David Broder of *The Washington Post* to give him background on the strategic implications of the speech and he ran a story. Panetta correctly assumed that I had given Broder the story. Throughout my tenure at the White House, I never leaked information unless I was told to and generally confined my press contacts to periodic background meetings meant to give reporters a better understanding of the president's moves and policies. Now, with this slipup, the old guard on the staff sensed a chance to inflict some punishment and brought the article to the president, protesting that I had said too much. Clinton called me by phone and chewed me out so vehemently that I had to hold the receiver away from my ear. I sensed that an audience in the Oval Office was watching with satisfaction as I received my punishment. I knew better than to respond. I assumed he was showing the rest of the staff that just because I had won this one battle, I was not free to act as I pleased.

In later conversations, the incident never came up. The president maintains a balance in everything. If one side or another gets too far up, he brings it down a little. This is his way.

Scrambling for Position: The Budget Wars Begin   I don't think the public ever understood what was at stake in the budget fight that lasted from September through December 1995. We never mentioned it, and the Republicans certainly never admitted it. On the surface, the fight appeared to be about whether and how to balance the budget and how deeply to cut taxes. But these were not the real issues at all in my opinion.

The Republicans said that certain cuts were needed to balance the budget, but Clinton had shown that the budget could be balanced without cuts. Seeing the transparency of the Republicans' position, many commentators assumed that they really wanted a massive tax cut. But as backroom negotiations progressed, the GOP abandoned its huge tax cut and accepted, in principle, a budget cut only slightly larger than the one the president had advocated.

The final positions of the two parties were astonishingly close. The Republicans sought to cut Medicare by $167 billion, whereas Clinton, though publicly committed to $124 billion, would probably have backed premiums on the high-income elderly to bring his cuts to $134 billion—only $33 billion below the Republican figure, and this amount to be spread over seven years. On Medicaid cuts, the differences were even narrower. Clinton's final offer was $54 billion, whereas the Republicans held out for $72 billion, again a minor gap.

So why did the Republicans insist on these differences at the risk of spoiling their chances in the election? Trent Lott gave me some insight when I pushed these questions during a meeting in November 1995. "It's not balancing the budget, it's not cutting taxes that we're all about," he said. "It's cutting government spending."

"Come on," I replied. "The difference between your position and ours is so narrow that it's ridiculous. Why won't you guys pull the trigger and get a deal?"

"It's not really the spending either," he said. "It's the entitlements. We've got to cut the entitlements."

"But we're so close on Medicare and Medicaid. Why can't we just split the difference between us on the entitlements?" I asked.

"We have to get basic reform of the entitlements," Lott answered. "Cuts aren't enough. We have to change the structure and get basic reform. Otherwise as soon as we leave here, the Democrats will go right back to their deficits again."

Confused, I asked Clinton what Lott had meant.

"It's what I've been trying to tell you for months," he said heatedly. "They don't want to balance the budget; that's just an excuse. They don't want to cut taxes, either; that's just an excuse. They don't want to cut government spending; that's just an excuse. What they want, what they really, really want is to end all middle-class entitlements.

"They would like to end *all* entitlements, but they know they can't do it. They know they need a political safety net. But they want to end all middle-class entitlements. That's why they are trying to turn Medicare into a welfare program by creaming off all the younger, richer, healthier elderly into private health-insurance pools—medical savings accounts [MSAs]. When they have only the sick and the old and the poor in traditional Medicare and everybody else is in private insurance through MSAs, Medicare will be a welfare program. It's why they also want to cut college scholarships and student loans. They don't want any middle-class entitlements."

I thought of France, where welfare is rarely a political issue since everybody gets it. Poorer people get a larger cash transfer than richer people do, but almost everybody gets something—just as with Social Security and Medicare in the United States. The Republicans wanted to end middle-class entitlements in the United States so that entitlements would go to *them*—the poor—not *us,* the rest of the nation. With entitlements earmarked for the poor, the funds would be easier to control, contain, and cut, just as those for welfare itself have been.

By proposing a way to balance the budget, cut taxes, and reduce entitlement spending without making dramatic changes in the structure of the middle-class entitlements, Clinton had taken away the Republican camouflage.

"You always have to remember that their goal, their goal"—the president repeated his words and further emphasized his point by thrusting his fist back and forth in a thumbs-up motion—"their *goal* is to dismantle Medicaid and Medicare and spending on federal education and environmental enforcement. Balancing the budget? Cutting taxes? Those are just means to the end."

I was more explicit in my next conversation with Lott, this one by phone: "What you guys are really saying is that you know we can balance the budget with our plan or something close to it. You know the overall numbers will work out. But you won't do it unless you can get to cut Medicare further."

"Well, not exactly," Lott replied cagily. "We all *hope* that your numbers are right and that it comes out the way you want, but until we can get entitlements under control, we can't be sure."

I pressed him further: "But you're really saying that the bottom line for you is to cut entitlements. Not only to balance the budget, not only to cut taxes, but simply because you want to cut entitlements."

"Controlling entitlements is our bottom line," Trent concluded.

As the budget fight moved into the fall of 1995, we found that the balanced-budget speech of June had given us the credibility to attack the Republican budget cuts. No longer were we opposed to a balanced budget; we were now opposed to *their* balanced budget and in favor of our own proposal. The speech let us attack the details of the Republicans' proposed cuts while showing that they weren't necessary to balance the budget.

All the president's advisers were united for once on the need to oppose the Republican budget. Panetta, Stephanopoulos, and I were of one mind. At a strategy meeting, I borrowed a quote from Winston Churchill when he became prime minister during World War II: "You ask what is our policy? I will say it is to wage war."

The entire linchpin of the Republican budget strategy was to favor a balanced budget and tax cuts while assuming that the administration, like the Democrats in Congress, would fight each cut and battle for each program. The Republicans could then shrug their shoulders and say, "We know these cuts hurt, but we have to balance the budget."

The balanced-budget speech had changed all that. Now the issue was not whether but how to balance the budget, not whether to cut taxes but which ones to cut and by how much. The Republicans were unprepared for this fight. No longer able to say that their party was the only one in town that wanted to balance the budget and cut taxes, they had no way to argue for deeper cuts than the ones we had proposed.

In discussing the reasons for President Clinton's triumph in 1996, after his prospects had seemed so bleak in 1994, many ascribe his success to his stand against Gingrich and the Republicans in the budget battle. They often forget that the president could stand firm only because he had staked out politically defensible ground. By boldly breaking away from Democratic orthodoxy in June of 1995 and proposing a balanced budget, the president co-opted what had been the GOP's exclusive ground. Only after the battle became one of *how* to balance the budget could the president attract public support for his position and build opposition to the Republican program. Had he mouthed the position being urged on him by the congressional Democrats and much of the White House staff—mere opposition to the GOP cuts without proposing a budget that was balanced without them—he never would have won the fight, even had we doubled our spending on advertising.

Leon and George now saw the need to use our zero-deficit budget plan with its modest tax cut as the context in which to criticize the Republicans. I sensed that they may have felt, in retrospect, that the president had been right to give the speech, but we never discussed it and I never asked.

Erskine Bowles set up a Budget Response Team, headed by Gene Sperling, to compare our budget proposal and theirs. Sperling, who had been with Clinton since the '92 campaign, was as intense as I am. Short, dark, and focused, he would make his points ponderously but with force and a vast command of economic data. Day after day, Gene would release damaging information about the consequences of the Republican budget plan. Articles and TV news segments appeared throughout the country documenting the impact of the Republicans' proposed cuts. Gene had our weekly polling information on the cuts that were most deadly to the GOP, and he called me excitedly from time to time to report on yet another lurid cut he had found in the Republican proposal and ask me to test it to see whether it would work as fodder for our ads.

In September '95, I met with Trent Lott again, and we discussed the budget debate. I emphasized how unpopular the Republican budget was and what a political disaster it would become. "Get the hell out of the way," I advised my friend and former client.

Lott was now mystified at the total refusal of the Republicans to incorporate political reality into their planning. While he continued in our meetings to espouse the virtues of their budget and miss no opportunity to deride ours as "phony" and balanced with "blue smoke and mirrors," he now recognized how politically indefensible the Medicare cuts had become. He sounded to me like a practical politician who had suddenly learned that his colleagues had secretly joined a religious cult and were lining up to drink spiked Kool-Aid.

But Lott also had an exquisite sense of political timing. While he claimed to be a helpless participant in the GOP leadership's self-destruction, I suspected he realized that, as the number-two Republican in the Senate, he had only to wait for this process to run its course. Then he would inherit the leadership and pick up the pieces.

For the president's part, it became clear as we studied his polls that his movement away from Democratic orthodoxy helped, but something was lacking. Voters told our poll takers that "Yes, Clinton means well, he's for the right things, bless his heart, but he can't get anything done. He's too weak. He's too ineffective." The president's balanced-budget speech had begun to repair his liberal image, but now we had to over-come the perception of weakness.

I began to see that the budget and Bosnia were the two keys to re-pairing the public's perception of the president's weakness. On both fronts, the president was doing what he deeply felt was right and was strongly standing up for his position.

Leon and George agreed that the president must stand absolutely firm on the budget, but they, like the rest of the White House staffers, were afraid that he would flinch, as the Republicans, too, anticipated.

"He won't cave," I assured Leon and George. "He won't even blink." The president had prepared this ground for a year. In late 1994, he had outlined a tax-cut program of his own in a national address. His gener-ous State of the Union message, urging bipartisan cooperation, had been rudely spurned. He had responded in his Pile of Vetoes speech by setting out where he would compromise and where he would veto. Fi-nally, in his balanced-budget speech, he had laid out the position on which he would stand. He had carefully reviewed every program and every expenditure and figured out which made substantive and political sense and which could be cut. He had planned well, whereas the Re-publicans, surprised to find themselves in control of Congress, had sim-ply offered a budget that suited them ideologically, but whose impact on the voters they had not tested.

The previous February the president and I had discussed the sanc-tions he had threatened to impose on China to make it stop the piracy of American films and CDs. He compared his success with China to his failure to settle the baseball strike. "I need a lever," he had said. "I need a weapon. When I have a lever, as I did in China, I can use it, and stand firm forever. Where I don't, as in baseball, I can't."

I tried to explain to Leon why the president could be counted on not to budge. "He knows his turf. He's happy with his position. He's got air cover—the ads are running. And he's got a weapon—the veto. He's not going anyplace."

Leon did not believe it. He and George were constantly afraid that the president would give everything away in a late-night phone call. I feel they now saw me as vaguely useful: my ads were helping them win their budget war with the Republicans, and even if they couldn't figure out why, the president seemed to value my advice and feel firmer in his positions because of it.

The only real difference between my advice to Clinton and that of other consultants is that theirs tended to deal only with the daily flow of specific problems, while I focused more on strategy. Sometimes I would call the president to discuss with him a change in the overall plan. He would happily talk about it for hours, until I had modified it to suit his views. In all these talks, I learned to listen carefully.

At the beginning, I often listened to my own words, not the president's. Clinton doesn't raise his voice over important things. When he does raise his voice, it's usually over a relatively trivial irritant. Instead, his style requires you to listen hard to what he is saying. You have to watch his body language, and over the phone you must listen to his pauses to gauge his attention span. Above all, you must watch his responses and notice when he doesn't react at all and when he keeps coming back with the same question—indications that he isn't buying what you propose and that you had better rework it to his satisfaction. The president is very intelligent and very subtle. You have to listen and watch carefully to pick up his cues.

Once I caught on to this process, we both knew exactly what the strategy was. Decisions became a lot easier. I may have appeared in the press to have a mystical capacity to predict his actions or influence his decisions, but what White House staffers didn't grasp was that he and I had already agreed on a theoretical or a strategic level, and I was just presenting him the blueprint upon which we had already tacitly agreed.

As the budget debate proceeded, the president continued to stand firm. He knew he had a superior political hand to play. But he nevertheless wanted to play his hand to negotiate a deal that was pretty close to his priorities. Throughout the budget debate, the president wanted an accomplishment, while his party in Congress wanted an issue.

At the president's direction, I kept open the channel to Trent Lott, who sensed the political weakness of his party's hand and was anxiously trying to avert a standoff. Lott knew that his rabid allies in the House, especially the freshmen, were naïve to think that Clinton would fold and sign their budget rather than risk a government shutdown. I told Trent in almost weekly meetings that when the crunch came, we weren't going to blink. I explained that we were winning the battle for public opinion and made him understand that we didn't *need* to blink.

Trent was terribly frustrated. He began to refer to the House freshmen Republicans, the radical purists, as the ayatollahs. While in basic agreement with their conservative views, he had a professional politician's contempt for their naïveté. Their refusal to compromise seemed to Lott to be a repudiation of what congressional and presidential government was all about. (In a way, his difficulties with the young freshmen were like Clinton's with "the children who got him elected.") Lott knew these freshmen would soon learn the ways of the world. Until then, without real power in the Senate and with no power in the House, he had to watch his ship sail off the edge of the earth.

To the country, the fight was about Medicare versus tax cuts.

To the press, it was Clinton versus Gingrich.

But to the experts, it was about the president's OMB estimates versus Congress's CBO assumptions.

At the time, though, no one could be sure what the economy would do, and the radical right-wingers at CBO held firm to their numbers. Had they shown more flexibility, Gingrich and Dole would not have had to impale themselves on such drastic cuts and Dole might be president today. Clinton, however, saw what was happening. He realized that the Republican conservatives were insisting on the CBO numbers not because they necessarily believed they were right but because they offered an excuse for major cuts in programs they had always wanted to kill. They could balance the budget and cut taxes by using the OMB projections, but those numbers didn't justify the budget cuts the Republican conservatives wanted.

Lott, however, wanted a budget that the Republicans could take to the public in the 1996 congressional elections, which meant that he wanted an agreement with the White House. He was open to considering use of the OMB projections. His theory was that once you got a balanced-budget deal on the table, you could always make more cuts if the numbers fell short. A supreme pragmatist, he told me, "Look, nobody has the faintest idea what is going to happen next year, let alone seven years down the road. This is all pie in the sky. Let's just work a deal on the best numbers we can find, each side gives a little, and we work it out."

Like the president, Lott very much wanted a deal.

But the Republican freshmen didn't. To them, a deal was anathema. They wanted a surrender, and they didn't comprehend that they weren't going to get one.

Within the administration, George Stephanopoulos was most opposed to a deal. A strong ally of House minority leader Dick Gephardt, he wanted the Medicare issue alive and well for the next election. Panetta, on the other hand, wanted a deal because he is ultimately an insider who wants government to work. But he was also sufficiently sympathetic to the needs and the wishes of the executive departments and agencies to oppose what the Republicans were proposing.

A more subtle difference existed between Clinton and Gore. Both wanted a deal. Both wanted a balanced budget in order to take the issue away from the Republicans. But Clinton wanted a compromise, whereas Gore wanted a deal that all but completely protected his priorities: the environment, technology, and so forth. Gore is more interested in specifics than in themes. So he believed a deal was desirable but not possible, whereas until the very end Clinton believed a deal could be worked out.

We all agreed, however, that the cuts required by the CBO estimates made compromise almost impossible.

Lott felt that the right-wingers had trapped Gingrich into taking the CBO numbers. "He needs a way to save face," Lott said.

We explored the possibility of asking Gingrich to appoint economists to review current economic data to see if the CBO estimates, arrived at six months before, still made sense. This would have given him an out. But word leaked out that the Republican leaders were considering "fudging" the CBO estimates. The House ayatollahs confronted Gingrich and Dole and raised hell. In the ensuing purge, all elements of reasonableness were dethroned. Gingrich now insisted that Lott and I stop talking, which muzzled Trent in his dealings with me, an occurrence that satisfied the no-dealers on both sides of the aisle. The president and Trent grimaced in private, but neither could do anything.

It looked as if a clash was inevitable. I watched in frustration as the negotiations dragged on. I worried that we were not flexible enough, and wondered why the Republicans were so politically unrealistic. Vice President Gore grasped the point I was missing: there was no budget deal because the two sides had opposing goals. We wanted to balance the budget with as few cuts as possible; they wanted to cut entitlements as much as they could.

I met with the vice president because I thought he was taking too tough a line against the Republicans.

"Don't you agree that a budget deal is the key to our putting this election away?" I asked. "It's the only thing that can anchor a good enough margin to carry us through election day."

From behind his desk, the vice president looked up at me with humorous, quizzical eyes. Then he opened them wide as if an idea had just come to him. "I've got it," he cried. "Maybe if we all hold hands around the desk," he said slowly, pronouncing each word distinctly, "and if we all concentrate real hard, and close our eyes, then maybe we can get a budget deal."

With no deal in sight, I felt that the president had become so involved in the fight that he looked more like a legislative whip, or even an accountant, than a president. He shared my concern. "I look like a congressional leader," he complained to me in early October, "going out there day after day, issuing our latest pronouncement on the budget. I've got to go back to being president."

I agreed with him and urged a strategy of "lift and loft." "Stay above the battle," I said. "Be president while the others squabble."

We outlined a vigorous program of executive action and advocacy to get us above the battle.

The president's foreign policy achievements played a significant role in this process. The bombing of Bosnia and the subsequent cease-fire, the signing of peace accords between Israel and the Palestinians, and Clinton's welcoming Pope John Paul II upon his arrival in the United States on October 4, all helped him rise above the tit for tat of the budget debate.

Gore had similar thoughts. He summoned me to his office and said I had done a good job in working with the president. We were taking all the right positions on the issues now, the ones the president had wanted to take but that liberals on the staff had opposed. But he suggested that the key need was for the president to show how strong he really was and what a dynamic leader he could be.

"I've seen Clinton when he really *is* a leader," Gore remarked. "I remember when he spoke to that black church in Memphis. He was a leader that day." The vice president stood up to reenact the scene. "He looked the people in the eye and said that the Reverend Martin Luther King did not live and he did not die 'to see thirteen-year-old boys get automatic weapons and gun down nine-year-olds just for the kick of it. That is not what he came here to do.' When he said that, he was a leader."

Gore cited other examples: "When he stood up in Austin, Texas, and talked about racial equality and when he defended affirmative action when everybody urged him to fudge the issue, then he was a leader. When he spoke out in Oklahoma City and rallied America, he was a leader."

The vice president concluded: "He knows you longer than he knows most of us. He trusts you. You have to help the president summon the leadership that is so obviously within himself."

I was startled with the candor and urgency with which Gore spoke. His faith in Clinton was apparent, as were his frustrations. My relationship with the president had ten more months to run, and throughout that time, I always kept the vice president's words in mind.

Indeed, the president had already begun strengthening his leadership when Gore spoke to me. Month after month, the president spoke out more and more both on domestic and on foreign affairs.

With Gore's comments in mind, I spoke to Clinton privately after our October 11, 1995, strategy meeting, drawing a generational parallel to show the changes in his public image over the years. I drew on conversations with Naomi Wolf, who had talked to me about the country's hunger for a good-father role model. I spoke to Clinton about how Arkansans saw him as their son who lost his way in 1980 but came back to the fold in 1982. As he succeeded, they became prouder of him, for he was still their child. In the '92 campaign, Clinton was America's buddy. Down-to-earth, riding buses to campaign events, conducting town meetings, eating at McDonald's, going one-on-one with people, appearing on MTV, and playing the saxophone—he was a regular guy. "But now," I told the president, "it's time to be almost the nation's father, to speak as the father of the country, not as a peer and certainly not as its child."

I urged him to stress family issues: the enforcement of child-support payments, the establishment of violence ratings for TV, improvements in education. These fit the image of a father concerned about America's children in a time when two-career families were stretched to the breaking point, growing fearful that their children were beyond their control.

"We've done a lot of that," he noted, "but we should do more."

I criticized the way he handled himself in public: "You explain yourself too much. Fathers don't. You seem to care too much about what others think of you; that's not a father's way. Don't have conversations with your audiences; speak *to* them. Don't complain in public about not getting recognition for your achievements. Don't be self-deprecating. Don't ask questions in speeches; give answers."

The president took notes. "I like this," he said. "I think what I've done recently in foreign policy and appearing with the pope will help along these lines."

By now, Squier and Knapp had begun to attend our strategy meetings, and at the next one, with Bob Squier's assistance, I showed the president a film of a speech he had given recently in Iowa. We contrasted the good and the bad by showing selected clips in a particular order.

In one clip, he spoke of the political risks he took when he challenged the tobacco industry and emphasized how others had urged him to play it safe. "That's not what a father says," I criticized. "It's not presidential."

Another clip had him speaking in a self-deprecating way about how he had lost in 1994 and noting that "probably many of you didn't think I had much chance back then." Again, not the father image—too much the peer or the child.

With each criticism, Clinton would say that he knew the line didn't sound right when he gave it. He kept detailed notes. He never made the same mistake twice.

Even his wardrobe came under our scrutiny. He favored light-colored suits and ties whose intricate patterns were distracting. "You don't look presidential in light-colored suits; adopt a red tie and navy suit as standard," I urged intrusively in a late-October memo. The next month, when Eileen and I were in Paris on vacation, we bought him some bright-red power ties. The president sent her a handwritten note thanking her for serving as his "chief outfitter."

In the fall of '95, he asked me to watch each of his speeches on C-SPAN and phone him that night with a critique. He seemed to enjoy this new way of working.

His achievements were a problem. In strategy meetings, he often complained that he had created seven million jobs and cut the deficit but nobody seemed to notice. In speeches, he referred to the achievements awkwardly. Our polls showed audiences either already knew about them or didn't believe they were true.

At one strategy session, Bob Squier suggested a better way to draw attention to what he had done. The key, Squier explained, was to cite the achievement while talking about something he was going to do. For example: "The hundred thousand extra police we put on the street can't solve the crime problem by themselves; we need to keep anti-drug funding for schools in the budget and stop the Republicans from cutting it." Or: "The seven million jobs we've created won't be much use if we can't find educated people to fill them. That's why I want a tax deduction for college tuition to help kids go on to college to take those jobs."

These changes may have been superficial. But in Bill Clinton's case, they made a real difference. The more he presented himself as America's father, the more he became it.

The Government Shuts Down During November 14–19, 1995, the passport office—closed. The national parks—closed. The museums—closed. The Social Security office—closed. The government—closed. It reminded me of an episode on *Candid Camera* decades ago in which actors dressed as policemen stopped motorists as they crossed the Delaware-Maryland border and informed them, with official briskness, that they were sorry but they would have to turn around because "Maryland is closed today."

During this siege, the White House was organized for daily combat. We worked frantically to shape the night's television news by stressing (1) the president's commitment to balancing the budget, (2) the drastic cuts the Republicans sought in Medicare, Medicaid, education, and environmental protection—the hot buttons, and (3) the Republicans' attempt to try to blackmail the president into approving their cuts and the president's staunch resistance. The response team was headed by Stephanopoulos and included Sperling, Panetta, Baer, Penn, and me. I communicated with the president several times a day, to discuss adjustments in the message.

One of my notes to the president, for example, said: "Our commitment to a balanced budget is getting lost in the partisan confrontation over who is to blame for the shutdown." In response, the president used the phrase *balanced budget* fourteen times in his statement that day. "Medicare cuts are not getting enough attention," another day's missive warned, and so on.

Every night at the height of the budget crisis we polled to measure the public's reaction. Our interviewers started phoning at seven in the evening and continued until one the next morning, eastern time, to catch West Coast voters before they went to bed. At about four in the morning, I would awaken to the sound of my fax machine as it spit out the poll results that had been collected only a few hours earlier. Each morning at seven-twenty, I called George with the data from the previous night's interviewing so he could report to the daily seven-thirty meeting that Leon held with the top White House staffers (which I never attended). When the president was awake, he'd take my call, so he could start his day with a summary of the latest polling information.

We watched the polling numbers climb day after day, until they had reached new highs for the three years in which Clinton had been in office. Voters got our message perfectly and were deeply sympathetic to our position. When the president vetoed the Republicans' balanced-budget bill on November 13, 1995, and the Republicans shut down the government, Clinton worried that eventually Washington itself would be blamed for the chaos. "Right now they're siding with me over the Republicans," he said over the phone in mid-November. "After the shutdown, I'll still do better than the Republicans, but we're both gonna drop because government will look a mess that no one in Washington can sort out." In unusually long phone calls, he expressed his anxiety to me, and I used the numbers from our daily polling to reassure him. There were no great strategic insights to be had. This was an old-fashioned goal-line stand, and the only strategy was firmness.

As the president saw that he was surviving the fight and then winning it, he calmed down. He went to the White House briefing room every day to do battle and return to continue his work as president. Our advertising solidified our public support and the president gained stature each week as he stood firm in the face of the Republican offensive.

On October 24, Gingrich said he would let Medicare "wither on the vine." On the same day, Dole told a conservative group that "I was there, fighting the fight, in 1964, voting against Medicare." These remarks proved Clinton's point and confirmed what Lott had seemed to be saying: that the Republicans refused to budge not because they wanted to cut taxes, but because they wanted to cut Medicare. The real target of those conservative Republicans was federal government itself. They didn't like it and they didn't want it.

We debated how to use the remarks of Gingrich and Dole in our ads. The president called me into the Oval Office for an unusual private chat. We often talked alone in the White House residence late at night, but ever since the June tête-à-tête with Leon, he was reluctant to see me alone in his office and did so only three or four times. "I don't want to run the Dole Medicare quote in our national ad buy," he confided.

"You worried that it'll hurt him too much and he'll lose the nomination?" I asked.

"Aren't you?" he countered. I was. We wanted to run against Dole.

So in early November we featured Gingrich's quote but not Dole's. We ran the ad for three weeks in about 40 percent of the country during the shutdown. The average voter in these swing states saw three showings of it every week, nine all told.

Despite the public's disapproval of a government shutdown, the Republicans persisted in this attempt to blackmail us. I was aghast. I had recently seen the movie *Gettysburg,* and told the president that it looked like Pickett's charge to me, that last gallant gasp of the Confederacy in which, with perfect discipline and unity, the rebels marched suicidally into the lead of Union fire and fell in even rows.

Newt Gingrich then made an even worse blunder. On Air Force One, with the president and other government officials and legislators, the Speaker of the House flew to Israel for the funeral of the slain leader Yitzhak Rabin. During the long round-trip flight, he apparently felt snubbed that he was seated at the back of the plane and was not invited to the front to talk with the president (presumably about the budget). Later, in the heat of the budget fight, he cited this as one of the factors that contributed to his intransigence in the budget negotiations. We all loved the next day's New York *Daily News,* which splashed CRY BABY over a cartoon of an infant Newt holding a toy and sobbing.

The shutdown, the Medicare quote, and the plane incident all effectively silenced Gingrich and dethroned his authority on the national level.

After a six-day shut-down, the Republicans caved. They indicated that they would allow the government to reopen for a month if we agreed to the principle of balancing the budget in seven years (not in the ten we had originally proposed or in the nine we now said was possible) and if we would accept the revenue and inflation estimates of the CBO as the basis for negotiations.

Two months before, the Republican insistence on using CBO's pessimistic numbers had been a deal breaker. Now it wasn't. As the OMB had predicted, the economic situation had improved a great deal, and even the CBO had to revise its numbers to include a lot of additional revenue that its economists hadn't counted in their earlier estimates. With the new CBO numbers, we could commit to balance the budget in seven years. We could now make a deal without sacrificing our core priorities.

A few days before the offer came through, our polls had shown some impatience with the continued stalemate. While the data reversed itself immediately before the Republicans' proposal, I was shaken by the poll and urged acceptance of the deal, provided our enumerated priorities were still protected. Harmless language either way.

I had shown Trent Lott too much of my hand when I told him about the poll showing the public was tiring of the standoff, and this emboldened the Republicans. It was a slip, and I apologized to the president. Leon and George think it weakened our hand in the negotiations, and they may be right.

Erskine Bowles kept in touch with me while George and Leon led our negotiators on Capitol Hill. We were greatly surprised when the Republicans surrendered by offering to reopen the government without getting a budget deal and without any commitments from us other than to balance the budget in seven years based on CBO numbers. We all knew this was GOP surrender, but to be sure the press interpreted it in that light, we insisted that the Republicans confirm that we intended to protect Medicare, Medicaid, education, and the environment.

Bowles called me on November 19 at my home in Connecticut, where Eileen and I were hosting a party for seventy guests to celebrate my birthday. I kept ducking in and out to take Erskine's calls, trying to hear him talk above the din. Bowles and I agreed with Panetta and Stephanopoulos that it was a good deal and a solid win.

Vice President Gore, on the other hand, was against taking the deal.

Flying home from Japan where he had filled in for the president at an official government reception, Gore told me from his plane that we were "giving away far too much." He felt we could have held out for a much better deal.

The president, however, was inclined to take the deal, pocket his winnings in the polls, and get up from the table. "You've accomplished your political purpose, and to drag on the shutdown further will risk a backlash—a plague on both your houses," I said.

The president was as surprised as everyone else in the White House that the Republicans had given up so much.

Once we had agreed to reopen the government, I urged us to put on the table a plan for a balanced budget in seven years with CBO assumptions to show that even under the ground rules the Republicans had laid down, we could still protect our major programs. The president listened to my suggestion impassively. George Stephanopoulos, Harold Ickes, Leon Panetta, and oddly, Vice President Gore all saw my proposal as fatally flawed. "Why should we give up our bargaining cards by suggesting deeper cuts than we have already put out on the table?" Gore said. "Let's hold our concessions for the negotiations."

Unaccustomed to debating Gore, my usual ally, I replied that "we can take the moral high ground by proving that vital priorities need not be cut even with CBO numbers and a seven-year deadline."

George said he didn't see how we could do it.

I outlined how I thought we could.

George's challenge was sharp: "Your numbers are full of shit. You don't know what you're talking about."

I replied heatedly that my numbers came from Alice Rivlin (director of OMB) and I was unaware that George had a Ph.D. that equipped him to challenge Rivlin's numbers.

The entire room joined in attacking me. One after another, Panetta, Ickes, and Stephanopoulos denounced my proposal. Ickes said it betrayed a total lack of understanding of the bargaining process. Panetta said it would trigger a whole round of denunciations from congressional Democrats.

The president sat silently by while the diatribes continued. Finally, he interrupted the one-sided debate by saying, "Dick is making a very good point. We must show that we can balance the budget with CBO numbers in seven years; otherwise we'll lose the high ground we seized in the June [balanced-budget] speech."

That quieted the mob, and the meeting ended a few minutes later.

The president did indeed then issue a new proposal to achieve balance in seven years using the CBO numbers that gave him the high ground he wanted: it kept the debate focused on *how* to balance the budget, not on *whether* to balance it.

A second attempt by the Republicans to have their way in the budget war led to a second shutdown of the government, this one between December 17 and January 6. It was even more absurd than the first shutdown, since the Republicans knew we wouldn't cave and they must have known the price they'd paid for the first shutdown. Most people don't commit suicide twice, but Gingrich did.

The deadlock ended when Dole broke ranks with his party and the Senate passed the resolution reopening the government. Now isolated, even the Republican freshmen knew it was time to fold.

Dole himself would probably have agreed to a more reasonable settlement much earlier. Had this pragmatic legislator been in charge, he would not have held out on so absurd a position for so long. But his hold on the conservative primary voters was tenuous, as subsequent events proved, and he was paralyzed by the fear that Senator Phil Gramm would beat him out on the right if he budged an inch.

The budget battle left the president in good shape. He had shown that he was both a moderate and strong—willing to stand firm and take the heat. Our polls indicated that he was now seen as *better* than the Republicans on two key issues: balancing the budget and fighting crime.

We had succeeded, as 1995 closed, in fulfilling the mandate I had sketched out at the start of the year: to take their own issues away from the Republicans and seize the political center. These gains set the stage for the dramatic jump that Clinton achieved after his State of the Union Address at the end of January 1996.

The budget battle left the Republican party humiliated and drastically weakened. We left the year holding a lead over Dole that generally ran about 47–38, still under 50 percent in our vote share and only eight points ahead, but at last we were back on track and had taken the lead.

While the budget battle raged, Mark Penn and I were fighting a lonely battle within the administration about how to describe the state of the economy.

Democrats had become pessimists by habit. After running presidential races based on predictions of economic disaster in 1984, 1988, and 1992, the party had become addicted to prophecies of doom. Throughout the 1980s, Democrats welcomed bad economic news and were depressed when times were good, believing that prosperity undermined their chances against Republican incumbents. By contrast, the Republicans welcomed good economic news.

The Democrats reminded me of the famous Jewish writer Harry Golden, who said, "if the roof caved in, the tenants would sit in the debris and laugh like hell because it meant trouble for the landlord."

Though the Democrats controlled the White House, the old pessimism remained. The president echoed this view in September 1995 when he noted that America was in a "funk" during a chat with reporters. As soon as I heard his comment, I knew he had made a mistake akin to President Carter's admission that America suffered a "malaise," a comment that helped lead to his defeat.

When Clinton says something that basic and important, there is only one way to try to change his mind: with polling data. So, we polled American attitudes toward the economy even as the president flew home after his "funk" remark. Our data awaited him on his return.

It showed a surge of optimism likely to equal the "feel-good" highs that animated Ronald Reagan's 1984 reelection campaign. People felt that the economy was better than it was when Clinton took office and would be even better in the future. More important, the polling reflected that Americans believed that their children would be better off than themselves by a margin of two to one.

In telling the president of the data at a September 1995 strategy meeting, I claimed that we had found a definite correlation between economic optimism and how people vote. Before revealing the data, I asked for a show of hands from the group.

"How many feel that optimists are more likely to vote for Dole?" I asked. Every hand in the room except one went up.

"And how many believe that economic optimists are more likely to vote for Clinton?" One hand, that of the president himself, was raised. He was right. By two to one optimists voted for Clinton. Pessimists backed Dole by the same margin.

Thereafter, Mark and I campaigned to discourage economic pessimism and make sure the administration spoke optimistically and positively about economic news. "Every time we say things are not going as well as we would like or call growth anemic," I said, "we are creating pessimists who will then have a two-out-of-three chance of backing Dole for president."

The president solved the problem by adding equal doses of optimism and pessimism in his speeches. Tom Freedman, my staffer on the road with the president, reported that Clinton would speak of our great economic successes but then would talk about wage stagnation, layoffs, and income inequality. Every week, we took what the president said and read it to voters in a poll. Then we asked a second question, taking out the negatives and dwelling only on the positive parts of his speech. We asked whether the statement made them more or less likely to vote for President Clinton. By omitting the bad news we usually gained an average of twenty points. Voters found the good-news-only statements more believable than the good/bad statements.

Clinton stressed economic recovery and spoke optimistically about reversing wage stagnation and inequality in income growth. As data confirmed that real wages were, in fact, starting to rise for all levels, it became easier for him to shift his emphasis.

But some never got the point. Bob Reich, secretary of Labor, for example, seemed to hunt for sour news, about wage stagnation, for example, and give it top billing in his department's press releases. I would always send them to Clinton and forward our latest polling data about economic optimism to Reich. Eventually, even Reich ran out of bad news. The country was enjoying a cyclical upswing in 1995–96 after years of sluggish growth. I saw no reason for the president to emphasize weakness in the economy.

How I Came to Be
a Bird Perched on Clinton's
Left Shoulder

The president, red-faced, turned toward me, jabbed me with his forefinger, and yelled, "*You* are the cause of the factionalism around here. *You* are. Ever since you insisted—*insisted*—on hiring Squier and made the vice president your employee . . . You are the one creating factions and friction around here. *You* are." He stalked off angrily to attend the evening's events in Washington.

His outburst was right after the first government shutdown on December 7, 1995. We had just ended a strategy session, and I was astonished by the outburst. I said to myself, He's right I am the cause of factionalism at the White House—damned right. But my faction was one that Clinton himself had created. He brought me in so that we could change course and save his happy liberals who screwed things up for two years from going over the cliff hand in hand. My forming a faction, I thought, is called trying to win the election.

There's a time to stay and a time to quit. And this was the time to quit. I said good-bye to the astonished Mark Penn, Doug Schoen, and Don

Baer, who had witnessed the president's outburst, and set out for Connecticut, sending word to the president that I had resigned.

The explosion had been building for a long time. After the June '95 meetings with Panetta, Gore, the president, and me, things had gone well. Leon, George, and I worked as a team with both Clinton and Gore and it seemed to me this was the way the White House should be run. We all gave the president the exact same advice: stand firm on the budget. I hoped this harmony could last forever.

The successful outcome of the budget battles should have reinforced the virtue of unity among the White House staff, but it had the opposite effect. My adversaries saw it as a chance to get rid of me. They no longer needed my help in getting Clinton to resist the Republican budget proposals, and now they geared up for a final push.

Why? Because no matter how well we had worked together, I was an intruder in their world, as David Gergen, Mack McLarty, Mickey Kantor, and Eli Segal had been. Now I was to go the way of these others: down the chute.

I began to see signs that suggested to me that Harold Ickes was making trouble. My New York friends told me that Ickes had boasted that "Morris will be out by Christmas." A reporter from *The Washington Post* called about my minibar bill at the Jefferson, which I was said to have charged to the campaign. Actually, I did not bill my minibar charges to the campaign, and I strictly honored the rule against seeking reimbursement for alcoholic beverages. Only someone with access to the campaign's accounting records could have leaked that story, and those records were directly under Ickes's supervision.

Suddenly, the press clamored for the disclosure of my outside sources of income, information I had not been obliged to divulge because I was not on the public payroll and because I did not have a hard pass giving me access to the White House. But my predecessor of sorts, James Carville, who did have a hard pass, had filed a financial-disclosure form. So the White House counsel ruled that I was also obliged to do so.

Originally, the counsel's office also demanded that my wife file such a form as well. Eileen refused, saying she did not work for Clinton and would not file a disclosure form just because her husband had to. "I don't work for them, and it's none of their business who my clients are or how much money I make," she said. Sensing that she was not about to budge and unwilling to make a public issue of it, the counsel's office backed off and asked only that I file the form. Although the form was called "Confidential Disclosure Form," it was immediately distributed to the press. None of the forms filed by the other consultants was released.

The form I completed revealed, among other things, that I had lent my polling expertise to Tom Puccio, a defense lawyer who represented a young Connecticut man, Alex Kelly, who was accused of two date rapes a decade ago. The pretrial publicity concerning Kelly's flight while on bail and the ten years he spent in Europe before turning himself in—with the police on his trail—had been intense. My polls showed that he was unlikely to get a fair trial in Stamford, and suggested two or three other Connecticut towns where knowledge of the case was much less widespread. I reported my findings to the court and recommended a change in venue. The Dole campaign briefly demanded my resignation for "defending rapists," and some Republican congresswomen held a press conference about my involvement, but not much came of it. First, Kelly wasn't a rapist until the jury said he was. Second, I wasn't trying to get him off; I was trying to show that the state ought to move the case to another part of Connecticut, where Kelly could get a fair trial. Such testimony is commonplace in legal cases. I was doing nothing unusual.

Another incident in this campaign of harassment—the most unusual incident—arose from a leak to Ann Devroy, the White House correspondent for *The Washington Post*. According to the leakers, I had rented pornographic movies in my hotel room and billed them to the campaign. Devroy asked me about it, and said she had gotten the information from the accounting office of the campaign. None of my hotel bills, in fact, showed movie rentals of any kind. I provided her copies of all of the bills I had submitted to the campaign and asked the manager at the Jefferson to confirm that I had never rented a movie.

I presumed the leaks were part of the harassment against me by Harold Ickes and James Carville, Clinton's consultant in 1992.

James was grateful for my having recommended him to Clinton, and we had been friendly during the first two years of the president's term. In 1993, when I complained to him about liberals playing too large a role in the White House, he replied that "liberals are like fucking water damage; they just seep in all the time."

For two or three months in the fall of 1995, I consulted with James. He told me that he would do anything for the president and didn't mind not being at the core of the campaign. He asked me, however, not to let on that he played no role in the strategic or consulting groups, so that he could continue to pull down large speaking fees by seeming to be closer to the center than he actually was.

I found James's advice useful, but I later broke off our regular meetings when I began to suspect him of inspiring some of the negative press about me. Someone told me, for example, that he had seen Carville lunching with Devroy the day before one of her negative stories broke, and Mary Matalin, his Republican wife, accused me on the air of renting pornographic movies. Carville always seemed to play this game with Mary: often when he wanted to punch some Democrat in the nose—like me—I suspected he'd get his wife to do it for him. Perhaps he returned the favor for her. It was like dealing with Edgar Bergen and Charlie McCarthy.

Such constant assaults were wearing me down. The Republicans joined in, as eager to have me removed from the Clinton campaign as Ickes was. I appreciated the implied compliment—that I was doing a good job for Clinton—but sometimes their tactics were a touch hamhanded. Another Friday (these attacks usually surfaced at 3:00 P.M. on Friday) Devroy called to say that Alex Castellanos, a Republican media man, had told her—on the record—that when Clinton was governor, I had procured women for him whenever he visited New York. Alex claimed that I told him that I personally "delivered" women to the Waldorf-Astoria Hotel. The story was wild, totally ungrounded in any possible fact at all. I offered to take a lie detector test to show it was untrue and produced evidence for Devroy that Clinton rarely stayed at the Waldorf when he was governor. Usually he stayed with friends. Devroy, a diligent reporter, always fair and honest in her dealings with me, did not run the story.

Despite all the smear attempts, the White House remained tolerable because one man made it so: Erskine Bowles. My guide to the bureaucracy and my confidant, Erskine helped me avoid White House infighting. I used to say that the president had two deputy chiefs of staff, one in charge of making my life work (Erskine Bowles) and the other in charge of making it hell (Harold Ickes). But Bowles had wanted to resign in the fall of '95, and extended his tenure only at the president's request.

As Erskine prepared to leave Washington at the end of 1995, Ickes was clearly planning a major move against me now that I was about to lose my only ally. I had expected Bowles to be replaced by someone sympathetic to my point of view—my survival depended on it—but now this was looking less certain. Ickes pressed to eliminate the "other" deputy chief of staff position, the one Bowles had occupied, leaving him as Panetta's only deputy. Then Stephanopoulos wanted the job.

When he asked me to support his promotion, I declined: George was a colleague—a valued one—but not my ally, we both knew it.

In late November, when the president named his former deputy press secretary, Evelyn Lieberman, to succeed Bowles, I was astounded. Lieberman and I hadn't had much to do with each other, and I was under the impression that she was very close with Ickes (I later learned that she was closer to Hillary than anyone). In fact, Evelyn turned out to be warm and helpful to me most of the time. But I didn't know that in November. What I knew was that she was no Erskine Bowles and not likely to be my ally on critical matters.

I also learned that plans were afoot to name as campaign manager Kevin Thurm, an Ickes protégé and, I was told, a former college roommate of George's. My encirclement now seemed complete.

Evelyn Lieberman's appointment was announced immediately before one of our weekly strategy meetings in the Map Room of the White House residence. The meeting went well enough, but before it was over, I handed the president an angry note: "I just don't get how you expect me to do my job when you keep appointing people who have exactly the opposite strategic and political worldview from yours and mine." It was this note that triggered the president's explosion.

As I recovered from the unexpected sting of the president's 1995 explosion, I pondered Clinton's words. I couldn't understand his accusation that I had made Vice President Gore my "employee." It was true that I worked closely with Gore. I may at times have come close to being *his* employee, but certainly the reverse was not true! The president may have been referring to my frequent dependence on the vice president to press my views on him during their weekly lunch meetings. It became evident that he resented being lobbied this way.

It is true, as the president had noted, that I had fought hard to hire Squier to do our ads. And I'm glad I did. Those were the ads that had brought us within sight of victory. His ideas often led to friction but this hardly accounted for the president's eruption, which implied an entirely contrary view from mine of the White House operation.

At eleven P.M., hours after I had returned to Connecticut that December 7, the president called to apologize. He was surprised that I had gotten home "so fast." I said anything was possible when you really want to "get the hell out of town." Eileen sat at my side as I poured my soul out to the president. I had never spent a lot of time bothering him with complaints about his staff, but at that moment, I did.

Months before, I had asked former White House adviser David Gergen for advice on the politics of the place. Gergen had sought to move the Clinton administration more to the center in his brief stint with the White House in 1993–94 and had been forced out by many of the same people who were now on my case. "I never complained to the president about what they were doing to me," Gergen said. "I considered it my job not to waste his time with complaints. But now I realize I should have brought my case directly to him." Now that I had the president's attention I took Gergen's advice.

"There are two fundamental camps in your White House: the New Democrats and the Old Guard Democrats. If you don't get it, you're the only one in Washington who doesn't," I began.

Clinton professed ignorance of the depth of the split.

"I can't believe you don't see it," I said. "But let me explain what's going on." I went on to sketch the liberals' hope for a return to the old Democrat-versus-Republican fight based on class warfare and their hostility to a new moderate third way. I told him of Ickes's daily schemes to undermine me and recounted several instances of harassment. Only Bowles, I said, made the situation livable, and he was being replaced by someone who was unsympathetic at best and hostile at worst.

Clinton said I was misjudging Lieberman and that I should give her a chance. "Obviously, I have confidence in you," he said. "I've turned the campaign over to you."

I imagined his long hand circling an imaginary globe in front of him as he illustrated his feelings.

I told him that I was leaving the campaign unless he let me help him get elected. "I will walk away from this, the prestige and the power," I added for emphasis, "rather than watch these people drag you down the same rabbit hole they dragged you down before I got here. These are the same sons of bitches that almost destroyed you over health-care reform and who *masterminded* the congressional elections of 1994. If you want 'em, you can have 'em."

The president said he wanted me to stay and that we would talk soon about how to make it work.

I was surprised—and doubtful—that the existence of White House factions was news to Clinton. No one is more perceptive of what is going on around him. Usually he knows what you are thinking before you do. At any rate, I had brought the matter out in the open and forced him to deal with it. I agreed to return.

In a subsequent meeting, Clinton said that he had told Evelyn Lieberman her first job was to end the factional fighting. Consequently, she fussed over me, wanted to know how my digestion was, whether my dog needed walking, and whether I had enough office supplies, anything to comply with the president's mandate. She was kind but she had no power.

Unfortunately, little really changed at the White House. In early December, I told Erskine that I would leave right after the State of the Union speech. Ickes was still trying to frustrate my every move. I asked Erskine to tell Clinton that "I had never leaked a single negative story about Ickes or sought to embarrass him." I asked him to say that "I'm quite happy to run the message and let Ickes run the mechanics."

Bowles passed this message very effectively and from then on Clinton made himself more accessible. From speaking five times or so a week, we were soon speaking several times a day. He returned my calls in ten minutes, not four hours. Bowles told me that Clinton had said that while he couldn't change his staff, he would show by the access he granted that he valued me.

Kevin Thurm was not appointed, and Lieberman tried her best to be the staff's one human face. Still, it was obvious that I had to head off the Ickes offensive.

To do this I relied on advice from Charles de Gaulle. He believed that when a situation is beginning to be untenable, you should quit before you are forced to leave. For de Gaulle, resignation was a way to gain power. *If* it works, fine. If not, your departure saves your reputation and you can fight again another day. This is why de Gaulle resigned at the height of his power when he saw its erosion as inevitable, "I decided . . . to . . . withdraw from events before they withdrew from me."

If you see that a downfall is inevitable, resign while you still have your power. But you have to mean it. Be prepared to go (I was), but make your move while you still have power and credibility.

I called the president in early January and said, "I feel that I've had a wonderful time working for you. I'm very proud of what we've done together in 1995. It's been a great year for me, but now it's time for me to pull out and let Harold take you the rest of the way."

"No, I need you; I need you to stay," he answered. "A lot can happen in 1996."

"Well," I said, "it will likely be without me."

He understood my game, but he also realized that unless things changed, I was in earnest. I told my fellow consultants that I expected them to resign with me so that Ickes "could have a clean shot at screwing up the campaign." They agreed to follow me.

My threat was crucial. The president had to understand that I was ready to leave the money on the table and not stay for the huge payday in 1996 which would, among other things, greatly enhance my career. I hoped he would see that if I was to forgo this power that I must want him to win for other and better reasons.

My offer to resign was, in other words, the ultimate statement of my good faith.

Then Eileen supplied an insight that became central to my relationship with the president. She had flirted with psychology as a profession and remained interested in it.

She was aware of my tendency to form symbiotic relationships and believed that Clinton and I had one. She observed that the terms of my relationship with Clinton were unusual. I would have complete access to him and he would feel free to take my advice, if he agreed with it, as long as I kept the relationship secret.

"He seems to explode with rage whenever you become known and the rules of secrecy in the relationship change," she said. "He knows Ickes can't run the campaign. He's told you so. Anybody can see that. But he uses Ickes to express his rage against you for altering the ground rules of your symbiosis, and that rage gives Ickes his power."

This ingenious synthesis of Freud and Machiavelli made sense to me. I'd lived this relationship with Clinton for almost two decades.

Eileen's advice: "Remind him that you can leave the campaign. You can't work under these conditions and you know it." She was right. My health and mental well-being were affected by the guerrilla war with Ickes while I was trying to concentrate on the Republicans. I was prone to diverticulitis, a stress-related intestinal ailment that can cause serious illness and even death should an attack go untreated, and now I was suffering monthly attacks as debilitating as they were threatening. My condition had worsened and I was scheduled to undergo surgery, right after the State of the Union speech later that January. This could not continue.

Eileen's other advice presented the solution: "I think that he's telling you he wants to restore the symbiosis. Do it. Give in to it. I know you've spent a lifetime trying to avoid symbiotic relationships because usually they don't work, but here, go with it. It's what he wants, and it'll work."

She reminded me how happy Clinton and I were as we worked on the 1995 State of the Union Address. "That's what he wants," she said. "He wants you to work quietly and directly with him, at his shoulder, in his sphere, but not beyond it. He doesn't want you to work with his staff or be known to the press." She advised me to stay away from staff meetings at the White House. "They're only a distraction and they provide the White House staff with early warnings of your ideas. This gives them time to undermine you, leak to the press, and, ultimately, undermine your relationship with the president."

By abjuring the White House staff, and working only with the president, I could get things done without the emotional turmoil.

I took her advice. In mid-January 1996, I entered the Oval Office for my crucial meeting with the president (a rare daytime one-on-one meeting). He was sitting in his desk chair with its unusually low back—little more, really, than a chair you might see at a kitchen table. He towered over the chair, the desk, and me. I sat in a similar chair beside his desk, at right angles to him, about four feet away. We were alone. As he studied me closely I came right to the point. "You have sent me two messages in the past two weeks," I began. "First, you have systematically staffed your office, your staff, and your campaign with people who oppose not only my ideology and strategy but your own, people who want to destroy me and who, the minute your back is turned, will try to move the campaign in the opposite direction of where you told me to take it."

He began to object, but I said, "Please let me finish.

"They are the same guys who ran against the Contract with America in 1994 even though you didn't want to. The same people who were supposed to line up support for your health-care plan and didn't. The ones who told you not to back a balanced budget. Do you need to be misled by them a fourth time? Meanwhile, you have opened your access to me wider than the Champs-Élysée. What do I make of it?"

He kept silent and looked on curiously, wondering where I would go.

"I think you are telling me that you don't want me to run your staff or your campaign office, that you want me to handle the ads and the polling. You've appointed Baer so that I can oversee the message operation. But beyond that you're telling me that you don't want me to be part of your staff, empowering them against you. You want me to be on your side, empowering you against them."

He nodded, apparently satisfied with this analysis.

Clinton kept a distance from his staff. He made his decisions alone. Normally he is extroverted and talkative. But in the White House, he had taught himself to be introverted, like a southpaw who has taught himself to throw right-handed. He kept his own counsel. He made himself elusive. At meetings he would often say nothing. Nothing. He would let others talk, keep a poker face, and leave his visitors with no impression at all of the decision he intended to make. The blank stare. He trusted no one.

I pointed to his left shoulder. "You want me to sit right there, on your left shoulder, like a bird, and whisper in your ear, three, four, five, ten times a day. Then, if you choose, you can use my advice to control your staff, your campaign, your dealings with Congress, your dealings with the NSC, to empower you."

He smiled broadly and said, "You got it. I'll take what I want, and I'll discard what I don't want, but leave it with me; don't do it yourself. Work through me."

It wasn't a bad offer. He was asking me, in effect, to cross the space that separated him from everyone else who worked for him. In return, I would ignore White House politics and work only through him. This had been his intention all along. That was the message he had been trying to send me by backing up Ickes and letting him fill the staff with his people. He didn't want me to take over his staff or even be part of it. He wanted me to work for *him*.

The president's usual method of control was to appoint people who were not likely to get along, much as FDR had done. For both presidents, conflict among staff sharpened the options. A harmonious staff, on the other hand, soon became a bureaucracy, with everyone in step but in the wrong direction.

I had told the president that I couldn't be part of such conflict. I couldn't fight case by case. I lacked the temperament and the stamina.

So the president agreed I would no longer exhaust myself battling with the staff in the mud-wrestling pit. I would whisper in his ear. When he took my advice he would argue with them himself. He would still be in control without the mind-numbing conflicts.

The arrangement suited Panetta. Leon was well used to the whims of the president. He considered it his honor and his duty to cater to them. That is what being chief of staff is all about. It was his duty to decode the puzzling signals he received from the president and relay them in comprehensible form to the staff. He had no need to worry about my whims.

From then on, everything worked fine. I withdrew completely from intra–White House combat and even stopped attending meetings, except for the weekly strategy sessions. Rather than let Panetta or Ickes cut me out of the loop, I withdrew into my world whispering from the president's shoulder.

At first, Panetta, Ickes, Stephanopoulos, and the others may have thought they had got rid of me. But they soon realized that the president and I were a team.

"The White House staff is like the moon," I hypothesized to my fellow consultants. "It cannot shine without the rays of the sun, the president. If those rays don't illuminate it, nobody knows that the staff is even there.

"The constant fear of any White House staff," I explained, "is to lose its president. Yet this president makes a specialty of elusiveness. He comes to a meeting, but he won't tell you what he's thinking, he won't tell you whether he agrees with you or not, and he certainly won't fight you up front. He just won't be there when you expect him to be."

Under the new arrangement, if I didn't like a speech they presented, I'd draft my own and give it to the president to do with as he wished. If I didn't agree with what they wanted the president to do that week, I'd give the president my alternative plans and leave it up to him. Gradually, the staffers, led by George, got the message and made a point of checking with me before they proceeded. Usually, I'd say what I thought but not push the matter. If I really disagreed, I'd just go to the president.

In the same Oval Office meeting in which the president and I discussed our relationship and, by implication, my future with him, Clinton also clarified his attitude toward Gore. Undoubtedly feeling awkward after his earlier accusation that I had made the vice president my "employee," he said, "I just want you to know that I will work ceaselessly, ceaselessly, to be sure that Al Gore is the presidential nominee of the Democratic party in 2000, without a primary if at all possible. Ceaselessly." His long fingers curled up, and in one of his characteristic gestures he pounded his fists up and down, inches from his chest, as he pronounced the last word: cease—less—ly.

I noted that in 1960, Eisenhower had hung Nixon out to dry when asked at a press conference whether his vice president had ever made an important contribution to any of the decisions he had made as president—Ike replied that if you gave him a week, he'd think of one.

"Yes," Clinton said, smiling broadly and laughing. "I do guess that might have hurt Mr. Nixon."

Later, the president handed Gore another token of his esteem by naming Gore's former staff director, Peter Knight, his campaign manager, giving the VP a measure of control over the campaign. He also gave me what I had sought all along: a campaign manager who would not be

Ickes's stooge. President Clinton could give me this now because I had joined *his* team and wasn't either trying to be part of his staff or talking to the press.

When I repeated the president's words to Gore, as Clinton had doubtlessly intended me to do, the vice president said, with a pixyish lilt, "Did he really say that? Oh my!"

Before our Oval Office meeting ended, I told the president that I had one important request: I wanted my own person on the campaign plane so that he could pass my messages to the president while they were in the air without risking conversations over the relatively open phone lines on Air Force One.

When the president was in the White House, communication was no problem. In time, we came to speak by phone pretty much every night. During the day, I would send him three or four brief notes, which were put directly on his desk by Nancy Hernreich or Betty Currie, who sat outside his office. Both women understood how inaccessible the president was and did all they could to facilitate my access to him.

Often my messages related to a meeting that was actually taking place as the message was carried in. I might, for example, be warning him of a move I expected one of the participants to make that would be contrary to his interests. Or I might remind him to press one of the people in the meeting to move in a certain direction, for example, in a direction we had discussed the night before on the phone. These messages could be as direct as I wanted them to be, for we had agreed that nobody but the president himself would ever see them. It was how he wanted it.

When Clinton was traveling, however, he was usually scheduled for dawn-to-midnight events and meetings, and communication was difficult. I asked that Tom Freedman, my chief of staff, be on the plane with him. Torn about losing Tom because he was so valuable to me, I told Clinton, "I'm giving you my firstborn son." The president came to like Freedman and worked well with him. Tom kept me abreast of the latest gossip on the plane and helped me shape my moves.

I had hired Tom in the fall. Tom is tall and angular, with a dry wit and a sense of the absurd—a trait I found especially useful in the White House. A basketball player, he is both brilliant and intensely loyal. Eileen and I came to value immensely his friendship and good judgment. Editor-in-chief of the law review at Berkeley, he had Clinton's ability to note the subtlest signals and understand what someone really thought behind their mask of approval. Frequently, when we left meetings, he would describe what had really happened, translating changes in body language and ambiguous comments he had noted, making it clear I still had much persuading to do. I was too busy talking to note what was actually happening around me. Tom kept me out of a lot of trouble and was a source of good ideas for presidential action. Each week, he would come to me with ten new proposals, many derived from an intense search of discarded bills introduced in Congress, some of which we used to great effect.

Traveling with the president, Tom told me what the president was saying in speeches. Clinton will toy with an idea and then will try it out in a speech to see what response he gets. Since Tom had helped develop our strategy, he knew the language I had suggested to Clinton. When he found the president developing new lines and approaches, Tom would tell me and I'd test them in the next poll. When I reported the results to the president he would suggest further variations. I'd test again and again until the theme he wanted was fully developed.

Sometimes, Tom Freedman would catch a mistake in one of the president's speeches and alert me. I'd raise it immediately with the president so he didn't repeat the error in the next speech. Had the Dole campaign been alive and kicking, they could have diverted us from our agenda at least a dozen times by exploiting these mistakes.

For example, in early August 1996, the president likened teen gangs to church congregations. His point was subtle and a good one. He compared the sense of belonging that animates churchgoers with the perversion of that same feeling among violent gang members. He argued that if we want kids to drop out of gangs we needed to give them something else to belong to. But who wanted to go on the defensive with that kind of explanation just as the Republican convention prepared to fire its guns? Fortunately, the GOP was asleep at the switch and never pounced on the comment.

Another time, Clinton said he was "confused" by the changes happening in our society. Good God, I thought when Tom told me this. If "funk" got us in trouble when he said it in September '95, this comment in the spring of '96 could sink us. Once again, Dole's people were too busy fighting among themselves to notice and the slip passed by.

▲

It was obvious what the president needed from me: he needed options.

As a president sits in his office, he may easily be overcome by the day-to-day details. He therefore relies on his staff to present him with possible courses of action; he has no time to develop them himself. He can issue whatever orders he wants to issue, but the alternatives are suggested to him by the staff. This—as I have said—is how the staff controls the president. He can't easily fire his people because they might turn around and savage him from the outside and give him even bigger problems than he started with. Besides, at least in Clinton's administration, each staffer represents a constituency, and by firing the staffer, the president would also fire the voters, or the donors or the politicians the staffer represents.

This is why Clinton is such an avid reader of magazines, journals of opinion, editorials, and columnists in preference to reading the news. After all, he *was* the news. He needed his reading hours to canvass advisers, and get opinions that amplify options.

Freedman recruited a staff of four top people—Brian Lee, Mary Smith, Matt Levine, and Marc Schwartz—paying them only a thousand dollars a month (the modern equivalent of dollar-a-year men) to monitor the nightly news. They also checked out TV talk shows, twenty-five regional newspapers, and dozens of periodicals to bring me whatever noteworthy ideas they found. I tried to develop policy alternatives for the president to deal with the issues these media outlets raised.

I also depended on an informal network of policy people. In government I consulted regularly with Education secretary Dick Riley, HUD secretary Henry Cisneros, Labor secretary Bob Reich, and Trade Representative (and then Commerce secretary) Mickey Kantor. Elizabeth Holtzman and Eliott Spitzer from New York advised me on crime and women's issues. On the White House staff, I regularly met with Rahm Emanuel on crime, Bruce Reed on welfare, Katie McGinty on the environment, Gene Sperling on tax and fiscal policy, and, above all, Bill Curry, who provided endless ideas on developing community schools, using computers in classrooms, fighting teen gangs, reforming health care, restraining lobbyists, and managing the devolution of government to communities. I also worked with Naomi Wolf, a new mother herself, whose advocacy helped persuade me to pursue school uniforms, tax breaks for adoption, simpler cross-racial adoption laws, and more workplace flexibility. She often said that the candidate who best understood the fatigue of the American woman would win.

I regularly brought their ideas to the president. The Cabinet secretaries could, of course, have called the president directly, but they welcomed my mediation because it helped to focus the president's attention on their ideas.

This new modus operandi survived a trial by fire in late January 1996, when I was scheduled to enter the hospital, just after completing my work on the State of the Union speech. This wasn't the best time to be hospitalized, but I happily anticipated an end to the diverticulitis. With the president's best wishes (and having allayed his fear that I actually had cancer and wasn't telling him), I set off for Mount Sinai Hospital in New York.

As I awoke from the anesthesia, I remembered that something important had happened to me and I needed to find out how it had come out, but I was so fixated on politics that the first question I asked the puzzled recovery room nurse was: "How did the State of the Union speech go?"

In the preceding months, the president and I had vainly hoped to pressure Lott or Dole or Gingrich into moving on a budget deal. I felt we needed one to get our voter share up over 50 percent—it had hovered in the mid-forties for months, and the ads didn't seem to be doing it. We needed real accomplishments, like a balanced budget, to pull off a large victory.

"No president has ever won reelection in a landslide without some major achievement," I reminded Clinton. "Roosevelt had the Depression and the war; Eisenhower ended the war in Korea; Johnson passed the civil rights bill; Nixon pulled off a Vietnam peace (or so it seemed on election day in 1972); Reagan cut taxes. We need an achievement on that order of magnitude, and the budget deal is it."

The president strongly agreed and was anxious—some would say desperate—to try for a deal. Every night we'd talk about how we could bend and fold the budget numbers to accommodate a deal. The president asked me to work with OMB director Alice Rivlin to keep abreast of budget numbers, but most of all he wanted to know about my sessions with Trent Lott.

Panetta and Stephanopoulos wanted to cut off my dealings with Lott; Leon wanted control and George didn't want a deal. George told me that he was going to ask Leon to order me to stop these contacts.

"George," I admitted, "I'm not freelancing here. I'm not flying solo. This isn't only my idea," implying what was the case: that the president wanted the relationship to continue.

As I have said, the positions held by the two sides in the budget debate were not far apart. After Leon skillfully negotiated an appropriations deal with Congress for 1996, ending threats of more government shutdowns, we were closer than ever. But Trent told me a deal wasn't possible. "Dole is so nervous about losing to Gramm that he's not even going to look at a budget deal until he's got the nomination. He's scared to death that he'll work out a deal with Clinton and then get zapped by Gramm, who would charge that Dole had sold out by compromising too much. Even if Dole wanted a deal, he's too distracted, and he won't let me in the room to get it done because he doesn't trust me, probably on account of you."

Dole was slipping badly in Iowa and New Hampshire, losing ground steadily to Forbes and Buchanan, with only weeks left before the primaries. I knew that he was falling because the Republican primary voters felt he couldn't get anything done. With authorization from Sosnik and Ickes (who had to approve any new poll), I surveyed Republican primary voters in those two states and found what I expected: that if Dole did a budget deal—even one in which he was attacked by Gramm and Buchanan for caving in to Clinton—he'd wrap up the two primaries. Republican voters wanted a tax cut and a balanced budget and were willing to vote for Dole in droves if he could produce them even if the right wing attacked him for it.

I briefed the president on the numbers. Then, I made my mistake: on the morning that I left for Mount Sinai, after fasting for thirty-six hours, I gave Dole's people a written memo explaining why a budget deal would wrap up the primaries. I assumed this would encourage Dole to agree on a deal with us. I figured Dole was so desperate to bolster his sagging candidacy that he wouldn't mind helping Clinton by agreeing to one. Politicians generally think only as far as the next election.

I passed the memo through Paul Manafort, a partner of my old friend Charlie Black. Manafort was a Dole intimate and eventually managed the Republican National Convention at Dole's behest. He was in Europe at the time, and so, as I later learned, passed the memo without telling me to Scott Reed, then his contact in the Dole camp. Manafort later told me that Reed gave the memo to Jill Hanson, one of his top aides, who also happened to be a close friend and protégé of Mary Matalin. How the memo got from Hanson to Ann Devroy of *The Washington Post,* I can't say, but a friend later told me that Carville and Devroy were seen together before the story broke.

I learned a week later that my memo to Dole had been leaked and was about to appear in the *Post.* I quickly called the president and accused George of the leak. I had prepared only two copies of the memo. One I gave to the president; the other I sent to Manafort. I couldn't believe that Manafort had been so careless or malicious as to let the message leak out, so I surmised instead that Stephanopoulos had found it and given it to Carville, who passed it to Devroy. George was Devroy's usual source.

There was, however, a slight difference between the copy I gave Clinton and the one I sent to Manafort, and it turned out that Ann had Manafort's copy, not the president's. I had blundered by blaming George so swiftly. George huffily responded to my proffered apology by saying, "I do not accept it."

McCurry let the press know that the president had chewed me out and I was "in the doghouse."

In private, the president, after an initial show of anger, tried to reassure me. His main concern was that Dole couldn't possibly do a budget deal now, since it would be seen as a political move based on my advice.

After a few weeks, the storm passed. Wolf Blitzer of CNN asked me, as I walked into the White House in February, whether I was still in the doghouse, and I pointed to the building and said, "That's no doghouse."

By now my relationship with the president had grown still closer. In mid-February, the president told me he had summoned a meeting of his top staffers, including Ickes, of course, and told them, "You want me to choose [between Morris and you]? I'll choose. But I don't advise you to make me choose. You won't like the choice I'm going to make. I think that other than Al and me, two people are responsible for the turnaround I've had—[fund-raiser] Terry McAuliffe and Dick Morris, so I advise you—don't make me choose."

After this all the infighting stopped for a while. Now I faced the only adversary whom I could not defeat: myself.

American Values

How did President Clinton gain an unbeatable lead? Popular comment suggests that it was either because he "moved to the center" in his proposal for a balanced budget and welfare reform or because he had the public on his side when Gingrich and the Republican Congress shut down the government.

These were important moves, but they are inadequate to explain what happened. They put us back in the game—but they were not what put us over the top. When the budget battles were over in mid-January, Clinton held a narrow lead over Dole in a two-way contest without Ross Perot. That was significant, but it does not explain why this lead ballooned after the president's 1996 State of the Union Address to 53–36 percent and stayed there until the election.

The reason lies in the president's unveiling of a "values" agenda in the State of the Union speech. His elaboration on that theme in speeches and ads throughout 1996 and the emphasis on it in his speech at the convention increased his lead and enabled him to hold it.

The Republicans had a values agenda, but it was largely negative: it was anti-gay, anti-sex, anti–single mothers, anti-abortion, anti-everything-but-the-nuclear family. We offered something different: an agenda of positive values. The public responded far better to our positives than to their negatives. A national consensus has formed out of our varying experiences of the Bush laissez-faire years, the early activism of Clinton, and the Gingrich reaction. We identified and spelled out this consensus in our polling. Naomi Wolf independently endorsed our findings as she noted in American culture a renewed sense of spiritual concern, one incompatible with rigid dogma. Massive majorities consistently rejected the doctrinaire views of both the left and the right and embraced an amalgam of conservative and liberal positions:

On abortion: keep it legal and safe, but regulate it, require parental involvement, and encourage adoption as an alternative.

On welfare: require recipients to work, limit the time on the rolls, but provide day care, job opportunities, education, and training to be sure those who can work, do.

On the deficit: balance the budget in the near future, cut the deficit year by year, but don't violate core priorities, like Medicare, Medicaid, education, and protection of the environment.

On government regulation: streamline regulations, allow businesses more flexibility in finding ways to comply with them, but maintain strict controls on the environment, clean drinking water, food and drugs, and safety.

On crime: mandate tough sentences, capital punishment, more police, and controls on handguns and assault weapons but not on hunting rifles used by sportspeople.

This consensus was apparent in virtually every poll on all these issues.

The American rejection of politics today is largely rooted in the government's failure to implement these common beliefs. Voters are saying to public officials, "Pass the stuff and move on!" But beyond these issues voters are deeply troubled by other developments in our society. They beg for guidance from political leaders on how to address them, and they get little attention:

How can we get absent fathers to meet their financial responsibility to support their families?

How can we stop television from leading our children to enjoy and possibly express violence?

Can we prevent our teenagers from becoming addicted to cigarettes?

How can health insurance be protected when we change jobs? And can pensions be secured for those fortunate enough to have them?

Will medical care be available when we need it, despite its high cost?

Will our schools adopt new technology as business has?

What can government, business, schools, and parents do to motivate and discipline today's children?

How can we balance the demands of work and family? How can we get the time to do both?

Will college be widely financially accessible as a way to escape poverty and ascend the middle-class ladder?

How do we put more cops on the street and get the guns off the block?

Voters beg for government help with these problems. They are largely ignored by our political process or trivialized by the media, yet our polls showed these to be the issues that preoccupy the average voter.

Robert Frost once wrote that poetry is about grief, and politics is about the grievances. In his State of the Union speech in 1996, President Clinton discussed many reasons for grief and outlined an agenda of grievances he would seek to redress. In this, he transcended the normal political dialogue.

Many have questioned my advocacy of a values agenda at the same time as I was seeing a prostitute. My sexual conduct was indefensible, but that is now a matter between myself and my loved ones. My personal failings should not prevent me from helping to get power into parents' hands to control the TV images aimed at their children, to keep their children from becoming addicted to tobacco, or from giving them more time off from work to be good parents. We all have our personal demons. But we need not let our struggles with them prevent us from doing whatever good we can manage to do in the larger scope of our lives.

▲

The president's concentration on positive values began with the Oklahoma City bombing of April 1995.

I learned about the bombing of the Alfred P. Murrah Federal Building in Oklahoma City while Eileen and I were vacationing in Paris over Easter. I had spoken with the president earlier that day, then decided to call him about something else early on the evening of April 19. He was distraught, almost in shock. "Haven't you heard what happened?" he asked, his voice trembling. "A terrorist blew up the federal building in

Oklahoma City, and dozens, maybe even hundreds of people, were killed."

I asked him if foreign terrorists were involved, but he was noncommittal. In the next few days, it became clear that men with links to domestic militias were involved. I urged the president to propose bold steps to counter domestic terrorism in an address to the nation, but he replied that "the FBI says that if I do that, I might bring on a second attack. I've got to move carefully here. This is a dangerous situation."

As Oklahomans dug out the rubble, the president was totally absorbed. He personally examined the entire range of anti-terrorism measures at the government's command. He delivered a moving eulogy in Oklahoma City and later in an interview on *60 Minutes,* he articulated a cogent anti-terrorism program calling for new laws to identify and control terrorist groups. In these appearances, he reached America in a way he never had before. He spoke for America, expressing our outrage with great power. He spoke as an American president, not as a partisan.

President Clinton is not given to private displays of emotion. Rarely have I seen his emotions—other than anger—come to the surface. But Bill Clinton is a deeply empathetic man. He can sense the most subtle emotions in others and respond to them as he cannot to his own feelings.

I originally saw the president's response to Oklahoma City in political terms, as a way to emphasize the menace of right-wing extremism. I felt the Republicans had made a serious political error by opposing key parts of the president's anti-terrorism package. But as it turned out, Oklahoma City was not a topic for partisan politics. It was, however, a turning point for Bill Clinton. Now, as president, he spoke to America's heart while before he had addressed only its head.

The president has always nurtured a deep sense of spirituality. I saw it occasionally but not often. It had little to do with politics, and he rarely advertised it to the public. He usually separated the realms of public policy from those of personal spirituality. But as the Oklahoma City shock passed through him, he began to speak more often in private about the values we, as Americans, needed to share.

The president felt that there are many voters who, like him, spurn the religious right but deeply embrace religion. Our polls showed that more than half the voters who identified themselves as "deeply religious" rejected the Christian Coalition. The president wanted to find a place in our politics to speak to these voters in new ways.

He decided to try it on July 6, 1995, in a speech at Georgetown University. The president was vague about his plans, and I could tell his ideas hadn't really taken shape. I didn't know what he intended, and he could tell I was confused. He had stayed up most of the night before, working on his speech, which he said would be a dialogue with the students—a dialogue in which he would do all the talking, I thought.

On his way to Georgetown, Clinton called and asked that George Stephanopoulos and I watch the speech on cable TV. "Don't just read the text; watch it live," he ordered. He'd never requested this before, so I was wondering what he was planning. George, Tom Freedman, and I sat on a couch in Bill Curry's office. As Clinton spoke he spelled out what he had been thinking since Oklahoma, the president absorbed the facial reactions of the students and responded to them so that there was something of a dialogue. It was a revelation.

He related the political issues of the day to our values. He explored, for example, the antipathy of gun owners to the Brady bill's requirements of waiting periods and background checks. He compared these with the inconveniences of airport security. "You don't gripe when you go through a metal detector at an airport anymore because you are very aware of the connection between this minor inconvenience to you and the fact that the plane might blow up and you don't want that plane to blow up or be hijacked." He appealed to Americans to think as members of a community, not just as individuals, and to focus on the good of all. He noted the common ground of our national consensus and called for politicians to respect it rather than try to shatter it for political gain.

George and I were quizzical. "Where's the news peg, the sound bite, in that speech?" Stephanopoulos wondered.

At first, I didn't see one either. What was the point of the speech? After about fifteen minutes, it dawned on me, "Don't you see what he's doing?" I said to George, "He hasn't been able to put these ideas together in his head and explain them to us, but in front of a thousand kids he can figure out how to say it in a way that reaches them, and he wants us to hear him, understand what he is saying, and figure out where it fits politically." This was the birth of the values agenda in our political thinking.

Republicans had always formed their ideology around individualism and personal liberty. Taxes, regulations, and big government were dangerous because they limited individual freedom. Now Clinton was offering an alternative: a focus on community.

He tapped into a conclusion many people have reached in their personal lives: that the impediment to a better life is not primarily one's economic performance but communal problems—the quality of life for everyone. Such problems as too little time for family life, crime, environmental damage, the high cost of college, ubiquitous TV violence, the drug subculture, and teen smoking, can be addressed only if we band together as a community. Sometimes the community acts through government, but more often, through voluntary religious, business, or civic organizations.

If the GOP was laying claim to "I," Bill Clinton was advocating "we."

Ever since Richard Nixon's Silent Majority of the Vietnam era rejected flag burners, pot smokers, and bra-less women all in the same breath, Republicans have made the social issue their own. Democrats normally focused on economic concerns and left the values to the Republicans. But now the Republican social-values agenda had become too negative to have much political appeal. Republicans were saying, "Don't do this, don't do that, and don't even think about doing the other thing," a strategy without positive focus, focus on what we *should* be doing to promote our values as a people. The president was creating a Democratic values agenda.

Mark Penn, our pollster, supplied interesting evidence of how important the values issues were. Penn had asked a national sample of voters five so-called values questions:

1. Do you believe that sex before marriage is wrong?
2. Do you believe that homosexuality is morally wrong?
3. Is religion very important in your life?
4. Do you personally ever look at pornography?
5. Do you look down on people who have affairs outside of their marriage?

About a third of the country was socially conservative, and gave moralistic answers to at least four of the questions. Another third answered conservatively to three of the five. The rest gave conservative answers to only one or two of the questions or, in some cases, none.

When Penn correlated these results, he found that they accurately predicted whom the respondents would vote for in the presidential election! Those who answered conservatively were overwhelmingly for Dole. Those in the middle split about evenly. The rest heavily favored Clinton. Penn compared this "values index" with other measures for predicting voters' behavior and found that it was more accurate than income, education level, gender, or age. Only political party and race forecast a voter's decision better in a Dole-Clinton race.

The inference was clear. We had to get the values voters back.

At a strategy meeting in July, Penn explained it rather harshly to Clinton, "If someone is single, we can count on their vote. If they've been married and divorced, separated, or widowed, they'll vote for us, but not quite as heavily. Once voters marry, we begin to lose them. Once they have children, they're likely to be for Dole." This was a damning analysis.

Penn further refined his model by age. He concluded that older social conservatives were largely lost to us unless they voted for Clinton over Republican Medicare cuts. Boomers, those of Clinton's and my generation, were not very socially conservative. But younger social conservatives, in their twenties and thirties trying to raise children, were up for grabs, and our values issues were crucially important to them.

We began to take the president's positions and articulate them in terms of values. We polled to ask people whom they trusted more in each value area: Clinton or Dole. We found there were five value areas where they favored Clinton over Dole:

1. Providing opportunity for all
2. Carrying out our duty to our parents
3. Standing up for our country
4. Doing what's right even if it's unpopular
5. Respecting the common ground of America's values

We resolved to focus our presentations in the budget debate not on numbers or even on programs but on these values instead. Where once the president would speak of his desire to raise spending on education or double funding for Head Start, he now spoke of providing opportunity for young children. Or of carrying out our duty to our parents by protecting Medicare. Or of honoring the common ground of Americans by saving the environment. The chord he had touched in his Georgetown speech required him to learn a whole new language.

The liberals on the White House staff were slow to grasp this new thrust. For them, the creation and distribution of wealth was the key concern. Wage stagnation, economic inequality, the fear of layoffs— these issues dominated their thinking about what our focus should be. But by the fall of 1995 people felt increasingly good about the economy. We learned that we could reach these voters not through "pocketbook" issues, but rather through their concerns about values.

The president was way ahead of Penn and me on understanding values. He had intuitively seen what we labored to reconstruct through polling: that Americans wanted to hear more about values and less about materialistic gain. He decided to speak out accordingly.

Clinton insisted on first addressing the problem of religion and morality in our schools. Traditionally, Republicans had monopolized this concern with their support of a constitutional amendment to allow school prayer, which the Supreme Court had banned as a violation of the separation of church and state.

I warned of the potential danger in addressing an issue in which the public overwhelmingly backed the Republican position, but the president was determined. He wanted to explain to school administrators the steps that they could legally take to promote religious observance and moral values on public-school grounds. He ordered Education secretary Richard Riley to circulate a list of steps, such as allowing religious clubs to meet in schools and teaching morals or ethics, that the First Amendment, as interpreted by the courts, seems to allow. His point was that rather than backing a constitutional amendment that might blur the separation of church and state, why don't we achieve many of the goals of such an amendment within the law as it stands?

His speech on school prayer defused much of the Republican initiative in this area. Few voters wanted to go beyond what the present legal limits allowed anyway. And the entire issue seemed to go away.

Affirmative Action   For months Clinton, George, and I had argued about affirmative action. George wanted the president to hold firm against Republican attacks and defend affirmative action. I feared this would permit Republicans a clear shot at us. I suggested basing affirmative action on income and residence in poor areas, not on race or gender. The president knew that supporting affirmative action might cost him conservative voters who would otherwise support him. But there was a political calculation on the other side. He knew if he wobbled on affirmative action he would be susceptible to an electoral challenge from Jesse Jackson, either as an independent or in the Democratic primaries. The political calculations balanced out, but Clinton ended up disregarding politics altogether. He grew up in the south and saw racism every day of his life. This was what made him determined to hold fast on affirmative action. He knew that racism in America is our mortal enemy. At the core of Clinton's being is his impoverished childhood. When he has to do things that hurt the poor—like budget cuts or welfare reform—he suffers physically with headaches and stomachaches. His mind accepts reason and politics, but his heart cannot.

He defused the issue politically by promising to reform affirmative action to eliminate racial quotas and assure that unqualified people are not hired. In this way he addressed America's core ideals, providing opportunity for those who would normally be passed by, but insisting on special privileges for none.

Race played no role in the 1996 presidential election even though anti-immigrant and anti-affirmative-action ballot propositions threatened to make it the most racial of recent contests. But Clinton helped to avert this polarization by addressing our values. In a survey right after his speech on affirmative action, we found that over three quarters of blacks *and* three quarters of whites felt that Clinton did not favor one race over the other.

Tobacco   Throughout the spring and the summer of 1995, I fought hard to extend the values agenda to include a ban on advertising tobacco products to teenagers. On other issues I raised with the president, I spoke as a political consultant, suggesting ways to help him win. But on tobacco, I was a zealot. My mother had smoked since the age of fourteen and died of cancer and heart disease. Vice President Gore's sister was another victim of the habit. He told me, in the summer of 1995, the same moving story of her death that touched so many Americans who heard his speech at the Democratic National Convention in August 1996.

In the meantime, David Kessler, commissioner of the Food and Drug Administration—FDA—had taken steps to evaluate whether nicotine is an addictive drug, and whether cigarettes as a drug-delivery vehicle, should be subject to federal regulation. Gore was following the issue closely and keeping the president briefed.

But tobacco controls the politics of North Carolina and Kentucky and heavily influences Tennessee, Virginia, and Georgia. Furthermore, the advertising industry is quite dependent on tobacco's four-billion-dollar-a-year ad budget. Advertising income from tobacco is vital to the survival of many newspapers, some of which may be inhibited by the connection. Through its lawyers, tobacco forced TV networks to trim their coverage of the issue rather than face huge legal fees. Convenience stores and some supermarket chains are also strong tobacco advocates. Yet tobacco kills hundreds of thousands of Americans a year.

At this rate, tobacco needs new addicts each year to replace those who have died. The most likely market is teenagers. About a million children start smoking each year, and a third of them eventually die of it.

Our polling revealed a broad public consensus that the tobacco industry should be barred from advertising to teenagers. People understood that tobacco ads are not aimed at persuading people to switch brands but toward encouraging children to pick up the habit.

I urged the president to challenge the industry to stop directing its ads to our children. I faced opposition among the president's inner circle. My budget-fight ally, Deputy Chief of Staff Erskine Bowles, is from North Carolina, and disagreed strongly. Well aware of the power of the industry in his home state, Erskine counseled against "fooling with them."

In the president's comeback, we had played only defense so far, dealing with Republican issues, like balancing the budget and reforming welfare. But as Winston Churchill said upon receiving England's praises for the brilliant evacuation of Britain's army from Dunkirk in World War II, "Wars are not won by evacuations."

"We must go on the offensive," I said to the president at our strategy meeting on July 12, 1995. "We need a new issue to make our own." I urged the president to support Kessler's likely conclusion that nicotine is addictive and take steps to restrict advertising directed at children.

The president was sympathetic. His mother, too, had died of cancer. But he was worried that "I'll make a speech, get applause, and then everyone else will forget about it, and I'll lose five states." He didn't realize how important a national issue tobacco would become if he gave it national exposure. I argued that this was not a one-day story. "This will be one of the three or four most decisive issues in the campaign," I predicted. "Once you elevate this to the level of a presidential decision, you will start a national crusade to stop teens from smoking."

Clinton was wary. "It'll cost me whatever chance I had in North Carolina. I won't win Virginia anyway. But I'm most concerned about Kentucky and Tennessee. I need those states."

Then Gore spoke up: "I can only speak for Tennessee, but when I voted to require warnings on cigarette packs, everyone said it would be my political death, but I went out and explained, 'This isn't good for you. It especially isn't good for kids, and I think we should warn everyone about the health hazards.' I remember I gave that speech in a small Tennessee town right in the middle of tobacco country, and they were nodding their heads as I spoke."

Doug Schoen was conducting polls at the time for Paul Patton, the ultimately successful Democratic candidate for governor of Kentucky. "Patton is afraid of the tobacco issue," Schoen said, "but my polling indicates that even in these tobacco states, as long as you are dealing only with advertising aimed at children, voters will strongly support you."

I showed the president survey data from each tobacco state indicating he could do well in those states even if he opposed children's access to tobacco. He assigned Bowles to learn how far the tobacco companies would go voluntarily. He wanted to see whether an agreement could be worked out. I was worried that the companies might agree to a limited package of measures and then not honor the agreement. I learned that their track record in living up to their commitments was not good.

Kessler formulated a series of strong measures, including a ban on all billboard ads featuring attractive come-ons, like Joe Camel, the Marlboro man, and thin Virginia Slims women. He wanted to restrict cigarette advertisements to black and white only and to words, not pictures. The FDA wanted to ban all displays in stores near schools and all promotions and giveaways, like T-shirts and caps, aimed at teenagers. It was a tough package and worth fighting for.

"You can make tobacco your equivalent of the drug issue," I said. "The public knows the guts it takes to fight this industry, and they will understand that you are breaking new ground."

Leon Panetta provided an important idea in June: "Since we can't get much through Congress," he said, "we should do what we can to take action on our own through executive orders."

I agreed and tried to help. This was the only way Clinton could exercise presidential power on domestic issues without the cooperation of Congress. Tobacco would be our first effort.

The problem was getting it done.

As usual, the best prod in Washington was the chance that you might lose control of the issue if you didn't act. David Kessler and the FDA scientists were ready to conclude that nicotine is, indeed, a drug and that cigarettes are therefore a drug-delivery device. Kessler was ready to propose far-reaching regulations to curb teen smoking. It became increasingly clear that the tobacco companies were not coming across with voluntary measures. They felt Clinton was certain to lose in 1996 and were waiting for a pro-tobacco Republican, like Dole, to win. So the time was right for presidential action.

And Clinton acted. He endorsed all the FDA regulations, in the summer of '95, and said that unless Congress enacted them as is, he would allow the FDA to assume jurisdiction over smoking.

Over the next few months, he came to see tobacco more and more as a major fight, which he was determined to win. As he learned more about the nexus of the Republican right and its links to the National Rifle Association and the tobacco industry, he began to see similarities between the battle against handguns and cigarettes: both were crucial efforts to protect children. His initial trepidation, natural for a president behind in the polls, gave way to courage and vision as he focused national attention on tobacco.

New evidence emerged suggesting even more strongly that tobacco companies had for decades deliberately concealed their knowledge of the addictive and harmful effects of smoking. Even more harrowing was the report that tobacco companies deliberately manipulated the level of nicotine in cigarettes to sustain addiction.

"You know," Clinton told me early in 1996, "I think we'll eventually get all our regulations approved in court, but I'll bet we drive teen smoking down anyway, just because of the attention we've focused on the issue."

"You'll have saved a couple of hundred thousand lives," I said. "It's just like with health-care reform. You said you wanted to cut the rate of medical inflation, so you asked for a huge reform package. Congress didn't pass a thing. But medical costs have dropped a lot since then, and I think you caused a lot of that by focusing public attention on the issue."

"I'll never get credit for that," he said glumly.

▲

The values agenda emerged fully in the president's 1996 State of the Union Address. This was a speech that changed everything. Before the speech, Clinton's rating was 50 percent favorable; after, it was 60 percent, and his job-approval rating rose from 55 percent to 60 percent. He moved from 47 percent of the vote and a nine-point margin to 53 percent of the vote and a seventeen-point margin. When he entered the House of Representatives to speak that night, he was a minority president; when he left, he was a majority president. And the changes lasted. Thereafter, until just before the election ten months later, the president never lost more than a few points of his share of the vote, his lead over Dole, his favorability rating, or his job-approval percentage. Polls following the State of the Union speech in January of 1996 revealed roughly the same numbers as in the fall general election. Through Whitewater, filegate, travelgate, Hillary's supposed seances, three terrorist bombings, reversals in the Middle East, the Republican primaries, the Republican Convention—through all the ups and the downs of Clinton's presidency in 1996, the numbers remained basically the same.

In following the values agenda, the president was really treading a path the First Lady had mapped out years before, with her focus on children's issues, women's concerns, and education. Her book, *It Takes a Village,* presaged many of the issues Clinton raised in the speech.

The public was tired of the budget battle and I had little difficulty in persuading the president that we should change the subject. Clinton was surprised at first when I urged him to spend only a few moments in his State of the Union Address on the budget, but soon realized this was wise. People were bored by it.

I had more difficulty emphasizing values over economic issues. Ever since the New Deal, the economy had been the basis of the Democratic party. For Democrats to run on social-values issues, as opposed to economic concerns, was like feeding the donkey peanuts and the elephant hay.

But polling showed that 65 percent of voters thought that "values" issues such as crime, school discipline, TV violence, and curbs on tobacco advertising were the most important. Only 30 percent felt economic issues like wages, benefits, jobs, wage stagnation, and imports were more important. The polling also showed we already had the votes of those who felt the economic issues were important—they were our base. But we were still losing among those who gave values preference. They were the voters we had to persuade.

Over the months, the focus of the administration shifted more and more to values and away from the traditional economic arena. ‚

In the end, the values agenda succeeded in laying out a new plan of action for the country, one that America focused on during the months before the election. But deciding what ideas to promote and how to present them was not easy in the Clinton White House.

I wanted us to address the values agenda three or four times a week. First, though, we had to identify through polls which values were important to Americans. Once the president gave his approval, we developed concrete proposals to support each value with government action. Then came the hard part: getting our proposals approved by the relevant agencies and White House staffers. After that, we'd have to schedule an event at which the president could speak. We'd review the issue with press secretary Mike McCurry so he could underscore its importance to the press.

Each issue presented unique problems. Here are a few:

Handguns and Domestic Violence   Tom Freedman showed me legislation being introduced in Congress by Senator Frank Lautenberg and Congressman Bob Torricelli, two New Jersey Democrats, to prohibit the sale of handguns to anyone with a felony or misdemeanor conviction for domestic violence. Since tens of thousands of incidents of domestic violence are committed with guns every year, the issue was a natural for us. Under the current law, felons are not allowed to buy handguns, but since most domestic-violence convictions are misdemeanors, convicted wife abusers, for example, are not barred from buying this type of firearm. We knew that by extending the handgun issue into the realm of domestic violence, we could develop a family-friendly issue that Dole couldn't embrace because of his ties to the NRA—the National Rifle Association, the leading opponent of gun controls.

Voters strongly approved, and I brought the issue up at a meeting.

The president said he liked the idea, but worried that the NRA could arouse voters by maintaining that this was another step down the "slippery slope of gun control." Someone else was worried that it would be unfair to bar someone from owning a handgun if the conviction was far in the past. HUD secretary Cisneros worried that this stand would further inflame rural voters' against the president.

In the next week's polling, I composed an argument for the NRA's opposition to the measure, saying it was a step toward banning all guns, but even in this light the proposal won the voters' enthusiasm. The polling showed, however, that voters felt the restriction would be fairer if limited only to persons convicted of domestic violence in the past ten years rather than to any person with a conviction. I reported all this at our next meeting.

Cisneros had by then tested the idea on a recent trip to the West and, as a result of his findings, endorsed the concept. Clinton, though, was still nervous.

I did not know why the president hesitated until I read the text of his most recent stump speech and followed his tortuous explanation of why the Brady bill and the assault-weapons ban would not stop any legitimate hunter from owning a rifle. I raised the issue in a phone call a few nights later, and in a third poll I included, almost verbatim, the concerns Clinton had expressed. They had no basis in political reality.

At our next meeting, the president approved the idea.

Now, to air it. Originally, I suggested that we announce it at a meeting of the NAACP in North Carolina. Dole was boycotting this forum and had recently tried to reverse his long-standing commitment to repeal the assault-weapons ban. I reasoned that it was good to seize a high-profile opportunity to strike back with this issue. But Alexis Herman, an African-American aide in charge of outreach to constituency groups, felt that to make this proposal at a meeting of a black organization would suggest that domestic violence is a special problem for the black community—and would touch on the sensitive O. J. Simpson case. So I backed down.

We next proposed to announce it during a West Coast tour in June. But Rahm Emanuel, who handled our law-and-order issues, had been in touch with police groups who told him they might not endorse Clinton because many policeman might be affected by this proposal. Rahm subsequently explained that police officers themselves would not be subject to this ban if they otherwise qualified for police work. The police groups relented, but only after Clinton's California trip.

Finally, we made the issue the centerpiece of the first day of the president's August train trip to Chicago for the Democratic National Convention. It was well received but soon faded. I hope a Democratic Congress passes it eventually.

Television Violence   In the seven months following the State of the Union Address, President Clinton laid out a program concerning families, children, and safety.

One priority was to curb TV violence. Tom Freedman first introduced me to the work of FCC chairman Reed Hundt, who is leading the most sweeping effort to reform television programming since the days of Newton Minow. Vice President Gore took the lead in convincing the TV networks to adopt a voluntary rating system to help parents choose which violent and sexually explicit programs to screen out using the V-chip—the violence chip—which the president succeeded in requiring in all new television sets. Two television networks, ABC and CBS, had recently merged, Capital Cities/ABC with the Walt Disney Company and CBS with Westinghouse Electric Corporation. We reasoned that Disney would not want to be seen as taking an anti-family position by rejecting the voluntary-rating proposal. But negotiations went nowhere, and the networks tenaciously resisted our suggestions to upgrade their programming or initiate a self-structured rating system.

On the values issues, each medium had its bias. Newspapers were often wary of our attacks on tobacco. For TV news, attacking tobacco was fine because cigarette ads are banned from television. But when it came to criticizing TV programming, the networks had an enormous capacity to work against us.

I suggested that we play hardball by using the State of the Union speech to call network executives to a summit meeting with the president and the vice president at the White House, even without any private commitments from them to adopt the voluntary rating system. I felt that if we put them on the spot before the entire nation, they would bow to public opinion. I reasoned that if the networks agreed to a rating system, we would get the credit. If they resisted, we could scold them publicly. At a strategy meeting my proposal was greeted with derision. An anonymous leaker placed an item in one of the papers citing the idea I had proposed as an example of my folly. Many who attended the strategy meeting were concerned that we would alienate the networks and would regret it during the campaign. There was a tremendous fear of "taking on the networks." McCurry even wondered whether our pressure in this area would discourage the TV networks from letting the president address the nation on national television in the future.

At first, Gore felt that he could achieve more by negotiations, but ultimately he came around to backing the idea of putting the stations on the spot by inviting them to a summit during the State of the Union Address. The device worked, and when the TV executives came to the White House on February 29, 1996, they fell all over themselves to show how eager they were to institute a rating system.

Many doubt that parents will actually use the V-chip. But I think they will. Our polls showed extensive parental concern about TV violence, more than enough to induce the average mother or father to overcome technophobia and use the chip. Will the kids outsmart their parents? Certainly, and the technology race will resume.

But on our second demand, that the networks offer a minimum of three hours of educational programming per week for children, they were intransigent. With cutbacks in public broadcasting, it was very important that the commercial networks create programs like *Sesame Street* to help educate children. In the spring of 1996, Andrew Barrett announced his impending retirement from the Federal Communications Commission, giving Reed Hundt, the commission's progressive-minded chairman, a working majority on the board once the president made the next appointment. It was only the threat of this change in the balance of the FCC that induced the TV networks to announce a program of "voluntary" compliance with the three-hour requirement.

Still outstanding are the administration's request for a family viewing hour between eight and nine every night, when the programs would be devoid of sex and violence, and its request that networks censor programs aimed at very young children—like *Mighty Morphin Power Rangers*—to reduce the amount of violence they depict. I became aware of the monstrous violence in shows like this when Mary Smith, of my staff, recorded the number of deaths and the form of death in each ten-minute segment of the program. The casualties mounted and each was portrayed more hideously than the one before. Yet, TV networks continue to oppose these reforms, but with the pro-reform Clinton appointees controlling the FCC, their opposition is likely to be overridden.

College-Tuition Tax Credit   The enormous public support we had found for the president's proposal to make college tuition tax deductible remained very much in the president's mind as he constructed his values agenda. "We just never penetrated with that proposal," he said. "It got lost in the debate about how large the tax cut should be. But I still think it's a great idea; we should talk about it more."

I told the president that I thought we should simplify the idea. "About two thirds of the people don't even file long forms with the IRS," I said. "They don't understand tax deduction. It's free or it isn't."

With this in mind, I asked Education secretary Dick Riley about college tuition, and was surprised to find out that on average, community colleges generally charge only about twelve hundred dollars a year for tuition. Based on this information, we came up with the idea of offering a twelve-hundred-dollar-a-year tax credit for the first two years of college instead of a tax deduction. Later the proposal grew to a fifteen-hundred-dollar-a-year tax credit for each of the first two years of college.

I reported this to the president, saying it "makes it possible for you to extend the frontier of free public education up to the fourteenth grade." I compared our initiative to Horace Mann's nineteenth-century advocacy of free public schools.

The president was intrigued by this way of urging that everyone go to college.

"We should say that high school isn't enough anymore and that college must now become as universal as high school," I argued.

"Education has now replaced race or gender as the best predictor of future income," Clinton, drawing on his photographic memory, retorted. "I really like this idea."

"What if we emphasize educational standards by requiring a B average in high school to get the tax credit?" I suggested.

"Or make them maintain a certain average in college to keep the credit," the president replied. "I think it's better if we let everybody in but make them keep up their studies to stay in."

I took the president's ideas back to Riley, my best friend in the Cabinet. He is delicate, aristocratic, and formal but friendly, my idea of a southern gentleman. In his department, policy was often shrouded in the jargon of social scientists and educators, but he cut through it and made sure his goals were expressed in plain English, a language not always used by federal bureaucrats.

The president's economic advisers—National Economic Adviser Laura D'Andrea Tyson; Treasury secretary Robert Rubin; Labor secretary Robert Reich; Budget Director Alice Rivlin; and Joseph Stiglitz, chairman of the Council of Economic Advisers—reviewed the idea. Then the objections began. Tyson and Rubin felt it was opening the Treasury door to pass out goodies before the election. Rubin didn't see the point of giving the aid through a tax cut or a credit. "If we want to help people go to college, let's just increase the scholarship program," the Treasury secretary told me.

"Politically," I replied, "people want us to downsize government, so we are developing ways of cutting taxes but achieving social good at the same time."

Rubin argued that tax cuts are an inefficient way of providing help. He said scholarships could be better targeted. I answered that more scholarships would add to bureaucracy, that we needed to seize the public's imagination, not with a scholarship they might or might not get but with a way to make the first two years of college free.

Rubin dismissed the idea as "political"—the most venal word in his vocabulary.

So was the GI Bill, I said to myself. A major national program that opened wide the doors of community colleges would encourage hundreds of thousands of new students and give us a way to defeat Dole's tax-cut plans. "Politically," I argued, "we need a tax cut to beat the tax cut we expect Dole to propose. We can't outbid him because we're not willing to cut taxes without identifying how to pay for them. But a college-tuition tax credit will be a whole lot cheaper and a lot more attractive than an across-the-board tax cut."

Rivlin worried about setting the academic requirements too high. Riley worried that states that had kept their tuitions low might raise them to the level allowed by the tax credit and pocket the extra money. Reich proposed that anyone returning to community college as an adult for extra job training get the same tax credit. The president loved the Reich idea and modified the plan to include it.

Eventually, everyone had talked himself or herself into wanting to postpone the idea for further study—everyone except the president and me. I met with Tyson and her staff, who argued that this was a bad idea and should be considered without any deadline pressure. I said I had the impression the president wanted to go with it, but this seemed to make no difference. They kept on debating the finer points. I repeated that the president wanted to go ahead. Still no response. Finally, I said that the president—"You remember him—tall, gray hair, southern accent?"—wants to do this and would appreciate your help. One of Rivlin's staffers walked out in a huff and I suspect that he later leaked to the press that the president was putting political considerations first and that I wanted to raid the Treasury to get him reelected.

The controversy simmered until Gene Sperling prepared a formal memo for Clinton. Sperling knew that the president wanted to go ahead with the plan, so he included some options to that effect. Clinton swept all objections aside and announced the plan, with minor modifications, in a speech at Princeton University's commencement exercises in June 1996. The program became a centerpiece of his campaign—and a great example of presidential leadership.

In the meantime, these battles with the White House staff were changing my personality. I was becoming harsh and inconsiderate. Eileen noticed it but felt powerless to change it. I was becoming a different person.

Family Leave   The idea of allowing family and medical leave from work—without pay but without losing the job, either—has long been popular with Americans. Current law allows parents to take up to twelve weeks off to be with a newborn or adopted child or with a sick child or an elderly relative, but we wanted to improve it.

We found a way in an amendment the Republicans tried to use to defeat the minimum wage increase we wanted and they opposed. They tried to tack three amendments onto the bill hoping these poison pills would force a veto. Two were bad ideas: barring union money for campaigns and letting employers set up bargaining units of employees. The third amendment, however, was good: it allowed workers the option of receiving overtime in either money or time off.

I brought the idea up with the president, who liked it immediately. I polled it, and the voters agreed. But the unions raised hell. Articulating their case at a strategy meeting, Ickes, who had been a labor lawyer, said, "Employees won't ever get to take the time off. They'll be bullied by their employers into turning down the overtime pay, and when they want to take time off, the bosses won't let them have it."

But the president said, "I don't agree with all these theories that the workplace is crawling with plots and conspiracies. I think most employers are in good faith, and I think most workers are too. With some protections, this can work out just fine."

Ickes said the unions might think twice about helping Democrats if this bill passed and the president signed it. With some heat, Clinton turned to him and said, "I'm the president around here. It's my decision. If anybody wants to make threats, they can go to hell. I want us to do this."

I applauded inwardly. As the months passed, the president spoke more and more bluntly. In 1995, he let people talk and tried to guide them toward his way of thinking. In 1996, more confident, presidential, he told them what he wanted them to do in sharp, aggressive terms.

We decided to couple this initiative with an expansion of family and medical leave. I proposed that we cover businesses with twenty-five to fifty employees (the law now covered only those businesses with more than fifty workers). Senator Chris Dodd of Connecticut, who joined our strategy meetings in 1996, warned about the impact on the small-business vote. I did some polling and found that owners of small businesses didn't feel the proposed change would be much of a burden and that about 20 percent of voters worked for businesses with twenty-five to fifty workers.

But with the flak the president was receiving on the overtime proposal, I didn't press the issue. At Mark Penn's suggestion we did propose expanding family leave to include four hours off every month for children's doctor's appointments or parent-teacher conferences. Tyson objected, saying that four hours per month was too much; she wanted a cap at two hours per month. I felt she was being unreasonable. Why shouldn't parents have this extra time to care for their children? We compromised on four hours in any one month, but with an annual cap of twenty-four hours per year.

Teen Pregnancy   Sometimes we chickened out. I was interested in seeing whether voters had matured on issues relating to sexual matters to the point where they would accept birth-control programs in schools. In Arkansas, Clinton had shown real courage in implementing a program to distribute condoms in high schools to children whose parents had consented. I hoped a similar program would be popular nationally. "Until we get real and give out birth control in schools, you'll never crack teen pregnancy," I said to the president.

"We've got to couple it with an abstinence program to encourage kids to postpone sex," he answered.

"Politically, sure," I said, "but abstinence is hopeless. Kids will have sex whatever anybody says."

"It's got to be in the program," Clinton concluded.

I polled it and found that about 60 percent of the respondents favored condom distribution, and when we coupled distribution with parental permission and with promoting abstinence, 64 percent of respondents were in favor.

Clinton liked the idea of parental permission "except in dysfunctional families," he interjected. "You've got to have an exception for families that don't work right."

When I asked voters which they would favor more, programs that promoted abstinence or those that distributed birth-control materials, they backed the birth-control program by two to one.

But now I lost my nerve. I told Clinton that it was an important idea, but we could not dare to go into an election urging birth-control distribution without at least 70 percent support. "After you are elected, I think this should be one of your top priorities," I urged, "but it's too risky now." The president agreed.

Education Standards   The president's recommendation that communities consider curfews—which he framed by saying that his mother told him, "When the lights come on, be home, Bill"—was widely acclaimed. He suggested school uniforms, an idea he warmed to slowly. "As I go around and see what difference these uniforms make," he said, "I think we're really on to something. There are no gang colors, and the girls don't dress in tight clothes. It's a good idea, I'm really getting into it."

But his recommendation, delivered at the National Governors Association meeting on March 26, 1996, that states adopt mandatory statewide student testing as a precondition for promotion or graduation was a cop-out. The president really wanted to *require* states to pass such tests, but found that there wasn't the base of public support for such enforcement. So we confined ourselves to urging states to adopt testing requirements.

Where we really defaulted, though, was in not demanding an end to tenure for schoolteachers. If the Republicans had run on this plank, rather than bashing teachers' unions and calling for school choice, they could have taken the education issue away from us, a key step for Dole. Polls showed that people fiercely resent tenure. When teachers' wages were low, tenure made sense, but now teachers in some states earn more than sixty thousand dollars a year on average. Voters resent this and want to be able to demand top performance from well-paid teachers— tenure or no. But the teachers' unions were too powerful for Clinton to oppose, and we never seriously considered this important idea.

Dole's proposal for school vouchers for private and parochial schools scared Clinton. He realized that this, combined with his veto of the late-term abortion prohibition, could cause major Catholic defections. My initial polls showed that voters backed Dole's plan by about 55–35. The president and I spent an hour on the phone one day pondering what arguments we could use to oppose Dole's plan. The president never thought of flipping on the issue and backing vouchers, but he did want to know how to defeat the proposal in debate. We found that when voters realized that the money for the private and parochial schools would come from the elimination of the Department of Education, voters rebelled and quickly turned against the plan. Voters felt that aid to Catholic schools and other religious or private schools was fine as long as it didn't come from funds that would otherwise go to public schools. The president used this argument effectively in the second debate with Dole to answer the voucher plan.

It was a big battle to get White House approval for the president's early July '96 proposal for federal funding for school construction. Though the public strongly backed this program and the president was keen to do it at once, virtually everyone else was against it. Even Secretary of Education Riley worried that brick and mortar was not the place to put education dollars. Treasury secretary Rubin and Laura Tyson opposed providing federal school construction aid. Gene Sperling, who piloted the idea to eventual approval, worried that the funds might subsidize existing construction and not result in new building. As he was doing more and more often in 1996, the president brushed aside these objections and announced the program with few modifications, although he did require that funding go only to new projects rather than projects already under way.

Crime   The biggest problem we encountered in getting tough criminal-justice measures approved was the attorney general, Janet Reno. Repeatedly, Reno and other Justice Department officials set up roadblocks. It was hard to understand why.

I proposed and the president agreed to the requirement that a trigger lock be purchased along with firearms so that children wouldn't kill one another or themselves when playing with their father's guns. The Justice Department opposed this idea.

Then the president wanted to increase penalties for persons under twenty-one found carrying a handgun. Reno said no and, I was told, even threatened to resign if the idea were promoted.

She also opposed the suggestion of a constitutional amendment giving crime victims rights equal to those of the defendants, but the president endorsed it over her strenuous objections—and those of Senator Chris Dodd.

For years, U.S. attorneys had been using the RICO (Racketeer Influenced and Corrupt Organizations) Act to go after teen gangs, as they have used it to tackle mob and drug-cartel cases. The Justice Department killed a proposal for a press conference in which the president wanted to highlight this strategy and recommend it to other U.S. attorneys. On this, though, the attorney general later relented.

Perhaps the most vivid example of Clinton's difficulties with Reno came in June 1996, when the FBI, concluding a special analysis, found that the juvenile murder rate was actually dropping, contrary to the widespread view that it was skyrocketing. Rahm Emanuel planned for the president to make a statement about juvenile crime at the same time the FBI released this data. It was to be a big California event.

Earlier in the week, though, Rahm had urged us to announce a gun-tracking program, having forgotten, as we all had, that we had already announced such a plan. We tried to cover our tracks by explaining that this was a stepped-up plan, but still we were embarrassed. Rahm was one of the only people who fought to get ideas out to the public, and this was one of his very few missteps.

Reno, nevertheless, was angry. She felt *her* Justice Department had been misused for political purposes. So she withheld the data on juvenile crime. "She'll come across with it next week," Rahm assured me; "she just wants to screw up Clinton's trip to California so she can punish us for the gun-tracking story." His prediction was accurate.

I have never understood why she opposed these steps. I never asked her directly, but every time we came up with a tough crime proposal, we'd worry that Reno would try to shoot it down.

Gay Marriages The president was deeply committed to laws protecting gays against discrimination, but he supported allowing states to ban gay marriages if they wanted to, saying this was none of Washington's business. When the Republicans introduced legislation giving states the right not to recognize gay marriages sanctioned in other states, Clinton was determined to sign it. The issue arose because Hawaii was on the verge of allowing gay marriages and thus, without legislation of the kind proposed, the other forty-nine states must accord marital rights to gays married in Hawaii but living in other states.

At a strategy meeting, I suggested that if the president wanted to sign the bill, as he said he did, then he should say so publicly right away. "Now the Republicans have a bill we can sign. But if we wait to back it, they'll probably tack all sorts of anti-gay amendments onto it that you'll find difficult to sign," I said to the president. "So before they go to committee and add all kinds of other restrictions to the bill, let's get on record as favoring the principle."

George Stephanopoulos said that some White House staffers might oppose the president's position. "I think we can work it out," George said, "but we need some time to smooth it out."

The president responded unusually sharply. "Well, I get a vote, don't I? I mean I'm the president, so I get a vote, don't I? Don't I?" he persisted. "Well my vote says I'm going to sign that bill, and I want to announce it right away so there's no confusion about my position. And if there are people here who don't like it, well, I've created seven and a half million new jobs and maybe it's time for them to go out and take some of them."

The room quieted. Press secretary Mike McCurry announced the president's position a few days later.

▲

This values agenda, which stretched over eight months, was the mainstay of Clinton's reelection campaign. Trivialized in the press as "small bore," it nevertheless showed voters what an activist president could do for the average person with the help of Congress and often without it. With each of these proposals, Clinton delivered a message of relevance to the lives of the people that had not really been offered in more than a decade.

I told the president, "We'll have our hundred days, just as FDR did, but ours will come at the end, not at the beginning."

In seven months, at breakneck pace, the president spoke of curfews for teenagers, uniforms for schoolchildren, and truancy enforcement. He proposed government funding for a massive program to renovate and build schools. With little funding but by catalyzing private contributions, he wired most California schools for computers and set a course for completing the job nationwide by 2000. To promote state standards in education, he urged that students be required to pass standardized tests to graduate or be promoted. Through tuition tax credits, he extended the frontier of free public education through the end of "the fourteenth grade." He called for schools to be open nights and weekends to serve as community centers. And he called for a massive program to ensure that children could read by the time they were in the third grade.

Community watch groups were given cellular telephones by the telecommunications industry at the president's prompting to report crimes in progress. Men with sex-crime records were tracked across state lines. Deportations of illegal aliens were set to double from 1992 levels by the end of 1996. The president proposed a constitutional amendment to protect the rights of victims. He said he'd withhold federal funds from states that didn't regularly drug-test parolees.

Clinton issued an executive order requiring teen mothers on welfare to work or be in school and to live at home. He signed legislation assuring a tax credit for adoption. He urged that hospitals allow women to stay more than twenty-four hours after giving birth.

Homeowners saw Federal Housing Authority closing fees lowered by one thousand dollars. The president proposed that employees be able to choose time off rather than extra pay for overtime, and he called for the expansion of family leave to provide time off for a child's medical needs or for school visits.

Deadbeat dads will now have their photos displayed in post offices, their federal benefits can be garnished, and Clinton has asked that the IRS be permitted to pursue them.

Meat inspection was upgraded for the first time in decades to permit microscopic inspection. Tougher pesticide restrictions were enacted, and a major bill for cleaner drinking water was signed into law. Yellowstone Park was saved from mining, and the president doubled the cleanup of superfund toxic-waste sites.

All in seven months.

Many proposals, however, didn't make it through the vetting process.

I wanted to cut the capital-gains tax to 20 percent. Deputy Treasury secretary Larry Summers suggested it and said that it would cost nothing because it would stimulate sales of assets and would actually net an extra ten billion dollars over seven years as long as it was not retroactive. It made political and financial sense. Senator John

Breaux, a friend and ally, checked it out with congressional tax experts, who agreed it would cost nothing but were less optimistic about revenue growth. I couldn't see why we shouldn't repeal a tax that yielded no money. Liberals argued it was important to maintain the tax, but I never really grasped why. The idea died when the president signed welfare-reform legislation. I agreed that cutting benefits to the poor while cutting taxes for the rich seemed too Republican a package for us.

I wanted to announce a "voluntary" agreement by banks to institute new safety standards at automatic teller machines—ATMs. Criminals often wait at night to prey on those who leave these machines with their wallets full. The safety standards are simple. Former Brooklyn district attorney—and former client—Elizabeth Holtzman, herself a victim of ATM crime, suggested video cameras that work and are out of reach, proper lighting, and windows through which passersby can see what is going on inside. Treasury secretary Rubin was supposed to pressure banks to agree to these standards, but he never really did, and the idea never went anywhere.

Panetta objected to the furious pace of these proposals and pleaded for a slowdown to allow more time for vetting. But the president wanted a constant flow of ideas, so Leon sped up the approval process to get it done.

Bill Clinton was always puzzled by the public's appetite for government to help while, at the same time, claiming to want less government. One evening at a strategy meeting he told us about a "speech" he planned to give offering assistance to a state after a particularly bad storm. Grinning, he read his "statement":

My fellow Americans, I know how much damage and devastation you have suffered as a result of the recent storms in your state. I know that many of you have lost your homes or your businesses. There has even been some loss of life. Everything in me cries out for giving you the most assistance I can offer in helping you to rebuild your lives. But I know how you vote, and I know how you think. I respect your opinions. I know that you believe that government, particularly at the federal level, cannot help people and always just gets in the way. I know that you believe that the less government the better, and I don't want to ask you to violate your principles at a time like this. You want government to leave you alone, to stay out of your lives. So tonight I say to you, Good-bye and good luck.

▲

Why didn't the Republicans adopt the values agenda as their campaign idea, especially as they saw us steal the center on their traditional fiscal, welfare, and crime issues? Why didn't Republican pollsters tread the same path I did?

I believe that the reason is that Republican consultants are not accustomed to breaking new ground on issues. Bill Buckley's writings of the 1950s, the themes of the Reagan Revolution, and the Contract with America were their substantive texts. There was no need to add on. Republican consultants generally confined their advice to strategic and tactical questions of how to sell their agenda and candidates. They never got a mandate to develop policy or programs.

But Clinton was exploring new turf, an expansion in the agenda of his party. He was not confined by any preexisting dogma and used polling extensively to pinpoint public concerns and test approval for his proposed solutions. My mandate clearly involved the development of policy options and program alternatives for the president to consider as he made his decisions.

I came to love our weekly polls of America. I saw them as a chance to chat with the country. In over a hundred polls, I got to know Americans very well. It was one of the most exciting opportunities to learn I have ever had.

Baiting the Radical Right   As we articulated a values agenda, I wanted to make the traditional Republican social priorities less attractive to voters. While generally I urged moderation in the president's positions, I strongly backed aggressive and confrontational positions on abortion, gun control, and the militia movement. By showing the right wing at its very worst, we undermined the Republican claim on the center.

I strongly urged a firm stand in favor of the confirmation of Dr. Henry Foster for Surgeon General and a veto of the partial-birth abortion prohibition passed by the Republican Congress. In both cases, the Republicans lost ground simply by raising the issue and demonstrating their hardheaded opposition to allowing women freedom of choice.

I worked hard to expand gun controls in areas where the public wanted them. Beyond the proposal Clinton made to prohibit those convicted of domestic violence from handgun ownership, I pushed recommendations that the President has not (yet) embraced. One was my suggestion that the purchase of trigger locks be required with all gun sales. At the urging of my staffer Matt Levine, I suggested a federal law akin to a Virginia statute prohibiting the purchase of more than one handgun per month to stop residents of tough gun control states from coming to states with weaker laws and stocking up with firearms for illegal resale back home. Finally, I suggested that special "arsenal" licenses be required for those who owned more than a certain number of guns.

These positions were designed to bait the right-wing hate and pressure groups for greater activity, so they would influence public perceptions of the Republican Party. I also felt that the more enraged and energized these organizations became, the more likely they would be to dominate the Republican nominating process and give us an opponent whom we could challenge over these issues.

The Republican Party has the same problem today that the Democrats had in the 1980s—anyone who can win the election can't win the Republican nomination. It is as trapped by its right wing as the Democratic Party of 1972, 1984, and 1988 was by its left. Centrist figures like General Colin Powell and Lamar Alexander will likely have to remain on the sidelines as more conservative candidates like Jack Kemp win the nomination and lose the election.

The very positions that make right wingers attractive to Republican Primary voters turn off the general electorate. While Nixon played his silent majority off against images of youthful flag-burners, draft-dodgers, and pot-smokers, Democrats can play off extreme pro-lifers, handgun-owners, tobacco-lobbyists, and militiamen.

The Presidential Vacation

Sometimes I carried polling too far. One good example was my insistence on using data to give the president unsolicited advice on what he should do during his August vacation. "This is the one time the public really gets to see you with your family without any overt message," I enthused.

In a previous vacation, the president had gone to Martha's Vineyard, where photos of him on a yacht with Jacqueline Onassis did not help his populist image one bit. I was on a populist kick, having just finished reading *The Populist Persuasion* by Michael Kazin, which traces the history of populism through the past hundred years. I gave the president the book, in which I had marked the key pages I thought he should read with special focus.

Kazin identifies nine populist eras in our history. Three of these—the original populism of the farmers and William Jennings Bryan, their advocate in the 1890s; the formation of unions in the trade crafts, which culminated in the American Federation of Labor (AFL) in the early years of the century; and the development of unions in steel, coal, and other basic industries in the 1930s, which became the Congress of Industrial Organizations (CIO)—the author calls "economic populism." I would have added the tax-rebellion populism of the 1980s Reagan era to the list.

Kazin also identifies six "social populist movements": Prohibition in the '20s, Father Coughlin's Catholic populism of the '30s, McCarthyism in the '50s, the student rebellion of the '60s, George Wallace and his racist cohorts of '68, and Nixon's Silent Majority in the '70s.

Democrats base their party on economic populism while Republicans use social populism instead. Kazin's basic point is that economic populism is declining, while social populism is rising. The enemy of economic populism is wealth and privilege. The enemy of social populism is the intellectual and cultural elite.

"By yachting off the Vineyard with Jackie O and Carly Simon, you offend the social populists," I stressed.

Mark Penn noted "you are doing badly with married people with kids. This is the time to show your family all together doing the things the average voters would do."

Penn wasn't going to leave this to chance, either. He had a theory that we could identify swing voters for an especially intensive phone and mail campaign we were planning. But swing voters are hard to find. The constitutional requirement of a secret ballot makes their identities a matter fit for a private detective. The usual way of finding them is by examining the past voting histories of the smallest election units possible—precincts, or election districts. If the voters in such a small area—usually about a city block—vote for a Republican one year and a Democrat the next, they are likely to be swing voters, the ones most easy to persuade.

But Penn had a unique way of finding swing voters. In his corporate consulting he had used lifestyle preferences to help identify customers most likely to switch brands. Market researchers have divided Americans into more than forty lifestyle groups, and have given them special names: Pools and Patios denotes middle-income, white, married suburbanites with children; Caps and Gowns refers to urban intellectuals generally living near universities. The marketing industry has even checked out the census tracts—very small units; again, about as big as a city block—in which the various lifestyle clusters reside.

So now Penn proposed that we do a huge national survey—ten thousand interviews—questioning people on specific aspects of their lifestyles. How often do you go to the movies? What movies do you like? Do you bowl? Are you a hunter? Do you play tennis? What is your attitude toward religion? Have you been divorced? And so on. His idea was to place each of the ten thousand interviewees into one of the lifestyle categories. Then he would ask the respondents whether they preferred Clinton or Dole. From this data, he would determine which five or six of the lifestyle clusters comprised swing voters. For example, he might find out that Caps and Gowns were overwhelmingly Clinton voters—no need to target them. But he might also find that Pools and Patios were evenly divided between Dole and Clinton—exactly the type of voter we were looking for. Using a map that identified where each of these lifestyle clusters were located, he could find the swing voters and reach them before election day.

The president was intrigued. He laughed at the plan's pretensions even as he believed it would work and he appreciated the technology and the psychology that made it possible. It was Gore, though, who most appreciated Penn's work. He and Penn talked on and on about the capabilities of this system—anything involving technology captured the vice president's attention. He's a grown-up computer geek, I thought.

Once when I had gone to the vice president's office about something I found vitally important—as usual—he had said, "Look at this," ignoring my urgency as he tapped on his computer keyboard. "See," he said. "Let's see if there are any stories today about Dick Morris." He tapped my name into his machine and pushed a button. Nothing happened. Embarrassed, he sat at the machine, determined to make it work. After three of four minutes of grunts and snorts, he gave up and began our now hurried meeting. But for the next five minutes, he might as well not have been there; I could see that he was trying to figure out what he had done wrong with his computer.

Now, as Clinton pondered his 1995 vacation, we put Penn's system to use. We learned that hunters were, of course, for Dole, MTV viewers for Clinton. But baseball fans were swing voters. So were hikers and people who love technology. Camping out was a favorite for swing voters.

At substantial risk of rejection and ridicule, which would have been appropriate, I presented the strategy group with a list of approved presidential activities for his coming vacation. I urged that he take a mountain vacation, that he hike and camp out in a tent. Golf, though a Dole-voter activity, was a presidential necessity, and so we compensated by noting that we would have to publicize the high-tech gear the president would be using on his vacation.

Clinton was not happy. This was carrying things too far. "Can I golf?" he asked in a question dripping with sarcasm. "Maybe if I wear a baseball cap?" he bargained.

"You're going to golf anyway," I answered glumly.

He began to pose hypotheticals. "What if I hike, set up my campsite, and go fishing but I don't catch anything? Will that be OK?"

I deserved the ribbing. This advice was the ultimate in carrying polling to a mindless extreme. Nevertheless, on his vacation he did camp in a tent. He did hike in the national parks. But, damn, he also golfed! No wonder at this stage we were still behind Dole!

"That's the first vacation I've taken that didn't help me in the polls," Clinton said irritably upon his return. "The first one. After all my *other* vacations, I've always risen a point or two. *This* vacation I didn't go up at all." He was rubbing in that I had gone too far with my poll-driven advice and I took his complaints in good spirits.

But, I felt, he was also bitter about the way his public life had intruded on his private time, especially his time with Chelsea. I heard more than sarcasm in his complaints; I heard pain, and I regretted having contributed to it.

Also in the interests of maintaining the president's populist image, I tried to keep him away from Hollywood and the jet set. In 1996, he and Hillary were invited to Martha's Vineyard for the wedding of their longtime Hollywood friend Mary Steenburgen, formerly of Arkansas, and Ted Danson of *Cheers*. At a meeting with Panetta I groaned when I heard about this. Leon helpfully suggested that it was hurricane season and maybe the president wouldn't be able fly up there. Then Stephanopoulos and I began plotting. But there was no way to talk Hillary out of it. I tried and got burned in the process. "We're their friends, and we're going," she said.

We did succeed in limiting the time they were on the Vineyard and arranged to follow the visit with a trip to the Boston area and with a statement about protecting police officers. I also asked Hillary's advance people to try to avoid photos of the president or First Lady with any of the many film stars present.

Leon's meteorological instinct worked the best. There was, indeed, a hurricane. The storm didn't stop the Clintons from going to the wedding, but it did force their early return. Coverage of the wedding was all but drowned out by the focus on Hurricane Opal.

During the president's 1996 vacation in the Rockies Clinton called me and asked, "I want to take Chelsea rafting. She really likes it. Do you think it's OK?"

"Is it dangerous?" I asked. I didn't know what he was getting at.

"No, there's no danger," he said, "but do you think they'll make a joke of it?"

I was dense, but then I got it. "You mean about white-water rafting?" I ventured.

"Yeah."

"No sir, go rafting. Even if they joke about it, they'll have to write that you went rafting, and that will be good for you politically."

Chelsea is as unaffected by her parents' status as it is possible for a president's daughter to be. She has a clear sense of herself, of who she is, and she marches to her own beat. For virtually her entire life, she has been either a governor's daughter in a small state where the governor is the center of attention or the president's daughter. Yet there is no trace of conceit, arrogance, or class consciousness about her. She knows that her status is temporary and that it is based on her parents' achievements, not her's. She knows that she'll have to make her own way in the world when all this is over.

I have known her since she first trotted into our meetings at the Arkansas governor's mansion. She had beautiful curly blond hair. As a teenager, she is good-natured, smart, and mannerly. When I called the president at the White House residence and she answered the phone, she always dutifully checked to see whether her father could come to the phone, and she took down messages precisely.

During a meeting I was having with the president in 1993, she and a friend burst into the Oval Office, soaking wet. As a Secret Service guard trudged after the pair, Chelsea excitedly announced, "We were kayaking and we capsized."

The president laughed at the sight of his bedraggled daughter and corrected her firmly but nicely. "Are you going to say hello to Mr. Morris?" he asked.

The Secret Service man did not appear amused.

During Christmas week in 1995, I had an appointment to see the president in the White House residence for a political chat, and I asked permission to bring our niece, Katie Maxwell, with me to meet the president. Hillary was delighted.

Katie, a fourteen-year-old all-American-kid-type child, entered the residence with me, and together we waited in the Map Room for the president, who silently, almost unnoticed, wandered in. He comes into a room like that. You assume his every entrance will be announced by bands and drums, but it isn't. He is quiet and unobtrusive. He doesn't call out to those in the room to attract their attention to him; he just enters and waits to see what's going on and to be noticed.

Katie almost bumped into him, startled to see the president standing there smiling. He seemed smitten with Katie's charm—it's hard not to be—but he soon turned to leave the room, saying he'd be right back with us. A few minutes later, Hillary came in, looking radiant. I introduced Katie, explaining that since Eileen and I have no children together, Katie is the closest thing.

Hillary insisted on introducing Katie to Chelsea, who was making bread with a machine she had been given for Christmas. Katie effortlessly joined in, having used such a machine at home. A friend of Chelsea's joined them and they all baked bread together for the hour or so I spent with the president.

▲

Chelsea's unpretentious manner very much mirrors her father's. Recently I visited a former client whose ego was the opposite of Clinton's. In addition to offering me a Coke, he insisted that I endure a lecture on his life, showing off one by one all the pictures on the wall of him with famous people and all the trophies and awards he had ever received. Visiting Bill Clinton, you have none of that. He never gives anyone the sense that he feels he is anybody important. He doesn't deprecate himself, but he just lets the fact that he's president speak for itself, and he moves on to other subjects. Lyndon Johnson once replied to a soldier's statement that "the president's helicopter is over there" with the comment, "They're all my helicopters, son." Not Bill Clinton.

Often he said of an official duty, it's "something I have to do because I'm president," distinguishing Clinton the man from the presidency. He doesn't resent the ceremonial aspect of his job—much of it he enjoys—but he knows that it's the job, not him, that commands attention. He doesn't, as Churchill once accused someone of doing, let his brains go to his head. Humility is Clinton's least recognized virtue.

Instead of a taste for pomp, Clinton has a morbid appetite for criticism. Although sensitive to partisan attacks, he wants criticism from people he meets and feels insecure unless he gets it. This is partly a legitimate need for feedback, to help him understand his shortcomings.

But much of it reflects insecurity. Unless you bounce criticism back to him, he can't locate you on his radar. Until he knows what you *don't* like about him, he doesn't feel that you *like* him at all.

Don Baer never got from Clinton the credit he deserved for his speechwriting or for his subsequent direction of the overall communications effort. The president never was at ease with Baer and only reluctantly, after much badgering, did he agree to promote him to director of communications. After Baer took that job and organized the White House message operation, Clinton still never praised him or made any effort to get to know him personally. I told Don that I thought this was because Baer never criticized Clinton to his face.

At an Oval Office meeting about the '96 campaign, Baer presented a concise, well-structured, and effective draft stump speech to the president. Clinton read through it and then talked about all the other things he was thinking of that day that might go into the speech. I was about to say that his stump speeches lacked discipline and that he should focus on the speech text Baer had given him. Instead, Baer jumped in, trying to please the president, and instead of defending the excellent speech he'd just presented, offered to include all of Clinton's meandering thoughts in a revised version. I watched the president's face as Baer spoke. It reflected the feeling that Don had caved in too easily, that he should have stood his ground. Clinton wants to be challenged. Subordinates who give way unnerve him.

If in the first five minutes after you meet Clinton, you don't mention something he's done wrong, you've lost him. He's bored by what he's doing right. But he'll try to fool you. He'll come on bright-eyed and eager and tell a story about how well he did in this debate or that speech. Don't let him con you, the answer he's looking for is, "The speech was pretty good, but I didn't like the part where you . . ."

▲

One of the more memorable moments of the president's 1995 vacation took place on August 16, when Senator Bill Bradley of New Jersey announced that he would retire from the Senate at the end of his term. There was speculation that he was planning to run as an independent for president or challenge Clinton in the primaries. He left both options open—though I didn't think he would do either, especially since he had barely defeated an underfunded Christie Todd Whitman in his last race. For some weeks, he allowed the speculation to continue, probably to emphasize his condemnation of Washington politics.

The president was agitated and called me on my beeper the day after the announcement.

You can't speak to the president or the vice president on a car phone or a cell phone; the dangers of interception are too great. Once or twice I spoke to the president over such "soft" lines, but only in emergencies and only after I warned him where I was calling from. Eileen and I were driving up Shore Road in Ogunquit on our way to our summer rental. "Clinton's on vacation, it will be quiet," Eileen had predicted somewhat inaccurately.

I had to find a phone quickly. I looked down the country road and saw no pay phones and no stores. Eventually, I came to a lobster stand, and explained to the proprietor that I had to make an urgent phone call. He showed me to his phone in the back of a building full of tanks of lobsters.

When you call the president, you first dial the White House switchboard. If your name is on the right list, the operator puts the call through, but if the president is away, the operator transfers you to "signal," the president's communications organization, and you tell "signal" that you want to reach the president, and "signal" will forward your call. Someone at the remote signal location then answers the phone, saying, depending on where the president is, "Wyoming White House" or "Paris White House," or whatever. At first, I didn't understand this system and wondered whether we had secretly placed little White Houses around the world. Later a friend warned me never to have the president visit my home because "signal" has to drill so many holes in the walls to set up its special communications operation that afterward the house won't be worth living in.

All this took some time as I waited amid the lobsters. When we were eventually connected, the president's first words were, as usual, "Where are you?" I described the building I was in and my companions. I noted that the phone was a hard line; we could talk.

He was worried about Bradley. I told him that I doubted Bradley would run and that the best thing to do was to say nice things about him so as not to make him angry. Clinton agreed, but he was in a foul mood.

These moods were inevitable on his vacations, for despite the press photos of Clinton happily golfing, the president hated vacations. He loves his work and dislikes being exiled from it. But he doesn't know this about himself; he thinks he likes them—until he is on one. Then he becomes cranky, anxious, nervous, overwrought, and desperate for contact with the real world. If he appears rested as he returns from a vacation, it's usually because he is thankful that it is over and he can get back to his regular life.

The president doesn't sleep well on vacation, but he thinks he should. After all, he's on vacation, isn't he? So he complains that someone or something is spoiling his vacation. He broods, turns nasty, and starts lacing into people.

After the '95 vacation, he was much more relaxed deciding what to do about Bosnia, fighting the budget battle with the Republicans, and jousting with Dole as the presidential race came into focus. Compared to his vacation, he found these activities relatively stress free.

T   h   i   r   t   e   e   n

Foreign Channels

While my renewed association with President Clinton began in September of 1994 with the telephone call about Haiti related in the opening chapter, I was not personally of any great significance in his conduct of foreign affairs. That is an important preface to this chapter. Foreign affairs is not my specialty. But I do want to describe my limited role for what insight the incidents may offer into the president's decision making in foreign policy. I found I could be of some use to him in this area as a conduit for the advice of outside experts and in helping to explain a decision to the American people in a compelling and persuasive way. It is also in this area that the president's personal evaluation and growth is most apparent.

When President Clinton took office, his experience in foreign affairs was limited, though it was not as bad as Bush had insinuated when he joked that Clinton's international experience was only at IHOP—the International House of Pancakes, where he was known to dine. Clinton knew foreign relations issues, but as a student not a participant. He was, however, determined to make a priority of domestic affairs. As a candidate, he had attacked Bush for spending too little time on these issues. Though hardly an isolationist—Clinton deeply believes in America's international role—he left many foreign issues to Secretary of State Warren Christopher and National Security Adviser Tony Lake. When I joined the president he had no special vision of his foreign policy. He reacted, more or less reluctantly, to global concerns when they intruded so deeply into America's politics that he had to do something. His intervention in Haiti, for example, was largely a reaction to his fear of the domestic implications of a massive flow of Haitian refugees into the United States. He saw many foreign crises—such as those in Rwanda, Liberia, and Cambodia—as blown out of proportion by an internationalist press trying to drum up support for more U.S. action and involvement in areas where the American people had no concern. The incessant TV coverage of scenes of depravity in Bosnia prompted him to remark, "They keep trying to force me to get America into a war." Only in foreign trade, about which Clinton knew a lot coming into the White House, did he seem to have an agenda he was pursuing. Here he often had to back up Trade Representative Mickey Kantor when the foreign policy types tried to prevent Kantor from taking tough stands against Japan and other trading partners.

The president's episodic interest in foreign policy in the early days of 1995 was reflected in the organization of his White House. The NSC staff, headed by Tony Lake and Deputy National Security Adviser Sandy Berger, was separated by a castle moat from the rest of the White House staff. Even Panetta had very little to do with foreign issues, and George Stephanopoulos often complained to me that he was "shut out" of what the NSC staff was doing on important decisions.

The NSC has its own speechwriters. Don Baer and his speechwriting staff had to wait anxiously for the "foreign policy stuff" to descend from the NSC for the president's 1995 State of the Union Address. The draft arrived on stone tablets. Spelling and punctuation could be corrected if a dictionary or style book proved them wrong, but that was about it.

If the White House staff had limited access to the NSC, you can imagine how little access I had. Whenever I came too close to NSC issues, the foreign policy staff honked like geese on a pond, warning one another of an approaching dog. Tony Lake, deeply idealistic but highly territorial, thought political advice was unchaste. His deputy, Sandy Berger, is more of a political creature, with a long track record in campaigns. Solidly built, like a football tackle, Berger tried to thrust a sense of political reality into NSC deliberations, but his political perspectives weren't always right. But at least he tried.

The president wasn't happy with his foreign policy staff. In December of 1994, shortly after I came to work for him, he asked me whether I thought he should change secretaries of State. "How about Sam Nunn?" he suggested.

"You'd lose that Senate seat in Georgia," I countered. "No Democrat could win that seat with our current poll ratings."

"I think he's going to retire at the end of his term in 1996, anyway," the president predicted accurately.

"He'd be a very good choice," I said, "but would he be loyal to you? Wouldn't he freelance?"

"He might." He thought for a moment and changed the subject. Still, his reference to Nunn was no endorsement of Warren Christopher.

A few weeks later, Christopher having heard what Clinton was thinking, publicly offered to step aside. That forced the president's hand. Since he had no ready replacement in mind he said he wanted Christopher to stay. The ways of Washington!

Clinton contemplated appointing Bill Cohen, the moderate Republican senator from Maine, as head of the Central Intelligence Agency. I asked Trent Lott about Nunn and Cohen, and he was positive about both men. "Tell the president those would be excellent choices that would send the right signals to the Congress."

By March of '95, I felt I was close enough to the president to tell him what I thought about how he was letting his appointees run foreign policy. "You know," I said, "I think I'm beginning to see how Lake runs foreign policy around here. There's a regency," I said, referring to the way European monarchies appointed adult ministers to guide underage kings. "You're too young now to run your own foreign policy, so Lake and Christopher have to do it. But when you turn twenty-one they'll let you take it over."

The president stiffened slightly at my characterization but said only, "I never get other options; I never get other information."

Clinton faced the same problem in foreign policy that most other presidents have faced, even those more experienced in foreign affairs. His information came only from his own bureaucracy; what the State Department or the CIA or the Pentagon or his own NSC said might vary, but essentially all his information and advice about his realistic options came from one source.

Clinton needed outside views and outside advice. He also needed a political perspective on foreign policy. The charade, carefully preserved by Lake, that foreign policy in a democracy could or should be determined without regard to "politics" was, in my view, nonsense. To implement major foreign policy in which any kind of heavy lifting is required—a commitment of manpower or of money—you must have public support. Political considerations need not intrude in the president's dealings with two hundred countries on routine matters, but when Americans are asked to risk their lives in Haiti or Bosnia or to commit significant financial resources to Mexico or Russia, the president had better make sure they understand and support his decision.

Those who formulated Vietnam policy apparently didn't care what the American people thought. Henry Kissinger and others may not have cared whether the American public agreed with them or not. They assumed we would automatically accept whatever scrapes the foreign policy oligarchy got us into as long as communism was the enemy. It was said of Metternich, who guided Austria's international relations through the first half of the nineteenth century, that he regarded Austria not as the nation he served but as a diplomatic term. I wondered whether this elitist attitude had dug too deeply into our own foreign policy establishment.

Bill Clinton did care what America thought. He cared not just so he would get reelected but because he too recalled Vietnam and knew that without popular support no policy would work. He was not, in this respect, a prisoner of polls. He rarely consulted them to decide what foreign policy should be. He used polling instead to discover what arguments would be most persuasive in getting popular support for a decision. In Bosnia, for example, he led America to the right conclusion despite adverse polling data that warned against American involvement.

▲

My polling showed that a core of almost 40 percent of America was really isolationist, opposed to having much of a foreign policy at all. In one poll, we posed three options: to intervene overseas to protect our interests and values and to act as a global police officer; to act as a peacemaker, doing what we can when we can to promote peace without overtaxing our resources; to focus primarily on our domestic needs without spending much time at all worrying about the problems of other nations. Only 14 percent opted for the police-officer role, whereas 43 percent backed the flexible peacemaker role. Ominously, 37 percent rejected any real role at all. Isolationism was very, very strong.

The NSC didn't understand that getting majority backing for a specific U.S. intervention abroad required political skills since 37 percent of the country opposed any action at all.

A key divergence between my approach and that of the NSC in presenting our foreign policy to the nation was their predilection for justifying our actions by citing our commitments to other nations, our national security interests, and our economic interests. I believed that the public was much more interested in promoting America's values than in advancing its self-interest. For example, when the president asked me to conduct a poll to help him figure out how to explain to a skeptical nation why he was sending troops to Bosnia, we found that the people were willing to send troops to stop the killing of women and children and to stop the practice of genocide. They were not particularly persuaded by the NSC arguments: the strength of the NATO alliance, the need to help out Europe so Europe would help us fight terrorism, and the global credibility of the United States. Above all, Americans were committed to the idea of American exceptionalism—the notion that the United States is a special nation, a fair and a just one trusted by other countries because we act out of a sense of justice, not in order to satisfy the national self-interest. Yet the NSC tended to regard such rhetoric as dangerous and likely to alienate our allies by suggesting a moral superiority they would resent.

The Japanese pride themselves on teamwork, the Germans on efficiency, the French on culture, and the English on grit. Americans value their fairness. By attributing our involvement in Bosnia to "national interest," I felt we were asking people to believe something that was not only hard to prove—that our safety or economic interests depended on Bosnia—but that also undermined the only reason that people approved of our involvement: that we would be fair because we had nothing to gain.

Our polling showed that the most formidable difficulty to be overcome in justifying our actions in Bosnia was that Americans didn't understand the difference between peacekeeping and combat. Two thirds of Americans felt that our troops were being sent to Bosnia as peacekeepers in name only and that they were really being sent to defeat the aggressors and force a peace through military action. So when the president announced his decision to send troops to Bosnia, he had to explain how peacekeeping differs from war making.

While the speech the president delivered to the nation on May 27, 1995, did contain NSC references to our interests, including the need to keep faith with our allies, the president carefully explained how peace-keeping differed from combat. The speech also stressed the idea of American exceptionalism. The president said, "It is the power of our ideas, even more than our size, our wealth, and our military might, that makes America a uniquely trusted nation." The line I feel most privi-leged to have ever suggested to the president summarized the idea of the peacemaker. "We cannot save all women and all children, but we can save many of them. We can't do everything, but we must do what we can."

▲

One day I asked Clinton what role he wanted me to play in foreign pol-icy. His instructions were strict, and I followed them closely: "Never talk to me about foreign policy in the presence of a third person. Always do it one-on-one with me."

We agreed that we would meet alone, before or after our strategy meetings, to discuss foreign policy and that I would cover it in a private memo to him and the vice president at our weekly meetings.

I began to consult outside experts and to channel their advice directly to the president. These included: John Ruggie, Columbia University's dean of the School of International Relations; Mat Nimitz, former U.S. negotiator and mediator in Cyprus and, more recently, in Macedonia; Jamie Rubin, press secretary for U.N. ambassador Madeleine Albright; Russian expert Lindsay Madison; and, starting in mid-1996, Bosnia ne-gotiator Richard Holbrooke. I kept Clinton closely informed of this net-work, and made sure that he knew who gave what advice. I never sought or got security clearance and never received classified information from any of these advisers. Nor did the president share secret material with me. He often alluded to something "I can't tell you about" as he strictly honored the procedures of confidentiality.

From my role as a conduit, I learned how Clinton gradually put his own stamp on foreign policy, making it *his* policy, not the mere product of bureaucratic momentum.

▲

My first involvement with foreign issues came right before election day in 1992. As Clinton moved closer to victory, Roger Stone, a Republican political consultant with whom I had often worked, called to tell me that former president Richard Nixon wanted to open a foreign-policy chan-nel to Clinton.

Two days after his victory, when the president-elect graciously called to thank me for my efforts over the years, I sounded him out on Nixon. I thought it was an invitation worth taking up. Could he receive Nixon publicly without political risk? he asked. "Only Nixon could go to China," I replied. "Only Clinton can go to Nixon."

He laughed. "I guess you're right. Ford, Reagan, and Bush couldn't go near him, but I don't have any of that stain because I'm a Democrat, so I can. Besides, I've always liked Nixon. He takes what they dish out and keeps on coming."

Clinton waited a while before calling Nixon. Every few days, Stone called with another insight Nixon had asked him to pass on, all in an attempt to induce a phone call from Clinton. For example, Nixon advised the president to appoint Republicans to his Cabinet and, in particular, his New Jersey neighbor, and Roger Stone's other client, former governor Tom Kean. I passed Nixon's ideas on to Clinton and heartily endorsed his recommendation of Kean, suggesting him for Education secretary.

Ultimately, Nixon and Clinton talked directly, and Monica Crowley has reported it from Nixon's side in *Nixon Off the Record.* I think Nixon had a great deal to do with Clinton's obsessive focus on Russia and Yeltsin. Nixon had warned President Bush that Russia was in danger of reverting to Communist control, and if it did, the big domestic political question would be, Who lost Russia? Nixon was qualified to utter this assertion since he gained momentum in his career in the 1940s and '50s, with the accusation that Harry Truman had "lost" China. Now Nixon repeated his warning, suggesting that Clinton could be defeated in 1996 by the question, Who lost Russia? Clinton got the point. Russia became to the president's foreign policy what California was to his domestic political strategy: the one place he couldn't afford to lose.

▲

After I became the president's campaign strategist, we discussed his May 9–12, 1995, trip to Russia. Looming over the Kremlin meeting was Russia's announced intention of selling nuclear reactors to Iran. Despite U.S. protests that such a sale would assist that terrorist regime in developing nuclear weapons, Russia planned to proceed because it desperately needed the money.

At our weekly strategy meeting before the trip, Vice President Gore raised serious concerns about the political implications if the president failed to convince the Russians to cancel the reactor sale. Republican senator Alfonse D'Amato was scoring points by demanding a cutoff of aid to Russia unless the deal was killed. I conducted a survey to see how people felt about the Iranian deal and about a cutoff in aid to Russia.

The poll revealed that voters were tremendously concerned about the sale of reactors to Iran but also were sympathetic to the complexities of U.S.-Russian relations and they wished to see the diplomatic discussions continue. People were not willing to put our relations with Russia on thin ice just to kill the reactor deal, but they would demand that aid to Russia be cut off if the Iranian deal ultimately went through. The administration knew, however, that cutting off financial aid would seriously undermine democracy in Russia and might permit a Communist comeback.

The president was determined to kill the reactor and keep aid flowing to Russia. Lindsay Madison, a seasoned Kremlinologist, told me that the real need was to get funds to Russian nuclear scientists who were now down on their luck because of the end of the Cold War. With such help, they wouldn't need to sell reactors. I passed the point on to the president and vice president. Both told me that they found it very helpful. The reactor deal was set back at the Russian summit and was further sidetracked as a result of Gore's skillful follow-up diplomacy.

On his return from Russia, the president told me that he had developed a new relationship with Yeltsin. "When we met before, I had the feeling we were each just saying our piece, talking past each other through the interpreters. But this time I got to really talk to him, really talk with him. He wants to run for reelection and is going to focus on winning it." Then he added, with a bemused chuckle, "He really thinks he can win."

Yeltsin's poll ratings were even more dismal than Clinton's. Less than 10 percent of the Russian people were saying they'd vote for him. His approval rating wasn't much higher. I suppressed the urge to point out that Yeltsin might have laughed too if he told his daughter (who ran his campaign) that Clinton was thinking he could win reelection in America.

The president was under increasing fire in the winter of 1995 for the sense of drift on Bosnia. He had criticized President Bush for steering clear of the mess—a three-sided war, largely a result of Serbian aggression against two other former members of the former Yugoslav federation: Bosnia and Croatia. Slobodan Milosevic, ruler of Serbia, was determined to fulfill his dream of a "greater Serbia" and annex much of the territory of his two neighbors. He set up a puppet regime among

Serbs living in Bosnia that soon acquired a life of its own. Headed by Radovan Karadzic and General Ratko Mladac, the Bosnian Serbs were waging a vicious war of conquest and "ethnic cleansing" that recalled Hitler's pogroms.

Like Bush, Clinton at first assumed a backseat to the Europeans; Britain and France had ground troops in Bosnia under a U.N. peacekeeping mandate. Peacekeeping, however, became a joke as the Bosnian Serbs used threat to the U.N. forces to restrain the U.N. and NATO from stopping their aggression with air power.

Towns that had been designated U.N. safe havens for refugee Bosnian Muslims fell before Bosnian Serb bombardment and ground assaults. Pressure for action grew. Television showed nightly images of carnage and destruction. As Clinton did little, Bosnia had become a metaphor for his weakness in America's mind.

Clinton had always been wary of ground involvement. So that the Bosnian Muslims could be armed to protect themselves, he favored lifting the international arms embargo that blocked weapon sales to all sides in the war. But the Europeans, with their forces on the ground, opposed this stance strongly, arguing that it would only escalate the conflict, while their troops were in the middle of it. The president backed off, hoping the Serbs would begin to want peace as sanctions against them caused more hardship. But this passive strategy was inappropriate, given the scale and nature of the killing. Then things got worse. At the U.N.'s request, NATO bombed Bosnian Serb positions to retaliate for the Serbian seizure of the Muslim refugees' safe havens. The Bosnian Serbs retaliated by capturing U.N. peacekeepers and tying them to trees, as hostages, near Bosnian Serb military installations.

Secretary of Defense William Perry took the president by surprise. He said, in public, that U.S. ground troops would likely be needed in Bosnia before too long. On May 31, 1995, as he traveled to Colorado Springs to speak at the Air Force Academy, the president heard of Perry's statement. The story dominated the news, and Clinton knew he would be confronted with it when he landed.

The president tried to limit the damage he thought Perry had done by stating the circumstances under which the United States might become militarily involved in Bosnia. "We should be prepared to assist NATO," the president said, "if it decides to meet a request . . . for help in a withdrawal or a reconfiguration and a strengthening of its forces." The president then specified that he would "carefully review any requests for an operation involving a temporary use of our ground forces."

The story was no longer what Perry said, but what the president was saying.

The national storm was savage. No groundwork had been laid for this hurried statement, and the nation was not prepared for a military involvement reminiscent of Vietnam. The president's ratings dropped, threatening to erode the gains he had maintained since Oklahoma City. Then the situation grew even more critical. An American F-16 piloted by one Scott O'Grady was shot down over Bosnia. As soon as the president returned from Colorado, I called him at the White House and shared my concern that his statement had been made without preparing the public. Noninvolvement in Bosnia had been a central element in my advice. "You don't want to be Lyndon Johnson," I had said early on, "sacrificing your potential for doing good on the domestic front by a destructive, never-ending foreign involvement. It's the Democrats' disease to take the same compassion that motivates their domestic policies and let it lure them into heroic but ill-considered foreign wars."

Now, at ten or eleven on Friday night, I suggested that in Clinton's Saturday-morning radio address he say flatly that there was very little chance of any ground involvement in the Bosnian war and that the possibility was so remote that nobody should stay up nights worrying about it—in other words, he should backtrack from his Air Force Academy speech.

"Fax me a draft of what you think I should say. Send it to the residence right away," he ordered.

As he requested, I sent it to the residence—not the office, where others might see it.

The next morning on the phone he went over the draft with me line by line, making a lot of changes but keeping the spirit of the original.

In his radio address, Clinton made clear that the U.N. faced a choice—either strengthen its forces or get out. If "our allies" decided to stay, he said he would use ground forces only "if there is a genuine peace with no shooting and no fighting." If they decided to get out, the president said we would help them. He contemplated actual military involvement only if Britain and France and other countries were "stranded and could not get out of a particular place in Bosnia," a possibility he called "highly unlikely."

The speech ended the uproar but Scott O'Grady was still missing.

I was with Clinton at the White House residence on the evening of June 7, 1995, after our strategy-group meeting had broken up. We sat in the president's dressing room, off his bedroom, as he played solitaire and we talked about whether he should give the balanced-budget speech. As it neared midnight, the president took a call. As he talked, a smile lit up his face. "You got him? You got him?" he exclaimed and then stamped his feet in glee, like a basketball fan watching his team score a shot in overtime to win the match. He pulled his fist toward himself and shouted: "*Yes!*"

When he hung up, he told me that the rescue had been a success, but we couldn't announce it until O'Grady was back on the ground. He slumped in his chair and a look of vast relief spread over his face. He touched his chest and rubbed it, as if rubbing a sore on his heart. "I was so worried all night about it. I knew we found him, but I didn't know until now that we were able to get him out."

Then, with relish, he told me how brilliant O'Grady had been. "It turns out this wasn't any ordinary pilot. At school, his top subject was exactly this—how to avoid capture and survive in enemy territory if you're downed." The president didn't know yet that O'Grady had eaten berries to survive and had come within a few yards of being discovered and captured.

Tony Lake came in as I was leaving and took the president aside. The national security adviser was so thrilled with the news that he didn't take the time to give me the evil-rodent look he bestowed on me whenever we met in the hallway.

But Bosnia remained a tough question for the president.

I passed on the advice of outside experts that we should retaliate against the Bosnian Serbs with massive air attacks. "I don't mean the current stuff," I said, "where NATO sends in only a few planes. I mean an air strike that continues until they give up."

"The U.N. has the decision to use air power so tied up in knots that nobody can do anything," he complained. "Boutros-Ghali won't let them," he added, referring to the U.N. secretary general.

Virtually every expert outside the government with whom I had spoken had told me that he or she believed the president must loosen the restraints on the use of air power and should reach out personally to French president Jacques Chirac and British prime minister John Major to get it done. Yet I found that every time I discussed Bosnia with the president, we ran into this word *can't* over and over again. "What do you mean *can't*?" I said in one meeting. "You're commander in chief; where does *can't* come from?"

The fact was that the president, distracted by domestic issues and eager for Bosnia to go away, had permitted what seemed to me a massive encroachment on his constitutional authority. What began as a tacit agreement to let Britain and France take the lead in what was, after all, a regional European problem had grown to a formal delegation of the United Nations as the triggerman for air strikes. And, the president told me, Boutros Boutros-Ghali was very reluctant to use that trigger. "He just doesn't get it," Clinton said. "He's too weak; he won't stand up and take action."

I told the president that rather than proceed at the foreign-secretary level, he should, as the experts had advised me, deal directly with Chirac and Major to negotiate new rules for air strikes. I suggested that he get Chirac onboard by appealing to the new French president's desire to show a firm military hand. Once he got Chirac, Major would probably follow.

As the month wore on, the president often seemed tired and almost groggy. "I was up all last night talking to Chirac," he would say. "It's getting there.

"Chirac has this idea of sending in ground troops in a kind of strike force or swat team," he reported. "That's not realistic, but I'm bringing him around to the idea of massive air power."

I warned, "France always loves the glory of the gallant but doomed effort. It's more a question of honor than of success with the French."

Because of his intensity, Bill Clinton focuses on one or, at most, two major things at a time, but rarely more. Now the president was focused on Bosnia by night and by day was preparing a balanced budget for his upcoming speech. He wasn't yet thinking much about other issues like tobacco or deciding whether to run campaign ads on welfare reform. It was not their turn.

Then the president got what he wanted from Chirac and Major. In late June, the allies announced a new policy on air strikes that gave NATO power over the trigger and to specify when and where it would attack.

On August 28, 1995, the Bosnian Serbs tripped the wire that brought on NATO air strikes by shelling the central Sarajevo market. The air strikes followed, between August 30 and September 14. They were massive and were followed up with cruise-missile attacks. The missiles finally broke the will of the Bosnian Serbs, and they agreed to a cease-fire, one that really held this time.

When the time came to send twenty thousand peacekeeping troops to Bosnia, the president recognized, as he told me, that he had to do it even though our polling showed that Americans opposed the move by 38–55 percent. He set out to persuade America and was effective enough to move the public to a 45–45 tie. As Americans saw the real difference between war making and peacekeeping and as they saw few if any casualties, public opinion gradually shifted even further.

▲

In 1996, the key foreign affairs challenges centered on three elections: in Israel, Russia, and Bosnia. In Israel, the challenge was to keep the peace process going. In Russia, it was to prevent a Communist takeover. In Bosnia, it was to demonstrate, by free and peaceful elections, that nation building was working.

Clinton was quick to grasp that we were entering a new era in foreign affairs, in which most of the world would be governed democratically. In an era of authoritarian regimes, President Eisenhower had sought to spread U.S. influence and fight communism by covert CIA actions that destabilized hostile governments and helped our friends retain power, whether or not they had been elected. Now that we were dealing with democracies where once we had dealt with dictatorships, the question became: how do we influence their people and their politics?

It was a challenge to Clinton's extraordinary gifts of public persuasion. In Israel, where he wanted Shimon Peres to defeat Benjamin Netanyahu, we had a special advantage. Several months before his death, Rabin took on Doug Schoen as his consultant.

A headline at the time of Rabin's death declared: RABIN DIDN'T NEED A DICK MORRIS. The columnist noted that Rabin had succeeded in leading Israel courageously despite opinion polls. I didn't doubt Rabin's courage, but I also knew that he did, in fact, have a Dick Morris named Doug Schoen.

When Shimon Peres took office, he kept Schoen's services, without, I gather, understanding at first the pivotal role Schoen was playing in Clinton's presidency. As the race unfolded, Schoen became a regular, informal channel to Clinton, and both the president and Peres welcomed it. Clinton wanted Peres to win so the peace process would continue, and he was delighted to hear about the prime minister's campaign. Late at night, after our weekly strategy meetings, Schoen would tell Clinton about the political situation in Israel.

For my part, I actively urged the president to bring his enormous popularity to bear on behalf of Peres. Schoen's polls showed Clinton to be the most popular international figure in Israel, more popular than either of the candidates seeking the prime minister's seat. The president did all he could to appear with Peres, in Israel and in the United States, to bolster the image of his Israeli ally.

As the election approached, Peres made a request of Clinton through Schoen. He said that Israelis would feel much better about the peace process if the United States formally guaranteed we would support Israel if it were attacked. Although the United States has always been ready to defend Israel, there was no formal commitment. Peres specifically said he was not asking for a commitment of U.S. troops, just one of military aid and other assistance.

The president favored the idea, but his ardor cooled when Israel attacked Lebanon to punish guerrillas based there for attacking Israel. The world community was particularly outraged when the Israeli army shelled a refugee camp, causing many casualties among innocent women and children. Israel claimed the attack was a mistake, indeed a setup, but some evidence suggested otherwise.

After the attack, Clinton was harsh in his private condemnation of Peres's inability to control his forces and noted that this made it a lot harder to help him in the Israeli election. The president played with the idea of extending a guarantee to Israel "if she took risks for peace." In other words, if Israel went the extra mile in concluding peace agreements with Syria, the United States would then guarantee to protect borders Israel had exposed in the search for peace. In the end, no formal treaty was concluded, but before the election, Clinton pledged U.S. support for Israel if it took risks to achieve peace as he came as close to endorsing Peres as he felt he could.

The election itself was very close, and for a while it appeared that Peres had won. I jumped to the premature conclusion that he was victorious and urged Clinton to congratulate him at once. I felt that the president deserved credit for what he had done for peace in the Middle East and I was determined that he should take it. Determined and dead wrong. It turned out that Benjamin Netanyahu won—by a few tenths of a percent. Stephanopoulos, Berger, and other cooler heads prevailed, and I was thankful that the president had avoided embarrassing himself—and me—by following my advice. I resolved never to jump the gun again.

The president was bitterly disappointed by Peres's defeat, but philosophical about it. "You can't push people faster than they are ready to go. If they're not ready for peace, there's not much you can do about it. It's the price of making foreign policy in a world increasingly composed of democracies. You can't get too far out ahead of the people, or they bring you up short."

I was angry that the Israelis had let "Arab terrorists" control their vote by reacting to the bombings whose sole purpose was to elect Netanyahu and begin an era of confrontation the Arab rejectionists wanted.

When the president asked how he stood with the Jewish vote, I asked Schoen to poll it. Clinton was winning almost 80 percent of the Jews and was even stronger among Orthodox Jews even though they had tended to support Netanyahu.

Ever the optimist, Clinton closed this conversation by hoping that Netanyahu, the hawk, had the credibility with the militant forces in Israel to make peace, just as Nixon, the anticommunist, had made the opening to China.

A few days later Clinton said that he felt the big loser in the Israeli elections was Yasir Arafat, and he told me that he feared for the Palestinian leader's life. "A lot of the Arab countries are worried that his people may try to assassinate him."

I was more directly involved in the president's efforts to help Boris Yeltsin in Russia. My former business partner, Dick Dresner, had been hired as part of a team of American consultants to handle the race for Yeltsin. Dresner and I had been best friends during the '70s and mortal enemies during most of the '80s. Our relationship was now friendly but devoid of the harsh emotional extremes that characterize business partnerships and business divorces.

When Dick was hired by Yeltsin, he called me and asked whether I was interested in keeping in touch about the race. I checked with Clinton, who gave his approval, and virtually every other week in March, April, and May and weekly in June, I got a poll briefing from Dresner, which I passed on to the president.

The relationship was particularly useful when Clinton visited Russia on April 19–21, 1996. Many in the State Department and the NSC had suggested that the president remain above the Russian election, in order to keep his options open. But Clinton thought he should help Yeltsin, as recommended by Deputy Secretary of State Strobe Talbott, his long-time friend, whose advice he most often took on Russian issues.

Clinton asked me to sound out Dresner on what his people thought the president could do to help Yeltsin's election chances. Dresner returned to Russia, polled the electorate, and called me with his recommendations. Because I felt insecure about talking over Russian phone lines, we used a code in which we referred to Yeltsin as the governor of

Texas and to Clinton as the governor of California. When I reported the results to the president, he was en route to Russia, and we used the same code. Dresner suggested that it would help Yeltsin's election most if Clinton did three things during his visit:

1. Praise Yeltsin's world role and campaign with him, since Yeltsin's standing as a world leader was an important element in his appeal to Russians.
2. Indicate that he regarded the Chechen war as an internal affair of Russia's.
3. Praise Russia's recent economic progress.

It's likely that the president would have done this on his own. He wanted to campaign, American-style, with Yeltsin, but Yeltsin backed out at the last minute, and Clinton was left to shake hands alone.

The major impact of the communications from Dresner was to overcome the objections of those who felt Clinton should keep Yeltsin at arm's length, either out of fear that he would lose (which most people in Washington predicted) or for fear that Yeltsin's showing himself to be close to Clinton might open Yeltsin to Communist charges that he was an American puppet. Dresner's Russian polling showed the opposite was true and that a link with Clinton would help, not harm, Yeltsin. This probably gave the president more confidence in his natural inclination to remain close to Yeltsin.

Of course, the major impact the Clinton administration had on the Russian elections had little to do with my efforts or Dresner's. It was the massive outpouring of economic aid to Russia that the U.S. provided directly and through international organizations that created the economic atmosphere for a Yeltsin victory. It allowed him to increase pensions and wages when both had massive electoral significance. Yeltsin won through patronage and pork-barrel politics at their American best.

The Russian election was held in two rounds. In the first, Yeltsin had to overcome the splintered forces of reform. Grigory A. Yavlinsky, his deposed economic reformer, was also running, as were quasi reformers General Alexander I. Lebed, who had opposed the Chechen intervention, and Svyatoslav N. Federov, an eye surgeon. They all took votes away from Yeltsin.

At the start, Dresner's polling had Yeltsin far down, shedding potential support to all three other candidates due to the Russian president's lack of popularity. Dresner told me—and I passed it on to Clinton—that Yeltsin was seen by most Russians as drunk, corrupt, and incompetent.

"Russia is a weird place," Dresner told me. "They are willing to vote for Yeltsin even though they hate him to keep the Communists from coming back. Fear of war is the leading reason they don't want the Communists. In one focus group," he continued, "all the voters said flat out, 'If the Communists win, there will be a war.' " Dresner's analysis showed Russian voters would back a candidate they didn't like in order to avoid an even worse outcome. I noted that Russians were used to backing leaders they disliked to avoid darker dangers.

As Yeltsin closed the gap with the Communists in the weeks before the election, I think the president felt more strongly that Yeltsin could win and was determined to take whatever steps were necessary to promote that result.

Clinton reminded me of the question Nixon had posed to Bush: What if the issue of the decade becomes who lost Russia? "It won't be me," Clinton said.

Dresner's strategy was, essentially, for Yeltsin to scare the country half to death with the fear of a Communist return. At one point, there was talk in the Yeltsin camp of canceling the elections for fear of a Communist victory. The president thought it odd that such speculation came from sources close to Yeltsin. Dresner explained that the story had been planted to raise fears of a Communist victory and thus move support away from the other reformers toward Yeltsin.

In the end, Dresner's strategy worked well, and his polling accurately predicted the outcome.

▲

Looking back on the Netanyahu victory in Israel and the Yeltsin win in Russia, Clinton noted that the Israeli victor did a better job of advertising his candidacy on television than Peres did. Summarizing the outcomes in the two countries, he noted, "The candidates who used American-style polling and media won."

In Israel and Russia, President Clinton tried to influence the outcome. In Bosnia, in order to declare our mission a success and withdraw our troops, he wanted an election that the world's observers would consider fair and free.

My involvement began in the spring of 1996 when, at Doug Schoen's prompting, I met Dick Holbrooke, the U.S. negotiator who worked out the Dayton peace accords. I invited him to my hotel and asked him to work secretly with me. I was impressed with Holbrooke. Unlike so many foreign policy people, he speaks clearly and understands instinctively how to seize the initiative and exert power.

Holbrooke told me that he was under consideration for a diplomatic mission to Bosnia but noted that some senior officials at State and NSC "had not yet pulled the trigger and recommended his mission to the president." He did not say so, but I suspected that perhaps Lake might be a bit jealous of Holbrooke's return to government service to work out a solution to the Bosnian situation that had so far proved elusive.

I was astonished to learn from Holbrooke that he had practically no contact with the president. He told me that he had had only one short audience with Clinton prior to the negotiations at Dayton. I had checked with Clinton and was able to tell Holbrooke that the president would welcome any input he cared to provide through me. I told him that the president was eager to hear his ideas directly without having them filtered through State or NSC.

Radovan Karadzic, the Bosnian Serb leader, was wanted by the International Court of Justice to stand trial for war crimes but refused to step down, as had been required by the Dayton accords. The U.S. and international press was irate. With Karadzic firmly in control of the government, there seemed no prospect of fair elections, and it even seemed likely that the indicted war criminal himself would control the elections. U.S. efforts to persuade Karadzic to step down had failed, and Slobodan Milosevic was unwilling to pressure his Bosnian Serb satellite government to oust Karadzic.

Holbrooke felt that the United States was not exerting enough pressure to influence Milosevic—a politician who understood power. "You have to go in and threaten to re-impose sanctions," Holbrooke said. "Milosevic is scared to death of economic sanctions. They crippled his economy before and would do so again. He'll back down if he faces sanctions." As soon as Holbrooke left my room, I called the president and told him of the conversation.

"Holbrooke's right," Clinton said; "sanctions are the only thing that will work."

"I think you have to have Holbrooke out there," I said. "He knows those guys and how to push their buttons. He understands power."

"Let me take care of it," Clinton said.

Holbrooke was sent to Bosnia. Before he left, we spoke again. "I still have no authority to threaten sanctions," he said. "They are sending me over there with an empty holster. If I walk in and see Milosevic and don't yell and scream and threaten sanctions, he'll know I'm bluffing in an instant, and I won't get anything out of him." Holbrooke told me that the NSC was considering half measures, like barring Serbian athletes from competing in the upcoming Olympic Games. "That won't get it done," he warned. "I have to put it directly to him: 'Play ball or face full and immediate re-imposition of sanctions.' "

I told him I'd call the president and get back to him.

"You tell him that if Milosevic doesn't play ball, we'll impose sanctions so fast he won't know what hit him," the president snapped at me. "We don't even need to go back to the United Nations," he added, echoing a point Holbrooke had made earlier; "we think we can do it through our military commanders."

I relayed Clinton's exact words to Holbrooke, and he said tersely, "Now I've got something to deal with."

The meeting with Milosevic was successful. Karadzic finally stepped down, and played no overt role in the elections, which were held peacefully in September 1996. Karadzic's Bosnian Serb followers elected Momcilo Kiajisnik, but at least the indicted war criminal himself did not make an explicit mockery of the Dayton peace accords.

Afterward, Holbrooke told me, "Without those words of the president's that you passed to me, I would never have been able to get it done."

▲

Sometimes I was able to bring the president the right idea from one of the outside experts. In the case of the U.S. response to Cuba's attack on two civilian planes piloted by members of a Cuban exile group, U.S. Brothers to the Rescue, the idea came from John Ruggie, dean of Columbia's School of International Relations.

I happened to be talking with Ruggie on the phone when the news of the Cuban attack broke, and I asked him for his advice. The president was greatly concerned about the attack, which took place in international airspace and clearly violated international law. It represented a departure in U.S.-Cuban relations, which had appeared to be heading for a thaw as Fidel Castro aged and his political isolation increased. When I met Ruggie the next day, he told me that he had thought my question over in the shower that morning. He advised against intrusive actions like retaliatory air strikes. It would be risky, he told me, to send U.S. air escorts along on future flights. "Why don't we put some ships offshore, well within international waters," he suggested, "and threaten to shoot down any Cuban aircraft that interferes with these kinds of refugee flights in international airspace? It won't escalate the situation but will be seen by Cuba, the world, and the exile community as an appropriate response."

The idea made sense to me. I borrowed Ruggie's phone and called the president. He came on the line at once. Clinton was silent for a few seconds as he considered the idea. "That might just work, that might just work. Thank him for me. I'll check it out."

A few days later Clinton did, indeed, send ships to protect the next flight of refugee planes. There have been no further attacks.

▲

After the tragic attack on U.S. troops in Saudi Arabia, which left nineteen American soldiers dead, Dick Holbrooke expressed his frustration to me with the government's apparent inability to determine who had been responsible for the outrage. In July of 1996 we spoke again.

"Our troops are terribly exposed out there," Holbrooke noted. "They're sitting ducks, in the middle of cities in high-rises exposed to terror attack."

I had not realized that the troops were still vulnerable and was horrified by the prospect of yet another attack.

Holbrooke had an answer: "The president should order those troops out of the cities and into the desert, where they can erect a combat perimeter against further attacks."

I told Clinton what Holbrooke had suggested and he said, "We met on this last night. We're meeting again tomorrow morning. We're moving in that direction, but I think we're moving too slowly. I've got to speed it up."

I stressed the urgency in Holbrooke's tone and then stated the obvious: "The country won't be as forgiving if there is a second attack that might have been averted had we absorbed fully the lessons of the first one."

"I know," Clinton said. "Thank you very much for calling. This is very important and very useful. I'll get on it right away." And he did redeploy our forces in Saudi Arabia—perhaps more swiftly because of our talk.

▲

Spurred by the experts I consulted, I had long been suggesting bolder moves against terrorist nations. A poll I had conducted ranked this issue as the main foreign policy concern of the American people: it ranked in the nineties; stopping drug-exporting nations from getting drugs into the United States was second, in the eighties; trade and economic issues scored only in the low seventies; Russia and China in the fifties; the Mideast was in the forties; Bosnia in the thirties.

The issue was especially hot since Senator Alfonse D'Amato, in one of his few positive moments, had been pushing for legislation to punish foreign companies for investing in Iran's oil industry by denying them access to U.S. markets. But the NSC and the State Department were suspicious of both the D'Amato bill and a companion measure introduced by Jesse Helms that applied this policy to Cuba. After Cuba shot down the exile group's airplanes, the Helms bill passed with the president's support, if not his enthusiasm, but the NSC and State remained wary of the Iran bill. Sandy Berger asked me, "What are we going to do? Keep the Reichsbank out of the United States market because it does business in Iran?"

But Clinton liked the bill. After it was modified to allow him to impose a broad range of sanctions against foreign companies and to choose inaction when he felt the national interest required it, he backed the bill and signed it. The law exposed Libya to sanctions as well. I remarked to the president that the bill might give him the means of dealing with reluctant allies as well as enemies, if they proved too eager to cut side deals with terrorists instead of confronting them. I liked the lineage of the idea going back to Thomas Jefferson, who tried to apply an embargo as an alternative to war. The president told me he looked forward to applying the bill "the first chance I get."

▲

In all these incidents, I emphasize again that I knew nothing of what went on between the president and his NSC, Defense Department, CIA, and State Department. I do not want to give the impression that my contributions were themselves decisive. They hardly could have been given his prodigious sources. But I did see the effect on the president of his work on foreign policy. It changed him probably more than his involvement in any other aspect of the presidency. As commander in chief he used the power of his office decisively. Hobbled by the Republican Congress, he found a chance here to grow personally and develop his own style of leadership.

The world has moved away from the bipolar struggle that marked decades of the twentieth century toward multiple but unrelated crises in which world peace and human values are, to some extent, at issue. In the bipolar world, the tools of confrontation were clear: armament, military action, head-to-head negotiation, propaganda to win public opinion, threats of the use of force, and rival alliances.

President Clinton grasped the essential point that we need new tools to cope with the more varied crises we now face. The key is flexibility and innovation—developing new ways of coping with each problem area tailored to its particular circumstances.

Politically, foreign policy and defense were expected to be major areas where Dole could score, but it did not turn out that way. Clinton took the issue away from Dole by redefining the job of president as it related to foreign affairs. Under Cold War presidents, the job description could have read: WANTED, FOR FOREIGN-POLICY POSITION, QUALIFICATIONS: STRENGTH, LEADERSHIP, MILITARY KNOWLEDGE, TOUGHNESS, STRONG NERVES. EXPERIENCE NECESSARY.

But, for the Clinton presidency, the advertisement might have read: WANTED, FOR FOREIGN POLICY POSITION, QUALIFICATIONS: CREATIVITY, FLEXIBILITY, INNOVATIVE STYLE. MUST BE GOOD AT POLITICS, DYNAMIC, CHARISMATIC. TOUGHNESS AND STRENGTH NEEDED, BUT ALSO SENSITIVITY AND EMPATHY.

▲

In both the budget battle and in foreign affairs, Clinton met the accusation of weakness by showing confidence and strength—and by producing results.

Thus, of the two conceptual negatives he confronted at the start of 1994—character and weakness—the values agenda addressed character, and his strength abroad and in the government shutdown addressed weakness.

By mid-1996, he was perfectly positioned to take on all comers.

How Dole Could Have Won

Republican presidential candidate Lamar Alexander wore a checkered shirt when he campaigned and reported the acronym ABC, "Alexander Beats Clinton." Nobody in the Republican primary electorate believed him. But he had two big converts in the White House: Bill Clinton and Al Gore. Both were scared of Alexander. Other than Colin Powell, he was the one man Clinton didn't want to face in November.

"He's too much like me," Clinton claimed. Both were southern, both essentially moderate, both charming, telegenic, young, attractive, and former governors, and both had made education the theme of their governorships. For Clinton it would have been like running against himself.

Gore, like Alexander, was from Tennessee, and he was even more obsessed with ABC. When I talked about attacking Dole during the budget fight, Gore would lean forward anxiously, furrow his brow, and say, "What if it's Alexander?" referring to the danger that Alexander could emerge as the winner of the Republican nomination.

I never shared their night sweats. Alexander couldn't be nominated, and I told them so. Once at a strategy meeting, I told the president and the vice president, "Alexander is to you two as inflation is to Alan Greenspan," referring to the chairman of the Federal Reserve Board, who had slowed the economy to a crawl for fear of inflation. "Greenspan spends his whole life worrying about inflation that isn't there and shows no signs of coming back, and you spend your days worrying about Alexander, who won't be the nominee.

"The Republican party is essentially a monarchical institution," I lectured these two lifelong Democrats. "It has a lot more in common with the Conservative party in England than it does with the Democratic party in the United States. The key word for Republicans is not *conservative* or *pro-life* or *pro-gun* or even *fiscal conservative*. The key word is *legitimate*. They look at elections and ask, 'Whose turn is it to run?' "

I recounted the history of Republican succession to the presidential nomination much as if it were in the Book of Genesis: "In the beginning, there was Eisenhower. Eisenhower begat Nixon by making him vice president. Then it was Nixon's turn. Nixon begat Ford by naming him vice president. Then it was Ford's turn. Reagan lost to Ford, but then it became Reagan's turn. Bush lost to Reagan, and then it became Bush's turn. Dole lost to Bush, and then it became Dole's turn. That's how they think. Phil Gramm? Lamar Alexander? Even Colin Powell? It's not their turn."

These brave words were uttered in the equanimity of October '95, before the Republican primaries had begun. As the primaries played out, I panicked and revised my predictions this way and that, as most political consultants do. But at the end of the process, Clinton told me, "It was Dole all along; he's the legitimate one, just as you said way back."

In his fantasies, Clinton would have loved to run against Pat Buchanan. He regarded the religious-right candidate as a real danger to the United States, turning us inward and playing upon our paranoia. He felt that Buchanan was basing his campaign on destructive ideas: racism at home, supernationalism abroad, and economic isolation. But he never took Buchanan seriously. Republicans, he knew, don't nominate nuts for president. But in the real world, Bob Dole was the man Clinton wanted to run against. Clinton had taken Dole's measure as Senate majority leader in their conferences and negotiations and the president found the senator weak.

"You can see in the budget talks how much he wants to make a deal, but he doesn't have the courage to do it," Clinton once told me. "Al or Leon suggests some compromise on Medicare and his head's nodding.

But then Gingrich or Armey speaks up, and he pulls his head in like a turtle and says nothing. He really lets those guys run him."

Clinton believed Dole was manipulated by his Senate caucus and really stood for nothing on his own. Clinton saw Dole as Clinton's detractors saw Clinton: wishy-washy, indecisive, unwilling to take stands. Clinton felt he was more decisive than Dole was. "I make decisions. I take stands: Bosnia, balanced budget, affirmative action," Clinton ticked them off. "Dole is all over the map. He was for banning assault weapons, but now he's not. He was for affirmative action, but now he's not. He used to be for a constitutional amendment on abortion; now he's not sure. Once he hated supply-siders; now he's running with one. But they say *I'm* the flip-flopper. I just don't get it."

During the budget debates, the president did not dislike Bob Dole. He saw Dole as a professional trying to score points. He seemed to feel that if Dole were left to his own devices, without the burden of running for president, the two of them would manage a budget deal in a few hours. I think he initially regarded his opponent as a fair and decent man.

But the accusations against Hillary in the Whitewater affair made Clinton a harsher partisan than he had been before. When the blows became very personal, he responded by vilifying the Republicans, including Dole.

President Clinton eventually believed—or persuaded himself—that Bob Dole was evil. After Elizabeth Dole's memorable praise of her husband at the Republican National Convention, he felt the Kansas senator was getting a free ride and he worried that I was unwilling for him to attack Dole often or vehemently enough. While on vacation in Wyoming, he screamed into the phone at me, "He's an evil, evil man." I envisioned his face contorting as he slowly pronounced the word—*eee-vvv-illl*. "He *likes* cutting food stamps. He *likes* it. He enjoys [*en-joooyyys*] cutting Medicare. He *relishes* slashing education. He *loves* cutting immigrants. It's how he gets his kicks. This is not a good man. This is an eee-vvv-illl, eee-vvv-illl man."

At first, I think he liked Gingrich. He saw Newt as an intellectual soul mate with whom it was fun to match wits. He looked forward to talking with Gingrich and often came back from their calls with a shy smile on his face. Leon and George were afraid that between his relationship with Gingrich and mine with Lott, Clinton would sign a budget deal not to the administration's advantage.

But by the end of '95, after Gingrich practically ordered his committee chairmen (no need to say chairpeople, there were no women) to investigate Clinton, the relationship soured. At first, I think neither man thought the fighting was real. But when Newt saw his reputation and his career destroyed by our ads and Clinton saw how close to home the Whitewater and FBI-file scandals' shells landed, each reconsidered and came to dislike the other.

Though I was pretty sure he'd eventually pull it off, I also feared Dole might fall apart in the early primaries. I'd seen too many front-runners count themselves elected before the first votes in the first caucus were cast. It's called overconfidence, but it's always misunderstood. Overconfidence doesn't mean you don't work; it means you don't take risks. You don't take strong positions to define yourself, but try to be popular with everybody.

Here's how it works. As more and more people support you, your success seems inevitable. But with each element of support comes a shackle. You can't talk about labor corruption because the teamsters gave you money. You can't take on environmental issues because of utility support. Health care? No, the drug companies are for you. Ultimately, your constituencies become your guards, and you are left with nothing to say. Plenty of support, plenty of money, but no message.

That's how front-runners fall. The public looks at them in the early primaries and realizes they aren't saying anything. Nobody told the voters that the election is over already, so they go to the polls and vote for the candidates who have something to say. In the Republican race, both Forbes and Buchanan had original thoughts. And they won the early primaries.

We made it harder for Dole by taking away his key issues: balancing the budget, crime, welfare reform, toughness in foreign affairs, and cutting taxes.

This was the crystallization of the strategy Clinton and I had mapped out in late 1994 based on the model of Mitterrand's defeat of Chirac in 1987. We had succeeded in accomplishing much of Dole's agenda. The deficit was way down. Welfare reform was in the offing. Clinton had tamed Bosnia, crime was down, and the president had proposed specific tax cuts. The popular frustration and anger that Dole needed had been soothed by Clinton.

Left without the Republican hymnbook, Dole had to improvise, but after thirty-five years in Congress singing the same hymns, he had lost whatever creativity he may once have had.

Even so, Dole could have won the election. Here's how:

There was always a way for Dole to beat us, right through September and October of 1996. Reporters would ask me what Dole should do or what weaknesses I saw in Clinton. I would always joke that I had sent Dole my last memo. Now that the ballots are cast, I can answer that question.

Dole could have defeated Clinton if he had simply articulated new ideas on the values issues as we were doing. We had stolen such issues from him as balancing the budget and reforming welfare because Clinton was president and could do something about them. He could have stolen our advocacy of values issues because he was a Republican and had a better claim to them than we did. Why didn't Dole call for curfews? Or school uniforms? Or letting employees take time off instead of pay for overtime? Or demand TV self-censorship of violence? Many of these issues were his before they became ours.

Once Dole came close to the right answer—when he attacked Hollywood for violence in May of '95, and in mid-1996 when he seized an issue that had been on our agenda when he advocated that prisoners be required to pay for their incarceration through prison jobs. Had he gotten ahead of us on these issues, he could have beaten us. Values issues were a fumbled football that lay on the fifty-yard line, equidistant from either party's traditional agendas. We scooped it up and ran it back for a touchdown. Dole could have done so just as easily.

But Dole's handlers always got it wrong. They thought the key to winning the values vote was adjectives, not verbs. The adjectives—Dole's *honesty, honor, reliability,* his *feel* for traditional values—dominated the convention in San Diego. But voters see through adjectives; they want action, they want results, they want specifics. They want *verbs.* By announcing specific actions day after day, President Clinton preempted the values agenda. In politics verbs beat adjectives.

The Republicans made another crucial error. They assumed that to beat Clinton they had to destroy him. The GOP's entire view of the political process is that each candidate has a certain level of positive support or negative opposition. They believe that to defeat an incumbent, they need to lower his support and raise his negatives. So they use negative attacks and ads to bring about this result.

They're off track. You don't always win by making incumbents unpopular. You can often win only by ignoring the incumbent and articulating your own positive ideas. If your ideas are more compelling, you can win without attempting to lower your opponent's popularity.

It's like the old concept in naval warfare of crossing the "T." Both fleets begin by cruising on parallel courses as in a foot race until one fleet outdistances the other and crosses its path, thereby forming a "T." This was potent because the fleet crossing the "T" had its broadside—half its guns—trained on the fleet sailing forward, while the oncoming fleet had only what firepower it could bring to bear off its bow.

In politics, you race alongside your opponent with positive issue-oriented ads. The side that can make the most compelling affirmative case for its candidacy gradually develops a lead. When it has a significant lead, it has, in effect, crossed the "T," while the other campaign has no choice but to go negative. In modern politics, with its quick TV advertising response to negative ads, the side throwing the negative is at a gross disadvantage. Voters have become so suspect of negative ads that the side counterpunching in rebuttal has the advantage.

These are the tactics we used to defeat Dole. Our positive, affirmative program was a lot better than his: deficit reduction, welfare reform, strength abroad, and less crime. Then we articulated a new set of issues—the positive values agenda—that was more compelling than anything Dole had ever advocated. By contrast, Dole's tax-cut plan came too late and, in any case, never caught on.

By the time we had taken the lead in January and February and held it through the winter and spring of '96 with our values issues, we crossed Dole's "T." We wanted him to think that the only way to win was to sail right through us with negative advertising. I worried that he wouldn't take the bait and would begin his race with positive ads. Early in the Dole advertising, he did run a particularly effective biographic ad and could have given us trouble if he had extended this approach into positive-issue advertising. But he didn't. He pulled the positive ad and went on the attack. Once on the attack, we could—and did—rebut each of his charges and then counterpunch with negatives of our own.

Had Dole put out his own values agenda and had he done it earlier, he could have gained a lead against Clinton and crossed *our* "T." But GOP strategic doctrine says:

1. Don't do early ads, they are a waste of money.
2. Don't rebut, it lets the other side control the agenda.
3. To defeat an incumbent, you have to raise his or her negatives.

Each idea is wrong in most races and, hobbled by these preconceptions, couldn't win. In fact, sometimes, you can defeat an incumbent more by first *praising* him and then articulating, better than he can, where we need to go next. Had I been running Dole's campaign, I would have said, "President Clinton did a fine job of helping to get our economy in order. He did well to set us toward a balanced budget. But now we must turn to the *new* issues we face, the values issues." Then I'd have focused on a host of issues that the president was afraid to touch or that his interest-group support wouldn't let him touch—ending teacher tenure, school choice, school prayer, an end to school busing, the balanced-budget amendment, a moratorium on immigration, passage of a federal right-to-work law, a ban on porn on the Internet. I'd have piled it on.

The personal attacks on the president never interfered with his use of the values agenda. Voters didn't care as much about what he *had done* in his past as they cared about what he *would do* about their everyday concerns. But a war hero like Dole with no scandal to worry about would have had an easier time running on a values agenda, had he only articulated one.

The values agenda was also our armor against Whitewater and other character attacks. "Public values defeat private character attacks" was the mantra Mark Penn and I recited every week to the president.

To test this supposition, we prepared a savage ad attacking Clinton. The president asked to see it to get a taste of the worst that could hit him. He turned white as he watched it on the TV set we always brought to the strategy meetings to show our ads and squirmed as the ad referred to Paula Jones, Gennifer Flowers, the draft, pot, Whitewater, filegate, and travelgate. "Oh!" he said after its thirty seconds of vitriol had been poured over him. "I don't guess I want to see *that* on TV anytime soon." He never asked to see it again.

When we played this hostile ad to audiences at shopping malls followed by an ad about the president's values agenda—tobacco, family leave, tuition tax credits, welfare reform, and so forth—the president's ad won out. We showed a net gain among the voters in our tests. Later, in June of '96, we had a chance to prove our predictions based on the mall tests with a national audience. Our tests proved to be an accurate predictor of the public's reaction to the two messages.

The values issues became our means of protecting Clinton from character attacks over Whitewater, filegate, Paula Jones's sexual-harassment suit, the travel-office scandal, and so on. Had Dole preempted this agenda, he could have removed our protection and left us vulnerable.

To further assess our position, Penn divided the electorate into age groups. He stressed that the opinion of younger social conservatives that the president was helping them raise their children the "right" way influenced their votes more than abstract observations about the president's character. "When you first hire someone to work for you," Penn said, "you look carefully at his résumé. But when he's been on the job for four years, you look at his job performance." Did Clinton duck the draft? Who cares? The real question is, What kind of a commander in chief has he been? Did he inhale? Well, check out how aggressive he has been as President in fighting drugs. Was his sexual behavior inappropriate? Well, as president, is he fighting to cut teen pregnancy? Does he want curfews for teens? Each of the scandal attacks in other words is seen through the prism of his record as president.

Republicans failed to focus on the fear that Clinton would veer to the left in a second term since he would never have to face the voters again. Our polls showed this was our Achilles heel. Dole tried this argument, but soon reverted to character attacks instead—a bull attacking the cape, not the matador.

I constantly warned that Dole could appropriate our values agenda to defeat us.

I warned Clinton of this at an early-February strategy meeting at which Leon and Mike McCurry had objected to my strategy of launching a new values issue nearly every day.

"It will all be a blur to the press," McCurry said. "Better to load up a big idea and trot one out every week than to do small-bore stuff every day."

I answered that on the day we launched our big shot, a plane might crash or there might be an earthquake or a riot in Bosnia. Such events, I argued, would wipe out our story and kill our entire week.

Leon said the White House was overloaded from having to vet ideas at the pace I was suggesting them. "We're going to make a mistake one of these days," he warned.

I replied that we hadn't made a mistake yet and that our biggest mistake would be to lie back and let Dole steal our issue. "If we go slow," I said, "we leave that much more for Dole to steal. Once the primaries are over, Dole can come to his senses and steal the values issues from us. We'd be dead then if we hadn't already made these issues our turf. We got a good, solid head start with the values agenda in the State of the Union Address, but we have to keep at it each day to retain the edge."

Leon muttered that it was a good thing Lincoln didn't have to conduct the Civil War by the polls.

▲

Throughout the campaign, I constantly imagined what Dole might do. I would stage an argument with myself to see how vulnerable we would be to a particular strategy that Dole might adopt. As a result I often responded to threats that seemed quite real at the time.

I needn't have worried. During the primaries Dole found that we had preempted traditional Republican messages and his handlers failed to come up with an alternative. His candidacy temporarily fell victim to the two men who had something to say: Pat Buchanan, with his jingoistic isolationism, and Steve Forbes, with his pro-growth flat tax.

Buchanan's revanchist ideas of isolationism and reaction has a continuing but sharply limited appeal among Republicans. I repeated to the president what I had said to him in October 1994, when he was considering invading Haiti, "Racism and isolationism are the two most deadly, poisonous forces in our politics."

We saw that Buchanan's radical agenda could win 20 percent of the vote easily and if he fought hard, as much as 33 percent. But he couldn't get more. The game for Dole was to win the Republican nomination by getting Buchanan one-on-one in the later primaries and forcing the other 67 percent to vote for him as the more moderate candidate.

After Gramm had immolated himself by getting caught in a low-turnout Louisiana caucus contest with Buchanan and Dole, and as Alexander failed to take off, Steve Forbes was the only obstacle in the way of a Dole-Buchanan race.

Forbes's single-idea candidacy was initially attractive in a field of candidates with no ideas of their own. His message stood out because, apart from Buchanan's, it was the only message. Voters respond when the other candidates are saying the same thing and you are saying something different. What you say doesn't even have to be that good; it just has to be different.

What Forbes was saying wasn't that good at all. The flat tax never overcame voters' suspicions that it was a way of lowering taxes for the rich and transferring the burden to the average family. When Forbes then combined his flat tax with a tax cut so as not to transfer the tax load but reduce it, he tripped over the deficit issue and never recovered.

Forbes might have come closer had he kept his wits about him. Instead, he proved fragile—the political glass jaw—vulnerable to a knockout punch. After he finished a close second in Iowa, he was euphoric. But that set him up for disappointment when he finished fourth in New Hampshire, where Dole's negative ads destroyed him. He won Delaware and Arizona. This seemed to buoy him, but he had failed to spend money heavily enough and early enough in the later-on states—like Illinois, Michigan, California, and Wisconsin—to win delegates there. He just withdrew. He might have done very well, since Dole's early heavy spending had brought him very near the caps on pre-convention spending set by federal law. This left him with little ability to compete with a strong Forbes media blitz in these big states with so many delegates.

Neither Buchanan nor Forbes could have been forced out of the race in the usual way: by donors withholding money as their prospects dimmed. Buchanan didn't need money to get his message across; his ideas were so outrageous the press publicized them for him. Forbes had his own money. Had he hit Dole in state after state, he would have piled up a large stack of delegates.

Clinton was amused by how Forbes had been "finessed out of running negatives by Dole." The president noted that "Dole was the one running all the negative ads, but he gets on Forbes's case about all the negatives Forbes is running and shames Forbes into pulling the negatives while Dole continues to eat his lunch." Bill Clinton's lesson: if you need negative ads to win, never let yourself be so embarrassed that you quit running them.

Ultimately, Forbes would not have had enough delegates to win anyway because the Republican party's rules are stacked against outsiders. Many states, like New Jersey, select their delegates by district, without even putting the name of the presidential candidate next to the delegates supporting his candidacy. This is done so the well-known politicians in the district (the congressmen, the state legislators, and so forth) will attract voters to their own names as delegates and win no matter whom they are supporting for president. Some states don't even use primaries at all but name their delegates at a state convention—a laydown for the insider. These factors would have stopped Forbes from winning outright or even from denying Dole a majority. But Forbes would have gone to San Diego with a large block of delegates. Not a majority, but a lot.

When Dole faltered, Forbes could have mounted an effort to force him to step aside, citing his ineffectual candidacy. As they gathered in San Diego for their convention in August of '96, the Republicans were so afraid of losing the election with Dole as their nominee that Forbes might have found it possible to cream off enough nervous Dole delegates to win. In any case, Forbes could have inherited the "on deck" slot for 2000 and begun to capture the legitimacy so vital for Republican presidential candidates just as the '76 defeat set up Reagan, the '80 defeat set up Bush, and the '88 defeat set up Dole. But Forbes showed that he was an amateur by folding after Arizona and mounting weak efforts in the remaining states.

▲

As the primaries zigged and zagged through Dole's bad days and good days, our strategy sessions were consumed with guessing who would win what. I was wrong as often as anyone else. Bob Squier rightly lectured me to keep my predictions about "other people's races" to myself. "Just get it right in predicting the one he's paying you to predict—Clinton's race," he urged.

In any event, when Dole emerged as the nominee, we entered the campaign with about the same lead we had held ever since the State of the Union Address—seventeen points. Now the task was to hold this lead as Dole launched his campaign.

We waited for the onslaught of Republican issue advocacy ads. As early as September 1995, the president had been worried that in a massive ad buy, wave after wave of GOP media would drown out our message, overwhelming our one- to two-million-dollar-per-week expenditure. Our worries gave way to incredulity as the Republicans remained off the air throughout the primaries and stayed off the air even after Dole wrapped up the nomination. "Where is their money?" I kept asking. Twice a week, I would nervously call Jamie Sterling, our ad buyer, and ask if there had been "any sign yet" of a Republican buy. Nope. Soon I was calling every day and, by April, even more often.

I'd run out of reasons to explain their inactivity. They had plenty of money they could have spent. Why weren't they?

As the enemy guns remained silent we had the airwaves to ourselves and we used them to highlight legislative issues actually in play in Congress where Dole's and Gingrich's positions were unpopular. Right after Dole clinched the nomination in March, his ratings rose to all-time highs as people decided to learn more about him, now that he was one of the two November finalists. If Dole had shaped an initially positive impression, he would have sustained it throughout the year, but if he acquired negatives, he would be dragged down permanently. By ceding the airwaves to us during this period, the GOP lost whatever chance it may have had to win the election. By the time the Republicans advertised in June, Dole was finished. By then we had locked up the race.

The opposition had given us twelve months of unanswered, unob-structed access to the airwaves. By the time the Republicans ran their first ad, we had spent about thirty million dollars on issue-advocacy ads without any opposition. Thirty million dollars is about three quarters of the *total* amount of money either Bush or Clinton spent on media in all of 1992, primary and general elections combined.

In December 1994, our polling showed us at only 33 percent of the vote in a two-way contest against Dole. By the end of February 1996, we were at 53 percent against Dole in a two-way race and at 50 percent in a three-way race with Perot. The president ultimately received 49 percent of the vote—about what our polls predicted eight months before the election. For all the ups and downs, the fact is that President Clinton had just about the same share of the vote when Dole got the nomination as he had on election day itself.

The entire Dole campaign, in other words, did not drop Bill Clinton's vote at all.

Yet, whenever we asked specific questions about Clinton—Is he a strong leader? Is he effective? Does he stand up for what is right even if it is unpopular?—his ratings were poor. On average, only about one third of the voters gave the president consistently high marks on these questions, while another third gave him poor ratings. The rest were in the middle. I warned that these ratings were our soft underbelly. But we found that when we measured Clinton against Dole on any of these questions, the president consistently outscored the Republican nominee. "Let's stop running against perfection," I urged. "Let's just run against Dole."

We implemented a strategy of compare and contrast. Developed by Penn and Schoen, the idea was to pit Clinton's legislative-issue positions against Dole's in all our ads so as to make the contrast clear. When measured not against utopia but against a real opponent, Clinton looked quite good.

This idea violated a key part of the conventional wisdom. A president is not supposed to put himself and his opponent in the same ad on the same level. If you are president of the United States, this is thought to be a double error—it means you are giving your opponent stature and downgrading yourself.

Nevertheless, that's exactly what we did. Our ratings rose sharply. Voters may not have found Clinton especially effective, but they found him more effective than the hapless, ad-less Dole—stronger, a better leader, more willing to do what's right, standing more for America's values.

Meanwhile, we were pouring it on with an intensity born of our conviction that this election would be decided early. "This race will be over by May," I predicted. "After that, not much is going to happen at all. The voters will lock in. A few points here or a few points there. But by May it will set in a pattern. Now, not in the fall, is the real campaign!" I fought, loudly and successfully, the week-by-week battle to stay on the air to highlight the positions that separated us on the questions before Congress.

Ickes groaned his disapproval.

Dole's ineffectiveness in the Senate visibly injured his campaign. At first Dole was planning to campaign from his Senate seat. This was a gigantic blunder, as he soon recognized. George Stephanopoulos said it best: "He's campaigning from quicksand." The Democrats used the procedural rules to twist the majority leader into a pretzel. He couldn't get anything passed or even defeat anything as the Democrats tied up the floor with filibusters that required sixty votes to break, and he had only fifty-four.

George explained the press situation to me vividly. "He'll walk up and down the Senate office and cloakroom corridors all day long, and reporters will line up and ask him questions. They'll stick microphones in his face, and he'll answer, We'll pounce on the answer, and that will be the story of the day, not what he wants the story to be." It was like a fraternity hazing, and it worked just as George predicted it would.

As I watched George deftly maneuver the Democratic congressional forces to stalemate Dole on the Senate floor, my admiration grew. He would call every morning to say, "Dole is giving us a gift today," and he would explain what the hapless Republican was planning and how he had arranged to counter the move. Each day it would happen as George had predicted.

▲

Even after I had fought hard and lobbied successfully for Stephanopoulos's inclusion in our strategy meetings, I still had the sense that the president worried that he was leaking to the press. According to White House rumors, Clinton was particularly incensed at what he felt was George's role in helping Bob Woodward with his devastating critique of the first years in the Clinton White House, *The Agenda*. For his part, George vehemently denied hurting Clinton and maintained that his role with Woodward resulted in a far more positive book than would otherwise have been written. I side with Stephanopoulos on this one.

Earlier, in the autumn of '95, the president had exploded at me over a *Washington Post* story that revealed some of our polling data. I told him that I had not spoken to any press person on or off the record about that insight.

"I know you don't talk to the press," Clinton said, "but you talk and you talk and you talk and you talk, and your words end up in print. You talk to my staff and they talk to the press. It's as bad as if you had called a reporter directly." He asked me whom I had discussed the issue with. I mentioned George and Rahm Emanuel. "You *only* told George and Rahm. Jesus Christ, why didn't you just issue a press release?" the president blustered. "Why didn't you just send it out over the AP wires? You *just* spoke to George and Rahm. Don't you get it, that that's all it takes around here. I don't say anything I don't want to see in print. Were you born yesterday? Do I have to spell it out for you?"

But I am still inclined to think that George didn't leak. At one point, the president asked me to deal directly with Trent Lott to see whether a budget deal was possible. I asked George to provide me with budget data so that I could handle my end of the discussions with the Republican senator. In response, he kept up a flow of helpful and accurate information—and no one ever read about any of this in the papers. I kept the president closely posted both on my talks with Lott and on George's role in providing me with the data.

At a strategy meeting in June of '96, I gave a memo to the president and the vice president commenting on several White House staff members. When we were alone after the meeting broke up, I reviewed these notes with Clinton.

The first comment concerned Gene Sperling, noting how he had ensured that the college-tuition and school-construction initiatives the president wanted survived Laura Tyson's efforts to kill them. "Gene has done a first-class job," the president said, stabbing his finger at Gene's name to make his point. "A first-class job."

Next I complimented Rahm Emanuel on his prodigious efforts to strengthen our crime program, usually in the face of Janet Reno's objections. The president nodded reversing his earlier criticism saying, "Rahm has really come around. He's doing good work."

Next I mentioned that George Stephanopoulos seemed a bit depressed lately and that I felt he sensed that the president didn't fully appreciate his efforts. I said that George's rapid-response efforts were "keeping us in the game," and I urged Clinton to reach out to George.

Despite his generosity toward Sperling and Emanuel, he was stonily silent at the mention of George's name. He looked at me, with a fixed expression, and kept his mouth tightly closed.

After an awkward silence, I moved on to the last name on my list, David Shipley. I praised his eloquence in speechwriting, citing his work in preparing the president's speeches in Austin on social tolerance and at the service for Ron Brown. Clinton opened his mouth, the lockjaw in remission, and resumed his generous praise. "Shipley has written some of my best speeches," he declared.

Still, the president looked to George as his chief adviser on the White House staff. George attended most of the president's meetings in the Oval Office and usually played the key role—apart from Mike McCurry, of course—in preparing the president for press conferences. The president very much valued George's judgment, and rightly so. It would have been impossible to have turned around Clinton's presidency without the professional skills of George Stephanopoulos.

▲

As April and May unfolded, the president was still trying to get a budget deal and was offering to negotiate with the Republicans anyplace, anytime. When the question was put to him as he hurried by in a Senate hallway, Dole suggested that he and Clinton sit down, one-on-one, to work it out. At George's suggestion, we accepted the offer; it was what we'd been seeking, and Dole's staff had to backtrack fast.

Dole looked worse each day. He was off stride and off message. He tried to repeal the gas tax Clinton had raised as part of his 1993 deficit-reduction package. This 4.3-cent-per-gallon hike had not meant much while gas prices were low, but after the oil scarcity and price increases of the winter and spring of 1996, it looked like a big bite to the motorist. Seizing on a tax issue, Dole trumpeted his desire to repeal the tax. We answered that he had voted for increases of more than ten cents over the years and opposed this one because it had been Clinton's bill.

For once, the Democratic congressional leadership played it perfectly, tacking the minimum-wage increase, a favorite among Democrats, on to the gas-tax repeal. Then, when the Republicans objected to the coupling, the Democrats filibustered and refused to permit any other business to be transacted on the Senate floor until the minimum wage was added to the gas-tax repeal.

The minimum-wage increase was about the only traditional Democrat-versus-Republican issue I found that resonated deeply with the voters. Although most workers would never be affected personally, single mothers who were working for $4.25 an hour and tried to support their children would benefit. As much as voters abhorred the welfare ethic of getting something for nothing, they disliked the idea of low wages that meant getting nothing for something.

Our polls also indicated that voters were not upset by the gas-tax issue. They knew that Dole was using it to try to get back in the race, and they learned, through our ads, that he had always supported gas-tax increases in the past. Except in the West, where miles add up quickly, voters gave the gas tax only a passing glance.

As the year unfolded, I noticed the difference between issues that appealed to self-interest and those that appealed to the voters' sense of fair play. Once again the conventional wisdom was wrong. It held that the closer an issue got to a voter's pocketbook, the more salient it became. But the opposite proved true. Issues that would directly benefit voters tended to be of less interest to them than those that would help others who needed the help more. It was politically more effective to raise the minimum wage for ten million single mothers and their kids than to cut a few cents off everyone's gas spending.

Clinton got the idea immediately. "It's exactly what I find when I'm out there speaking," he said when I explained the comparison in a May '96 strategy meeting. "They care a lot more about the other person than they do about themselves. It shows what we're made of as a people."

Based on this data, I advised Clinton to hold firm and demand the minimum wage as the price of a gas-tax repeal. Since Dole wouldn't turn his back on his business supporters, the minimum wage stayed down for the moment and the gas tax stayed up.

By mid-May, the president was soaring, with Dole still on the ground. Our ads remained uncontested. Our values agenda was firing up the voters. In May alone the president called for:

- a tax credit for adoption
- funding for AIDS research
- an end to discharges of new mothers within twenty-four hours of giving birth
- a crackdown on teen gangs
- a set of guidelines for corporate responsibility in handling employees
- a teen curfew
- a new program for Vietnam-era victims of Agent Orange
- a new anti-drug strategy

- emphasis on computer literacy in schools
- approval of the far-reaching Wisconsin welfare-reform plan

While Clinton and I were focused on getting a budget deal—our fruitless quest for the Holy Grail—nothing seemed to move Dole from his determination to run against the deficit rather than cure it, even though the numbers between the two sides on the budget were very, very close.

The money was there for the deal. But there was no agreement because Gingrich, Dole, Gephardt, and Thomas Daschle (the Republican and Democratic leaders of Congress) agreed on only one thing: they wanted the issue for election propaganda—Medicare for the Democrats and the deficit for the Republicans—more than they wanted the problem solved.

Clinton didn't feel that way, nor did Trent Lott, but Lott had no power. Yet.

When Dole left the Senate, it was clear that Trent Lott would take his place as the majority leader. I called my old friend and told him I would do him the favor of staying far out of his way and off his phone while the race was in play. But when Oklahoma senator Don Nickles announced that he would not run for the position, but settle for the number-two job—majority whip—it was clear that Lott had the votes he needed. Only Trent's fellow Mississippian, the senior senator, Thad Cochran, ran against him, out of pure envy that Trent was vaulting over him even though he had been in office ten years longer.

At my next meeting with Gore, he inquired anxiously whether I could find time to help Clinton and him while I was going to be so busy running Lott's campaign for majority leader. My relationship with the vice president had been tense ever since late November, when the president had accused me of making Gore my "employee."

At root, I believe Gore sensed my absorption with Clinton after my January '96 meeting with the president had revived our close relationship. Thereafter Gore saw me as the president's consultant, not his.

Dole's people saw they were in trouble, and Dole saw it most of all. With Dole's dramatic announcement of his resignation from the Senate on May 15, 1996, they regrouped. This stirred the press to wonder if his new role as private citizen heralded a new race. As a result, Dole got four weeks of publicity. At the time of his May announcement and again around his June 11 departure from the Senate, we watched grimly as the news featured five to ten minutes of praise each night for the senator from his colleagues in both parties. Basking in this adulation during his month-long operatic death scene, Dole must have thought he was moving rapidly up in the polls in response to the outpouring of flattery.

But he forgot something. He forgot to advertise during this period. We responded, in our ads, with a commercial showing moving crates and boxes from Dole's Senate office stacked high on a desk that was adorned only with Dole's nameplate and an old photo of the lonesome senator. The announcer noted that Dole was "quitting the Senate, leaving behind the gridlock he and Gingrich created." In the next scene, Clinton was active and in color, fighting hard to do the unfinished business of America—balancing the budget, reforming welfare, raising the minimum wage—now that Dole had run off to campaign full time. It was a devastating ad conceived by Marius Penczner. It captured all the cynicism of Dole's resignation and his abandonment of the very commitments he promised to meet if he were elected.

Clinton loved it, changing only a few words here and there. But he left the word *quitting* in place. Then, with Memorial Day approaching, Deputy National Security Adviser Sandy Berger called to urge that the word *quitting* be dropped from the spot. "He'll come back surrounded with veterans all around him and say, 'I never quit a fight in my life. Who is draft-dodger Bill Clinton to call me a quitter?' " I told Sandy that we had tested exactly this comeback and that it made no difference in our polling.

Unconvinced, Sandy must have called the president. Early the next morning, Clinton paged me as he traveled to his plane, asking whether the ad had been "shipped out" yet. I told him that it had been but that we could change it at the stations if he really wanted.

"You've got to get the word *quit* out of the ad," he said excitedly, almost breathlessly; "it'll bring up the draft thing, and the ad would be just as good if you used *left the Senate* instead."

I agreed that it wouldn't make much difference but said I didn't think it was a good idea to call attention to it by changing the ad once it was at the stations.

"Well, who cleared the text?" he asked angrily.

"You did," I answered and reminded him that we had played it twice for him two days before, at our strategy meeting.

"Well, it went by too fast for me to catch the word *quit*." He reminded me that an earlier ad had used the *q* word and he had ordered it changed. "Why didn't you listen and do the same thing here?"

I said that the newspapers were all using the words "Dole quits Senate" to describe what happened.

He hung up distressed.

The ad worked beautifully and largely blunted the impact of the Dole resignation. A few papers talked about the *q* word, and Dole mentioned it a few times, but nothing much came of it.

Still, Clinton would return to the "quit" episode whenever he wanted to show that our ads were less than perfect.

▲

Before the San Diego convention, we had a second Colin Powell scare, this time with speculation that Dole would choose the hero general as his running mate. Our polling showed that this choice would make a considerable difference, as much as seven to eight percentage points for Dole, enough to knock our lead below 10 percent. The president reacted as usual to Powell: with terror.

Penn, Schoen, and I huddled. We tested four or five different approaches to a Powell choice. All but one did little to dent the general's popularity. The exception worked not to hurt Powell but to stop Dole from taking advantage of his popularity. We found that if we contrasted Dole's opposition to affirmative action, handgun controls, and abortion with Powell's support of these issues, Powell would not help Dole's vote at all.

So we composed a sample ad announcing the "great presidential debate of 1996—not the one you think, the debate between Bob Dole and [drum roll] Colin Powell." By noting that it was the president, not the vice president, who made the important decisions, we underscored how little it meant to have a good vice president if you didn't have a good president. Gore would shift uncomfortably in his seat when we made that argument.

The Scandals of June '96

At the end of May and throughout all of June, the Republicans tried to break Clinton's grip on the race by dominating the news with hearings on scandals concerning Whitewater and the FBI files. I stayed away from the administration's efforts to rebut the scandal stories. It was the one conference call in which I never participated. I used to joke that "my job is to run the pump and the engines, not to patch up the hole people felt there was in the bottom of the boat."

I know nothing about the factual basis of the varied accusations or the lawyers' or administration's strategy in rebutting them. I did give three basic pieces of advice to Clinton in handling Whitewater:

1. As the attacks escalated, I urged him to increase his public focus on the values issues to offset the impact of the negatives.
2. Our polling found that Special Prosecutor Kenneth Starr and congressional hit men Alfonse D'Amato and Bill Clinger were especially vulnerable to the charge that they were trying to discredit the president

for partisan purposes. I advised Clinton to hammer at the link between
Starr and his tobacco clients.

3.   I urged the president himself never to mention Whitewater or any of
the other supposed scandals and to leave the rebuttals to his lawyers,
staff, and spokespeople. By talking about these scandals, he would have
identified himself with them. Otherwise, the public would feel they concerned only his staff at most or his wife at worst.

The Whitewater and FBI-file charges and the drumbeat of hearings
deeply disturbed the president. Each night's television news dedicated
about 40 percent of its time to one or another of the subjects. Tom Freedman recorded a three-to-one ratio of *negative* over positive TV news coverage of Clinton. For Dole, it was the opposite. He got a two-to-one ratio
of *positive* coverage in June, the period that included Dole's resignation
from the Senate.

In late May and June, Governor Jim Guy Tucker of Arkansas and Jim
and Susan McDougal were convicted in Kenneth Starr's first contested
Whitewater trial. The president's best friend, White House staffer Bruce
Lindsey, was named an unindicted co-conspirator by Starr in the trial of
Arkansas banker Herb Branscombe. And to cap off the month, it was
revealed that two junior White House staffers, Anthony Maresca and
Craig Livingstone, had examined FBI files of prominent Republicans,
including former secretary of State James Baker, a violation of their
right to privacy.

As Republican congressman Bill Clinger conducted hearings on the
matter, the implication was that the files had been studied, at least in
part, in an effort to get dirt on Billy Dale, whose dismissal from the staff
in 1993 had led to the travel-office scandal. Dale was indicted for financial irregularities in handling the office's affairs but was subsequently
acquitted by a jury.

Then Senator D'Amato's committee issued its report attacking the
White House for its handling of Whitewater and the investigation of
Vincent Foster's suicide.

Next, the press accused Hillary of secretly communicating with the
spirit of Eleanor Roosevelt, and a former FBI agent turned author accused the president of womanizing and drug use.

Quite a period.

When the story of Hillary's alleged séances with Eleanor Roosevelt
broke, we polled its impact. We found that while 25 percent of America

believed that such communication was possible, voters believed by
three to one that Hillary had been simply imagining Eleanor and what
she would have said if she were alive now.

I told the First Lady about this data, and she seemed relieved. We
chatted for a while, and she asked me, chirping and chipper, in her
high-pitched asking-an-innocent-question voice, "By the way, Dick, is
there anyone I can call for you? I thought maybe you'd like to speak
with Machiavelli or someone?" I asked if she would tell Metternich to
beep me.

"No problem," she said.

The president dealt with his and his wife's troubles with less good
humor. The constant pounding on his wife concerned him personally
and the tempest in general worried him politically. It is hard to over-
state the emotional beating Hillary took during this offensive by the
Republicans as they attacked her daily with insinuations of dishonesty.
The anger and pain the president felt as he saw his wife pummeled was
profound.

He exploded at a strategy meeting on July 3, 1996, after a month and
a half of bad news on Whitewater and the FBI-file scandal. "You can't
tell me this drip, drip, drip isn't having an effect!" Red in the face and
full throated in his cry of pain, he continued, "Every innocent person
they drag through the mud, every honest mistake they call a shocking
scandal, every item of information they twist out of all proportion—you
can't tell me that's not killing me out there." He raged on at the astonished members of the group, who accepted this display of presidential
emotion with averted glances. The president appeared to be scolding
them, but he was, of course, scolding me, seated immediately to his left,
catching a side view of his rage as he projected it toward everyone but
me. "The hammering, the pounding, the garbage, the lies, the dirt, the
innuendo, the stuff they make up and they throw at me, at my wife, at
my friends, at my staff—you can't tell me that's having no effect. You
can't tell me that!"

He was challenging my repeated assertion that none of these accusations would have the slightest eventual effect on his vote share. I knew
he was berating the group as a way of testing me to make sure I stood
my ground. He wanted to know how deeply I was convinced that the attacks had no effect. He wanted to quiet his worries and soothe his pain.
So I said what he was expecting me to say. Sitting up in my chair as tall
as my five-foot, six-inch frame would allow and summoning the adren-

aline I'd need, I said to the president, "I not only can say it, I will say it.
None of this is having any effect on you, and it won't have any effect no
matter how long it continues."

Clinton probed further. "How can you say that? How can you say
that? It's on the air all the time, they cover nothing but that. They have
an endless appetite for the most inconsequential, innocent, tiny little
grain of so-called evidence. How can you say it's having no effect? How
can you say nothing ever will have an effect? How can you say that?" he
raged, this time directly at me.

"All right, all right," I said with my hands held high, as if I was being
robbed in a TV Western. "You're right." I shrugged my shoulders for effect and shifted my tone to a singsong Yiddish inflection. "You're right.
When you're right, you're right." Then I pushed the argument to its
ridiculous extreme. "If you," I said, pointing right at him, "you, *you* are
indicted and *you* are convicted and *you* are impeached and *you* are removed from office, they won't vote for you again."

Laughter erupted, the president joined in, and the tension was broken. The president slumped back in his chair, emotionally spent.

Through all such alarms, our campaign held true to its task· to promote the president's values agenda. We did this by issuing statements
several times a week in which we made new proposals and announced
executive actions and by running ads, thereby controlling the dialogue
in the campaign.

George Stephanopoulos, in charge of "rapid response," handled the
task of day-to-day rebuttals of opposition mischief. My job was to keep
the "paid" and "free" media messages coming out every day through
press ("free media" in political jargon) and ads ("paid media" in consultant lingo).

Our campaign's momentum was, astonishingly, protecting the president's lead from serious damage. The articulation of exciting issue ideas
for the country was central to our ability to swim above the effluent.

During June, the president proposed or announced, one day after the
other: a cut in FHA-insurance closing costs for home buyers; allowing
employees to take overtime in time off, not just in extra pay if they
wished; the distribution of fifty thousand cellular telephones to community watch groups; tuition tax credit; the garnishee of federal benefits
checks for deadbeat dads; posting deadbeat dads' photos in post offices,
support for a constitutional amendment to protect the rights of crime victims; a national gun-tracking system to track handguns across state lines;
and extension of family-leave benefits to include time off for children's

medical care and parent-teacher conferences. With such a daily barrage of proposals important to everyday people, Whitewater seemed far away.

▲

The Republicans launched their long-awaited air attack in the last few days of May. Their effort was, however, curiously limited and out of focus. While our ads ran in about half the country, theirs sought to reach only a third. Their choice of markets indicated that they were more focused on winning House and Senate seats than on electing Dole. Often they would buy markets in states where they had no chance of losing (Mississippi, Texas, or South Dakota, for example) in an effort to influence congressional races. Moreover, their ads were terrible.

First, they ran a commercial that showed Clinton promising to balance the budget in ten years, then seven years, then nine years, then between seven and nine years. The point was that he wasn't sincere in his balanced-budget promise. This was a variant of an ad the Republicans had produced during the budget wars and had run only on a token basis. We tested it at the time it was first produced and retested it in shopping malls when it was actually aired. It hadn't worked then and didn't work now.

Their idea was that the ad would coincide with congressional action, for the second time, on a balanced-budget amendment, which Clinton had always opposed. We answered it with one that restated our budget priorities in terms of values. Our reply ad said that Clinton wanted to "do our duty to our parents by protecting Medicare" and "wanted to provide opportunity for all by improving education."

In our mall tests, we invited shoppers, one at a time, to watch the Republican attack ad and then watch our rebuttal commercial. Before and after they had seen the two ads, we asked them a series of questions on how they would vote and how they felt about Clinton and about Dole. Our tests showed that we gained, rather than lost, votes in the exchange of the two ads.

So we aired our commercial and waited for the Republicans to pull their ad and redo it to counter ours. They never did. They ran their ad for three weeks in May and June without altering it in the slightest to take account of our response. What idiocy! The Republicans were spending some five million dollars to run an ad, but they wouldn't spend thirty thousand dollars to test how it would run against our response.

Next, the Republicans ran a commercial that tried to capitalize on the immigration bill as it moved through Congress. It pictured Clinton as unwilling to cut off "benefits" to illegal immigrants. In fact, the president backed the denial of benefits to illegals but did believe that their children should be allowed to attend school while they were here. By including education under the rubric of benefits, the Republicans implied, falsely, that Clinton favored giving welfare to illegal immigrants. Mall tests showed this ad would hurt us badly if left unanswered.

We immediately prepared a reply that pointed out that the president had opposed welfare for illegals, had dramatically increased border patrols, and had increased deportations. We also noted that Dole opposed legislation to stop illegals from taking American jobs. Our polls suggested this ad would completely nullify the Republican assault, but HUD secretary Henry Cisneros objected to it because we featured film of Hispanic illegal aliens being handcuffed and arrested.

I pointed out that the Republican attack ad showed refugees running past the border with the word *Mexico* bright and visible for all to see. We were replying to a racist ad. Nevertheless, Cisneros warned of a backlash among Hispanics. I told Cisneros that I didn't care "if the film was of a blue-eyed Norwegian sailor"; I just wanted to illustrate that we were making arrests. We reenacted the arrests with Anglo actors and used the revised footage.

Cisneros was a tremendous help in the campaign and a good ally. His creative ideas on issues were prolific and insightful. Once he proposed that the president push a button and detonate an explosive, blowing up an old public housing project, one of the redbrick slums that dot our cities. Then the president would travel a few blocks and cut the ribbon on a new low-rise public housing project. We never got to do the event, but I came to like Cisneros very much.

In any case, the Republican immigration attack fared no better than their assault on Clinton's stand on the balanced-budget amendment. Our lead remained stable.

▲

Still, I was nervous each week as we got our polling results back. Surely *this* must be the week that the scandals hit us and dropped our vote share. But each week the lead generally held steady, dropping only three points over the six-week pounding.

In June, the nation was outraged by the burning of black churches in the South. The president was personally offended by these fires and determined to stop them. I saw them as a political opportunity to stand up to racism and capitalize, at a time when he was under such intensive partisan fire, on the president's well-deserved reputation for racial fairness. But, more important, I saw a moral opportunity for the nation. Naomi Wolf had been urging me to translate into policy our themes of reconciliation and restitution. I urged specifically that Clinton call out the National Guard to protect the churches from damage. I advised: "By acting boldly, in the tradition of Kennedy in Alabama and Mississippi, you will generate a national outpouring of support for the churches. It will give voice to our national repudiation of racism."

"I think Dick's onto something," Clinton told Gore after one strategy meeting. "It may not be feasible, but if it checks out, I'd like to do it."

The Pentagon and the NSC did everything they could to block such a deployment. First, they warned of disastrous political consequences if we interrupted the lives of so many guardsmen, regularly civilians, calling them out to protect the churches. Our polls showed the opposite, however; they showed that the country would rally behind such an effort and be inspired by such bold action. Then, they said it would interrupt the Guard's summer training. Finally, they said that we could not call out the Guard without the approval of the governors, except in a moment of insurrection, a justification Kennedy had invoked in federalizing southern Guards during the violence against civil rights protesters of the early '60s.

I urged the president to protect the churches by working with the southern governors to deploy the Guard or other federal resources, such as FBI or Alcohol, Tobacco, and Firearms officials. It is hard to convey the indifference to my proposal on the part of any agency of the federal government—the White House staff, the Justice Department, or the Pentagon.

George Stephanopoulos, unlike most of the staff, favored bold action and suggested that we convene a summit of southern governors to discuss how to deal with the burnings; Don Baer worked into the president's schedule frequent appearances in front of churches. But strong government action was always assigned a low priority, despite the president's wishes.

Finally, Clinton became fed up with the lack of action and directed FEMA, the Federal Emergency Management Agency, which supervises disaster relief, to coordinate help for the churches. He allocated extra money to FEMA to hire guards for many of the churches. The president chose to give the money to FEMA because the agency was headed by his old Arkansas friend, James Lee Witt. "He was the only one I could count on to get it done," he told me. "I couldn't count on any other agency to treat it as important."

Thankfully, the burnings decreased, perhaps in response to the president's efforts. He and the vice president then shifted their attention to reconstruction. The president was successful in channeling a vast amount of national aid into the project. Gore arranged for voluntary efforts to rebuild the churches and faced down insurance companies that threatened to cancel their coverage.

Why did Whitewater have so little effect on the president's political standing? The most important reason is that voters were not prepared to jump to conclusions about a president whom they saw every day doing good important things to help them in their own lives.

The second reason for Whitewater's failure to affect the campaign is that the voters distrusted the accusers far more than they distrusted the accused. We regularly polled voters' attitudes toward D'Amato's Whitewater investigation in the Senate, Clinger's FBI-file investigation in the House, and Special Prosecutor Kenneth Starr's grand jury probe into Whitewater. Consistently, a large majority of voters said that each of these investigations was "a politically motivated attempt to embarrass and discredit the president before election day" rather than a "serious and fair investigation into the charges." The voters felt these three forums were "kangaroo courts" and regarded their output with deep suspicion.

As the election approached, voters' cynicism about Starr, Clinger, and D'Amato increased, escalating in tandem with the increased stridency of their charges. Starr's deep involvement in the tobacco industry and D'Amato's own past ethical problems made them particularly inappropriate spokesmen for an attack on the president.

S   i   x   t   e   e   n

Let's Pass Everything

For three weeks in July 1996, four months before voters went to the polls, government finally worked as it should have done for the preceding two years. Trent Lott and Bill Clinton got bills passed into law and made history. I was the secret intermediary.

As soon as Lott had secured his victory as Senate majority leader, I called him at home to congratulate him, my first contact in several weeks. "We both done pretty good," Lott said, mimicking down-home talk.

"Sure have," I replied. "Remember when you and I sat together on your front porch in Pascagoula and looked out over the Gulf of Mexico?"

"Yessir," he said.

"Well, I've got my end under control, and it looks like you've got yours," I said.

"So what do we do with it?" Lott asked.

"Let's pass everything," I answered.

"Sounds good to me. Let's get started," the senator replied.

Lott had taken to calling me Mr. Prime Minister when we spoke, though of course I was simply carrying out the president's wishes. I called Lott HMO (His Majesty's Opposition).

I sketched through what was pending and asked HMO how to proceed. "We have to get minimum wage off the floor so it doesn't block everything," he began. The bill had stalled in the Senate for months, the Democrats holding out for a "clean" bill without crippling amendments, the Republicans refused to let such a bill come to a vote. "It'll take me a while to get my people in line on that," said Lott, "but I'll promise you that we'll let there be a fair vote on the minimum wage by itself, up or down. If it passes, it passes. But let me get it off the floor so we can do business. Let's get some momentum for getting things passed."

HMO outlined the next steps. "We'll get a deal on Kennedy-Kassebaum and try to pass that. We'll get pesticide and clean water out. Then we see if we can tackle welfare reform."

"How about a balanced-budget deal while you're at it?" I suggested, returning to our perennial topic of discussion.

"Not this summer, but if we get that far, maybe immigration reform, and maybe we could pull off a balanced-budget deal,"

Excitedly, I reported Trent's comments to the president. He was wary, as always, of news from Lott. "Can he deliver Gingrich?" he wanted to know.

"My bet is that he can," I answered. "Gingrich is depressed and, from what I hear, kind of out of it anyway. Also, Trent was Newt's mentor in the House. He gave Gingrich his start on the leadership ladder when Lott was minority whip."

Gingrich was facing a strong challenge from his majority leader, Dick Armey of Texas, who was then thought likely to try to wrest power from Gingrich after the November elections. In my day-by-day dealings with Lott, HMO seemed able to deliver House support. I never directly asked what was going on with the senator's erstwhile protégé from Georgia, but I got the distinct impression that all was not well.

The president had to take Lott on faith and persuade the Democrats in the Senate to allow the minimum-wage bill to go to the conference committee so that other business could proceed. This was risky for the Democrats. Their price for allowing the Senate to move again had been simple: a Republican commitment to pass the minimum-wage bill on the Senate floor and let it make its way through the conference committee without amendments which might force the president to veto it.

But Trent was too new to the majority leader's job at this point to make such a commitment. He could commit himself only to allowing a floor vote on a "clean" minimum-wage bill. As for its ultimate fate in conference, he could guarantee only his "best efforts" to allow a bill without veto-bait amendments to reach the president's desk.

Clinton decided to trust Lott and, through the president's new legislative director, John Hilley, persuaded the Senate Democrats to let other bills proceed without interference.

Hilley was new to the president's staff, but had extensive experience in Congress. A former aide to Senate minority leader Tom Daschle, he knew its ways. He had served on the staff of the usually bipartisan Budget Committee, so he knew not just the Democrats, but, more important, the Republicans. I worked very closely with Hilley and the president invested heavily in him as he fashioned his moves in the summer of 1996. Hilley, a superb diplomat, got along well with Panetta and Stephanopoulos and could negotiate the cross currents of the White House with skill.

But would Lott deliver? The first step was to pass the Kennedy-Kassebaum bill, which was stalled over the side issue of Medical Savings Accounts.

Named for its sponsors, Democratic Senator Ted Kennedy of Massachusetts and Republican Senator Nancy Kassebaum from Dole's own Kansas, the bill provides for "portable" health insurance, obliging insurance companies to extend the same protections to a worker in a new job that he had in his old one, despite any preexisting conditions. Now that Clinton had abandoned his desire to solve all the health-care problems in America with one bill and had embraced the idea of gradualism, the Kennedy-Kassebaum bill seemed like a logical next step.

Republicans, however, were obsessed with their concept of medical savings accounts—MSAs—the last remnant of the Gingrich revolution and its discredited Contract with America. MSAs are individual plans, modeled on IRAs, by which people can put a sum of money aside, tax free, for medical expenses. Out of this sum—four thousand dollars per year, for example—they pay for whatever health insurance plan they wish to buy and all deductibles, copayments, or uncovered health-care costs. If the costs exceed this sum, they would have to reach into their pockets for more. But if the costs are less, they keep the difference, tax free. In Republican free-market theory, this gimmick was supposed to reduce needless use of health services and give the patient a stake in keeping costs down.

Clinton, however, was far more worried that MSAs would "cream off" the wealthy and the healthy, who would set up MSAs and then buy insurance with high deductibles, protecting themselves only from catastrophic health-care costs. The president said, "This will leave only the old, the sick, and the poor in traditional fee-for-service insurance. All the healthy people will be in MSAs, keeping their money instead of using it to pay for treating those who are sick." The president had proposed an MSA regional experiment, but Lott rejected the idea, saying that the Republicans wanted to take credit for putting MSAs into effect nationally. I proposed to the president and Lott a national experiment (to satisfy the Republicans) with numerical caps on how many people could join. Both agreed on the compromise conceptually. The problem now was to work out how many could participate and on what basis.

As the actual talks over the details of the bill unfolded, the president found that my relationship with Lott was getting in the way. He worried that I intimated to Lott too many of his ultimate intentions and thereby undermined his ability to bargain with a poker face. He worried that I had let Lott know how keen he was on the Kennedy-Kassebaum bill, and was increasingly concerned that I had forfeited his leverage in fighting the MSA experiment.

He had a valid point. I realized that I would have to withdraw from the detailed negotiating process and use my relationship simply to bring Lott to the table with the president with suggestions to each on the general parameters that might work.

When I was alone with the president, however, I regularly complained that we were losing the chance for a major accomplishment as we haggled over the details of how many people would be in the MSA experiment and on what terms it would operate. "Health care is the single biggest unkept promise of your administration," I said. "It is your biggest black eye. If you can get Kennedy-Kassebaum passed, it will get rid of all that. Who cares whether the MSA experiment is exactly right? Who cares how many it covers? The point is to give portability to two hundred fifty million Americans." I told him I felt it was like the Arab-Israeli talks, haggling for weeks over each detail. But the president felt the rules of the MSA pilot program were critical to his fight to protect Medicare.

Clinton would listen patiently and then say, "It's going to come out all right; just let Hilley and me handle it, and—*stay out!*"

After weeks of wrangling, they finally agreed to cap the MSA experiment at seven hundred thousand people and to ground rules that made the experiment a fair test of the concept.

The MSA deal that emerged, after weeks of intense effort by Hilley, Lott, and the president, was one of the few successful instances of give-and-take between the executive and the legislative branches of government during the 1995–96 session of Congress. It was also the maiden voyage of Lott's leadership and pointed to a successful future. With the MSA deal, the Kennedy-Kassebaum bill passed easily.

As Lott began to move the legislative agenda with alacrity, many speculated on his motives. Substantively, Lott simply said that it was time to start passing bills for America. Politically, he let the press know that he was worried that Republican incumbents might have to face the electorate with slim records of achievement and lengthy records of what they had failed to do. Lott reasoned that Dole was not showing the kind of long coattails the Republicans had hoped for and that it was unreasonable to stop bills from passing just to give Dole ammunition to shoot at Clinton in the '96 election.

It was this decision by Lott that probably won the Senate, and likely the House too, for the GOP in the '96 election. Had the Republicans remained totally obstinate, the public would have rejected them decisively. But when Senator Lott assumed the majority leadership and made it clear that the deadlock was over, he sent signals to the electorate that the GOP would hereafter work to influence legislation, not to kill it. He also showed that the Republicans had their fill of extremism by moving in the direction of the president's agenda—welfare reform, health-care portability, environmental protection, safe drinking water, and the minimum wage. This is not to say that once Lott had shown a degree of reasonableness the Senate would inevitably go Republican. I believe it was errors at the end of the Clinton campaign that caused the Senate to fall to the GOP. But without Trent's compromises, the Republicans would have had no chance at all.

True to his word, Trent allowed the minimum wage to come to a vote. It passed, to nobody's surprise, and headed for a conference committee. There Lott succeeded in guaranteeing a smooth passage, and the bill ended up on the president's desk unmolested.

Now the majority leader dared disentangle welfare reform and send it on its way. Previous attempts at welfare reform had failed. Fearful that the president would actually agree to it, thus robbing them of one of their dearest issues, the congressional Republicans had cynically tied the bill to the elimination of free health care for poor children and nursing-home care for the elderly, requiring that these Medicaid entitlements be replaced by block grants to be used at the states' discretion. They knew the president would never go along with these harsh cuts, and they looked forward with glee to his third veto of a welfare-reform bill. Their legislation would fail so their campaign issue might live.

But things were changing. I had predicted, earlier and prematurely, that the Republicans would split into hunter-gatherer groups. Now White House Political Affairs Director Doug Sosnik said the prediction was coming true. More interested in ensuring their own reelection than in sacrificing themselves for a lost presidential race, Republican legislators were now eager to enact laws they could take back to their districts as they campaigned.

Sensing the changed mood, Lott unlocked the welfare bill from its Medicaid cage and sprang it loose on the Senate floor.

In twice vetoing Republican welfare-reform proposals, Clinton had objected to the inadequate amount for day care. The bill now allowed for enough day care. He had complained that too little was available for welfare funds should a recession come. The contingency funds were now increased. He had protested that school lunches and child protection services should not be subject to state whim in a block grant and now they were not. Food stamps were restored as entitlements for U.S. citizens. These were substantial changes, but the president wanted more. He was under intense pressure from child-advocacy groups, particularly the Children's Defense Fund, on whose board the First Lady had once served. Protesting that a million children would still be cast into poverty by the bill, they lobbied hard for improvements. But what counted more than this outside pressure was the president's internal pressure—the constant demands of his own conscience fueled by his personal memories of poverty.

Most of Congress basically accepted the ideas of requiring work in exchange for welfare and limits on the length of time for which welfare could be collected, the core of the bill. The president advocated these changes. Over the objections of children's advocates and liberals, he also agreed to end the entitlement for welfare so that Washington would make block grants that the states would administer. "What sense does it make to call it an entitlement now," he asked me, "when Texas can pay one hundred eighty dollars a month and another state pays seven hundred? What kind of entitlement is that?"

The two big areas of controversy were the bill's cutoff of welfare, Medicaid, Social Security, and food stamps to legal immigrants and its failure to provide vouchers for diapers and other child-care necessities to children of mothers who had been on welfare and were cut off.

"Mr. Prime Minister, you're moving the goalposts," Trent said when I brought these protests to him. "You said you wanted school lunches fixed, and we did that. Then you wanted day care. Then you wanted a contingency fund. Then you wanted it separate from Medicaid. Now you're moving the goalposts back with a whole new set of demands. We've caved in on almost everything, and each time you all come back with more, more, more."

Lott knew that Clinton was in a difficult position. The majority leader figured no matter what the Republicans did on these new issues, the president would probably have to sign the bill or face the anger of the electorate for yet another veto. "Why shouldn't immigrants be cut off from benefits? They came here to be self-supporting, and if they're not, do we have a responsibility to pay for them?" Lott asked. He was open to the idea of a voucher for child-care needs for those who had exceeded the time limit, provided "it doesn't pay for anything a welfare mother herself can wear or eat."

For his part, Clinton was even more passionate in his disagreement. "An immigrant comes here legally, pays his taxes, works hard, and gets hit by a truck, and they want to cut off disability benefits to his child? Is that fair?" Whenever he talked about welfare reform, I could sense what Jefferson called the "war between his head and his heart."

Clinton's heart felt for poor children cut off from benefits because their mothers were irresponsible, as his own stepfather had been. He worried endlessly about immigrants, here lawfully and paying taxes, temporarily thrown out of work, and unable to get medical care for their children because of Medicaid cutbacks. This was no abstract issue to him; it was real human suffering. He would conjure up the most specific examples as he discussed his doubts about the bill, speaking of families he had met as he campaigned across the country. In the privacy of the room in which we sat alone, with no audience present, he told me of an immigrant who had waited on him when he spoke at a New York hotel. "What's going to happen to his children? That guy can't afford health care."

His head, though, responded that the basic parts of the bill—work for welfare and time limits—were critically important to end welfare "as we know it," which he had pledged in his campaign and deeply believed he must do.

I told him flatly that a welfare veto would cost him the election. Mark Penn had designed a polling model that indicated that a welfare veto by itself would transform a fifteen-point win into a three-point loss. Of all the developments that could realistically happen to affect the race, a welfare veto and Powell as Dole's VP ranked the worst in their impact on the president's fortunes.

"What good will you do if you lose?" I asked the president. "If you veto that bill and lose, what will the Republicans do then to the very people you want to help?"

The Senate restored Medicaid funds for legal immigrants but kept the cuts in welfare and other programs. Although they refused to provide vouchers for child-care needs for mothers whose time limits have expired, they did allow funds for child-protection agencies to help children in such situations. They also provided that states could waive the cutoff in many cases.

The president was still deeply concerned by the cuts that remained in place.

So was the First Lady. I made it a point to meet with Hillary at least every other week throughout 1996. In one such session in May she told me flatly that she did not want to become involved in the welfare-reform issue. "We have to do what we have to do, and I hope our friends understand it. It's OK to require time limits and work requirements. I've always felt so, and I still do," she had said. But now that the actual cuts in aid to immigrants and children whose mothers were cut off from welfare were to be presented to the president, she was unhappy. She noted, with some resignation, that I was advising a signature, not a veto, and said she supposed it was my job to look only at the politics of the issue. "I know the politics, I know the numbers, but it still bothers me deeply," she said.

My argument to the president made a similar point. He was in a foul mood when he called late in the evening on July 31, 1996. He was deeply unhappy with the welfare bill and showed it. I had given him cause to believe that Lott would produce a somewhat better bill than finally emerged. I thought that Trent was weakening on vouchers and food-stamp benefits for legal immigrants, but I was wrong. The final bill did grant Medicaid to legal immigrants, but the other cutoffs remained. Now he denounced Lott in the harshest of personal terms. "He *loved* cutting off children. You should have seen his face. He was *delighted* that he could savage them, *delighted,*" the president shouted.

Then he attacked me. "You've just given me biased polling on this bill. Did you ever ask if they want me to sign or veto a bill that would let three-year-old children starve, go hungry in the street, because their mother was cut off? You didn't ask that, did you? You didn't want to know the answer, did you? Did you ask if they wanted a father who waits his turn, waits for years to come here, comes here, works hard, is always employed, and suddenly gets hit by a truck. Did you ask if they wanted me to cut off benefits to his six-month-old baby now that he can't work? Did you ask that? I'll bet you didn't."

I pointed out that it was possible to stack any poll question so it came out one way or another, and I staunchly denied that I had ever tilted the polls in favor of his signing the welfare bill. "You know that my job is giving purely political advice," I replied. "I'll tell you what I think is the objective political reality and then talk substance if you want." Rival pollsters have often accused me of "cooking" poll data to support my own point of view. I don't and I never have. The simple answer to this kind of charge is that I would have failed if I had disregarded the public's true feelings in my polls and replaced them with my own.

The president seemed almost to collapse at the other end of the phone, his rage spent. He had unburdened himself of his deep emotional pain at the cuts the welfare bill imposed and wanted me to see it first-hand. Now he was ready to listen.

I was genuinely moved by his agony. It wasn't a political anguish, a concern about offending liberals or moderates. It was not that at all. The politics pointed one way and one way only: toward signing. On balance, I knew the president felt that work requirements, day-care funding, and time limits were vital to reducing welfare dependency in America. But the cuts tortured the poor boy he had once been and he needed to show the pain.

I argued back: "I think you have to see the bill as the start of a process, not as a stand-alone piece of legislation. You'll never get a bill with strict enough cutoff requirements out of a Democratic Congress to have any real credibility. You'll get this end of the equation—the 're-sponsibility' end—only from a Republican Congress. So take it while it's on your desk. Then win the election. Once you win—and hopefully carry Congress with you—"

"You think I'll carry Congress if I sign this bill?" he interrupted.

"If you sign this bill and don't screw up the rest of the campaign, I think you'll win by twelve to seventeen points. If you do that, I think you'll carry Congress." I continued, "Then you can get to stage two: fixing the bill to delete the onerous cuts on legal immigrants and get some child vouchers passed. Then, later in your second term, you can go to stage three, and provide the 'opportunity' part of the equation by proposing a massive program of inner-city jobs for people getting off welfare. But if you veto the bill, there'll never be a welfare reform period."

"Bruce Reed made the same point in today's meeting," the president replied. "He said welfare reform is a process, not just a piece of legislation." Reed, a staunch "New Democrat," was one of my closest allies in the battle for welfare reform. Almost alone among the insiders on the White House staff, he fought hard to get the president to sign the bill. Bruce knew a lot about welfare reform and used his knowledge to debunk the claims of liberal staffers who suggested the bill was worse than it really was.

"Do you think that when I sign this bill, I can say exactly what changes I will seek in my second term? Can I spell it out?" he asked.

"Absolutely. Shout it from the rooftops. You're right that these cuts are not what America wants; the Republicans are getting it wrong again. You can sign the bill and still attack the cuts. The country will be behind you now and they will be behind you when you fix the cuts next year," I said.

"That's a good point," he said, the head winning over the heart. "It's a process, and we're just starting out." Then he added, "Bruce made another good point today. He says this is a good welfare-reform bill buried in a bad budget-cut bill. After all, the welfare parts of it are OK: work requirements, time limits, day care, Medicaid unchanged, a contingency fund if we hit a recession—not large enough, but by the time a recession comes, they'll probably add more money. It's not a bad bill. It's got all the things I've been fighting for over the years. But then they added all these cuts that have nothing to do with welfare reform, like the cuts on aid to immigrants. That's really a budget bill, and we can change it when we get back in January. Might be able to change some of it in the immigration bill this September."

I replied, "I believe that your signing of this bill, coupled with the recent cuts in the crime rate, will usher in a sixties-like era of commitment to helping poor people. The burrs under the saddle that drove America mad—the welfare mothers who don't look for work but collect checks, the high crime rate with token punishments—these irritants are fading. And the normal American spirit of generosity and equality is winning out. This bill will hasten the process and will make possible a commitment to providing jobs and good schools for the inner city that was not possible before."

The president was impressed by these arguments and probed each one. "You really think this will improve racial attitudes, don't you?"

"I do, and after you sign it, I think the turnaround will be self-evident," I replied.

I cited a poll we had conducted months before to test the impact of welfare reform. "We polled two identical samples and asked them both the same series of questions about how much spending on poor people and inner cities they would support. We asked questions like, Would you favor a major increase in government spending on inner-city schools? and, Would you support a big tax incentive for businesses to get them to hire people now on welfare? But in the first sample, we asked only the questions. In the second, we prefaced the questions by saying, 'Please assume that Congress has passed and the president has signed a welfare-reform bill requiring welfare recipients to work and setting time limits for how long people can stay on welfare.' "

I reported the results: "We found that the sample which assumed welfare reform had passed were fifteen points more willing to see spending in the inner cities increased than were the others. The welfare-reform group backed these measures by an average of about sixty-five percent, while only about half of the control group supported them."

"Those are good points," the president said as he hung up. "Good points."

The next day, as I held my breath, he announced he would sign welfare reform, repeating his argument that this was a good welfare bill inside a bad budget bill.

The White House staff deeply resented my role in urging the president to sign the bill. I believe that both Panetta and Stephanopoulos thought Clinton would veto it at the last minute and assumed that it was my advice that had "turned him around."

The truth was very different. The president required no turning around at all. He had always known that if a welfare reform bill that included adequate day care, nutrition programs, and the like came to his desk, he would sign it. The provisions penalizing immigrants were unfortunate, in his view, but he would not sacrifice the reforms for them.

He was also persuaded that welfare reform was a long process and that this was the first step. The defects in the bill could likely be fixed after the election. He also trusted my political judgment that he would carry Congress if he signed this bill.

An hour after his press announcement, he phoned me and asked how I thought he did.

"Splendid," I said.

"I want you to know I signed that bill because I trust you," he told me.

Trust me? I knew what he meant. He signed the bill because he believed that I could help him win by a sufficient margin to bring in a Democratic House and Senate to help him change the bad features of the bill. That day I felt he had given me a second mandate: not just to assure his election, but to work to elect a Democratic Congress as well.

After the welfare announcement, I began to see the large shifts in public opinion that our polling had predicted. Voters were willing to open their hearts and their government's checkbook to be sure that welfare reform succeeded. In one survey, we asked rural voters in Republican states like the Dakotas, Nebraska, Iowa, Kansas, and rural Missouri if they would be willing to give up the ethanol tax break, which is dear to all corn growers, if the revenues could be used instead to provide jobs for inner-city welfare recipients. Over 80 percent of the voters in these areas, where there are few inner cities or minorities, said yes, they would be willing to see their own tax loopholes closed to make welfare reform work.

The president was thrilled by the news. Energized, he began to see welfare reform as a major task for his second term, not as a bill to be signed and forgotten.

In early August after his announcement that he would sign the legislation I told the president that I felt Americans were becoming committed to a grand social contract. "The middle class understands that the poor are doing their end of the bargain. Crime is down. Welfare is down. Welfare reform has passed. Affirmative action is being cleansed of quotas. Now they'll accept their end—to provide the jobs, schools, day care, and training to make welfare-reform work."

Clinton was fascinated with the idea at our meeting and referred to it constantly in the remaining weeks we were together. More than anything else, I wish I had been able to stay on long enough to help advance this new social contract. But it remains as a new political reality. Politicians who would oppose jobs programs for welfare recipients and want to punish welfare mothers rather than help them find jobs misread the temper of America. Welfare reform is the achievement of a generation of effort, and voters are determined to make it work.

But, of course, President Clinton now faces a Republican Congress. I feel badly about his not winning Congress, especially after my reassurances. When I made these predictions I believed I was setting a task I would have worked on myself that, with luck, might have been attainable. But I never got the chance.

But Clinton did win overwhelmingly, as he might not have done if he had vetoed the welfare bill. I will discuss later why he won by eight points, not the larger leads he held during much of the race.

▲

Toward the end of my tenure, our conversations changed from only daily politics to the larger ideas of social trends and presidential turning points. On Sunday morning, August 4, 1996, I began my telephone call matter-of-factly, as he liked it. "Mr. President, if you have a moment, I have some ideas that might be interesting in a broader context. I was thinking last night about our great presidents and about where you fit in. Do you have a minute to talk about it?"

"Sure do," he replied, and I could hear him settling into a chair in the White House residence.

"I can think of eighteen outstanding presidents," I began. Since Clinton is the forty-first person to be president,* twenty-two presidents didn't deserve ranking, in my estimation.

"Let's hear the list," he urged.

"In the first tier are presidents who did great things but also did them in great times. I don't think you can get onto the first tier unless you have the right backdrop."

"You mean a war or something like that?" he asked.

"Right, so I have Washington, Jefferson, Lincoln, Wilson, and Franklin Roosevelt on the list in my first tier," I said.

"Wilson?" he questioned.

I conceded, "I thought a lot about that one, but when you add in the New Freedom agenda, the creation of the Federal Reserve, and then the idea of world law and the League of Nations, I'd put him up there."

"Makes sense to me," Clinton answered. "What about Theodore Roosevelt? And where do you put Truman?"

"I put them both in the second tier. They did great things, but the backdrop was not quite as compelling as Lincoln's or Washington's," I answered.

---

* He is called the forty-second president because Grover Cleveland was elected twice, but not sequentially.

"Yeah, I think you're right," the current president replied. "And who else is in your second tier?"

"I put Jackson, Polk—for doubling the size of our country—and Ronald Reagan," I continued, emphasizing the last name to elicit Clinton's comments.

"Polk's a good choice," he began. "I agree with your list, but why Reagan?"

"He won the Cold War, and he probably permanently lowered the tax rates in America. He began an era of less government. But mainly his defeat of communism; that's what really does it for me," I answered.

"Hummm," he pondered, "maybe. Third tier for Reagan, I think."

"OK," I conceded. "My other third tier choices are James Madison, for winning the war of 1812; Andrew Johnson, for standing up to Congress and preserving the presidency; Chester Alan Arthur, for the civil service system; Grover Cleveland, for breaking out of the boss era and making integrity a yardstick for government; John Kennedy, maybe out of sentiment, but he did begin the end of the Cold War with his test ban treaty with Khrushchev and set a tone for an entire generation. Then I put in Lyndon Johnson. I think he deserves second tier for the civil rights bill and the Great Society, but Vietnam knocks him down by a tier."

"Right, he did some great things, but with Vietnam, I think you're right. What about Nixon?" he asked.

"He's also third tier for me. Deserved second tier for China, but Watergate drops him down," I answered.

"And don't forget his environmental laws and legal services and a lot of his domestic legislation," Clinton added. "You skipped Eisenhower."

"Yeah," I answered, "he didn't do anything. Popularity doesn't get you on the list. And I don't know how you feel about it, but I put Bush in third tier because he set up a new global role for the United States in the aftermath of the Cold War and handled the Russian transition pretty well."

"I agree," he said with surprising alacrity and generosity. It was the fourth or fifth time I'd mentioned Bush to him, and he was always uniformly kind to his defeated predecessor.

"Good list," he said, "where do I fit in?"

"Right now, to be honest, I think you are borderline third tier. It's too early to rank you yet, but you are right on the cusp of making third tier."

"I think that's about right," he said.

"You know what's interesting about this list?" I continued. "It doesn't matter much what the economy was doing while the president was in office."

"Yeah, it has so much to do with whether you get reelected or not, but history kind of forgets it," Clinton agreed.

"The economy and crime," I continued, "seem to be cyclical, and it doesn't really matter from a historical point of view. These are the two leading issues people care most about, but they don't make history."

"What do you think I need to do to become first tier?" he asked.

"You can't be first tier"—I broke the bad news to him gently—"unless unanticipated historical forces put you there."

"Like a war," he agreed. "OK, second tier?"

"I would say three big things and four medium things," I answered.

He asked me to wait while he got paper and a pen. "OK, what are the big things?" he asked as he returned to the phone.

"First, I think you have to make welfare reform work. That's what got me started on all this last night," I answered. "You signed the bill, now you have to fix the bill, and then you have to implement the bill so that it really works. If you can end the welfare underclass—not just punish it like the Republicans want, but really end it by providing the jobs and the schools to go with the work requirement and the time limits—then I think that would do more than anything else to qualify you for second tier."

"You know, so many people have come up to me and said, 'When you talked about welfare reform as a process, not as a bill, I didn't think of it that way, but you're right.' "

"FDR tried and failed. Johnson tried and failed. And the country understands that if you fail too, we've got a permanent underclass in this country that will drag us down," I said.

"What's the second thing?" the president prompted.

"I think you have to implement the balanced-budget plans you've laid out. Ever since Roosevelt started to pile up deficits, we've never been able to live within our means, within our revenues, if the president is an activist."

"FDR always said he was going to balance the budget, but he never did," Clinton said.

"He ran saying he would," I pointed out.

"But never did," Clinton repeated.*

I pressed on: "Eisenhower ran surpluses, but he didn't do anything much. So did Truman when we were demobilizing. But you'll be the

* In 1936 he tried. It was a disaster, precipitating another depression.

first one to show that government can be activist, do things, and still live within our means. Deficits are not the inevitable price of activism."

"I agree with that," Clinton responded.

I deeply believe that one way or another, President Clinton, in his second term, will eliminate the budget deficit.

"Finally," I said, "I think you have to break the international back of terrorism by economic and military action against the terrorist states. You had hoped to do it with the peace process, but Peres's defeat closed that door. Now you have to smash it militarily and through sanctions," I added, finishing the list of the top three achievements that I thought would qualify him for a place in the second tier of presidents.

"That's a good list," Clinton commented. "It puts things into perspective. What are your four medium achievements?"

"Tobacco—setting it on the path to extinction by cutting back on teen smoking. Education—developing the notion of a federal responsibility for setting national standards that are consonant with local administration. It's ridiculous that the second most important issue voters cite is not a federal responsibility, at least insofar as standards are concerned."

"Damn right," he agreed.

"Health care—a step-by-step process. Kennedy-Kassebaum took the first step. Insurance for the unemployed will be the second step, and coverage for all children the third step."

"I think we can get children covered by the end of the second term," he ventured.

"I agree," I said. "Finally, moving your values agenda by improving the everyday lives of people through presidential—but not necessarily governmental—action." I wanted to emphasize this last point, so I continued. "In a way, it's a lesser issue than with Theodore Roosevelt's extending government responsibility into conservation and protection of the consumer and far less than FDR's extending the government mandate to include the economic well-being of its citizens, but it's in the same category. You can make the presidency permanently concerned with noneconomic lifestyle issues, as Nixon did with crime."

"Good list," he concluded. "I've got it down; I'll think about it a lot," he promised, and we hung up.

This was the first time we had been able to rise above the day-by-day political and look ahead substantively. I was following Gore's advice to "encourage him to lead." I didn't know that my departure was only twenty-five days away.

On the Right Track

Something significant happened to America in July 1996.

The most important question pollsters ask in their surveys is: Would you say that the country is on the right track, or have things gotten off on the wrong track? The ratio of right track to wrong track responses is the fundamental statistic upon which politics is based. Are voters happy or unhappy with the way things are going?

Since the end of the Gulf War and the subsequent recession that choked off our patriotic optimism, voters have told pollsters that America is on the wrong track. At first, Clinton exploited this concern to defeat Bush and win as an insurgent promising change. But except for a brief flurry of optimism right after the '92 election, this underlying dissatisfaction overshadowed Clinton's presidency.

When I first started working for Clinton, only 30 percent of the voters said things were on the right track, and over 60 percent said we were on the wrong track. By June 1996, after eighteen months of better economic news, reduced budget deficits, falling welfare rolls, and foreign policy successes, only 36 percent felt things were going well and 54 percent of the voters still felt things were going wrong. It wasn't that they thought the Republicans could do better. The president was ahead in the polls. People were just clinging to their depression.

It seemed hopeless to think we could ever persuade voters that things were going well enough to reverse this four-and-a-half-year-old pessimism. Good economic news, which usually encourages a right-track view, seemed to have lost its traditional impact. Lifestyle issues, such as we were addressing in our values agenda—like crime, fears about retirement, concerns about affordable medical care, and a sense of unease about the values and education of the younger generation—overcame personal economic optimism and left most voters with a wrong-track view of things in general.

But in July 1996, it all changed. And it changed fast.

Just before the Republican National Convention, voters had flipped from a 36–54 right track–wrong track ratio to a 46–44 edge for the right track—a huge change in a short space of time.

The Republican Convention, with its insistence that all was wrong in America, restored the wrong-track plurality, but the right track soon reaffirmed its dominance in the weeks that followed and continues through this day

What caused the turnaround? The Olympics had a lot to do with it, but so did the firming up of good economic news and the sudden break in the paralysis in Congress with the almost simultaneous passage of welfare reform, the Kennedy-Kassebaum health reforms, the minimum-wage increase, the Safe Drinking Water Act, and pesticide-control legislation.

Doug Schoen, Mark Penn, and I heralded the dramatic mood shift in our strategy meetings in late July and early August. "You see this kind of shift in this space of time very, very rarely," Doug Schoen told the president in July.

The swing set an entirely different context for the presidential race. In the short term, it permitted Clinton to recoup quickly the three-point decline he had suffered during the June FBI-file and Whitewater hearings, restoring his lead to a healthy seventeen points.

But more permanently, it ushered in a new national willingness to get things done. In discussing this change with the president, I cited Arthur Schlesinger's masterful study, *The Cycles of American History* (1987). The Schlesinger book, updating observations of the author's father, notes that Americans seem to swing from periods of exhaustion to periods of rapid activity, from inertia to intervention. Schlesinger argues that this almost manic-depressive cycle in social attitudes may be discerned throughout our history. Exhausted by the depression, World War II, and Korea, we collapsed into the passive arms of General Eisenhower. By the 1960s, he writes, we had recovered our vital force. We plunged into an era marked by protest and activism, by the civil rights movement and the Great Society, only to be exhausted again by Vietnam and Watergate, which led to a passivity that lasted through the Reagan and Bush years.

Whether Schlesinger's observations about the past cyclical nature of our history explains everything is something the president and I had discussed frequently before. Now it seemed that his prediction of an up cycle was coming true right before our eyes in July.

The Olympics played very well in America, not so much because America won, but because of television's emphasis this year on individual stories of heroism, the courage of specific athletes, American and foreign, and the resilience displayed after the bombing. We had polled the themes people would most want to see featured in the Olympics. The idea of taking individual responsibility for self-improvement and overcoming obstacles and handicaps to reach high levels of achievement resonates deeply within the American consciousness. The president underscored these themes. But the change of mood came primarily from politics, not sport. The break in the gridlock in Congress was crucial and Bill Clinton and Trent Lott can take credit.

It was against this renewed optimism that Bob Dole and the Republicans sought to build a case based on national disillusion. It was the wrong message, delivered by the wrong messenger at the wrong time.

Historical analysis warned us that since 1960 the average convention had produced a ten-point "bounce" in the polls. Our trick, I said, must be to hold our loss to ten points or less and recoup at our convention. I calculated that once the conventions were over, the average change in vote share between Labor Day and election day would be less than six percentage points.

If we held the Republican convention to a ten-point bounce and recouped it at our convention, we stood little chance of losing the election.

We had two fond hopes for the Republican Convention as it began in San Diego in the first few days of August: that it would be ultra-right-wing, like the 1992 Houston convention, and highly negative toward Clinton. Our polling showed that a right-wing convention that featured abortion and drove moderates out of the party would work greatly to our advantage. It also showed us that people were tired of negatives and wanted, instead, to hear what the presidential candidate was going to do if he was elected.

The Republican polling must have reflected the same result because the convention presented a moderate image, and a largely positive message.

But the Republicans did one thing wrong: they sent the wrong message. They bet all their chips on a 15 percent tax cut launched by Dole just a week before they met. His idea was that economic growth was flat and that a tax cut would get the country moving again.

He sought to borrow themes from those John Kennedy had used to push his successful tax cut in 1961, which did, indeed, usher in a period of high growth and low unemployment. But to watch seventy-three-year-old Bob Dole imitating a forty-three-year-old John Kennedy was pitiful.

In his advocacy of such tax cuts, Dole was betraying a lifetime of opposition to cuts that could not be offset by spending reductions. He had castigated the supply-siders who hoped fervently that tax cuts would stimulate so much growth and new revenue that the deficit would go down too. It hadn't worked out that way in the '80s when Reagan tried it. The deficit scared away investors and dried up capital. Economic growth did increase slightly, but not nearly enough to offset the jump in the deficit. The deficit's growth created a long-term hangover that depressed the economy far longer than the buzz from the tax-cut cocktail stimulated it. But here was Dole pushing the same discredited theory. Americans found it odd.

Anticipating Dole's move, we had run ads for three weeks heralding the good economic news and criticizing Dole for taxes he had increased during his thirty-five-year career. After telling voters that Dole had voted for nine hundred tax increases, the announcer in one ad summarized them by saying, "Bob Dole, thirty-five years of higher taxes."

When Dole announced his tax cut, George Stephanopoulos and Gene Sperling cast doubts on the cut, pointing out, for example, that over two hundred billion dollars of the tax cut lacked offsetting spending cuts. Our polling showed that people approved each of the tax cuts that Dole was proposing, but they thought the whole package was too big, would increase the deficit, and was an election-year stunt by a desperate candidate. Voters did not believe that Dole had undergone a conversion to supply-side economics and would not approve it if he had.

These results illustrated one of my favorite rules of politics: if you change positions, the people who once agreed with you will hate you for it, but the people who used to disagree with you won't believe that you're sincere, so they'll still dislike you. Nothing is gained by changing positions.

The most interesting discovery we came across is that people firmly believed that less is more when it comes to cutting taxes. We asked voters whether they would rather see a $550-billion tax cut (Dole's proposal) or a $110-billion tax cut (Clinton's proposal). They voted, in our poll, two to one for the smaller tax cut.

"It's like the old joke about Atlantic City," I told the president. "First prize is four days in Atlantic City. Second prize is a month."

Voters felt the larger tax cut would mess up the economy. But in my opinion, the voters were making a more profound statement. The polling, I told the president, suggests that "voters don't want to vote their own pocketbooks at this point in our history. They want to vote what they think is right and just. It's of a piece with the increasing commitment to jobs for welfare people. They aren't motivated by self-interest nearly so much as they are by the public interest."

I pointed out, for example, that more people wanted a tax cut for businesses that created jobs for welfare recipients than wanted the capital-gains tax cut for people who sold their homes. "The second tax cut will benefit the sixty-five percent of Americans who own their homes and may someday want to sell. The welfare tax cut won't benefit the overwhelming majority of people at all, but it will help solve the welfare problem. They prefer the welfare tax cut to the homeowners' tax cut because they are focusing on the public interest, not on themselves."

Clinton was fascinated by the observation. "So when they say people vote their pocketbooks, they really don't?" he asked.

"That's right. Dole is fundamentally misreading them. When he offers everyone a fifteen percent tax cut and you say no and offer a tax cut to people trying to go to college or to low-income workers or to families trying to raise children or to businesses hiring welfare recipients, they prefer your approach even though it benefits them directly much less than Dole's approach is supposed to."

For months, we had waited impatiently for Dole's tax-cut plan, knowing that voters preferred the "targeted" tax cuts Clinton was offering. The Republican walked right into the trap.

Once again, the decade of the 1990s was showing itself to be the "we" decade.

"It's a form of triangulation," I said to the president. "Old Democrats don't want to cut taxes at all. Republicans want to cut them in order to roll back the public sector and let people keep more of their own money. We want to cut taxes to do specific things for specific deserving people. Just as we targeted our spending when government was growing, we should target our tax cuts when government shrinks."

Unable to punch through before the convention with his ideas and engulfed by a bitter platform fight over abortion, Dole did not gain a single point in the run-up to his convention. We waited with some anxiety for his choice of running mate.

I was most alarmed early in August when the president called to say, "I have it on good authority that Dole offered the VP spot to Bill Bennett." That scared me. As former education secretary, drug czar, and bestselling author with his book on virtues, Bennett could compete with us on our basic issues: children, values, and schools. He would have made a tough opponent. I assumed that the president's source was Bill Bennett's brother, Bob, who is also Clinton's lawyer. The next day I learned from the president that Bill Bennett had turned Dole down. I heard Dole renewed the offer and still Bennett refused. Had Bennett accepted and persuaded Dole to run on values, we would have been in trouble.

Now we had Kemp. On Friday, August 9, Dole began to put real gains up on the board. His announcement of Kemp as his running mate caught America—and us—by surprise and gave his candidacy new life. Kemp is better liked nationally than Dole. He could probably have defeated Dole for the nomination. His designation now seemed to say that Dole was open to new ideas and new people. Even if Dole couldn't be exciting, maybe his appointees could be. Our polling showed that Clinton's lead had fallen by three points.

As the Republicans opened their convention, their run at our lead continued. Ahead by seventeen points before their convention, we slipped to fourteen after Kemp's announcement and dropped another point after Nancy Reagan's Monday-night performance and General Colin Powell's moving speech that same evening. Our polls suggested that voters saw the Republicans as reaching out to moderates and rising above partisan calls to the faithful.

Then on Tuesday night the Republicans stepped all over themselves. Susan Molinari's cheerleader performance in the keynote address struck voters as juvenile and sophomoric. She was seen as a nice, enthusiastic person, but not someone to listen to on something as serious as choosing a president. What really turned voters off, though, was Texas Senator Kay Bailey Hutchison's negative speech earlier on Tuesday night. It received the worst ratings of any major speech by any speaker at either convention.

When the Texas senator rattled off her chain of adjectives to describe Clinton—"high-taxing, free-spending, promise-breaking, Social Security–taxing, health-care-socializing, drug-coddling, power-grabbing"—voters turned sour. All of our polling showed that voters wanted a positive convention. The Republicans scored no gains from their Tuesday-night name calling, and their convention was seen unfavorably by a plurality of voters.

Then Elizabeth Dole's electrifying speech reached America in a big way as she descended from the podium to stand amid the audience to recount her husband's struggle to overcome a disability. She had flown in under the voters' bullshit detector, and her style resonated deeply. Elizabeth Dole had left politics and talked to America in a different way.

After her speech, our polling showed a further three-point gain for Dole, reducing our lead from thirteen points to ten. As much as Tuesday night's ludicrous performance by Hutchison heartened me, Wednesday night sent a chill through my body.

I called the president every morning during the Republican Convention as he vacationed in the Grand Tetons, where he studiously avoided watching the convention. In the hopes of blunting the Republican Convention gains, I had pushed successfully to have him announce on Monday, right before the convention opened, an agreement to save Yellowstone National Park from mining. This may or may not have accomplished my goal, but it did shorten the president's vacation by a day and left him in a foul mood as the Republican Convention began. Each morning, I lifted his spirits by showing that the Republican gain was well within our predictions and about average for a party at a convention. Each day he groused that he hadn't slept well the night before, doubtless because he worried about what he wasn't watching on TV.

The weekend before the convention, he was even worse. He called me ten times in three days to suggest a new line of attack against Jack Kemp. "Check out his record at HUD." "What's the impact on the voters of Dole's criticism of Kemp's supply-side economics?" "Kemp endorsed the gold standard; do voters think that's wacky?" And so on.

Then I made a mistake. I called the president on Wednesday night, right after Elizabeth Dole's speech. My purpose was to reassure him that we'd get the points back during our convention. Instead, I stepped on a land mine. The vacation had not been going well at all, and Clinton blamed me for calling him at night, interrupting "the first good night

I've had since this damn vacation started. You shouldn't be calling me like this at night when I'm out here trying to have a vacation. You ought to be ashamed of yourself, intruding on my privacy like this."

"I'm sorry, sir, I didn't—"

"Well you ought to be," he continued. "We talk every morning, but now you want my evenings too. I haven't been sleeping well, and today I had a good game of golf, and for once, for the first time on this vacation, I'm really able to sit here at night and try to relax, and you call me and screw it up."

God, get me out of this, I thought. "I really apologize—"

"Well, you should apologize," he said. "I have a right to a vacation, just as anybody else does. *You* take vacations. *You* go to France all the damned time. Why can't I have a vacation *too* without your calling and interrupting me."

It continued like this for literally five—count 'em, five—minutes. That's three hundred seconds. Eventually, he let me hang up.

After he had settled down, he called me back, about an hour later, to apologize. Eileen answered the phone, furious at how he had treated me when I was trying to assuage the worries I knew he must have had. As usual, the operator said the president was calling. "He won't take the call," Eileen said irately. "He's gone to sleep."

"But, ma'am," the operator said in disbelief, "it *is* the president himself calling."

"He still won't take the call," my valiant wife said as I took the phone from her and said hello.

She went back to sleep, and I went to the next room to talk.

Clinton was contrite as I was about calling at night during his vacation.

We talked about the Republican Convention and the impact it was having. "I'm really worried that we're not getting on top of them," he began. He questioned my recommendation to avoid negatives during our convention and focus instead on values-related positives. "I don't know what all this happy talk you have planned will accomplish," he said testily. "What's happened to you? What's gotten into you? You used to believe in negatives. You used to be the best negative campaigner around. Have you gone mellow? Are you losing touch?"

I assured him I was still as capable of nastiness as ever, when the situation called for it. We discussed the plans for our convention for half an hour and had a productive call.

Had Bob Dole followed his wife's speech with an appeal to independents and with an upbeat message, he could have turned the election around that night. She had teed it up for him. All he had to do was swing hard and get a hole in one. But as usual, Dole failed to rise to the occasion.

Terrified that he would do well, I watched his speech in my hotel room with Doug Schoen and Bill Knapp. We had been constantly on the phone with Tom Freedman, who was with George in San Diego, and had gotten an advance text of the speech. George and I were vastly relieved at its partisan oratory: "It's not a ten," Stephanopoulos said prophetically.

Dole blundered badly. His delivery was good, but his content was terrible. Rather than discuss the future, he offered to be a bridge to the past, a line that is destined to live in the history of convention faux pas.

Instead of talking about how he'd help the average American, he spoke of his own honor, courage, truthfulness, and integrity. Good talk for older male voters, who switched to him in considerable numbers that night, but of absolutely no interest to anybody under fifty. Far from building on the image of compassion that Liddy Dole had set for him, he came across as somewhere between grumpy and unsympathetic as he mirrored the rigidity of his party's ideological doctrines.

George called as Dole was saying good night. "What did you think?" he asked.

"It's a time warp," I replied. "His crack about bridges to the past was the greatest mistake at a convention since Goldwater's defense of extremism."

George agreed and went out to spin the press with that line.

"His speech—and their whole convention—was about *him*, about Dole, about their party," I told the president the next morning (no more night phone calls for me while he was on vacation). "It's their vulnerability. Our convention will be about *you* the voter and what we will do to help *you*, not about how great we are."

Dole blew it. The polls dutifully recorded a further three-point decline in our lead, down to seven points, as a result of the sheer weight of press coverage. But I was confident that Dole had missed the mark completely and that we would get all those points back and then some.

Why was Dole so inept? Why was his campaign, from beginning to end, one of the worst in our history?

I had studied the Republican party from within as one of their consultants. If you are in their field of fire, they are deadly. Raise taxes, go soft on crime, oppose work for welfare, weaken the military? They're all over you yelling "liberal." If you wander into their line of fire, they're going to kill you every time. But they have no other game plan, no other way to win. If you come around behind them or alongside and don't raise taxes, if you're tough on crime and want to reform welfare, use the military effectively, and cut spending, they can't hit you. A tank can rotate its turret—a Republican can't.

The president evaded the Republican fire through triangulation, which made it impossible for anyone to label him a liberal. But the Democrats who ran for Congress were linked to labor money and Democratic orthodoxy in the minds of many voters. Unable and unwilling to triangulate, they were mowed down by Republican charges of liberalism.

On election night, as the Senate went Republican and the House did too, I thought, *There but for triangulation goes Clinton.*

The president contemplated his ten-point drop after the Republican convention with surprising equanimity. After his outburst on Wednesday night, he calmed down and believed we would get the points back.

The Conventions

We had been planning our convention for months, based on Mark Penn's polling and a lot of practical suggestions from Tom Freedman and Naomi Wolf. Our approach was to demonstrate to Americans that we were a party of values, dedicated to restoring and strengthening in concrete, practical ways the values on which they base their lives. Then we would show how Dole opposed the values issues we stood for: gun controls, limits on tobacco marketing to teenagers, family and medical leave, and so on.

Penn began our planning by noting that his polling indicated "we have nothing to gain by identification with the Democratic party. We are seen by the voters more favorably—more fiscally responsible, more values-oriented, more compassionate, more of everything—than the Democratic party as a whole. We don't want this convention to be about the party. We want it to be about Bill Clinton."

These insights drew enthusiasm for Harry Thomasson's idea of the president's pre-convention whistle-stop train tour. Harry is a bearded

Arkansan who moved to California and, with his wife, Linda Bloodworth, became successful in television production. Harry paints scenes in the air with his hands to demonstrate his ideas. He had been active in Clinton's '92 campaign and, with his wife, had produced *The Man from Hope,* which eloquently introduced Clinton to America. I liked and admired him from the start. The Clintons, especially Hillary, consider him a dear friend.

Penn, who pointed out that "every vote we need to win the election is within five hundred miles of the convention center in Chicago," worked with Harry to structure a train route that would take us by the front yards of a good portion of these voters' homes in Ohio and Michigan.

Hillary was worried the ever-zealous Secret Service would stop train and car travel in all directions to let the president's train pass. She was right to be sensitive. We learned that if we had kept to our original plan and gone to Pittsburgh by train, we would have tied up the entire eastern seaboard's rail network, which apparently operates out of that city. We averted that disaster by starting in West Virginia instead.

The Clintons presided over our first meeting to discuss the convention. Someone asked whether Hillary should join her husband on the train. The First Lady rarely attended political meetings, and this was the first full strategy meeting she had attended since I began working for Clinton two years earlier. She had been taking an awful pounding in the press, over the Whitewater and FBI-file scandals, and the president was deeply sympathetic. As we discussed whether Hillary should go on the train, the president reached over and took her hand, held it in his lap, and said, "I don't want to spend three days on a train without you." The room fell silent, and a tender moment passed between them. It was one of those moments the voters would dismiss as political posturing if it occurred in public. The president bit his lower lip; she looked serene and happy. They looked into each other's eyes. But this was not a public performance. There was nobody there but hard-eyed professionals long since committed to working for the Clintons. The emotions were real and we knew it.

Once before, in 1994, when Hillary was on the grill for her high profile, I said to her on the phone, "People just don't get it. It's that you really love him; that's all." She broke down and sobbed into the phone. She was alone, crying her eyes out.

Now, as we talked about the train trip, I said it would be an empty gesture if we did not dignify it by announcing substantive initiatives each day. If we could keep attention focused on the train during the day and on the convention at night, we would be holding two conventions at once, one at six (eastern time) on the evening news and another later, when the convention was broadcast live. We just needed to be sure we had something to say from the train.

The president approved enthusiastically.

We decided that on Monday we would announce our backing of legislation prohibiting the sale of handguns to anyone with a conviction for domestic violence.

Then I met with Secretary of Education Dick Riley and his staff. Our polling put education near the top of the voters' agenda, a new development, since it used to be seen only as a state or a local problem. I suggested that we propose establishing a universal prekindergarten year of schooling, an option for all children. Riley suggested the literacy project instead: a commitment that every American child be able to read independently and well by the third grade. Riley thought this program made the most sense for children. Polling confirmed the popularity of this idea, and we scheduled it for the second day.

To plan an environmental event for the third day, I met with Katie McGinty, head of the Council on Environmental Policy, which Gore had got Clinton to set up in the White House. Accustomed to being last on everybody's agenda, McGinty was thrilled at my insistence on pushing environmental initiatives. She developed a number of proposals, which became the basis for Wednesday's announcement.

The most exciting idea for Wednesday night came from Eileen, who told me that in Connecticut, liens are frequently placed on defendants' property at the beginning of a trial to stop them from selling their assets before a judgment is awarded and paid in full. With assistance from Bill Curry, we developed a program to put liens on the property of polluters at the start of litigation to ensure that they clean up their mess. These liens would block sales or mergers or takeovers of the offending corporation until the pollution was cleaned up. In one stroke, it seemed to me, this concept would make polluters want to resolve environmental claims quickly rather than let them drag on for decades, as they now try to do. Gore and McGinty loved the idea. It was announced from the train, and I hope that one day it becomes law.

The Republicans had sliced ten points off our lead, but they had tripped badly by failing to send the president the welfare-reform, minimum-wage, and Kennedy-Kassebaum bills until after their convention. The Constitution gives the president only ten days in which to sign a bill, but allows Congress to take whatever time it likes to send the bill to the president after it has been passed. The GOP waited three weeks to send Clinton the controversial welfare-reform bill, forcing him to sign it—or not sign it—right before the Democratic Convention met. The Republicans hoped that if he signed the bill the Democratic left would go berserk, turning the convention into a repetition of the confrontational 1968 Chicago convention.

The plot backfired. It gave Clinton the opportunity to sign the three popular bills immediately after the Republican Convention on succeeding days. And on the fourth day, he announced that tobacco-marketing restrictions aimed at protecting teenagers, which he had endorsed the year before, would now take effect. The impact of these signings, one day after the other, was so immense in rekindling the public's feeling of optimism and America's sense of being on the right track that it actually cut four points from the Republican gains even before the Democratic Convention began. By the time the convention was gaveled into session, our lead had risen from seven points back up to eleven.

Press secretary Mike McCurry urged me to do a few on-the-record interviews with newspapers and magazines before the convention started. Until then, I'd resisted such interviews. The election is about the candidate and his staff, not about his consultants, and I always felt it was wrong for a consultant to detract attention from his boss.

But Mike told me that if I maintained my vow of silence, the press would haunt me at the convention. Cameras would follow me, and reporters would shout questions. I didn't want to become the Howard Hughes of political consultants, a distant figure invisibly calling the shots, so I did an interview with Frank Clines of *The New York Times,* which worked out well, and one with Eric Pooley of *Time* magazine. I had developed a good rapport with Pooley's editor, Walter Isaacson; I've read and admired his two books and concluded it was a very good idea for an historian to edit a newsmagazine.

I called Walter on Thursday, August 22, to check on some quotes of mine for *Time*'s convention issue on Monday. Walter dropped the information that I was to be the cover of that issue.

"You mean on the cover?" I asked.

"No, I mean *the* cover, just the best picture you've ever seen of yourself, smiling away, with the heading THE MAN INSIDE THE PRESIDENT'S MIND."

I was horrified. "How the hell can you run *my* picture when it's the president's convention. What about *his* picture?" I asked.

"We've had him on the cover a lot; it's you we want to run," Isaacson replied.

"Oh, my God, Walter. You'll kill me. He'll fire me. I won't be able to breathe, let alone talk to you guys again. You never said cover. I specifically asked that I not be on the cover," I said.

I agreed that they had not promised to *not* put me on the cover and repeated: "It'll kill me."

McCurry called Isaacson who said he was thinking, as an alternative, of a caricature of Clinton with a hinge in his head and an opening, with a cartoon of me standing in his brain—actually *in* his brain.

"You call that an improvement?" I said to Isaacson late Thursday night. "That says that I am his brain. I'm not. That's totally unfair to him and totally lethal to me."

I called the president and briefed him on Isaacson's cover.

"That's a disaster," he said.

"I know," I replied. "They were going to run a full-page cover of me, but I think this is even worse."

At midnight I called Walter again. He told me he had decided that the final cover would show me sitting on Clinton's shoulder, not in his head, and that the heading would be THE MAN WHO HAS THE PRESIDENT'S EAR.

I didn't like that either. My only leverage was that I had asked not to be on the cover but, foolishly, had received no commitment.

At twelve-thirty I called Clinton again and described the cover to him. "That's OK; you do have my ear," he said. Then the president, as I have mentioned, commented on our relationship.

"I realize that our relationship is a subject of legitimate historical interest." he said. "It's unique in American history. I don't think any president has ever had someone as close as you are to me. Maybe Louie Howe."

Howe was Franklin Roosevelt's political manager, who piloted FDR's course when he was flat on his back with polio in 1921 to the New York State governorship in 1928 and to the White House in 1932. There was just one problem. "Louie Howe died after the first term," I said. I'd hoped to live a little longer.

Clinton laughed. "Well, Harry Hopkins then." He had replaced Howe as FDR's confidant.

"He was more Eleanor's than Franklin's," I reminded the president.

"Until he moved into the White House and started messing around with women," Clinton commented.

We laughed.

Then the president said, "But I do understand the legitimate historical interest in our relationship. I just ask you two things if you write a book. First, hold it until after the election, and second, when you tell it, be sure it's right for me and right for you. Right for Bill Clinton and right for Dick Morris."

"You got it," I said.

While I was talking to *Time* and to the president, the prostitute whom I'd been seeing for a year was on the balcony outside my door. As I usually did, I'd asked her to leave the room while I spoke to the president. I came out between calls to say I was sorry she'd had to wait and ask if she'd like a drink. That was when *Star* magazine shot its photograph; just as the president was discussing our relationship, it was ending. I just didn't know it at the time.

For himself, Clinton was finally committed to the idea that unless he remained popular with the voters, not just on election day but throughout his term, he couldn't govern. He needed good polls not just to win, but to succeed in Washington. When his poll numbers had fallen, he couldn't get a health-care bill passed even with a Democratic Congress. When his numbers improved, he was able to sign a welfare bill, a health-care reform, and a minimum-wage bill, all largely to his specifications, with a Republican Congress.

He saw himself as a good man, his virtue enhanced by his skill at keeping the people behind him. And he increasingly saw me not as a political medicine man but as an adviser who could develop programmatic ideas to express concretely his idea of where he wanted to lead America.

After I left the campaign, he dismissed the notion that he had needed me to find the political center, but he did tell *The News Hour with Jim Lehrer* that "what I miss the most is his creativity, his ideas, his energy—he would come up with lots of ideas. I'd go through them and pick the ones I wanted and discard the others, but I miss his ideas."

I'll always treasure those words and wonder whether the recent discussions we'd been having about history and his ultimate goals would not have characterized our relationship to come, now that he had restored his majority for the election.

It was not to be. I failed myself, my wife, and him. For all my advice about virtue, I wasn't good enough to continue with the president.

▲

Harry Thomasson conceived of opening the convention with a completely nonpolitical night of nonpartisan speeches focused on values. Penn and I agreed. "Let the Republicans be partisan from the beginning," I argued; "let's have a night without politics, just values, to show the people where our priorities lie."

The president liked the idea in the abstract but worried about Harry's suggestion to invite Billy Graham to address the convention on Monday. Harry argued that he would be nonpolitical and that while he would never mention the president's name, his presence would signal our commitment to values.

Hillary liked Graham but warned that "he is a dedicated evangelist. He'll get up there and talk about abortion being evil and the way of Jesus Christ being the right way." I worried about how Jews and others might react. I asked Hillary whether she felt he could be secular. She noted that while he had done splendidly in his speech at Oklahoma City, she didn't know what he would say at the convention.

We flirted with the idea of asking Walter Cronkite to speak, but when he criticized us for being slow to take up journalist Paul Taylor's idea of accepting free time to appear with Dole throughout the campaign, we backed off.

I had long felt that Christopher Reeve would be an ideal choice. His courage, I felt, would resonate deeply. Although the president and the vice president liked the idea, I had to fight hard to convince the others that only nonpolitical speakers should speak the first night—heresy to the politicians. Finally we agreed that Gore should invite Reeve to speak. He accepted, provided he could write his own speech.

We all agreed to invite Sarah Brady to speak on Monday night, and her appearance with her husband, timed to coincide with our domestic-violence handgun proposal, was electrifying. Monday night gained us two points as we expanded our lead to thirteen. We had now recaptured six of the ten points the Republicans had gained at their convention. And our heavy guns hadn't spoken yet.

We debated whether Hillary should speak or not. Thomasson, in a rare misjudgment, proposed that the First Lady not speak but appear on the video screen, welcoming the delegates to "my hometown" and then conduct a tour around her old neighborhood, her old school, candy store, and so forth. "Too precious," said Hillary and she rejected the idea.

Hillary was emphatic in rejecting efforts to enhance her image, which she felt could not convey a true picture of who she really is. Once I recommended changes in her wardrobe. Experts had told me that an open-necked look suggested more openness than the high closed collars she usually wore. But Hillary said: "I get colds frequently, and I need to keep my neck warm to avoid them." The same experts got me in further hot water by telling me that earth tones like brown and beige were more soothing than the brightly colored outfits she liked. She angrily replied: "If my husband cannot get elected president because people don't like the way I dress, he'll have to win without me. I will dress as I please. When he first became president, I promised myself always to be myself and that's what I'm going to be."

I told Hillary that I felt she should speak at the convention and focus on what she had done for her entire career: be an advocate for children. She agreed, and when Elizabeth Dole spoke so effectively for her husband a few weeks later, we were all thankful she had made that decision.

Hillary is warm and friendly as an individual but relatively rigid as a political figure. She's good at marching straight ahead to fight for what she's always fought for: health care, children, women's rights, education. But she doesn't share her husband's adaptability. She's not good at curves or changes or subtlety. She is basically not a manipulative person.

Many people have asked me if Hillary is a liability for her husband. She isn't. She's an asset politically. While the press tends to focus on her antagonists, she has a huge base of support for her battles for children and women's rights. I used to tell people who asked if she was hurting the president's ratings: "Dole has 51 percent favorable and 46 percent unfavorable. Hillary's ratings are almost identical. Hillary hurts Bill no more than Dole hurts Dole."

The key is to let Hillary be Hillary, to ask her to talk about what she believes in and to fight for children and women. Do that and she's great. Try to change her and it doesn't work.

I rejected the conventional wisdom that Hillary would seem too powerful or too liberal if she spoke about children. While I always feared that she would hurt the president by seeming to be too powerful, I also felt that the more she spoke about her genuine passion for children, the better she would do and the better the president would do.

Hillary has great power in the White House but not in the Machiavellian way many believe. It is not pillow talk or ideological nagging that sways the president when she speaks. Her fights for children evoke the president's memory of his own childhood. She taps directly into the poor boy that lingers in the president's soul. She speaks to the needs of that young child with an abusive stepfather, a distracted and harassed mother, and a town without opportunity. The president sees his own childhood in her views and her speeches.

The American people appreciate the positive advocacy of the public Hillary even as they suspect the hidden power of the private Hillary. The truth is very different. The private Hillary is very private and nonpolitical. She is a wife and a mother in very traditional senses of the words. When, in the privacy of their home, the First Lady advises the president about government issues, it is the *public* Hillary, the one we like, who speaks, the advocate for children and women and education. When she wants her husband's attention on a matter of policy, she doesn't whisper in his ear and pull his strings, she gives him the same speeches she gives us from her lecterns.

Once when she complained to me about my efforts to move to the center, I replied with a metaphor. My home in Connecticut was being painted at the time by what seemed to be live-in painters who manifested such care on every millimeter of our walls and ceilings that I doubted if Michelangelo had taken such care with the Sistine Chapel. Now I used the painters as a metaphor in my reply. "Hillary," I said, "we've worked together for almost twenty years. I thought you would have gotten it by now." She smiled slyly, suspecting what was coming. "I get called in every two or four years to paint the house. Before you call me, you arrange the furniture just as you like it, the couch over there, the wing chair here, and so forth. But when you called me, you knew I'd want to put the furniture in the center of the room. The center, the middle," I repeated to be sure the metaphor was not lost on her. "Then I cover it up with canvas, and I paint the walls and ceiling." I made a painting motion with my hand, adopting a shoulder-shrugging posture of an I'm-doing-my-job-don't-bother-me housepainter. "When the walls are painted and the paint is nice and dry, I take off my canvas covering and leave the house. I go away. Then you have four years to put the furniture back exactly as you and your husband wish."

"You sweet-talking devil, you," she said with a forgiving grin.

Only when she is forced against the wall by snapping wolves does she sometimes overreact by seeing enemies where there may be none.

The president celebrated his fiftieth birthday at a fund-raising party a few days before the convention. At the end of the evening, the gathering was disrupted by gay and anti-welfare-reform hecklers who shouted during the president's remarks. They were removed by the police while the president, anxious that they not be treated roughly, called after the officers to treat them with respect. "Remember, they have rights too," Clinton said from the podium.

Hillary cited this episode a few days later and told me she felt the Republicans may have planted the hecklers in the audience. "How could they afford five-hundred-dollar tickets?" she asked. She warned that the Republicans might use similar tactics at our convention and that we had to be careful to screen the people who got tickets. I ignored her comment because it seemed to demonstrate her tendency to overreact.

The blunt truth is that Hillary is no damn good at subtle infighting. What she's great at is advocating her beliefs, whether before a thousand cheering students or to the president over breakfast.

I worked closely with Hillary's speechwriter, Lissa Muscatine, on the First Lady's convention remarks. As I saw Lissa work, I realized that being Hillary's speechwriter is unlike any other writing assignment. Hillary is constantly thinking of new ways to express her beliefs. Lissa's job is not so much to write the speeches as to collect Hillary's variations each time she speaks, like a recorder of oral history, keeping them in a notebook and recycling them in the next day's text. Hillary's speeches are composed of a bit she gave here or a riff she used the other night and a sequence she explored last week in Kentucky. From these scraps, an effective speech emerges, as it did on Tuesday night at the Democratic National Convention.

Hillary's speech that night was very effective and it picked up yet another point for her husband, so that now we were only three points away from recapturing the Republican Convention bounce.

I proposed a radical idea—that Gore should speak a night before Clinton spoke, rather than on the same night, as the vice president has always done. I felt it would be good for Gore and Clinton for the VP to have his own night.

But the vice president's commitment to tradition runs deep in his psyche. He was suspicious that I was selling him out. He imagined that I wanted to minimize his role in order to let some other speaker enjoy the glory of speaking right before the president did.

"The vice president doesn't simply speak at the convention," he lectured me; "he accepts the nomination of his party for the office of vice president. That's very important to me, and it's very important to the process. By speaking before the roll call, you alter that tradition and reduce me to the level of yet another convention speaker."

His focus on the procedural decorum blinded him to the central reality: that if he was the featured speaker on Wednesday, he would do a whole lot more for himself and for Clinton than as an also-ran on Thursday, when his speech would be lost in the enthusiasm for the president's address.

I had given up on the idea until the magnitude of the Republican convention bounce alarmed me. It was one thing to speak blithely of a traditional and normal ten-point bounce for the other party, but these were points we had gained with blood and determination and couldn't, wouldn't, mustn't let them slip away. Ever.

I revisited the issue with Gore, hammering home my message. "This speech will define you. It will be the very basis of your candidacy in 2000. People will talk about your speech for four years if you give it right." I deeply believed this and worked desperately to talk some sense into Gore. He's a stubborn man.

But "give it right"? That was the real sticking point. Gore began to talk about what would happen if he didn't give a good speech. Where would he be then?

I finally understood—Gore wasn't fully confident of his own rhetorical ability. He'd read too many articles about his stiffness and coldness and he was beginning to believe them.

Tipper knew better. When Gore returned from his July 1996 visit to an ailing Yeltsin to congratulate him on his election, commentators noted how pale and rigid the Russian president had seemed. We now know that he had suffered a heart attack after his first June victory and had been ill during almost the entire runoff. Tipper told Al at the time, "Next to Yeltsin, you didn't look stiff at all, dear."

I told Gore I thought he would give a great speech and that he should go for it.

The president also hoped Gore would switch to Wednesday night so we could have a great program that evening. He insisted that Gore could do anything he wanted on Thursday night, even speak again if he wished, but the key was to make Wednesday night a winner, as Elizabeth Dole had done at the Republicans' convention.

After much shoving and pushing, Gore finally agreed to speak on Wednesday.

But would Tipper speak too? I had suggested that Mrs. Gore precede Hillary on Tuesday night, but she was reluctant. I quizzed the vice president, trying to learn if he was worried that if Tipper spoke on Tuesday relations between her and Hillary might suffer. He turned rigid, like a Soviet Politburo member trying to avoid exile to Siberia, and said, "There is no tension between Tipper and Hillary."

OK. Got it. Actually, Hillary was amenable to having Tipper speak before her, especially when I proposed that Tipper not just introduce her but speak substantively about her own lifelong crusade against sex and violence on TV.

I urged Tipper to speak, citing polls that showed she was the most popular of the foursome. The president's favorable/unfavorable rating was 60–38, Gore's was 54–34, and Hillary's was 51–46, and Tipper's was 48–21. This reflected the fact that the other three had absorbed a lot of media punishment and she hadn't. When she finally realized that Hillary had no objection and that she could be of help, she agreed.

I suggested to Gore that he enumerate in his speech what the president's values agenda has meant for people day to day, hour to hour. I called the speech "rock around the clock." It began when your children brushed their teeth with clean water and ate fruit without dangerous pesticides. It continued through a trip to school without passing by the tobacco billboard anymore. The husband was taking computer courses at the community college for free, thanks to Clinton. The younger son was able to go to college on a scholarship, and so on. He liked the idea and used a lot of it in his speech.

I was sobbing with everyone else as Gore described his sister's painful death from smoking. He was magnificent. His speech closed two more points—leaving just one to go.

By the time Gore spoke on Wednesday night, the *Star*'s accusations about my affair with the prostitute had already broken. I knew I was finished. I sat in my hotel room in tears as I watched Gore on television. I was proud that I had helped plan this convention. Clinton had recaptured all that the Republicans had gained, and the race would be locked into a pattern for the last two months.

The president spoke the next night. I watched it on TV from my Connecticut home, having fled Chicago one step ahead of the press posse. It was a speech I had written, Don Baer had improved, and Mark Penn had protected from the president's distracted attempts at revision when his attention was focused mainly on each day's train event.

The concept of the speech had been bold, and the president rose to it magnificently. Three months before, I had suggested to the president that he give a second State of the Union speech at the convention in Chicago. Citing the results of the '96 State of the Union speech, which gave him his seventeen-point lead, I suggested he rekindle that passion and commitment. He was in full accord and eager to see a draft. Every week, at our strategy meetings, we would review new ideas and issues for him, adding some to the May-June-July speeches but reserving others for the convention acceptance speech.

So much good could be done in the second term. The IRS collecting child support and seeing to it that every single mother got her child's due; the literacy program; the restrictions on handgun ownership; the environmental programs announced from the train and recounted in this speech; most of all, the plan for creating jobs for welfare recipients, the boldest such plan in decades, designed to create a million jobs for welfare mothers. Children's TV programs could be self-censored to reduce violence; criminals in state jails could be required to serve 85 percent of their sentences; homeowners could avoid capital-gains taxes when they sell their homes; two thirds of all Superfund toxic-pollution sites could be cleaned up—all this and more the president identified as his second-term agenda, the agenda we had created together.

I watched in a daze. From afar, I learned that the convention had exceeded my fondest hopes. Not only had we recaptured the ten points the Republicans had gained at their convention, but we had added four more points and now led by twenty-one.

But it was the Clinton campaign, of which I was no longer a part, that led by twenty-one points. I had destroyed my career and, perhaps, wrecked my marriage.

Downfall

On Wednesday, the third day of the convention, I sat huddled with my media team—Squier, Knapp, Schoen, Steinberg, and Freedman (Penn was on the train with the president)—to design a post-convention advertisement. I had proposed earlier that we recall the threats the Republican budget had posed to our national well-being. Marius Penczner and Bill Knapp designed a heart-stopping ad featuring the president's desk in the Oval Office. As images of Dole and Gingrich were superimposed on the screen over the desk, the announcer spoke of their proposed cuts in extra police, Medicare, school-drug programs, Head Start, and the environment. The ad noted that President Clinton had vetoed these excessive cuts, but warned, "If Dole is elected president, and Gingrich controls Congress, there'll be nobody there to stop them."

The ad used Gingrich's control of Congress as a weapon against electing Dole. More broadly, it knocked Kemp out of the picture and symbolically replaced him with the man we had spent a year making Dole's real running mate—Newt Gingrich.

As I worked on the ad, my pager went off. I checked the number. It appeared to be in suburban New York since it had a 914 area code, but I didn't recognize the number. Then the pager repeated its summons. This time, the message read: "*Star* magazine calling." All week I had been fending off press calls. *What do they want?* I wondered. Then, a few minutes later, the pager vibrated again sending the message that *Star* magazine was calling about the prostitute I had been seeing in Washington. It used her name.

My mind cast desperately about for options, but I saw, in that instant, that there were none. What had begun with a telephone page from Clinton in September 1994 had now ended with this page. My work with Clinton was over, along with my career. But, more poignantly, I thought my marriage was probably over as well.

As soon as I knew the *Star* and the *New York Post* were going to publish the story, I told Eileen. She was furious in private and fiercely loyal in public. When I was attacked, she rallied to my defense. When we were alone, she frankly expressed the deep pain I had caused her.

She had not wanted me to work for Clinton in the first place. She felt that our lives would be permanently disrupted and that the glare of national attention would make privacy impossible. Now, because I had not only ignored her advice but had acted idiotically as well, her life was turned upside down. She couldn't go anywhere without being recognized as "the woman" whom I had betrayed.

After the convention closed on Wednesday night, Erskine Bowles visited me, alone, in my Chicago hotel room. He said he had been sent by the president to ask me whether the allegations against me were true.

"Yes," I answered. "Not all, but basically, yes."

We talked about whether I should resign.

I was shocked, hurt, and devastated. I recognized the seriousness of the situation, but still hoped that somehow I could stay. "Why?" I asked. "What the hell did I do that he wasn't accused of doing in the exact same magazine four years ago?"

"You've admitted it's true," Bowles replied.

An angry exchange ensued and Bowles went back to talk with the president.

Three hours later Bowles returned with White House counsel Jack Quinn, by now my long-term ally, since his days as Gore's chief of staff. They confirmed the president's desire that I resign, although they offered me a leave of absence as an alternative. I knew it was all over.

When Bowles and Quinn returned the next morning, Eileen battled for me like a tigress. When Erskine said that Leon Panetta wanted me to come downstairs to his room at the hotel, Eileen said: "No, he's not going." The truth was that when I tried to speak, I could only sob. Bowles suggested that Panetta come up to our room. Eileen again said no. "He *is* the chief of staff," Erskine prompted.

"Not to Dick anymore, he isn't," Eileen replied.

"I think he wants to convey a message to Dick," Bowles said.

"Tell him to do it the way he usually does, through leaks to *The Wall Street Journal*," she said.

My voice broke whenever I tried to talk to my fellow consultants. Before I left Chicago I wrote a letter to them on my laptop computer that they could pass around for each of them to read. Tom Freedman and the other members of my staff helped shield me from the press as we left the hotel for the airport on Thursday morning. At our home in Connecticut, we were surrounded by over a hundred camera people.

We were under siege for the rest of that day and into the next. Reporters and photographers were held at bay by the three Redding police officers in our driveway—half the Redding constabulary. But some photojournalists had made their way through the woods in back of our house and were shooting pictures through the windows.

Eileen suggested that maybe if we agreed to a photo session—with no questions—outside our home, the reporters would go home for the Labor Day weekend. She went outside and approached them. They all wanted to go home and would accept the ground rules. The picture of us together went around the country. At the last minute, our three-year-old golden retriever, Dizzy (short for Disraeli), sauntered up to us and got into the picture. "She's a publicity hound," I said.

The press dispersed and did not return.

Some interpreted Eileen's public loyalty as stupidly "standing by her man" without question. But the fact is that, along with her anger, she felt sorry for me, and worried seriously about the possibility of suicide. As she sheltered me, she shared her own deep pain. As yet we have no firm understanding of our future.

Somehow absurdly, cruelly, *her* conduct was scrutinized and criticized. Should she stay with me? Was she being naïve? Was she afraid to leave? She had been absolutely loyal and supportive for two decades—and especially in the months after the scandal. Now she was savaged for it by busybodies who didn't know either of us.

We both decided to protect what little privacy we had left, knowing how hard it would be to confront such a massive betrayal of trust in marriage. I can cite only my inadequacies and neuroses by way of explanation, and make promises that seem hollow after those I had made before and failed to keep.

But I know that I've changed.

I am learning how to control my compulsions. I look back on who I had become by August 28, 1996, and hope that I will have the strength never to lose my personal bearings again. I'm struggling to fix what was broken inside me.

One reporter asked whether I felt I had betrayed the president. I said, "No, he's doing fine. He's way ahead. I didn't take an oath of office to him, but I sure did take marriage vows, and I have certainly betrayed them. That's the betrayal that I'm focused on right now."

The president, the vice president, and the First Lady all called me on Thursday afternoon in New York, as we returned to Connecticut. The president's call came only a few hours before his speech. All were gracious, but Hillary was the most understanding and sympathetic. I sensed she was genuinely worried about me.

For weeks, I watched the presidential campaign unfold, reading the papers every day. The staff at the White House and the campaign workers and consultants had been instructed by Panetta not to speak to me. Campaign manager Peter Knight was designated the only person I could contact.

The most important thing I had helped achieve in my life was this victory in 1996. When I felt it was in danger, I did what I could to protect it.

I took advantage of my channel to Peter Knight to pass on advice to my former colleagues. I complained that the president was spending too much time campaigning and not enough on the kind of values-oriented presidential actions that had created his large lead in the first place. This advice was similar to that which I had offered in October 1994 after the president returned from the Middle East.

"The reason we held our lead," I told Knight on September 20, 1996, in my first call, "is that we made the incumbency more exciting than the campaign. In a campaign, Republicans and many independents will naturally gravitate back to Dole. It's a partisan event. But if their attention is riveted on what we are doing in the White House, they will tend to stay with us, not as a Democratic candidate, but because we keep their attention focused on his presidency."

I ran through a list of ideas that lay on the shelf after my departure and suggested people who could develop them.

The president pursued his values initiatives: declaring Red Rocks a national monument, requiring drug tests to get a driver's license, and enforcing child-support. Afterward, Bill Knapp said: "Thank God you left the tank full."

On election night, I am sure my former colleagues were distressed to see the president's lead crumble to single digits. The drop in his margin of victory was due largely to the tendency of those who had registered as "undecided" in the polling to switch to Dole at the last minute.

This is an inevitable fact of politics. The undecideds *always* vote against the incumbent. They are undecided only in that they have not decided on which alternative to the incumbent to back. In almost every case, they vote against the person in office.

When Perot entered the race, I hoped that he would soak up the un-decideds and deny them to Dole. In 1992, Perot picked up four of the five undecided percentage points and I thought he would do the same in 1996. But when Dole's people excluded Perot from the debates, he was out of the race and could no more keep those votes away from Dole than any other fringe candidate could.

In retrospect, the decision that probably cost Clinton the margin he needed to deliver a Democratic House and Senate was his willingness to abide by the decision of the Presidential Debate Commission and en-gage in a two-way debate with Dole. Had he insisted on a three-way de-bate, Dole would have had no choice but to go along. Nobody would believe that Clinton was afraid to debate Dole and most would sympa-thize with his decision to open the process to include all candidates who received federal matching funds.

My former partner Dick Dresner says that the key question to ask in any campaign is, "What are you going to do differently in the last two weeks?" During this period, those who have followed the race all along are likely to get restless and bored unless you change your campaign. Those who are just starting to follow the election need to get up to speed. In my opinion, Clinton should have issued a few bold executive actions or proposals during the final fourteen days to hold the nation's attention and keep the excitement and electricity flowing into his incumbency.

I would have suggested four ideas:

- Give anyone who cares for an elderly relative who might otherwise have needed nursing-home care a tax credit to make the burden lighter.

- Announce a new program for a voluntary thirty-three-cent postage stamp. The extra penny would go to any one of five or six charities the purchaser selects—such as breast cancer, AIDS, the homeless, and others. The stamp would be designed to celebrate this voluntary contribution. It would have made for a more generous Christmas.
- Move to get the FCC to demand that TV stations self-censor excessive violence out of their programming for young children, including shows like *Mighty Morphin Power Rangers.*
- Require trigger locks on all guns that are sold in America to reduce gun accidents involving children.
- Make restitution to victims a condition of a criminal's release on parole.

But while these steps, which I suggested to Peter Knight, may have stopped the president's vote from dropping, they would have done little to move undecided voters to Perot instead of Dole.

To keep undecideds from voting for Dole, the Clinton campaign should have changed its ads from the overused and, by then, threadbare comparison of Clinton and Dole on Medicare and tax policy to ads that compared them on new issues like child immunization, aid to reduce class sizes in schools, and on Dole's proposal to exempt polluters from paying for toxic-waste dumping if the offense took place before 1980.

These comparisons would probably have driven Dole's negatives up to a point where the undecideds would likely not have switched to him.

When I was at the campaign, the president wanted to do "endorsement" ads in which ordinary people whom he had helped would speak of his efforts and defend his character. I was always wary of such ads. Americans don't take anybody's word for anything when it comes to politics and even highly popular figures find that their endorsements mean little. In 1986, the Republicans lost the Senate, in my view, because they insisted that all Senate candidates run an ad in which President Reagan endorsed their candidacy. His endorsement didn't work nearly as well as the effective last-minute ads their opponents ran. I think Clinton may have dug his own ditch by insisting on firing blanks in the final weeks.

Finally, I think the Clinton campaign violated its basic policy—answering opposition attacks through paid media and then counterpunching. When the Indonesia fund-raising controversy erupted, Clinton's paid media should have generated a more effective advertising response. My own choice would have been an ad emphasizing Republican hypocrisy by featuring a playful travelogue identifying the countries Dole got money from. Without access to the polling, I cannot say precisely what might have been most effective. The campaign decided to use a Common Cause quote attacking Dole on campaign-finance reform, but deleted the organization's equally fierce attack on Clinton over the same issue. I think a clearer factual contrast between Dole's and Clinton's position on the specifics of finance reform might have been more appropriate.

These ideas become most clear in hindsight. I hope those who had the day-by-day responsibility for conducting the campaign will forgive my armchair quarterbacking.

I think the election was a watershed in U.S. politics. It points, in my view, to an emerging national consensus, to a redefinition of the power of the presidency, and to a new role for polling in the American democracy, one so well understood by the victor and so little appreciated by the vanquished. For good or ill, these issues and others I have touched on in this narrative will affect the conduct of American politics well into the twenty-first century.

Polling Versus Leadership   The emphasis on polling—in this book and in the recent election—naturally gives rise to the question of whether it has become a substitute for leadership. Voters have never much liked the idea that candidates merely spout what pollsters have told them the public wants to hear. It smacks of opportunism. But Clinton used polling for a different purpose: as a tool for governing, as a technique to facilitate progress in a democracy. Polling for him was not a onetime test of opinion. It was a way of conducting an extensive dialogue with the public. As for leadership, he never used polling to determine what position on an issue he should take. Never. He used polling primarily to choose which of several of his current or contemplated positions were popular. When the polls indicated that his position on an issue was unpopular, he would usually ask for a study of how he could convince people of his point of view. Several examples illustrate this distinction:

1. Clinton had decided to oppose a constitutional amendment to allow school prayer, but the polls showed that the public supported the amendment. Deadlock? No. Our polling identified the specific religious, spiritual, and moral activities the public wanted in schools, activities that had been subsumed under the rubric of "school prayer." But we found that prayer itself was not high on the list; people really wanted schools to teach values, ethics, and morals. Armed with this information, Clinton

explained that the First Amendment did not limit the teaching of any of these subjects and that there was therefore no justification for tinkering with it. The demand for a prayer amendment abated.

2. The right wing demanded an end to affirmative action. The polls then, and since in California, showed that voters agree with the demand, yet the president decided to resist. His was not a hopeless cause because the surveys also noted that what voters objected to were quotas, layoffs based on race or gender, and unqualified people getting preference. Knowing this, Clinton proposed "mending," rather than ending, affirmative action so that the specific objections would be met while the principle would be retained. His acuity in relieving these three anxieties has largely crippled the repeal movement at the federal level. California did not try to mend its program and ended up losing it.

3. President Clinton recognized that he had to send troops to Bosnia if peace was to have any chance there. Crude polls showed massive public opposition to this action, but more thorough research suggested that he could win broad popular support if he could distinguish peacekeeping from combat. His explanation of what peacekeeping entails succeeded in securing public support. Without that research, a lesser president might have been tempted to run away from the issue.

Polls, used in this way, are not the instrument of the mob; they offer the prospect of leadership wedded to a finely calibrated measurement of opinion.

Triangulation: Opportunism or Progress?   Triangulation is much misunderstood. It is not merely splitting the difference between left and right. Clinton's objective was to combine the best theme from each side: "opportunity" from the left and "responsibility" from the right. And he rejected the worst of each: the tendency of conservatives to ignore the problems of the less privileged, and the liberals' tendency to be naïve. This "third way" rises above the other two and forms a triangle.

In a related triangulation, the president discarded both the idea of "they"—that the federal bureaucracy should be the agent of social progress, and the idea of "I"—that the government should withdraw and leave individuals to fend for themselves. He focused instead on "we"—on how the local and volunteer sectors can become agents of social betterment.

Triangulation is a dynamic process. No three-way matrix can ever be permanent in what is essentially a two-party country. Politicians will adapt. The votes in 1996 seem to have indicated that those who triangulated won and those who did not lost. President Clinton won. Senate Republicans expanded their margin of control because they were willing, under Senator Trent Lott's leadership, to compromise with the White House on health care, welfare, and the minimum wage. But congressional Democrats who resisted triangulation forfeited their chance to ride Clinton's coattails to power. House Republicans paid for their stubbornness and partisanship by seeing their margin of control eroded. Should future elections bear out the trend of 1996, the Democratic party is likely to gradually adopt Clinton's position—as it shows signs of doing already. The triangle will once again become a straight line between the two parties.

The Power of the Presidency   In my work with President Clinton, it became clear that the four primary instruments of presidential power have been diminished. First, a president's power to spend money has been limited by a divided government, popular opposition to taxes, and the demand for an end to deficit spending. Second, though the president's authority to promulgate regulations escaped the formal curtailment sought by the Contract with America, this authority is more restricted than it was when Philip Howard's *The Death of Common Sense* exposed the absurdities of rigid regulation. Third, the chief executive's role as commander in chief has been reduced. Americans may well tolerate military action if the casualties are limited, but it is nearly certain that they will never again accept a war with casualty levels approaching anything near those of Korea or Vietnam.

Finally, the power of the president—and the power of Congress—over the economy has been eroded by a consensus that the Federal Reserve Board is the best qualified manager of the variables of inflation, interest rates, economic growth, investment, and employment. This delegation of the hottest topic in politics to a panel of experts suggests that the United States is becoming Japanese in elevating a consensus of experts over political decisions.

There are four other areas, however, in which the power of the presidency has grown, or will grow, significantly.

First, the explosion in media coverage of news has amplified the bully pulpit of Theodore Roosevelt. A president has unparalleled ways of making the public focus on the issues he is concerned with. Sustained presidential leadership can therefore lead all elements of society to work toward a solution, regardless of government intervention.

The health-care debate is a case in point. The president's general proposals were defeated, but the two years of obsessive national attention to these proposals provided a climate in which companies could restrain health costs with their employees' cooperation. The president's regulations aimed at discouraging teenage smoking may not survive a court challenge, but the concern he raised will contribute to a reduction in teen smoking. Similarly, Nancy Reagan's Just Say No campaign surely played a part in the decade-long drop in drug use in the 1980s.

Second, the president, with Congress, will discover a new tool in the targeted tax cut. It is the obverse of the power traditionally accruing to the big spender. That source of power declines as big government shrinks, but a tax cut or a tax credit can be mobilized to achieve the same ends. Instead of expanding the state-run bureaucracy for administering college scholarships, for instance, a tax cut or a tax credit for students or their families works just as well. The across-the-board tax cuts Republicans favor weaken the public sector, but targeted tax cuts strengthen it.

Third, the international prestige of the president has grown enormously since the end of the cold war. Catholic republics have long been accustomed to having two leaders, a president, who is chosen by the nation's electorate, and the pope, who is chosen in Rome by the college of cardinals. In a sense, the president of the United States has become a secular, global pope. He can reach over the heads of warring leaders and speak directly to the people to plead for peace and harmony. President Clinton did that in Bosnia and, notably, in a Northern Ireland beset by Irish Republican Army and Protestant terrorists. He spoke directly to the voters in Russia with the message that the world would stand behind them if they rejected communism and fascism in favor of democratic reform. Where the president's military legions can't go, his voice can, to great effect.

Finally, a new area of presidential leadership has emerged from President Clinton's outspoken advocacy of social reforms that directly affect the lives of Americans. By addressing family leave, time off in lieu of pay for overtime, educational standards, handgun control, student discipline, TV violence, and tobacco advertising, Clinton has enlarged the concerns of the president.

Entitlement Reform   These will be watershed years, with a vengeance, for entitlement reform. As my narrative has made clear, I believe Republicans will try to end entitlements for all but the poor. They want to ax food stamps and tax credits for the working poor. Their leaders have already tried to introduce medical savings accounts to cream the middle class off Medicare, so that only the poor, the old, and the sick would be left in the traditional fee-for-service system. And the party wants to use IRAs and private retirement plans to induce many in the middle and upper classes to leave the Social Security system.

Why? To denude these programs of their political protectors—middle-class voters—and leave them with no supporters but the low-voter-turnout poor. The reduction of Social Security benefits, cuts in Medicare coverage, and a rollback of student aid become possible when only the poor are affected. But is this exclusionist approach the right answer for a civilized society? There are other ways to tackle the serious cost problem. As a first step, in Medicare there is obvious mileage to be gained in the president's plan to hold down payments to providers of service, forcing efficiencies. States using managed care have cut the growth in Medicaid spending to approximately 4 percent after years in the double digits, so a second step would be to encourage the elderly to enter managed care voluntarily by offering incentives, such as free prescription drugs. A third step would be to cut health-care costs in all segments of society by continuing the anti-smoking campaign. All three steps combined will very likely reduce the rate of inflation of Medicare costs. There is no need for MSAs.

With Social Security, so well-examined by Peter Peterson in *Will America Grow Up Before It Grows Old?,* the answers are more difficult, but we have more time.

If I were still sitting on the president's shoulder, this is what I would whisper: "There are three root causes of impending bankruptcy.

"The first is the indexing of benefits to increases in the cost of living—back reform of inflation measurement to cut this cost increase. The second is longer life expectancies. What indexing has wrought, indexing can undo. Consider indexing the retirement age to life expectancy. Medical care has not merely extended the life span; it has extended the time during which we can expect to be fit and energetic. Everyone should be entitled to rest at the end of his or her life, but when should that rest begin? The actuarial tables tell us that the average person can look forward to many more years of life after reaching the Social Security retirement age. Pegging retirement age to life expectancy seems a sensible thing to consider.

"The third is low earnings from the Social Security Trust's fixed investments. Expand the range of possible investments beyond government bonds. Voters oppose the investment of Social Security funds in the stock market in general, but I believe they would be willing to endorse some limited equity holdings if there were safeguards, as there are in many private pension funds."

The Emerging National Consensus   The success of the president's third-way fusion seems to me to reflect a growing national consensus. Possibly, it will resolve the debate between the advocates of big government and their opponents. Certainly it will be the mission of the second term of the Clinton presidency and the Lott Senate majority leadership to tear down the Berlin Wall of partisan division that has dominated our domestic debate. They will try to stand on the bipartisan common ground so clearly identified in the last election. The hundred years' war over the role of government really began in 1901 with Theodore Roosevelt's activist presidency and raged through the New Deal, the Fair Deal, the New Frontier, the Great Society, the Reagan Revolution, and the Contract with America. As the century ends, the emerging consensus is that the role of government is to provide opportunity for those who take responsibility, especially through tax incentives rather than bureaucratic programs. The government will shrink, but it will remain an essential catalyst for individual and community efforts.

A Last Word

The final weeks of the election campaign were the hardest of my life. I had gone home to heal my marriage, engage in some soul-searching, and face myself and what brought me to my moral crisis. I passed on ideas for the campaign when I could, but I was depressed. I had not yet awakened to what gives life meaning when power, ego, and self-gratification are stripped away. On October 7 I left a message for the president. I said I would appreciate a call because I was in "a bad way." I wanted to speak to him "as a friend."

He came back to me the next day and we talked for half an hour.

He had returned from a trip late the night before, and called my New York apartment at about ten-thirty in the morning, shortly after he woke up. I gathered he was still in bed. "I'm not angry with you," he said. "There's nothing you have done to make me angry. I feel gratitude and affection, not anger," he said generously.

I told him about my pain and the daily struggle to make it to tomorrow. He asked about Eileen, and I told him I hoped our marriage would survive but that I couldn't be certain or even confident. He said he hoped we'd both make it through this.

"We all have to fight the disintegration of our personal lives in this business. It's a very lonely business. You sleep in a different hotel every night, and if you don't work hard to hold your personal life together, it just disintegrates on you," he said.

I complimented him on his campaign. "We're basically following your game plan," he said kindly. "It's working well."

I criticized his performance in the first debate with Dole. "I felt you talked about 1995 and he talked about 1993 and 1994, but neither of you talked about the future, about 1997. That's what the voters want to hear about."

He said, "I agree. Did you see how I opened the debate speaking about the values issues and the future, but then I got off the track?"

"Dole pulled you off by attacking your programs and your budget positions. He lured you into a point-by-point defense so you couldn't rise above it all and talk about the future. You didn't need to give that defense as much as you did. You fell into his trap."

"Right," he responded. "I did. But then I realized what was going on about two thirds of the way through the debate and got it back onto the future again."

I agreed.

"My answer on education scored," he related.

"That's because education is America's number-one issue now, replacing crime or the balanced budget. And you spoke about the future. You need to do that more in the second debate," I advised.

We returned to my personal crisis. I apologized once again and mentioned that I had let the prostitute hear only a moment of his voice in a phone conversation with me. "I didn't think you let her eavesdrop," the president responded. "I trust you."

We talked about the book. "I think you'll find it interesting," I said. I mentioned a few of my observations, including how much he liked to campaign because he needed the stimulus of public approval. "That's why you have to stop going out on the road all of the time right now and issue executive actions as president."

"I got your messages through Peter, and we're doing it," he said.

"I'm very, very touched that you aren't mad. It means a lot to me," I said. "I think our relationship had developed a new dimension, and I so desperately wanted it to continue."

"You can. It will. I'll give you access to me all the time," he said.

"You ought to read some of Saint Patrick's writings. You know, the Irish saint. He writes about a different kind of Christianity, more like the kind Jesus intended."

"Not Saint Paul or Saint Augustine, with their unforgiving sternness?" I ventured.

"No, the opposite," he said. "Forgiveness."

A p p e n d i x

Agendas

This appendix contains the actual texts of the briefing materials that the political consultants in the 1996 campaign presented to the president and the vice president at our weekly campaign strategy meetings in the White House residence. Called the agendas, these documents contain much more than a list of topics for discussion. Rather, they were the documents through which we briefed President Clinton on polling data, proposed advertisements, and suggested political and substantive policy initiatives. They were the central organ of communication in the Clinton campaign between the consultants and the president. Most of the events which animated his presidency between 1995 and 1996 found their origin in these pages.

The agendas were distributed at the start of each of the weekly strategy meetings which were usually on Wednesday or Thursday evenings. The copies were collected at the end of the meeting and only the president and Deputy Chiefs of Staff Harold Ickes and Evelyn Lieberman were permitted to keep theirs. The vice president, Cabinet members, and Chief of Staff Leon Panetta dutifully handed in their agendas before they went home.

The meetings were held each week except when the president's travel schedule precluded them. The first meetings were held in early December 1994 between only the president, the First Lady, and me. In January 1995, Hillary stopped attending and others began to be included. By March, the vice president, Panetta, Ickes, and Deputy Chief of Staff Erskine Bowles, the vice president's chief of staff Jack Quinn, and pollster Doug Schoen had joined the sessions.

There was no written agenda for these early meetings, but as the group grew and the discussions became longer and more complex, I began to write the agendas before each meeting. The first agenda presented here is for the strategy meeting of February 17, 1995. The last is for August 20, 1996, shortly before I left the campaign.

The meetings grew as the president reached out to other advisers and eventually came to include:

the president
the vice president
Chief of Staff Leon Panetta
Deputy Chief of Staff Harold Ickes
Deputy Chief of Staff Erskine Bowles and his successor, Evelyn Lieberman
Secretary of Commerce Ron Brown
U.S. Trade Representative and then Secretary of Commerce Mickey Kantor
Secretary of HUD Henry Cisneros
Senator and Democratic National Committee Chairman Chris Dodd
Former Chief of Staff Mack McLarty
Counsel to the President George Stephanopoulos
Communications Director Don Baer
Legislative Director John Hilley
Press Secretary Mike McCurry
Political Director Doug Sosnik
Chief of Staff to the First Lady Maggie Williams
Campaign Manager Peter Knight
Campaign Communications Director Ann Lewis
Deputy National Security Adviser Sandy Berger
Chief of Staff to the Vice President Jack Quinn and, later, Ron Klain
Political consultants Bob Squier, Bill Knapp, Doug Schoen, Mark Penn, and me

Before each meeting the consultants would conduct extensive polling and would begin the meeting by presenting the results. A summary of these results is included in each week's agenda. Then the consultants would proceed to discuss the advertising campaign and present suggested new ads for approval. The discussion would then broaden to policy proposals, political analyses, strategic insights, and themes for upcoming speeches.

During the 1996 campaign, Special Prosecutor Kenneth Starr subpoenaed these agendas. My attorney argued that the need to protect campaign confidentiality during the election superseded Starr's need for the material. The issue was not resolved by election day and, afterwards, Starr dropped his request for the agendas.

While it was important to protect the confidentiality of the agendas during the campaign, it makes no sense to wait to release them until after the president leaves office. They would just gather dust in a presidential library, enlivening the day for the occasional presidential scholar. In the spirit of open government it is appropriate to publish them while Clinton is still in office, especially in light of the controversies that swirl around him. When the need for secrecy has passed, so should the secrecy.

This appendix contains the actual texts from thirty-five of the agendas. About a dozen others are not in my possession and are not included. Demands of space have forced some abridgment, but the sections that are included are presented here exactly as they were shown to the president, with no editing.

To make sense of the agendas, they are preceded by short narratives to explain their contexts. But to fully grasp their content, it is best to read them in connection with the rest of this book.

February 17, 1995
Defining Where to Confront Gingrich
(See chapter 6)

When the Republicans took control of the House and the Senate in the elections of November 1994, they announced a legislative program as sweeping as any ever put before Congress. Touching on virtually every area of public policy, they planned a total change in budgetary priorities, social programs, entitlements, anti-crime measures, environmental policy, education funding, land use policy, and every other area of federal regulation.

The dazed Democrats who were left in Congress after the 1994 massacre rejected the GOP initiatives across the board. Determined to fight to preserve every inch of the status quo, they resisted virtually every Republican proposal from the line-item veto to the balanced-budget amendment.

But the president wanted to move to the center of the political spectrum and meet the GOP halfway. In his State of the Union speech of January 1995, he defined the broad outlines of his positions, accepting some cuts and rejecting others. In the strategy meeting of February 17, 1995, we discussed how to define more clearly where Clinton should compromise and where he should fight. The agenda reflects the centrist advice of the consultants, which contrasted sharply with the more confrontational course urged by Chief of Staff Leon Panetta who squirmed uncomfortably in his seat, suspicious of any departure from a united front of opposition to the Republican legislation.

TO   THE PRESIDENT

Date February 17, 1995

AGENDA FOR MEETING

1. Week of February 18th

    a. lobbyist regulation (possibly in radio address)

        1. best done in radio speech which goes over head
          of press and while congress is home to limit
          mocking reactions

    b.unfunded mandates veto threat over effective date

        1. Republicans will cave over this one, make the threat
          before they can cave in quietly

(I proposed as a backup for the radio address.)

2. Week of February 25th

    a. Line Item Veto Filibuster

        -make this the most theatrical and longest running drama
          possible

        -prepare list of things you would veto if you had line item
          to release each day of the fight

FEBRUARY 17, 1995

3. Paid Media Plans

    a. Recommendation of team headed by Squier with
       Hank Sheinkopf and Marius Penczner as members

      -please review video tapes

    b. Recommendation for TV buy in March/April

4. Longer term actions

    a. Plan Affirmative Action Speech in late March

      -develop consultative plan so as to consult, but not to risk
       leaking

      -find appropriate setting for major address

    b. Work with agencies to get popular regulations written so as to
      justify veto of moritorium

      -designate staff member (Curry?) to work with agencies
       to assemble list

    c. Oppose welfare bill only over work requirements being too
      limited. (only requires 2% to work new while 7% actually

work and only requires that 20% work by 2003)

-make explicit veto threat over this work requirement --
attack the bill only from the right

-6

-do not fight over: entitlements,
need for growth in payments
legal immigrants
counter cyclical stimulation
no state matching
cutoff for extra children
no benefits for under 18 unwed mothers
formula for division of block grants

-work quietly with Senate to eliminate as many of the above
as you wish, but make public issue only over work
requirements being inadequate.

d. Foster nomination

a. agree to tacit curb on discussion to give other issues
a chance to be heard

b. but never agree to pulling nomination

-if we don't have the votes, then just lose rather than
withdraw. Process is more important than
outcome.

c. fire people involved in vetting process to shed image
of Presidential incompetence.

FEBRUARY 17, 1995

e. California Quake Aid -- make public fight over all disaster aid remaining off budget -- cite Florida and Midwest floods too.

-7-

f. Crime Bill -- continue to hang tough on 100,000 cops and on nothing else

1 don't be tempted to join any other fight such as on search and seizure or the 85% prison rule, etc.

2. let Reno fight on these if you want, but keep your involvement and the veto threat squarely targeted at the 100,000 cops

3. Stress how 100,000 cops is almost a 20% increase over current total of 550,000 cops nationwide (better check number, it comes from the press)

4. Senate will cave -- when they do, predict victory and then crow from the rooftops to show how we won.

(he loved the clarity with which his posiiton had been seen. I said that it retroactively changed the 94 debate over the bill from pork and gun control to extra cops whee he had wanted it all along. I said was the exemplificaiton of my idea to get credit for hsi past acheivments as the republicans tried to repeal them)

FEBRUARY 17, 1995

h. Foreign Policy Legislation -- let your cabinet fight it, but don't get personally involved and don't be high profile on it

   1. deal should be possible without a lot of posturing by us

   2. a lose/lose issue politically

      -most don't care
      -democratic isolationists offended by our position
      -too technical for these of nation

I. Government re-organization Republican Initiatives

   1. don't threaten veto over anything including:

      -state department consolidation
      -elimination of 4 cabinet departments

   2. just try to get the best we can in the Senate.

   3. If publically high profile opposition, it will dominate media since it is about govt. departments and we shouldn't be seen as opposing cuts in bureaucracy

J. Education

   1. center advocacy on two ideas: college deduction and

Americorps and student loans

2. Do not dillute the focus by spending much time on

-dept of education
-goals 2,000
-etc.

-9-

3. Only possible other fight over cuts in school aid, but let
them make the budgetary move first

K. Tax cuts

1. Push negotiations with Republicans over package

-their own inability to produce moderate Republican
votes on this makes them vulnerable.

2. Advocate capital gains tax to set up deal for minimum
wage without setting up class warfare

3. I lold the line for tax cuts as opposed to deeper deficit
reduction unless republicans come up with more
cuts.

FEBRUARY 17, 1995

L. Lawsuit Limitations

    1. stay out of it, let the trial lawyers lead the fight

-10-

M. De regulation

    1. articulate fight not over general rules like impact studies, legal standing to sue, representation on boards, right to be informed of enforcement action, etc.

        -as matters of general principle, we lose on them all

    2. Vent opposition by demanding exceptions for --

        -environment
        -OSHA
        -FDA
        -Safety regulations

N. Immigration

    1. see attached package

        -no drivers licenses for illegals
        -El Paso border enforcement
        -more immigration judges to speed deportation

March 2, 1995
A Plea for Advertising
(See chapters 6 and 7)

Throughout February, the cavalcade of Republican legislation continued its march through Congress, seemingly without obstacle. The president's attempts to define a "third way" of accommodation of some
GOP ideas and opposition to others was largely drowned out by the partisan rhetoric on both sides.

In the March 2 meeting the consultants proposed that the president
begin TV advertising to hold the Republicans in check and to define the
president's "third-way" position. Concerned that it would be impossible
to fund an adequate TV effort within the financial limits which would
bind the president if he accepted federal matching funds, the consultants proposed that he turn down federal funds, freeing himself of such
limitations.

Clinton well remembered how his failure to advertise had led to vast
public misunderstanding of his healthcare reform program. Without ads
to defend his position, the insurance industry defined the Clinton program. With clever appeals featuring a dialogue between "Harry and
Louise," a typical American couple, the industry succeeded in making
America believe a falsehood—that the Clinton plan would deprive
Americans of the right to choose their own healthcare plan. Clinton's
program sank beneath the waves.

Determined to avoid such a fate in the face of the Gingrich-Dole contract agenda, the president readily agreed that advertising was crucial,
but did not yet know how to pay for it.

This agenda reflects our insistence on keeping one team in charge of
the campaign without yielding to the centrifugal pressures that a multiplicity of consultants at cross-purposes had brought to the 1992 campaign.

The balance of the agenda deals with the continuing attempt to define
a centrist course in the face of Democratic orthodoxy on the one hand
and Republican extremism on the other.

TO: THE PRESIDENT

Re: Agenda For Meeting -- March 2, 1995

| Campaign Overview |

1. Use of paid media -- major use of paid media different from other Presidential races

   A. Need not to take federal funds

      -- With federal funding, $37 million likely total, $7.5 for fund raising. Probably less than $20 million for TV

      -- With federal funding, no ability to do TV in key primary states

         -- If assume half available for media and half for field/Pres visits:

STATE	TOTAL LIMIT	MEDIA POINTS
Iowa	$914,000	2500
New Hamp (include MA)	$2,600,000	2800
Arizona	$1,210,000	3300
South Carolina	$1,160,000	2400
Colorado	$1,100,000	4400
Georgia	$2,100,000	4200
Idaho	$552,000	2800
Maryland	$1,600,000	2100
Minnesota	$3,000,000	7142
Utah	$552,000	3200
Washington	$1,600,000	3500
New York	$4,500,000	3500

(holding 1/4 for New Jersey & Connecticut)

(In three earliest primaries, less than 3 weeks of decent media coverage)

-- Limits Presidential appearances in early states, too

I

MARCH 2, 1995

359

2. Polling

A. Need to identify theme. See attached questionnaire

- New Covenant vs. traditional Dem and Rep lines
- Historical context -- vs. old Democratic programs
- Historical context -- vs. Reagan cuts
- Social context -- generational analysis
- Biographical context -- poor state/alcoholic father
- Biographical context -- made it on my own
- Presidential record as New Covenant
- Republican issues with New Covenant spin
- Disagree with both parties -- triangulation
- Middle class theme
- Doing it myself
- Hillary

3

B. Tracking and new issues. See attached questionnaire

    -- Affirmative action
    -- Clinton getting better
    -- Republican budget cuts
    -- No public funds for Clinton
    -- Cut NASA
    -- College loans
    -- Medicare and HMOs
    -- Parents liable for gun acts of children
    -- Baseball strike tracking
    -- Superfund changes Republicans want
    -- Whitewater
    -- Russia/Iran
    -- Foster tracking

C. Next step:

-- Identify 20% of vote that is up for grabs

    -- Personality tests and type of ads
    -- Issue appeals
    -- TV shows
    -- Radio music habits to construct network
    -- Locations and demographics
    -- Identify key variables

3. Consultants

A. Media Creators

-- Use Bush-Ailes '88 model

-- Need for early decision

    -- Get full time media person, not divided with other races

    -- Go on air early

-- Importance of centralized and well controlled team

4

-- Squier at head

    -- Media expert for 30 years
        -- talk show commentator
        -- strategist of first order -- best in Dem party
    -- Did Clinton ads in '92 (read my lips)
    -- Best overall media in Dem party
    -- Widest variety of ads
    -- Close working relationship
    -- National credentials, well respected
    -- Gore and Senators will love it
    -- Ongoing advisor on free and paid communication
    -- Client list -- 52 senate and governor

Gore

Sens: Graham, Rockefeller, Bryan. Byrd,
        Akaka, Heflin, Pell, Mitchell,
        Lautenberg, Biden, Simon, Hart,
        Burdick, Harkin, Lieberman, Sasser(not
        his loss), Muskie

Govs: Bayh, Richards, John Y. Brown,
        Florio(not loss), McWherter, Winter

-- Suggest inclusion in Thursday meetings

-- Assisted by:

-- Hank Sheinkopf

    -- Very emotional media
    -- Different type of media

-- Marius Penczner

    -- Country MTV producer
    -- Very varied cinema techniques

-- Tony Schwartz for radio

    -- See Anastasia Somosa ad

5

B. Consultant Mix

-- No two teams -- one group only

-- Premises of Squier-Morris-Schoen team

      1. Expand vote share v fortify base

         -- focus on expanding base, not just strengthening it

      2. Use issues to win v use images and visuals

      3. New Covenant vis-à-vis old Dems and old Repubs v liberal
         neo-populism

      4. Middle class focus v poor-rich class war

      5. Record of successes for you v '94 debacle

      6. Have vast experience

         -- A combined total of 94 senate or governor races:
            Squier (52), Schoen (17), Morris (26)

         -- End use of leaks to set up team: Times, Time, AP

MARCH 2, 1995

363

4. Issues

    A. Line Item Filibuster

        -- Our recovery from balanced budget issue

        -- Make sure filibuster is dramatic, round the clock, controversial

        -- Play leading role in fighting for cloture

        -- Ready list of vetoes you would do if you had the line item

            -- Release one per day during debate

    B. Tax Cut Deal

        -- Act 2 of our recovery

        -- Negotiate with Packwood

        -- Try for minimum wage/capital gains deal based on indexing

8

C. Rescissions

    -- Praise Republicans for helping in search for cuts
    -- Take cuts under advisement
    -- Quietly, privately lobby to kill bad cuts
    -- Publicly only take on education cuts:

        -- Drug free and safe schools
        -- WIC
        -- School to work
        -- Goals 2000
        -- AIDS prevention

    -- Total of less than $1 billion of $20 billion, stress low amount

    -- You and Hillary visit cut children's programs

D. Regulatory Moratorium

    -- Make explicit veto threat

    -- Make fight over three regulations:

        -- Probe for e coli microbes in food inspection

           -- Replacing smell, touch, feel "test"

        -- Drinking water regulation

           -- Cryptosporidium no requirement for testing it

               -- But in Milwaukee, made thousands sick and
               killed many
               -- Milwaukee wants tests imposed

        -- Air commuter safety

           -- New York Times critique of current regulation
           -- Recent crashes. No effective anti-icing regulations
               specially designed for commuter craft in US
               conditions

        -- If Republicans claim exempt from moratorium, cite
litigation which blocks enforcement

9

E. Welfare Reform

    -- Fight over work requirement

        -- Modified in House to 90% by '98

            -- But if not, penalty on state in form of aid cut
            -- We want people who won't work thrown off welfare

            -- "Seeking work" covered, blast loophole

        -- They are modifying bill as fast as we can read it, get going with criticism soon

F. Affirmative Action

    -- Move immediately or risk being eclipsed

    -- No need to supply details, just leave it to agencies to make proposals

        -- Add advisory committee to vet proposals

G. Lobbyist Reform

    -- Wash hands:

        -- No lobbyist money in '96
        -- No DNC lobbyist money in '96
        -- Refund $13,000 in defense fund money

    -- Then proceed with executive orders:

        -- Ban contacts between executive branch and foreign lobbyists
        -- Ban gifts from lobbyists to executive branch
        -- Require reports of each contact by lobbyists from executive branch officials
        -- Badges for lobbyists in executive branches

    -- Finally, draw up legislation making the above applicable to Congress

10

March 16, 1995
Proposal for the "Pile of Vetoes" Speech to Define Centrist Response to Gingrich
(See chapter 7)

By our meeting on March 16, 1995, the president's poll numbers were dropping sharply. After his long but excellent State of the Union address earlier in the year, his job approval had begun to show signs of recovery, but as gridlock and partisanship engulfed Washington, it fell back again.

In this agenda the consultants stress that Clinton should run more as an incumbent than as a Democratic partisan. While the conventional wisdom pitted Gingrich and Clinton against each other in a zero-sum game where a gain by one necessitated a loss by the other, the agenda stresses that both the Speaker of the House and the president are incumbents whose fate is closely tied to the general impression of success or failure in Washington. It notes that Clinton's "ratings and Dole's and Gingrich's are joined at the hip. We go up or down together." Voters wanted Washington to succeed in addressing the nation's problems and were determined to punish all or reward all based on their collective performance.

To define a response to the Contract with America's cuts, the agenda proposes that the president lay down the boundaries of what he would sign and what he would veto in a major policy address. The title of the speech—Pile of Vetoes—would come from its sound bite in which the president proclaimed, "I was not elected to produce a pile of vetoes or a stack of issues for the next election."

In the agenda the consultants suggest a variety of compromises to offer to the Republicans and propose a sharp departure from the knee-jerk rejection of all the Contract with America proposals by Gephardt and the orthodox Democrats in Congress.

The agenda also proposes a new approach to the Affirmative Action issue. It recommends basing preferences not on race or gender but on objective facts like income or residence in a poor area. This third-way proposal received a chilly reception from White House liberals, who ultimately killed it as the threat of a Jessie Jackson primary challenge to the president's renomination loomed.

Also notable in the agenda was an initial attempt to define a third-way welfare reform position, embracing Republican ideas for time limits and work requirements for welfare clients and the Democratic demand for day care and job training. Ultimately, the president moved to the left of the position suggested in his agenda, but the broad outlines are quite similar to the highly successful welfare reform bill that he signed in 1996.

The First Lady had chosen to withdraw from the weekly strategy meetings by January. She had come to realize that her up-front public role was creating the impression that she ran the show and that the president was weak and easily manipulated. Her withdrawal from the public stage was, however, too complete. In this agenda the consultants propose that she begin to write a weekly newspaper column to raise her visibility, a proposal she soon adopted.

2. Declining Poll Ratings -- Due To Partisanship And Populism

A. Public Perceptions of Gridlock and Partisan Bickering

    1. We win each issue, but lose the overall game

    2. Our ratings and Dole's and Gingrich's are joined at the hip. We go up or down together

    3. You live in a Democratic culture that applauds moves that attack Republicans and defend Democratic values, but which come back to haunt you in ratings

        a. If it feels good to your circle, be suspicious of it

    4. Speeches are too diffused, each contains everything, needs more focus so press has to cover the message we want, not the Rep vs. Dem message they are inclined to cover

        a. Suggest standing orders to run speech drafts by Curry (and, through him, me) at every stage of the process -- not just a few days before. Curry and Bahr are developing a good rapport

B. Attacks on Republicans and anti-rich populism was right for Feb and early March

    1. We needed to demonstrate Republican monstrosity to get sufficient public backing to force compromises

    2. But we needed to switch gears right after defeat of balanced budget amendment

    3. Lesson: It is taking too long to turn around our battleship

4. The cities speech on Monday shows that when New
Covenant rhetoric and anti-Republican rhetoric are side-
by-side, the press will ignore New Covenant and only
cover attacks on Republicans

    a. Just as Friday's Press Conference showed that when
anti-rich comments are mixed with New Covenant,
only populist comments get covered

    b. Therefore: need to discipline speeches to showcase
only one push at a time -- conciliatory or
confrontational, not both at once

C. Now we need major effort to break gridlock and get bills passed

    1. Effort is not enough, we actually need to sign laws

    2. Point one of strategy: let the wave exhaust itself by its own
successes

    3. Frustration will lead to energized Republicans in 96

D. Proposal for "Pile of Vetoes Speech" and White House-Senate "conference committee"

   1. Give speech with drama and flair to mark important point of \ departure from Feb-March rhetoric

      A. Summary Of Speech

         1. Americans demanded change in 92 and 94
         2. At first we worked together
         3. Now: Partisan gridlock
         4. "I was not elected...to produce a pile of vetoes or a stack of issues for the next election"
         5. Resume momentum for change
         6. Sketch out common ground
         7. "Ideological purity is for dictatorships, compromise....and negotiation are the substance of democracy"

         -- Then review areas and direction of compromise -- see next page (2-E: "Outline of Likely Deals")

   2. Be sure all White House staff is on board for new line

   3. Cut deals on everything with Senate and confront House with fait accompli

      a. Name "conferees" to negotiate

      b. Suggest Curry's inclusion so I can keep my hand in

      c. Suggest Griffin, Galson, Rasco, MacLarty, and Curry as conferees

   4. Weekly meetings with Congress leadership

      a. Majority leaders included to get in Lott

MARCH 16, 1995

E. Outlines of likely deals:

    1. Taxes: 65-100 billion

        a. Give way on capital gains

        b. Get our way on middle class limits on $500/child

        c. Get our way on college education

        d. Leave minimum wage out of it

    2. Regulation

        a. 45 day override for moratorium

        b. Cost v health standard for regs, not cost v cost
           -- Roth Bill

        c. Some alternative dispute resolution to avoid
           strangulation in courts
           -- Make 45 day override permanent
           -- Have exec-leg commission rule within a year on
              appeals from regs (or within 3 months if
              "urgent")
           -- Special courts like immigration courts
           -- No injunctive relief possible in regular federal
              court system

    3. Line item veto: win it

    4. Term limits: berate House for failure to pass

        a. Press for statute allowing states to act

5. Unfunded mandates

    a. Sign it with hoopla

6. Litigation reform

    a. Let Senate chop it to pieces

        -- Modify loser pays for expedited ruling at start of case

        -- Punitive damages are to deter future abuse

            -- So, set up four levels based on judicial determination, after hearing evidence, on severity of damage if defendant's conduct is not deterred and on likelihood of each dollar level constituting sufficient deterrence to avoid repetition
            -- 250,000 normal maximum
            -- 500,000 if "significant chance of injury to others similarly situated if defendant's conduct is not deterred"
            -- 1,000,000 if "real danger to life, health, or safety is found for others similarly situated if conduct is not deterred"
            -- Up to 10,000,000 if standards for 1 mil is met, but judge finds that larger reward is necessary to deter conduct in future

    b. If entire bill doesn't pass Senate, that's OK

7. Peacekeeper bill

    a. Delete provisions cutting UN aid by amount of US spending

    b. Delete other provisions you find obnoxious

8. Crime bill

    a. Veto over 100,000 cops and gun control

    b. Encourage version you can sign

F. Preparing Senate Democrats for Compromise

    1. Extended dialogue with moderate Dems

    2. Push hard on line item veto

    3. Start with Dems who voted for balanced budget amendment

    4. Walk them through compromises and actively participate in negotiations between them and Republicans

3. Paid Media

A. Ratings improve after major speeches -- Ads will have same effect, but permanent

B. Need decision on No Federal Funds

    1. Will poll rationales (see polling section)

C. Need actual fund raising for May buy

    1. $2.5 million for 700 points

    2. Crime -- 100,000 cops likely theme

D. If exempt from federal limits, heavy push in NH, Ariz., Iowa

MARCH 16, 1995

375

5. Affirmative Action -- A New Approach:

A. General Principles

    1. Government should be color blind and gender neutral unless there is specific statistically based evidence of discrimination

    2. Affirmative Action programs should be based on need so as not to discriminate against poor white males

B. Specifics:

    1. Law should be color blind

        a. No racial or gender criteria, only needs based criteria

    2. If evidence of discrimination, can use race or gender based affirmative action

        a. If statistical evidence of disproportionately low hirings or promotions of minorities or women, affirmative action by race and gender can be used, but only insofar as it is necessary to end this discrimination

          -- Specific acts of discrimination not necessary to show, just statistical evidence

    3. No matter whether discrimination or not, all affirmative action programs must benefit all people below poverty level, regardless of race or gender

C. THEREFORE:

    1. If no discrimination found by statistical evidence, then no basis other than income is possible

    2. If discrimination is found, then affirmative action based on race, gender, and poverty can be employed, but such programs must not exclude poor white males.

D. Evidence and argument:

    1. Unfair to exclude white males in poverty
    2. Need to fight discrimination
    3. Affirmative action must be color blind unless there is discrimination

E. Rhetoric

    1. By basing racial preferences clearly on discrimination, we put rightist opponents of these preferences in the position of defending discrimination.

        a. Dole says he's against discrimination. Use this position to press him on affirmative action where discrimination exists

2. By extending benefits to white males in poverty, we
   demonstrate compassion and equal playing field for white
   men.

   a. 13.4 million children in poverty are white male headed
      households out of a total of 23.2 million total
      children in poverty

      -- 3.6 million children in black households
      -- 2.9 million children in Hispanic households
      -- 2.3 million children in female white headed
         households

      -- Included in 13.4 million children in white male
         headed households are 500,000 children in
         single male headed households

3. By excluding color or gender from affirmative action, unless
   discrimination is present, we articulate the idea of color
   blind affirmative action as the ultimate goal.

   a. MLK was moving in that direction at the end of his life
      when he made common cause with Memphis
      sanitation workers and, in a host of speeches,
      urged economic empowerment and a class based,
      not merely race based, coalition

   b. Jesse Jackson's rainbow coalition articulated same
      notion

      -- Use rainbow to neutralize Jesse

         -- If oppose your stand, was he kidding about
            rainbow?

4. Racially or gender based affirmative action is only a

temporary expedient to remedy discrimination, not a permanent fixture.

   a. If affirmative action is temporary or transitional, as now supposed, it will terminate as discrimination ends. Discrimination is clearly in retreat and the end is in sight

   b. Key change in concept of affirmative action

5. Affirmative action should continue to exist, on a needs basing only, after discrimination is remedied. color blind affirmative action for poor people is societal imperative

   a. Affirmative action is a permanent necessity to fight poverty and can continue to exist if we base it on need, not discrimination

F. Changes:

1. Affirmative action is permanent to help poor, not simply as expedient to remedy discrimination

2. White men in poverty will now be helped

3. The ultimate ideal of color blind is now clearly before us

G. No changes:

1. Still use affirmative action to remedy statistically proven discrimination

H. On Set Asides

   1. Base on geographic location of firms in poverty areas

      and

   On former poverty status of employees

      and

   On ongoing involvement with and residence in poor areas
   of senior management

   2. Argument

      a. Set asides are too often basically phony. They
          benefit people who are minority or female, but
          have nothing to do with poor people or inner
          cities. By requiring location and ongoing
          involvement with poor communities, as
          opposed to racial or gender criteria, we
          assure that set asides help poor areas, not
          upper income areas.

      b. 2/3 of all black and Hispanic people are not
          poor. We must assure that scarce resources
          go to people and communities genuinely in
          need, not to those who can make a historic
          case of discrimination

I. Differences from Democrats

   1. Target communities, not minority rich -- end phony set-
       asides

   2. Set goal of no affirmative action by race

   3. Help white men in poverty

J. Differences from Republicans

    1. Affirmative action is a permanent necessity to help poor people

    2. Affirmative action based on race and gender is necessary to fight discrimination where evidence proves there has been discrimination

    3. Set asides that target poor communities necessary to help save cities.

6. Policy Suggestions

A. Lobbyist Reform

    1. Unilateral actions for immediate announcement

        a. Renounce all lobbyist contributions for 96 campaign

            1. Would also include overt lobbyist sponsorship of fund raising

            2. Can't have events at lobbyist homes

            3. Would not include lobbyists helping to raise money from other sources, just not overt sponsorship of events

        b. Announce a parallel policy for the DNC

        c. Refund the $13,000 collected from lobbyists for defense fund

        d. Refuse to hire any lobbyists on campaign staff or include them in any advisory board in campaign

    2. Executive Orders

        a. Since no legislation is contemplated in this phase -- and wouldn't pass if it were -- we are reversing the process to regulate employees of executive branch, not lobbyists. An inside out approach to regulation, but effective nonetheless

b. Ban all contacts between executive branch employees and lobbyists who represent a foreign government

    1. Law currently requires registration of all such lobbyists

    2. Law currently requires full report of each contact by lobbyist

    3. Law would now preclude such contacts with all executive branch employees

    4. Practical effect: end foreign lobbying

c. Require all executive branch employees to disclose all contact with lobbyists. Including date of contact, name of lobbyist, interest represented, and substance of call

]

    1. Pattern report after that which lobbyists representing foreign governments now must file after each contact with govt official

    2. Because there is no executive branch registration for lobbyists:

        a. Employee must ask if person is a lobbyist for a party in the matter under discussion (or if his firm is)

        b. If yes: must file report as noted above

        c. If no: must send name to Ethics office for vetting. If found to be a lobbyist, then reporting requirement would trigger for all contacts with that person including that which has already taken place

B. Welfare Reform

    1. Overall Attitude -- Positive, good beginning on welfare reform

        a. Main Objection -- Needs tougher work requirements

            1. Throw off if won't work (poll 73-23 supp)

            2. Eliminate looking for work loophole -- furnish public jobs if private not available

        b. Things We Like

            1. 5 year cutoff (but would rather have 2 years)

            2. Block grants for child care (but oppose caps)

            3. Cutoff to legal immigrants (poll 50-47 split)

            4. Work requirement for food stamps

            5. Electronic card for food stamps

            6. Cutoff for welfare for extra children while on AFDC (poll 64-32 supp. cut)

            7. Block grant for foster care

            8. No disability for drug addicts or alcoholics

            9. Child support registry

c. Things We Want That Aren't In The Bill

    1. No drivers' license if no child support

    2. 2 year cutoff, not 5 years (poll 55-39 supp cutoff 2 yr)

    3. Stiffer work requirements (main objection)

d. Things We Strongly Oppose That Are In The Bill

    1. Food stamp caps (poll 42-55 opp cut)

    2. Nutrition and school meals block grants and caps (poll 22-76 opp cut)

e. Things We Don't Like But Are Willing To Look For Middle Ground

    1. Block grants for welfare, end of entitlement (poll 58-35 supp)

    2. No cash for most disabled, just services

    3. No welfare for teenage mothers (poll 44-35 opp cut)

C. Immigration -- Deportations

  1. INS issue monthly body counts of deportations and increase number -- bring Presidential pressure for higher body counts

    a. Now 50,000 a year (half criminal, half civil)

    b. Too little emphasis on deportation, too much other policy

  2. 100 more immigration judges to increase deportations

    a. 125,000 backlog of cases

    b. Bottleneck is number of judges

    c. Separate asylum requests from immigration judges

  3. Extend El Paso System to three other corridors

    a. One in Arizona, one in Texas, one in California

    b. Guards or infra-red detectors at least every 500 yards

      1. Working well in El Paso
      -- Initially committed to drop in arrests as measure of success. Stupid measurement.
      2. 14 corridors in Southwest. Now guard San Diego and El Paso. Would extend to three more
      3. No new funding. Can be done through transfers and funds under last year's crime bill

4. Make States issue drivers' licenses which expire when Visa does

    a. Half of illegals are Visa overstays

    b. Automatic referral to be required from motor vehicles to INS with no licenses if designated as license based on Visas

    c. Condition of highway funds, like 55 speed limit

5. Automatic deportation from criminal justice system

    a. Completely implement vis-à-vis prison discharges and non-prison guilty verdicts

    b. Implement deportations for not-guilty verdicts or dismissal of charges

MARCH 16, 1995

G. Hillary

    1. Radio show

        a. Guests with dignity: Cronkite, Kirault, Bennett

        b. No ratings grabbers: Rosanne Barr, Charles Barkley

    2. Expensive Drugs

        a. Interface with drug companies to raise funds
        b. Possible TV ads promoting fund

    3. Suggest weekly newspaper column have submitted memo to her on this

H. Term Limits

    1. Push issue harder
        a. Attack need for constitutional amendment as attempt to kill it

        h Push for statutory action

March 23, 1995
Triangulation Is Born
(See chapters 5 and 11)

For decades America had been polarized by the sterile debate between the two parties. Voters felt forced to swallow ideas they hated in order to get what they wanted from their government. Those who sought relief from taxation by voting Republican had to stomach a pro-life agenda in the bargain. People who wanted to protect the environment and voted Democrat to do so usually had to put up with higher taxes as part of the deal.

As a candidate in 1992, Clinton had campaigned as a "new Democrat"—a fiscal conservative, tough on crime, but a devotee of traditional Democratic concerns for the three E's: education, the elderly, and the environment. Now, as the pitched battle raged between Democrats and Republicans over the Contract with America proposal, the president groped for a way to express his "third-way" alternative to both Republican cuts and Democratic spending.

At the March 23 meeting the consultants proposed the idea of triangulation—the development of a fusion alternative embodying the best elements of the traditional Republican and Democratic positions, but rejecting the extremes of each party. This agenda outline first articulated what triangulation meant by discussing how this positioning varied from the stereotypical agendas of either party. The agenda is particularly interesting in that it presents triangulation as an extension of Hegelian philosophy, with its emphasis on the triangle of thesis/antithesis/synthesis—an analysis which struck home with the well-read president.

In the spring of 1995 most press attention was focused on the hardened band of right-wing ideologues who were driving the Contract with America agenda through the House of Representatives without compromise or any effort at conciliation. In the March 23 agenda, the consultants propose that the president focus on crafting a moderate block of Democrats in the Senate as a counterpoint. Eventually, the legislation emerging from the House would have to pass the Senate. With the GOP in control of a simple majority, but well short of the sixty votes needed to cut off debate and move legislation, the influence of these moderate Democrats on legislation loomed as decisive.

This refashioning of the Democratic minority in the Senate was designed to give de facto leadership to the moderates like Connecticut's senator Joseph Lieberman and Louisiana's John Breaux, rather than to the liberals like Kennedy and Moynihan who usually held sway. By becoming the key block between the Republicans and the liberal Democrats, these moderate Democrats, although small in number, were able to wield a disproportionate influence, deciding which bills to pass to Clinton for signature and which to kill through never-ending debate.

Also notable in the March 23 agenda is the first discussion of anti-tobacco regulations. As yet, we had not focused on teen smoking as the target, but were still groping to find our way.

TO: THE PRESIDENT

RE: Agenda for meeting on March 23, 1995

1. CONGRESSIONAL ACTION -- AVOIDING VETOES, ACHIEVING COMPROMISE

    A. Premise: We Need To Show That Government Works

        1. We seem to poll regularly in the low fifties except for screwups, now, while before, we polled in the low forties except for successes

            a. Due to policy of accommodation

            b. After toning down partisan and populist rhetoric, our ratings, USA/CNN showed a 4 point gain between 2/29 -- 3/19

    B. Crafting A Moderate Vote Democratic Bloc In Senate

        1. Basic to your capacity to govern

            a. Stem charges of Presidential irrelevance

            b. Make the House irrelevant through ideological rigidity

            c. Way to get credit when you win Congressional fights

C. Issues Coming Up In Senate Before Recess

    1. Line Item Veto

        a. Make enough noise to get credit

        b. Get moderate Dems used to working together under your leadership

        c. Get press used to covering "President's Party" in Senate -- moderate Dems

        d. Use perception to gain Presidential relevance again

    2. Recissions

        a. A veto would be a disaster

            1. Would show us vetoing first real spending cut after 94 elections

            2. Even if we win the rhetorical fight, the price in government-doesn't-work would be too high

b. Formulate narrow list of objections to Republican
cuts

1. Suggest objecting to:

a. Anti-drug in schools ($482)
b. Housing for AIDS patients ($186)
c. Goals 2000 ($174)
d. Public school grants - low inc. ($140)
e. Anti-drug in public housing ($32)
f. Anti-school drop-outs ($28)
g. WIC food ($25)
h. Counselors for child violence ($14)
I. Americorps cut ($416)

(Total restored: $1.5 billion)

2. Lesser priority: 33% restore in:

a. Summer jobs ($1.7 bil)
b. Low income heating assistance
($1.3 bil)
c. PBS ($141)
d. Technical training ($108)
e. Trade adjustment aid ($99)
f. National Inst. Stand Technology ($27)
g. Rental aid to poor ($2.7 bil)
h. Operate housing projects ($404)
i. Comm devel block grants ($349)
j. Job trainining for youths ($310)
k. Lead paint removal ($90)

(Total cuts -- $7.2 bil. assuming 33% restoration --
$2.4 bil cost)

c. Total Restorations: $3.9 billion

d. Cuts I see no political problem with

   1. Grants for clean water projects ($1.3 bil)
   2. Modernization of public housing ($1.2 bil)
   3. Public housing & devel and acquisit ($690)
   4. Improvements to public house ($523) (we OKed it)
   5. Local aid adoption, foster care ($150)
   6. Mass transit projects ($132)
   7. Pell grant surplus ($104)
   8. School construct ($99) (we OKed it)
   9. FAA construct ($70)
   10. Highway construct ($70)
   11. Solar energy res ($34)
   12. Food and homemaking ed ($34)
   13. Library const ($15)
   14. Nat'l Endow Human and Arts ($5)
   15. Reading program for inmates ($5)

   (Total no problem: 4.6 bil)

   (Unaccounted for: 3.7 bil -- assume we will want to restore 1 billion = 5 bil)

e. Present alternative list of cuts for $5 billion

   1. Be sure that they are not too partisan

      a. Largely structure around cuts already in recommended budget

      b. Clear them in advance with Lott

      c. Avoid defense

f. Negotiate with Senate to get bill we can sign

3. Regulatory Moratorium

    a. 45 day congressional override to be made permanent

        1. Pres could veto override of a reg
        2. Then it would take 2/3
        3. We can certainly live with that

    b. Let's try to make 45 day rule all that we need to do in this area

        1. Lott says the Rs may buy that

    c. Political reality: Congress would never override most of the regulations

    d. Let's use moratorium to kill reform package

D. Items Coming Up After Recess In Senate

    1. Telecommunications - urge greater involvement by Gore

    2. Regulatory reform

        a. Just cutting regulations won't be enough

        b. Should avoid a veto

        c. Moratorium idea of 45 day veto may provide the key to dispute

            1. Lott says if it were permanent, that might be all we need to do

            2. May not need any new standards for passing a regulation at all

MARCH 23, 1995

    d. If 45 day override is not enough, then urge focus on alternate dipute resolution mechanisms to avoid litigation delays

    e. Should be easy to negotiate a cost weighed against science, health, and cost -- if 45 day is not enough

3. Litigation reform

    a. Urge negotiations on punitive damages assigned by judge

    b. Idea of damages paid to court was very attractive

4. Tax cuts

    a. Need to rejoin debate -- with Republicans split, you can be tax cut hero

    b. Use remarks to articulate third way

        1. Take on deficit hawks
        2. Take on excessive cuts
        3. Urge targeting education

4. ANALYSIS OF NEW THEMES APPROACH

A. It is not enough to be the Democrat who isn't a spendthrift and the Republican who isn't cruel. Affirmative positioning vital

B. Three formative events in recent political history

    1. Recession made Reagan-Bush inactivism intolerable

      -- Result: Clinton's election

    2. Health Care, Gun Control, and Tax Changes made Clinton's governmental activism unpopular

      -- Result: Gingrich-Dole victory

    3. Draconian Republican Cuts in School Lunches and other compassion programs make less government suspect

      -- Result: A hunger for a new synthesis

C. Two paths for '96: Bifurcation -- refighting the dialectic

vs.

Triangulation -- create synthesis

    1. Refighting dialectic (populism and partisanship) won't

MARCH 23, 1995

work because it merely reignites impetus for '94
Republican victories

2. A little populism steals headlines and drowns out your
New Covenant message

    -- Experience of Friday press conference

    -- Like a drop of ink in water, it takes over

3. Synthesis builds on history, does not attempt to alter it

4. The triangulation of the new synthesis mirrors the
individual conclusions of most voters and all swing
voters

    -- Harnesses "plague on both your houses" vote

    -- Perotist appeal

D. Articulation Of Synthesis: New Covenant

1. Learning process is key

    Reinvent New Covenant as the product of
    evolution from '92 and '94 dialectic

    -- Walk people through their own learning
       experience

    -- Revisit defects of past proposals:

        -- Bush passivity
        -- Clinton big government (I've learned)
        -- Gingrich compassion cuts (without personal
           attacks)

2. Express Triangulation On Each Issue

a. Taxes:

> Old Dem: -- no tax cut
> Rep: -- tax cut for wealthy & with
> no purpose
> Us -- aim at middle class &
> catalytic of better raising and
> educating of children

b. Balanced Budget:

> Old Dem -- raise taxes or don't do
> it
> Rep -- cut everything in sight
> Us -- bring down deficit more
> gradually so as not to cut
> children and education
> investments

c. Regulatory Reform:

> Old Dem -- don't
> Rep -- no govt regulations
> Us -- change code napoleon
> itemization to a common
> law/common sense
> approach based on:
>
> > - flexibility
> > - empirical experience
> > - differing vehicles of
> > dereg depending
> > on the issue
> > - taking account of
> > feedback

d. Welfare Reform:

> Old Dem -- don't

Rep -- punish
Us -- change to a system of
incentives and disincentives
to move people off. Use
welfare to get people off
welfare

e. Crime:

Old Dem -- don't toughen laws
Rep -- toughen courts
Us -- toughen courts and
community policing and drug
treatment and job training,
etc.

f. Affirmative Action:

Old Dem -- preserve it
Rep -- end it
Us -- continue, but base on need

3. Relate To Other Contexts In Speeches

a. Biographic

-- Alcoholic father = standards
-- Small town boyhood = opportunity

b. Societal

-- 40s and 50s = self-sacrifice/old Dem
-- 80s = narcissism/Rep
-- 90s = responsibility/new Dem

c. Programmatic

    -- Great Society failures
    -- Self-defeating cuts
        -- housing cuts = homelessness
        -- school cuts = crime, joblessness
        -- job training cuts = unemployment
    -- Intelligent cuts needed
        -- cut welfare, not investments

6. GENERAL POLITICAL

A. Tobacco Suit   3/23/95

  1. Suggest Federal intervention in five existing suits over Medicaid

    a. Medicaid enforcement is delegated to the states

    b. Five states -- Mississippi, West Virginia, Florida, Massachussetts, and Minnesota are suing tobacco companies for reimbursement for Medicaid costs in treating tobacco cases

    c. Suggest Federal government intervene as co-plaintiff in these suits

    d. Suggest Federal encouragement of other states to join lawsuit

    e. Suggest Presidential statement at Tallahasee dinner on Thursday, March 30 to call attention to the suits and urge their success

      1. In attendance at dinner: Chiles, Mike

3/23/95
cont.
          Moore, Miss. Attny General who is
          bringing the suit

  2. Kessler is laying basis for regulations against tobacco

      a. Suggest he use same counsel as is handling
         these suits to defend his regulations in court

         1. Would permit information for state suits

         2. Would tap into mainstream of anti-smoking
           suits

      b. Main lawyer: Dick Skruggs (Trent Lott's brother-
         in-law) is handling Miss. and Fla. suits.
         Suggest he meet with Kessler re: this

B. Be sure Dems don't follow Reps in making Louisiana
   primary early

     1. Not as good a state for us as Iowa and NH

C. Keep calling date V-J day: could explode if we rename it

     1. Special DOD committee is doing arrangements and
       Washington Times reports its conidering changing
       name to end of war day

D. See David Broder's column for confirmation of December
   predictions on our strategy

     1. GOP gets little credit as bills whiz by

     2. Dems rename bills and focus attention and
       disagreements

E. Gramm's attack on corporate welfare

     1. Identify corporate welfare to be cut

MARCH 23, 1995

402

   a. He'll be against user fee increases

   b. He'll be against tax expenditure curbs

   c. But he'll likely favor cuts in spending for export, marketing, etc.

  2. I'll pass list to Gramm and see if there is common ground

F. Hillary

  1. Need for more exposure

  2. Suggest weekly column

   a. Need to push it, get it going

G. Baseball strike -- NLRB

April 5, 1995
A Turning Point. Clinton Agrees to Do Pile of Vetoes Speech
(See chapters 10 and 11)

Until the April 5 meeting the president had only experimented with the idea of a "third way," parting company with the Democratic front of rejection of the Republican initiatives. While he included the occasional centrist remark in his speeches, the red meat of partisan attacks against GOP cuts in Medicare or the school lunch program dominated his comments. It became evident throughout February and March that his acquiescence in the Democratic front of partisan opposition had consigned him to the sidelines and made him little more than a soldier in the Democratic army. In the agenda for the April 5 meeting, the consultants call for an end to the "miniaturization" of the president and urge him to strike out in a new direction.

Frustrated by stagnant or dropping poll ratings and by his inability to project a centrist message, at the April 5 strategy meeting Clinton decisively turned away from the confrontational tactics urged upon him by his staff. Instead the president took the first clear steps to embrace centrist triangulation as his political theme by deciding to deliver the Pile of Vetoes speech we had suggested in March, outlining areas for possible compromise and warning where he would use his veto to make a stand.

The president used the early April meeting in Dallas of the newspaper editors as a forum to deliver this message. Panetta wanted the speech to focus on education cuts and to use it to continue pounding away at the Republican cuts. He felt that Democratic opposition to the cuts in the Contract with America was making headway in the country and that we had to keep up the fire.

Clinton sharply disagreed and emphasized the need for a course between rejection and surrender in which he would carefully outline where he would compromise and where he would veto legislation if he were forced to do so. After the meeting the president ordered speechwriter Don Baer, White House staff member Bill Curry, and me to draft the Pile of Vetoes speech. The centrist course it defined eventually became the key to the president's national political positioning.

The meeting was also notable for its discussion of how the president should use the weekly Saturday morning national radio addresses he had been giving. The tradition, inherited from President

Reagan, offered what seemed to us to be a wonderful opportunity to make news in the Sunday papers. Unfortunately, the address had been largely devoted to platitudes and ceremonial pronouncements. In this agenda we ask that the addresses be targeted for their political impact and that they become a key way to communicate the Clinton agenda. Increasingly, the radio address became a central way of projecting the president's ideas.

The April 5 agenda also marks the introduction of the idea that the president might advocate a balanced budget but reject the GOP demand that balance be achieved in seven years. Eventually this proposal proved the key to allowing the president to have his cake and eat it too—to propose to eliminate the deficit but also to avoid the harsh cuts proposed by the Republicans.

TO: THE PRESIDENT
RE: AGENDA FOR MEETING ON APRIL 5 *95*

---

1. OUR STRATEGY IS NOT DOING ENOUGH TO IDENTIFY THE PRESIDENT WITH CENTRIST REFORM

A. The vast bulk of our rhetoric is anti-Congress and anti-Republican

   1. Getting involved in a zero-sum game with Congress is a very bad idea

   2. Congress is winning the PR war

      a. Congress' ratings are pretty good. 58-35 approval of first hundred days in CNN/USA poll

      b. 49-39 say Congress is doing right amount of cutting not going too far

B. Even if we define the Congressional Republicans as bad, we are not doing enough to define Clinton as good

   1. We are being folded into Democratic rhetoric of rich v. poor and harsh cuts v. rich tax cuts

      a. It makes us old Democrats, not new Democrats

      b. It reinforces idea that voters must choose one either Republicans who cut too much or Democrats who spend too much

APRIL 5, 1995

406

2. The new Clinton positions are receiving short shrift and are getting submerged in a two way Dem v. Rep fight

    a. Welfare Reform has been submerged in our concerns about school lunches

    b. Tax Cut proposals have been submerged in our concerns about tax cuts for the rich and deficit cutting

    c. Our commitment to state empowerment has been submerged in our attack on block grants

    d. Our progress in cutting government size is being submerged in our opposition to Republican budget cuts

    e. Our regulatory reform is being submerged in our opposition to Republican regulatory cuts

3. Even Clinton's centrist accomplishments are getting no attention -- drowned out by partisan rhetoric

    a. Line item veto -- no credit at all

    b. Budget cuts are becoming exclusively Republican in their perceived origin

    c. Tax cuts we proposed are forgotten, Republicans are now the tax cutters

    d. Cuts in regulations are getting little attention

C. Even if this produces short term gains by hurting Republicans, its long term cost in tying Clinton to Democratic orthodoxy is too big a price to pay

D. Ultimately, this strategy demands vetoes which will undermine central element of strategy -- that we exhaust the wave and permit Republicans to become satisfied

    1. Rhetoric will trap us into vetoes to show strength and consistency

    2. Our failure to articulate third way alternatives and to negotiate them will lead to vetoes

    3. The more the public sees these issues in bi-frucated terms the more vetoes will be evidence of commitment to Democratic Party orthodoxy

    4. Unless we articulate third way solutions in the crucible of the current controversies, the more they will become irrelevant and inadmissible later on

E. The result of this responsive, anti-Congressional Republican Strategy is the miniaturization of the Presidency

    1. Makes Initiatives Hard To Sustain

        a. Like Minimum Wage, it gets marginalized

        b. Like Reinventing Government, it is seen as irrelevant in face of more drastic Republican action

    2. If Clinton is always seen as responsive, it is hard to switch into a pro-active mold when needed

    3. The perception of an inactive Presidency likely reinforces idea of weakness

F. Doug Schoen's Focus Group Research

    1. Focus groups conducted with swing Dems and Ind voters

        a. San Francisco, Louisiana, Minneapolis, New York, Florida over last two months

    2. Major findings of research:

        a. Impetus still with Republicans in Congress

            1. Voters want to give them a chance

            2. Believe that, while there are excesses in Rep agenda, excesses are part of any drastic change

            3. More willing to forgive Rep excesses to accomplish goals

        b. Clinton not perceived as having changed since November

            1. Function of Dems in Congress and lack of visibility since State of Union address

        c. Welfare reform idea tests well

            1. Work elements are critical -- voters are willing to forgive women for a mistake, but feel that government must help them rejoin the workforce

            2. No sense that Clinton is fighting for this welfare reform package

  d. Affirmative action remains key sore point

    1. Among downscale whites, more acceptance of need-based affirmative action

    2. Upscale whites less favorable to entire concept of affirmative action

2. PROPOSALS FOR SPEECHES

 A. Use recess to regain initiative

 B. Pile of Vetoes -- Friday at Editors Meeting (see draft attached)

   1. Seemed like we were working together -- but now becoming too partisan, too divided

   2. We have lots of common ground -- deficit, tax cut, welfare reform, cut regulations, etc.

   3. Danger of inflexible ideologues taking over debate

   4. Call for summit to negotiate compromises

   5. Tax cut

    a. Must cut taxes to share prosperity and recovery

    b. Not $200 bil, that imperils balanced budget

    c. So target: Education, Middle Class

APRIL 5, 1995

410

6. Welfare

    a. Agree on work, time limits, state empowerment

    b. Disagree on:

        1. How to build in work

        2. Cutting off children of teenage mothers

        3. Entitlement: Possible compromise by leaving up to states

    c. Don't let welfare become campaign issue -- get reforms passed

7. Deficit reduction and balanced budget

    a. Amendment is dead, so now let's balance the budget

    b. Avoid cuts I have to veto, like lunches, and make cuts I can sign

    c. Avoid riders like strikes, prevailing wage, clean water, abortion -- veto bait

    d. Avoid artificial date, set a date where budget can be balanced without huge harm

        1. Dates are for campaign speeches

        2. Annual progress toward zero

        3. 2005, not 2002 more realistic

8. Line item veto

9. Regulatory reform

   a. Need fewer regs, more common sense

   b. Approve of 45 day override

   c. No strait jacketing of regulation -- that's a veto

   d. Sit down and figure out way to restore common
      sense regulation

10. Legal reform

    a. Needed,

    b. Trust judges on punitive

    c. No loser pays

11. Environment takings bill

    a. No negotiation, just veto

12. Health Care

    a. Common ground, one step at a time

    b. Pre-existing/Portability/Voluntary pool

13. Crime

    a. 2 vetoes: guns and 100,000 cops

    b. Then sign rest of bill with some changes

14. Peacekeeper

    a. No hamper Presidential authority

    b. Don't undermine UN

    c. Never put troops under UN in combat

15. Historic Opportunity

    a. Crossroads between confrontation and progress

    b. No pile of vetoes -- pile of laws

C. Tax Cut Speech

1. We have two deficits: fiscal and educational

    a. We must use tax cuts to remedy educational
       deficit even as we limit size of cuts to cut fiscal
       deficit

2. Need tax cuts to distribute fruits of recovery

3. Third leg of deficit hawk v. tax cutter debate: targeted,
limited tax cuts

APRIL 5, 1995

4. STYLE AND SPEECHES

    A. One subject per speech

        1. Don't give press a smorgasbord -- they'll choose the wrong issue

        2. Anytime we offer an attack on Republicans mixed with anything else, it's the attack that will get covered

    B. Use radio address for tactical intervention in story of the day

        1. We get more coverage when we make news

        2. Keep subject matter flexible until last minute to adjust to targets of opportunity

        3. Avoid pre-charted subjects -- too rigid for response to news currents

    C. Never be Undecided on a veto or signing after bill comes to you -- always know in advance

        1. We look very weak when we are undecided

        2. It highlights tough and close calls and makes too much out of them

        3. It gives interest groups too much time to work us over and become invested themselves

5. OTHER ISSUES WE SHOULD GET UNTRACKED

A. Health Care

    1. Still our core issue

    2. Must show progress

    3. Press Republicans for deal

        a. Pre-existing
        b. Portability
        c. Voluntary pools

    4. These achievements will loom very large to average person

B. Deportations

    1. Monthly "body count"

    2. More immigration judges to relieve bottleneck

    3. Drivers' license expire when visa does

    4. Better interface with prisons and courts

C. Lobbyist reform

    1. Key wedge issue against Dole

    2. Personal reforms

        a. No lobbyist money in 96

        b. No DNC lobbyist money

        c. Give back $13,000 legal defense fund

APRIL 5, 1995

415

3. Executive orders

    a. Disclosure of lobbyist contacts
    b. Ban on contacts with foreign govt. lobbyists

4. Legislative proposals

    a. Apply to Congress things we have already done
       in Executive
    b. Extend disclosure to all of government

    c. Extend ban on contacts to Congress

5. Don't let cynicism about our past relations with
   lobbyists stop us from using the issue

    a. Measured by newspapers against perfection, we
       may seem wanting, but measured against
       Dole, we'll look great in 96 on this if we set it
       up now

D. Balanced budget deal -- by 2006

1. GOP is not wed to 2002. Doesn't want to have to walk
   the plank to make it by then

    a. In Senate particularly there is willingness to
       extend it out years

    b. Republicans don't want to do the Medicare cuts
       they'd have to do to make 2003 work

2. Suggest floating later deadline

    a. But clearly indicate year-by-year progress toward
       goal

    b. Not a curve where most of progress is in out
       years

E. Medicaid

    1. Back managed care

        a. In Mass, only a 1% increase under managed care

        b. Distinguish welfare (Medicaid) from Medicare and Social Security

F. Medicare

    1. Oppose premium increases except on rich

    2. Be willing to consider reduced premiums for HMOs and managed care incentives

        a. But oppose raised premiums for current type of care

            1. i.e., back incentives, not punishments

        b. Oppose required HMOs and managed care -- use freedom of choice of doctor issue

H. Smoking

    1. Join lawsuits on Medicaid

    2. Launch lawsuit on Medicare

    3. Encourage other states to join suit

APRIL 5, 1995

417

April 27, 1995
The Political Impact of the Oklahoma City Bombing
(See chapter 11)

In the aftermath of the tragic bombing of the Federal Building in Oklahoma City, the president provided moral and spiritual leadership to a grieving and worried nation. The intimacy he achieved with the average American in that hour of sorrow was deeper and more profound than at any previous moment of his presidency.

But the bombing afforded an important political opportunity as well by demonstrating so vividly the danger of right-wing extremists. While the GOP leaders were not themselves extremists, it was evident that they would have to mute their denunciations of ultra-right groups. With the presidential primaries looming, no GOP candidate could afford to alienate so large a group of voters in his own party. Proposals for controls on explosives or weapons the radical right might use were particularly difficult for the Republican candidates because the National Rifle Association, with its formidable campaign clout, was unalterably opposed to such legislation.

Any attempt to link Republican leaders like Dole and Gingrich to the radical groups advocating violence would backfire. The consultants proposed a "ricochet" theory where the president would advocate executive and legislative measures to counter right-wing hate groups and limit their access to weapons of destruction. Reluctant to alienate part of their political base, the Republican leaders were certain to rise in opposition. By doing so, the consultants argued in the April 27 agenda, the GOP would link itself to the extremists.

In the agenda the consultants argue that much the same tactic was used against the Democrats in 1952, the Goldwater Republicans in 1964, and the New Left in 1968.

TO: THE PRESIDENT
RE: Agenda For Meeting On April 27, 1995

1. AFTERMATH OF OKLAHOMA CITY BOMBING

A. Temporary gain: boost in ratings -- here today, gone tomorrow

B. More permanent gain: Improvements in character/personality attributes -- remedies weakness, incompetence, ineffectiveness found in recent poll

C. Permanent possible gain: sets up Extremist Issue vs. Republicans

   1. Past experiences with extremist/violence issue --

      a. 1952 communism issue against Democrats
      b. 1964 extremism issue against Goldwater
      c. 1968 riots issue against Humphrey

   2. Common elements:

      a. A common national enemy from one side of ideological divide

         1. 1952 from left
         2. 1964 from right
         3. 1968 from left
         4. 1996 from right

      b. Groups heavily feared by the nation

         1. Communist party in '50s
         2. Birch Society -- Minutemen in 1964
         3. Ghetto rioters/student demonstrators in '68
         4. Bombers/paramilitary/skinheads in 1996

      c. Flirtation with extremists by mainstream party

          1. Civil libertarian stance by liberals in 1950s
          2. "Extremism is no vice" statement by
             Goldwater
          3. Kerner Commission/antiwar by '68 liberals
          4. Pro-gun stance by Republicans in 1996 --
             and protection of extremist groups
             against Federal intrusion

D. How to use extremism as issue against Republicans

    1. Direct accusations will not work

        a. Attacks on Republicans as extremists will
           provoke media backlash against President
           exploiting issue

        b. Republican leaders don't act like extremists, and
           it will be impossible to make them look
           extremist

    2. Ricochet theory -- the approach that will work

        a. Stimulate national concern over extremism and
           terror

           1. Metaphor: McCarthyism, '64 Birch Society
             concern, '68 ghetto riots/student protests

           2. When issue is at top of national agenda,
             suspicion naturally gravitates to
             Republicans

              a. Just like it did in '64
              b. Just like it attached to Dems in '52
                and '68

b. Implement intrusive policy against extremist
groups

  1. Necessary to prevent terrorism/extremism

  2. Reject "tombstone" approach which only
     acts after terrorism has happened.
     Instead, call for preventative surveillance
     and public disclosure of terrorist group
     activities to save lives before criminal
     actions are committed

  3. Will provoke outrage by extremist groups
     who will write their local Republican
     congressman

  4. This will provoke criticism by right-wing
     Republicans which will link right-wing of
     the party to extremist groups

  5. In Republican Presidential primary, this will
     create competition among candidates for
     this voter bloc

  6. Net effect: Self-inflicted linkage between
     party and extremists

     a. Metaphor: Liberal defense of
        Hollywood in '52
     b. Goldwater quote "extremism is no
        vice" in '64
     c. Humphrey defense of students and
        blacks in '68

3. How to implement ricochet theory

    A. Create "President's List" of extremist/terrorist organizations

        1. To warn public against well-intentioned donations which might foster terrorism
        2. To warn Americans against cooperation with such groups
        3. To warn communities of groups like these in their neighborhoods

    B. Require public disclosure of membership lists and donor lists by such organizations

        1. To aid in investigative process
        2. To let public know what is happening and get it out in the open

    C. Do not prohibit such groups, as this will trigger backlash

4. Use cultural differences with radical right to separate it from the norms of American culture

    A. Historical metaphors

        1. McCarthy hit liberal/communist/Hollywood elitism against religious bias of anti-communism
        2. Johnson stressed dangers of extremism against hotheads and paranoids of the right
        3. Nixon stressed patriotism and mainstream values against culture of demonstrators

B. Clinton needs to stress lawfulness and decency against vigilantism and brutality of terrorists

    1. Stress weird lifestyles, paranoia, and aberrant behavior of these groups

    2. Develop cultural norm issues against these groups, such as hatred and commitment to violence

2. THEMES VIS-À-VIS CONGRESS

A. Experience during Feb-March was very bad

1. White House Staff thought compassion attacks, like on school lunches, would work

a. Ratings dropped as liberal identification increased

b. Fusion with orthodox Democratic ideology

2. Broad gauge commentary on New Covenant, without reference to Congressional agenda provoked sense of ineffectuality and weakness

B. Differences between my suggestions for May-June and conduct during Feb-March

1. Core message

a. I suggest social and fiscal conservatism

b. As opposed to anti-Republican

2. Sense of accomplishment

a. I suggest key focus on making it all work together

b. As opposed to attacking Republican initiatives

3. Relevance of commentary

    a. I suggest commentary specifically tied to legislative action

    b. As opposed to Presidential speeches expressing philosophy and broad, elevated views on the one hand, and, on the other hand, orthodox comments parroting Democratic views

4. Leadership in debate

    a. I suggest we call on Congress to move in a certain direction

    b. As opposed to criticizing what they have done already

5. Reaction to Republican proposals

    a. I suggest acceptance of fiscal core and attack on non-fiscal periphery

        1. In general, cooperate on budget cutting
        2. In general, fight on environment, regulatory safety, loser pays, etc.

    b. As opposed to making fight on fiscal/compassion issues

6. Claiming credit

    a. Claim credit for compromises and for forcing moderation on Dems and Republicans

        1. Surface with recognizable position early enough to stake out claim so you get credit when your position is adopted

    b. As opposed to letting Daschle get credit for forcing compromise or letting moderate Republicans get credit for modifying House demands

    c. Increase public identification of President with moderate bloc of Dems in Senate under Lieberman and Breaux so their moves are seen as part of the President's moves

        1. Engender overt attitude of close cooperation between White House and moderate bloc

        2. Heighten self-identification of moderate bloc as balance of power in Senate

7. Push our own package of legislation

    a. I suggest we push

        1. College tuition deduction
        2. Anti-terrorist
        3. Deportations
        4. Lobby reform
        5. Health care
        6. Minimum wage

    b. As opposed to either responding to contract or waxing elegant about philosophy

3. PAID MEDIA

   A. Urge freedom from limits

   B. Decide on media creator now.

   C. Fund raising for $2.5 million in June

4/27/95

4. SPEECHES COMING UP -- NEED FOR HIGH PROFILE TO SUSTAIN PRESIDENTIAL INITIATIVES IN FACE OF RETURN OF CONGRESS

   A. Saturday Radio (to be taped on Friday afternoon)

      1. Criticize Supreme Court decision overturning ban on guns within 1,000 feet of schools

      2. Propose, instead, new legislation requiring a gun ban as precondition of receiving federal school funding

         a. Justification for linkage: We cannot encourage good education if firearms may be present. Therefore, we can withhold school aid unless state provides a gun-free school

         b. Precedent: Federal Highway funds denied unless states pass 55 mph speed limit

      3. Release text and proposals on Friday to get Saturday press. (Do not want to step on coverage of Williamsburg speech proposed below which will be on Saturday)

E. Emily's List (Monday)

    1. Pattern of violence spreading throughout America

        a. Domestic violence

        b. Child abuse

        c. Teenage gangs

        d. Operation Rescue

        e. Oklahoma

        f. Hate and bias crimes

    2. Violence is interlocking and catalytic

        a. Cannot pursue a selective war against violence --
           have to oppose it in all of its forms

        b. Attack "liberal" toleration of violence

           1. Criticize knee-jerk reaction against criticism
              of Hollywood and TV as a free speech
              issue (even though no government
              coercion is being suggested)

           2. Criticize liberal opposition to anti-crime
              measures, like more cops, longer
              sentences, and greater freedom of
              action for police

              a. By "counterscheduling" like this, you
                  show strength and refute those
                  who charge you with "saying what
                  they want to hear"

APRIL 27, 1995

428

    c. Attack conservative toleration of violence

        1. Anti-abortion

        2. Wanton possession of firearms

3. Demeaning value of human life -- treating people as things, not as humans (this echoes religious right rhetoric usually used to justify opposition to abortion and pornography, but here, we turn it around to serve our agenda)

    a. To gangs...people are customers or rivals

    b. To wife beaters...people are subjects to dominate and depress

    c. To child abusers, people are sex objects to gratify prurient sex drives

    d. To Operation Rescue....people are targets in ideological war

    e. To street criminals, people are prey

4. Need to assert belief in humanity of each individual

    a. Show how violence has consequences

        1. Death is the beginning of misery, not the end of the story...after you pull the trigger come the orphans

        2. Need to show that violence threatens all, not just immediate victims

    b. Stress human worth and value of each life

F. Aging Conference (Wednesday)

    1. Counterscheduling lecture on need to control Medicare and Medicaid costs

        a. Again, show strength by counterscheduling

    2. Attack on Republican remedies, which include higher premiums, deductibles, and penalties unless elderly join managed care

    3. Embrace incentives for managed care on Medicare like lower premiums and more services if join managed care reflecting cost differences

    4. Encourage alternatives to nursing home care like home care

    5. Different treatment for Medicare and Medicaid

        a. Stress Medicaid as part of welfare reform

            1. Medicaid recipients are welfare recipients

            2. We have every right to require managed care as many states, i.e. Massachusetts, now do

        b. Stress Medicare is earned right with individual empowerment to make choices

            1. Reject coercion and penalties to embrace incentives

May 4, 1995
The Blueprint for Campaign Strategy
(See chapter 9)

With the president pursuing a centrist agenda in the aftermath of the Pile of Vetoes speech, the basic strategy we would follow in 1996 was becoming clear. The May 4 agenda articulates it perhaps more clearly than any other.

The basic proposition was that the Republican Party is limited to five fundamental political messages—crime, defense, fiscal, racial, and social. Its history and ideology make it more attractive than the Democrats to voters who are concerned with reducing crime, strengthening national defense, or who focus on fiscal issues like holding down taxes or balancing the budget. Racial resentments over welfare, immigration, and affirmative action have also traditionally drawn disgruntled white voters to the Republican Party. Finally, GOP traditional orthodoxy on social issues like abortion, gay rights, and gun control make it an attractive option for social conservatives.

It is very hard to imagine a Republican candidate straying outside these issues by trying to run to the left of a Democrat on issues like education, consumer protection, the environment, or help for the elderly. Unless a Republican can win on one or more of these five basic issues, he can't win.

From these insights flowed the basic strategic goal of the campaign—to neutralize the four basic issues of crime, defense, fiscal policy, and race, thereby forcing the GOP to run on its social issues where its conservative positioning would ghettoize its appeal and keep marginal or swing voters away.

How to neutralize the four basic issues? Take away the fiscal issue by cutting the deficit and cutting taxes. Remove the defense issue by acting decisively abroad and never hesitating to show and use power. Neutralize the crime issue by cutting crime through a combination of gun controls, more police, and tougher sentencing. Finally a strategy was proposed to relieve racial resentments by curtailing illegal immigration, reforming affirmative action to eliminate its abuses, and moving people from welfare to work.

Merely taking away the Republican issues, however, won't win an election. The other part of the strategy was to use the extreme cuts in the GOP's Contract with America to make differences over the three traditional Democratic E's—education, the elderly, and the environment—the key contrasts in the campaign.

In the agenda of May 4 the consultants propose the first of many, many plans to solve the budget gridlock and reach a deal with the Republicans. This elusive goal, the holy grail of the 1996 campaign, held us all in its thrall. When the deal was finally cut in 1997, its terms closely paralleled the proposals in this and subsequent agendas.

2. STRATEGY FOR VICTORY

A. Republican Party is based on five messages

1. Fiscal/Economic
2. foreign/defense
3. racial
4. crime
5. social

B. When Republicans are Reduced to Only Social Message, they lose

1. not national majority issues

a. abortion and guns are minority issues
b. gays are majority issue, but not high enough profile

2. Republican strategists know this and work to avoid having social issues only

a. they work hard at structuring other issues so as not to be left with only the social issue

b. examples

a. Sundquist in Tennessee used income tax to cover abortion
b. Ridge in Pa used crime-pardons to cover up abortion differences

2

C. But, when stripped of all other issues and left only with social issues, Republicans lose example: Bush 92

    1. denied other issues

        a. fiscal by his tax increase
        b. economic by recession
        c. foreign/defense by his own success in ending cold war and by leaving Saddam in power
        d. racial and crime by his 88 campaign and the legacy of Horton issue and by his own inaction on this from in four years as Pres
        e. left only with social issues

    2. social issue didn't work for him

        a. Houston convention was a disaster

            1. no bump at all

        b. Family values issue didn't gain traction

            1. except as negative on Clinton re: Flowers

D. Stripping the Republicans of their issue appeals:

    1. Republicans start without access to crime issue

        a. crime bill of 94
        b. 100,000 cops
        c. signing of crime bill of 95
        d, 1,000 FBI agents, anti-terrorism, death penalty

    2. Republicans can't access economy as long as prosperity

        a. ~~appoint good people to Fed Res Bd~~

3

3. Republicans can access foreign/defense, but who
   cares

   a. not high in public priorities
   b. when an issue rises to the level of public
      priority, take bold, strong action
      ~~1. Iran is only one up that high now~~
      ~~2. don't show weakness with Russia~~ on
        ~~Iran~~

E. All the Republicans have left is racial, fiscal, social

   1. Counter their racial appeals. We must take this
      issue away from them

      a. counter affirmative action with our plan

            1. at first, present plan as balanced between
               goal of color blindness on one hand and
               use of aff action to remedy
               discrimination on the other

            2. After filing dates for primaries pass, move
               emphasis to the right and stress color
               blindness

            3. all along stress reform of set asides which
               both blacks and whites like poll shows

      b. counter immigration racism by deportations

   2. Counter their fiscal issue by reaching deal with
      Republicans in Congress

      a. balanced budget glide path
        (see Section 3 for How to do it)
      b. deficit reduction
      c. tax cut deal

   3. All they'll have left is social -- *check mate* !

4

MAY 4, 1995

3. How to Reach Fiscal Deal

A. Deficit Reduction/Balanced Budget

1. Give absolute political priority to making a deal

a. stop partisan shots

1. short term benefit of stinging them is minor tactical advantage compared to strategic windfall of getting these issues off the American agenda and giving Clinton credit for fiscal conservatism

b. most cuts never hurt politically

1. see Weld example

2. hide behind cover of Republicans wanted to go further

c. get staff to focus on deal making, not fight picking

d. Conflict of Interest with Congressional Dems

1. Gephardt-Dashle want no fiscal deal, so they can say Republicans didn't deliver

2. Gramm, etc want no deal so they can say Dole didn't deliver

3. But Dole wants deal to show he can deliver (despite hurt in general)
4. Gingrich wants deal for same reason

e. "Congressional loyalists" on white house staff can't force us into vindicating Gephardt's

6

Elements of the Deal:

1. We give Republicans cover to back incentives for managed care and rich people premium hikes on medicare to save $120-$150 billion

    a. we force them to divulge their budget, first

        1. but avoid rhetoric that makes deal impossible

    b. then we come back, in private, with incentive non-penalty program for HMOs

        1. elderly support such an option, with no coercion or penalties

        2. And offer backing for increases in premiums for upper income elderly (also has elderly backing)

2. We go along with heavy managed care ~~coercion~~ in Medicaid

    a. make it a welfare issue

    b. distinguish from medicare

    c. even with elderly on medicaid, be tough

        1. they are in nursing homes, so it is not an anti-elderly stance, but an anti-nursing home stance

        2. stress cost controls on providers, not cutting of services

        3. stress cheaper home care alternative

8

6. Paid Media Themes for June

A. Crime/Terrorism

1. 100,000 cops
2. tough sentences, limit parole
3. 1,000 FBI agents

B. Not Gun Control

C. Factual Style of Ad -- Infomercial, not rhetoric, but facts

E. Timing -- must be in June

1. summer levels of TV down
2. need pre-summer shot in "nonpolitical" season

F. Money and Location

1. $2.5 million enough to reach half of country 7 times
2. will provide media market list by:

a. developing scale including Clinton margin of
   defeat or loss per media market. (stress
   closest markets)

b. includes chances of carrying state (stress closest
   92 margins)

c. electoral vote of state

d. cost per point of ad

e. will integrate all 4 in a recommendation

MAY 4, 1995

May 16, 1995
The Push for the Balanced-Budget Speech
(See chapter 9)

Until the president outlined an alternative to the Republican budget plan, which imposed such harsh cuts on Medicare, Medicaid, education, and the environment, he was at a perpetual disadvantage. The GOP could and did reply to any Democratic criticism of its proposed cuts by saying simply, "We know they're tough, but they're the only way to balance the budget."

The agenda for the May 16 meeting makes the case for a speech outlining the president's proposed alternative for balancing the budget. Led by the liberal trio of Leon Panetta, George Stephanopoulos, and Harold Ickes, almost every senior member of the White House staff opposed such a speech. Among the staff the lone advocates of a balanced-budget speech were Erskine Bowles, Don Baer, Bill Curry, Alice Rivlin, and Bruce Reed. Of course the president and the vice president turned out to favor giving the speech, but their support was not evident at the beginning.

The debate over whether to propose a balanced-budget alternative raged with fury and fire until the president eventually gave the address in late June of 1995.

By the May 16 meeting it was clear that the president was going to need paid advertising over the budget issues to have a hope of winning the battle that was to grip the nation in 1995. In this agenda the consultants press urgently for television advertising to get the president's issues before the public.

Despite the president's move to the center in April of 1995, the White House staff, under Panetta, continued to do all it could to block middle-of-the-road ideas from reaching the president's desk, much less his podium. The May 16 agenda echoes the frustration the consultants felt at this gridlock. As recounted in this book, the president and the vice president took direct action to break this deadlock, culminating in a private meeting between them, Panetta, and me in which the president told his chief of staff that he was so far behind the Republicans that he "had to throw long."

AGENDA FOR MEETING ON TUESDAY, MAY 16

1. SUGGEST PRESIDENTIAL SPEECH ON BALANCING THE BUDGET

    A. Need to take fiscal issue off the table

        1. Key to winning election -- remove fiscal issues
        2. Keep attention focused on social issues

            a. Ricochet theory is working very well

                1. But Republicans could move back to center if we go too left on fiscal issues
                2. Don't let Republicans get mainstream again

    B. Error of past week -- too orthodox Democrat

        1. Created clear impression: Clinton opposes balanced budget

            a. He submitted a budget in deficit
            b. He opposed balanced budget amendment
            c. Now he's attacking Republican bal budget plans
            d. Conclusion: if it talks like a duck, walks like a duck, and looks like a duck, its a duck -- Clinton is fiscal liberal

        2. As in Feb and March we became irrelevant

            a. Shared impotence of Dems in Congress
            b. With no plan, Clinton was reduced to carping

    C. Need to set out markers for presidential position -- Now

        1. Can't wait until summer or September

            a. Can't be on sidelines on major issue of the day

                1. If we are not on the map, Republicans can present us with take-it-or-leave-it fait accompli, which we can't veto politically

                2. Republicans can present us as marginalized players -- part of impotent Democratic Congressional opposition

MAY 16, 1995

440

b. We're on the map as liberals, anti-balanced budget

    1. Unless we move off that position, we'll be stuck

    2. We have no other choice

        a. Back Dashle, Gephart, we stay liberal
        b. Back Dominici-Kasich, we're irrelevant
        c. Shut up and we breed irrelevance and confusion and weakness
        d. Must have a position clearly staked out to play in the game. Price of not playing is shrinking Presidency talk

2. Give speech, not a budget

    a. Not all the numbers, but the direction
    b. Will be Presidential, not accountant-like
    c. Will avoid much specific criticism over details

D. Outlines of plan in speech (draft of speech attached)

    1. Commitment to a balanced budget

        a. Clear, unambiguous statement of need for zero deficit plan to be passed this year
        b. Praise for Republicans for finally leaving speechmaking behind and now joining serious work of budget balancing

    2. Invitation to negotiate to Congress

        a. Invitation to budget summit during summer

            1. Puts us into negotiations
            2. Makes White House central actor
            3. Sets up forum for deal making

        b. Call for each side to abandon extreme positions to achieve historic opportunity to balance budget

    3. Section by Section Outline of Markers

        a. Medicare

            1. Cuts needed

2. Managed care the best route
3. Incentives only for managed care
    a. No requirements
    b. No penalties or disincentives
    c. Only position incentives; lower premiums,
    more coverage, lower deductibles
4. Higher premiums and deductibles for upper income
elderly
5. Re-invest half the savings in Medicare
    a. Trust fund
    b. Home care services
6. Must accompany Medicare cuts with health reform
    a. Portability
    b. No exclusion for pre-existing conditions
    c. Voluntary purchasing pools

b. Medicaid

1. Needs major cuts through managed care

2. Can require managed care, is welfare based
program

3. But must have better home care alternative (see
under Medicare 5-b)

4. End "spend down" of elderly assets for Medicaid

    a. Accord benefits on same basis as Medicare
    b. Higher premiums and deductibles for
    wealthy elderly

c. Welfare

1. Agreement with broad cost cutting features
of Republican program

2. Need to add back job training, day care money

3. Need to preserve some form of entitlement

    a. Leave to states the option of entitlement v.
    block grants

           1. Just as benefit levels are left to states
           and vary dramatically

    4. Need to cover children of teen mothers

        a. Require that they live at home with grandparents

        b. Require mothers and kids be in school and then go
        to work

d. Tax loopholes -- corporate welfare

    1. Attack how Republican plan ignore these

    2. Seeks cuts in tax loopholes but don't spell out in speech

        (for private info-adds up to 90 bil):

        (a. Puerto Rican business (20 bil)
        b. Depreciate bus advertising costs, no expensing (19
        bil)
        c. End deferral of tax on income of American run
        foreign corps until repatriation of income (6 bil)
        d. End 15% export income exclusion granted US
        firms until expatriation (8 bil)
        e. Cut private purpose revenue bonds (10 bil)
        f. End exemption of credit union income (3 bil)
        g. Various energy cuts (21 bil)
            -expensing drilling, explore
            -end special tax credit for non conventional
            sources
            -depletion cost recovery
            -alcohol fuels tax credit)

e. Opposed to any cola cut

    1. Breaks social security pledge
    2. Politicize issue

        a. Leave door open to truly technical adjustments of
        minor magnitude
        b. Attack .6 cut in rep bill as political

f. Discretionary spending

1. Favor cut, but not of same order of magnitude as Republican cuts
2. Specific markers
    a. Don't cut public school aid
    b. Don't eliminate key Clinton programs
    c. Specify areas where cuts are fine or where we need to go further
        1. Reinventing govt initiatives

  g. Attack 2002 deadline

    1. "A date off a bumper sticker"
    2. Attack prolonged delay, but suggest 2003 or 2004 might be more reasonable
    3. Demand that we show year-by-year progress deficit reduction

  4. Tax cuts

    a. Attack Dominici no tax cut plan

      1. Need tuition deduction
      2. Need IRAs
      3. Need $500 per child for mid inc people

    b. Attack Gingrich tax cut plan

      1. Too much money
      2. No substantive targeting
      3. Improperly aimed (avoid populist rhetoric)

2. NEED FOR TELEVISION ADS

  A. Need to run ads in June

    1. Free media can only go so far in permanent increase in ratings
    2. Need to get basic messages out to the public in the spring before political season is too far along
    3. TV use drops in summer, need to move in spring

  B. Subject of ads should be Crime/Television

    1. 100,000 cops
    2. Death penalty extension

3. 1,000 FBI people on terrorism
4. Show presidential toughness

C. Specialized media in specific markets where useful

D. Need to begin scripting/storyboarding now. Further delay is tantamount to saying "no" for June

E. Request approval for Squier to move ahead

3. IMMEDIATE SPEECHES COMING UP

A. Need better vetting/approval process

1. Current process has resulted in too many "pulled teeth"

a. Deportations package without drivers license

1. Got almost no coverage
2. Justice never really objected on legal grounds just was worried about too many cases
3. Unfunded mandates was never issue, program would be voluntary

b. Japan speech without aggressive rhetoric

1. Got no coverage at all
2. Lost huge opportunity to regain momentum after trip

c. Anti-crime/terrorism speech without 4 part program

1. Very little coverage
2. Justice's constitutional objections surfaced late Sunday night -- in effect they pocket vetoed the speech
3. Holtzman's legal justification of constitutionality was Oked by Larry Tribe, Burt Newborne (NYU) and Irwin Chemerinsky (SoCal) and handed to President 10 days earlier

d. Net effect: a trip not bracketed with hard domestic hits. break in momentum. Congratulations to the vettors, a few more like this and we can hang it up

1. Need new vetting process
    a. Suggest it be centered in Bowles and that he be empowered to set deadlines for dept memos and for my responses

    b. If continue bad vetting, we destroy news days and frustrate efforts to appear strong

    c. Need to vet NOW the proposed speeches below

    d. Request my close involvement in vetting and that of Bill Curry

B. School to Work Speech on Wednesday

    1. Do not use for fight on cuts -- that will get all the press

    2. Use it to announce job training voucher

C. Japan trade sanctions

    1. Announcement must be made by President personally

    2. Tough language is the true way to solidify and recapture "the base" trade issues, not fiscal ones

D. Budget Speech or Press Conference --

    1. See attached draft

    2. Suggest press conference for statement Thurs or Fri

    3. Need to do it soon so we aren't locked into impotence or fiscal liberalism and so we are on the playing field when budget target votes take place

E. MADD photo op May 19

    1. Call for enactment at federal level of MADD's program (or parts of it we support) as condition of highway money (precedent 55 mph speed limit)

    2. I will have specifics at meeting

F. Radio Address for 5-20

    1. Deportation: Motor vehicles license proposal

    2. Specifics:

        a. Voluntary, not mandate
        b. We invite illegal alien state govs to White House meeting to present the idea
        c. We invite each to pass a law prohibiting licenses for illegals and making licenses expire when visa does for legal stays
        d. We set up computer system to vet names of people cops pull over to determine legal status
        e. We move to deport those who are not legal

4. GENERAL   5/16/95

  A. Tobacco

    1. Check with Reno on joining Medicaid suits seeking tobacco company reimbursement for Medicaid costs

    2. Check with Kessler on other anti-tobacco measures

        a. Ban on vending machines where children can access

MAY 16, 1995

447

5/16/95 cont.

b. Ban on cigarette advertising aimed at children

c. Assumption of authority would relate to finding that nicotine is addictive drug

B. WACO and Idaho Hearings

1. Strongly condemn them

2. Defend your local cop theme to our presentation

3. Attack hearings as giving aid and comfort to terrorists

C. Affirmative Action

1. Prepare speech

2. Base speech on conceptual changes, not just slicing a few programs

3. To repeat:

a. Move all affirmative action programs to race and gender neutral

b. Continue race and gender based aff act where there is statistical evidence of discrimination until discrimination is remedied, then go race and gender neutral

c. No unqualified person is ever hired

d. All white males below poverty line are automatically included in all affirmative action programs, even those to remedy discrimination

e. Set asides are converted to geographic basis, not race or class basis

f. Certain job categories retain race and gender base due to their nature (i.e. police, teachers)

June 21, 1995
Pressing to Move Ahead on Tobacco
(See chapter 11)

The president's balanced-budget speech won wide applause from America, but sharp condemnation from congressional Democrats. The June 21 meeting began, appropriately, with some crowing about the positive impact of the speech on Clinton's ratings. But the bulk of the meeting focused on whether to propose broad-based anti-teen-smoking regulations. The decision to take on big tobacco scared the president and he felt that it might lead to the loss of Tennessee, Kentucky, Georgia, and North Carolina. To allay his fears, we polled the issue in these states. As the agenda for this meeting suggests, the polling determined that taking the offensive against teen smoking would not hurt in these key states and might even help.

Despite the loud and insistent warnings of Harold Ickes that such an expenditure would be premature and a waste of money, the president okayed the first flight of television advertising at the July 21 meeting. The ads focused on GOP opposition to curbs on assault rifles and on its attempts to revoke funding for the 100,000 extra local police the president had won in 1994.

This agenda reflects our unsuccessful effort to persuade the president to reform Affirmative Action to base it on objective measures like income and residence in poor areas rather than on race and on gender. George Stephanopoulos, who had not yet been invited by the president to these weekly meetings, ultimately prevailed in killing this idea.

AGENDA FOR MEETING WITH PRESIDENT ON JUNE 21, 1995

I. BUDGET SPEECH WORKED VERY, VERY WELL. NOW, MOVE ON.

    A. Immediate aftermath poll data reflects 58% approval, 3% gain favorability --nearing glass ceiling

        1. Highest in Presidency, except for one or two peaks which were short lived

        2. Sustained approval in mid fifties for eleven weeks

           a. reaching for a new plateau -- likely there

    B. More Important --- definitely, probably, possibly vote for Clinton up to 42-44

        1. Two months ago was 34-54

        2. Two weeks ago was 34-48

        3. We are now within reach of being able to win

    C. Gain may have continued and accelerated

        1. Last night poll data -- 1500 interviews (not at your expense) in Kentucky, Tennessee, North Carolina, Georgia, and Virginia shows 53% approval AND 42% def/prob/poss vote for Clinton

           a. If those numbers in these five states are national numbers, based on differention in past surveys will likely put re elect numbers up in mid or high 40s!

    D. Move on

        1. Not much public criticism of speech

        2. Metaphor: its like Israeli-Syrian talks, public knows both sides are moving closer, but don't follow each minute move.

        3. Republican attacks have been muted

           a. CBO-OMB hit was on back pages over weekend

           b. no attack on ten years--they may need it

        4. Demo attacks have been loud, but not well covered -- drowned out with positive press and editorials

[handwritten in left margin: "important", "lib pos.", "not", "neg."]

E. Negotiate with Republicans

    1. Most important thing is to get balanced budget passed

    2. If possible, do separate deal on NDD items

II. Run TV Ads Now

handwritten: June 21, 1995 p2

A. People's minds are open to new centrist info about you in aftermath of speech

B. Only 43% of voters know about assault rifles (and only 33% about death penalty). Fill that void

    1. Facts will stay in public's mind. Just as NAFTA, gays in military, pro choice, Haiti and health care will stay there

    2. Arkansas experience with early media -- great recall

handwritten: 26- early august

    3. Take crime away from Republicans as issue

    4. During Whitewater hearings, use paid media to keep up vote share and approval

    5. We now may have the numbers we need to enter election with. We are certainly very close. Now, keep approval in high 50s and vote in mid forties and let it sink in and become baseline

    6. Do it through DNC and take Republican complaint which we probably win

III. NEGOTIATIONS OVER WELFARE -- NOTHING MORE IMPORTANT THAN BI-PARTISAN PASSAGE WITH OUR BACKING.

    --we can't really veto in any case, so cooperate and provide Dem support for compromise bill

    -- don't go crazy over winning each detail -- passage is a lot more important.

A. Entitlement

    1. Move toward state choice of entitlement vs block grant

        a. CBO will score it if we cap total welfare spending year by year so if too many choose entitlement, it won't go up by too much

B. Maintenance of Effort

    1. Not likely to cause severe problems

C. Child Care

    1. Expand dollars for this as Hatch wants,

        a. even if we have to tradeoff education and job training funds

D. Contingency Economic Downturn

    1. Fold into entitlement issue

E. Teen mothers

    1. Vouchers instead of cash

    2. Have to live at home

    3. Some give on incentives on illegitimacy ratio

        a. but not punishment of states

    4. Agree to Florio bill of cutoff of aid for more than two children

F. Allowance for growth in population by states

G. Performance bonus if work requirement are met

V. NEXT IDEAS   6/21/85

   A. Tobacco

     1. Poll finds strong support for all anti-smoking in children measures in tobacco states

     2. Polled Ky, Tenn, NC, Geo, and Va. 1500 interviews

        -only 8% either make their living from tobacco in any way or feel that their personal financial fortunes would be hurt if tobacco sales dropped

        -76% report "no effect at all" and another 15% report very little effect

     3. Back reduce teen smoking by govt action by 64-8

        -backs no vending machines near areas where kids have access 82-14

        -backs fining storekeepers who sell to minors by 79-20

        -backs new warnings for kids on packs by 79-16

        -backs no package decoration to encourage teens by 70-24

        -backs ban on ads that appeal to kids like Joe Camel by 69-24

JUNE 21, 1995

453

4. Proposals

    -FDA initiatives on above issues

    -amicus brief in medicaid suits

        -in 5 states, back amicus by 49-41

        -in 5 states back amicus as alternative to
          deeper medicaid cuts by 55-37

        -in Mississippi, back suit by 62-31
          in Florida back suit by 59-32

B. Index minimum wage for index capital gains

6/21/95 con̶t.

July 26, 1995
The Planning for the Budget Fight
(See chapter 9)

The president, the vice president, Leon Panetta, and the consultants discussed the strategy for confronting the Republicans over their budget cuts on July 26. Until this meeting, the administration recoiled in horror at the prospect that Republican intransigence might lead to a government shutdown—a scenario we called "the trainwreck."

But at the July 26 meeting, when we played out the trainwreck scenario, it didn't look all that gloomy. As a strategy emerged for surviving and winning the trainwreck, it increasingly appeared to be the way for Clinton to recover from the defeats of 1994. Reflecting this view, the agenda advises the president to make clear that "we won't sign a bill with Republican cuts." It notes that such a posture would "force Republicans to inflict massive pain in order to get cuts okayed." Boldly, it predicts that a "shutdown will be seen as the immediate manifestation of all the Republican cuts the public has been reading about" and would represent a "clear way to focus national anger at the cuts." This is about how the issue played out six months later.

We realized that paid advertising was essential to explain how drastic and unnecessary the Republican cuts were to the goal of balancing the budget. Only through ads could we get out the message that Clinton had proposed a way to avoid them and still eliminate the deficit. The excellent public reaction to the July anti-crime ads encouraged us to push for more. In this agenda the consultants propose that advertising focus next on Medicare cuts and the GOP budget plan. Since our goal was to weaken the support for the Republican budget, the agenda proposes targeting the ads in states with key swing Republican senators.

At the meeting of July 26 the consultants embraced a proposal from Panetta that we switch our focus from congressional to executive action. Stymied by the Republican majorities in Congress, we suggest a series of presidential actions which would not depend on House or Senate approval. These include requiring that federal contractors disclose any pollutants they were emitting, reform of lobbying within the executive branch, teen tobacco regulations, and federal waivers which would permit states to reform their own welfare systems. Over the balance of the summer, President Clinton announced each of these actions, creating a sense of momentum even though Congress refused to act on his proposals.

I. Budget

    1. CI committed to bal bud 59-36
    2. Reps more committed 53-39
    3. wish they'd stop fighting and do it 93-4

    4. Republicans cut too much med, ed, env 68-26
    5. R just cutting what need to bal the bud 51-41
    6. R cutting more than need for bal bud, but they want
        huge tax cut too 57-31
        7. R should cut enough to bal the bud and not
            try to pay for huge tax cut too 57-31

    8. tax cut is mainly for people richer than me 67-24

    9. can't afford tax cut as big as R want 63-23

2. SWITCH RHETORICAL FOCUS FROM BUDGET TO EXECUTIVE ACTION

A. The press isn't giving it much coverage

    1. no front pages
    2. partisan visuals from Medicare speech
    3. no TV from Monday speech at all

B. We look too partisan. too mired in budget details

    1. look at damage Dole is sustaining from this

JULY 26, 1995

July 26 '95 p 4

1. very good chance that good faith can prevail here
2. opportunity to begin to "pencil in" consensus
3. must be personal effort by President

B. Pressure campaign aimed at Swing Republican Senators
   on medicare during recess

1. Target recess paid media, funded by DNC, to
   aim at key moderate Republican Senators

   a. Hit small states with moderate Republican Senators

   Ashcroft, Missouri
   Bond, Missouri
   Chaffee, RI
   Cohen, Me
   Snow, Me
   Dominici, NM
   Hatfield, Oregon
   Packwood, Oregon
   Jeffords, Vt
   Kasselbaum, Kansas
   ~~Murkowski, Alaska~~
   ~~Stevens, Alaska~~
   Bennett, Utah

   b. 1,200 Points in these states would cost
      $500,000

   c. Use DNC to pay for it, we control production

   d. In 1983, RNC did ads on inflation in March & July

2. Get constituency groups to bring pressure

3. flesh out Republican ideas and educate media

C. Announce veto of all appropriation bills until across the
   board deal is signed

1. we don't want to have to come up with alternate

ways to achieve a fixed magnitude of cuts in
each separate bill

2. in trainwreck, we want Republican as well as
Democratic programs to be hit

3. encourages negotiations before veto

4. must be communicated soon to Dems in Congress
so we avert separate deal making

5. we came close to this yesterday when we called
all the bills "unsignable"

6. should be Panetta statement so as not to mire
Clinton in budget quagmire

D. Trainwreck Scenerio

1. Debt Limit

a. the true nuclear war

1. govt defaults, nothing is paid, etc.
2. Immediate impact on national
interest rates, bank stability,
adjustable rate mortgages,
state and local financing,
corporate bonds, stock market
3. could bring on depression

b. explain impact of debt limit weapon to
Wall street and have them pressure
Republicans to take it out of their
hands

1. make it like nuclear weapons I the cold
war, there but unuseable

2. Closing Govt Down

1. Strategy: amplify pain, don't mute it
2. Use pain to demonstrate how bad
   Republican cuts are

3. Our position: we won't sign a bill with
   Republican cuts

   a. if we get a continuing resolution at
      current levels or our proposed
      levels, we'll sign it.

   b. If it is any less than that, we veto it.
      we wont sign a bill with cuts

   c. forces republicans to inflict massive
      pain in order to get cuts Oked

4. Left won't hit us on it, they will back not
   signing

5. Republicans can't attack closedown and
   defend cuts at the same time

6. shutdown will be seen as immediate manifestation of all the Republican cuts public
   has been reading about

   a. the republicans cut the budget and now
      section 8 housing people are on
      streets, homeless shelters are
      full, etc.

   b. clear way to focus national anger at
      the cuts

4. Tobacco — no negotiations, just regulate   7/26/95

   A. clear importance of clean break with companies so we
      can run agaisnt them

   B. massive popular issue which will help us carry every

2/26/95 cont.

state, including tobacco states

C. Tobacco Companies are enemy, like polluters or
   asbestos companies. can't negotiate

D. Tobacco can't be trusted

    a. Pertschuk letter – companies lied

    b. left will attack negotiated settlement as unenforceable

        1. like Japan, only worse

E. Need to show strength from the inception

F. can't afford 2 front war of left and right against each other

JULY 26, 1995

August 3, 1995
Tobacco Reform and Budget TV Ads
(See chapter 11)

By August 3 it was time to shelve bipartisanship and declare war on the Republican Congress. Now that Clinton's Pile of Vetoes and balanced-budget speech had staked out centrist ground, it was time to attack the Republicans and move them to the right. As the agenda notes, polls showed that the Republican position on Medicare cuts was their key weakness. It was time to open fire.

For the moment, bipartisanship would have to wait. The agenda predicted that the attacks on the GOP over Medicare would give Republicans a "bad odor" and noted that it was "not [a] good idea to be seen [with them] in public." With the president happily issuing executive orders, he did not need bipartisan cooperation with the GOP, but could generate a sense of lofty action for the country by himself.

The crucial phase of the war would be through TV advertising. The agenda presses for these ads and defines clearly their goal: "to raise the heat to such levels that Republicans (a) abandon their plan, (b) try to postpone everything until November, and (c) eventually feel the heat so much that they demand a quick resolution, a reconciliation on the president's terms to lower their political heat." Some have said that these ads were but thinly disguised reelection commercials. No way. They were undisguised attempts to win the battle of the budget.

The August 3 meeting was held a few days before the president made his historic announcement of federal regulations to curtail tobacco advertising aimed at teenagers. The air was thick with talk of negotiation with tobacco companies and we were deeply concerned that the regulations might never be issued. By stressing the possibility of FDA Commissioner David Kessler criticizing any inaction from the left, we hoped to ensure that Clinton would act.

AGENDA FOR MEETING WITH PRESIDENT ON AUGUST 3

1. BUDGET STRATEGY – MEDICARE CUTS DERAIL REPUBLICANS

    A. Polling on Medicare briefing by Doug

        1. solid opposition to Republican Medicare cuts

            a. 25-68 on virtually all the tests after almost
               any argumentation

            b. bankruptcy argument only gets 43% to be more
               likely to back cuts while 50% still oppose them
               and has no impact at all on head to head

            c. all other arguments work less well for them then
               bankruptcy

            d. opposition by all voters is only slightly less than
               among elderly – about 68 for all vs 72 for all
               voters -- not a special interest issue

        2. Move away from bipartisan strategy and substitute
           lift.

            a. Republicans are about to acquire bad odor, not
               good idea to be seen in public

            b. Instead of centerism, we need lift

               1. run an anti-medicare campaign with
                  paid media and surrogates

               2. keep President doing Presidential
                  events like: affirmative action,
                  tobacco, prayer, etc. were this
                  month.

AUGUST 3, 1995

462

B. Strategy -- fold out

1. Step one: Ads

   a. run ads in moderate Republican states to pry
      loose swing Senators -- $700,000

      1. Iowa, Des Moines Grassley
      2. Kansas, Wichita, Kassebaum
      3. Maine, Portland, Snow, Cohen
      4. Missouri, Spring, Col, St. Joe, Bond,
         Ashcroft
      5. NY, upstate small, D'Amato
      6. NM, Alb., Domenici
      7. Oregon, Port., Packwood, Hatfield
      8. R.I., Providence, Chafee
      9. S.D., Sioux Falls, Pressler
      10. Tenn, Nashville, Thompson, Frist
      11. Vt. Burlington, Jeffords,

2. Step One: Free Media

   a. In N.H., have Ann Lewis start a pledge
      movement

*aug 3
'95
p2*

AUGUST 3, 1995

b. publicize CBO scoring of managed care

    1. hold their feet to fire so they can't score
       vouchers higher than they now do

3. Step Two: Paid Media

    a. continue marginal republican senate ads

    b. begin swing state ads

    c. aim media at targeted seniors

    cost of all three: $3.5 mil for 1,000 pts
    likely cost will equal $5 million for 1500 pts

    d. ads which respond to republican answers and
       developments in political situation

    e. goal: to raise the heat to such levels that
       Republicans

       1. abandon their plan

       2. try to postpone everything until Nov.

       3. eventually feel the heat so much that they
          demand a quick resolution, a reconciliation
          on the President's terms, to lower their
          political heat

f. Splitting the Republicans

       1. as pressure mounts on moderate
          senators and GOP generally
          they will split and blame each other

       2. Gramm may open a populist front against
          Dole

       3. Wilson, Alexander will hit Dole on medicare

       4. eventually, Republicans will break into
          small groups, a la how we were on
          health care in August, 94

P 3
aug 3
'95

August 10, 1995
Defining a Welfare-Reform Position
(See chapter 7)

The president never felt any hesitation in vetoing the Republican budget in 1995. But he agonized over his veto of welfare reform legislation. He instructed us to poll to find what justification would convince the public that he had to veto the bill. As the agenda indicates, nothing really worked. As long as the legislation required welfare recipients to work in order to get benefits, the public wanted Clinton to sign it.

Fortunately for the president, the cup passed from his lips when the Republicans made a fatal mistake by linking their welfare reforms to their other spending cuts, particularly their Medicaid reductions. This blunder gave the president all the justification he needed for a veto. Had they passed a stand-alone welfare reform bill, he would have been hard-pressed to veto it.

3. WELFARE REFORM– A REPUBLICAN ISSUE

    1. They want welfare reform – mainly work

        a reform welfare very impt 74, somewhat 20 not 2

        b. work very important – 69%   (overall 91-8)
        c. time limits very import –45%   (77-20)
        d. block grants very import – 33% (61-30)

    2. Republicans get the credit

        a. more committed to reform Cl 26 Reps 44

        b who agree on welfare Cl 35 reps 43

    3. Only veto issue is job training and that is inaccessible

        a. If no worker training, veto-60 sign-36

            1. but favor block grants by 61-33
            2. If block grants cause job training to
                lose money, oppose it by 33-58
            3. But chances of winning that arguement
                in traffic without ads is nil
            4. and, if veto would mean no work or
                time limti reforms, favor signing by 54-35

        b. if no child care sign 45 veto 52

        c. if no work incentives to states s-45 v-48

d. if no recession hedge s-50 v-46

e. if time limit cutoff if mom looks for job, but can't
find one s-53 v-44

f. if llump sum   s-61 v-33

g. if maintenance of state effort not required, s-63 v-31

h. overall, with these items s-63 v-28

I. and half of veto support for each catagory
leaves if told welfare reform won't pass

4. Political consequences of veto:

a. losing welfare reform

b. racism over aff action can't be controlled

5. Strategy on Welfare

a. Brag about cuts in AFDC levels

b. try to increase identification with reform

1. attack Dole of not passing bill

c. try to get Dems to hold line in Senate on key veto
issue 3, so you don't have to

d. never, never veto it. - Rs don't need this bill. They'd
gladly accept defeat for blame on you

September 7, 1995
The Push for More TV Advertising
(See chapter 8)

In late August, Democratic National Committee soft-money TV ads rained down on the states of moderate Republican senators and congressmen. The ads depicted the GOP Medicare cuts in harsh terms and laid the blame squarely on Gingrich and Dole. The polling we reported to the president in the September 7 agenda shows the effectiveness of the ads.

Encouraged by this data, the consultants presented the president with a plan for $50 million in advertising before the August 1996 Democratic National Convention. The program relied on $33 million in issue ads from the DNC financed with soft money and $17 million in hard-money ads paid by the campaign. (The final totals were very close to these projections.) The advertising expenditure is carefully divided between the two pots of money in accordance with the recommendations of campaign lawyers so that no law is broken.

The meeting kicked off a month-long debate which pitted the consultants against Harold Ickes in arguing for the advertising as essential to our "air cover" in the battle of the budget.

AGENDA FOR MEETING WITH PRESIDENT ON SEPT 7

I. IMPACT OF ADS -- EXCELLENT, BUT MORE IS NEEDED
TO HAMMER POINT HOME

   A. 38% recalled seeing the ads

      1. good show for 1000 points

   B. Of those who saw ads:

      1. swings of +15 in our ratings and -14 in there's on
         helping to protect Medicare
      2. swings of +10 in our ratings and -8 in there's on
         helping elderly parents
      3. swings of +11 in our ratings and -3 in there's on
         wants to balance the budget

II. AD RECOMMENDATIONS -- KEEP UP PRESSURE

   A. Stress President's commitment to balanced budget

      1. the more the public believes we are for balanced
         budget, the more ability we have to insist on
         our terms

      2. the opposite of the welfare debate (where lack of
         public belief that we are for reform, makes it
         harder to insist on our version of reform)

   B. Shift focus to Education, the key appropriations battlefield

   C. Run Medicare spots in swing state markets along with
      education ads to bring public up to speed

III. HOW TO PAY FOR ADS WITHOUT BUSTING FEDERAL CAPS

   A. I propose about $50 million of pre-convention ads:

      1. $10 billion to win the budget fight

Sept 7, 1995

a. now-Nov 15
b. all DNC payable

9/7/95

P 2

2. $10 million to take credit for bal bud and welfare

    a. Nov 15-Jan 31
    b. all campaign paid

3. $15 million to ~~interpose~~ in Republican Primaries

    a. Feb 1- Apr 15
    b. half to protect us against Republican hits in
       swing states (all campaign)
    c. half to hit Republicans candidates ~~to arse~~
       ~~~~ (all DNC)

4. $15 million to hit Republican nominee

    a. Apr 15-August 1
    b. all DNC

5. Total DNC: $33 mil   Total Campaign: $17 mil

B. Key Questions

1. Can campaign hold down other spending to allow it
   to spend additional $17 mil ($20 mil total) on ads?

    a. with no primary fight, why not?
    b. travel more on official business.

2. Can we raise an additional $33 mil for DNC

    a. in addition to about $20 mil we have to raise
       for them already to meet their budget

    b. total to raise for DNC=$50 mil

    c. less about $5 - $10 mil through better direct
       mail targeting using Penn's data

d. equals net of about $40- $45 mil to raise
e. almost all soft money (enough mail to
    cover hard proportion)

f. if we could raise $20-$24 million in six months
    at $1000 caps, why can't we raise $45 mil
    in 12 months with no cap??

3. Can we stop DNC from spending the money on
things other than our ads

9/7/95

$3

September 25, 1995
Laying the Basis for the Budget Battle
(See chapter 9)

With the ultimate battle of the budget looming, the consultants set out the themes the president should push during the contest. Noting that "we are winning the rhetoric on Medicare," the agenda presses for a full-scale paid media campaign during the budget crisis. At that meeting the president gave final approval for the advertising campaign to begin and the epic battle with the Republicans was joined.

AGENDA FOR THE PRESIDENT FOR SEPT 25, 1995

1. REPORT ON RECENT POLLING DATA

    A. Finally, a gain to 57% approval

    B. Head to Head with Dole: 45-38

        1. it is too early to "force" the leaners by pressing them, but, if you did, you'd be only 2-3 pts below 50

    C. Three way with Powell is beginning to draw more from Republicans than from us

        1. last week: 28-28-28

        2. now its Cl 30 P 29 D 24

    D. We are winning the rhetoric on medicare

        1. we are "more likely to protect medicare and insure that it exists for future generations" 52-31

    E. Support for bombing Bosnia went up ten from 59-33 to 69-20

    F. Probably, possible, or definitely vote Clinton up since early August from 35 to 38 to 41

    G Probably, possibly, or definitely vote against down since early August from 37 to 35 to 32

        1. net swing from -2 to +9

    H. All the elements are present for a big forward move in the next few weeks if::

        1. We get a balanced budget, tax cut, and welfare reform

        2. In reality, they do not cut education, environment, or raise medicare premiums

3. In perception, if the public perceives that it got done and that you were a key element

    a. we don't need a "win" vs the Republicans, we need an accomplishment that is not a "loss"

3. STRATEGY FOR THE KEY PERIOD AHEAD

   A. Get the message right

      1. Clinton wants to stop borrowing money and living off future generations, so he wants to balance the budget

      2. Clinton believes we have a duty to care for our elderly parents so he won't cut medicare

      3. Clinton believes in our duty to nurture our children so he won't cut education

B. Punch the message through over paid media *Sept 25 '95*

NS

   1. Our history -- doing good things and getting no credit

      a. sometimes we don't ever get credit

         1, jobs, economy
         2. deficit

      b. sometimes a win gets presented with too much ambiguity to generate credit

         1. trade sanctions

   2. We need paid media to set up the battle in the public's mind -- education, medicare, balanced budget

      a. while fight is in play and free media ratification is there

      b. with the repetition and simplicity only paid media can

      c. sets up criteria for a win: education, environment, medicare -- not tax cut size or capital gains or ten years or other NDD cuts

   3. Then we need paid media to narrate the play-by-play of the fight

      a. win game of chicken on budget

      b. assign responsibility for any crisis

      c. show tough President standing firm

   4, Finally, show achievement and declare victory over paid media

      a. even in ambiguous press, move credit for achievement and lay basis for future

   5. In any event, don't let Republicans get their message

across through their ads without answer

6. Cost

    a. immediately, to answer Republican ads: $300,000

    b. to get our point across to swing states: $1,200,000 per week

        1. California, Oregon, Washington, Colorado, Missouri, Tennessee, Arkansas, Ohio, Illinois, Michigan, Wisconsin, Pennsylvania, 1/3 of N.J. Florida, and Kentucky

        2. also, to impact moderate Republican Senators: Rhode Island, Vermont, parts of NY, New Mexico, Iowa,

    c. reaches   GOP Senators and   GOP congressmen

SEPTEMBER 25,1995

476

October 3, 1995
Reacting to the O. J. Verdict
(See chapter 11)

The acquittal of O. J. Simpson intruded on our preparations for the budget battle as September drew to a close. The president was very concerned that the verdict might trigger a right-wing backlash. Our polling found sharp disagreement between whites and blacks over whether or not O. J. was guilty. But it also found broad agreement that the police had been racist and had handled the case badly. The agenda outlines a variety of steps Clinton could take to blunt right-wing anger.

Within a few days of the verdict we were pleasantly surprised to learn that while whites continued to believe in Simpson's guilt, they also felt that the prosecution had failed to meet its burden of proof. In a few days the public had learned the difference between innocent and not guilty.

AGENDA FOR MEETING WITH PRESIDENT ON OCTOBER 3 *9)*

I. OJ VERDICT -- Acquittal is enormous danger and great opportunity

    A. Danger:

        1. new symbol for racist whites

        2. new litmus test by Republicans

        3. replaces welfare, affirmative action and immigration
            as wedge issue

    B. Opportunity -- gives us the chance to channel and lead
        white protest

        1. polling shows that white and blacks agree

            a. that cops were racist

            b. that cops messed up

            c. gives us a chance to appeal to whites over the
                process, while avoiding attack on jury system in
                analyzing the verdict

                1. we can't comment on verdict, in appropriate
                    for a President

                2. positive themes:

                    a. respect for law and order
                      -WACO, Idaho, FBI, cops

                    b. reform of police to promote respect
                      -only way to allow future convictions
                      -technical training in DNA, crime
                          scenes
                      -sensitivity training and Civil Rights
                          investigations to purge racism

                    c. violence against women

OCTOBER 3, 1995

478

October 11, 1995
Two New Themes Emerge—Optimism
and Clinton as Father
(*See chapter 9*)

As the Republicans seemed to be headed for a budget confrontation, our advertising was etching deeply in the public mind the enormity of the budget cuts they were proposing.

But more immediate concerns dominated the October 11 meeting. The month before, the president told the press on Air Force One, as it returned to Washington one night, that he sensed a national "funk" over the new challenges of the information age and corporate downsizing. This remark reminded everyone of Jimmy Carter's self-destructive description of America as afflicted with a "national malaise."

To stop his perception of a national mood of pessimism from getting out of hand, the consultants reported to him on their polling. The verdict surprised the consultants and Clinton equally: there was a mood of vast optimism. The polling showed that voters believed, by 53–21, that their children's lives would be better than their own and felt, by 49–12, that the economic positions of their families would improve. The October 11 meeting marked the beginning of a year-long effort to switch Clinton's emphasis from America's problems to its success in coping with them. With the Democratic Party's historic orientation toward pessimism, this was no easy task.

But the October 11 meeting is notable for an even more basic shift in strategy. The agenda calls for a determined effort to project Clinton to America as a father, rather than as a son or even a peer. In Arkansas, the "boy Governor" seemed to be everyone's son—a young man in a hurry and of whom the state was very proud. As a candidate in 1992, Clinton had run as everyone's buddy who travelled on buses, jogged in ill-fitting shorts, and loved Big Macs. Now, the consultants said, he should position himself as above the country, as its father.

The agenda calls not only for an emphasis on "fathering" issues like child support enforcement, education standards, and children's TV but for a change in the president's platform style. "Don't explain yourself overly—fathers don't," the agenda warns. "Don't complain." And it urges him to stay away from the "Blues Brothers" image he had lately projected when he played the sax wearing sunglasses on MTV. In the weeks following, the president's style and image changed dramatically.

AGENDA FOR MEETING WITH PRESIDENT ON OCTOBER 11

I. POLL DATA FROM OCTOBER 10 -- ~~SCHOEN~~

   A. Overall numbers

      1. Lead over Dole from 1 point on Sept 14 to 10 points on Oct 10

         a. among independents went from 41-40 to 43-29

         b. Our vote went from 44 to 46 in total sample -- 4 to go!

      2. Job approval Aug: 54-44 Sept: 55-43 Now: 57-39

      3. Biggest change in last month: foreign policy from 45-51 to 54-43

      4. Clinton vs Republicans:

         a. Balance budget June 48-28 Aug: 44-31 Sept: 50-32 Oct: 43-39

         b. bal bud fair to all cl-47 reps-38

         c. protect medicare from budget cuts cl-61 reps-25

         d. in touch with my values up 4

         e. down 7 on helps education -- need to put message up

         f. .losing cutting taxes comparison by 35-48

         g. fight crime cl 42 reps 44 --- same as after ads ran in July --
           no diminution. Media lasts and lasts.

         h. Are Republicans just cutting enough to balance budget or
           are they cutting so much they seem to be mean spirited?
           50--cutting just enough 40--mean spirited

         I. among elderly we went from 48-36 to 59-27 vs Dole

   B. Impact of Ads

      1. VIRTUALLY ALL THE GROWTH WAS IN MARKETS WE
         ARE ADVERTISING IN

2. Almost no changes on attributes outside of buy areas -- inside of buy areas:

    a. Protect med from cuts up 9 in buy areas up 3 in non buy areas

    b. values up 9 in buy areas   up 1 in non buy areas

    c. clear stands on issues up 8 in buy   down 1 in nonbuy

    (This is not just of seen ads -- its of markets as a whole)

3. Optimism --- Very high no national funk

    a. Will your career improve (57) get worse (8) same (33)

    b. Future children improve (52) worse (21) same (20)

    c. eco position of you and family improve 49 worse 12 same 35

    d. Amer econ in general improve 38 worse 22 same 32

        --no pessimism and 2-1 positive

    e. Areas where more worse than better only health care minus 11
                                  avoid war minus 2

    f. Technology is our friend: helps more than hurts by 69-24

    g. ON ECONOMY -- OPTIMISM ABOUT SELF, CAUTIOUS OPTIMISM ABOUT NATION, MINOR PESSIMISM

    h areas of real worry are: values, families, crime, health care, retirement

II. BUDGET SITUATION -- WE ARE WINNING   KEEP UP PRESSURE

    A. Republicans in bad shape and bad position

1. We have closed gap on trust more to bal the budg from 18 to 7 to 4

2. We are now 9 points ahead on bal the bud in a way that's fair

3. Bankruptcy argument is gone

4. All the Republicans have to "inevitability" as their argument

B. Need to continue ads *Oct 11, '95 p3*

    1. Ads are producing important movement and we need to continue them

    2. If "train wreck" ads give us reason to hold firm

    3. If "deal" ads give us criteria for victory and basis for getting credit

    4. During negotiations, ads give us a context to see moves as means to an end, not flip flops or weakness

    5. Reaching 97 Republican and 71 Democratic Congressional Districts

C. Content

    1. Stay on cuts until Republicans signal negotiations -- keep up pressure

    2. Put on education ad in rotation with medicare and, later medicaid

        a. slippage on education, need to get it back in the game

    3. Then, move to conciliation ads to set up pressure on Republicans for making a deal and laying basis for taking issue away

        a. these ads context negotiations and don't make them flip flops

D. Weight

    1. First two weeks were $1.25 million each, recommend next week at $1 million. Then, when negotiations start going back up to $1.25

        a. Go to $1 million for next week to save money so buy can stretch through mid December

        b. Go back up to $1.25 million in third week becaus that is likely

III. PRESIDENTIAL STYLE

    A. The Father Image vs Peer vs Child

        1. In Arkansas, image was of their child

            a. promising at first, then chasened, then reformed, then excelling
and making them proud

        2. In campaign, image was of peer

            a. down to earth -- bus rides, town meetings, one on ones

            b. contrast with starchy formality of Bush

        3. Now, increasingly, image must be of father

            a. country craves fathers -- Cosby, Lion King,

            b. women crave men who act responsibly -- Romance novel
themes are now of woman done wrong and rescued by
Mr. Right

        4. Images of Father

            a. literal fathering through personal experiences

                1. don't have to tell about Chelsea, but can describe your
own feelings doing homework with her, camping
out, etc.

            b. Issues about fathering: personal responsibility, child support,
education, child TV

            c. Fathering style in speeches and Q & A

                1. don't explain yourself overly -- fathers don't

                2. don't complain (about lack of credit for accomplishmnts,
for example)

                3. no contemporary images like Blues Brothers

                4. Correct style: Memphis speech

                5. don't have peer group conversations with audience --
speak to them

6. don't be self-depricating

7. don't ask questions -- give answers

8. don't be around unkempt kids, they need to show
   respect

9. maintain sense of distance not eye to eye

10. lecturn should be small enough to tower over it

OCTOBER 11, 1995

October 25 and November 1, 1995
The Mandate to Stand Firm
(See chapter 9)

With the budget showdown coming to the wire, most Washington observers were betting that the president would flinch in his game of chicken with the GOP. Republicans were agreed that if they stood firm, Clinton would fold. Panetta and Stephanopoulos were equally concerned. The consultants argue in the agendas of October 25 and November 1 that Clinton must not cave in, but needs to stay the course.

To bolster the president's determination, the agenda reports how solidly the public backed his course of action, in part because of the advertising that was running. Americans, by 64–31, wanted Clinton to stand firm and not compromise. They wanted the Republicans to compromise and not stand firm—by 20 (stand firm) to 76 (compromise). If a breakdown in negotiations were to come, the poll reported that the public would blame the Republicans rather than Clinton, by 58–25. The agendas counseled "tenacity, stubbornness, no concessions."

If a government shutdown was to come, we believed that advertising was the key to winning it. Both agendas include strong pushes for more advertising to shore up the president's hand in the coming shutdown.

AGENDA FOR MEETING WITH PRESIDENT ON OCTOBER 25   *95*

I. POLLING DATA -- CONTINUES UPWARD MOVEMENT

    A. Clinton vote (vs Dole) up from 44 to 45 to 46 to 47(now)

        a. Margin over dole now 11 pts (up from 10 last poll)

            1. where we are advertising, we are ahead by 14
              ...where we are not advertising, we are ahead by only 9

    B. Clinton re-elect number from 38 to 40

    C. Definite against Clinton from 37 to 35 to 32 to 33 to 30 (now)

    D. Approval steady at 57% (but could be higher based on limited sample)

II. THE BUDGET SITUATION AS POLLED

OCTOBER 25,1995

486

C. Polling on Default and Negotiation

    1. should Republicans pass budget as is without negotiating 11-86

    2. If Reps say they will pass bill without compromise: Cl veto 65 sign 25

        a. strong belief reps must be flexible

    3. Statement of Clinton principles followed by: should Clinton stand on
        principles or should he compromise?   64 stand firm 31
        compromise

        a. but Clinton should not be flexible

    4 Statement of Rep principles follow by: should reps compromise after
        a veto or stand firm.   20 stand firm 76 compromise

        a. Republicans must give, Clinton should not -- perfect

    5. Should Republicans pass short term resolutions to prevent default or
        should they stand firm for their budget cuts before they pass
        such resolutions 62-28 they should pass short term resolutions

        a. Republicans will be seen as unreasonable

    6. If a breakdown, who is to blame Cl 25 reps 58

    7. Final result of budget fight

        a. If Clinton forces Reps to agree to his principles and budget

           Cl 62 Dole 28

        b. If Stalemate continues for 90 days

III. ADVERTISING -- THE KEY TO CONTINUED GROWTH AND BUDGET WIN. *04 25 '95 p 3*

A. Despite week of tax increase comment flap and 7 year flap, we moved up

B. Manage debate, cover moves on budget, set up end game

C. Budget for Ads

    1. Spent already: $4.2 million through November 1

    2. Proposed: November 2-21 spend $5.4 million through Dec 1

        1. Nov 2-8: $1.8 mil   Nov 9-15 $1.8 mil   Nov 16-33 $1.5 mil
           Nov 27-30 $300,000

        2. In November: Expand from 28% of America in current buy
           to 40-45 percent of country

        3. And go up from current 325/week to 400/week

        4. Left for December: $400,000.

           a. if we need to run in December, likely cost would be
             about $2.5 million or $2.1 mil more

D. Targeting Media -- Presentation by Penn

E. Ads -- Presentation by Squier

OCTOBER 25, 1995

488

IV. THE BUDGET STRATEGY — TENACITY, STUBBORNNESS, NO
   CONCESSIONS

   A. Preconditions allow extreme expression of strength and uncompromising
      determination

      1. public believes we should stand firm 64-31 and they should cave 20-76

         a. partially that we are right and partially that they are pig-headed

         b. so you don't have to be open minded

      2. public thinks our budget plan is OK and theirs' is terrible

         a. so you can't shouldn't and mustn't give an inch

      3. public gets that you are for welfare reform and a balanced budget

         a. on balanced budget trust we are behind by only 5
         b. on balanced budget fair to all we are ahead by 9
         c. welfare reform we are ahead by 7

         d. therefore: we don't need a win. indefinite continuation of
            process is enough
         e. so you can veto it without losing the issue

      4. we are on paid media and that is doing everything to shape public
         attitudes

         a. so we can be forceful and strong in public and even err on the
            side of rigidity because our media is showing people why
            we are taking so hard a stand

OCTOBER 25, 1995

AGENDA FOR MEETING WITH PRESIDENT ON NOVEMBER 1, 1995

I. SUMMARY OF POLL DATA

    A. Approval is now 58-37 -- up from 57 two weeks ago and 55 a month ago

        1. highest level we have ever recorded

    B. Clinton vs Dole 46-36

        a. in markets advertised: 48-31
        b. rest of nation: 45-39

    C. Clinton vs Powell 45-31

        a. in markets advertised: 38-38
        b. rest of nation 28-47

II. BUDGET STRATEGY -- NEED TO RESIST NEGOTIATING OR CALLS TO NEGOTIATE

    A. Republicans will plead for negotiations -- they are "withering on the vine"

    B. Opinion Leaders and Editorials will say we are being unreasonable.

        1. that is the way to show strength

        2. criticism over inflexibility is the way to show firmness

            a. the criticism would have to go on for months for
              it to have anything but a positive effect
        3. public wants a veto

            a. Question: "last week the Republican majority in Congress
              passed bills they say will balance the budget in 7 years
              The bill contains $270 bil in cuts in medicare spending,
              $70 bil cuts in education spending, major cuts in
              environmental programs, and tax changes which would
              raise taxes on some working families, but lower them
              on others support-33 oppose 63

b. Do you think Clinton and Republicans are just engaging in normal political bickering or are important issues at stake in the budget debate such as the future of medicare

bickering 29   important issues 61

c. more or less likely to vote for Clinton over a veto

more likely 46   less likely 15

4. public does not want us to compromise -- they want them to compromise

a. We stated pure Republican principles. Do you want Repubs to compromise or stand firm?
Compromise a lot-38 vs Stand Firm-15
(44% said compromise a little)

b. We stated pure Clinton principles. Do you want Clinton to compromise or stand firm?
Compromise a lot-17 vs Stand Firm-21
(59% said compromise a little)

c. in ad markets: Repub 47 compromise a lot vs 9 stand firm
rest of country Repub 35 compromise a lot vs 17 stand firm

5. Don't float rationales for compromise or ideas for compromise in public or in private. If you whisper it, it will make its way out

6. Republicans only weapon is debt limit and CR and the public will hate them for using blackmail once they start to do it even more than they hate their cuts

NOVEMBER 1, 1995

491

December 7, 1995
Aftermath of the Government Shutdown
(See chapter 9)

Incredibly, the Republicans fell for our carefully baited trap and shut down the government at the end of November. The results were as predicted—a tremendous growth in Clinton's personal image and a dramatic falloff in perceptions that he was weak or wishy-washy.

The GOP did not, however, get the message. They shut the government down again over Christmas. The damage to Republican popularity was enormous.

But now, as the agenda for December 7 indicates, we had come up against a glass ceiling. With Clinton's approval ratings at sixty percent, his vote share was not likely to rise much above the fifty-percent mark (it was unrealistic to expect Clinton to win the votes of everyone who approved of his conduct in office). As the agenda notes, the undecided vote usually went against the incumbent president.

The December 7 agenda stressed the importance of reaching a budget deal with the Republicans to punch through this ceiling. In these efforts, Clinton failed. But punch through he did, as a result of his January 1996 State of the Union speech and its values agenda.

▲

Some agendas for December, January, and February are missing. These largely dealt with the upcoming State of the Union address which catapulted the president into a double-digit lead over Dole. For a discussion of this period, see the Values Agenda chapter in the book.

I. TRACKING POLL DATA -- CONTINUATION OF HIGH RATINGS
           DESPITE DISCONTENT OVER BOSNIA
           LESSENING OF WEAKNESS NEGATIVE

A. Basic ratings hold basically firm

   1. Approval at 58-41 (steady)
   2. Head to head at 49-35 (down from 51-36 pre speech)
   3. Re-elect number at 40 (down from 42 pre-speech

B. Tremendous Growth in personal ratings -- more positives,
      a lot less weakness

   1. For the first time, open ended mentions of Clinton
      personal positives equal mentions of personal
      negatives (33 positive vs 35 negative)

      a. In the past, it ran 21 positive vs 43 negative

      b. major positive mentions:

            cares/compassionate 7%
            honest/integrity 7%
            strong leader 6%
            tries hard   6%

            others 3% or more: energetic/active, doing
            better, appearance, adaptable/compromises,
            fairness, intelligent

   2. Weakness mentions down from 33% to 25%

   3. Personal Clinton positives now equal issue positives
      in open endeds 33% personal vs 36% issue

      a. in the past, a 3-1 ratio of issue vs personal
         positives

DECEMBER 7, 1995

4. In ratings, about a 10 point improvement among Dems and Inds.

    a. strong leader: up 8 among Inds
    b. takes clear stands, up 8 among Inds
    c. In touch with my values: up 9 among Inds
    d. effective: up 6 among Inds

II. OVERALL STRATEGY -- BUDGET DEAL ESSENTIAL TO ADEQUATE VICTORY MARGIN

A. Partisan divide in America is basically 40-20-40

    1. more or less the Clinton-Perot-Bush vote

    2. even now, 40% say they will definitely-probably-possibly vote against Clinton

B. We are currently at roughly 60% approval / 50% vote share

C. We are unlikely to be able to improve those numbers much in the normal course of events

    1. We haven't moved beyond these ratings in six weeks

    2. Polling predicts these numbers without a budget deal

DECEMBER 7, 1995

D. At a 60% approval, we cannot do better, consistently, than 50% vote share

   1. How can we count on getting more than 83% vote share among approvals? We can't

   2. But at a 50% vote share, we are locked in a tie race

   3. Remember -- Incumbent always loses undecideds

      a. Gallup analysis of undecided distribution:

1956	Stevenson: 3	Eisenhower: 0
1964:	Goldwater 7	Johnson: 0
1972	McGovern 3	Nixon: 0
1976	Carter: 4	Ford: 1
1980	Reagan 2	Carter 0
1984	Mondale: 2	Reagan: 2
1992	Perot/Clnt 5	Bush 1
TOTAL	CHALLENG: 26	INCUMB: 4

E. What is standing in our way of passing 60/50?

   1. Perception of weakness acts as a drag

   2. Huge partisan divide acts as a ceiling

F. First step -- overcoming weakness-drag` -- well on the way to getting done

-5-

G. Second step -- blowing off the partisan cap

    1. Budget deal is essential for this

    2. Without a national consensus like we had in 1984,
       incumbent cannot be re-elected by large enough margin
       to breathe easily

    3. Unless national consensus is reached on balanced
       budget, tax cuts, and welfare reform, we are
       capped at 60/50...and a tough race

DECEMBER 7, 1995

February 22, 1996
Values over Economics
(See chapter 14)

Unfortunately, since the agendas for the period right before and right after the 1996 State of the Union speech are missing, it is impossible to recount here how dramatic was the improvement in Clinton's image following this magnificent speech. The ratings that the president has enjoyed in the middle years of his incumbency all date from that remarkable speech.

In the State of the Union message the president addressed a new kind of issue in modern American politics. He broke away from the traditional focus on economic issues and talked instead about "values" issues like teen pregnancy, domestic violence, child support, teen smoking, TV violence, and welfare reform.

The February 22 agenda ranks the popularity of the proposals the president made in his address. In the months and years that followed, it often seemed as if the president was daily consulting this list. Its priorities became the focus of his presidency to a startling degree.

But the most interesting part of the agenda is its discussion of the need for a conscious shift in priorities from economic to values issues. By 60–37, voters wanted to hear about values issues more than about wage stagnation or layoffs. By 55–42, they wanted to focus on values more than on jobs and growth.

More to the point, the voters who demanded a focus on wages, jobs, and the economy were already voting for Clinton by a whopping 57–27 margin. It was the voters who wanted a discussion of values issues whom we had to reach. They were only backing the president by a slender 45–39 margin.

To the extent that the president did discuss the economy, the consultants urged him to stress optimism and growth, not the problems of wage stagnation or layoffs. The advice was clear: "Stress values . . . stress growth . . . stress optimism."

II. Ad Presentation -- Squier and Knapp

A. Ranking of State of the Union Values Message

1. First Tier:

% much more likely

—health insurance reform	60%
—reform welfare	56
—teen pregnancy	56
—fathers care for kids	55
—teach values in school	54
--domestic violence	52
--serve 85% of sentence	51

2. Second Tier:

—pension portable	48
—job training vouchers	47
—foreign lobbyists	47
--deduct tuition	46
--challenge for corporate responsibility	46
—no tobacco ads for kids	45
--wire schools for computers	45
--superfund	44
--campaign finance reform	42

3. Third Tier:

—$1,000 scholarship	38
-- V chip	37
— evict from public housing	36
—TV ratings	34
—school uniforms	31
--environmental right to know	29
--downsize govt	28

III. ECONOMIC MESSAGE -- VALUES MORE IMPORTANT THAN
                        ECONOMICS; GROWTH IS KEY
]   ECONOMICS MESSAGE
                        ---Mark Penn

   A. Values does better than Economics as Message

        1. Values v Economics (defined as wage stagnation, layoffs
                        insecurity)

           -- 60-37

        2. Values v Economics (defined as jobs and growth)

           --55-42

   B. We have Economics voters already and need values voters

        1. Of economic driven voters:

            Clinton: 57   Dole 27

        2. Of values driven voters:

            Clinton: 45   Dole 39

        3. Swing voters are values driven

        4. THEREFORE: stress values, but don't ignore
                        economics

   C. Growth beats Addressing Income Gap

        1. Voters back "stronger economic growth" over "closing
           the gap between rich and poor" by 74-23

FEBRUARY 22, 1996

499

2. Voters back "faster economic growth and expanding educational opportunities" over "encouraging higher pay for lower-skilled people facing stagnating wages" by 71-24

3. Even voters who put economics over values favor growth as the answer by 70-29

4. Among voters who want growth: Cl-45 Dole-41
   who close income gap Cl-66 Dole-17

   a. go after marginal voter, not after base

5. THEREFORE: stress growth polices

D. Economic Optimism Remains Strong

1. No real fear of job loss:

   a. very afraid: 8%,
      somewhat afraid: 15

   TOTAL AFRAID: 22%

   TOTAL NOT AFRAID: 68%

2. Optimism about career

   a. improve in 5 years: 52%
      get worse: 11%
      stay the same: 34%

3. Optimism about economic position:

   a. improve: 46%
      get worse: 16%
      stay the same: 34%

4. Children better off:

    a. improve: 47%
      get worse: 26%
      stay the same: 20%

5. Economy to get better:

    a. improve: 37
      get worse: 26
      stay the same: 30%

6. pessimism creates Dole voters, optimism creates
    Clinton voters

7. THEREFORE: Stress optimism

FEBRUARY 22, 1996

501

March 6, 1996
Mapping Strategy against Dole
(*See chapter 14*)

By early March it had become clear that Dole would be Clinton's opponent. The March 6 meeting focused on how to defeat him. Clearly, the battleground would be the "values oriented" voters. The agenda recommends that we attack Dole on family values issues, stressing his opposition to family leave legislation and curbs on tobacco advertising, plus his failure to support education funding and expansion of scholarship aid.

The meeting of March 6 featured a broad philosophical discussion of how to win elections. The consultants noted that Republicans believed primarily in relying on negative ads to produce a victory. We advanced the idea that positive ads and rebuttal advertising, responding to negatives, were more effective. Once the Republicans began their advertising in early June, the Clinton campaign deliberately went over to the defensive. In a kind of "rope a dope" strategy, we let the Republicans punch themselves out, rebutting each of their attacks as they came but resisting the temptation to run our own negative ads.

The immigration issue threatened our hold over California and our chances in Florida. To cope with the expected GOP attacks on this front, the agenda tests rebuttal themes and notes that the president's progress in strengthening the border and deporting aliens worked well in offsetting attacks over the issue.

AGENDA FOR MEETING WITH PRESIDENT ON MARCH 6 '96

IV.. Media Doctrine -- Squier and Morris

    A. Republicans believe in negatives mainly

        1. they see positives as "pretty pictures and music"
        2. they see rebuttals as a "getting off message"

    B. We believe in dialogue

        1. We see positives as key to winning race
        2. We see rebuttal and counterpunching -- dialogue --
           as way to nail a race down

MARCH 6, 1996

VI. DOLE NEGATIVES -- Doug Schoen

A. We revisited Dole negatives, as requested by President, to
reflect thematic negatives without specifics that
cross cut in different directions

1. We found that anti-family negatives
worked when used in this context

2. caveat: we asked Clinton
positives before asking Dole negatives. That
likely bumped up the Clinton vote from the 53%
baseline to the 57-58% range most achievements
scored.

MARCH 6, 1996

B. Ranking of Dole Negatives

   1. Best: family issues

      (Dole not pro family. anti-student loan. tax increase
      on 8 million working families earning less than $30,000,
      anti-family leave)

      a. moves head to head to 64-30

      b. rebuttal: (Dole fought in WW II for families,
         balanced budget, keep pay not send to Wash
         in taxes, $500/child tax credit, pro-life,
         school prayer, film industry attack)

      c. moves head to head to 61-33

   2. Second best: Washington insider

      (half of life in Wash, deals, self-advancement, six
      pay raise votes include 23% increase in 91, $25,000
      expense account, created own PAC and raised
      $20 million while voting against PACs)

      a. moves head to head to 61-30

      b. rebuttal (experienced, break gridlock, works with
      Dem and Rep Presidents, tax reform of 86 cutting
      taxes).

      c. moves head to head to 61-32

   3. Third best: Medicare

      (voted against Medicare in 65, cuts $270 billion
      raises premiums)

      a. moves head to head to 60-30

b. rebuttal: (protect medicare, big spending liberals
bankrupt it. increases spending on medicare
more than inflation. makes medicare sound)

moves head to head to 59-31

4. Fourth: No New Ideas

(running for 20 years, no new ideas. Kassenbaum
says Dole blows whichever way the wind blows"
no clear reason to run, no agenda, ambition and
nothing else, cant be sure where he stands

a. moves head to head to 59-35

b. rebuttal: (Dole knows time to end liberal policies
of past. power to states and local, shape own destiny
eliminate Dept of Ed, get IRS off backs,

c. moves head to head to 56-38

5. Fifth: Flip Flops vs Always Conservative

(flip flop. promised no taxes, then voted to raise them
by $137 billion. attacks Hollywood but opposes V chip,
anti-cable child tv protections, flipped on affirmative
action)

a. moves head to head to 55-35

b. rebuttal (beware of sudden new conservatives. Dole
has always fought for conservative values. balanced
budget amendment, spending cuts, bal bud plan 7
years, anti Hollywood, war hero, in touch with our
values

moves head to head to 56-34

6. Sixth:Special Interest Captive

(captive of special interests, anti-assault rifle ban,
cut environmental enforcement, opposed family leave
changes abortion position, appease far right

a. moves head to head to 55-37

b. rebuttal (Dole will bring change we need, doer, not
talker, effective leader, stand up to special interests,
bring Americans together, fights for America

moves head to head to 52-40

7. Summary: Key vulnerability is anti-family, all others
move numbers unconvincingly

X. IMMIGRATION -- ~~Debate~~

A. People don't feel situation is getting better

1. Illegal immigration has increased (65%) not decreased(4%)
or stayed the same (25%)

2. But they do feel the are more deportations (43%) not
less (10%) or stayed the same (35%)

B. We have no edge on issue, but Republicans have lost their
edge

1. Clinton better: 42%   Reps in Cong better: 44%

C. Immigration Measures

1. Stepping up border patrols, electronic equipment

--26% much more, 31% somewhat more likely to vote
for Clinton if he backs this (57% more likely total)

2. proof of citizenship for drivers license, deny licenses to
   illegal aliens

   —24% much more, 31% somewhat more (55% more)

   —works even if we delete traffic cop enforcement
      piece which caused all the problems. Just
      make life unattractive in US to illegals—works
      by itself

3. unannounced raids of businesses employing illegals

   —21% much, 25% somewhat (46% more)

4. speeding up deportations to 30 days

   —16% much, 26% somewhat (42% more)

D. Immigration after Arguments

   1. deportations up 30%

      —Clinton: 53   Republicans in Congress: 38

   2. illegal immigration cut 30% by border guards

      Clinton: 61   Republicans in Congress: 41

   3. cut in immigration more remarkable because of Mexico
      economic problems

      -- Clinton: 51   Republicans in Congress: 39

   4. Counter: Dole says enforcement too lax and prompts
      Mexicans to try to come here

      -- Clinton: 48   Republicans in Congress: 42

MARCH 6, 1996

April 1, 1996
A Daring Strategy: Abandon Incumbency Advantage and Invite Comparisons with Dole
(See chapter 14)

"Don't ever mention your opponent's name" was FDR's advice to incumbents. In 1972 Richard Nixon departed from this conventional wisdom and ran effective negative ads against Democratic nominee George McGovern. Now the Clinton strategists went a step further. They urged that the president deliberately invite side-by-side comparisons with Republican nominee Bob Dole.

This radical departure stemmed from the fact that Clinton perpetually fared poorly when voters were asked to rate his attributes. But when compared with Dole, he looked just great. For example, while only thirty-six percent of the nation believed that Clinton was "a strong leader," fifty-two percent felt that he was stronger than Dole. The key to making Clinton look good was to use Dole as the comparison. Clinton ads were to feature direct comparisons between the president and his Republican challenger, even though this strategy seemed to surrender our advantage of incumbency.

AGENDA FOR MEETING WITH PRESIDENT ON APRIL 1   '96.

(DISCLAIMER: Nothing in this memo is intended to be construed as a
celebration of the rites of April 1st)

I   GOALS OF THE PRE-CONVENTION PERIODS- TO COMPARE AND
CONTRAST CLINTON VS. DOLE

A) Voters Have Seen an extensive, updated view of Clinton in 1995-1996.

1) Values Orientation

2) Decisiveness- No Flip-Flops

3) Sure hand in foreign Policy

4) Upbeat, optimistic assessment of economy

5) Centrist positioning on welfare, tax cut, balanced budget, crime

6) Pro-Values Differences with extreme Republican initiative in these
areas.

B) But Clinton Still falls far short of perfection- especially when measured
against their high hopes of 1992

1) Current Poll Data:

1. in touch with my values 39-39

2. does things because they are right 39-35

3. strong leader 36-33

4. effective 29-33

5.Ratings are no better than OK, and certainly
don't reflect a 52% vote share

2) However, when measured against Dole, Clinton's ratings
acquire a new buoyancy:

Dole- Time tested, mature/ Clinton- young, immature
True- 28%   Not true -51%

Dole- Strong, decisive leader/ Clinton- weak and flip-flops
True- 30%   Not true- 52%

Dole- Practical and down to earth/ Clinton- too abstract
True- 26%   Not true- 52%

Dole- Doer/ Clinton- Just a talker
True- 21   Not true- 51%

Impact of above on head to head: NONE

C) The Mission: To contrast Clinton and Dole

    1) Dole: To express Clinton's achievement, positioning and personal skills
    in the context of Dole's weakness'

        a) Economy- contrast 91-91 recession with current
        prosperity

            1) Show Dole's absence of economic
            program in 91 when the country
            needed it.

        b) Achievements: Stress how Dole opposed Clinton's
        achievements

            1) Student loans, immunizations, family
            leave, Brady Bill

        c) Positioning on Budget: Express how Dole tried to
        destroy America's values by
        extremism in budget debate:

            270B in Medicare cuts
            Medicare premium increase
            Entitlement for Medicaid children
            Nursing homes
            Head start
            College scholarships

Federal help for schools
Environmental policies
EPA enforcement
Toxic waste
Tax cut for working families
Tuition deductibility

    d) Advocacy: Contrast Clinton and Dole differences over
       ongoing issues:

V-Chip
Federal role in education and education
    standards
Tobacco/smoking
Minimum wage
domestic violence
100,000 cops
Campaign finance reform,

D) Overall Conclusions:
   1) To show Dole's inadequacies:

      a) Dole lacks generational perspective to embrace new era.

      b) Dole is too much of a worn-out insider to seek dynamic change.

      c) Dole is too much of a Washington figure to understand real
        values issues.

      d) Dole embraces Republican passivity and inaction in the face of
        economic difficulty.

   2) To show that Clinton has the right vision for America

      a) Clinton is generationally suited for a new look at America's
        problems at turn of the century.

      b) Clinton is an active, energetic proponent of new ideas.

      c) Clinton embraces the values of America as it copes with change

      d) Clinton actively and vigorously seeks to foster economic growth

F) Free Media Implementation of Above Strategy- Presidential

    1) Continue positive exposition and elaboration of the State of Union agenda into our basic message:

        Tobacco,
         education standards
        television violence
        teen gangs,
        going to college,
        corporate responsibility
        pension reform
        health care portability
        job training vouchers
        responsible parenting,
        criminal sentencing,
        anti-terrorism
        domestic and spousal abuse
        education technology,
        environmental protection
        school uniforms...

    2) To highlight economic optimism and current economic growth

    3) To accomplish closure on conservative themes of budget balancing, tax cuts, welfare reform, crime, immigration reform.

    4) To highlight international role as peacekeeper and statesman

    5) The goal of Presidential free media activity is not and should not be to raise Dole's negatives.

G) Free Media Implementation of Above Strategy-- Non-Presidential

APRIL 1, 1996

1) To interfere with the elaboration of Dole's message with tactical hits as opportunities arise

2) To use the Senate Floor to show Dole's lack of leadership and inability to be an effective President.

3) Force Dole into a position which exemplify the issues outlined above.

4) To distract Dole and break his momentum by tactical intervention in his campaign and in his legislative leadership.

H) Summary: (What do we want people to remember about Clinton and Dole)

1) Dole is too old, stuck in another era, but Clinton is current and with it.

Single word translation- Generational

2) Dole is too tired and mired in the status quo to permit him to seek change. Clinton is active, energetic and committed to change.

Single word translation- Status Quo

3) Dole is a Washington insider who does not get the fundamental values of America. Clinton is embracing those values in his program and politics.

Single word translation-Values

4) Dole is committed to passive economic policy while Clinton dynamically seeks growth.

Single word translation -Growth

I) RECAP; Generation, Status Quo, Values and Growth

April 24, 1996
Using Public Values Issues to Beat Clinton Scandals
(See chapter 14)

In retrospect, the April 24 strategy meeting may have been the single most important in the Clinton presidency. It was there that the strategy team adopted the tactic of using "public values to defeat private scandal."

As Clinton was pounded by sexual, draft, drug, and financial scandals, it was clear that Americans were splitting into three groups. Voters over fifty were highly critical, reflecting their own strict value standards and upbringing. Only Medicare brought them back to us in any quantity. Baby Boomers between thirty-five and fifty were more relativist in their value perspectives and cared less about Clinton's misdeeds, perhaps because they remembered their own.

That left the Generation-X voter as the key. Far more moralistic than Clinton and more critical of his behavior than their boomer relatives, the voters under thirty-five were, however, more concerned about raising their own children than they were about the president's character. To win their support and get them to ignore the scandals, it was important to stress how the president's agenda was making their own parenting easier.

We discovered this strategy of using public values issues to offset private scandal in the polling that is reported in the April 25 agenda. We asked voters questions like this one:

"Some say that Bill Clinton has shown that he does not have the character to be president, when you consider the charges that he ducked the draft and had an affair with Gennifer Flowers. Others say that while these things should have been considered three years ago when Clinton did not have a track record, now he has shown his real values in office by pressing for child support enforcement, fighting against violence and sex on TV, and cracking down on teen smoking. Which point of view comes closest to your own?"

We found that the values issues brought us back the Generation X voters we had begun to lose over scandal. The conclusion, expressed in this agenda, is: "Any attack on [Clinton's] private character and conduct can be met by reference to . . . our values agenda issues and defeated in the context of these actions showing [Clinton's] real values."

Reduced to the formulation that "public values defeat private scandal," this strategy for coping with scandal remains a mainstay of the Clinton administration.

IV. CHARACTER ISSUE --- ACQUIRING IMMUNITY BASED ON PUBLIC
LEADERSHIP ON VALUES ISSUES

    A. Our agenda of public values issues has become a highly effective response to
        attacks on the President's character

        1. people increasingly see the President's public
            values agenda as a more relevant indicator of his character
            than the allegations of personal prior conduct

APRIL 24, 1996

2. Even when subjected to a harsh set of attacks, the public values
   agenda beats them back

    Format: Some people say that Bill Clinton has shown that he does
   not have the character to be President when you
   consider.............Others say that while these things should
   have been considered three years ago when Clinton did
   not have a track record, now he has shown his real
   values in office by................

    a. negatives: failed promises, Whitewater, draft

      vs.: assault weapons, education, Medicare, tobacco, TV ratings,
   Oklahoma City, Rabin

        bad character: 35
   has real values: 63

    b. negatives: failed promises, Whitewater, draft

      vs. assault weapons, education, medicare, tobacco, TV ratings --
   no Okla or Rabin

        bad: 36
   values: 61

    c. negatives: womanizing, pot smoking, sexual harassment suit

    vs. peace in Bosnia and Mid east, tax cuts for working families,
   Brady Bill,

        bad: 35
   values: 60

    d. negatives: womanizing, port smoking, sex harassment suit

    vs. domestic violence, truth in sentencing, health portability

        bad: 34
   values: 63

3. Conclusion: Any attack on private conduct and character can be met
   reference to virtually any of our values agenda issues and defeated
   in the context of these actions showing his "real" values

B. President's character perceptions are highly competitive with Dole.

    1. We do best on public values and do OK on private values

    2. Question: Does this apply more to Clinton or Dole?

        a. Works to help majority of people Cl 57 D 33

        b. Inspiring: Cl-52 D-29

        c. Doing right even if unpopular 53-37

        d. Keeps campaign promises: 41-31

        e. Someone you would leave your kids with 40-33

        f. responsible 45-44

        g. represents basic American values 46-46

        h. decent 44-45

        i trust 44-46

        j. strong on defense 39-52

    3. Analysis:

        a. big progress in leads on doing right and promises

        b. good progress in break even on personal character stuff

            1. margins like this are not the basis for a campaign against us.

V. RESPONSE TO DOLE ATTACKS

    A. Generic Goals:

    1. Make Dole seem nasty

        a. take away his ability to wage a negative campaign by making him pay with nastiness adjectives for each shot he takes

2. Make Dole seem incompetent

    a. by peddling the story that his attacks aren't working or are a blunder, make him seem incompetent

    b. put him through the same ringer we went through in the opening months

3. Stress Dole hypocrisy

    a. by contrasting proposals with past positions, make him seem flip floppy. Take away affirmative advocacy as an option

4. Use to showcase our accomplishments

    a. Just as we used Republican

VI. GENERATIONAL THEME -- THE BASIC STORY WE HAVE TO TELL

A. We tested two story lines on generational issues.

1. Clinton vs Clinton --

Clinton is the first of a new generation to hold the Presidency. He was young and inexperienced at the start but now he really understands how to govern and has become a solid leader who will be even better in the second term

vs

He is typical of young people who lack discipline, character, and maturity. He doesn't understand or respect how the older generation worked to make the country what it is and we need to bring back leadership that understands he old ways and has greater maturity and understanding

Good Clinton -59 Bad Clinton: 36

2. Clinton vs Dole

Clinton is the first of a new generation to hold the Presidency. He was
young and inexperienced at the start but now he really understands how to
govern and has fresh ideas. Dole represents the older generation trying to
take back power just as the younger generation is coming into its own and
doing a better job. It would be wrong to let Dole turn back the clock
on America's leadership and its new direction

vs

He is typical of young people who lack discipline, character, and
maturity. He doesn't understand or respect how the older generation
like Bob Dole, worked to make this country what it is. We need to
bring back leaders who understand that our old values are still
useful and give people like Bob Dole. who understand those values,
one more turn to lead us in the right direction

Clinton: 56   Dole 37

XIV. INTEREST GROUP RATINGS

We tested each of six interest groups to determine who had worst image

Tobacco Companies priority to cut power: 56   importance of group: 49

Lawyers: priority: 43   importance: 61

News media   priority: 43   importance: 72

NRA   priority: 40   importance: 47

Christ. Coalition   priority 27   importance: 41

AFL and labor priority: 24   importance: 41

Analysis: Good offense possible against tobacco and NRA, but not against
            Christian Coalition

            Worry about attacks on lawyers but not on labor

Need: to develop a defense to lawyer attack apart from specific issues like
       tort reform

XV. OTHER ISSUES

    A. Smoking

        Zero tolerance for smoking on school property or at events like games
        or dances. smoke detectors in bathrooms. Smokers told to leave activity
        strictly enforced:

            more likely vote Cl: 63   less likely vote Cl 30

            great, lets do it

    B. Welfare Reform

        Require Teenagers Moms to stay in school to get AFDC -- exec order

            more likely Cl:81   less likely: 13

        Bruce says we can do by exec order, lets do it.

    C. Child abuse/neglect

        Denying free legal counsel that is currently available to parents who
        have been found guilty of child abuse and are seeking to regain
        custody of their children, often on grounds that they have changed their
        ways

            agree: 55   disagree: 37

            too close for comfort

    D. Spouse Abuse

        1. Half of insurance companies deny coverage for spousal abuse
        injuries. Require coverage.

            more likely: 89-8

        2. Calling on the ABA to encourage lawyers to offer free order of
        protection services to anyone who is threatened

        no polling, well worth doing, obviously popular

E. Tax Credits for Adoption/Marry Single Mothers

>Offering an additional tax credit for people who agree to take on the support obligations for a child that is not their own either by marrying a single parent or through adoption of a child

>more likely vote Cl: 74   less likely: 19

F. Deadbeat Dads

>Garnish veterans checks, social security, disability if recipient is delinquent in his or her child support payments

>more likely: 80-16

G. Community Watch Volunteers

>100,000 community watch volunteers to match the 100,000 new cops to serve as added eyes and ears of police in spotting crime.

>more likely: 76-21

H. Buy American

>Urges all Americans, including every govt agency, every business every consumer to go out of their way in looking for the made in USA label whenever possible as a way to stimulating our economy and showing the pride we take in American workers

>more likely 74-20

I. Community Service

>Community service for high school seniors working in their communities at hospitals, shelters, nursing homes, and other places to earn credits they could use to pay for college tuition

>more likely 86-13

>I have in mind urging colleges and high schools to do this voluntarily

K. Out of wedlock children

> Major speech on 1/4 children out of wedlock, creates social problems, need to reverse policies to encourage children to have the su.~port o^two parents

> more likely 88-16

J. Intimidation of Federal Officials

> crime to intimidate govt officials through threats of violence

> strong agree: 57
> some agree: 23

> total agree: 80

K. College:

> If Clinton said higher education was key to competing international economy. National goal every student have opportunity for some college. High school isn't enough anymore. At least some community college is necessary and we need to give everyone opportunity for college as we did for high school diplomas years ago

>> more likely Cl: 73   less likely: 26

> basic new theme for campaign

L. Employer-Employee Duties

>> 1. Support that employees have a duty to make company more profitable, not just do their job by 72-23

>> 2. Support that employers have a duty to make employees more valuable through job training not just to provide a paycheck by 82-14

>> 3. Support "employees have a duty to make a company more profitable and employers have a duty to make employees more valuable by 93-6

May 9, 1996
Politicizing the Olympics
(See chapter 14)

The 1996 Summer Olympic Games in Atlanta seemed to be a golden opportunity for the president. Ronald Reagan had used the 1984 Los Angeles Olympics to sell the idea that America was on the way back. In the May 9 agenda the consultants suggest that Clinton should emphasize how "the real meaning of these Olympics is that it shows us examples of what happens when individuals take on personal responsibility for self-improvement."

Clinton, indeed, focused on this theme during his participation in Olympic events, only to have it overshadowed by the terrorist bombing which disrupted the games.

In the meantime, Bob Dole had finally found an issue. With a sharp run-up in gas prices, Dole's campaign began to demand repeal of the gas tax increase Clinton had passed in 1993. We needed to find a counter. On May 9 we presented one: raising the minimum wage. While this would seem to be comparing apples and oranges, our polling had demonstrated that voters cared much more about the minimum wage than they did about the gas tax. As a result of this polling, Democrats in the Senate attached a minimum-wage increase rider onto any Dole attempt to lower the gas tax.

This surprising finding was the forerunner of a key element of the 1996 campaign strategy—the realization that voters were more idealistic than they were self-interested. While the gas tax affected each voter and the minimum wage applied to only about a tenth of the electorate, the American people were more interested in raising the minimum wage than in getting a break on gas taxes. As the tax-cut debate sharpened during the remainder of 1996, this emphasis on helping others as opposed to helping oneself became a key point of departure between the Clinton and Dole campaigns.

AGENDA FOR MEETING WITH PRESIDENT-- MAY 9 　96

I. TRACKING-- DOLE FAVORABLITY SINKS, HEAD TO HEAD STEADY
CLINTON APPROVAL UP

Dick Morris

 A. Head to head steady at 18 pts 53-35 (54-36 last week)

 B. Job approval up to 60(from 57 last week)

  1. renewed stress on positive message and new ad

 C. Favorability up to 59 (from 58)

 D. Re-elect at 50, up from 49

 E. Dole favorability down to 45-50 (from 47-46 last week)

  1. Our negatives are cutting him deeply

  2. Now, we need to push hard to try to move his unfavorables to an
   unelectable range

 F. Hillary Favorable at 50-40 (from 47-45)

 G. Budget tracking

  1. Who is most to blame for failure to reach a deal: Cl: 30 Reps. 53

   a. up from last week's 33-50

   b. But Dole v Cl on blame: D-39 Cl-36 (down from 41-33 last
    week)

MAY 9, 1996

526

II GAS TAX --- LINKAGE TO MINIMUM WAGE IS THE WAY TO GO

    A. Recall of the issue is up to 69%

        1. growing too fast not to act

    B. Dole is seen as initiating the repeal rather than Clinton by 35-24

    C. If Clinton urged repeal, they'd back repeal by 56-36

    D. If Clinton urged repeal, they'd be more likely to vote for him by 51-35

    E. If it were repealed, credit would go to Clinton over Dole by 26-17. but most
       would give credit to both (15) or neither (32)

        1. They don't like Dole and don't like to give him credit for anything

F. But, Clinton's support of repeal would be seen as "political gimmick" and
   "flip-flop" as opposed to due to change in gas prices and cut in deficit
   by 58-36

    1. When any politician's motives for anything are probed, swing voters
   will never give him the benefit of the doubt, only his core partisans

    2. Dole was seen as hypocrite on the issue by 65% last week

    3. Neither of these factors will stop either candidate from reaping positives
   or negatives from whichever side he takes on the issue

    4. This will be used in Republican ads and we cannot give them a clear
   shot at us by vetoing the repeal

    5. It is just too precise and clear that 4 cents a gallon costs a driver 50
   cents to fill up his 12 gallon tank each time.

    6. You know how these car issues can work (1980)

G. Repeal gas tax now or link to minimum wage increase

    Repeal: 35   Link to Min Wage: 57

H. If Clinton favored gas tax repeal without conditions: 52-43

I. If Clinton favored gas tax repeal only if guarantee pass through and pass
   minimum wage: 75-23

    1. past polling indicates that pass through is not the key element, minimum
   wage is

III MINIMUM WAGE

A. Strong support for minimum wage continues--

    a. An unbelievably strong issue. Much more important than any issue
   now in play including gas tax.

    Support-- 81-18 (Strongly support- 63))

MAY 9, 1996

B. Strong electoral connection- Clinton favors, Dole opposes

        more likely--63   less likely--27

C. Argumentation: Automation, cut in teen jobs, increase EITC instead of minimum wage vs. living wage, adjusted for inflation, don't hit taxpayers with burden

        Support minimum wage increase-- 70-26

        More likely Clinton-- 64-32

IV RESPONSE TO DOLE ADS -- NEED FOR INSTANT PRESIDENTIAL APPROVAL OF SCRIPTS

A. We need instant access to the President for script approvals in answering Dole ads.

    1. When an answer is needed and I call the President for script approval, I would request that he authorize Betty to tell him immediately and request that he either take the call or return it within a few minutes

B. General Procedure:

    1. Republican ad sighted in morning of day 1.

    2. Response ad anamatics are generated for mall tests on the evening of day 1

        a. they are digitally conveyed to mall test sites

        b. They are fact checked during day 1

        c. script writing is coordinated with Sosnik

    3. President is called on morning of day 2 for approval of script that worked in mall tests

        a. need immediate access as per above

    4. Ad is produced on day 2 and satellited to stations

VII OLYMPIC THEMES

A. Our participation in the Olympics should be guided by a substantive theme rather than just identification with the event.

    1. We should use Olympics as metaphor for our positive theme and return to it again and again in our Olympic involvement.

B. Testing of Themes:

    1. Best theme : Assuming responsibility and self-improvement

        73-20 (37 much more likely)

"The real meaning of these Olympics is that it shows us examples of what happens when individuals take on personal responsibility for self improvement. It shows what happens when we better ourselves and concentrate our energies on achieving a task. As each of us watches these athletes strive and win as a result of their training, we should be inspired to continue our education, get new job skills, to go back to college and to get degrees to finish HS so we can make the most of our own lives."

2. Second best theme: Race and gender don't matter

72-20

"The true meaning of the Olympics is that race and gender and other superficial differences don't really matter. We are Americans under the skin, all working together, all competing together to help our country win. When the pole vaulter clears the bar we don't think of it as a man or woman, or if he or she is Black, White, Asian or Hispanic- we think that that person is an American and we burst with pride at their successes."

3. Third best theme: AMERICA WINS
70-22

"What the Olympics mean is an example of how America can win if we all pull together. If we train hard. If we set our minds at tasks. If we disregard our differences and work together as one team. When I see Americans winning in the Olympic Stadium, I think of how we can win at global trade, in improving our society and creating more jobs and in Strengthening our families- if we only apply the Olympic spirit of Team America working together."

4. Fourth best theme: Peace
65-26

"The key meaning of the Olympics is that it shows a world at peace where nations put down their guns and their suspicions, and engage in wholesome athletic competition. Let the spirit of peace go from these games to the Middle East, to Bosnia, and to other places where the spirit of war causes to children to die."

MAY 9, 1996

5. Worst theme: America united

60-26

"The Olympics is about how this country's strength can be found in working together, because when we are united, we never fail. Through these games we, as a nation, will reach across all of our differences of color, creed or station in life to give those who are willing to work hard a chance to succeed. I believe that this summer the world will see one America, a place where individuals are realized through common efforts. A place where different points of view and different heritage's are held together by the shared values that keep this country great and strong."

VIII MISCELLANEOUS

A. Voters support targeted tax cuts over across the bard tax cuts.

1. Across the board tax cut v. targeted tuition, raising children, low income workers back targeting 59-36

2. More likely Clinton if he backs targeting- 61-34

MAY 9, 1996

532

May 15 and May 24, 1996
Dole's Retirement from Senate
(See chapter 14)

With his campaign dead in the water, Dole decided to jump-start his lagging effort by retiring from the Senate to campaign full-time for the presidency. Frantically, we set about polling to develop an answer. In the May 15 agenda we reported that we had found one: Rather than let Dole characterize his departure from the Senate as an act of dedication and commitment to his candidacy, we should portray it as abandoning his job in the Senate while major issues were still on the line.

We proposed an ad featuring a pile of moving boxes stacked up on Dole's desk being carried off by moving men. The announcer said: "He promised change. Said he'd balance the budget, reform welfare. But now he's leaving the Senate, quitting with the job still undone, leaving behind him only the gridlock he and Gingrich have created." The ad went on to feature a hard-working President Clinton battling to solve America's pressing problems.

But Clinton was afraid to take on the Dole retirement so directly. His advisers at the May 15 strategy meeting, particularly Sandy Berger, emphasized caution. By May 24 Dole was achieving significant gains through his projected retirement. Only a major dose of pessimistic poll data made the president reconsider and agree to airing the anti-Dole ad.

Building on the "help other people, don't help me" theme we had discovered in using the minimum wage to counter the gas tax increase, the May 15 and May 24 agendas recommend that Clinton counter Dole's proposals for tax cuts with targeted tax cuts of his own aimed at Americans in particular need. Tapping into the feeling of charity and generosity which was common in the America of 1996, these targeted tax cuts had a much greater appeal than did the across-the-board reductions.

The most interesting aspect of the May 15 and May 24 agendas was their discussion of what would be Dole's best stategy to defeat Clinton. Dole was constantly attacking Clinton as a liberal and ignoring his move to the center in 1995 and 1996. When we war-gamed how Dole might win, it became clear that his best attack would be to dismiss Clinton's recent moderation as just politics and warn that Clinton would revert to liberalism if reelected. Only late in the 1996 campaign did Dole realize this weakness in Clinton's armor and, when he did seize on it, he succeeded in closing the gap between them substantially.

II. DOLE'S RETIREMENT FROM SENATE

A. Superficially the "right decision" voters feel:

> "Some people say Dole made the right decision by stepping down as majority leader because running for President is a full time task that requires all of a candidate's effort. Others say that it is wrong for Dole to step down and abandon his responsibility as majority leader leaving behind much unfinished business in Congress"

right decision: 56
wrong decision: 34

B. We must make this a huge mistake on Dole's part:

1. as we get things done in government, he is on the fringe

2. he has no positive message to sustain him on the stump

3. the Republicans in Congress who remain have their own leaders and as he fades, their own agenda of achievement

4. We must keep in the voters' minds the huge failure that has been the Republican Congress for which he bears responsibility.

   5. we cannot let him become born again as a candidate with no past and no responsibility for 95-96

C. Dangers

1. We must avoid Washington trap by executive actions and values messages

2. Comeback by underdog

   a. stop it by denying him a message which he needs for traction

D. Free Media Strategy

1. Press Congress for action

2. Progress vs Partisanship -- getting it done while he wants to campaign

3. Send Dole and Gingrich off on the road and get it done here in Washington

4. Vigorous program of public action and statements to highlight contrast between President getting it done for America and Dole running for office

E. Paid Media Strategy

1. Pour it on to thwart his initiative. If he is still 20 points behind after this has run its course, they are dead and they know it

2. Stress themes that work in polling tonight in positive ads

3. Get it done for America, politics can wait. Dole (insert hit) But The President says balance the budget and get it done.

MAY 15, 1996

IV   HANDLING DOLE ATTACKS

    A. We have war gamed three likely Dole attacks and developed answers
        that work for each one

       1. Taxes and Promises

          a. attack ad

              middle class tax cut promise--tax hike
              end welfare promise -- welfare veto

          b. response works that hits Dole tax hikes and praises
            Clinton tax cuts

       2. Character attack

          a. attack ad

              --Dole from Heartland; Clinton gays in military
              --Dole hero, wounded; Clinton draft dodger,
                 demonstrated in London
              --Dole values Clinton: partial birth abortion,
                 sex harassment suit, Whitewater

          b. response works that contrasts Clinton and Dole on "values"
            issues

       3 Welfare attack

          a. attack ad

              --end welfare as we know it vs two vetoes
              --blocking replace welfare with work
              --rewards illegitimacy and dependency
              --actions louder than words

b. response ad

      --quiet revolution in welfare reform
      -- exec order on teen moms
      -- 37 states
      -- day care
      --1.1 million off welfare
      --Clinton vetoed old way
      --moving people from welfare to work on his own

4. Also tested gas tax attack ad and found it did no real damage

V   SECOND TERM CRITIQUE-- THE MOST DANGEROUS DOLE CHARGE

A. Most devastating attack on Clinton is that he is "really a liberal who, for the past two years has been running a re-election campaign to appear more moderate. But, if elected, he will never have to answer to voters again and will go back to being liberal on issues like gays and taxes"

      more likely Clinton: 43
      less likely Clinton: 47

1. Similar to 51-46 agreement in last week's poll

B. Best Answer. Respond with Time Flow of Clinton Moderate Actions

  1. Over Crime: --promise cut crime
                  --crime now down
                  --Brady, assault
                  --100,000 cops, 1,000 fedl terrorism agents
                  --will get tougher in second term

    more likely: 75-21

  2. Over Welfare: --end welfare as we know it
                  --37 states waiver
                  --teen moms
                  --EITC
                  --second term: move to work, jobs in poor
                      areas

    72-24

MAY 15, 1996

3. Over Budget: --promise to cut deficit
                        --cut in half
                        --proposed bal budg plan

65-29

C. Next best: show how Clinton has changed Democrats to
more focus on balanced budget, tax cuts, crime, welfare
reform. From government is answer to opportunity, won't
go back to old liberal approach

66-27

D. Third best: contrast Clinton and Dole positions over
gun control, extra police, EITC, budget cuts

63-30

VI DOLE AND THE AGE ISSUE

A. Voters break narrowly, disagree that Dole is too old to be President: 44-53

B. When told that Clinton always spoke of Dole's "old approach" in his
ads, and that the press criticized Clinton, saying this was a way
of getting voters to oppose Dole because he was too old, it had
little effect on voter attitude on Clinton

More likely to vote for Clinton-- 18
Less likely to vote for Clinton-- 29
No Difference-- 52

C. Even if voters perceived that Clinton is saying that Dole is too old to be
President, the fact that Clinton is making the allegation has little effect
on the likelihood of vote for Clinton.

More likely to vote for Clinton-- 14
Less likely to vote for Clinton-- 29
No Difference--   57

VIII   TAX CUT- A TRAP FOR DOLE

    A. If Dole advocates an "Across the board" tax cut, he will fall into a major
        trap.

        1. Voters support Doles proposal for a 15% across the board tax
            cut by 48-42

            a. very tepid margin

MAY 15, 1996

2. It, however, has little impact on the race

More likely to vote Dole-- 41
Less likely to vote for Dole--50

Clinton--58   Dole--35

3. When Dole's support for tax cuts is argued (let people keep their own money, spur job growth) it fails in the face of each of two different responses.

    a. When Medicare, Medicaid, Education and Environment cuts are cited in opposition to Dole's tax cut, the tax cut fails by

39-53

    b.. When targeted tax cuts like tuition, per child, working poor, are cited as an alternative, Dole's tax cut fails by

34-62

    c. Given the list of possible alternatives in targeted tax cuts, voters back:

Two-years free Community College-- 73-23

Four-year tuition tax deduction-- 74-22

Increased tax cut to businesses that locate in
    low income areas to create jobs for
       former welfare recipients-- 82-16

$1,000 tax credit per child ($500 this year and $500
    next year)-- 78-20

4. Therefore, if Dole advocates across the board cuts, we should initially hit him over '95 budget arguments, but then move the debate to a grand referendum over whether tax cuts should be across the board or targeted.

    a. Dole can't say the money isn't there for our targeted tax cuts because he proposed the tax cut first.

XII WHITEWATER -- ALL DEVELOPMENTS POSITIVE DESPITE
     TESTIMONY AND HEARINGS

A. Is President Clinton involved in serious wrongdoing?

    31% yes (37% yes on 4-23)

B. Is Hillary Clinton involved in serious wrongdoing?

    45% yes (49% on 4-23)

C. Is D'Amato's hearings:

    fair inquiry 23 (was 27 on 4-23)

    politically driven to discredit Pres. 67 (was 64)

    Continued downward slide.

D. Is Starr's investigation

    fair inquiry: 26

    politically driven: 59 (was 56)

    He is now where D'Amato was three months ago

E. After testimony adamantly denying asking Hale for loan:

    Strongly believe Clinton: 21
    somewhat believe Clinton 33

    total believe Clinton   54

    somewhat believe Hale: 16
    strongly believe Hale   12

    total believe Hale   28

    based on testimony: more likely to vote Clinton: 46
                        less likely to vote Clinton: 47

F. If Starr loses current case close investigation because politically driven during election or complete investigation because good prosecutor and get all the facts out

      close investigation 44
      complete investigation: 50

G. Should Starr resign, conflicts, paper company, RTC

      resign 48-35

H. If McDougal's and Tucker are found guilty is Pres involved in serious wrong doing:

      35% (up. 4)

    1. Hillary-- 46 (up 1)

MAY 15, 1996

Dick

AGENDA FOR MEETING WITH PRESIDENT ON MAY 24, 1996

I. TRACKING - DOLE IS ESCAPING FROM THE CELLAR...WE ARE LETTING HIM DO IT

    A. Vote at 54-37-- 17 points. Up 1 for Clinton, up 3 for Dole from last week.

    B. Clinton Favorability at 62-- a new high.

    C. Dole Favorability up 50-45-- 5 point gain from last week's 48-48.

    D. Clinton job approval at 61 and re-elect at 51-- tied with past for record high.

    E. Analysis

        1. Dole has his best week through resignation. While his gains appear modest, the hardest thing to do in politics is switch direction and he did it successfully

        2. Clinton moved to record high due to effectiveness of paid media.

        3. Dole is escaping from the box in which we had him and may be getting off the mat.

    F. Dole gains from last weeks lows in almost all adjective categories.

        1. <u>Adjective</u>

Effective	Dole gains 5 (Cl ahead by 4)
Strong Leader	Dole gains 10 (Cl ahead by 4)
Touch w/ values	Dole gains 3 (Cl leads by 10)
On my side	Dole gains 3 (Cl leads by 15)
Clear stand on issues	Dole gains 20 (Dole leads by 10)
Balancing the budget	Dole gains 11 (Cl leads by 10)
Peacemaker	Dole gains 10 (Cl leads by 36)
New Ideas	Dole gains 17 (Cl leads by 16)

MAY 24, 1996

Does things cause they're right	Dole gains 10	(Cl leads by 10)
Flip- Flops	Dole gains 17	(Cl trails by 38)
Vision for future	Dole gains 11	(Cl leads by 19)
Does right thing even when unpopular	Dole gains 10	(Cl leads by 4)

2. Issues

Handling economy	Dole gains 17	(Cl leads by 2)
Crime	Dole drops 2	(Cl leads by 8)
Foreign Policy	Dole gains 5	(Cl leads by 9)
Welfare	Dole gains 7	(Cl leads by 13)

Taxes	Dole gains 17	(Cl trails by 4)
Health Care	Dole gains 18	(Cl leads by 22)
Education	Dole gains 13	(Cl leads by 25)

Analysis: Adjectives are the lead indicator, favorability is the next indicator, vote share is the lagging indicator

Dole is about to break this race wide open and slash our lead to single digits.

We must not let him

II. REACTION TO DOLE'S RESIGNATION

    A. As time has progressed, more people support Dole's decision.

        1. On Thursday, the day after, voters back decisions by 67-16

        2. On Tuesday and Wednesday night, support grew to 71-19.

    B. After argumentation, still support Dole's decision-- 65-28.

    C. However, Dole is highly vulnerable on the implications of this decision

        Attack on Dole

            Leaves behind gridlock Dole pushes budget cuts in medicare
            etc.

            Much less likely Dole-43%   Total Less likely Dole-61%

Dole gives tearful speech, then runs negative ads

Much less likely Dole-40%   Total Less likely Dole-60%

Dole no leadership, proposed stuff, then flip flopped and left

Much less likely Dole-37%   Total Less likely Dole-59%

Dole pension

Much less likely Dole-37%   Total Less likely Dole-58%

Clinton leads to do things, Dole won't work with President

Much less likely Dole-36%   Total Less likely Dole-58%

Bob Dole leaves country in lurch when key bills come up

Much less likely Dole-35%   Total Less likely Dole-58%

Text of Empty Ad without visuals:

Much less likely Dole-39%   Total Less likely Dole-57%

Congress and Dole did nothing, now he quits

Much less likely Dole-34%   Total Less likely Dole-57%

Bob Dole leadership failed, now quits   President?

Much less likely Dole-36%   Total Less likely Dole-56%

Clinton says that politics can wait. Now pass welfare etc

Much less likely Dole- 32%   Total Less likely Dole-56%

Dole failed to campaign from Senate desperate bid to revive campaign

Much less likely Dole-34% Total Less likely Dole-55%

Dole is highly vulnerable and let's hit him right now to reshape views about his resignation

IV. STARTEGY OF ENGAGEMENT-- FREE MEDIA PHILOSOPHY

    A. We do best when we are showcased next to Dole

        1. Don't avoid engagement by trying to be above the battle – join it

        2. seek out side by side coverage on news

        3. comparison with dole is a relief to people who are used to judging us vs perfection

    B. Need one announcement by the President every Monday, Tuesday, Wednesday, and Thursday. We benefit by contrast with Dole.

        1. the theory of doing 2-3 a week, not every weekday night is unsound because we can't predict when events will force us off the air

        2. We need to put out a message, by the President, every single weekday night except Fridays (no good TV news)

        3. Can do events in Washington to minimize impact on President's time

        4. Can do events with minimal visuals, if necessary, the key is to do it--

MAY 24, 1996

547

--whether or not it can be done with good visuals

5. Don't do major initiatives over weekend radio address

    a. TV more important than print and no Saturday TV

    (compare impact of Meagan -- done on weekday -- vs welfare Wisconsin waiver done on Saturday radio

6. Suggest 8:30 conf call on positive message, like 9:00am call on rapid response

C. We have a higher bar than before on making statements and getting them covered on the networks

    1. must either be bold and important policy proposal

    2. or major campaign move vis a vis Dole

    3. or important executive initiative

V. A DOLE TAX CUT MOVE-- THE ONLY WAY DOLE CAN WIN

    A. Dole's two issue gambits have not worked

    1. Gas tax got him nothing.

        a. Minimum wage/strategic petroleum reserve tactic worked.

    2. Welfare offense so far has done little.

        a. We still hold 13 point edge on welfare

            i. even though he gained 7 points on this issue.

        b. In the absence of paid media, only 28% heard of his welfare move

        c. 27% heard of our Wisconsin waiver which constituted effective blockage.

B. In going to a tax-cut move, Dole is making his third bid for a breakout.
--his third long bomb

C. A tax cut move that we do not defend can put him right back in the race.

    1. When told Dole proposed "major across the board tax cut" the head to head dropped to 45-45. A 17 point gain for Dole.

        a. this represents the first time in any simulation in the past four months that we found an issue that gets him back to even

        b. tax cut moves always do better in reality than in surveys

            1. witness Whitman's "failed" tax cut proposal that eventually powered her past Florio

    2. We have never had the credibility on the issue of tax cuts that we have acquired on balancing the budget, fighting crime or reforming welfare

        Our lead on... Welfare-- 53-40

                Crime-- 49-41

                Balanced 44-34
                Budget

        But Dole wins Taxes by 41-45.

        a. Therefore, any Dole move on tax cuts must be handled from a pro tax-cut position.

            i. Just like welfare, balanced budget and crime are all addressed from a pro-welfare reform, pro-balanced budget and anti-crime position.

            ii. Cannot be perceived as Democratic opponent of tax cut.

D. Opposition to across the board tax cut and support for targeted tax cut must be the lynch-pin of our position.

    1. When voters are asked who they would support if Dole advocated an across the board tax cut and Clinton backed targeted tax cuts for families with children, tax incentives for business to create jobs in

empowerment zones and tax deductions to help finance a college education,

Oppose by 30-64

2. Tactical response to Dole proposal should be hypocrisy and pandering.

   Dole is a hypocrite and is pandering...Dole has consistently voted for billions in tax increases

Oppose by 36-57

   a. Dole has a lot better rating on hypocrisy than we do, argument is up hill

   b. We are seen as taxers, so it is the bad vs the hypocrite even if we succeed

   c. Hypocrite is a short term, limited gain, harassing response to Dole's tax cut NOT the key to winning the issue

3. Medicare, Medicaid, education environment cut defense must be used very, very gingerly since it suggests opposition to tax cuts.

Oppose only by 41-54

   a. We must use this argument only to attack the size of the Dole tax cut and support smaller tax cuts which are targeted.

   i. In this debate, a straight liberal opposition to tax cut <u>or even leading with the Medicare argument</u> would be a disaster since we have not established sufficient credibility for our own desire to cut taxes.

E. We can fight all election season on the BIG issue of targeted vs. across the board tax cut.

   1. The argument is played on their side of the field, how best to cut taxes, so gains come out of their hide. This argument permits us to address democratic goals- education etc...- with Republican tools- tax cuts- and leaves us in perfect positioning.

a. We must seek to make this the big issue over which we fight the election.

    i. In the argument of across the board vs. targeted tax cut we have a tax cut equivalent to the debate over welfare vs. targeted education and environment spending and investments

    ii. like 1993 spending vs investment distinction

2. It inoculates us against their best charge: that we are high taxers and gives us antibodies against 1993 tax hike hit

    a. If we are always debating how to cut taxes, it is hard to sell that we want to raise taxes

    b. but, if we use medicare etc to oppose a tax cut, then our propensity to raise taxes becomes highlighted

3. Conclusion

    a. use homeowner event next week to move first tax cut proposal

        1. no cap gains for home sales up to $500,000

    b. use Princeton speech on June 4 to move big idea of free community college through refundable tax credit

VI. FEAR OF CLINTON SECOND TERM LIBERALISM

A. A very potent issue and they are onto it

B. Will Clinton be too liberal in second term?

    concerned-56   not concerned-41

C. Will Dole be too conservative in first term?

    concerned-59 not concerned-36

D The answer: raise fears of Dole's first term to overshadow Clinton's second term

    Clinton too liberal v Dole-Gingrich pass medicare, guns, environment

(11)

fear Clinton 37   fear Dole 54

E. If you knew that Dole's agenda included: medicare cuts, assault weapon repeal, environmental cuts, eliminate Dept of Educ

less likely vote Dole 74 much less likely 52

a. best we have ever seen in hypothetical

F. WE MUST USE DOLE'S OVERT AGENDA TO OFFSET FEARS OF CLINTON'S HIDDEN AGENDA

MAY 24, 1996

May 29 and June 6, 12, and 20, 1996
Scandal Engulfs Clinton
(See chapters 13–15)

The advertisement featuring moving cartons piled on Dole's desk worked and blunted the Republican's rise.

Despite this good news, May and June were nervous months for the Clinton campaign as scandals took a larger and larger toll with each week. At the end of May, Arkansas governor Jim Guy Tucker and Clinton's former Whitewater partners Jim and Susan McDougal were convicted in a prosecution brought by Kenneth Starr. In June the FBI-file scandal erupted when it came out that Clinton aides had kept FBI files on prominent Republicans in the White House, presumably for political use. Clinton was on the ropes. His ratings slid almost continuously during June. This agenda and the ones that follow reflect our scampering to try to stop the bleeding and restore Clinton's ascendancy.

As the FBI scandal grew in intensity, it became clear that the public refused to believe the administration's explanation that the files were in the White House by mistake. Voter concerns over Whitewater increased and, as June unfolded, the president's lead dropped from seventeen to fourteen points.

The growth in Republican ratings was triggered, in part, by the fact that the GOP finally began its national advertising at the end of May. This agenda, and the ones to follow, constantly tests the ads the Republicans were running and suggests answers and rebuttals to blunt their thrust.

By the middle of 1996, Clinton's foreign policy performance had metamorphosed from a negative into a positive. In the June 6 agenda the consultants rate the various foreign achievements of the Clinton years and probe for Dole's foreign policy weaknesses. We suggested that Dole could be portrayed as out of touch with a changing world, a cold warrior in a global economy. On the positive side of the ledger, the agenda highlights the importance that voters attached to Clinton's ongoing determination to use force when necessary to contain Iraq and other terrorist nations.

The relentless pounding Clinton was taking in the press continued as the nation riveted its attention on the emerging FBI-file scandal. A review of the TV news networks for the week preceding June 20 showed that thirty-two minutes had been devoted to anti-Clinton coverage while only fourteen minutes focused on Clinton positives.

We worked on countering the firestorm against us by focusing on protection of black churches in the South which had been the object of racially inspired arson. The agenda for the June 20 meeting celebrates our ability to hold the polls steady despite the savaging Clinton was getting in the media.

AGENDA FOR MEETING WITH THE PRESIDENT--May 29, 1996

I. TRACKING -- DOLE RISE BLUNTED; WHITEWATER HURTS US

    A. Head to head down 1 (us down 2, him down 1) to 52-36

    B. Job rating up to new high of 62

    C. Favorability down 2 to 59

        a. personal negatives, not job performance

    D. Re-elect down 2 to 49

    E. Dole favorability down from 50-45 to 48-46

    F. Dole drops, we rise on all most adjectives

ADJECTIVE	Last week	This Week	Change
(Clinton v Dole)			
effective	46-42	50-40	+6
strong leader	47-43	51-43	+4
in touch with my values	50-40	51-39	+2
is on my side	50-35	52-34	+3
takes clear stands on issues	37-47	41-46	+5
doing a lot to bal the budg	44-34	45-34	+1
peacemaker	61-25	67-21	+10
new ideas	50-34	54-32	+6
does thing because they're right	47-37	49-36	+3
flip flops	61-23	61-24	+1
vision for future	52-33	53-33	+1
does right even when unpopular	44-50	48-48	+6

    Because our ad is a personal character hit, it reverses Dole's rise on all
    adjectives

ISSUES

economy	48-46	48-45	+1
crime	49-41	48-43	-1
foreign policy	50-41	53-35	+9
welfare	53-40	50-42	-5
taxes	41-45	47-40	+11
health care	57-35	58-32	+4
education	57-32	61-30	+6

We gain in all areas of issue comparisons because of basic trend set in motion by the ad; Dole gains only in welfare and crime, the two areas he hit specifically this week.

II. WHITEWATER

A. Have you heard of verdict convicting Tucker and McDougals

yes 67

1. Did you watch TV news tonight?

yes 31

B. Rating on Clinton wrongdoing in Whitewater

34% wrongdoing -- up from 31, but not at historic high of 37

MAY 29, 1996

C. Rating on Hillary wrongdoing

    44% wrongdoing — down from 45%, not at historic high of 51

D. Did Clinton tell truth in his testimony at Whitewater trial

    yes 39-34

    a. Huge undecided of 27%. Key swing in this controversy

E. Is Starr's inquiry a serious, fair inquiry or is it politically driven?

    serious fair — 38   political -- 52

    (down from 26-59 two weeks ago)

    a. this is the major impact, a move up for Starr's credibility and ability to act on other fronts

F. Does this verdict make you more/less likely to believe Clinton's involvement in Whitewater

    more: 24   less: 8   no effect: 65

G. ....Hillary's involvement

    more: 26   less: 9   no effect: 60

H. Does verdict make you more/less likely to vote for Clinton

    more: 25   less: 46

    Impact is important, especially since our historic high in vote share is 54 and 46% are less likely due to the verdict

I. Clinton was a witness for the defense and testified that he didn't pressure Hale to make a loan to Susan McDougal. Does the jury verdict question the credibility of the President or do you think the jury found the defendants guilty on the basis of other evidence without contradicting what the President said?

    verdict questions credibility: 21
    found them guilty on other evidence: 48

MAY 29, 1996

L. Paula Jones --

1. Did you hear about Clinton invoking the Soldiers and Sailors relief act to seek to delay a sexual harassment suit brought against him by Paula Jones.

yes: 45

2. Paula Jones is suing Clinton for sexual harassment which she claims took place in a motel room in Arkansas. Clinton is asking the court to delay the lawsuit until after he has left office as president. Should or should not delay lawsuit?

delay: 49   don't delay: 44

a. We do surprisingly well on this. I never would have imagined that we would break even on the issue of delay. It shows how much the voters want to protect the President

3. Lawyers for Paula Jones say that she is entitled to justice now and that delaying the suit might mean that she never gets a fair trial because witnesses forget, die or move away. Lawyers for Clinton say that the president is too busy to participate in a trial and that having to devote the time to it would interfere with his job as president. Should court delay until after Clinton leaves office?

delay: 48   don't delay: 48

4. President Clinton's lawyers recently said that as Commander in Chief of the armed forces, Clinton is protected from civil suits by the Soldiers and Sailors Relief Act which provides that members of the military may not be sued while they're on active duty. This law was passed in 1940 to protect servicemen on active duty. Do you agree that this law should apply to President Clinton...

agree: 44   disagree: 49

5. Republicans attack President Clinton for using this law to delay the suit saying that since Clinton ducked the draft and never wore a uniform, it is hypocritical for him now to claim protection as Commander in Chief. Does this make you more likely to vote for Clinton...

more likely vote Clinton: 34   less: 49

MAY 29, 1996

6. Clinton's lawyers say they are not relying on this statute but just used it as an example of how sometimes the President is protected from lawsuits under various statutes, of which this was one. Does this make you more likely to vote for Clinton...

more likely: 35   less: 49

7. Effect on head to head: no effect

Analysis: not a significant flap. A phony issue, not serious.

All this draft-war stuff is just way overrated by people who think in a certain mindset and cannot believe other people think differently

P9   May 26 96

If we run our ad and they run their ads for a week at a $2 million for us and $3 million for them levels, we will emerge with a decisive win in the exchange

2. Supporters of helping parochial schools say they educate millions and we should help them get a quality education, no constitutional violation if only physical facilities. Opponents say violates separation of church and state and unconstitutional to use tax money for helping parochial schools

> Doesn't violate/help schools build--44

> Violates church and state/no tax dollars--46

> Don't link it to parochial schools, it costs too many points.

C. Comp time

1. Bill pending require employers to offer employees choice of cash overtime payments or time off

> Support--68   Oppose--23

> We should support this and bill it as Family Leave part II

2. Labor unions oppose bill saying workers in minimum wage jobs would be scared to death to ask for money for overtime and this will permit bosses to intimidate them so that they ask for time off even though they need the money. Supporters of the bill say that many employees want the time off to be with their families as opposed to the cash and this bill permits them to ask for it.

> Support--66   Oppose--27

> Argument doesn't work, still support.

3. Some oppose this bill saying that employees can be fired before they use the compensatory time and boss will constantly pressure them to postpone using the time off saying that they can't be spared right now. But supporters of the bill say that it requires employers to pay cash whenever 48 hours of compensatory time has been accumulated by an employee.

> Support--64   Oppose-30

This is the fourth argument we have run against it and none work.

AGENDA FOR MEETING WITH PRESIDENT ON JUNE 6, 1996

I. TRACKING -- SLIGHT SLIP IN HEAD TO HEAD AND OTHER RATINGS
DOLE FAVORABLE DROPS SLIGHTLY

A. Head to head lead down to 15 from 16 -- from 52-36 to 52-37

1. Had been 19 pts three weeks ago, then to 17 two weeks ago, then to
16 last week, now to 15

B. Other internals drop slightly

1. Job approval at 58 (down from 62)

a. some cause for concern in drop, but other numbers are pretty
good

b. historic norm in this measurement is 59, so slight drop

2. Favorability down to 58 (from 59)

a. historic norm has been 58

3. Re-elect number steady at 49

a. historic norm is 49

F. Whitewater

1. President and First lady are at their all time high in perception of
wrongdoing

a. Hillary up to 50 wrongdoing

1. one above historic high

b. President up to 37% wrongdoing

1. at historic high

2. Jury verdict made voters less likely to back Clinton

less likely: 48%

JUNE 6, 1996

III   THE CHARACTER ISSUE

    A. Dole statement: Race is about character to be President. War record, hospital bed, Clinton ducked draft, womanizing, sex harassment, Whitewater convictions

        more likely Dole: 47 more likely Clinton: 46

    B. Clinton reply: Character issue is who will do the most to help America's children grow up with character to preserve our values. Family leave, tobacco ads, assault rifles, V chip, head start, school anti-drug, Dole opposed each. That's the real character issue

        more likely Dole: 37 more likely Clinton: 56

      —the character attack does little in the first place, and we can take it back by hitting them on public values vs. private character

    C. Republicans attack Clinton for stealing their ideas

        true v untrue: 44-51

        more v less likely to vote for Clinton: more: 49 less:36

      —may or may not be true, but its a compliment if it is!

    D. Republicans attack Clinton for talking conservative and governing liberal

        true vs. untrue: 45-38

        more vs. less likely to vote for Clinton: 45-45

      —blunted the impact

6.

JUNE 6, 1996

E. Republicans say Clinton promised balanced budget, tax cut, welfare reform but instead raised taxes, vetoed bal budg and welf ref. Clinton says Repubs went too far so he vetoed, Clinton broadened death penalty, 100,000 cops, teen mothers in school, ratings for TV, conservative steps

More likely Clinton: 59   less likely: 34

— values win out over flip-flop

F. Thus, the values agenda permits us to defeat -- in an exchange -- the two leading negatives that have dogged us: character and flip-flop

VIII   FOREIGN POLICY

A. What are important issues?

1. Voters think nuclear terrorism, drugs, and Iran-Iraq are important

2. Strong isolationist sentiments

JUNE 6, 1996

563

3. Trade decidedly less important than terrorism issues, but more important
than traditional country issues like Russia, China, Korea, etc

4. Moral values like human decency and freedom more important than
national interests and political values like spreading democracy and
freedom

Importance of Global Issues

	% Extremely Important
Keeping nuclear weapons out of the hands of terrorists	92
Stopping nuclear weapons from going to nations like Iran	84
Stopping the flow of drugs into the U.S.	84
Protecting values of human decency and freedom	74
Opening foreign markets to American products	66
Protecting American workers from foreign trade competition	60
Stopping Japan from taking advantage of us	60
Stopping Russia from returning to Communism	58
Coping with the threats posed by China	58
Stopping war from breaking out in Korea	56
Protecting America's interests abroad	55
Spreading democracy and liberty abroad	43
Stopping trade wars between us and our trading partners	41
Helping Eastern Europe become democratic and free	30

Summary of Importance of Global Situation

	Importance
Terror-- Iran-Iraq	84-92
Drugs	84
Isolationist responses	74-80
Values	74
Trade	60-66
Illegal Immigration	58
Making Mexico pay	59
Russia-China-Korea	56-58
Middle East	47
Spreading Democracy and Liberty	43
Eastern Europe	30
Mexico-economy	24

12.

B. What has Clinton Achieved

    1. Taking strong action to protect America, as in the Gulf against
       Iran works best

    2. Voters don't believe we did much on nuclear proliferation and opening
       foreign markets

    3. Voters believe we did good things in Bosnia, Mideast, Ireland. and
       Haiti, but they aren't very important to them

Credibility and Importance of Clinton Accomplishments

	Credibility	Importance	Index
Clinton took strong action to defend America by giving it the tools it needs and by using force when necessary, such as deterring Iraqi threats in the Persian Gulf.	53	68	172
Clinton reduced nuclear threat, making unprecedented progress in curbing proliferation of nuclear weapons in the former Soviet Union and North Korea.	35	69	139
Clinton advanced peace in Mid-East and Northern Ireland playing a crucial role in helping people in these regions reach their first-ever peace agreements.	42	54	138
Clinton stopped fighting in Bosnia, ending four years of terror, war. and ethnic cleansing.	39	57	135
Clinton restored Democracy to Haiti, effectively ending the violent and oppressive regime which encourages the dangerous flow of refugees to U.S. shores.	40	54	134
Clinton cracked open foreign markets, creating high wage for American workers and benefits for American business through agreements such as NAFTA.	36	60	132

13.

Also tested: Is Clinton losing the respect of world leaders: 43-52 he isn't

Only Strength really works as accomplishment

C. Comparison of Clinton and Dole

    1. Adjusting to change, Innovation, and Strength work best for us
       as comparisons

    2. Only making tough decisions is close

Clinton/Dole Comparison

	Who would do better job?	
	Clinton	Dole
Adjusting to new situations as they develop throughout the world	59	35
Innovation in foreign policy	57	37
Strength in foreign policy	56	39
Steadiness in foreign policy	51	38
Judgment in foreign policy	51	35
Making tough decisions about foreign policy	49	47

Big win for foreign policy effort that strength goes for us

14.

JUNE 6, 1996

D. Dole Negatives

    1. What works is: rigid-inflexible/ can't inspire youth/ doesn't get
       peacekeeping/ not modern world leader

<u>Dole Negatives</u>

	Credibility	Importance	Index
Dole will be too rigid and inflexible.	51	64	166
Dole won't be able to appeal to the young people of the world to follow America's example and our leadership.	46	66	158
Dole won't understand how American military must excel at peacemaking, not just at winning wars.	35	71	141
Dole won't be a modern world leader.	37	65	139
Dole won't be able to adjust enough to changes as they take place throughout the world.	34	59	127
Dole is too much of a legislator to be an effective world leader.	33	61	127
Dole, too often, will act unilaterally, with the United States going it alone and not taking account of world opinion and the views of our allies.	31	54	116
Dole won't be able to inspire other countries to follow our policies.	26	64	116
Dole lacks actual, hands on experience in foreign policy.	29	57	115
Dole will be too dominated by his right wing colleagues like Jesse Helms.	32	48	112

15.

	Credibility	Importance	Index
Dole won't understand global economy and won't be able to advance American interests in it.	23	66	112
Dole won't be able to tame the isolationists in his party.	32	44	108
Dole will bring a cold war mentality to international situations.	24	58	106
Dole too often will respond with only the military and not use other tools like economic sanctions and persuasion often enough.	21	63	105
Dole won't be able to adjust to the realities of the post cold war world.	28	46	102
Dole won't pay enough attention to trade issues.	19	59	97

16.

JUNE 6, 1996

AGENDA FOR MEETING WITH THE PRESIDENT, JUNE 12, 1996

I. TRACKING -- THE SLIDE CONTINUES -- WE STAY STEADY, DOLE RISES

    A. Clinton not down, Dole is up. Head to head from 52-37 to 53-39

        1. Since May 14, race has gone from 54-35 to 53-39

            a. We lost a point we had not really solidly gained
               (just one prior week at 54)

        B. But Dole has gained steadily from 35 to 39

    B. Clinton's positive ratings are not down, but are actually up slightly

        1. Job approval up from 58 to 60

        2. Favorability up from 58 to 61

        3. Re-elect number up from 49 to 51

        4. FBI has not hurt much at all

        5. Our ads, tuition, curfews, church burnings issues are all moving us up

    C. But Dole is rising. We are letting him get off the mat

        1. Dole favorability up from 48-48 to 51-45

        2. In a three way race, Perot drops from 14 to 11 as rumors that he won't run
           Mount. Dole picks up all these votes rising form 31 to 36 in a
           Three way (was 48-31-14; now 47-36-11)

    D. Adjectives reflect Dole's rise

	Last week	This Week	Change
Big Dole Gains:			
Clear stands on issues	43-41	39-46	minus 9
Doing a lot to balance the budget	44-34	43-41	minus 8
Doing right even if unpopular	49-34	46-39	minus 8
Flip flops	60-25	65-22	minus 8
Strong leader	50-41	47-45	minus 7

JUNE 12, 1996

569

III. FBI FILES -- PUBLIC DOESN'T BELIEVE US AT ALL

   A. Was there a White House Coverup of Watergate like activities or was it simply
      a mistake and the white house asked for the wrong files

                      Watergate-style coverup   52
                      Simple mistake   26

   B. With Argumentation --

      Even with argumentation, people are inclined to disbelieve what we say

      1. First we tried summary argument:

            If Army investigator who asked for files swears that he got them as part of
               routine security work and got wrong files

            Coverup -- 46
            Mistake-- 42

      2. Then we tried Republican attack --

            Among files was Bill Dale, Republicans charge white house trying to dig
            up dirt.Clinton supporters say was bureaucratic error

            Agree Republicans   50
            Agree Clinton supporters 38

      3. Last, we tried extensive explanation. It did no better than short one

         White house says error was because the needed to review files of who had access
         to the White House. But got an old list of those who had access under Bush. By
         the time the guy reviewing the files realized the mistake he had gotten up to G.
         Dale's file was, as a result, one of those examined. Repubs say convenient
         mistake and Clinton always stonewalls

            More likely Clinton: 43
            More likely Dole: 42

      4. Conclusion: the issue a loser for us no matter how we argue it. Best course is
         to distract attention with other issues

JUNE 12, 1996

V. DOLE'S MOVE TO THE CENTER-- CREDIBLE AND EFFECTIVE

A. Dole moderating conservative views and moving to center as he runs for Pres or has he always been a moderate

Always moderate: 49
moderating views to run: 39

People buy his move to the center

B. but it is a device to get votes--

Device to get votes 53
was always a moderate: 40

C.Liklihood of vote for Dole based on move to center

More: 41
Less: 50

Does him some good, performs above vote share

D.Answer: remind them of his record

Critics of Dole say he says he's in the center and moderate, but Medicare cuts, Medicaid cuts, education, environ--meant it when he cut it and should be held responsible now

More likely Dole: 25
Less likely Dole: 66

VII. CRIME VICTIMS AMENDMENT

A. Support constitutional amendment by 87-10 (69 strong support)

B. Argument: don't need amendment, can use statute vs. If give criminals const rights, must give same to victims

61-31 support amendment

C. If Dole for Amendment and Clinton opposed:

Agree Dole: 53
Agree Clinton: 37

VIII. CAPITAL GAINS TAX CUT

A. Support 64-24

B. Argument: will generate jobs, make up for lost revenue, cost no money

Vs

Not realistic, won't pay for itself, fuzzy thinking, lead to deficits
Little new investment or jobs, just make rich richer

Still support: 52-39

C. If Clinton backed capital gains cut

More likely: 51
Less likely: 35

JUNE 12, 1996

572

NEW IDEAS

    A. Expand family leave -- broad support

        1. Now only for 50 or more employees, expand to all businesses

            Support 64-31 (strong support 49)

        2. Expand to businesses with 25 or more

            Support 73-24

        3. Argument: supporters say basic right; opponents say huge hardship for
           Business with one or two employees

IX. CONVENTION

    A. Theme nights:

        1. Idea has been suggested of theme nights for the 7-9 PM period each night
        of the convention. This is pre-network and the idea is to attract
        viewers by the nature of the theme

        2. Ranking of likelihood of watching it theme is:

        (ranked by much more likely to watch)

            1. Improving the lives of children: 56
            2. Improving education: 55
            3. Fighting Crime: 49
            4. Reforming welfare: 49
            5. Helping families: 42
            6. Protecting the environment: 41
            7. Protecting medicare and medicaid: 40

B. Speakers

Who would make you more favorable to Clinton if they spoke at convention.

Walter Cronkite	32
John Kennedy Jr	30
Bill Gates	27
Oprah Winfrey	26

(We did not ask about Christopher Reeve but he tested very well
In previous poll)

Caroline Kennedy	23
Maya Angelou	22
Michael Douglas	22
Ray Charles	21
Sally Ride	21
Aretha Franklin	19
Whitney Houston	19
Tom Hanks	18
Magic Johnson	16
Michael Jordan	16
Garth Brooks	15
Reba McIntyre	15
Lily Tomlin	14
Gloria Estefan	13
Garrison Keilor	12
Travis Tritt	10
Michael Bolton	9
Tricia Yearwood	9

JUNE 12, 1996

AGENDA FOR MEETING WITH PRESIDENT ON JUNE 20, 1996

I. TRACKING POLL DATA -- AMAZINGLY, NO SLIPPAGE DESPITE POUNDING

A. Head to head steady at 52-38

    1. both dropped a point from 53-39 last week

    2. first week since May 7 without any slippage

    3. In our media buy 54-37 (17 pts)
       Out of media buy 51-39 (12 pts)

        a. out of buy includes areas where ads started on Tues

    4. Published polls:

        CNN (today) 19 pts
        Wash Post   20
        NY Times   19
        CNN-old   6 (now repudiated, in effect by new poll)

B. Job approval at historic high of 61

    1. except for one week at 62, this is our highest level

C. Favorability of 60-40

    1. two points below all time historic one week high of 62

D Hillary Favorability is at 47-46

    June 19: 47
    June 11: 48
    June 5: 49
    May 28:47
    May 22:54
    May 14 51

    1. After drop in May, no real change in past few weeks

E. Whitewater-FBI

    1. 65% had heard of FBI story but it made only 37% less likely to

vote for Clinton

2. 43% had heard of Freeh saying he was victimized by White House, but it made only 31% less likely to vote for Clinton

3.. Was President Clinton involved in wrongdoing? - 32 yes

    a. answers on this question have ranged between 31-37

    b. so 34 represents no increase

4. Was Hillary involved in wrongdoing? - 48 yes

    a. her range has been 44-50

    b. so this represents no increase for either

5. Did investigations show the Clintons are responsible for a lot of wrongdoing?   -Yes 39, No 35

    a. not cutting very much

6. Voters regard D'Amato inquiry as partisan

    a. Do you think that Congressional hearings by D'Amato are a serious fair inquiry into Whitewater or are they politically driven to try to discredit the President by keeping old stories in the news as the election approaches

        serious, fair: 23
        politically driven: 68

        Clinton base: 7-74
        Swing I   13-78
        Swing 2   28-52
        Dole base: 61-30

    b. For Starr:

        serious, fair: 31
        political driven: 59

        Clinton base: 6-86
        Swing 1:   13-78
        Swing 2:   30-58

Dole Base: 59-30

7. Who are the voters who are less likely to vote for Clinton because of

FBI files issue:

Clinton base: 14%
Swing I: 6%
Swing 2: 28%
Dole Base: 71%

a. Only people affected are those against us anyway

8. Net of exchange on Whitewater didn't hurt with swing I and base

does the Whitewater committee report challenging Hillary's
credibility and charging a pattern of coverups surrounding her role
make you more likely Clinton or Dole

total	34- Cl	44-D
Clinton base	77	3
Swing I	45	21
Swing II	11	54
Dole base	4	85

9. Lindsay as unindicted coconspirator could present a problem

1. makes 56% less likely to vote for Clinton, including 32% much
less likely

2. People break even on whether this is a political trick by Starr
(41%) or shows serious wrongdoing (43%)

F. But ... Dole favorability rose again to 52-43

1. Closing gap in favorability

2. Rise in recent weeks:

June 19: 52
June 11: 51
June 5: 48

May 28:48

3. But Dole rise in adjectives has basically stopped

    a. Dole Gained: 4   Clinton gained: 3 No change: 5

    b. Dole gained:

        Strong leader Dole gained 7
        Vision for future: gained 6
        effective   gained 5
        in touch with my values: 2

    c. No change:

        on my side
        takes clear stand on issues
        doing a lot to balance the budget
        offers new ideas
        does things because they are the right thing to do

    d. Clinton gained:

        Peacemaker Clinton gained 2
        Flip flops Clinton improved 1
        Doing right even if unpopular 1

4. On issues, Dole move also stopped

    a. Clinton gained on 3, Dole gained on 4, No change on 1

    b. Dole gained:

        education +11
        foreign policy +10
        crime +7
        economy +2

    c. no change on defense and military

    d. Clinton gained

        welfare +5
        taxes +2
        health care +1

V. COMP TIME -- URGE WE DO IT IN NASHVILLE

    A. Great issue--

        Makes people more likely to vote for you by 64-24

    B. Garrin did a phony poll for labor on the issue. He biased the question by
        phrasing it as if employers would decide which to give employees
        overtime pay or time off. Even so --

        people backed it in our version of his poll by 56-39

    C. But when told that the employee would have the option, not the employer

        people backed comp time by 76-16

    D. With argument:

        some say employers could pressure employees to take time not money
        (32)

                    vs

        employees would, as a practical matter have free choice (62)

    E. If comp time required to pay time if they lay off workers or he leaves

        more likely Cl 52 less likely 14 no difference 23

    F. If labor doesn't come off its opposition, it is just time for you to declare a bit
        of independence here. They don't own you. We're glad they're
        advertising. But most of it is congressionally aimed and we can do more
        for our members and insurgents by winning by a big margin than by

VI. CHURCHES

    A. This issue is holding us afloat and aloft almost by itself

    B. Our event yesterday was the fourth straight event in which we really didn't propose anything of substance

    C. Must revisit issue to make clear that we are going to protect churches, not just investigate arson

    D. Urge a definite plan, state-by-state, which we tell the media all about each day to defend and guard churches

        1. Use Dems like Hunt and Chiles to set up models. Then press Repubs to join in implementation

        2. Feed lots of stories of federal agents and local cops deploying to protect churches

    E. If arson continues, then we should use this to escalate our actions leading to the inevitable, which is use of the Guard in concert with Governors

        1. If Governors don't cooperate, and arson continues, we can isolate the Governor and lay a case which leads to federalization

            a. don't forget, many are racist Republicans -- like Fordice -- with no more national credibility than Wallace or Barnett or Faubus had.

JUNE 20, 1996

XII. WHAT WAS CLINTON'S FIRST TERM ALL ABOUT -- WHAT HE'LL DO IN
        SECOND TERM

   A. Best summary of what Clinton did in first term -- Opportunity and
       Responsibility:

      1. BEST THEME: He worked to provide citizens with opportunity and
            demanded from them personal responsibility -- 70% more likely

          a. Best specifics behind it:

                immunization
                V Chip/ TV Ratings   •
                Tobacco Ads
                Deadbeat Dads
                College scholarships
                Family leave

                (with specifics: 79% more likely

2. Other themes:

-- Maintained America's leadership at home and abroad - 64
-- Protected children - 61
-- Prepared us for 21st Century - 59
-- House was in disarray, straightened it out - 58
-- Transcended brain dead choices of past with new approaches -
56
-- Stopped rt. wing Repubs from ruining country - 55
-- Seemed like sunset for America, but Clinton stepped in and
prepared us for next century - 53

B. Agenda for Second Term -- in order of popularity

1. Deadbeat Dads: 55 much more; 86 total likely to vote for Clinton

2. Welfare Reform -- Work for Welfare: 50 much more; 87 total more

3. Education standards -- tests for promotion 50 much; 83 total more

4. Empowerment zones, create jobs for welfare to work: 46/77

5. Cut corp subsidies and use funds to shore up Medicare, Soc Sec 43/77

6. Tobacco ads 43/76

7. Balance the budget 42/77

8. Worker training 41/79

9. School construction 40/78

10. tuition tax aid 40/75

11. Go after teen gangs 40/75

12. Computers in school 38/76

13. Cut abortion by making inter-racial adoption easier 34/74

14. Extend family leave 33/71

C. Great Agenda

1. Is this enough?

    too much -- 18
    enough --   41

    not enough -- 28

2. Is it realistic

    can make progress -- 50

    not realistic -- 49

    (pretty good given cynicism)

XIII. WOODWARD BOOK WILL SAY YOU GOVERN BY POLLS

A. Here is list of unpopular actions you have taken despite polls --

    Flag burning amendment
    School prayer amendment
    Bal budg amendment
    anti busing amendment
    Bosnia
    Mexico bailout
    Nafta
    Affirmative Action
    Prop 187
    Haiti
    China MFN
    Wouldn't deny aid to unmarried mothers
    Wouldn't deny ed to illegals
    Preserved benefits for legal immigrants
    opposed term limits
    vetoed partial birth abortion
    opposed restricting US participation in peacekeeping under UN
    Product liability veto
    Securities reform veto

June 25, 1996
Setting the Second-Term Agenda
(See chapter 15)

By the end of June, Clinton had stopped his free fall and was poised for a July comeback. The June 25 meeting was largely focused on setting forth a second-term agenda for the campaign. Every incumbent likes to recite his achievements and Clinton did more than most. But he realized that he could best defeat Dole by portraying himself as the candidate of the future while Dole wallowed in the past.

In the June 25 agenda we rank the Clinton second-term issues in order of their popularity. The list and the rankings will sound familiar to anyone who has studied the issues that Clinton, in fact, focused on in his second term. Deadbeat dads, welfare reform, education standards, healthcare for the unemployed, shoring up Social Security, cutting teen smoking, and balancing the budget headed up the list.

As noted in the upper left corner of the first page, this agenda was the one actually used by the vice president during the meeting.

2.
Vice- President
Gore

AGENDA FOR MEETING WITH THE PRESIDENT, JUNE 25, 1996

I. TRACKING -- THE ANTI-GRAVITY CONTINUES

    A. Head to head -- no change from last week or week before -- 52-38

        1. Slide which began on May 22, seems to have ended on June 11

            a. since then, notable for its stability

        2. ~~In May   54-37~~
          ~~Out Only   49-42~~

    B. Internals solid

        1. Job approval at 60 (down 1)

        2. Favorability at 59 (down 1)

        3. Re-elect number at 52 (new record high--up 3)

    C. Dole favorability drops 2 to 50 after three week rise

        1. May 7   45
           May 14   48
           May 22   50
           May 28   48
           June 5   48
           June 11 51
           June 19 52
           June 24 50

IV. CLINTON'S FIRST TERM ALL ABOUT --WHAT HE'LL DO IN SECOND
TERM

A. Best summary of what Clinton did in first term -- Opportunity and
Responsibility:

1. BEST THEME: He worked to provide citizens with opportunity and
demanded from them personal responsibility -- 70% more likely

a. Best specifics behind it:

Immunization
V Chip/ TV Ratings
Tobacco Ads
Deadbeat Dads
College scholarships
Family leave

(with specifics: 79% more likely)

2. Other themes:

-- Maintained America's leadership at home and abroad - 64
-- Protected children - 61
-- Prepared us for 21st Century - 59
-- House was in disarray, straightened it out - 58
-- Transcended brain dead choices of past with new approaches -
56
-- Stopped rt. wing Republicans from ruining country - 55
-- Seemed like sunset for America, but Clinton stepped in and
prepared us for next century - 53

B. Agenda for Second Term -- in order of popularity

1. Deadbeat Dads: 55 much more; 86 total likely to vote for Clinton

a. They feel increasing child support a lot is realistic 71-29

2. Welfare Reform -- Work for Welfare: 50 much more; 87 total more

a. They feel making welfare recipients work is realistic 77-21

3. Education standards -- tests for promotion 50 much; 83 total more

13

JUNE 25, 1996

4. Empowerment zones, create jobs for welfare to work: 46/77

5. Health care benefits for 6 months after person loses job 44/71

6. Cut corp subsidies and use funds to shore up Medicare, Soc Sec 43/77

7. Tobacco ads 43/76

8. Balance the budget 42/77

9. Worker training 41/79

10. School construction 40/78

11. Tuition tax aid 40/75

      a. They feel expanding number of children in college is realistic - 60-37

12. Go after teen gangs 40/75

13. Computers in school 38/76

14. Cut abortion by making inter-racial adoption easier 34/74

15. Cutting teen pregnancy 34/63

      a. Is it realistic? 48-50

16. Extend family leave 33/71

C. Great Agenda

    1. Is this enough?

        too much --   18
        enough --   41
        not enough -- 28

    2. Is it realistic?

        can make progress -- 50
        not realistic -- 49

        (pretty good given cynicism)

E. Brady Bill Expansion

    1. Bar handgun purchases by anyone who has been convicted of a
       Misdemeanor offense under domestic violence law?

          75-21 (61 strong support)

    2. Argument:

       Domestic violence usually misdemeanor, but law now only bars felons
       No spousal abuser should have a gun--62

          Vs

       Misdemeanor is minor, long time ago, not grounds to deny a gun -- 30

    3. If amendment barred handguns to anyone with a 10 year old or less misdem
       conviction?

       68-25

    4. This issue comes from a bill by Lautenberg.

       --He says every year, there are 150,000 domestic violence crimes
       committed with a gun

    5. Great new issue! Recommend we go with it. Keeps gun control alive and
       takes it directly into violence against women

JUNE 25, 1996

H. School Construction

    1. Support major program to provide funds to localities for school
       construction and repair

        81-12 (includes 52 strong support)

    2. $8 billion for school construction and repair to build or renovate
       25% more schools a year for the next four years?

        76-18 (incl 51 strong)

    3. Support/oppose if aid conditioned on being open throughout day and
       into evening as community center for youth and elderly

        71-21 (incl 42 strong)

    4. Support/oppose if aid conditioned on raising educational standards and
       kids must pass state-formulated tests to promote?

        74-19 (incl 50 strong)

    5. Program great, money works, community center tack works.

       --may be a way into education standards issue with federal mandate, but we
       will poll to develop it more

          a. I was surprised, it's the first federal mandate on educ that works
           but we need more testing to check it out with arguments

JUNE 25, 1996

589

July 3, 1996
Recovering from the Damage of June
(See chapter 15)

After a difficult month wrestling with the FBI-file scandal, the consultants were relieved that Clinton still led Dole by fourteen points—a slippage of only three points during June. In a particularly interesting section of the July 3 agenda, the pollsters asked voters who felt that Clinton "did something illegal in Whitewater" but who voted for him anyway in the trial heat with Dole, why they were voting for Clinton. One-third said it was because they disliked Dole, one-third said it was because he was a good president promoting good values, and the remainder said it was because "he didn't do anything really bad."

The agenda is also notable for its analysis of "how to expand [Clinton's] lead." It suggests that the president needed to pass five bills: Kennedy-Kassenbaum (for portable healthcare coverage), an increase in the minimum wage, welfare reform, immigration reform, and comp time (allowing workers to take time off instead of extra pay for overtime). "If we do all these," the agenda notes, "I think we will see our head-to-head move over fifty-five percent and stay there."

In fact, Clinton did pass the first three of these bills and his head-to-head vote share moved as predicted.

The July 3 meeting was conducted after the terrorist attack on American troops in Saudi Arabia. The polling shows how most people did not blame the president and approved of Clinton's handling of the situation. The agenda refers to polling data collected the previous Friday (July 3, 1996, was a Wednesday) when the public was much more critical of Clinton on the bombing. This comparison is interesting in that it shows how we used polling to monitor the public's reaction to crises and to suggest ways of addressing them more effectively.

Analysis: Still losing on the scandals, but holding race due to issues

1. More important to have President who does good than good character

    a. Is doing right things for people   68
       Highest moral character   27

    b. Cares about people like you   62
       Highest moral character   34

    c. Shares your values   59
       Highest moral character   35

    d. Once again: public values beats private character

2. Did President Clinton do something illegal in Whitewater
    Yes: 43
    No   37

    Of those who say yes, but vote Clinton anyway, Why--

        33   Dislike Dole, better than Dole
        27% good Pres, values, parent
        27   He didn't do anything really bad

    Reason we are holding up:

        a strategy of contrast with Dole

        b. Positive values message

        c rapid response team defensing scandals

3. Did Hillary do something illegal in Whitewater

    Yes: 52
    No: 28

4. Did President Clinton do something illegal in FBI

    Yes: 36
    No: 41

5. After argument, they oppose security privatization

    a. Initially they break even 41-45; but reject idea after argument:

        --only FBI has authority to do thorough review--55
        --privatize would remove abuse of power--31

        (5)

IV. HOW TO EXPAND LEAD

    I believe we must move head to head up over 55% on a sustained and stable basis. The only way to do this is legislative accomplishment. So lets keep our eye on the ball. We need to work on passing and signing:

> --Kennedy Kassenbaum
> --Minimum Wage
> --Welfare Reform
> -- Immigration bill
> --Comp time

    IF we do at least these, I think we will see our head to head move over 55% and stay there

V. SAUDI BOMBING -- recovered from Friday and looking great

    A. Approve Clinton handling 73-20   Big gain from 63-20 on Friday

    B. Should keep troops in Saudi 58-35

        1. Argument that they contain Iraq works 61-33

        2. Argument that don't buckle to terrorists works 65-29

    C. Security was adequate 52-40

        1. But, should have known to expect bigger bomb and had
           stronger security in place

           55-36

        2. But its not Clinton's fault 18-76

July 18, 1996
Focus on Welfare Reform
(See chapter 15)

With welfare reform legislation headed toward passage, the question of whether or not to sign the bill increasingly dominated White House discussions. At the July 18 meeting the consultants presented fifteen possible events which could take place over the summer and measured the effect each would have on the president's lead over Dole.

The central finding of the exercise was to advise the president that "welfare veto would be a disaster"—tied only with Powell running as Dole's vice president in its impact on Clinton's chances. The poll predicts that a veto of welfare reform legislation would "cost us eight points."

I. TRACKING -- WE CONTINUE TO WIN JULY ... LEAD UP 1 TO 16 PTS

    A. Lead has grown to 52-36 (up from 52-37 last week)

        1. In three way race lead is also 16 (48-32-15)

    B.Clinton Ratings not changed

        1. Job Rating at 60 (down 1)

        2. Favorabililty steady at 59

        3. Re-elect at 51% (up 2)

    C. Dole favorability down to 49-47 (from 50-46)

        1 Continued decline:

            July 2 -- 53%
            July 8 -- 50%
            July 17- 49%

        2. Negatives are working

        3. Dole's favorability is much less intense than ours'

            a. In three way:

                Dole gets 60% of his favorables
                Clinton gets 75% of his favorables

            b. In a two way

                Dole gets 67% of his favorables
                Clinton gets 81% of his favorables

        4. Dole's unfavorability has same intensity as our unfavorabililty

                Dole loses 95% of his unfavorable in a 2 way
                Clinton loses 91% of his unfavorable in a 2 way

1

II. PREDICTORS -- WHAT COULD ADD TO LEAD OR DETRACT FROM IT

Event	Margin
Rep convention attacks Clntn character, Whitewater	+31
Gingrich and Buchanan speak at Convention	+26
No further Whitewater indictments	+25
Agree on Balanced Budget with tax cut	+24
Kennedy Kassenbaum passes	+21
Perot runs	+17
Minimum wage passes	+17
CURRENT HEAD TO HEAD	+16
Welfare reform passes	+15
Dole VP is Governor of Mich or Ohio	+12
Whitman runs as VP	+ 9
Whitewater indictments of high ranking official	+ 6
Dole economic plan with large tax cut	+ 2
Clinton vetoes welfare reform	- 3
Powell as VP	- 3
Moderate Republican convention, Family values, tax cut	- 6

Key points:

1. Welfare veto would be a disaster

2. Republicans can gain heavily by a good convention: positive, family, tax cut

3. Passage of budget deal, Kennedy Kassenbaum can expand lead

4. If Republican Convention can be made negative, attacking in media's eye, it will help us

VIII. GUN CONTROL

A. Extension of Ban on handguns to domestic violence misdemeanors -- wildly popular

1. People back extension of Brady bill ban on gun ownership to "people convicted of Misdemeanor offenses under the domestic violence law."

77-19 (66% strong)

2. Still support after argument that "just another step down the slippery slope of gun control that won't end until all guns face tight controls"

Ban will save lives	63
Slippery slope of gun control	32

12

B. Assault Rifle flip flop by Dole -- unpopular

    1. Statement by Dole "time to put repeal of ban behind us, no longer an important legislative priority for me"

        More likely: 30
        Less likely; 61

        Head to head: +19

    2. Statement by Clinton: House voted for repeal of ban. Doesn't matter if priority, Opponent won't say if veto. I would veto repeal

        More likely Clinton: 59
        More likely Dole: 35

C. Instant background checks unpopular compared to waiting period

    1. Dole quote: "I want instant background checks, no felony or mental illness buy guns"

        More likely: 52-42

    2. Clinton quote: "even people without felony records or mental illness should should not be allowed to buy handguns without 5 day wait imposed by Brady Bill. Heat of passion."

        More likely: 68-28

    3. Head to head: 57-38

D. Trigger lock -- good public backing

    1. Approve of require gun purchasers to buy trigger lock to stop child firing

    2. If Clinton got voluntary agreement from gun manufacturers to send trigger locks to all gun stores for distribution:

        More likely Clinton: 68-24

    3. If Clinton suggested a law making it a crime to store a gun in such a way that a child was injured

        More likely: 68-33

    4. If Clinton issued executive order requiring fedl employees to store firearms safely and use trigger locks

        More likely: 63-27

July 24, 1996
Preparing for the Conventions
(See chapters 16 and 17)

Barely had Clinton regained his large lead over Dole after the scandals of June had tightened the race, when the campaign had to brace for the Republican convention in early August. Since World War II, the average presidential candidate has gained ten points against his opponent as a result of his party's convention. If Dole gained ten points after the Republican convention and Clinton regained the ten points at our convention, the gains would cancel each other out. But if the GOP gain exceeded ten points or our gain fell short of the mark, the net change could spell trouble for the president's reelection. Once the two conventions had been held, history suggested that the race would pretty much stay the same. Historically, the average gain or loss by a presidential candidate between Labor Day and election day was only five points. So the results on Labor Day would likely be the same as the outcome of the election.

Anxiously, the consultants polled the likely results of the GOP convention. As the agenda for July 24 indicates, if the Republicans succeeded in projecting a moderate image and avoided a harshly negative convention, they would likely achieve the full ten-point gain. To counter this gain, the polling suggested that the best rebuttal would be to emphasize the linkage of Dole and Gingrich and to suggest that if one were president and the other controlled Congress that they would "pass bad bills and sign them." Specifically, the polling ratified the slogan that with Republicans in charge of both branches of government "there would be nobody there to stop them."

The consultants prepared an ad which they presented at the July 24 meeting to emphasize this theme. While a camera panned around an empty Oval Office, showing an empty chair behind the president's desk, an announcer warned of GOP plans to make drastic cuts in Medicare, Medicaid, education, and environmental spending. At the end of the ad the announcer says, menacingly, "If Gingrich runs Congress and Dole becomes president, there will be nobody there to stop them." The ad, which the president approved at the meeting and which ran as soon as the GOP convention ended, succeeded in wiping out about half of the gains the Republicans harvested at their convention.

Central to our plans for the Democratic convention were nonpolitical speakers, particularly during the first night. The poll and agenda detail some of the names under consideration—including Magic Johnson. Eventually we settled on Jim and Sarah Brady and Christopher Reeve.

The week before July 24 had been blackened by the crash of a TWA flight. Some suspected terrorism might be the cause. The agenda explores public attitudes on a host of air-safety measures and reflects their broad popularity. In the fall of 1996, Vice President Gore announced the implementation of many of these proposals.

AGENDA FOR JULY 24, 1996

I. TRACKING -- GOOD MOVEMENT UP. HEAD TO HEAD LEAD UP TO 18

    A. Head to head: 53-35 (up from 52-36 last week)

        1. We have now recouped all but 1 pt from the May slide from 19 ahead
           to 14 ahead.

        2. Three way is 47-31-13 -- 16 pts -- same as last week

        3. Gender gap: lead is +4 among men and +31 among women

           a. we are topped out among women; need to show toughness
              to get men over terrorism and Saudis

        4. Among Swing II we are 37 Dole -- 34 Clinton

    B. Ratings

        1. Clinton job approval up to 61 (from 60)

        2. Favorability holds at 59

        3. Re-elect number at 49, down from 51

        4 All three of these ratings have ebbed and flowed within 4 points for
           months

    C. Dole favorability at 47-48

        drop from:

        July 2: 53-45
        July 8: 50-46
        July 17: 49-47
        July 23: 47-48

    D. Hillary at 47-46

    E. Gore at 55-31

    F. Generic Congress ballot at 44-40

JULY 24, 1996

III.   CLINTON AND TWA/SAUDI ATTACKS

A. Is Clinton doing "all he can to investigate" TWA crash "and punish those responsible"

Doing all he can: 67
Could do more: 23

1. Approve of FAA handling of airport security, but just barely

53-42

2. good ratings because it just happened last week

B. But, on Saudis, public patience wears thin:

Is Clinton doing all he can to investigate Saudi bombing
and punish those responsible or is there more he can do

Doing all he can: 54
Could do more: 32

1. as event ages, it takes a heavier toll on Clinton.

C. But an attack on Clinton -- Works for Dole

Out of control. Two airline disasters, one linked to terrorism. FAA asleep at switch. Terror in Saudi Arabia. Bosnia could blow up. Mid east peace process faltering

More likely Dole: 44
More likely Clinton: 36

Head to head: 50-39

D. We tested two alternate defenses to this attack: Peacemaker or Toughness (toughness worked better)

7

1. Peacemaker:

Clinton is peacemaker. Brought together Arabs and Israelis. Ireland.
Bosnia cease fire. Use strength to bring about peace.

>More likely Clinton: 51
>More likely Dole: 39

>Head to head: 50-39 (no recovery of lost territory)

2. Toughness:

Clinton tough. Standup for American interests. Against foreign
companies doing business in Cuba. Sanctions against Iran. Anti-
terrorist legislation. Held up by Republicans. Prosecuted World
Trade Center bombers

>More likely Clinton: 54
>More likely Dole: 32

>Head to head 53-37 (recoups the entire lost ground)

E. Voters back tough measures and believe in their effectiveness:

	Sup/Opp	Effect/Ineffect
1. Modern X-ray machines at airport	90-7	50-12
2. More security personnel at airports	92-6	60-13
3. Picture ID for travelers	92-6	70-26
4. Wiretap on pay and hotel phones	70-26	49-24
5. Tagents	92-6	65-14
6. INS investigate and deport aliens suspected of terrorism	90-8	60-17
7. US Military domestic intervention to aid in anti-terrorism	82-16	57-18

(these effectiveness numbers are very, very high. They are on a five
point scale where voters normally use a "3" to describe their
ambivalence)

8

F. Dole's opposition to these measures hurts Dole

Clinton proposed expanding military role, wiretaps, tagents, but
Republicans including Dole killed these bills last year

More likely Clinton: 67
More likely Dole: 25

G. Anti-Militia Plan

1. Highlights successful Arizona arrests

2. Includes:

a. Advance notification of fedl and local authorities before
training or maneuvers: 77-19

b. Inventory of weapons 66-32

c. Toughen penalties against intimidation of govt officials 80-18

d. More FBI power to investigate militia 60-34

e. Government list of organizations the encourage terror 75-18

H. Recommended Plan:

1. Air Safety event

a. X rays
b. increased personnel

2. Anti Terror speech

a. wiretaps
b. tagents
c. Posse Comitatus
d. More INS money

3. Push for terrorist bill passage by recess at Mubarak visit

4. Push for militia package

9

V.   COUNTERING DOLE'S CONVENTION AND POST CONVENTION SURGE

  A. Does Powell, Bush, and Ford speaking about character, wisdom and
     determination of Dole make you:

          More likely Dole: 38
          Less likely Dole: 41

          Head to head: 50-40

11

B. At convention, Dole will share his vision of America's future and the need
   for America to renew its economy through tax cuts to stimulate growth

> More likely Dole: 49
> Less likely Dole: 41
>
> Head to head: 47-41

C. Conclusion: Dole can do himself a lot of good at his convention and probably
      will

   1. Evidence indicates that he is avoiding extremism and avoiding
      negatives

   2. We must anticipate a Dole bounce from the convention. It is quite
      likely

D. We tested rebuttals to Dole if he surges at his convention, as we expect

Rebuttal	Head to head	fav Dole	fav Clinton
1. Gingrich-Dole; budget, social			
Gingrich-Dole team, pass bad bills, sign them, budget cuts social legislation too: abortion, sex ed, assault weapons	58-33	34-58	67-37
2. Ging-Dole, budget			
Gingrich-Dole team, pass bad cuts: Medicare medicaid, ed, environ. If Dole wins nobody there to stop them	57-34	26-66	60-37
3 Clinton accomplishments			
Clinton accomplishments. Economy, ten million jobs, increase min wage. Kennedy Kassenbaum, welfare reform.	56-36	37-62	63-30
4. Dole historical opposition to programs			

12

Dole Record: anti establishing Medicare, anti-establishing student loans, anti setting up head start anti-min wage	56-36	26-67	60-30

5. Dole wrong on values issues

Dole's values wrong. tobacco, family leave, child immune, Brady bill, assault rifles, Medicare	55-36	24-68	59-32

6. Dole is negative

Dole too negative, character attacks, mean spirited	54-36	24-67	56-34

7. Dole out of date

Dole no 21st cent leader, age, younger, innovative, values on Medicare, medicaid ed, environ	53-38	26-60	52-39

8. Dole no experience/vision

Dole no vision. 35 yrs but no exper in administering, for pol, economy, outdated	53-39	29-59	53-37

9. Dole backs right wing

Dole backs right wing. const ban on abortion, assault rifles ban, Pat Robertson agenda, backs Reed and Christ Coalition	52-39	36-58	53-39

10. Powell and Dole disagree

Powell won't run with Dole, disagree on abortion, guns, Medicare. just loyal republican	51-40	29-58	50-37

13

August 1, 1996
The Impact of Signing Welfare Reform
(See chapter 17)

The days leading up to the August 1 strategy meeting were contentious ones at the White House, with the consultants supporting and the White House staff opposing the welfare reform legislation just passed by Congress. The president announced that he would sign the bill right before the August 1 meeting. His job approval rose to an all-time high of sixty-three percent—and largely remained there for the next two years. The signing seemed to pivot a national shift toward optimism as the percentage saying America was on the right track rose to the highest of Clinton's presidency.

The Olympic bombing injected a sour note into the week and the agenda probes the possible anti-terrorist legislation Clinton could push. It particularly highlights the damage to the Republicans from their NRA-induced resistance to legislation which would identify who bought and who sold explosives.

AGENDA FOR MEETING ON AUGUST 1, 1996

I. TRACKING -- LEAD HAD DROPPED TO 17, BUT AFTER LAST NIGHT'S INTERVIEWS RETURNED TO 18 (53-35)

    A. Head to head

        1. For Monday and Tuesday nights, lead was 52-35.

        2. Last night after welfare signing, it jumped to 54-35 (19 points)

        3. Combined head to head -- 53-35

            a. Welfare bill signing made voters more likely to vote for Clinton by 70-19

            b. Perhaps a bit of rally around the Chief was behind last week's gain to 18. This might be a normal correction.

            c. But all around positive news gives us good potential for growth

            d. Moment of uncertainty:
               --Atlanta, Saudi, TWA, legislative issues
               -- with accomplishments, investigative and legislative, vote should move up

    B. Job Rating is at new all time high of 63-36

        1. Strongly disapprove is down to all time low of 20%.

        2. Favorability at 61-38
            a. at all time high -- highest since June 11

        3. Re-elect is at 51 -- at its all time high

        4. Right track: wrong track is at 42-right and 49-wrong
            a. highest since Gulf War
            b. highest in your administration
            c. Olympics beat terrorism

        5. Dole Favorability holds at 47-48 (same as last week)
            a. continues to be held down below 50

        6. Hillary Favorability at 51-41

1

II. TERRORISM -- SOLUTIONS HAVE TO STAY AHEAD OF THE PROBLEMS

    A. Heard of/Impact of Stories:

        1. Bomb in Atlanta: 99%

            a. More likely Clinton v Dole: 34-20

            no political impact

        2. Investigators saying TWA was likely destroyed by bomb 97%

            a. More likely Clinton v Dole: 32-24

            no political impact

        3. Clinton's plan for airport security 94%

            a. More likely Clinton v Dole: 54-15

            answers work

        4. Clinton meeting with TWA families 84%

            a. More likely Clinton v Dole: 50-16

        5. Clinton's anti terrorist bill   67%

            a. More likely Clinton: 54-17

  B. Trust Clinton more than Dole by 48-33

  C. Approve of Clinton on terrorism 72-26

        1. Clinton is acting like a strong leader in response to terror 61-30

        2. Clinton is moving swiftly to counter terror vs. dragging feet 54-30

        3. But our efforts are seen as scattered

            a. Coordinated plan: 35 Scattered: 48

D. We are winning the personal battle for strength; but need to be seen as
        having more solutions and more coordination among solutions

    1. If we ever let problems get ahead of solutions, we risk Israeli
       precedent

    2. People now are not worried about their safety 23-74 (and 33-52 after
       argumentation designed to scare) but that could switch in a hurry
       unless we are out there with solutions--
       aggressively and constantly

E. Approve of three part formulation on terrorism:

    --international cooperation, sanctions on Iran and Iraq
    --expand FBI powers and death penalty
    --airport security

    75-16

    1. But, demand more measures beyond these by 62-33

F. Then, approve of three new measures:

    --wiretap
    --taggants
    --Defense Dept involvement

    84-14

    1. Still some appetite for even more: 48-45

G. If learned Clinton backed terror package and Dole, Gingrich opposed them:

    More likely Clinton: 63
    More likely Dole   27

    1. Huge negatives against Republican opposition on taggants. Big
      error.

    2. Suggest we get a wiretap bill passed now and keep pressing for
      taggants

7

a. Don't get political and anti-NRA, let the public do that, instead just stay on high road about how important taggants are

b. Constantly press for taggants

H. Possible new measures against terror:

1. Using undercover agents to infiltrate suspected terrorist organizations

   93-6   Effective: 60-11

2. Economic sanctions on countries that harbor terrorists or assist terrorists even if they didn't explicitly sponsor terrorist act

   82-16 Effective: 50-25

3. Military action against suspected terrorist installations in nations that harbor terrorists or assist terrorists even if they didn't explicitly sponsor a terrorist act

   77-21 Effective: 45-23

4. Use military domestically and abroad to pursue terrorists

   77-19   Effective: 39%

I. Possible new measures against domestic militia:

1. Context: We didn't lose lives in Arizona, or in Washington State, or due to the Georgia militia. We stopped them just in time. Now, enact bold anti militia agenda so we don't have to play this kind of roulette with the lives of our people.

   a. Advance notification of fedl and local authorities before training or maneuvers: 77-19

   b. Inventory of weapons: 66-32

   c. Toughen penalties against intimidation of govt officials 80-18

   d. More FBI power to investigate militia 60-34

   e. Govt list of organizations that encourage terror 75-18

8

2. This is the fifth agenda in which these ideas have been proposed. Please get Justice to get them moving

J. Attack on Clinton doesn't work as well as last week on terror:

1. "With Clinton in charge, things are out of control. Airline disasters, bad FAA, Saudi bombing, Bosnia could explode. Terror. Iran Syria (not updated to include Atlanta to provide comparability)

More likely Dole: 46   (last week was: Dole: 55
More likely Clinton: 47   Clinton: 45)

Head to head: 51-40   (had been 50-39)

a. Still is an anti-terror argument for Dole to aim at Clinton weakness

b. Must move debate to anti-terror bill so as to avoid allowing Dole to exploit our weakness on this

1. Recommend signing limited anti terror bill now; but as we do, continuing to push for perfect package when Congress returns

2. As long as there is an unfinished agenda looming, we have insurance against more attacks

V. THE BIG CHOICE: POST REPUBLICAN CONVENTION

    A. Republican Convention is likely to produce bounce:

        1. When told that convention would feature Powell, Bush, Ford and Dole would offer new tax cuts, vision of America, stimulate economy

            head to head   Clinton 49 Dole 40

    B. If Republican convention causes bounce, we have three alternate ways of fighting it:

        1. Attack Dole's plan (gets Cl vote to 59)

        2. Attack Dole-Gingrich link and program (nobody there to stop them) (gets Cl vote to 61)

        3. Stress Clinton Accomplishments: jobs, welfare, Ken Kassen, Min wage (gets Cl vote to 56)

    C. We need to poll this right after their convention to make decision.

    D. As things now stand, alternative 2 -- stop them has an edge

11

AUGUST 1, 1996

VI. SCHEDULE

August 1 Economic Data and Warning about Rocking the Boat

August 2: No Sweat Labels

August 3: Sign Pesticide or Clean Water Bill

August 5: Foreign Policy Speech

August 6: Sign A bill (Welfare, Ken-Kassen, Min Wage)

August 7: Girl Sports in High School (at Olympic ceremony)

August 8: Parent Responsibility for Crimes of their Children

August 9: Sign A bill

  (if we get min wage, welfare, and KK, we might need another bill day)

August 12: Yellowstone Park

August 15: Saudi Base Briefing and Action (right before Dole's speech. Makes
    evening news right before he speaks)

August 16: Utah Park Red Rocks

August 21. Meagan's Law; announcement of national network to track abusers

AUGUST 1, 1996

6 1 4

IX. STUMP SPEECH

We tested three paragraphs that you have been using ---

Summary:

    1. "election is about how we raise our children"   36 strng 70 total

    2. "opportunity, responsibility, community"   32 strng 70 total

    3. "We've got to do this together....magic is   29 strng 65 total
       helping each other do better"

      ---children and opptunty-resp-comm work best

      ---don't let unity eat up too much of the speech; it doesn't
         work as well

Full texts:

    1. Children:

      -help families raise children
      -Repub Congress not cooperated
      -tobacco ads
      -immunizations
      -environment laws
      -college tax credit
      -character and values of children

    2. Opptny Responsbty Communty

      -enduring values in new age
      -Offer opportunity, demand responsibility
      -mutual obligation come together as community
      -help families help themselves
      -govt can only help; Americans must do their part
      -meet responsibilities, take advantage of
         opportunities

    3. Unity

      -We've got to do this together
      -helping each other do better makes us magic
      -don't define ourselves by resentments or looking down on
         somebody who looks different
      -this makes us special

AUGUST 1, 1996

August 20, 1996
Recovering from the Republican Convention
(See chapter 17)

As predicted, the Republican convention, held in San Diego during the second week in August, triggered a ten-point gain for the GOP, knocking Clinton's margin over Dole to seven points from its pre-convention level of seventeen.

The August 20 agenda reflects the Clinton campaign on the comeback trail. With the president scheduled to sign legislation reforming welfare and raising the minimum wage, we expected to regain many of the lost points even before the Democratic convention was held in Chicago the next week.

The agenda analyzes the impact of the Republican convention and indicates that the GOP "achieved most of its objectives."

The most interesting part of the agenda is a page-long listing of issues and initiatives to be included in the president's speech at the convention. In the polling that ranked these issues, voters were asked if Clinton's advocacy made them more likely to back him at the polls. Based on this ranking, we formulated the president's speech which reflected many of his major second-term initiatives.

Hillary's convention speech, too, was shaped by a similar polling process. Those results are also reflected in the agenda.

AGENDA FOR MEETING ON AUGUST 20, 1996

I. TRACKING -- POST CONVENTION SLIPPAGE TO 11 PT LEAD IN 3 WAY

    A. 3 way head to head: 43-32-14

        1. Pre-convention was 48-31-12

            a. Perot absorbed all but one point of Dole rise

            b. Dole had shrunken 3 way to 43-35-11 on Friday poll, but
Perot's rise over the weekend took 3 pts away from him
to open up current result

    B. 2 way race in post convention is at 47-39 (8 pts, up from 7 on Friday)

    C. Dole's favorability has risen dramatically -- from 47 to 59

        1. now is 59-38 (was 47-46 before convention)

        2. Clinton favorability is 60 -- only 1 pt higher

        3. Kemp favorability at 56 (Gore at 58)

        4. Hillary at 50 (Eliz Dole at 60)

    D. Clinton ratings virtually unchanged -- negatives had little impact

        1. Job rating at 59 (from 62 pre convention)

        2. Favorable at 60 (from 58 pre convention)

        3. Re-elect at 48 (from 50 pre convention)

    E. Perot favorability up to 37 from 33

        1. each extra point puts that many Dole voters into plan

        2. Perot has now become Dole's opponent in the primaries

1

AUGUST 20, 1996

617

II. SUMMARY OF IMPACT OF REPUB/PEROT CONVENTIONS

A. Republicans achieved most of their objectives

1. Kemp is seen favorably 57-25

2. Convention was viewed favorably: 51-38

3. Convention was seen as moderate: 41 conservative: 41

(about the same as electorate's self-description)

4. Convention was seen as Reaching out to independents vs. partisan

reached for independents: 52
partisan   31

5. Convention was seen as positive: 42 negative: 40

6. Dole emerged as having a clear vision for future 49-38

7. Dole's favorability rose from 47 to 59

8. Voters switched from a right track +2 to a wrong track -7 on state of
the nation

9. Dole's economic plan rose from 54% approval to 60% approval

10. But, people did not feel Dole explained how pay for tax cuts by 12-51

5

B. Demographics of Republican Voter Gain:

    1. Gender:

        male: -8
        women -12

    2. Age

    3. Key Clinton losses/Dole gains

Women, 50 and over	-24
Weak Republicans	-22
Independents	-13
Married	-9
Elderly, total	-8

C. Impact of Bob Dole Speech

    1. 48% heard it

        a. more likely to vote for Dole: 26-14

        b. Backward looking 34
          Forward looking   37

        c. Painted a clear vision of his future actions: 49-37

    2. Creative nostalgia

        a. Appealed to Dole base and Swing II successfully

        b. Good job on taxes, less govt, immigration, crime, trade

        c. character based on war record

        d. school choice

        e. America paralyzed by problems

6

3. Flaw:

    a. few specific issues

    b. Little in the way of positive ideas -- other than plan -- to help regular people

D. But, Perot emerges as Dole's chief competitor for an expanded vote share

    1. Perot is the candidate who now faces Dole in the primaries

    2. Perot embraces the old Dole message vs. the new Dole message

    3. We need to be sure Perot is in all debates (contrary to Fowler statement)

    4. 17% heard Perot's speech

E. And, Clinton ratings are largely unaffected. Negatives didn't work

F. Key defect of their convention was that it was about them, not about the people

    1. Each speech was about redefining Dole and the Party; not about what relevance each had to the people

    2. Tax cut was only proposal. And its a slender reed for the future

III. DOLE TAX CUT PLAN AND HOW TO ANSWER IT

A. Tax issue really hasn't helped Dole yet:

    1. Who Trust on Taxes Clinton vs. Dole

	Aug 11	Aug 19
Clinton	46	44
Dole	46	45

    2. Of those (46%) who have heard of Dole plan more likely to vote for Clinton by 40-32 (about the same as our two way margin)

B. But the tax plan could still be a big win for Dole

7

1. Support for his plan has grown during the convention

    Support for Dole Tax and Economic Program
    (after being read its specifics in positive terms)

	Aug 11	Aug 19
Support	54	60
Oppose	39	34

    More favorable Dole: 54
    Less favorable Dole: 37

    Clinton: 48
    Dole: 43

2. Support would grow more if he linked fight over his plan to
    Clinton promises, middle class squeeze, and no no-tax pledge
    by Cl

    a. Dole attack on Clinton on broken promises and tax increases
       works well.

       after tax and broken promises attack:

            more likely Clinton   40
            more likely Dole: 51

            Clinton: 48
            Dole: 44

    b. We tested: Clinton says Dole plan balloons deficit, jeopardizes
                Med, med, ed, environ -- 48
                      vs
                Dole says: Cl broke tax promise, won't pledge no
                new taxes -- 43

    c. We tested: Clinton says he cut deficit, will cut taxes -- 45
                      vs
                Dole says economy not good. middle class squeeze
                Clinton will raise taxes -- 48

8

C. Strategy for winning tax/plan/economy issue

    1. Attack Dole plan

        a. by 56-23 voters agree it will raise the deficit

            --and we can't take the risk :48-39

        b. D'Amato says cuts are inevitable

            1. less likely to vote Dole 37-51

            2. horse race: 53-40

        c. Outside experts -- Time, Bus Week, Concord Coalition

            1. more likely Clinton: 55-34

            2. horse race: 53-40

    2. Do plan vs plan

        a. People prefer Clinton plan by 56-38

            1. head to head: 55-39

    3. Defend Clinton's tax record

        a. by 68-31 voters find believable that Clinton actually
           cut taxes for working people and has no intention of
           raising taxes despite no pledge

            1. and this statement makes people more likely Clinton by
               55-41

            2. It is not necessary to take no new tax pledge as long as
               rebuttal has four elements:

                a. EITC
                b. targeted tax cuts
                c. no intention of raising taxes
                d. irresponsible to make blanket pledge
                    example: extra $5 tax for air safety (80-15)

9

4. But key to safety is to attack Dole's tax record

    a. in effect says: you won't keep your no tax pledge

    b. When told of Dole tax increases: 54-41 more likely Clinton

        1. who trust more on taxes: Cl: 54 D: 36

        2. head to head: 55-39

IV. STRATEGIC GOALS FOR NEXT TWO WEEKS

  A. Pre-Convention

    1. Use bill signings to reverse wrong track/right track ratings to restore right track view of U.S.

    2. Use Ads to --

      a. Restore image of extremism via Gingrich

        1. particularly on medicare, abortion, education

          a. elderly, single women, married women

      b. Hit Dole plan and promote Clinton plan

      c. Set up tax negatives and hypocrisy argument against Dole

    3. Use free media attacks to savage Dole Plan and sell Clinton plan

    4. Ads:

      a. Oval Office

        1. Use Gingrich to reinject Repub extremism

        2. Use Medicaid to get elderly back

        3. Use abortion/education to get women back

        4. Use drug program cuts to get crime back

        5. Savage their plan

10

6. Sell our plan

7. Show Dole weakness vs. Gingrich

8. Argument in ad tested: less likely Dole: 35-60

b. Dole as Taxer

1. Defend Clinton tax record

2. Attack Dole tax increases

3. Attack credibility of Dole plan

5. Relative Quantity of Buys between conventions: *P 11   8/20/96*

Clinton ad buy: $4.2 million
Repub ad buy: 3.9 million

a. Knight says we are unable to add more hard money to the buy

1. If we could, it would be highly useful given need to make up ground

2. Suggest we wait on all possible hard money uses other than ads until after convention to augment buy to maximum extent possible

B. At Convention

1. Demonstrate that our convention reaches out to moderates and indpens

a. Moderate, American heroes on Monday

b. Use gun control and tobacco on Monday to reach out

c. Hillary/Tipper stress consensus agenda on TV, children, values

d. Bayh emphasizes family achievements

e. Gore stress impact on a family's day

f. Clinton proposes vision of life in 21st century

11

g. Avoid leftist rhetoric or speakers

2. Use Public values to defeat private character attacks

    a. values on Monday night

    b. Hillary speech

    c. Bayh enumeration of initiatives

    d. Gore on a family's day

3. Stress comparative visions of America

    a. by focusing on their opposition to values initiatives

    b. In Gore, Dodd, Gantt etc, speeches

    c. by invoking Gingrich and Dole whenever we can

4. Defeat their tax cut plan

    a. Bayh speech

    b. Dodd speech

    c. Cleland-Gantt-Morales speeches

    d. Clinton presents his alternative on Thursday

5. Highlight progress, accomplishments and promises kept

    a. Bayh speech

    b. Gore speech

    c. Ordinary people on Monday

    d. signs in hall

    e. allusion to them in Clinton speech (brief)

6. Unveil 21st century agenda

    a. Hillary speech

12

b. Tipper Speech

c. Gore speech

d. mainly -- Clinton speech on Thursday

7. Convention schedule

a. Sell Clinton accomplishments

b. Emphasize -- in restrained way -- Dole and Gingrich opposition
to our accomplishments

C. In Clinton's Speech

1. Create positive vision of second term

2. Fill people's minds with ideas of the future, so there is no time for
Republicans or for this election

a. let's hurry and get over this election so Clinton can get on with
it and continue to lead us to where we want to go

3. Relieve fears of second term liberalism

a. by stressing moderate issues

b. by being liberal where they want us to be liberal

1. environment
2. education
3. jobs for welfare recipients

D. After Convention

1. Hammer home positive proposals by Clinton in post convention ads
very much like our post state of the union ads

V. ISSUES FOR PRESIDENT'S SPEECH, TRAIN TRIP, GORE SPEECH

A. In this poll, we ranked every issue we are thinking of using by their likelihood
of making people vote for Clinton and then tested them for their
feasibility in accomplishing their goals

13

These 44 proposals all test above 60% and all but two test with
feasibility over 50%.

	Likelihood of Support for Clinton	Feasibility
Welfare to work	80-17	51-43 (cumulative)
Welfare/work in neighborhoods	79-20	51-43 (cumulative)
College tax credit	78-28	75-20
cop killer bullet ban	78-18	70-24
Track sex crimes	76-20	68-24
No guns for felons	74-23	57-40
Clean drinking water	74-21	68-26 (cumulative)
Enviro crimes/lien	73-22	64-30 (cumulative)
Adult college tax credit	73-24	77-18
Trigger locks	72-23	68-27
100,000 cops	72-23	71-24
3 hrs educational TV	72-22	76-21
Enviro right to know	72-24	70-25 (cumulative)
Ban racial preference in adoption	72-19	76-16
75% cleanup toxic waste	71-25	54-45
Welfare employee tax credit	71-25	51-43 (cumulative)
Education savings bonds	71-22	68-26
IRS deadbeat dads	71-27	74-21
School health clinics meet primary med needs of uninsured kids	70-28	
State standardized test for promotion	70-26	68-27
No tax deductions for deadbeat dads	69-28	72-22
Brady bill dom violence misdems	68-27	57-36
State standardized test/graduation	68-28	71-22
Fed govt standardized test/promotion	68-29	74-21
Welfare/placement bonus	68-27	51-43 (cumulative)
No guns under 21	68-24	53-43
Iran/Libya sanctions	68-25	49-45
50,000 literacy teachers	67-31	73-23
Welfare-staffed child care	67-30	51-43 (multi steps)
HMO Notification/alt treatment	67-26	
TV family hour	65-26	68-25

14

6 yr bal budget plan	65-29	61-33
Violence on kids TV	64-28	71-25
Ban cig ads at kids	64-31	59-36
Mandatory adoption if abuse	64-26	66-26
Targeted tax cuts	64-26	62-30
Health Ins for Unemployed	63-33	
No firing of HMO Doctor	63-26	
Penalize drug countries	62-31	44-48
Teen gangs RICO	61-33	50-43
No cap gains on home sale	61-33	52-39
Adopt after 1 year foster care	60-27	68-24
Ban Meth (drug)	58-33	52-34

B. Vetting Issues Remaining:

    1. Financial Issues:

        a. We need to include homeowner capital gains tax cut in program

            1. without that, we have too limited a targeted tax cut plan

            2. estimated cost: $2 billion

        b. We need tax exempt education savings in our plan

            1. we can't let Dole get to the left us with his proposal for tax exempt student loans

            2. likely low cost, although not yet estimated

VI. ISSUES FOR HILLARY SPEECH

Warm, stimulating child care	77-17
Hospital stays new mothers	75-19
Guaranteed child health care	73-19
Toll-free medical advice	72-19
Mentoring new moms/dads	71-19
Learning a daily activity	69-22
Employer child care	66-26
Stimulate first 3 years	65-25
Household instability	65-25

15

Note

The scandal which toppled me from leadership of the campaign hit during the Democratic convention. The strategy meetings reportedly continued throughout the campaign and through much of 1997 and 1998.
Hopefully, when the time comes, any agenda or other written material
associated with these sessions will also be released to the public.

Acknowledgments

I wrote this book during a difficult time.

It would have been impossible to do it without the steady and constant support of my wife, Eileen, support that she gave in the cruelest of circumstances.

My father, Eugene Morris, rooted for me and still does.

My special friends Bob Steingut, Frank Baraff, Dennis and Nancy Pels-Paget, Andy Brody, and Paul Feinstein helped me make it through.

I want to thank Harold Evans and Peter Matson for believing in me and what I had to say. Harold would make a great campaign manager.

The people at Renaissance have been helpful in guiding the preparation of this paperback edition with its agendas and new introduction. I especially want to thank Bill Hartley, the publisher, Michael Levine, acquiring editor, Anni Hartley, copyeditor, Arthur Morey, managing editor, and Lisa Lenthall, the designer. They have all shown great patience and enthusiasm and I appreciate it.

Index

and government shutdowns, 178,
183–86, 187, 207, 492
inflexibility of, 317–18, 340
issues preempted by Democrats, 38, 81,
86, 145, 159, 269–70, 274, 431
moderates in, 75
and 1994 congressional election, 18, 37, 90
no-government agenda of, 94–95, 97, 105
and presidential race, 133, 153, 156, 202,
267–70, 271, 273–77, 285, 297,
311–15, 321–22
radical purists in, 178–79, 184–85, 187,
233–34, 311
and social issues, 159, 236, 298–305
split in, 149–50, 298
and tax cuts, 81–83, 86, 146, 312–14,
341
and values agenda, 208, 211, 212, 214,
217–18, 225–26, 227–28, 230, 233–34
responsibility-opportunity mode, 60–61,
82–83, 92, 94–95, 120, 304, 311
RICO (Racketeer Influenced and Corrupt
Organizations) Act, 229
Ridge, Tom, 9, 19
Riley, Richard, 203, 214, 223, 224, 228,
321
Rivlin, Alice, 187, 204, 224
Rockefeller, Winthrop, 51
Romney, Mitt, 152
Roosevelt, Eleanor, 110, 286–87, 323
Roosevelt, Franklin D., 108, 199, 323
achievements of, 204, 230, 305
public image of, 140, 148
social programs of, 158, 307, 308
Roosevelt, Theodore, 5, 305, 308, 340, 343
Rubin, Jamie, 249
Rubin, Robert, 224, 228, 232
Rudman, Warren, 19, 31, 60
Ruggie, John, 249, 262, 262–63
Rules for Radicals (Alinsky), 44
Russia, 126, 250–51, 256, 258–60, 264,
341

Saffire, William, xxiv
Samuels, Howard J., 58–59
Sandler, Joe, 141, 146
Sasha (dog), 168
Sawyer, David, 49
Schlesinger, Arthur, 310–11
Schmitt, Jack, 60
Schoen, Doug, 190
and campaign ads, 146, 147, 277, 332
and foreign policy, 256–58, 260
poll on tax cuts, 85, 146
and presidential race, 24–25, 143, 145,
156, 284, 310, 317

and presidential speeches, 88
and values agenda, 216–17
and White House meetings, 26, 96, 114,
348
Schwartz, Marc, 203
Schwartz, Tony, 53–54, 107, 170
Segal, Eli, 191
Senate, *see* Congress; Dole, Robert J.; Lott,
Trent
Seward, William, 22
Shalala, Donna, 102
Shannon, Mike, 62
Sheinkopf, Hank, 141–42, 143, 144, 146,
147
Shipley, David, 280
Simon, Carly, 236
Simpson, Alan, 72, 73, 74
Simpson, O. J., 221, 477
Smith, Mary, 203, 223
Smith, Steve, 43
social issues:
and budget, 158
and community values, 85–86, 92,
211–12, 281–82, 302–4, 313
cycles of, 92
and Democratic party, 159, 165, 212,
219, 282
limitations of, 60–61, 91–92
and opportunity-responsibility mode,
60–61, 82–83, 92, 94–95, 304
populist movements, 236
and Republican party, 159, 236, 298–305
see also entitlements; values agenda
Social Security, 342–43
Sosnik, Doug, 26, 147, 154–55, 205, 298,
348
Sperling, Gene:
and budget, 175, 183
and campaign ads, 146
as economic adviser, 135, 203, 279
and school construction, 228
and tax cuts, 145, 312
and values agenda, 225
Spitzer, Eliott, 203
Squier, Bob, 190
and campaign ads, 141–44, 146, 147,
151, 194, 332
and presidential race, 276
and presidential speeches, 120, 169, 170,
182
and White House meetings, 26*n,* 348
Stanton, Edwin, 22
Star magazine, 324, 330, 333
Starr, Kenneth, 285, 285–86, 286, 292, 533
Steenburgen, Mary, 238
Stein, Andy, 152